ACCA

Applied Skills

Taxation (TX-UK)
(Finance Act 2019)

EXAM KIT

For June 2020 to March 2021 examination sittings

KAPLAN

PUBLISHING

British Library Cataloguing-in-Publication Data

A catalogue record for this book is available from the British Library.

Published by:

Kaplan Publishing UK

Unit 2 The Business Centre

Molly Millar's Lane

Wokingham

Berkshire

RG41 2QZ

ISBN: 978-1-78740-416-8

Acknowledgements

These materials are reviewed by the ACCA examining team. The objective of the review is to ensure that the material properly covers the syllabus and study guide outcomes, used by the examining team in setting the exams, in the appropriate breadth and depth. The review does not ensure that every eventuality, combination or application of examinable topics is addressed by the ACCA Approved Content. Nor does the review comprise a detailed technical check of the content as the Approved Content Provider has its own quality assurance processes in place in this respect.

The past ACCA examination questions are the copyright of the Association of Chartered Certified Accountants. The original answers to the questions from June 1994 onwards were produced by the examiners themselves and have been adapted by Kaplan Publishing.

CONTENTS

Section

Key features in this edition

In addition to providing a wide ranging bank of real past exam questions, we have also included in this edition:

- An analysis of all of the recent examinations.

- Exam specific information and advice on exam technique.

- Our recommended approach to make your revision for this particular subject as effective as possible. This includes step by step guidance on how best to use our Kaplan material (study text, pocket notes and exam kit) at this stage in your studies.

- A wealth of past real examination questions adapted to the new examination style with enhanced tutorial answers and packed with specific key answer tips, technical tutorial notes and exam technique tips from our experienced tutors.

- Complementary online resources including full tutor debriefs and question assistance to point you in the right direction when you get stuck.

You will find a wealth of other resources to help you with your studies on the following sites:

www.mykaplan.co.uk

www.accaglobal.com/en/student.html

Quality and accuracy are of the utmost importance to us so if you spot an error in any of our products, please send an email to mykaplanreporting@kaplan.com with full details, or follow the link to the feedback form in MyKaplan.

Our Quality Coordinator will work with our technical team to verify the error and take action to ensure it is corrected in future editions.

INDEX TO QUESTIONS AND ANSWERS

INTRODUCTION

All TX exams have been computer-based exams (CBEs) from the June 2019 sitting, if you would like further information on sitting a CBE TX examination please contact either Kaplan or the ACCA.

As a result of changes to the TX exam format over time, the majority of past exam questions in their original format are not representative of current TX examination questions. The questions contained in this exam kit are therefore based on past exam questions but it has been necessary to adapt them to ensure that they are representative of questions in the examinations. The adaptations have been made to reflect the new style of exam, new legislative changes in recent Finance Acts, Tax law changes and IFRS® Standards terminology. We have also included new topics brought into the syllabus in some questions.

Many of the questions within the kit are past ACCA exam questions, and the more recent questions (from 2005) are labelled as such in the index. Note that if a question within this kit has been adapted or changed in any way from the original version, this is indicated in the end column of the index below with the mark (A).

Also included are the marking schemes for past ACCA examination questions to assist you in understanding where marks are earned and the amount of time to spend on particular tasks. Note that if a question has been changed from the original version, it will have also been necessary to change the original ACCA marking scheme. Therefore, if a question is marked as 'ADAPTED' you should assume that this also applies to the marking scheme.

A number of questions included in the exam kit are referenced to two examination sittings e.g. March/June 2017. This is as a result of a change in policy made by the ACCA regarding the release of examination questions. Previously, examinations were released in their entirety. The ACCA now release a selection of questions from the March/June and September/December examinations. Therefore, questions referenced as such are taken from the sample released by the ACCA.

KEY TO THE INDEX

ANSWER ENHANCEMENTS

We have added the following enhancements to the answers in this exam kit:

Key answer tips

All answers include key answer tips to help your understanding of each question.

Tutorial note

All answers include tutorial notes to explain some of the technical points in more detail.

Tutor's top tips

For selected questions, we 'walk through the answer' giving guidance on how to approach the questions with helpful 'tips from a top tutor', together with technical tutor notes.

These answers are indicated with the 'footsteps' icon in the index.

Within the questions in the exam kit you will see the following icons, shown in the question requirements:

= word processing

= spreadsheet

The icons highlighting the constructed response workspace tool alongside some of the questions are for guidance only – it is important to recognise that each question is different and that the answer space provided by ACCA in the exam is determined by both the technical content of the question as well as the quality assurance processes ACCA undertakes to ensure the student is provided with the most appropriate type of workspace.

ONLINE ENHANCEMENTS

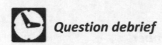 *Question debrief*

For selected questions, we recommend that they are to be completed in full exam conditions (i.e. properly timed in a closed book environment).

In addition to the examining team's technical answer, enhanced with key answer tips and tutorial notes in this exam kit, online you can find an answer debrief by a top tutor that:

- works through the question in full

- points out how to approach the question

- advises you how to ensure that the easy marks are obtained as quickly as possible, and

- emphasises how to tackle exam questions and exam technique.

These questions are indicated with the 'clock' icon in the index.

Online question enhancements and answer debriefs will be available on **My**Kaplan at:

www.mykaplan.co.uk

PRACTICE INCOME TAX AND NATIONAL INSURANCE QUESTIONS

KAPLAN PUBLISHING

PRACTICE CHARGEABLE GAINS QUESTIONS

PRACTICE INHERITANCE TAX QUESTIONS

PRACTICE CORPORATION TAX QUESTIONS

PRACTICE VALUE ADDED TAX QUESTIONS

ANALYSIS OF PAST EXAMS

The table below summarises the key topics that have been tested in recent exams.

Key:

Q   The question references are to the number of the question in this edition of the exam kit.

✓   Refers to questions which have not been included in the kit due to similarity to other recent questions.

*   Refers to topics that were included in the question when originally set, but with the adaptation of the question to the new style exam, this topic element has been removed from this question in the exam kit.

	Mar/Jun 2016	Sep 2016	Dec 2016	Mar/Jun 2017	Sep/Dec 2017	Mar/Jun 2018	Sep/Dec 2018	Mar/Jun 2019
Principles of taxation/Ethics								
Extra statutory concession			Q75					
Direct tax		Q71						
Income tax								
Exempt income					Q97			Q113
Basic income tax computation	Q95 Q104	✓	Q16		Q96	Q94 Q114	Q125	
Savings income				Q99			Q93	Q113
Dividend income		✓			Q96	Q94	Q125 Q93	
Reduction of personal allowance								
Property income	Q95		Q20	Q99		Q114	Q125 Q93	Q113
Furnished holiday lettings								
ISAs			Q127					
Residence		Q13	Q10		Q97	Q114		Q113
Qualifying interest				Q99		Q114		
Employed individual								
Employed vs. self-employed	Q104							Q113
Salary and bonus	Q95	Q116		Q99	Q97	Q94	Q93	Q113
Exempt benefits	Q95		Q92		Q97			
Car and fuel benefit			Q92				Q93	
Living accommodation								
Payroll giving							Q93	
Beneficial loan	Q95		Q92		Q97		Q93	
Use/gift of assets		Q30	Q92		Q97		Q93	
Mileage allowance		Q116		Q99	Q97			Q113
Professional subscriptions		Q116		Q99	Q97			
Removal expenses			Q92					

	Mar/Jun 2016	Sep 2016	Dec 2016	Mar/Jun 2017	Sep/Dec 2017	Mar/Jun 2018	Sep/Dec 2018	Mar/Jun 2019
Self-employed individual								
Adjustment to profits		Q116				Q114		
Capital allowances	Q95	Q116				Q114		
Basis of assessment rules	Q95							
Partnerships – allocation						Q114	Q93	
Tax planning				Q110				
Pensions								
Pension income								
Occupational pension	Q95	Q116		Q99	Q97			
Personal pension contributions	Q95	Q64 Q116	Q127					Q107
Annual allowance		Q64	Q127	Q99	Q97			
Income tax losses								
Relief against income		Q116			Q97	Q114		
Opening year loss relief		Q116						
National Insurance contributions								
Class 1	Q104	✓				Q96 Q94		
Class 1A			Q92					
Class 2	Q104							
Class 4	Q104	Q57	Q61					
Capital gains								
Basic CGT computation	Q95 Q174	Q171						
Exempt assets								Q169
Part disposal	Q174							
Shares		Q171	Q157 Q168					Q169
Wasting asset			Q140					
Insurance for destroyed assets								Q169
Husband and wife	Q174	Q134						Q169 Q107
Capital losses								Q169
Planning			Q168					Q107
Reliefs								
Entrepreneurs' relief			Q168					Q169
Principal private residence relief		Q149						
Gift relief	Q174		Q157					
Rollover relief		Q171		Q110				

	Mar/Jun 2016	Sep 2016	Dec 2016	Mar/Jun 2017	Sep/Dec 2017	Mar/Jun 2018	Sep/Dec 2018	Mar/Jun 2019
Self-assessment – individual								
Payments on account		Q85		Q110				
Compliance checks							Q93	
Interest and penalties		Q87					Q93	
Record retention			Q79					
Inheritance tax								
PETs	Q209	Q182 Q184						Q200
CLTs	Q209	Q184	Q203					
Exemptions	Q209		Q203					Q200
Diminution in value			Q203					
Estate computation		Q204	Q193					
After tax inheritance								
Reduction of tax	Q209	Q204						
Due dates		Q204	Q203					Q200
Transfer of nil rate band		Q204	Q199					Q200 Q107
Residence nil rate band							Q200	Q107
Corporation tax								
Residence			Q260				Q264	
Definition of accounting periods							Q264	
Adjustment to profits	Q263	Q214 Q249	Q260	Q252	Q259	Q251	Q264	Q250
Capital allowances	Q263	Q249	Q260	Q252	Q259	Q251		Q250
Lease premiums		Q249	Q260	Q252		Q251		
Basic TTP computation				Q252	Q96 Q259	Q251	Q264	Q250
Property income		Q249	Q221 Q260		Q259	Q251		
Interest income								
Chargeable gains		Q171 Q249		Q252	Q259	Q251	Q264	Q250
Long period of account								
Qualifying donations		Q249		Q252	Q259	Q251	Q264	Q250
Corporation tax losses								
Capital losses			Q260	Q252			Q264	Q250
Trading losses	Q263	Q222	Q260		Q259	Q251	Q264	Q250
Property losses			Q260	Q252				

	Mar/Jun 2016	Sep 2016	Dec 2016	Mar/Jun 2017	Sep/Dec 2017	Mar/Jun 2018	Sep/Dec 2018	Mar/Jun 2019
Groups								
Group relief	Q263				Q259		Q264	Q250
Capital gains group			Q231					
Group structure planning								
Self-assessment – companies								
Quarterly instalments			Q218	Q252				
Compliance check			Q212					
Value added tax								
Registration		Q291	Q294					Q288
VAT return computation	Q295		Q294					
Tax point				Q110				
Due dates		Q291	Q294					
VAT invoices		Q291						Q288
Default surcharge			Q294					
Errors in a VAT return								Q288
Pre-registration input VAT								Q288
Annual accounting scheme	Q295	Q283						
Cash accounting scheme	Q295							
Input VAT recovery			Q277 Q294					Q288

EXAM TECHNIQUE

GENERAL COMMENTS

- We recommend that you always read the questions and examination requirements carefully.

- **Divide the time** you spend on questions in proportion to the marks on offer:

  - one suggestion for this examination is to allocate 1.8 minutes to each mark available (180 minutes/100 marks), so a 10 mark question should be completed in approximately 18 minutes.

  - within that, try to allow time at the start to read the question and plan your answer (see P.24 below) and at the end of each question to review your answer and address any obvious issues.

- If you **get completely stuck** with a question:

  - flag the question in the CBE software and **return to it later.**

- Spend the last **five minutes** of the examination:

  - reading through your answers, and

  - **making any additions or corrections**.

SECTION A OBJECTIVE TEST QUESTIONS

- Decide whether you want to attempt these at the start of the examination or at the end.

- Stick to the timing principle of 1.8 minutes per mark. This means that the 15 OT questions in section A (30 marks) should take 54 minutes.

- No credit for workings will be given in these questions; the answers will either be correct (2 marks) or incorrect (0 marks).

- Work steadily. Rushing leads to careless mistakes and questions are designed to include answers that result from careless mistakes.

- If you don't know the answer, eliminate those options you know are incorrect and see if the answer becomes more obvious.

- Remember that there is no negative marking for an incorrect answer. After you have eliminated the options that you know to be wrong, if you are still unsure, guess.

SECTION B OT CASE QUESTIONS

- There is likely to be a significant amount of information to read through for each case. You should begin by reading the OT questions that relate to the case, so that when you read through the information for the first time, you know what it is that you are required to do.

- Each OT question is worth two marks. Therefore you have 18 minutes (1.8 minutes per mark) to answer the five OT questions relating to each case. It is likely that all of the cases will take the same length of time to answer, although some of the OT questions within a case may be quicker than other OT questions within that same case.

- Once you have read through the information, you should first answer any of the OT questions that do not require workings and can be quickly answered. You should then attempt the OT questions that require workings utilising the remaining time for that case.

- All of the tips for section A are equally applicable to each section B question.

SECTION C CONSTRUCTED RESPONSE (LONG) QUESTIONS

- The constructed response questions in section C will require a written response rather than being OT questions. Therefore, different techniques need to be used to score well.

- Unless you know exactly how to answer the question, spend some time planning your answer. Stick to the question and tailor your answer to what you are asked. Pay particular attention to the verbs in the question e.g. 'Calculate', 'State', 'Explain'.

- If you do not understand what a question is asking, state your assumptions. Even if you do not answer in precisely the way the examining team hoped, you should be given some credit if your assumptions are reasonable.

- You should do everything you can to make things easy for the marker. Your answer should:

  - have a clear structure

  - be concise.

  It is better to write a little about a lot of different points than a great deal about one or two points.

- **Section C Computations:**

  - It is essential to include all your workings in your answers. Many computational questions require the use of a standard format e.g. income tax computations, corporation tax computations and capital gains.

  - Be sure you know these formats thoroughly before the examination and use the layouts that you see in the answers given in this book and in model answers.

  - Adopt a logical approach and cross reference workings to the main computation to enable the marker to find them easily. Do not leave a large gap between your answer and the workings.

  - You will be presented with a blank spreadsheet. A number of standard spreadsheet functions are available via the menu and tool bar for you to use when responding to the question. It is important to practise answering questions using the CBE software and to familiarise yourself with the CBE functionality, particularly the spreadsheet functions.

- **Section C Reports, memos and other documents:**

  - Some questions ask you to present your answer in the form of a report, a memo, a letter or other document.

ADDITIONAL TIPS

- Do not attempt a CBE until you have completed all study material relating to it.

- On the ACCA website there is a CBE demonstration. It is ESSENTIAL that you attempt this before your real CBE. You will become familiar with how to move around the CBE screens and the way that questions are formatted, increasing your confidence and speed in the actual examination.

- There is an additional constructed response (CR) workspace on the ACCA website which you can use to practice questions from this exam kit in a CBE environment.

- Be sure you understand how to use the software before you start the examination. If in doubt, ask the assessment centre staff to explain it to you.

- Questions are displayed on the screen and answers are entered using keyboard and mouse.

- In addition to multiple choice type questions, CBEs will also contain other types of questions. You need to be sure you know how to answer questions of these types before you sit the examination, through practice. The types of objective test questions you could see in your CBE are as follows:

Question type	Description	Example exam kit question
Multiple choice	Select one correct answer from a choice of four	2
Multiple response	Select a given number of correct answers	31
Fill in the blank	Input a numerical answer	3
Drag and drop	Match chosen answer to chosen areas of the screen	145
Drop down list	Select one correct answer from a drop down list	156
Hot area	Select one or more areas in an image as a correct answer (e.g. true or false)	1

EXAM SPECIFIC INFORMATION

THE EXAM

FORMAT OF THE EXAM

The exam will be in **THREE sections**, and will be predominantly computational.

Section A will consist of 15 objective test questions, each worth 2 marks.

Section B will consist of three 10 mark questions which each comprise five objective test questions of 2 marks each.

Section C will consist of one 10 mark question and two 15 mark questions.

All questions are compulsory.

		Number of marks
Section A:	15 objective test questions of 2 marks each	30
Section B:	Three 10 mark questions covering any area of the syllabus	30
Section C:	One 10 mark question covering any area of the syllabus	10
	Two 15 mark questions, one focusing on income tax and one on corporation tax	30
Total		100

The **CBE** will be **3 hours** long and students will have up to 10 minutes to familiarise themselves with the CBE system before starting the exam.

Note that:

- Section A and section B questions can be drawn from any area of the syllabus.

- The two 15 mark section C questions could include a small number of marks in respect of other taxes.

- There is no set order for the section C questions. In the specimen exam the 10 mark question appeared before the 15 mark questions, but the examining team could change the order.

PASS MARK

The pass mark for all ACCA Qualification examinations is 50%.

SUGGESTED APPROACH TO THIS EXAM

Decide in advance whether you will attempt section A, B or C first so that you are not wasting time on this decision in the real examination.

- This is a personal choice and you have time on the revision phase to try out different approaches, for example, if you sit mock examinations.

- A common approach is to tackle the short section A questions first, so they are out of the way, then section B and finally the longer constructed response questions in section C.

- Others may prefer to tackle the longer section B and C questions first, as they will take longer than the individual questions in section A.

You should complete at least one mock examination under examination conditions to try out your chosen approach in advance.

Whatever your approach though, you must make sure that you leave enough time to attempt all questions fully and be very strict with yourself in timing each question.

READING AND PLANNING

Reading and planning are crucial elements of your examination technique and it is important that you allocate time in the examination to this. Spend time reading the questions carefully, particularly in sections B and C, where questions will be based on longer scenarios than the 2 mark OTs in section A.

Whatever happens, always keep your eye on the clock and do not over run on any part of any question!

As all questions are compulsory, there are no decisions to be made about choice of questions, other than in which order you would like to tackle them.

Therefore, in relation to TX we recommend that you take the following approach to planning your answers:

- **Note down the amount of time you should spend on each part of each question**.

- **Decide the order** in which you think you will attempt each question in sections B and C:

  A common approach is to tackle the question you think is the easiest and you are most comfortable with first.

  Others may prefer to tackle the longest questions first, or conversely leave them to the last.

  It is usual however for students to tackle their least favourite topic and/or the most difficult question in their opinion last.

  Whatever your approach, you must make sure that you leave enough time to attempt all questions fully and be very strict with yourself in timing each question.

- **For each section C question** in turn, read the requirements and then the detail of the question carefully.

  Always read the requirement first as this enables you to **focus on the detail of the question with the specific task in mind**.

  For section C computational questions:

  Note key numbers/information and key words in the question, scribble notes to yourself to remember key points in your answer.

  Jot down pro formas required if applicable.

For section C written questions:

Take notice of the format required (e.g. letter, memo, notes) and identify the recipient of the answer. You need to do this to judge the level of financial sophistication required in your answer and whether the use of a formal reply or informal bullet points would be satisfactory.

Plan your beginning, middle and end and the key areas to be addressed and your use of titles and sub-titles to enhance your answer.

For all section C questions:

Spot the easy marks to be gained in a question and parts which can be performed independently of the rest of the question. For example, writing down due dates of payment of tax, due dates for making elections, laying out basic pro formas correctly.

Make sure that you do these parts first when you tackle the question.

- As mentioned in the 'Exam Technique' section earlier, you should decide in advance of the real examination whether to attempt section A, B or C first.

 Always keep your eye on the clock and do not over run on any part of any question!

DETAILED SYLLABUS

The detailed syllabus and study guide written by the ACCA can be found at:

www.**acca**global.com/en/student.html

KAPLAN'S RECOMMENDED REVISION APPROACH

QUESTION PRACTICE IS THE KEY TO SUCCESS

Success in professional examinations relies upon you acquiring a firm grasp of the required knowledge at the tuition phase. In order to be able to do the questions, knowledge is essential.

However, the difference between success and failure often hinges on your examination technique on the day and making the most of the revision phase of your studies.

The **Kaplan study text** is the starting point, designed to provide the underpinning knowledge to tackle all questions. However, in the revision phase, pouring over text books is not the answer.

Kaplan Online knowledge checks help you consolidate your knowledge and understanding and are a useful tool to check whether you can remember key topic areas.

Kaplan pocket notes are designed to help you quickly revise a topic area, however you then need to practice questions. There is a need to progress to full examination standard questions as soon as possible, and to tie your examination technique and technical knowledge together.

The importance of question practice cannot be over-emphasised.

The recommended approach below is designed by expert tutors in the field, in conjunction with their knowledge of the examining team and the recent real examinations.

The approach taken for the Applied Skills Level exams is to revise by topic area. **You need to practice as many questions as possible in the time you have left.**

OUR AIM

Our aim is to get you to the stage where you can attempt examination standard questions confidently, to time, in a closed book environment, with no supplementary help (i.e. to simulate the real examination experience).

Practising your examination technique on real past examination questions, in timed conditions, is also vitally important for you to assess your progress and identify areas of weakness that may need more attention in the final run up to the examination.

In order to achieve this we recognise that initially you may feel the need to practice some questions with open book help and exceed the required time.

The approach below shows you which questions you should use to build up to coping with examination standard question practice, and references to the sources of information available should you need to revisit a topic area in more detail.

Remember that in the real examination, all you have to do is:

- attempt all questions required by the examination
- only spend the allotted time on each question, and
- get them at least 50% right!

Try and practice this approach on every question you attempt from now to the real examination.

EXAMINER COMMENTS

We have included the examining team's comments to the examination questions in this kit for you to see the main pitfalls that students fall into with regard to technical content.

However, too many times in the general section of the report, the examining team comment that students had failed due to:

- 'misallocation of time'

- 'running out of time' and

- showing signs of 'spending too much time on an earlier question and clearly rushing the answer to a subsequent question'.

Good examination technique is vital.

ACCA SUPPORT

For additional support with your studies please also refer to the ACCA Global website.

KAPLAN'S TX EXAMINATION REVISION PLAN

Stage 1: Assess areas of strengths and weaknesses

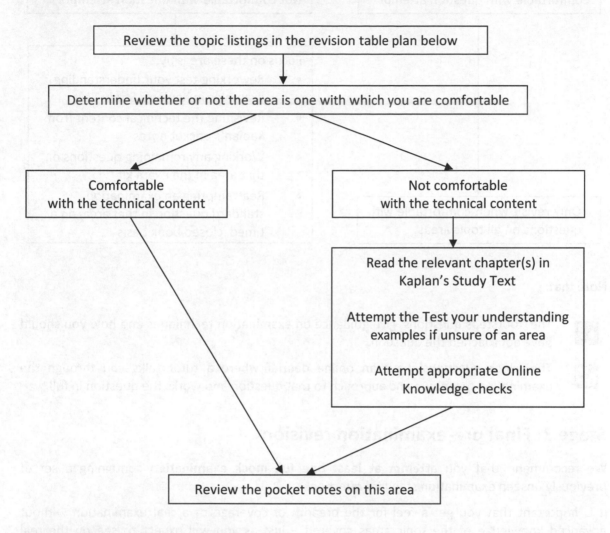

```
┌─────────────────────────────────────────────────────────┐
│     Review the topic listings in the revision table plan below    │
└─────────────────────────────────────────────────────────┘
                              │
                              ▼
┌─────────────────────────────────────────────────────────┐
│  Determine whether or not the area is one with which you are comfortable  │
└─────────────────────────────────────────────────────────┘
```

Comfortable with the technical content	Not comfortable with the technical content

Read the relevant chapter(s) in Kaplan's Study Text

Attempt the Test your understanding examples if unsure of an area

Attempt appropriate Online Knowledge checks

Review the pocket notes on this area

Stage 2: Practise questions

Follow the order of revision of topics as recommended in the revision table plan below and attempt the questions in the order suggested. Note that although the plan is organised into different subject areas, the real examination questions will cover more than one topic, and therefore some parts of the examination questions set below will be on topics covered later in the revision plan.

For each topic listed below you must also practice a selection of objective test questions covering that topic. Do bear in mind that some of the questions in this kit will take longer than 3.6 minutes each.

Try to avoid referring to text books and notes and the model answer until you have completed your attempt.

Try to answer the question in the allotted time.

Review your attempt with the model answer and assess how much of the answer you achieved in the allocated examination time.

Fill in the self-assessment box below and decide on your best course of action.

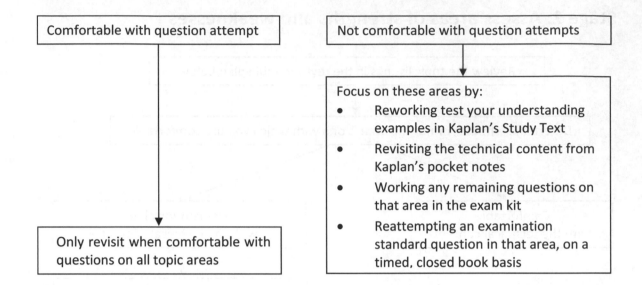

Note that:

 The 'footsteps questions' give guidance on examination techniques and how you should have approached the question.

 The 'clock questions' have an online debrief where a tutor talks you through the examination technique and approach to that question and works the question in full.

Stage 3: Final pre-examination revision

We recommend that you **attempt at least one full mock examination** containing a set of previously unseen examination standard questions.

It is important that you get a feel for the breadth of coverage of a real examination without advanced knowledge of the topic areas covered – just as you will expect to see on the real examination day.

Ideally this mock should be sat in timed, closed book, real examination conditions and could be:

- a mock examination offered by your tuition provider and/or

- the specimen exam in the back of this exam kit and/or

- the last released examination (available shortly afterwards on **My**Kaplan with 'enhanced walk through answers').

THE DETAILED REVISION PLAN

Topic	Study Text Chapter	Pocket note Chapter	Questions to attempt	Tutor guidance	Date attempted	Self-assessment
			Section B/C			
Personal income tax computation	2	1		Review the layout of an income tax computation and rates of tax.		
				Section C in the examination will include at least one question focusing on income tax, and it is crucial that you are comfortable with the pro forma.		
				Various aspects of income tax will also inevitably be tested in section A and possibly section B as well, and it is important to practice a cross-section of these questions.		
– Residence	2	1	97(a) 114(a) 113(a)	The rules to determine whether an individual is resident in the UK are relatively complex. Revise the rules from the pocket notes and practice this question, along with the relevant questions in Section A, where residence is most commonly tested.		
– Employment income and assessable benefits	5	2	97(b) 93 99 90 104(a)	A popular exam topic, almost guaranteed to form part of the exam.		
				There are many questions on this area.		
				Start with Q97 (b) which covers a number of employment benefits.		
				Follow this with Q99, and Q93 which are also past exam questions on this area.		
				Q104 (a) tests the rules for determining whether an individual is employed or self-employed and the consequences of this decision.		

Topic	Study Text Chapter	Pocket note Chapter	Questions to attempt	Tutor guidance	Date attempted	Self-assessment
			Section B/C			
				Q90 is an example of a section B case OT question. It is important that you practice these before your examination as you are likely to find it takes practice to isolate the information that you need for each individual question from the case information.		
– Property income	4	1	99 114	Property income is a small part of these income tax questions. It is often tested as one of a few sources of income for an individual in the examination.		
– Badges of trade	7	3	–	Revise the badges of trade rules from the pocket notes. You may be asked to apply the rules in the exam.		
– Adjusted trading profit, including capital allowances and cash basis	7 & 8	3 & 4	103 101 112(a)	An adjustment of profits calculation is almost certain to be tested in the exam, although it may form part of a sole trader/partnership or corporation tax question. Q103 tests many of the typical adjustments you may see, and having practiced this question you can then attempt Q112(a) to time. Q101 tests the cash basis of assessment.		
– Basis of assessment	9	5	108(a)(i) 109(a)	You may benefit from practising the test your under-standings from the study text before attempting these questions. The opening year rules are commonly tested and these questions provide good practice.		

KAPLAN PUBLISHING

Topic	Study Text Chapter	Pocket note Chapter	Questions to attempt	Tutor guidance	Date attempted	Self-assessment
			Section B/C			
– National insurance	12	8	104(b) and (c)	National insurance may form part of a section B or C question and can provide easy marks to a well-prepared student. It is also likely to be tested in Section A. This question covers NICs for both an employee and a self-employed individual.		
– Trading losses for individuals	11	7	118 117 116	These questions cover the range of ways losses can be tested – in an ongoing business, losses in the opening years and losses on cessation. Q118 also tests the cap on income tax reliefs. Losses are a popular examination topic and it is important to be familiar with each of the reliefs.		
– Partnerships	10	6	122(b) 123(a)	The allocation of profits between partners is a relatively straightforward computation, but does require practice.		
– Pensions	6	8	126 127	Like National Insurance, pensions is a topic which is likely to form a small part of a longer question, however the two questions listed here provide excellent practice of the various ways this topic could be tested.		

Topic	Study Text Chapter	Pocket note Chapter	Questions to attempt	Tutor guidance	Date attempted	Self-assessment
			Section B/C			
– Tax admin for individuals	13	9	128 130	Administration is highly likely to be tested in sections A and B as an OT question. It is vital to learn the dates for submission and payment as well as the potential penalties and interest.		
Consolidation of income tax			95 100 120	Having revised all of the above topics, attempt Q95, Q100 and Q120, these questions incorporate many aspects of the taxation of individuals. Don't forget to practice a number of section A questions on income tax if you haven't already done so.		
Inheritance tax (IHT)	24	18	205 207 210	IHT can be tested in all three sections of the examination and therefore it is important to study this area. Use your pocket notes to revise the key facts and techniques. Warm up with Q205 then practice questions 207 and 210.		
Corporation tax computation	14	10	–	Review the layout of a corporation tax computation and the rates of tax. One of the 15 mark section C questions will focus on CT, and it is crucial that you are comfortable with the pro forma. There may also be a section B question and certainly some section A questions as well.		

Topic	Study Text Chapter	Pocket note Chapter	Questions to attempt	Tutor guidance	Date attempted	Self-assessment
			Section B/C			
– Adjustment of profits and capital allowances	15	10	249 257 246	It is important to be comfortable with the differences between sole traders and companies for adjustments to profits and capital allowances. Use Q249 to check that you are clear about these differences, then attempt Q257, which is classic example of this type of question. Q246 is an example of a section B OT case question on corporation tax.		
– Property income	15	10	256	There are minor but important differences between taxing property income for individuals and companies. This question covers property income for a company.		
– Long periods of account	15	10	253	In order to deal with a long period of account, you need to learn the rules regarding apportioning different types of income between the two periods. Having revised these rules from the pocket notes, practice them using this question.		
– Corporation tax losses	16	11	254 259 261	Many students are daunted by loss questions, however a systematic approach is all that is required and practice is key. Remind yourself of the layout required using the pocket notes, and practice the test your understandings from the study text if you are not confident, before attempting these questions.		

Topic	Study Text Chapter	Pocket note Chapter	Questions to attempt	Tutor guidance	Date attempted	Self-assessment
			Section B/C			
– Groups	17	12	262 263 248	Groups are often tested as part of a corporation tax question. Q263 tests group relief and Q262 tests the rules for determining a capital gains group. Q248 is an example of a section B case OT question.		
– Tax admin for a company	18	13	265(b) 266(b)	Administration could make up part of a constructed response question so you need to be prepared for this. It is also highly likely to be tested in sections A and B as an OT question. It is vital to learn the dates for submission and payment as well as the potential penalties and interest.		
Chargeable gains for individuals	19	14	–	Chargeable gains could appear in section B or C and these questions will usually test a wide variety of the topics below. They are also likely to be tested in Section A. Revise the basic computation using the pocket notes before looking at the detailed areas.		
Chattels, shares, PPR, Entrepreneurs relief	20, 21 & 22	15 & 16	167 172 177	These questions demonstrate how various aspects of capital gains will be tested in one question. Few of these areas are technically challenging, however, it is important that you can tackle them all.		
– Deferral reliefs	22	16	173 174	Recognising which deferral reliefs apply and whether they are available in full is important These questions cover all these reliefs and provide excellent practice.		
Chargeable gains for companies	23	17	179	Remind yourself of the different gains rules for companies, and test your understanding using this question.		

Topic	Study Text Chapter	Pocket note Chapter	Questions to attempt	Tutor guidance	Date attempted	Self-assessment
			Section B/C			
– Quoted shares	21	15 & 17	180	A brief revision of the share pool and matching rules from the pocket notes may be useful. Then attempt this question which tests the capital gains rules for companies, including share pooling.		
Value added tax	25 & 26	19	289 291 297 299	Start by reviewing the examiner's VAT article. VAT could be tested in any of the three sections so it is important that you practise VAT questions from both sections.		
Scenario style exam questions	N/A	20	94 96 98 105 178 208	These questions test a range of subjects and the tax rules covered are not complex, however, the style of questions differs from the others in the kit. Look at the different styles of question using the chapter in the pocket notes, and then ensure you are comfortable with the different question styles by practicing each of these questions.		

Note that not all of the Sections B and C questions in the exam kit are referred to in the programme above.

We have recommended an approach to build up from the basics to examination standard Section B and C questions using a selection of the exam kit questions. The remaining questions are available in the kit for additional practice for those who require more questions on some areas.

It is also vital that you practice Section A questions on all topics.

TAX RATES AND ALLOWANCES

Tax rates and allowances will be produced in the examination for TX for the June 2020 to March 2021 sittings which will contain the following information.

SUPPLEMENTARY INSTRUCTIONS

1   Calculations and workings need only be made to the nearest £.

2   All apportionments should be made to the nearest month.

3   All workings should be shown in Section C.

INCOME TAX

		Normal rates	Dividend rates
Basic rate	£1 – £37,500	20%	7.5%
Higher rate	£37,501 – £150,000	40%	32.5%
Additional rate	£150,001 and over	45%	38.1%
Savings income nil rate band	– Basic rate taxpayers		£1,000
	– Higher rate taxpayers		£500
Dividend nil rate band			£2,000

A starting rate of 0% applies to savings income where it falls within the first £5,000 of taxable income.

Personal allowance

Personal allowance	£12,500
Transferable amount	£1,250
Income limit	£100,000

Where adjusted net income is £125,000 or more, the personal allowance is reduced to zero

Residence status

Days in UK	Previously resident	Not previously resident
Less than 16	Automatically not resident	Automatically not resident
16 to 45	Resident if 4 UK ties (or more)	Automatically not resident
46 to 90	Resident if 3 UK ties (or more)	Resident if 4 UK ties
91 to 120	Resident if 2 UK ties (or more)	Resident if 3 UK ties (or more)
121 to 182	Resident if 1 UK tie (or more)	Resident if 2 UK ties (or more)
183 or more	Automatically resident	Automatically resident

Child benefit income tax charge

Where income is between £50,000 and £60,000, the charge is 1% of the amount of child benefit received for every £100 of income over £50,000.

Car benefit percentage

The relevant base level of CO_2 emissions is 95 grams per kilometre.

The percentage rates applying to petrol cars (and diesel cars meeting the RDE2 standard) with CO_2 emissions up to this level are:

50 grams per kilometre or less	16%
51 grams to 75 grams per kilometre	19%
76 grams to 94 grams per kilometre	22%
95 grams per kilometre	23%

Car fuel benefit

The base figure for calculating the car fuel benefit is £24,100.

Company van benefits

The company van benefit scale charge is £3,430, and the van fuel benefit is £655.

Individual Savings Accounts (ISAs)

The overall investment limit is £20,000.

Property income

Basic rate restriction applies to 75% of finance costs relating to residential properties.

Pension scheme limits

Annual allowance	£40,000
Minimum allowance	£10,000
Income limit	£150,000

The maximum contribution that can qualify for tax relief without any earnings is £3,600.

Approved mileage allowance: cars

Up to 10,000 miles	45p
Over 10,000 miles	25p

Capital allowances: rates of allowance

Plant and machinery

Main pool	18%
Special rate pool	6%

Motor cars

New cars with CO_2 emissions up to 50 grams per kilometre	100%
CO_2 emissions between 51 and 110 grams per kilometre	18%
CO_2 emissions over 110 grams per kilometre	6%

Annual investment allowance

Rate of allowance	100%
Expenditure limit	£1,000,000

Cash basis

Revenue limit	£150,000

Cap on income tax reliefs

Unless otherwise restricted, reliefs are capped at the higher of £50,000 or 25% of income.

CORPORATION TAX

Rate of tax	– Financial year 2019	19%
	– Financial year 2018	19%
	– Financial year 2017	19%
Profit threshold		£1,500,000

VALUE ADDED TAX

Standard rate	20%
Registration limit	£85,000
Deregistration limit	£83,000

INHERITANCE TAX: nil rate bands and tax rates

Nil rate band		£325,000
Residence nil rate band		£150,000
Rate of tax on excess –	Lifetime rate	20%
–	Death rate	40%

Inheritance tax: taper relief

Years before death	Percentage reduction
More than 3 but less than 4 years	20%
More than 4 but less than 5 years	40%
More than 5 but less than 6 years	60%
More than 6 but less than 7 years	80%

CAPITAL GAINS TAX

	Normal rates	Residential property
Lower rate	10%	18%
Higher rate	20%	28%
Annual exempt amount		£12,000
Entrepreneurs' relief – Lifetime limit		£10,000,000
– Rate of tax		10%

NATIONAL INSURANCE CONTRIBUTIONS

Class 1	Employee	£1 – £8,632 per year	Nil
		£8,633 – £50,000 per year	12%
		£50,001 and above per year	2%
Class 1	Employer	£1 – £8,632 per year	Nil
		£8,633 and above per year	13.8%
		Employment allowance	£3,000
Class 1A			13.8%
Class 2		£3.00 per week	
		Small profits threshold	£6,365
Class 4		£1 – £8,632 per year	Nil
		£8,633 – £50,000 per year	9%
		£50,001 and above per year	2%

RATES OF INTEREST (assumed)

Official rate of interest	2.50%
Rate of interest on underpaid tax	3.25%
Rate of interest on overpaid tax	0.50%

STANDARD PENALTIES FOR ERRORS

Taxpayer behaviour	Maximum penalty	Minimum penalty – unprompted disclosure	Minimum penalty – prompted disclosure
Deliberate and concealed	100%	30%	50%
Deliberate but not concealed	70%	20%	35%
Careless	30%	0%	15%

TIME LIMITS AND ELECTION DATES

Income tax

Election/claim	Time limit	For 2019/20
Agree the amount of trading losses to carry forward	4 years from the end of the tax year in which the loss arose	5 April 2024
Current and prior year set-off of trading losses against total income (and chargeable gains)	12 months from 31 January following the end of the tax year in which the loss arose	31 January 2022
Three year carry back of trading losses in the opening years	12 months from 31 January following the end of the tax year in which the loss arose	31 January 2022
Three year carry back of terminal trading losses in the closing years	4 years from the end of the last tax year of trading	5 April 2024

National Insurance Contributions

Class 1 employee and employer's – pay days	17 days after the end of each tax month under PAYE system (14 days if not paid electronically)	22nd of each month
Class 1 A NIC – pay day	22 July following end of tax year (19 July if not paid electronically)	22 July 2020
Class 2 NICs – pay day	Paid under self-assessment with balancing payment	31 January 2021
Class 4 NICs – pay days	Paid under self-assessment with income tax	See self-assessment

Capital gains tax

Replacement of business asset relief for individuals (Rollover relief)	4 years from the end of the tax year: – in which the disposal occurred or – the replacement asset was acquired whichever is later	5 April 2024 for 2018/19 sale and 2019/20 acquisition
Holdover relief of gain on the gift of a business asset (Gift relief)	4 years from the end of the tax year in which the disposal occurred	5 April 2024
Entrepreneurs' relief	12 months from 31 January following the end of the tax year in which the disposal occurred	31 January 2022
Determination of principal private residence	2 years from the acquisition of the second property	

Self-assessment – individuals

Election/claim	Time limit	For 2019/20
Pay days for income tax and class 4 NIC	1st instalment: 31 January in the tax year 2nd instalment: 31 July following the end of tax year Balancing payment: 31 January following the end of tax year	31 January 2020 31 July 2020 31 January 2021
Pay day for CGT and class 2 NIC	31 January following the end of tax year	31 January 2021
Filing dates If notice to file issued by 31 October following end of tax year	Paper return: 31 October following end of tax year Electronic return: 31 January following end of tax year	31 October 2020 31 January 2021
If notice to file issued after 31 October following end of tax year	3 months from the date of issue of the notice to file	
Retention of records Business records	5 years from 31 January following end of the tax year	31 January 2026
Personal records	12 months from 31 January following end of the tax year	31 January 2022
HMRC right of repair	9 months from date the return was filed	
Taxpayer's right to amend a return	12 months from 31 January following end of the tax year	31 January 2022
Taxpayer's claim for overpayment relief	4 years from the end of the tax year	5 April 2024
HMRC can open an enquiry	12 months from submission of the return	
HMRC can raise a discovery assessment – No careless or deliberate behaviour – Tax lost due to careless behaviour – Tax lost due to deliberate behaviour	 4 years from the end of the tax year 6 years from the end of the tax year 20 years from the end of the tax year	 5 April 2024 5 April 2026 5 April 2040
Taxpayer's right of appeal against an assessment	30 days from the assessment – appeal in writing	

Corporation tax

Election/claim	Time limit
Replacement of business asset relief for companies (Rollover relief)	4 years from the end of the chargeable accounting period: – in which the disposal occurred or – the replacement asset was acquired whichever is later
Offset trading losses brought forward against total profits (income and gains)	2 years from the end of the chargeable accounting period in which the loss is **relieved**
Current year set-off of trading losses against total profits (income and gains), and 12 month carry back of trading losses against total profits (income and gains)	2 years from the end of the chargeable accounting period in which the loss **arose**
Surrender of trading losses to other group companies (Group relief)	2 years after the claimant company's chargeable accounting period
Election for transfer of capital gain or loss to another company within the gains group	2 years from the end of the chargeable accounting period in which the disposal occurred by the company actually making the disposal

Self-assessment – companies

Election/claim	Time limit
Pay day for small and medium companies	9 months and one day after the end of the chargeable accounting period
Pay day for large companies	Instalments due on 14th day of: – Seventh, tenth, thirteenth, and sixteenth month **after the start** of the chargeable accounting period
Filing dates	Later of: – 12 months from the end of the chargeable accounting period – 3 months from the issue of a notice to deliver a corporation tax return
Company's claim for overpayment relief	4 years from the end of the chargeable accounting period
HMRC can open an enquiry	12 months from the actual submission of the return
Retention of records	6 years from the end of the chargeable accounting period

Value added tax

Election/claim	Time limit
Compulsory registration Historic test: – Notify HMRC	30 days from end of the month in which the threshold was exceeded
– Charge VAT	First day of second month after the month when taxable supplies exceeded the threshold
Future test: – Notify HMRC	30 days from the date it is anticipated that the threshold will be exceeded
– Charge VAT	The date it is anticipated that the threshold will be exceeded (i.e. the beginning of the 30 day period)
Compulsory deregistration	Notify HMRC 30 days from cessation
Filing of VAT return and payment of VAT	One month and seven days after the end of the return period

Section 1

PRACTICE INCOME TAX AND NATIONAL INSURANCE QUESTIONS

PRACTICE SECTION A OBJECTIVE TEST QUESTIONS

INCOME TAX BASICS AND EMPLOYMENT INCOME

1   Said has made a number of investments during the tax year.

Tick the appropriate box to show which of the following investments will generate taxable income and which will generate exempt income.

	Taxable	Exempt
£400 in shares in the company he works for	✓	
£1,000 in an Individual Savings Account		✓
£800 in a NS&I investment account	✓	
£500 purchasing a NS&I certificate		✓

2   *Specimen exam June 2015 OT question*

Martina is self-employed, and for the year ended 5 April 2020 her trading profit was £111,900. During the tax year 2019/20, Martina made a gift aid donation of £800 (gross) to a national charity.

What amount of personal allowance will Martina be entitled to for the tax year 2019/20?

A   £12,500

B   £6,950

C   £6,550

D   £600

PA   12,500

Restriction (£111,900 – £800 – £100,000)= £11,100 ÷ 2 = (5,550)

£6,950

3 Fiona is a sole trader. During the tax year 2019/20 she had taxable trading income of £106,800 and received dividend income of £1,500. Fiona made a gift aid donation of £2,000 (gross) during the tax year 2019/20.

What amount of personal allowance is Fiona entitled to for the tax year 2019/20?

£ [   ]

4 Genna and Wayne are a married couple. In the tax year 2019/20 Genna had a salary of £5,000 and Wayne had property income of £40,650. They have made an election to transfer the fixed amount of personal allowance from Genna to Wayne.

What is Wayne's income tax liability for the tax year 2019/20?

A £4,380

B £4,130

C £5,380

D £5,880

5 **Tick the appropriate box to show which of the following items of expenditure are deductible in the calculation of an individual's taxable income.**

	Deductible	Not deductible
A contribution into a personal pension scheme		✓
A charitable gift aid donation		✓
A contribution into an employer's HM Revenue and Customs registered occupational pension scheme	✓	
A charitable donation made under the payroll deduction scheme	✓	

6 *June 2015 OT question*

For the tax year 2019/20, Chi has a salary of £53,000. She received child benefit of £1,789 during this tax year.

What is Chi's child benefit income tax charge for the tax year 2019/20?

A £1,789

B £0

C £1,252

D £536

7 Ifram has been employed for many years and has also recently become a partner in a partnership. He is in the process of completing his tax return and has asked your advice regarding the interest payments he has made.

Identify, by ticking the appropriate box, whether his interest payments represent qualifying interest and are deductible from his total income or are not qualifying.

	Qualifying interest	Not qualifying
Interest paid on a loan he incurred to purchase a laptop for use in his employment		
Interest paid on the mortgage for his principal private residence		
Interest paid on an amount he borrowed to finance the acquisition of 2,000 shares in a quoted company		
Interest paid on a loan he took to invest capital in a partnership in order to become a partner		

8 *June 2015 OT question*

Samuel is planning to leave the UK to live overseas, having always previously been resident in the UK. He will not automatically be treated as either resident in the UK or not resident in the UK. Samuel has several ties with the UK and will need to visit the UK for 60 days each tax year. However, he wants to be not resident after he leaves the UK.

For the first two tax years after leaving the UK, what is the maximum number of ties which Samuel could keep with the UK without being treated as resident in the UK?

A   One

B   Four

C   Two

D   Three

9 Bao spent 37 days travelling in the UK during the tax year 2019/20. He has never been resident in the UK prior to the tax year 2019/20.

Minh arrived in the UK from Vietnam on 10 November 2019 to work full time in the UK. Minh did not work full-time in Vietnam before arriving in the UK.

Identify, by ticking the appropriate box, who is treated as UK resident in the tax year 2019/20.

	Resident	Not resident
Bao		
Min		

10 *December 2016 OT question*

Which of the following will NOT cause Harper to be treated as automatically UK resident for the tax year 2019/20?

A   Harper spending 192 days in the UK during the tax year 2019/20

B   Harper renting a house in the UK to live in and then occupying it (as her only home) throughout the tax year 2019/20

C   Harper accepting a 15-month contract for a full time job in the UK on 6 April 2019

D   Harper's husband living in the UK throughout the tax year 2019/20 and Harper staying with him when she visits the UK

11   During the tax year 2019/20 Petra had trading income of £56,500 and she paid an annual charitable donation of £400 under the gift aid scheme. She received child benefit of £1,076 during the tax year 2019/20 in respect of her son, Kostas. Petra had no other income for the tax year 2019/20.

What child benefit income tax charge, if any, will be added to Petra's income tax liability for 2019/20?

£ [   ]

12   Matthew purchased £200,000 (nominal value) gilts, paying interest at 1%, for £211,000 on 1 September 2018. Interest is payable half yearly on 30 June and 31 December.

He sold the gilts on 1 December 2019 for £213,000 (including accrued interest).

How much will Matthew include in savings income in respect of the gilts in the tax year 2019/20?

A   £833

B   £2,000

C   £1,000

D   £1,833

13   **Identify, by ticking the appropriate box, whether or not the following individuals are automatically not resident in the UK.**

Eric, who has never previously been resident in the UK, was in the UK for 40 days during the tax year 2019/20.

Fran, who was resident in the UK for the two tax years prior to the tax year 2019/20, was in the UK for 18 days in the tax year 2019/20

	True	False
Eric is automatically not resident in the UK		
Fran is automatically not resident in the UK		

14 Ahmed purchased £10,000 (nominal value) gilts, paying interest at 2%, for £11,000 on 1 June 2019. Interest is payable half yearly on 31 March and 30 September.

He sold the gilts on 29 February 2020 for £11,400 (including accrued interest).

How much will Ahmed include in savings income in respect of the gilts in the tax year 2019/20?

A   £150

B   £165

C   £100

D   £183

15 **Identify, by ticking the appropriate box, the treatment of each of the following forms of savings income.**

	Taxable	Exempt
NS&I investment account interest		
Gilt edged security interest		
NS&I savings certificate interest		

16 *December 2016 OT question*

David received the following income for the tax year 2019/20:

	£
Property income	21,150
Interest from UK Government securities (gilts)	2,400
Dividends	1,250

What is David's total income tax liability for the tax year 2019/20?

A   £2,010

B   £2,104

C   £2,210

D   £2,304

17 Harrison's only income in the tax year 2019/20 was dividend income of £56,950.

What is Harrison's income tax liability for the tax year 2019/20?

£ [   ]

18   *September 2015 OT question*

Since 6 April 2019, Nicolas has let out an unfurnished freehold office building. On that date, the tenant paid Nicolas a premium of £82,000 for the grant of a 15-year lease.

How much of the premium of £82,000 is taxable as property income for the tax year 2019/20?

A   £59,040

B   £22,960

C   £82,000

D   £5,467

19   Amber is in employment earning an annual salary of £55,000. Her only other income is bank interest of £3,000. She received child benefit of £1,789 during the tax year 2019/20.

Select Amber's child benefit tax charge and method of collection for the tax year 2019/20, by selecting the appropriate box in the table below.

		Method of collection	
		Self-assessment	PAYE
Child benefit tax charge	£1,431	A	B
	£894	C	D

20   *December 2016 OT question*

On 6 April 2019, Melinda rented out a furnished room in her house to Jenny at a rent of £750 a month. Jenny continued to rent the room on the same terms until 5 July 2020.

Melinda continued to live in the house and paid for all of the living expenses, of which £475 a month related to the room rented out to Jenny.

What is Melinda's property income for the tax year 2019/20, assuming that any beneficial elections are made?

A   £1,500

B   £0

C   £3,300

D   £7,500

21   Hannah granted a 23 year lease on a warehouse to Mandy for £42,000 on 1 September 2019.

What is the property income assessable on Hannah for the tax year 2019/20?

£ [   ]

22 Maisy has a cottage which she lets out furnished for an annual rent of £9,600, payable monthly in advance.

She incurred the following expenditure, which was paid for on the dates shown:

		£
6 April 2019	Council tax (for the year to 31 March 2020)	900
6 October 2019	Insurance for the year ended 30 September 2020 (previous year £480 paid 5 October 2018)	540
9 December 2019	Replaced the refrigerator with a similar model	870

What is Maisy's property income for the tax year 2019/20?

A   £8,190

B   £7,290

C   £7,320

D   £8,160

23 Steffania's only income is from letting out furnished residential property, none of which is qualifying furnished holiday accommodation. For the tax year 2019/20 her taxable property income was £25,000, BEFORE adjusting for the following items.

(1)   Payment of £500 to replace a damaged kitchen unit in a fitted kitchen.

(2)   Interest paid of £12,000 on a loan to acquire one of the properties.

What is Steffania's taxable property income for the tax year 2019/20?

£ [   ]

24 Katie earned an annual salary of £55,000 throughout the tax year 2019/20. She used her own car for business travel, and she travelled 14,500 business miles during the tax year 2019/20.

What is Katie's assessable employment income, assuming her employer paid her 43p per business mile?

A   £55,610

B   £54,390

C   £54,710

D   £55,290

25 Christos, a higher rate taxpayer, is provided with the following benefits in the tax year 2019/20 by his employer:

(1) Free use of the staff canteen at lunchtime for 200 days during the tax year. The canteen is available to all staff and the average cost of preparing a meal is £4.

(2) Private medical insurance at a cost of £650 to his employer. Christos made a claim during the tax year 2019/20 and the insurance provider paid out £350.

(3) £3 per week for the additional household costs incurred when he works from home.

What is the assessable value of his benefits in the tax year 2019/20?

£ _____

26 Jo is provided with accommodation by her employer, which the employer purchased 35 years ago at a cost of £72,000. The property has an annual value of £2,600, and had a market value of £245,000 when first made available to Jo 8 years ago. Jo pays £250 per month to her employer to live in the property.

The accommodation does not qualify as job-related.

What is the assessable benefit for Jo in the tax year 2019/20?

A £0

B £3,850

C £3,925

D £2,600

27 Thiago is provided with a new diesel company car on 6 May 2019, which he used for both business and private purposes during the tax year 2019/20. The car has a list price of £28,000 and CO_2 emissions of 158 grams per kilometre. The car meets the RDE2 standard.

What is Thiago's car benefit for the tax year 2019/20?

£ _____

28 Woojin is provided with a loan, on which he pays interest at 1% per annum, by his employer. The loan was £100,000 when it was taken out on 6 April 2019 and he repaid £40,000 of the loan on 6 August 2019.

What is Woojin's beneficial loan benefit for the tax year 2019/20 assuming the average method of calculation is used?

A £2,000

B £1,267

C £1,100

D £1,200

29 Sanjay is employed. As well as his annual salary he is also paid a bonus in April each year. The amount of the bonus is based upon his performance to the end of the previous calendar year.

Identify, by ticking the appropriate box, the treatment of each of the following bonuses.

	Taxable in tax year 2019/20	Not taxable in tax year 2019/20
Bonus of £2,800 received on 6 April 2019 in respect of the year to 31 December 2018		
Bonus of £3,300 received on 3 April 2020 in respect of the year to 31 December 2019.		

30 *September 2016 OT question*

Max is employed by Star Ltd. On 6 April 2018, Star Ltd provided Max with a camera for his personal use. The camera had a market value of £2,000 on 6 April 2018.

On 6 April 2019, Star Ltd gave the camera to Max for free. The camera had a market value of £1,400 on 6 April 2019.

What is Max's taxable benefit in respect of the camera for the tax year 2019/20?

A   £1,000

B   £1,400

C   £2,000

D   £1,600

31 On 6 June 2019 Albert, a marketing manager, was reimbursed £500 by his employer, Generous Ltd, in respect of subscription fees he had paid to The Chartered Institute of Marketing, and £200 in respect of train fares incurred travelling to meetings.

Which TWO of the following statements concerning the tax treatment of the reimbursed expenses are correct?

A   The reimbursed subscription fees must be added to taxable pay and taxed through the PAYE system

B   The reimbursed travel expenses must be added to taxable pay and taxed through the PAYE system

C   The reimbursement of the subscription fees is exempt income so no action is required for tax purposes

D   The reimbursement of the travel expenses is exempt income so no action is required for tax purposes

E   Albert must include the reimbursed subscription fees on his tax return

F   Albert must include the reimbursed travel expenses on his tax return

INCOME TAX BASICS AND INCOME FROM SELF-EMPLOYMENT

32 Wilson is a sole trader. When calculating his trading profits, Wilson has deducted the following expenses:

(1) Gifts of food hampers for 10 customers costing £450 in total

(2) Christmas party for 3 staff members costing £630 in total

(3) Legal fees of £150 in respect of the acquisition of a 20 year lease of a property

(4) Employee parking fine whilst on business of £30

What amount must be added back when calculating Wilson's tax adjusted trading profits?

£ [   ]

33 Haniful has taken goods from his business for personal use. The goods cost £850 and have a selling price of £1,100. He has made no entry in his business accounts in respect of the goods except to record their original purchase by the business.

Haniful's trading profits prior to any adjustment required for the goods taken for own use were £247,500.

What is Haniful's tax adjusted trading profit after making any necessary adjustments in respect of the goods taken for personal use?

A £248,350

B £248,600

C £246,400

D £247,750

34 Fleur runs a sole trader business and on 1 January 2019 she paid a £25,000 premium for a 20 year lease on an office from which she will run her business.

What amount can be deducted in respect of the lease premium when calculating Fleur's tax adjusted trading profits for the year ended 31 December 2019?

£ [   ]

35 *September 2015 OT question*

Wan ceased trading on 31 December 2019, having been self-employed since 1 January 2005. On 1 January 2019, the tax written down value of her plant and machinery main pool was £6,200. On 10 November 2019, Wan purchased a computer for £1,600. All of the items included in the main pool were sold for £9,800 on 31 December 2019.

What is the balancing charge which will arise on the disposal of the main pool items upon the cessation of Wan's trade?

A £4,716

B £3,404

C £2,000

D £3,600

36 **Which TWO of the following assets bought by a sole trader will be allocated to the main pool for capital allowance purposes?**

A   Delivery van costing £12,500 with 25% private use by the owner of the business

B   Laptop computer costing £4,500 with 15% private use by the owner of the business

C   Motor car with CO_2 emissions of 105g/km costing £17,500 with 25% private use by an employee of the business

D   Motor car with CO_2 emissions of 135g/km costing £16,500 used solely for business purposes by the owner of the business

E   Factory air-conditioning system costing £110,000 with a 27 year expected life

F   Packing machine costing £105,000 and with a 24 year expected life

37 Andrew prepared accounts for the eight months to 31 March 2020. The tax written down value of the main pool on 1 August 2019 was £18,000.

On 15 January 2020 he purchased a new motor car with CO_2 emissions of 50g/km costing £12,260. It is used solely for business purposes by Andrew.

What are the maximum capital allowances Andrew may claim for the eight month period ended 31 March 2020?

£ ⬚

38 Ronald has always prepared his accounts to 31 March. On 31 March 2020 Ronald ceased trading. The tax written down value of the main pool at 1 April 2019 was £15,000.

On 1 January 2020 Ronald purchased a laptop solely for business use costing £4,500.

On 31 March 2020 all the items in the main pool were sold for £14,550 apart from the laptop which was retained by Ronald. The market value of the laptop at 31 March 2020 was £4,150. None of the items in the main pool was sold for more than its original cost.

What is the capital allowance/(balancing charge) for the year ended 31 March 2020?

A   £144

B   £450

C   (£800)

D   £800

39 Jacinta started trading on 1 August 2019 and prepares accounts to 31 December each year. Her trading profits for the first two periods are as follows:

5 months ended 31 December 2019   £10,500
Year ended 31 December 2020   £24,000

What is the trading income assessment for Jacinta for the tax year 2019/20?

£ ⬚

40 Lee decided to cease trading on 31 January 2020 after trading for many years. His tax adjusted profits for recent years have been:

Year ended 30 April 2018	£40,000
Year ended 30 April 2019	£10,000
Period ended 31 January 2020	£14,000

Lee has overlap profits of £3,000 brought forward from the commencement of trade.

What is Lee's trading income assessment for the tax year 2019/20?

A £11,000

B £14,000

C £21,000

D £24,000

PARTNERSHIPS

41 Elizabeth and Henry have been in partnership for many years, preparing accounts to 31 December each year.

Until 31 July 2019 profits were shared in the ratio 70:30 to Elizabeth and Henry respectively, with no salary allocated to either partner. From 1 August 2019 the profit sharing ratio was adjusted to 80:20 to Elizabeth and Henry respectively, after allocating a salary of £24,000 per annum to Henry.

The adjusted trading profits for the accounting year ended 31 December 2019 are £120,000.

How much of the profit for the year ended 31 December 2019 is allocated to Henry?

A £41,000

B £31,000

C £43,200

D £39,000

42 Albert and Jolene have been in partnership for many years, preparing accounts to 30 September each year. Albert and Jolene have balances on their capital accounts of £50,000 and £40,000 respectively.

The partnership agreement provides for Albert to receive an annual salary of £25,000 and both partners to receive interest on capital of 4% per year.

The agreed profit sharing ratio is 1:3 to Albert and Jolene respectively.

The adjusted trading profits for the accounting year ended 30 September 2019 are £80,000.

How much trading profit is assessable on Albert in the tax year 2019/20?

£ _____

43 Tim, Abhiroop and Angela have been in partnership for many years, preparing accounts to 31 December each year.

The partnership agreement provides for Tim to receive an annual salary of £15,000.

The agreed profit sharing ratio is 1:3:2 to Tim, Abhiroop and Angela respectively.

Tim left the partnership on 31 May 2019.

The adjusted trading profits for the accounting year ended 31 December 2019 are £360,000.

How much of the profit for the year ended 31 December 2019 is allocated to Tim?

A   £25,000

B   £30,208

C   £72,500

D   £23,958

44 Nazim and Laura have been in partnership for many years, preparing accounts to 31 October each year and sharing profits equally.

On 1 June 2019 Fabiola joined the partnership. The agreed profit sharing ratio was 2:2:1 to Nazim, Laura and Fabiola respectively.

The adjusted trading profits for the accounting years ended 31 October 2019 and 2020 were £240,000 and £300,000 respectively.

Which THREE of the following statements about Fabiola's trading income are correct?

A   Fabiola will be assessed on trading income of £20,000 in the tax year 2019/20

B   Fabiola will be assessed on trading income of £45,000 in the tax year 2019/20

C   Fabiola will be assessed on trading income of £45,000 in the tax year 2020/21

D   Fabiola will be assessed on trading income of £60,000 in the tax year 2020/21

E   Fabiola will have overlap profits of £25,000

F   Fabiola will have overlap profits of £60,000

TRADING LOSSES

45 *June 2015 OT question*

Naomi is self-employed. For the year ended 5 April 2020 she made a trading loss of £110,000, having made a trading profit of £24,000 for the year ended 5 April 2019. Naomi also had employment income of £92,000 for the tax year 2018/19.

What is the maximum loss relief claim which Naomi can make against her total income for the tax year 2018/19?

A £74,000
B £50,000
C £110,000
D £29,000

46 Brooke had been trading profitably as a sole trader for many years. However, in the year ended 31 August 2018 she made a trading loss of £65,000.

Brooke has the following income in the tax year 2019/20:

	£
Trading profit for year ended 31 August 2019	12,000
Dividend income	9,000
Property income (furnished holiday accommodation)	4,000
NS&I savings certificate interest	1,000

What is Brookes' net income for the tax year 2019/20 assuming she carries the trading loss forward?

£ ☐

47 Damyanti has been trading as a sole trader for many years. Her recent tax adjusted trading profits/(losses) have been:

Year ended 31 August 2018 £55,000
Year ended 31 August 2019 (£90,000)

Damyanti also receives bank interest of £14,000 each tax year.

What is the amount of trading loss carried forward to the tax year 2020/21 assuming that Damyanti makes a claim to use the loss in the current and prior tax years?

A £35,000
B £26,000
C £21,000
D £7,000

48   Sabine started to trade as a sole trader on 1 November 2017. Her tax adjusted trading profits/(losses) for the first two years are:

Year ended 31 October 2018   (£25,000)

Year ended 31 October 2019   £5,000

Sabine was employed until 31 March 2017 earning £45,000 per annum.

How much, if any, of the loss can be offset against Sabine's employment income in 2014/15?

£ [   ]

49   Sally has been trading as a sole trader for many years. In the year ended 31 July 2019 she made a trading loss of £45,000.

Sally's only other source of income is property income of £8,000 each tax year.

In the tax year 2019/20 Sally realised a chargeable gain of £32,000 on the sale of a necklace and a capital loss of £4,000 on the sale of a painting. She has capital losses brought forward of £18,000.

What is the amount of trading loss that Sally can offset against her chargeable gain in the tax year 2019/20?

A   £45,000

B   £37,000

C   £28,000

D   £10,000

50   Carol ceased trading on 30 September 2019.

Her recent tax adjusted trading profits/(losses) have been:

Year ended 31 January 2019   £39,000

Period ended 30 September 2019   (£24,000)

Carol had unused overlap profits from the commencement of trade of £12,000.

What is the amount of terminal loss available to Carol?

£ [   ]

PENSIONS AND NIC

51   *June 2015 OT question*

Which classes of national insurance contribution is an employer responsible for paying in respect of its employees?

A   Both class 2 and class 4

B   Class 1 only

C   Both class 1 and class 1A

D   Class 2 only

52   Hamid runs a sole trader business, in which he employs an employee who earns £40,000 per annum and is provided with a company car for private and business use.

For each class of NIC select whether it is paid to HMRC by Hamid and also whether it represents part of the total tax cost suffered by Hamid.

	Paid by Hamid to HMRC	Suffered by Hamid
Employee class 1 primary		
Employer's class 1 secondary		.
Class 1A		
Class 2		
Class 4		

53   *September 2015 OT question*

Lorna has the choice of being either employed or self-employed. If employed, Lorna's gross annual salary for the tax year 2019/20 will be £36,000. If self-employed, Lorna's trading profit for the year ended 5 April 2020 will be £36,000.

How much more national insurance contributions will Lorna suffer for the tax year 2019/20 if she chooses to be employed rather than self-employed?

A   £821

B   £924

C   £665

D   £1,080

54   *Specimen exam June 2015*

During the tax year 2019/20, William was paid a gross annual salary of £82,700. He also received taxable benefits valued at £5,400.

What amount of employee class 1 national insurance contribution (NICs) will have been suffered by William for the tax year 2019/20?

£ [   ]

55 Efe is a director of Mulch Ltd, and is paid an annual salary of £60,000. During the tax year 2019/20 he also received an annual bonus of £3,000 and free meals in the workplace canteen, open to all staff, at a cost of £1,040 to his employer.

What amount of employee class 1 national insurance contribution (NICs) will have been suffered by Efe for the tax year 2019/20?

A   £5,224

B   £5,245

C   £5,164

D   £6,524

56 Bob is an employee of Dibbit Ltd, and is paid an annual salary of £50,000. He makes contributions of £3,000 into the company's occupational pension scheme each year.

In the tax year 2019/20 he drove 12,000 business miles in his own car for which he was paid 50p per mile by Dibbit Ltd.

How much employer's class 1 NICs is Dibbit Ltd required to pay in respect of Bob for the tax year 2019/20?

£ ⬚

57 *September 2016 OT question*

Paloma has been trading for a number of years. Her tax adjusted trading profit for the year ended 31 May 2019 was £58,000 and for the year ended 31 May 2020 was £57,200.

What is the amount of class 4 national insurance contributions (NIC) payable by Paloma for the tax year 2019/20?

A   £4,371

B   £4,443

C   £3,867

D   £3,883

58 Kolo is an employee of Lapsang Ltd. He is paid a salary of £20,000 and has use of a petrol-driven company car for private purposes throughout the tax year 2019/20. The car has a list price of £15,000 and CO_2 emissions of 99g/km. No petrol is provided for private mileage.

How much class 1A NICs is payable in respect of Kolo's company car and by whom is it suffered? Select the appropriate box in the table below.

		Suffered by	
		Lapsang Ltd	**Kolo**
Class 1A	£476	A	B
	£3,236	C	D

59 Robin is a sole trader. His tax adjusted trading profit for the year ended 31 July 2019 is £70,000. In the year ended 31 July 2018 he had a trading loss of £20,000 which he decided to carry forward rather than offset against total income of the current or prior year.

Robin's other income in the tax year 2019/20 comprises £3,000 of savings income.

How much are his assessable profits for class 4 NIC purposes for the tax year 2019/20?

A £70,000

B £53,000

C £50,000

D £73,000

60 Mohammed, age 35, runs a sole trader business. In the year ended 5 April 2020 his accounting profit and tax adjusted trading profit were £5,400 and £6,800 respectively.

Nicole is aged 75 and receives the state retirement pension. She also has a sole trader business. In the year ended 5 April 2020 her accounting profit and tax adjusted trading profit were £5,900 and £6,400 respectively.

Identify, by ticking the appropriate box, who is required to pay class 2 NIC for the tax year 2019/20:

	Class 2 NICs payable	Class 2 NICs not payable
Mohammed		
Nicole		

61 *December 2016 OT question*

Sanjay commenced trading on 1 January 2019 and prepared his first set of accounts for the six month period ended 30 June 2019. His second set of accounts were prepared for the year ended 30 June 2020.

Sanjay's tax adjusted trading profits were:

| Six month period ended 30 June 2019 | £8,800 |
| Year ended 30 June 2020 | £24,400 |

What are the class 4 national insurance contributions (NICs) which Sanjay should pay in respect of the tax year 2019/20?

£ _____

62 Broadman Ltd provides employment benefits to its employees.

On which TWO of the following benefits is class 1A NIC payable by Broadman Ltd?

A   Occupational pension scheme contributions of 5% of the employees' salaries

B   Payment for a parking space in a public car park near the office

C   Annual summer event costing £200 per head

D   Provision of a smart phone for business and private use including the cost of private calls

E   Membership of local sports club at a cost of £400 per annum

F   Mileage allowance of 5p per mile for cost of travel between employee's home and the company's office premises

63 Isaac is self-employed and for the year ended 31 March 2020 he paid £40,000 (net) into his personal pension plan. Isaac's relevant earnings for the tax year 2019/20 were £110,000.

What amount of income tax will Isaac pay at the basic rate for the tax year 2019/20?

£ ☐

64 *September 2016 OT question*
Abena has made the following gross contributions to her personal pension scheme over the past three tax years:

Tax year	£
2016/17	42,000
2017/18	37,000
2018/19	28,000

What is the maximum gross contribution which Abena can make to her personal pension scheme for the tax year 2019/20 without giving rise to an annual allowance charge?

A   £53,000

B   £40,000

C   £55,000

D   £52,000

65 Austin, age 47, runs a sole trader business. In the tax year 2019/20 his trading income was £51,200. During the tax year 2019/20 he paid £22,400 (net) into a personal pension scheme.

Petra, age 45, has employment income of £120,000 in the tax year 2019/20. She has never been a member of a pension scheme until the tax year 2019/20 when she paid £50,000 (net) into a personal pension scheme.

Identify, by ticking the appropriate box, who has made fully tax relievable pension contributions in the tax year 2019/20.

	Fully tax relievable pension contributions	Not fully tax relievable pension contributions
Austin		
Petra		

66 Griff is employed by Gargoyle plc on an annual salary of £50,000. In addition Griff lets out two properties:

(1) qualifying furnished holiday accommodation which generates taxable income of £5,000 per annum, and

(2) a warehouse, let to a local business, which generates taxable income of £8,000 per annum.

In the tax year 2019/20 he made a £4,000 (gross) donation to a national charity under the gift aid scheme.

What are Griff's net relevant earnings for the tax year 2019/20?

A £51,000

B £63,000

C £59,000

D £55,000

67 Roger is employed on an annual salary of £145,000. His employer has an occupational pension scheme into which Roger pays 2% of his salary and the company pays 5% of his salary. Roger also made a payment of £20,000 into a personal pension scheme in the tax year 2019/20.

What is Roger's net income (before deducting the personal allowance) for the tax year 2019/20?

£ _____

68 Natalia's only income in the tax year 2019/20 is trading income of £100,000. She also has an annual allowance charge of £10,000 as a result of making gross personal pension contributions of £50,000 in the tax year 2019/20.

What is Natalia's income tax liability for the tax year 2019/20?

A £19,500

B £21,500

C £27,500

D £31,500

ADMINISTRATION AND ETHICS

69   Taxes can be either capital taxes or revenue taxes, although some taxes are neither type of tax.

Tick the appropriate boxes to show the correct classification for the following three taxes.

	Capital tax	**Revenue tax**	**Neither type**
Value added tax			
Inheritance tax			
National insurance contributions			
Capital gains tax			

70   *June 2015 OT question*

Which of the following statements correctly explains the difference between tax evasion and tax avoidance?

A   Both tax evasion and tax avoidance are illegal, but tax evasion involves providing HM Revenue and Customs with deliberately false information

B   Tax evasion is illegal, whereas tax avoidance involves the minimisation of tax liabilities by the use of any lawful means

C   Both tax evasion and tax avoidance are illegal, but tax avoidance involves providing HM Revenue and Customs with deliberately false information

D   Tax avoidance is illegal, whereas tax evasion involves the minimisation of tax liabilities by the use of any lawful means

71   **Tick the appropriate boxes to show whether the following statements about direct taxes are true or false.**

	True	**False**
Corporation tax is a direct tax on the turnover of companies		
National insurance is a direct tax suffered by employees, employers and the self-employed on earnings		
Inheritance tax is a direct tax on transfers of income by individuals		
Value added tax is a direct tax on the supply of goods and services by businesses		

72   **Which TWO of the following are true of tax evasion?**

A   Tax evasion means using the taxation regime to ones' own advantage by arranging your affairs to minimise your tax liability

B   Tax evasion includes not providing all relevant information to HMRC

C   Tax evasion is legal and does not involve misleading HMRC

D   Tax evasion utilises loopholes in tax legislation

E   Tax evasion encompasses any attempt to avoid or reduce tax by illegal means

F   Tax evasion includes utilising tax-free investments, such as ISAs

73   **Which of the following is true of a tax adviser?**

A   A tax adviser can only disclose information about the client to third parties with the clients' consent

B   A tax adviser must not assist a client to plan or commit any tax offences

C   If a tax adviser becomes aware that a client has committed a tax irregularity they must disclose it to HMRC

D   A tax adviser acting for a client has no duties and responsibilities towards HMRC

74   You are a trainee Chartered Certified Accountant and your firm has a client who has refused to disclose a chargeable gain to HM Revenue and Customs (HMRC).

Tick the appropriate boxes to show which of the following actions could be expected of your firm and which would be unacceptable.

	Could be expected	Unacceptable
Reporting under the money laundering regulations		
Advising the client to make disclosure		
Ceasing to act for the client		
Informing HMRC of the non-disclosure		
Warning the client that your firm will be reporting the non-disclosure		
Notifying HMRC that your firm has ceased to act for the client		

75   *December 2016 OT question*

Which of the following is the correct definition of an extra-statutory concession?

A   A provision for the relaxation of the strict application of the law where it would lead to anomalies or cause hardship

B   Supplementary information providing additional detail in relation to the general principles set out in legislation

C   HM Revenue and Customs' interpretation of tax legislation

D   Guidance provided to HM Revenue and Customs' staff in interpreting and applying tax legislation

76   For the tax year 2019/20, what are the latest dates by which a taxpayer, who does not wish to incur a penalty, should file a self-assessment tax return on paper or online?

Select the appropriate box from the table below.

		Paper tax return	
		31 October 2020	**31 October 2021**
Online tax return	**31 January 2021**	A	B
	31 January 2022	C	D

77   **Which of the following statements concerning self-assessment tax returns for individuals is true?**

A   Individuals with tax payable of less than £1,000 for a tax year are not required to file a tax return.

B   Individuals are only required to file a tax return for a tax year if they receive a notice to deliver from HM Revenue and Customs (HMRC).

C   All individuals who submit a tax return on time are able to have their tax payable calculated by HM Revenue and Customs (HMRC).

D   The tax return for an individual covers income tax, class 1, class 2 and class 4 national insurance contributions and capital gains tax liabilities.

78   Philip is a sole trader and is married to Harriet. Harriet is in employment. They jointly own a residential investment property which is rented out.

Select, by ticking the appropriate box, the latest date until which Philip and Harriet must keep the records which support their tax returns for the tax year 2019/20.

	Phillip	**Harriet**
31 January 2022		
31 January 2025		
31 January 2026		

79   *December 2016 OT question*

For what length of time after the end of the tax year for which a self-assessment tax return has been completed is a sole trader required to keep their accounting records?

A   12 months after the 31 January which follows the end of the tax year

B   12 months after the end of the tax year

C   60 months after the end of the tax year

D   60 months after the 31 January which follows the end of the tax year

80 For the tax year 2018/19, Willard filed a paper self-assessment tax return on 10 August 2019.

What is the deadline for Willard to make an amendment to his tax return for the tax year 2018/19, and by what date will HM Revenue and Customs (HMRC) have to notify Willard if they intend to carry out a compliance check into this return?

Select the appropriate box from the table below.

		Amendment	
		10 August 2020	**31 January 2021**
Compliance check	**10 August 2020**	A	B
	31 January 2021	C	D

81 *June 2015 OT question*

Abdul's tax liabilities for the tax years 2018/19 and 2019/20 are as follows:

	2018/19	2019/20
	£	£
Income tax payable	300	2,400
Class 4 national insurance contributions	320	1,260
Capital gains tax liability	240	0
	860	3,660

What payment on account will Abdul have to make on 31 July 2020 in respect of his tax liability for the tax year 2019/20?

A £310

B £1,830

C £430

D £0

82 Jeanette's income tax and capital gains tax liabilities for the tax year 2019/20 were £25,000 and £5,000 respectively. Of the £25,000 income tax liability, tax of £5,400 was deducted at source under PAYE. She made payments on account totalling £18,000 for the tax year 2019/20.

What is the balancing payment Jeanette should pay and when is it due? Select the appropriate box from the table below.

		Due date	
		31 January 2020	**31 January 2021**
Balancing payment	**£6,600**	A	B
	£16,400	C	D

83 *June 2015 OT question*

Quinn will not pay the balancing payment in respect of her tax liability for the tax year 2019/20 until 17 October 2021.

What is the total percentage penalty which Quinn will be charged by HM Revenue and Customs (HMRC) in respect of the late balancing payment for the tax year 2019/20?

A   15%

B   10%

C   5%

D   30%

84 Belinda paid the balancing payment of income tax of £7,400 for the tax year 2018/19 on 10 March 2020.

For each of the following statements select whether it is true or false:

	True	False
Belinda will have to pay interest on late paid tax from 31 January 2020 to 10 March 2020		
Belinda will have to pay a £100 fixed penalty because the payment is late		
Belinda will have to pay a 5% penalty because the payment is more than 30 days late		

85 *September 2016 OT question*

Eva's income tax liability and class 4 national insurance contributions (NIC) for the tax year 2019/20 are £4,840. Her income tax liability and class 4 NICs for the tax year 2018/19 were £6,360.

What is the lowest amount to which Eva could make a claim to reduce each of her payments on account for the tax year 2019/20 without being charged interest?

A   £4,840

B   £0

C   £3,180

D   £2,420

86 Florence filed her return for the tax year 2019/20, showing income tax payable of £6,500, 8 months late.

In addition to the initial £100 late filing penalty, what is the maximum further penalty that she can be charged for filing the tax return late?

£ [   ]

87 *September 2016 OT question*

Rajesh is a sole trader. He correctly calculated his self-assessment payments on account for the tax year 2019/20 and paid these on the due dates.

Rajesh paid the correct balancing payment of £1,200 for the tax year 2019/20 on 30 June 2021.

What penalties and interest may Rajesh be charged as a result of his late balancing payment for the tax year 2019/20?

A   Interest of £15 only

B   Interest of £36 only

C   Interest of £36 and a penalty of £60

D   Interest of £15 and a penalty of £60

88   Welan Ltd pays its employees monthly on the 15th of every month.

For each of the following statements select whether it is true or false:

	True	False
Under the Real Time Information PAYE system, Welan Ltd must submit income tax and NIC information in respect of the monthly salary payments to HM Revenue & Customs electronically by the 15th day of each month		
If Welan Ltd pays the income tax and NIC due on the monthly salary payments to HM Revenue & Customs electronically it must make the payment by the 22nd of the month following the month the salaries are paid		
Welan Ltd must provide each employee with a year-end summary form (P60) for the tax year 2019/20 by 6 July 2020		

PRACTICE SECTION B OBJECTIVE TEST CASES

INCOME TAX BASICS AND EMPLOYMENT INCOME

89   PHILIP & CHARLES (ADAPTED) *Walk in the footsteps of a top tutor*

Philip and Charles are father and son. The following information is available for the tax year 2019/20.

Philip Wind

Philip retired at the age of 55. During the tax year 2019/20 Philip received pension income of £15,000 and building society interest of £14,600.

Charles Wind

Charles is self-employed, and his tax adjusted trading profit for the year ended 31 December 2019 was £112,400.

During the tax year 2019/20 Charles made a gift aid donation of £800 (gross) to a national charity.

Charles has been a member of a registered personal pension scheme since May 2017. He made a gross contribution of £25,000 in the tax year 2017/18 but has not made any subsequent contributions.

1   **What is Philip's income tax liability for the tax year 2019/20?**

   A   £2,720

   B   £2,920

   C   £3,220

   D   £3,420

2   Charles is entitled to a personal allowance of £_____ for the tax year 2019/20.

   Select the appropriate answer from the options below.

   A   £12,500

   B   £6,700

   C   £6,800

   D   £5,800

3   What is the amount of class 4 national insurance liability in respect of Charles for the tax year 2019/20?

£ ☐

4   What was the total available annual allowance available to Charles for pension contribution purposes in the tax year 2019/20?

A   £95,000

B   £40,000

C   £135,000

D   £88,750

5   Charles had considered making payments of £6,880 into a personal pension scheme during the tax year 2019/20.

For each of the following statements select whether it would be true or false if he had made such a contribution:

.	True	False
His basic rate band for the tax year 2019/20 would have been increased by £8,600 in relation to this contribution		
His taxable income for the tax year 2019/20 would have been reduced by £8,600		
HM Revenue and Customs would have paid £1,376 into the pension fund on his behalf		
His personal allowance would have increased by £4,300 in the tax year 2019/20		

90   KIM BAXTER (ADAPTED) *Walk in the footsteps of a top tutor*

Kim is employed as a sales person by Sharp-Suit plc. During the tax year 2019/20 her employment package included the following benefits:

(1)   During the period from 1 June 2019 to 5 April 2020 Kim used her private motor car for business and private purposes. She received 36p for each business mile travelled from Sharp-Suit plc.

Kim's mileage during this period was as follows:

	Miles
Normal daily travel between home and permanent workplace	3,400
Travel between permanent workplace and Sharp-Suit plc's customers	9,200
Travel between home and a temporary workplace for one month	1,300

(2)   On 1 June 2019 Sharp-Suit plc provided Kim with a loan of £14,600, at an annual interest rate of 1%, so that she could purchase a new motor car.

(3)   On 6 April 2019 Kim purchased a television from Sharp-Suit plc for £50 when its market value was £200. The company had purchased the television for £800 on 6 April 2018 and Kim had used it at home since that date.

Kim's total employment income, including the above benefits/deductions, for the tax year 2019/20 was £25,650.

Other information

During the tax year 2019/20 Kim paid interest of £140 on a personal loan, taken out on 1 January 2019, to purchase a laptop computer for use in her employment with Sharp-Suit plc. She also paid a charitable contribution of £800 under the gift aid scheme. She had no other sources of income.

Kim's husband Richard stays at home to look after their children while Kim is at work. Richard's only income in the tax year 2019/20 was savings income of £11,700.

1   **What effect will the use of her car for business purposes have on Kim's taxable employment income in the tax year 2019/20? Select the appropriate box from the table below.**

		Effect on employment income	
		Allowable deduction	**Taxable benefit**
Amount	£845	A	B
	£945	C	D

2   **What is the taxable benefit in respect of the loan from Kim's employer for the tax year 2019/20?**

A   £219

B   £304

C   £122

D   £182

3   What is the taxable benefit in respect of the purchase of the television from Sharp-Suit plc in the tax year 2019/20?

£ ☐

4   What is the amount of Kim's taxable income for the tax year 2019/20?

A   £13,010

B   £13,150

C   £25,510

D   £25,650

5   Assuming that Kim and Richard make a marriage allowance election in respect of the tax year 2019/20, match the correct tax impact to each individual.

	Richard	Kim
Personal allowance reduced by £800		
Personal allowance reduced by £1,250		
Personal allowance increased by £800		
Personal allowance increased by £1,250		
Income tax liability reduced by £160		
Income tax liability reduced by £250		

INCOME TAX BASICS AND INCOME FROM SELF-EMPLOYMENT

91 FOO DEE (ADAPTED)

On 31 December 2019 Foo Dee resigned as an employee of Gastronomic Food plc and on 1 January 2020 Foo commenced self-employment running her own restaurant, preparing accounts to 30 September.

The following information is available for the tax year 2019/20:

Employment

During the period 6 April 2019 to 31 December 2019 Foo earned a salary of £38,000 and was provided with the following benefits:

(1)   A car with CO_2 emissions of 139g/km and a list price of £19,000. Foo was also provided with all diesel fuel for the car. The car does not meet the RDE2 standard.

(2)   Gastronomic Food plc paid Foo £6 per night to cover incidental expenses when she was working away in the UK for 14 nights.

(3)   The company contributed 6% of Foo's gross salary of £38,000 into Gastronomic-Food plc's HM Revenue & Customs' registered occupational pension scheme.

Self-employment

(1)   Foo's statement of profit or loss for her restaurant business for the nine-month period ended 30 September 2020 is as follows:

	£	£
Gross profit		202,054
Depreciation	3,500	
Legal fees (Note 2)	4,200	
Property expenses (Note 3)	12,800	
Other expenses (all allowable)	50,700	
		(71,200)
Net profit		130,854

(2)   Legal fees include conveyancing fees of £1,400 for the purchase of the restaurant.

(3)   Foo purchased her restaurant on 1 January 2020. She lives in a flat that is situated above the restaurant, and one quarter of the total property expenses of £12,800 relate to this flat.

(4)   On 30 September 2020 Foo purchased a motor car with CO_2 emissions of 105 grams per kilometre for £14,600. Private use of the car by Foo is 30%.

Foo never had to complete a tax return whilst she was employed by Gastronomic Food plc.

1   Which TWO of the following statements concerning the taxable benefits in respect of the company car for the tax year 2019/20 are correct?

A   Foo will have a car benefit of £4,417

B   Foo will have a car benefit of £4,987

C   Foo will have a car benefit of £6,650

D   Foo will have a fuel benefit of £5,603

E   Foo will have a fuel benefit of £6,326

F   Foo will have a fuel benefit of £8,435

2   How much is the total taxable benefit for the payment of the overnight expenses and the pension contribution by the company for the tax year 2019/20?

A   £0

B   £84

C   £14

D   £2,364

3   What is Foo's taxable trading profit before capital allowances for the nine-month period ended 30 September 2020?

£ [   ]

4   What is the maximum capital allowances claim that Foo can make in respect of the nine-month period ended 30 September 2020?

A   £1,380

B   £1,971

C   £1,840

D   £818

5   Foo has not previously been required to submit a tax return to HMRC.

By what date must Foo inform HMRC of her new source of self-employment income and what is the filing date for the first tax return that includes income from self-employment? Select the appropriate box from the table below.

| | | Inform HMRC of new source of income | |
		30 September 2020	5 October 2020
First tax return filing date	31 January 2021	A	B
	31 January 2022	C	D

PRACTICE SECTION C CONSTRUCTED RESPONSE QUESTIONS

INCOME TAX BASICS AND EMPLOYMENT INCOME

92   ARRAY LTD (ADAPTED) *Walk in the footsteps of a top tutor*

Array Ltd provides its employees with various benefits. The following benefits were all provided throughout the tax year 2019/20 unless otherwise stated.

Alice

Alice was provided with a petrol powered motor car which has a list price of £24,600. The motor car has an official CO_2 emissions rate of 108 grams per kilometre. Alice made a capital contribution of £5,600 towards the cost of the motor car when it was first provided to her by Array Ltd.

Alice was also provided with fuel for her private journeys. The total cost to Array Ltd of fuel for the motor car during the tax year 2019/20 was £1,500.

During the tax year 2019/20, Alice drove a total of 12,000 miles, of which 8,000 were for business journeys.

Buma

Buma was provided with a loan of £48,000 on 1 October 2017, which she used to renovate her main residence. Buma repays £1,000 of the capital of the loan to Array Ltd each month, and by 6 April 2019 the amount of the loan outstanding had been reduced to £30,000. In addition, Buma paid loan interest of £240 to Array Ltd during the tax year 2019/20.

The taxable benefit in respect of this loan is calculated using the average method.

Claude

On 6 July 2019, Claude was provided with a mobile telephone. The telephone is a smartphone which is mainly used by Claude for personal internet access. It was purchased by Array Ltd on 6 July 2019 for £600.

On 6 January 2020, Claude was provided with a home entertainment system for his personal use. This was purchased by Array Ltd on 6 January 2020 for £3,200. The market value of the home entertainment system on 5 April 2020 was £2,400.

Denise

During May 2019, Array Ltd paid £10,400 towards the cost of Denise's removal expenses when she permanently moved to take up her new employment with Array Ltd, as she did not live within a reasonable commuting distance. The £10,400 covered both her removal expenses and the legal costs of acquiring a new main residence.

During February 2020, Array Ltd paid for £340 of Denise's medical costs. She had been away from work for three months due to an injury, and the medical treatment (as recommended by a doctor) was to assist her return to work.

Required:

(a) State how employers are required to report details of employees' taxable benefits to HM Revenue and Customs following the end of the tax year, and the deadline for submitting this information for the tax year 2019/20. 🖥️ **(2 marks)**

Note: You should assume that the employer has not applied to collect tax on the benefits through PAYE.

(b) Calculate the taxable benefits which Array Ltd will have to report to HM Revenue and Customs in respect of each of its employees for the tax year 2019/20. ⊞

Note: Your answer should include an explanation for any benefits which are exempt or partially exempt. **(11 marks)**

(c) Calculate the class 1A national insurance contributions which Array Ltd would have had to pay in respect of its employees' taxable benefits for the tax year 2019/20, and state when this would have been due if paid electronically. ⊞ **(2 marks)**

(Total: 15 marks)

93 MARTIN (ADAPTED) *Walk in the footsteps of a top tutor*

Martin is employed by Global plc and he is also a member of a partnership. The following information is available in respect of the tax year 2019/20:

Employment

(1) During the tax year 2019/20, Martin was paid a gross annual salary of £144,000 in respect of his employment with Global plc.

(2) In addition to his salary, Martin was paid the following bonuses by Global plc:

Amount £	In respect of the six-month period ended	Date of payment	Date of entitlement
18,200	28 February 2019	31 March 2019	20 March 2019
21,400	31 August 2019	31 August 2019	20 September 2019
13,700	28 February 2020	30 April 2020	20 March 2020

(3) During the tax year 2019/20, Global plc provided Martin with the following petrol powered motor cars:

Period provided	List price £	CO_2 emission rate
6 April to 31 December 2019	16,400	113 grams per kilometre
1 January to 5 April 2020	36,400	26 grams per kilometre

Martin was not provided with any fuel for private use.

(4) On 6 April 2019, Global plc provided Martin with an interest free loan of £8,000 which he used to purchase a motor bike. No loan repayments were made during the year.

(5) Throughout the tax year 2019/20, Global plc allowed Martin private use of a home entertainment system owned by the company. The home entertainment system cost Global plc £7,400 on 6 April 2019.

(6)   During the tax year 2019/20, Martin donated a total of £1,000 (gross) to charity under the payroll deduction scheme operated by Global plc.

(7)   Martin paid an annual professional subscription of £560, which is relevant to his employment with Global plc. Martin also paid an annual membership fee of £1,240 to a health club, which he used to entertain Global plc's clients. Global plc did not reimburse Martin for either of these costs.

Partnership

(1)   Martin has been in partnership with Norma and Oprah since 1 January 2007. The partnership's trading profit for the year ended 31 December 2019 was £54,600.

(2)   Until 30 September 2019, profits were shared 40% to Martin, 30% to Norma and 30% to Oprah. Since 1 October 2019, profits have been shared equally.

Other income

(1)   During the tax year 2019/20, Martin rented out one furnished room of his main residence, receiving rent of £9,200 for the year. No additional expenditure was incurred as a result of the letting.

(2)   During the tax year 2019/20, Martin received dividends of £440.

(3)   On 30 November 2019, Martin received interest of £1,330 on the maturity of savings certificates from NS&I (National Savings and Investments).

Self-assessment tax return

Martin always files his self-assessment tax return online on 26 December, so his tax return for the tax year 2019/20 will be filed on 26 December 2020.

Because more than 80% of Martin's tax liability is paid under PAYE, he is not required to make self-assessment payments on account.

Required:

(a)   **Calculate Martin's taxable income for the tax year 2019/20.** ▦

        Note: You should indicate by the use of zero (0) any items which are not taxable or deductible.   **(11 marks)**

(b)   (i)   **Advise Martin of the deadline for making an amendment to his self-assessment tax return for the tax year 2019/20, and state how HM Revenue and Customs (HMRC) will calculate interest if such an amendment results in additional tax becoming payable.** ▭   **(2 marks)**

        (ii)   **State the latest date by which HMRC will have to notify Martin if they intend to carry out a compliance check in respect of his self-assessment tax return for the tax year 2019/20, and (assuming the check is not made on a completely random basis) the possible reasons why such a check would be made.** ▭   **(2 marks)**

                                                                                 (Total: 15 marks)

94 KAYA *Walk in the footsteps of a top tutor*

You should assume that today's date is 25 March 2020.

Kaya is the managing director of, and 100% shareholder in, Hopi Ltd. Hopi Ltd has no other employees.

For the year ended 5 April 2020, Hopi Ltd's tax adjusted trading profit, after taking account of director's remuneration and employer's class 1 national insurance contributions (NICs), is forecast to be £80,000. Hopi Ltd has already paid Kaya gross director's remuneration of £30,000 and dividends of £45,000 for the tax year 2019/20. Kaya does not have any other income. Based on these figures, the tax and NICs for Kaya and Hopi Ltd for the year ended 5 April 2020 will be:

	£
Kaya	
Income tax	12,975
Employee class 1 NICs	2,564
Hopi Ltd	
Employer class 1 NICs	2,949
Corporation tax	15,200

However, on 31 March 2020, Kaya is planning to pay herself a bonus of £25,000, but is unsure whether to take this as additional director's remuneration (the gross remuneration will be £25,000) or as an additional dividend.

Required:

Calculate the revised tax and NICs for Kaya and Hopi Ltd for the year ended 5 April 2020 if, on 31 March 2020, Kaya pays herself the bonus of £25,000 (1) as additional director's remuneration or (2) as an additional dividend. ▦

Notes:

1   **You are expected to calculate the revised income tax liability and NICs for Kaya and the revised corporation tax liability and NICs for Hopi Ltd under each of options (1) and (2).**

2   **You should assume that the rate of corporation tax remains unchanged**

(Total: 10 marks)

K 95   **PATIENCE (ADAPTED)** *Walk in the footsteps of a top tutor*

Patience retired on 31 December 2019, and on that date ceased employment and self-employment. The following information is available in respect of the tax year 2019/20:

Employment

(1)   Patience was employed by a private school as a teacher. From 6 April to 31 December 2019, she was paid a salary of £3,750 per month.

(2)   During the period 6 April to 31 December 2019, Patience contributed 6% of her monthly gross salary of £3,750 into her employer's HM Revenue and Customs' (HMRC's) registered occupational pension scheme. Patience's employer contributed a further 10% on her behalf.

(3)   During the period 6 April to 30 June 2019, Patience's granddaughter was provided with a free place at the private school run by Patience's employer. The normal fee payable would have been £4,600. The additional marginal expense of providing the place for the grandchild was £540.

(4)   On 25 June 2019, Patience was given a clock valued at £600 as an award for her 25 years of teaching at her employer's school. She has not previously received any similar awards.

(5)   Patience's employer provided her with an interest-free loan so that she could purchase a season ticket for the train to work. The balance of the loan outstanding at 6 April 2019 was £8,000, and Patience repaid the loan in full on 31 December 2019.

Self-employment

(1)   Patience was self-employed as a private tutor. Her trading profit for the year ended 31 July 2019 was £14,800. This figure is **after** taking account of capital allowances.

(2)   Patience's trading profit for the final five-month period of trading from 1 August to 31 December 2019 was £6,900. This figure is **before** taking account of capital allowances.

(3)   The tax written down value of the capital allowances main pool at 1 August 2019 was £2,200. On 10 August 2019, Patience purchased a laptop computer for £1,700.

On the cessation of trading, Patience personally retained the laptop computer. Its value on 31 December 2019 was £1,200. The remainder of the items included in the main pool were sold for £800 on 31 December 2019.

(4)   Patience has unused overlap profits brought forward of £3,700.

Personal pension contributions

During the period 6 April to 31 December 2019, Patience contributed a total of £3,600 (net) into a personal pension scheme.

Pension income

During the period 1 January to 5 April 2020, Patience received the state pension of £1,450, a pension of £6,000 from her employer's occupational pension scheme, and a private pension of £3,300. These were the total gross amounts received.

Property

Patience owned two residential properties which were let out unfurnished until both properties were sold on 31 December 2019. The following information is available in respect of the two properties:

	Property one £	Property two £
Rent received during the tax year 2019/20	3,600	7,200
Sale proceeds on 31 December 2019	122,000	98,000
Allowable revenue expenditure paid during the tax year 2019/20	(4,700)	(2,600)
Purchase cost	(81,400)	(103,700)

Patience has never occupied either of the two properties as her main residence.

Required:

Calculate Patience's income tax and capital gains tax liabilities for the tax year 2019/20. ▦

Notes:

1   You should indicate by the use of zero (0) any items which are not taxable or deductible.

2   The following mark allocation is provided as guidance for this question:

Income tax   **(13 marks)**

Capital gains tax   **(2 marks)**

                                                                                            (Total: 15 marks)

96   ALIMAG LTD *Walk in the footsteps of a top tutor*

You should assume that today's date is 15 March 2019.

You are a trainee chartered certified accountant dealing with the tax affairs of Gamila, who is the managing director of, and (currently) 100% shareholder in, Alimag Ltd.

For the year ended 5 April 2020, Alimag Ltd's taxable total profits, before taking account of director's remuneration, are forecast to be £180,000.

Original basis of profit extraction

Gamila originally intended to withdraw £125,000 of the profits as director's remuneration, and you have calculated that this approach would result in the following tax liabilities and national insurance contributions (NICs):

	£
Alimag Ltd	
Corporation tax for the year ended 5 April 2020	7,399
Class 1 employer NICs for the tax year 2019/20	16,059
Gamila	
Income tax for the tax year 2019/20	42,500
Class 1 employee NICs for the tax year 2019/20	6,464
	———
	72,422
	———

Revised basis of profit extraction

After a meeting with Gamila, a more beneficial approach to withdrawing £125,000 of profits from Alimag Ltd has been agreed for the tax year 2019/20:

(1)   Gamila will withdraw gross director's remuneration of £25,000.

(2)   Gamila's husband, Magnus, will become a 25% shareholder in Alimag Ltd.

(3)   Alimag Ltd will then pay dividends of £75,000 to Gamila and £25,000 to Magnus. Neither Gamila nor Magnus will have any other income for the tax year 2019/20.

Required:

Calculate the overall saving of taxes and NICs for the tax year 2019/20 if the revised basis of profit extraction is used instead of the original basis of profit extraction. ▦

Notes:

(1)   **You are expected to calculate the income tax payable by Gamila and Magnus, the class 1 NIC payable (if any) by Gamila, Magnus and Alimag Ltd, and the corporation tax liability of Alimag Ltd for the year ended 5 April 2020.**

(2)   **Alimag Ltd is not entitled to the NIC annual employment allowance.**

(3)   **You should assume that the rate of corporation tax remains unchanged.**

(Total: 10 marks)

97   DILL   *Walk in the footsteps of a top tutor*

Up to and including the tax year 2017/18, Dill was always resident in the United Kingdom (UK), being in the UK for more than 300 days each tax year. She was also resident in the UK for the tax year 2019/20. However, during the tax year 2018/19, Dill was overseas for 305 days, spending just 60 days in the UK. Dill has a house in the UK and stayed there on the 60 days which she spent in the UK. She also has a house overseas. For the tax year 2018/19, Dill did not have any close family in the UK, did not do any work in the UK and was not treated as working full-time overseas.

On 6 April 2019, Dill returned to the UK and commenced employment with Herb plc as the IT manager. She also set up a small technology business which she ran on a self-employed basis, but this business failed and Dill ceased self-employment on 5 April 2020. The following information is available for the tax year 2019/20:

Employment

(1)   During the tax year 2019/20, Dill was paid a gross annual salary of £270,000.

(2)   In addition to her salary, Dill has been paid the following bonuses by Herb plc:

Amount £	Date of payment	Date of entitlement	In respect of the four months ended
16,200	31 December 2019	1 November 2019	31 July 2019
29,300	30 April 2020	1 March 2020	30 November 2019

(3) Throughout the tax year 2019/20, Dill had the use of Herb plc's company gym which is only open to employees of the company. The cost to Herb plc of providing this benefit was £780.

(4) Throughout the tax year 2019/20, Herb plc provided Dill with a home entertainment system for her personal use. The home entertainment system cost Herb plc £5,900 on 6 April 2019.

(5) During the tax year 2019/20, Dill's three-year-old son was provided with a place at Herb plc's workplace nursery. The total cost to the company of providing this nursery place was £7,200 (240 days at £30 per day).

(6) On 1 June 2019, Herb plc provided Dill with an interest-free loan of £80,000 which she used to renovate her main residence. No loan repayments were made before 5 April 2020.

(7) On 25 January 2020, Herb plc paid a health club membership fee of £990 for the benefit of Dill.

(8) During the tax year 2019/20, Dill used her private motor car for both private and business journeys. The total mileage driven by Dill throughout the tax year was 16,000 miles, with all of this mileage reimbursed by Herb plc at the rate of 25p per mile. However, only 14,500 miles were in the performance of Dill's duties for Herb plc.

(9) During the tax year 2019/20, Dill paid an annual professional subscription of £560 which is relevant to her employment with Herb plc. She also paid an annual membership fee of £1,620 to a golf club which she uses to entertain Herb plc's suppliers. Herb plc did not reimburse Dill for either of these costs.

(10) During the tax year 2019/20, Dill contributed the maximum possible tax relievable amount into Herb plc's HM Revenue and Customs' (HMRC) registered money purchase occupational pension scheme. The company did not make any contributions on her behalf. Dill has never previously been a member of a pension scheme.

Self-employment

For the tax year 2019/20, Dill's self-employed business made a tax adjusted trading loss of £58,000. Dill will claim relief for this loss against her total income for the tax year 2019/20.

Other income

(1) On 1 November 2019, Dill received a premium bond prize of £1,000.

(2) On 28 February 2020, Dill received interest of £1,840 on the maturity of savings certificates from NS&I (National Savings and Investments).

Required:

(a) **Explain why Dill was treated as not resident in the United Kingdom for the tax year 2018/19.** 🖥 **(3 marks)**

(b) **Calculate Dill's taxable income for the tax year 2019/20.** ⊞

Note: You should indicate by the use of zero (0) any items which are not taxable or deductible. **(12 marks)**

(Total: 15 marks)

98   RICHARD TRYER (ADAPTED) *Walk in the footsteps of a top tutor*

Richard Tryer is employed by Prog plc as a computer programmer.

Richard has tried to prepare his own income tax computation for the tax year 2019/20, but he has found it more difficult than expected. Although the sections which Richard has completed are correct, there are a significant number of omissions. The omissions are marked as outstanding (O/S).

The partly completed income tax computation is as follows:

Richard Tryer

Income tax computation – 2019/20

	Notes	£	£
Employment income			
Salary		41,000	
Car benefit	1	O/S	
Fuel benefit	1	O/S	
Living accommodation	2	O/S	
		——	
			O/S
Property income	3		O/S
Building society interest			1,260
Dividends			5,800
			——
			O/S
Personal allowance			(12,500)
			——
Taxable income			O/S
			——

£		
37,500 at 20%		6,900
O/S at 40%		O/S
O/S at 0%		O/S
O/S at 40%		O/S
O/S at 0%		O/S
O/S at 32·5%		O/S
——		
O/S		
——		
Income tax liability		O/S
Less: PAYE		(19,130)
		——
Income tax payable		O/S
		——

Note 1 – Car and fuel benefits

Throughout the tax year 2019/20, Prog plc provided Richard with a petrol-powered motor car which has a list price of £17,900. The motor car cost Prog plc £17,200, and it has a CO_2 emission rate of 109 grams per kilometre. During the tax year 2019/20, Richard made contributions of £1,200 to Prog plc for the use of the motor car.

During the period 1 July 2019 to 5 April 2020, Prog plc also provided Richard with fuel for private journeys. The total cost of fuel during this period was £4,200, of which 45% was for private journeys. Richard did not make any contributions towards the cost of the fuel.

Note 2 – Living accommodation

Throughout the tax year 2019/20, Prog plc provided Richard with living accommodation. The property has been rented by Prog plc since 6 April 2019 at a cost of £1,100 per month. On 6 April 2019, the market value of the property was £122,000, and it has an annual value of £8,600.

On 6 April 2019, Prog plc purchased furniture for the property at a cost of £12,100. The company pays for the running costs relating to the property, and for the tax year 2019/20 these amounted to £3,700.

Note 3 – Property income

Richard owns a freehold shop, which is let out unfurnished. The shop was purchased by Richard on 1 October 2019. Richard spent £8,400 replacing the building's roof: the shop was not usable until this work was completed on 30 November 2019, and this fact was represented by a reduced purchase price.

On 1 December 2019, the property was let to a tenant, with Richard receiving a premium of £12,000 for the grant of a 30-year lease. The monthly rent is £664 payable in advance, and during the period 1 December 2019 to 5 April 2020 Richard received five rental payments.

Due to a fire, £8,600 was spent on repairing the ceiling of the shop during February 2020. Only £8,200 of this was paid for by Richard's property insurance.

Richard paid insurance of £480 in respect of the property. This was paid on 1 October 2019 and is for the year ended 30 September 2020.

Required:

Calculate the income tax payable by Richard Tryer for the tax year 2019/20. ▦ **(15 marks)**

99 **PETULA (ADAPTED)** *Walk in the footsteps of a top tutor*

Petula has been employed as a sales manager by Downtown plc since 6 April 2011. The following information is available in respect of the tax year 2019/20:

(1) During the tax year 2019/20, Petula was paid a gross annual salary of £230,000.

(2) In addition to her salary, Petula has been paid the following bonuses by Downtown plc:

Amount £	Date of payment	Date of entitlement	In respect of the six month period ended
21,200	30 April 2019	1 April 2019	31 December 2018
18,600	31 October 2019	1 October 2019	30 June 2019
22,400	30 April 2020	1 April 2020	31 December 2019

(3) During the tax year 2019/20, Petula used her private motor car for both private and business journeys. The total mileage driven by Petula throughout the tax year was 26,000 miles, with all of this mileage reimbursed by Downtown plc at the rate of 60p per mile. However, only 21,000 miles were in the performance of Petula's duties for Downtown plc.

(4)   Petula pays an annual professional subscription of £630 which is relevant to her employment with Downtown plc. Petula also pays an annual subscription membership fee of £1,840 to a golf club which she uses to entertain Downtown plc's clients. Downtown plc does not reimburse Petula for either of these costs.

(5)   During the tax year 2019/20, Petula paid interest of £140 on a personal loan taken out on 6 April 2018 to purchase a computer for sole use in her employment with Downtown plc.

(6)   Each tax year since 6 April 2011 (including the tax year 2019/20), Downtown plc has contributed £30,000 into the company's HM Revenue and Customs' registered money purchase occupational pension scheme on Petula's behalf. Petula has never personally made any pension contributions and her adjusted income in all tax years prior to 2019/20 never exceeded £150,000.

(7)   Petula owns a freehold house which was let out furnished throughout the tax year 2019/20 The total amount of rent received during the tax year was £12,000.

        During August 2019, Petula purchased a new washer-dryer for the property at a cost of £730. This was a replacement for an old washing machine which was scrapped, with nil proceeds. The cost of a similar washing machine would have been £420.

        During November 2019, Petula purchased a new dishwasher for the property at a cost of £580. The property did not previously have a dishwasher.

        The other expenditure on the property for the tax year 2019/20 amounted to £1,640, and all of this is allowable.

(8)   During the tax year 2019/20, Petula rented out one furnished room of her main residence. During the year, she received rent of £8,900 and incurred allowable expenditure of £2,890 in respect of the room. Petula always uses the most favourable basis as regards the tax treatment of the furnished room.

(9)   On 1 July 2019, Petula purchased £250,000 (nominal value) of gilts paying interest at the rate of 3% for £300,000. Interest is paid half-yearly on 30 June and 31 December based on the nominal value. Petula sold the gilts on 31 October 2019 for £302,500 (including accrued interest).

Required:

(a)   Calculate Petula's taxable income for the tax year 2019/20. ▦

Note: Your computation should list all of the items referred to in notes (1) to (9), indicating with the use of zero (0) any items which are not taxable or deductible.

(12 marks)

(b)   Advise Petula of the total amount of her unused pension annual allowances which are available to carry forward to the tax year 2020/21. 🖥   **(3 marks)**

(Total:15 marks)

INCOME TAX BASICS AND INCOME FROM SELF-EMPLOYMENT

100 CAROL COURIER (ADAPTED)

For the purposes of this question you should assume that today's date is 15 March 2019.

Carol Courier is employed by Quick-Speed plc as a delivery driver, and is paid a salary of £44,000 per year. She contributes 5% of her gross salary into Quick-Speed plc's HM Revenue & Customs registered occupational pension scheme.

As an alternative to being employed, Quick-Speed plc have offered Carol the opportunity to provide delivery services to the company on a self-employed basis.

The details of the proposed arrangement for the year ended 5 April 2020 are as follows:

(1) Carol will commence being self-employed on 6 April 2019.

(2) Her income from Quick-Speed plc is expected to be £47,000.

(3) Carol will also provide delivery services to other clients. Her income from these contracts is expected to be £13,000.

(4) Carol will lease a delivery van and 100% of the mileage will be for business purposes. The cost of leasing and running the van will be £4,400.

(5) When she is unavailable Carol will have to provide a replacement driver to deliver for Quick-Speed plc. This will cost her £2,800.

(6) Carol will contribute £3,000 (gross) into a personal pension scheme during the tax year 2019/20. This will provide her with the same benefits as the occupational pension scheme provided by Quick-Speed plc.

Required:

(a) **Assuming that Carol does not accept the offer from Quick-Speed plc and continues to be employed by the company, calculate her income tax and class 1 NIC liability for the tax year 2019/20.** (5 marks)

(b) **Assuming that Carol accepts the offer to provide delivery services to Quick-Speed plc on a self-employed basis from 6 April 2019 onwards, calculate her income tax, class 2 NIC and class 4 NIC liabilities for the tax year 2019/20.** (6 marks)

(c) **Advise Carol as to whether it will be beneficial to accept the offer to provide delivery services to Quick-Speed plc on a self-employed basis.**

Your answer should be supported by a calculation of the amount by which Carol's income for the tax year 2019/20 (net of outgoings, income tax and NIC) will increase or decrease if she accepts the offer. (4 marks)

(Total: 15 marks)

101 IDRIS WILLIAMS *Walk in the footsteps of a top tutor*

(a) Idris Williams has opened a small bed and breakfast and is considering whether to prepare his accounts to 5 April or 30 June.

Required:

Advise Idris of the advantages for tax purposes of choosing an accounting date of either 5 April or 30 June. 💻 **(4 marks)**

(b) Idris commenced trade on 6 April 2019 and has decided to prepare his first set of accounts to 5 April 2020.

The following information is available regarding his statement of profit or loss for the first year of trading:

	Notes	£	£
Revenue	(1)		49,910
Less: Food, utilities and other household goods	(2)		(17,660)
Gross profit			32,250
Expenses:			
Depreciation	(3)	1,250	
Motor expenses	(4)	9,340	
Other expenses	(5)	1,485	
			(12,075)
Net profit			20,175

Notes:

(1) Revenue includes £10,275 which is still receivable at 5 April 2020.

(2) Idris paid for 95% of his purchases of £17,660 by 5 April 2020 and the remainder in May 2019. There is no closing inventory at 5 April 2020.

Idris is living in part of the bed and breakfast and £4,500 of the purchases paid for during the period relate to Idris's personal use.

(3) The depreciation charge relates to furniture bought in the period for £3,500 and a motor car purchased on 6 April 2019 for £9,000. The motor car has CO_2 emissions of 105g/km.

(4) The motor expenses of £9,340 relate to Idris' car and in the period he drove 13,000 business miles and 20,000 miles in total.

(5) The other expenses are all allowable for tax purposes. £400 of these expenses was unpaid at 5 April 2020.

The cash basis private use adjustment for one occupant in a business premises for a 12 month period is £4,200.

Required:

(1)   Calculate Idris' tax adjusted trading profit for the year ended 5 April 2020, assuming he uses the normal accruals basis. ⊞   **(4 marks)**

(2)   State why Idris is entitled to use the cash basis and calculate Idris' tax adjusted trading profit for the year ended 5 April 2020, assuming he uses the cash basis. ⌨   **(6 marks)**

(3)   State which basis would be more beneficial for Idris for the tax year 2019/20. 💻   **(1 mark)**

(Total: 15 marks)

102 ETHEL *Walk in the footsteps of a top tutor*

Ethel Brown started to run a small bed and breakfast business as a sole trader on 6 April 2019. She prepared her first accounts for the year to 5 April 2020.

She has read about the cash basis of accounting and HMRC flat rate expense adjustments which are intended to simplify tax accounting for small businesses.

In the year to 5 April 2020 she has the following transactions:

(1)   Ethel earned income of £74,500 during the year. At 5 April 2020 £10,000 of the income was still outstanding.

(2)   Payments of £25,000 in respect of food, utilities and other household costs. She lives in part of the bed and breakfast premises with her husband and two children and 35% of the food, utilities and other household costs relate to their private use. The HMRC flat rate private use adjustment for four occupants of business premises is £7,800.

(3)   On 1 June 2019 Ethel paid a car dealer £14,000 by cheque for a car with CO_2 emissions of 105g/km. She also made payments totalling £3,000 related to the running costs of the car for the year. She has used the car 40% of the time for private purposes and she drove 11,000 business miles during the year.

(4)   On 1 March 2020 she acquired an item of kitchen equipment for £350 on credit terms. She paid the supplier's invoice on 15 April 2020.

Required:

(a)   Calculate Ethel's tax adjusted trading profit for the year ended 5 April 2020 assuming that she opts to prepare her accounts using the cash basis and the HMRC flat rate expense adjustments. Your answer should be supported with brief notes to explain how you have treated the transactions in Notes (1) to (4). ⊞

You should ignore VAT   **(6 marks)**

(b)   Calculate Ethel's tax adjusted trading profit for the year ended 5 April 2020 using the accruals basis. ⊞

You should ignore VAT   **(4 marks)**

(Total: 10 marks)

103 SAM WHITE (ADAPTED) *Walk in the footsteps of a top tutor*

(1) Sam is self-employed running a retail clothing shop. His statement of profit or loss for the year ended 5 April 2020 is as follows:

	Notes	£	£
Gross profit			190,300
Depreciation		7,600	
Motor expenses	2	8,800	
Patent royalties	3	700	
Professional fees	4	1,860	
Other expenses	5	71,340	
		———	(90,300)
Net profit			100,000

(2) During the year ended 5 April 2020 Sam drove a total of 25,000 miles, of which 5,000 miles were driven when he visited his suppliers in Europe. The balance of the mileage is 25% for private journeys and 75% for business journeys in the United Kingdom.

(3) During the year ended 5 April 2020 Sam paid patent royalties of £700 in respect of specialised technology that he uses when altering clothes for customers.

(4) The figure for professional fees consists of £1,050 for legal fees in connection with an action brought against a supplier for breach of contract and £810 for accountancy. Included in the figure for accountancy is £320 in respect of personal capital gains tax advice for the tax year 2019/20.

(5) The figure for other expenses of £71,340 includes £560 for gifts to customers of food hampers costing £35 each and £420 for gifts to customers of pens carrying an advertisement for the clothing shop costing £60 each.

(6) Sam uses one of the eight rooms of his home as an office. The total running costs of the house for the year ended 5 April 2020 were £5,120. This cost is not included in the expenses in the statement of profit or loss of £90,300.

(7) Sam uses his private telephone to make business telephone calls. The total cost of the private telephone for the year ended 5 April 2020 was £1,600, and 25% of this related to business telephone calls. The cost of the private telephone is not included in the expenses in the statement of profit or loss of £90,300.

(8) During the year ended 5 April 2020 Sam took goods out of the clothing shop for his personal use without paying for them and no entry has been made in the accounts to record this. The goods cost £820, and had a selling price of £1,480.

(9) The tax written down values for capital allowance purposes at 6 April 2019 were:

Main pool	£14,800
Motor car bought January 2018	£20,200

The motor car is used by Sam (see note 2) and has an official CO_2 emission rate of 190g/km.

Required:

Calculate Sam's tax adjusted trading profit for the year ended 5 April 2020. ⊞

Your computation should start with the net profit of £100,000 and should list all the items referred to in Notes (1) to (8), indicating with a zero (0) any items that do not require adjustment.

(10 marks)

✓ **104** **GEORGE (ADAPTED)** *Walk in the footsteps of a top tutor*

HIS CHORES
– Hours
– Integration
– Source of work
– control
– Holidays
– Obligation
– Risk/reward
– Equipment
– Substitutes

You should assume that today's date is 1 March 2019.

George, a software developer has accepted a one year contract to update software for Xpee plc.

(1)   The contract will run from 6 April 2019 to 5 April 2020, with a fee of £41,000 payable for the entire year of the contract. A condition of the contract is that George will have to do the work personally and not be permitted to sub-contract the work to anyone else.

(2)   George will work from home, but will have to attend weekly meetings at Xpee plc's offices to receive instructions regarding the work to be performed during the following week.

(3)   George will not incur any significant expenses in respect of the contract apart from the purchase of a new laptop computer for £3,600 on 6 April 2019. This laptop will be used 100% for business purposes.

(4)   During the term of the contract, George will not be permitted to work for any other clients. He will therefore not have any other income during the tax year 2019/20.

(5)   George's tax liability for the tax year 2018/19 was collected through PAYE, so he will not be required to make any payments on account in respect of the tax year 2019/20.

George has several friends who are also software developers. He understands that his employment status is not clear cut but that his income tax liability for the tax year 2019/20 will be the same regardless of whether he is treated as employed or as self-employed. However, George appreciates that there are advantages to being classed as self-employed.

Required:

(a)   **List FOUR factors which are indicators of George being treated as an employee in relation to his contract with Xpee plc rather than as self-employed.** 🖥

Note: You should confine your answer to the information given in the question.

(2 marks)

(b)   **Calculate George's income tax liability and national insurance contributions for the tax year 2019/20 if he is treated as self-employed in respect of his contract with Xpee plc.** ⊞ **(4 marks)**

(c)   **If George is treated as being an employee of Xpee plc instead of self-employed:**

(1)   **Explain why his income tax liability will be payable earlier.** 🖥 **(2 marks)**

(2)   **Calculate the additional amount of national insurance contributions which he personally will suffer for the tax year 2019/20.** ⊞ **(2 marks)**

(Total: 10 marks)

105 SOPHIA WONG (ADAPTED) *Walk in the footsteps of a top tutor*

You should assume that today's date is 15 March 2019.

(a) Sophia Wong has been self-employed as a lawyer for many years. For the year ended 5 April 2020 Sophia has forecast that her tax adjusted trading profit will be £80,000.

This will be her only income for the tax year 2019/20, and Sophia's total income tax liability and national insurance contributions (NIC) for this year if she continues to trade on a self-employed basis will be as follows:

	£
Income tax	19,500
Class 2 NIC	156
Class 4 NIC	4,323
	———
	23,979
	———

Sophia understands that she could save tax and NIC if she instead traded as a limited company, and she is therefore considering incorporating her business on 6 April 2019. The forecast taxable total profits of the new limited company for the year ended 5 April 2020 are unchanged at £80,000 (before taking account of any director's remuneration).

Required:

Assuming that Sophia Wong incorporates her business on 6 April 2019, advise her whether or not there will be an overall saving of tax and national insurance contributions (NIC) for the tax year 2019/20 if she withdraws all of the profits from the new company as:

(1) director's remuneration (after allowing for employer's class 1 NIC, gross director's remuneration will be £71,346) ▦, or (6 marks)

(2) dividends (after allowing for corporation tax, dividends will be £64,800). ▦
(5 marks)

Notes:

(1) For both alternatives, you are expected to calculate the corporation tax liability (if any) of the new limited company for the year ended 5 April 2020, the income tax liability of Sophia Wong, and the class 1 NIC (if any) payable by Sophia and the new company.

(2) You should assume that the rate of corporation tax remains unchanged.

(b) Since receiving your advice in (a) above Sophia has unexpectedly received a very generous offer to buy her business. This coincided with discussions she has been having with a major law firm who are interested in employing her.

She has therefore now decided not to incorporate her business but instead to sell it to an unconnected third party for £200,000, to be received in cash on 1 May 2019. The only chargeable asset of Sophia Wong's business is goodwill, the value of this asset has increased over a number of years to £150,000. The goodwill has a nil cost.

On 15 April 2019 Sophia sold a necklace realising a chargeable gain of £12,053.

Sophia will not make any other disposals during the tax year 2019/20. She will take a long holiday before starting her new job and her taxable income (after deduction of the personal allowance) for the tax year 2019/20 will be £20,000.

Required:

(1)   Calculate Sophia Wong's capital gains tax liability for the tax year 2019/20 assuming she sells her business on 1 May 2019 for £200,000 cash and she makes any beneficial elections. ⊞   (3 marks)

(2)   State the deadline(s) for making any elections you have identified as being beneficial. 💻   (1 mark)

                                                                                        (Total: 15 marks)

106   FERGUS   *Walk in the footsteps of a top tutor*

You should assume that today's date is 15 March 2019.

Fergus is currently self-employed, and if he continues to trade on a self-employed basis, his total income tax liability and national insurance contributions (NIC) for the tax year 2019/20 will be £32,379.

However, Fergus is considering incorporating his business on 6 April 2019. The forecast taxable total profits of the new limited company for the year ended 5 April 2019 are £100,000 (before taking account of any director's remuneration).

Fergus will pay himself gross director's remuneration of £20,000 and dividends of £40,000. The balance of the profits will remain undrawn within the new company.

Required:

Determine whether or not there will be an overall saving of tax and national insurance contributions (NIC) for the year ended 5 April 2020 if Fergus incorporates his business on 6 April 2019.

Notes:

(1)   **You are expected to calculate the income tax payable by Fergus, the class 1 NIC payable by Fergus and the new limited company, and the corporation tax liability of the new limited company for the year ended 5 April 2020.** ⊞

(2)   **You should assume that the rate of corporation tax remains unchanged. (10 marks)**

107   DEMBE (ADAPTED)

You should assume that today's date is 15 February 2020.

You are a trainee chartered certified accountant dealing with the tax affairs of Dembe and her husband Kato.

Personal pension contribution

Dembe is self-employed and her trading profit for the year ended 31 December 2019 is £130,000. She will not have any other income or outgoings for the tax year 2019/20.

Dembe is planning to make a personal pension contribution of £32,000 (net) before 5 April 2020, and would like to know the amount of income tax and national insurance contributions (NICs) which she will save as a result of making the pension contribution.

Sale of residential property

During March 2020, Dembe is going to sell a residential property and this will result in a chargeable gain of £67,000 if she makes the disposal.

Dembe wants to know whether it would be beneficial to transfer the property to Kato, her husband, as a no gain/no loss transfer prior to it being sold during March 2020. The transfer from Dembe to Kato will cost £2,000 in additional legal fees, and this cost will reduce the chargeable gain to £65,000 if the disposal is made by Kato.

Dembe has already made other disposals during the tax year 2019/20, which have utilised her annual exempt amount. Kato, however, has not yet made any disposals.

Kato's taxable income for the tax year 2019/20 is £21,150.

Inheritance tax

Dembe, who knows nothing about inheritance tax (IHT), is concerned about the amount of IHT which will be payable when she and Kato die. The couple's combined chargeable estate is valued at £880,000 for IHT purposes. The estate includes a main residence valued at £360,000.

Under the terms of their wills, Dembe and Kato have initially left their entire estates to each other. Then when the second of them dies, the total estate of £880,000 will be left to the couple's children.

The couple are not sure whether to change the terms of their wills so that assets worth £325,000 are left to their children when the first of them dies.

Neither Dembe nor Kato have made any lifetime gifts.

Required:

(a)   Calculate the reduction in Dembe's income tax liability and NICs for the tax year 2019/20 if she makes the personal pension contribution of £32,000 (net) before 5 April 2020. ⊞

Note: You are not expected to prepare full tax computations.   **(4 marks)**

(b)   Calculate the couple's overall saving for the tax year 2019/20, after taking account of the additional legal fees of £2,000, if the residential property is transferred to Kato and sold by him, rather than the property being sold by Dembe. ⊞   **(3 marks)**

(c)   Calculate the amount of IHT payable, if any, were Dembe and Kato to both die in the near future, and explain whether or not it might be beneficial to leave assets worth £325,000 to their children when the first of them dies. ⊞

Note: You should assume that the IHT rates and thresholds remain unchanged.

(3 marks)

(Total: 10 marks)

108 FANG, HONG AND KANG *Walk in the footsteps of a top tutor*

 Question debrief

(a) Fang commenced self-employment on 1 August 2017. She has a trading profit of £45,960 for the year ended 31 July 2018, and a trading profit of £39,360 for the year ended 31 July 2019.

Required:

(1) Calculate the amount of trading profit which will have been assessed on Fang for each of the tax years 2017/18 to 2019/20 (inclusive), and state the amount of any overlap profit. 🖾 **(3 marks)**

(2) Explain how Fang would have obtained relief for trading expenditure incurred prior to 1 August 2017 and for computer equipment which Fang already owned which was brought into business use on 1 August 2017. 💻 **(2 marks)**

(b) Hong has been in self-employment since 2008, preparing accounts to 5 April. For the year ended 5 April 2020 she made a trading loss of £45,800, and has claimed this against her total income and chargeable gain for the tax year 2018/19.

For the year ended 5 April 2019 Hong made a trading profit of £29,700. She also has property income of £3,900 for the tax year 2018/19. Hong has an unused trading loss of £2,600 brought forward from the tax year 2017/18.

During the tax year 2018/19 Hong disposed of an investment property and this resulted in a chargeable gain (before the annual exempt amount) of £17,800. Hong has unused capital losses of £6,200 brought forward from the tax year 2017/18.

Required:

After taking account of the loss relief claims made, calculate Hong's taxable income and taxable gain for the tax year 2018/19, and state the amount of any trading loss carried forward. 🖾

You should assume that the tax allowances for the tax year 2019/20 apply throughout. **(5 marks)**

(c) Kang, Ling and Ming have been in partnership since 2010, preparing accounts to 30 June. Ming left the partnership on 31 October 2018. Profits have always been shared equally.

The partnership had a trading profit of £148,800 for the year ended 30 June 2018, and a profit of £136,800 for the year ended 30 June 2019. Each partner has unused overlap profits brought forward of £29,400.

Required:

Calculate the trading income assessments of Kang, Ling and Ming for each of the tax years 2018/19 and 2019/20. **(5 marks)**

(Total: 15 marks)

 Calculate your allowed time and allocate the time to each separate part.

109 NA STYLE (ADAPTED) *Walk in the footsteps of a top tutor*

Na Style commenced self-employment as a hairdresser on 1 January 2017. She had tax adjusted trading profits as follows:

	£
Six months ended 30 June 2017	25,200
Year ended 30 June 2018	27,600
Year ended 30 June 2019	31,315

Other information

(1)   During the tax year 2019/20 Na received dividends of £5,200, building society interest of £700, interest of £310 from an individual savings account (ISA), interest of £1,100 on the maturity of a NS&I savings certificate, and interest of £370 from government stocks (gilts).

(2)   Na's payments on account of income tax in respect of the tax year 2019/20 totalled £3,200.

Required:

(a)   Calculate the amount of trading profit that will have been assessed on Na Style for the tax years 2016/17 to 2019/20 (inclusive), clearly identifying the amount of any overlap profits. **(6 marks)**

(b)   (1)   Calculate the income tax payable by Na Style for the tax year 2019/20. **(6 marks)**

(2)   Calculate Na Style's balancing payment for the tax year 2019/20 and her payments on account for the tax year 2020/21, stating the relevant due dates.

You should ignore national insurance contributions. **(3 marks)**

(Total: 15 marks)

110 ZHI (ADAPTED) *Walk in the footsteps of a top tutor*
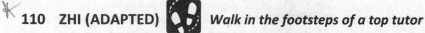

You should assume that today's date is 15 December 2019.

Zhi has been self-employed since 2003, preparing accounts to 31 December. On 1 December 2019, Zhi purchased a new freehold warehouse for £164,000 for use in his business, but this purchase has resulted in Zhi having cash flow problems. He has various tax payments becoming due over the next two months, and would like to reduce or postpone these payments as much as possible.

Income tax and national insurance contributions (NICs)

Zhi's income tax liabilities and class 4 NICs for the tax years 2017/18 to 2019/20 (inclusive) are, or are forecast to be:

	2017/18	2018/19	2019/20
	£	£	£
Income tax liability	25,200	27,600	18,000
Class 4 NICs	4,084	4,204	3,724

Zhi has not made any claims to reduce his payments on account.

Capital gains tax (CGT)

Zhi has a CGT liability of £12,860 becoming due for payment on 31 January 2020. This is in respect of a freehold office building which was sold for £210,000 on 10 December 2018, resulting in a chargeable gain of £76,000. The office building had always been used for business purposes by Zhi.

Zhi is a higher rate taxpayer. No claim has been made for rollover relief.

Value added tax (VAT)

Zhi has forecast that he will have to pay VAT of £20,200 on 7 February 2020 to HM Revenue and Customs (HMRC) in respect of the VAT quarter ended 31 December 2019.

On 12 December 2019, Zhi dispatched goods relating to an exceptionally large credit sale of standard rated goods of £45,600 (inclusive of VAT). He has not yet issued a sales invoice for this sale.

Because the customer is unlikely to pay until 28 February 2020, Zhi is considering not issuing a sales invoice until 1 February 2020.

PAYE and NICs

Zhi will have to pay PAYE and NICs of £5,594 electronically on 22 January 2020 to HMRC in respect of his two employees for the tax month running from 6 December 2019 to 5 January 2020.

This includes amounts for bonuses, which Zhi was planning to pay to his two employees on 1 January 2020, but he could delay payment until 10 January 2020. The bonuses are in respect of the year ended 31 December 2019, and they will be treated as being received on whichever is the date of payment.

The first employee has a gross annual salary of £20,000 and is to be paid a bonus of £1,500. The second employee has a gross annual salary of £55,000 and is to be paid a bonus of £5,000.

Required:

(a) Calculate the amount by which Zhi can claim to reduce his self-assessment income tax and NICs due for payment on 31 January 2020 without incurring interest or penalties. ⊞ **(2 marks)**

(b) Calculate the amount by which Zhi's CGT liability due for payment on 31 January 2020 will be reduced if he makes a claim for rollover relief based on the warehouse purchased on 1 December 2019 for £164,000. Assume that tax rates and allowances for the tax year 2019/20 apply throughout. ⊞ **(3 marks)**

(c)   Explain whether Zhi can reduce the amount of VAT payable on 7 February 2020 by not issuing a sales invoice for the credit sale of £45,600 until 1 February 2020, and, if so, by how much the payment will be reduced. 💻   **(2 marks)**

(d)   Calculate the amount by which Zhi's PAYE and NICs due on 22 January 2020 will be reduced if he delays the payment of employee bonuses until 10 January 2020, and state when the postponed amount will be payable. ▦

       Note: Your calculations should be based on annual income tax and NIC thresholds.
       (3 marks)

       (Total: 10 marks)

111   TIM BURR (ADAPTED) *Walk in the footsteps of a top tutor*

Tim Burr is a self-employed tree surgeon. His business has grown rapidly over the last few years and Tim is struggling to keep up with his workload.

On 1 December 2019, he is planning to bring a newly qualified tree surgeon, Hazel Grove into his business. Hazel will either be taken on as an employee, being paid a gross monthly salary of £3,300, or join Tim as a partner, receiving a 20% share of the new partnership's profits.

Tim has forecast that his tax adjusted trading profit will be £216,000 for the year ended 30 September 2020, and £240,000 for the year ended 30 September 2021.

Hazel does not have any other income for the tax year 2019/20.

Required:

(a)   Assuming that Hazel Grove is employed from 1 December 2019, calculate the total amount of national insurance contributions that will be paid by Tim Burr and Hazel Grove, if any, in respect of her earnings for the tax year 2019/20.

       You are not expected to calculate the national insurance contributions that will be paid in respect of Tim Burr's earnings. ▦   **(4 marks)**

(b)   Assuming that Hazel Grove becomes a partner from 1 December 2019:

       (1)   Calculate her trading income assessments for the tax years 2019/20 and 2020/21. ▦

              You are not expected to calculate any overlap profits.   **(4 marks)**

       (2)   Calculate the total amount of national insurance contributions that will be paid by Tim Burr and Hazel Grove, if any, in respect of her trading income assessment for the tax year 2019/20. ▦

              You are not expected to calculate the national insurance contributions that will be paid in respect of Tim Burr's trading income assessment.   **(2 marks)**

              (Total: 10 marks)

112 RICHARD FEAST (ADAPTED) *Walk in the footsteps of a top tutor*

(a)   On 6 April 2019, Richard Feast commenced in self-employment, running a restaurant. Richard's statement of profit or loss for the year ended 5 April 2020 is as follows:

	Notes	£	£
Gross profit			73,440
Expenses			
Motor expenses	1	7,660	
Property expenses	2	16,200	
Repairs and renewals	3	6,420	
Other expenses	4	10,960	
			(41,240)
Net profit			32,200

Note 1 – Motor expenses

	£
Cost of running Richard's motor car	4,710
Cost of running a motor car used by the restaurant's chef	2,670
Parking fines incurred by Richard	280
	7,660

Richard's motor car is used 70% for private journeys, and the chef's motor car is used 20% for private journeys.

Note 2 – Property expenses

Richard lives in an apartment which is situated above the restaurant, and one-fifth of the total property expenses of £16,200 relate to this apartment.

Note 3 – Repairs and renewals

	£
Decorating the restaurant	5,100
Decorating the apartment	1,320
	6,420

The property was in a usable state when it was purchased.

Note 4 – Other expenses

The figure of £10,960 for other expenses includes legal fees of £2,590 in connection with the purchase of the restaurant property. The remaining expenses are all allowable.

Additional information: Plant and machinery

The following motor cars were purchased during the year ended 5 April 2020:

	Date of purchase	Cost £	CO_2 emission rate
Motor car (1)	6 April 2019	14,000	109 grams per kilometre
Motor car (2)	6 April 2019	16,800	103 grams per kilometre

Motor car (1) is used by Richard, and motor car (2) is used by the restaurant's chef.

Required:

Calculate Richard Feast's tax adjusted trading profit for the year ended 5 April 2020. ⊞

Notes:

(1) **Your computation should commence with the net profit figure of £32,200, and should list all of the items referred to in Notes (1) to (4), indicating by the use of zero (0) any items which do not require adjustment.**

(2) **In answering this part of the question you are not expected to take account of any of the information provided in parts (b) or (c) below.**　　　　**(7 marks)**

(b) Richard's only employee is a chef who is employed throughout the tax year 2019/20 on a gross annual salary of £46,000. The chef was provided with a petrol powered motor car (see the plant and machinery information in part (a) above) throughout the tax year. The list price of the motor car is the same as its cost. Richard did not provide any fuel for private journeys.

Required:

Calculate the employer's class 1 and class 1A national insurance contributions which Richard Feast would have incurred in respect of the chef's earnings and benefit for the tax year 2019/20. ⊞

You are not expected to calculate the national insurance contributions suffered by the employee or by Richard in respect of his self-employment.　　　　**(3 marks)**

(c) Richard has not previously filed a self-assessment tax return, and therefore wants to know when he will have to file his return for the tax year 2019/20. He is not sure whether to file a paper tax return or to file the return online.

As this will be his first self-assessment tax return, Richard is concerned that HM Revenue and Customs might carry out a compliance check.

Required:

(1) **Advise Richard Feast of the latest dates by which his self-assessment tax return for the tax year 2019/20 should be filed in order to avoid a penalty.** ⌨
　　　　(2 marks)

(2) **State the period during which HM Revenue and Customs will have to notify Richard Feast if they intend to carry out a compliance check in respect of his self-assessment tax return for the tax year 2019/20, and the possible reasons why such a check would be made.** ⌨

You should assume that Richard will file his tax return by the filing date.
　　　　(3 marks)

　　　　(Total: 15 marks)

113 TONIE (ADAPTED)

Up to and including the tax year 2017/18, Tonie was resident in the UK for tax purposes, spending more than 300 days in the UK each year. Tonie understands that for the tax year 2019/20, she will again automatically be treated as resident in the UK, but is unsure of her residence status for the tax year 2018/19. For this tax year, Tonie was neither automatically resident in the UK nor automatically not resident. Throughout the tax year 2018/19, Tonie was travelling around the world and did not stay in any one country for longer than 30 days, although she did spend a total of 50 days in the UK. Tonie has a house in the UK, but it was let out throughout the tax year 2018/19. She is single, has no children, and stayed with a friend on the 50 days that she spent in the UK. Tonie did not do any substantive work in the UK during the tax year 2018/19.

The following information is available for the tax year 2019/20:

Employment

On 6 April 2019, Tonie, who is a software developer, accepted a one-year contract to maintain websites for Droid plc. Droid plc treated the contract as one of employment, with the payments to Tonie being subject to PAYE. However, Tonie thought that, because she was working from home, her employment status should instead have been one of self-employment.

(1)   For the term of the contract, from 6 April 2019 to 5 April 2020, Tonie was paid a fixed gross amount of £6,200 a month. During the term of the contract, Tonie was not permitted to work for any other clients. She was required to do the work personally, not being permitted to sub-contract the work to anyone else.

(2)   During the term of the contract, Tonie worked from home, but had to attend weekly meetings at Droid plc's offices to receive instructions regarding the work to be performed during the following week. During the period 6 April 2019 to 5 April 2020, Tonie used her private motor car for business visits to Droid plc's clients. She drove 2,300 miles, for which Droid plc paid an allowance of 60 pence per mile.

(3)   During the term of the contract, Tonie leased computer equipment at a cost of £180 a month. This was used 100% for business purposes.

Property income

(1)   Tonie owns a freehold house which is let out (this is not a furnished holiday letting). The total amount of rent received during the tax year 2019/20 was £10,080.

(2)   Tonie partly financed the purchase of the property with a repayment mortgage, paying mortgage interest of £4,200 during the tax year 2019/20.

(3)   During May 2019, Tonie purchased a new washer-dryer for the property at a cost of £640. This was a replacement for an old washing machine which was scrapped, with nil proceeds. The cost of a similar washing machine would have been £380.

(4)   During November 2019, Tonie purchased a new dishwasher for the property at a cost of £560. The property did not previously have a dishwasher.

(5)   The other expenditure on the property for the tax year 2019/20 amounted to £1,110, and this is all allowable.

(6)   During the tax year 2019/20, Tonie rented out one furnished room of her main residence. During the year, she received rent of £8,580 and incurred allowable expenditure of £870 in respect of the room. Tonie always uses the most favourable basis as regards the tax treatment of the furnished room.

Other income

(1)   On 1 July 2019, Tonie inherited £100,000 (nominal value) of gilts paying interest at the rate of 3%. The inheritance was valued at £120,000. Interest is paid half-yearly on 30 June and 31 December based on the nominal value. Tonie sold the gilts on 30 November 2019 for £121,250 (including accrued interest).

(2)   On 31 January 2020, Tonie received a premium bond prize of £100.

(3)   On 31 March 2020, Tonie received interest of £520 on the maturity of savings certificates from NS&I (National Savings and Investments).

Required:

(a)   Explain why Tonie was treated as not resident in the UK for the tax year 2018/19. 🖳   **(2 marks)**

(b)   List FOUR factors which are indicators of Tonie being treated as employed in relation to her contract with Droid plc rather than as self-employed. 🖳

Note: You should confine your answer to the information given in the question.

(2 marks)

(c)   On the basis that Tonie is treated as employed in relation to her contract with Droid plc, calculate her taxable income for the tax year 2019/20. ▦

Note: You should indicate by the use of zero (0) any items which are not taxable or deductible.   **(11 marks)**

(Total: 15 marks)

 **114   DANH**   *Walk in the footsteps of a top tutor*

Up to and including the tax year 2016/17, Danh was always automatically treated as not resident in the UK, spending fewer than 46 days in the UK each year. He is unsure of his residence status for the tax years 2017/18 and 2018/19. For these two tax years, Danh was neither automatically not resident in the UK nor automatically resident, having spent 100 days in the UK, with the remainder of each tax year spent in the same overseas country. Throughout both tax years Danh had a property in the UK and stayed there on the 100 days which he spent in the UK. Danh also did substantive work in the UK during both tax years. He does not have any close family in the UK.

Danh knows that for the tax year 2019/20, he will automatically be treated as resident in the UK. The following information is available for the tax year 2019/20:

Self-employment

(1) On 6 August 2019, Danh commenced self-employment as a sole trader. Danh's statement of profit or loss for the eight-month period ended 5 April 2020 is:

	Note	£
Income		96,400
Expenses		
Depreciation		(2,300)
Motor expenses	2	(3,300)
Professional fees	3	(1,800)
Other expenses (all allowable)		(18,800)
		———
Net profit		70,200

(2) During the eight-month period ended 5 April 2020, Danh drove a total of 12,000 miles, of which 4,000 were for private journeys.

(3) The figure for professional fees consists of £340 for accountancy and £1,460 for legal fees in connection with the grant of a new five-year lease for business premises.

(4) Danh runs his business using one of the six rooms in his private house as an office. The total running costs of the house for the eight-month period ended 5 April 2020 were £4,200. No deduction has been made for the cost of using the office in calculating the net profit of £70,200.

(5) The only item of plant and machinery owned by Danh is his motor car. This was purchased on 6 August 2019 for £14,800, and has a CO_2 emission rate of 110 grams per kilometre.

Partnership loss

(1) On 6 September 2019, Danh joined an existing partnership run by Ebele and Fai. For the year ended 5 April 2020, the partnership made a tax-adjusted trading loss of £12,600. Until 5 September 2019, profits and losses were shared 60% to Ebele and 40% to Fai. Since 6 September 2019, profits and losses have been shared 20% to Danh, 50% to Ebele and 30% to Fai.

(2) Danh will claim to relieve his share of the partnership's loss against his total income for the tax year 2019/20.

(3) During the tax year 2019/20, Danh paid interest of £875 (gross) on a personal loan taken out to purchase his share in the partnership.

Property income

(1) On 6 April 2019, Danh purchased a freehold house which was then let out. The total amount of rent received during the tax year 2019/20 was £14,400.

(2) Danh partly financed the purchase of the property with a repayment mortgage, paying mortgage interest of £5,000 during the tax year 2019/20.

(3) The other expenditure on the property paid during the tax year 2019/20 amounted to £1,480, and this is all allowable.

Required:

(a)   Explain whether Danh was treated as resident or not resident in the UK for each of the tax years 2017/18 and 2018/19. 🖥   **(3 marks)**

(b)   Calculate Danh's income tax liability for the tax year 2019/20. ⊞

Note: When calculating Danh's trading profit from self-employment for the eight-month period ended 5 April 2020, your computation should commence with the net profit figure of £70,200, indicating by the use of zero (0) any items which do not require adjustment.   **(12 marks)**

(Total: 15 marks)

TRADING LOSSES

115   NORMA (ADAPTED)

Norma, who had been in business as a confectioner since 1 May 2015, disposed of the business and retired on 31 May 2019. She does not intend to start any other business, but will be employed part time from 1 June 2019 on an annual salary of £11,400.

Her trading profits/(losses), as adjusted for taxation were:

	£	
Period ended 31 December 2015	21,000	Profit
Year ended 31 December 2016	27,000	Profit
Year ended 31 December 2017	16,900	Profit
Year ended 31 December 2018	9,835	Profit
Period ended 31 May 2019	(11,000)	Loss

Norma has received bank interest of £3,250 each year since April 2015. In addition, she realised a taxable gain (i.e. after the annual exempt amount), of £38,000 in June 2018.

The taxable gain does not qualify for entrepreneurs' relief and it is not in relation to residential property.

Required:

(a)   Calculate Norma's taxable income and gains for each tax year that she was in business before any relief for the loss arising in the period ended 31 May 2019. ⊞

(b)   Explain the options available to Norma to utilise the loss and explain the effect on her tax liability of the loss relief claims identified. 🖥

Assume that the tax rules, rates and allowances for the tax year 2019/20 apply throughout.   **(15 marks)**

116 ASHURA (ADAPTED) *Walk in the footsteps of a top tutor*

Ashura has been employed by Rift plc since 1 January 2016. She has also been self-employed since 1 July 2019, preparing her first accounts for the nine month period ended 5 April 2020. The following information is available for the tax year 2019/20:

Employment

(1)   During the tax year 2019/20, Ashura was paid a gross annual salary of £56,200, from which she paid 5% into Rift plc's HMRC registered occupational pension scheme.

(2)   On 1 January 2020, Ashura personally paid two subscriptions. The first was a professional subscription of £320 paid to an HM Revenue and Customs' (HMRC's) approved professional body. The second was a subscription of £680 to a health club which Ashura regularly uses to meet Rift plc's clients. Ashura was not reimbursed for the costs of either of these subscriptions by Rift plc.

(3)   During the tax year 2019/20, Ashura contributed £3,400 (gross) into a personal pension scheme.

(4)   During the tax year 2019/20, Ashura used her private motor car for business purposes. She drove 3,400 miles in the performance of her duties for Rift plc, for which the company paid an allowance of 55 pence per mile.

Self-employment

(1)   Ashura's tax adjusted trading loss based on her draft accounts for the nine month period ended 5 April 2020 is £1,996. However, this figure is before making any adjustments required for the cost of Ashura's office (note (2)), capital allowances (note (3)) and advertising (note (4)).

(2)   Ashura runs her business using one of the five rooms in her private house as an office. The total running costs of the house for the nine month period ended 5 April 2020 was £4,350. No deduction has been made for the cost of the office in calculating the profit of £10,198.

(3)   On 10 June 2019, Ashura purchased a laptop computer for use in her trade for £2,600. On 1 July 2019, Ashura purchased a motor car for £19,200. The motor car has a CO_2 emission rate of 137 grams per kilometre. During the nine month period ended 5 April 2020, Ashura drove a total of 8,000 miles, of which 2,400 were for self-employed business journeys.

(4)   Ashura incurred advertising expenditure of £800 in January 2019. The expenditure has not been deducted in calculating the loss of £1,996.

Other information

Ashura's total income for the previous four tax years is as follows:

Tax year	Total income
	£
2015/16	10,700
2016/17	10,400
2017/18	48,800
2018/19	54,300

Required:

(a) State TWO advantages for Ashura of choosing 5 April as her accounting date rather than a date early in the tax year such as 30 April.   **(2 marks)**

(b) Calculate Ashura's tax adjusted trading loss for the nine month period ended 5 April 2020. ⊞ **(6 marks)**

(c) Explain why it would not be beneficial for Ashura to claim loss relief under the provisions giving relief to a loss incurred in the early years of trade. 💻

Note: You should assume that the tax rates and allowances for the tax year 2019/20 also applied in all previous tax years. **(2 marks)**

(d) Assuming that Ashura claims loss relief against her total income for the tax year 2019/20, calculate her taxable income for this tax year. ⊞ **(5 marks)**

(Total: 15 marks)

117 DEE ZYNE (ADAPTED) *Walk in the footsteps of a top tutor*

On 5 July 2019 Dee Zyne resigned as an employee of Trendy-Wear plc. The company had employed her as a fashion designer since 2009. On 6 July 2019 Dee commenced self-employment running her own clothing business, preparing accounts to 5 April.

The following information is available for the tax year 2019/20:

Self-employment

(1) Dee's tax adjusted trading loss for the period 6 July 2019 to 5 April 2020 was £11,653. This figure is before taking account of the information in Note (2) and capital allowances.

(2) During the period 6 July 2019 to 5 April 2020 Dee paid patent royalties of £500 in respect of specialised technology that she uses in her clothing business.

(3) Dee purchased the following assets during the period ended 5 April 2020:

		£
10 July 2019	Computer	1,257
16 August 2019	Office furniture	2,175
13 November 2019	Motor car (1)	10,400
21 January 2020	Motor car (2)	17,800

Motor car (1) purchased on 13 November 2019 has CO_2 emissions of 105 grams per kilometre, is used by an employee, and 15% of the mileage is for private purposes.

Motor car (2) purchased on 21 January 2020 has CO_2 emissions of 135 grams per kilometre, is used by Dee, and 20% of the mileage is for private purposes.

Other information

(1) Dee's employment income for the period 6 April 2019 to 5 July 2019 was £29,875.

(2) Dee's total income for each of the tax years 2013/14 to 2018/19 was £80,000.

Required:

(a) Calculate Dee's tax adjusted trading loss for the tax year 2019/20. **(6 marks)**

(b) Describe the ways in which Dee could have relieved her trading loss for the tax year 2019/20 against total income, and explain which of these claims would have been most beneficial.

You should assume that the tax rates for the tax year 2019/20 apply throughout.

(4 marks)

(Total: 10 marks)

118 SAMANTHA FABRIQUE (ADAPTED) *Walk in the footsteps of a top tutor*

Samantha Fabrique has been a self-employed manufacturer of clothing since 2008. She has the following income and chargeable gains for the tax years 2018/19 to 2020/21:

	2018/19	2019/20	2020/21 (estimated)
	£	£	£
Trading profit/(loss)	21,600	(81,900)	11,650
Building society interest	52,100	3,800	1,850
Chargeable gains/(loss)	53,300	(3,400)	12,200

The chargeable gains do not qualify for entrepreneurs' relief and are not in relation to residential property.

Required:

(a) State the factors that will influence an individual's choice of loss relief claims.

(3 marks)

(b) Calculate Samantha's taxable income and taxable gains for each of the tax years 2018/19 to 2020/21 (inclusive) on the assumption that she relieves the trading loss of £81,900 for the tax year 2019/20 on the most favourable basis.

Explain your reasoning behind relieving the loss on the most favourable basis.

You should assume that the tax allowances for the tax year 2019/20 apply throughout.

(12 marks)

(Total: 15 marks)

119 MICHAEL AND SEAN *Walk in the footsteps of a top tutor*

(a) The UK Government uses tax policies to encourage certain types of activity.

Required:

Briefly explain how the UK Government's tax policies encourage:

(1) Individuals to save, **(1 mark)**

(2) Individuals to support charities, **(1 mark)**

(3) Entrepreneurs to build their own businesses and to invest in plant and machinery. **(2 marks)**

(b) You are a trainee chartered certified accountant and your manager has asked for your help regarding two taxpayers who have both made trading losses.

Michael

Michael commenced in self-employment on 1 July 2018, preparing accounts to 5 April. His results for the first two periods of trading were as follows:

		£
Nine month period ended 5 April 2019	– Trading loss	(24,600)
Year ended 5 April 2020	– Trading profit	7,100

For tax years 2014/15 to 2016/17, Michael had the following employment income:

	£
2014/15	44,500
2015/16	17,200
2016/17	51,000

Michael did not have any income during the period 6 April 2017 to 30 June 2018.

Sean

Sean has been in self-employment since 2009, but ceased trading on 31 December 2019. He has always prepared accounts to 31 December. His results for the final five years of trading were as follows:

	£
Year ended 31 December 2015 – Trading profit	21,300
Year ended 31 December 2016 – Trading profit	14,400
Year ended 31 December 2017 – Trading profit	18,900
Year ended 31 December 2018 – Trading profit	3,700
Year ended 31 December 2019 – Trading loss	(23,100)

For each of the tax years 2015/16 to 2019/20 (inclusive) Sean has property business profits of £12,500. Sean has unused overlap profits brought forward of £3,600.

Required:

For each of the two taxpayers Michael and Sean, identify the loss relief claims that are available to them, and explain which of the available claims would be the most beneficial. 📖

Notes:

(1) **You should clearly state the amount of any reliefs claimed and the rates of income tax saved. However, you are not expected to calculate any income tax liabilities.**

(2) **You should assume that the tax rates and allowances for the tax year 2019/20 apply throughout.**

The following mark allocation is provided as guidance for this requirement:

Michael	**(5 marks)**
Sean	**(6 marks)**
	(Total: 15 marks)

PARTNERSHIPS

120 PETER, QUINTON AND ROGER (ADAPTED) *Walk in the footsteps of a top tutor*

Peter and Quinton commenced in partnership on 1 January 2017. Roger joined as a partner on 1 January 2018, and Peter resigned as a partner on 31 December 2019. Profits and losses have always been shared equally.

The partnership's tax adjusted profits and losses are as follows:

	£	
Year ended 31 December 2017	40,000	Profit
Year ended 31 December 2018	90,000	Profit
Year ended 31 December 2019	(30,000)	Loss

All of the partners were in employment prior to becoming partners, and each of them has investment income. None of the partners has any capital gains.

Required:

(a) **Briefly explain the basis by which trading profits are assessed on partners when they join a partnership.** 🖥 **(2 marks)**

(b) **Calculate the trading income assessments of Peter, Quinton and Roger for the tax years 2016/17 to 2018/19 (inclusive).** ▦ **(6 marks)**

(c) **State the possible ways in which Peter, Quinton and Roger can relieve their share of the trading loss for the tax year 2019/20.** 🖥

Your answer should include a calculation of the amount of loss available for relief to each partner. **(7 marks)**

(Total: 15 marks)

121 AE, BEE, CAE, AND DEE (ADAPTED) *Walk in the footsteps of a top tutor*

(a) Ae and Bee commenced in partnership on 1 July 2017 preparing accounts to 30 June. Cae joined as a partner on 1 July 2019. Profits have always been shared equally.

The partnership's tax adjusted trading profits since the commencement of trading have been:

	£
Year ended 30 June 2018	54,000
Year ended 30 June 2019	66,000
Year ended 30 June 2020	87,000

Required:

Calculate the trading income assessments of Ae, Bee and Cae for each of the tax years 2017/18 to 2019/20 (inclusive). ▦ **(5 marks)**

(b) Dee has been self-employed for many years. The business has been loss making for the last two years. In the year ended 5 April 2021 she is planning to bring her sister, Eae, into the business as a partner, in an attempt to turn the business around. She anticipates that the business will make a small loss in the year ended 5 April 2021, but will make growing profits going forward.

Dee's losses have been as follows:

	£
Year ended 5 April 2019	5,000
Year ended 5 April 2020	165,000

Dee has savings income of £85,000 each year.

Required:

(1) **Explain how the loss in the year ended 5 April 2020 can be relieved, assuming Dee always claims relief for her losses as soon as possible.** 🖳 **(3 marks)**

(2) **Explain the claims available to Eae to obtain relief for her share of any trading losses in the year ended 5 April 2021.** 🖳 **(2 marks)**

(Total: 10 marks)

122 AUY MAN AND BIM MEN (ADAPTED) *Walk in the footsteps of a top tutor*

Auy Man and Bim Men have been in partnership since 6 April 2009 as management consultants. The following information is available for the tax year 2019/20:

Personal information

Auy spent 190 days in the United Kingdom (UK) during the tax year 2019/20. Auy was resident in the UK during the tax year 2018/19.

Bim spent 100 days in the UK during the tax year 2019/20 living in her holiday home in Devon. Bim also spent 100 days in the UK in each of the previous five tax years, and was treated as resident in the UK during each of the previous three years.

Statement of profit or loss for the year ended 5 April 2020

The partnership's summarised statement of profit or loss for the year ended 5 April 2020 is:

	Notes	£	£
Sales			143,880
Expenses:			
Depreciation		3,400	
Other expenses	1	1,800	
Wages and salaries	2	50,900	
			(56,100)
Net profit			87,780

Notes:

(1) The figure of £1,800 for other expenses includes £720 for entertaining employees. The remaining expenses are all allowable.

(2) The figure of £50,900 for wages and salaries includes the annual salary of £4,000 paid to Bim (see the profit sharing note below).

Plant and machinery

On 6 April 2019 the tax written down values of the partnership's plant and machinery were:

	£
Main pool	3,100
Motor car (1)	21,000

The following transactions took place during the year ended 5 April 2020:

		Cost
		£
8 May 2019	Purchased motor car (2)	10,150
21 November 2019	Purchased motor car (3)	14,200
14 January 2020	Purchased motor car (4)	11,600

Motor car (1) was purchased in March 2017 and has a CO_2 emission rate of 175 grams per kilometre. It is used by Auy, and 80% of the mileage is for business journeys.

Motor car (2) is a new car purchased on 8 May 2019 has a CO_2 emission rate of 50 grams per kilometre. It is used by Bim, and 80% of the mileage is for business journeys.

Motor car (3) purchased on 21 November 2019 has a CO_2 emission rate of 105 grams per kilometre. Motor car (4) purchased on 14 January 2020 has a CO_2 emission rate of 140 grams per kilometre. These two motor cars are used by employees of the business.

Profit sharing

Profits are shared 80% to Auy and 20% to Bim. This is after paying an annual salary of £4,000 to Bim, and interest at the rate of 5% on the partners' capital account balances.

The capital account balances are:

	£
Auy Man	56,000
Bim Men	34,000

Required:

(a) Explain why both Auy Man and Bim Men will each be treated for tax purposes as resident in the United Kingdom for the tax year 2019/20. 🖥 **(2 marks)**

(b) Calculate the partnership's tax adjusted trading profit for the year ended 5 April 2020, and the trading income assessments of Auy Man and Bim Men for the tax year 2019/20. ▦

Your computation should commence with the net profit figure of £87,780, and should also list all of the items referred to in Notes (1) and (2) indicating by the use of zero (0) any items that do not require adjustment. **(10 marks)**

(c) Calculate the class 4 national insurance contributions payable by Auy Man and Bim Men for the tax year 2019/20. ▦ **(3 marks)**

(Total: 15 marks)

123 DANIEL, FRANCINE AND GREGOR *Walk in the footsteps of a top tutor*

(a) Amanda, Beatrice and Claude have been in partnership since 1 November 2013, preparing accounts to 31 October annually. Daniel joined as a partner on 1 May 2019. Profits have always been shared equally. The partnership's recent tax adjusted trading profits are as follows:

	£
Year ended 31 October 2018	147,000
Year ended 31 October 2019	96,000
Year ended 31 October 2020 (forecast)	180,000

Required:

Calculate Daniel's trading income assessment for the tax year 2019/20. ⊞ (3 marks)

(b) Francine is employed by Fringe plc. On 1 August 2019, Fringe plc provided Francine with a loan of £96,000 to help her purchase a holiday cottage. On 1 October 2019, the loan was increased by a further £14,000 so that Francine could renovate the cottage. Francine pays interest at an annual rate of 1.5% on this loan.

The taxable benefit in respect of this loan is calculated using the average method.

Required:

Calculate Francine's taxable benefit for the tax year 2019/20 in respect of the loan from Fringe plc. ⊞ (3 marks)

(c) Gregor has been self-employed since 6 April 2006. He has the following income and chargeable gains for the tax years 2018/19 and 2019/20:

	2018/19	2019/20
	£	£
Trading profit/(loss)	14,700	(68,800)
Property income/(loss)	4,600	(2,300)
Building society interest	1,300	900
Chargeable gain/(loss)	(2,900)	17,400

Required:

On the assumption that Gregor relieves his trading loss of £68,800 as early as possible, calculate the amount of trading loss carried forward to the tax year 2020/21. ⊞

Note: You should assume that the tax allowances for the tax year 2019/20 apply throughout. (4 marks)

(Total: 10 marks)

PENSIONS AND NIC

124 JOHN BEACH (ADAPTED) *Walk in the footsteps of a top tutor*

The following information is available in respect of John Beach for the tax year 2019/20:

(1) John has been employed by Surf plc as a sales director since 1 December 1998. During the tax year 2019/20, he was paid gross director's remuneration of £144,000.

(2) During the tax year 2019/20, John contributed £28,000 into Surf plc's HM Revenue and Customs' registered occupational pension scheme. The company contributed a further £11,000 on his behalf.

(3) During the period 6 April to 31 October 2019, John used his private motor car for both private and business journeys. He was reimbursed by Surf plc at the rate of 60p per mile for the following mileage:

	Miles
Normal daily travel between home and Surf plc's offices	1,180
Travel between Surf plc's offices and the premises of Surf plc's clients	4,270
Travel between home and the premises of Surf plc's clients (none of the clients' premises were located near the offices of Surf plc)	510
Total mileage reimbursed by Surf plc	5,960

(4) During 2016 Surf plc provided John with a loan which was used to purchase a yacht. The amount of loan outstanding at 6 April 2019 was £84,000. John repaid £12,000 of the loan on 31 July 2019, and then repaid a further £12,000 on 31 December 2019. He paid loan interest of £1,270 to Surf plc during the tax year 2019/20. The taxable benefit in respect of this loan is calculated using the average method.

(5) Surf plc gave John an engraved gold watch costing £465 on 1 December 2019 in recognition of his long service with the company.

(6) During the tax year 2019/20, John made personal pension contributions up to the maximum amount of available annual allowances, including any unused amounts brought forward from previous years (see Note 7). These personal pension contributions were in addition to the contributions he made to Surf plc's occupational pension scheme (see Note (2)).

(7) John had an unused annual allowance of £1,000 in the tax year 2018/19 and each of the previous four tax years.

Required:

(a) **Calculate John Beach's income tax liability for the tax year 2019/20.** 田 **(12 marks)**

(b) **Calculate the class 1 national insurance contributions that will have been suffered by John Beach and Surf plc in respect of John's earnings and benefits for the tax year 2019/20.** 田 **(3 marks)**

(Total: 15 marks)

125 KAT (ADAPTED) *Walk in the footsteps of a top tutor*

You should assume that today's date is 15 March 2019.

On 6 April 2019, Kat will purchase a residential freehold property which she will let out. However, Kat is unsure whether to purchase the property personally or via a limited company. The limited company would be incorporated for the sole purpose of purchasing and letting out the property, and Kat would hold all of the shares in the company.

Regardless of whether the property is purchased personally or via a limited company:

(1)   The property will be let throughout the year ended 5 April 2020 at a monthly rent of £2,600.

(2)   The purchase of the property will be partly financed with a repayment mortgage. Mortgage interest of £12,000 will be paid during the year ended 5 April 2020.

(3)   The other expenditure on the property for the year ended 5 April 2020 will amount to £4,600, and this will all be allowable.

(4)   Kat will also have employment income of £60,650 for the tax year 2019/20.

If the property is purchased via a limited company, then the company's corporation tax liability for the year ended 5 April 2020 will be £2,774 and Kat will withdraw dividends from the company totalling £6,000 during the tax year 2019/20.

Kat will not have any other income for the tax year 2019/20.

Required:

(a)   **Determine if there will be an overall saving of tax for the year ended 5 April 2020 if Kat purchases the property via a limited company rather than purchasing it personally.** ▦

Notes:

1   **Your answer should include a calculation of Kat's income tax liability if she purchases the property personally and if she purchases it via a limited company.**

2   **You should ignore national insurance contributions (NICs).**   **(9 marks)**

(b)   **Explain ONE way in which the calculation of a future taxable gain on a property disposal made by the limited company would differ from the calculation of a taxable gain on a disposal made personally by Kat.** 🖥   **(1 mark)**

(Total: 10 marks)

126 ANN, BASIL AND CHLOE (ADAPTED) *Walk in the footsteps of a top tutor*

You are a trainee accountant and your manager has asked for your help regarding three taxpayers who have all made personal pension contributions during the tax year 2019/20.

Ann Peach

Ann is self-employed as an estate agent. Her trading profit for the year ended 5 April 2020 was £38,650. Ann received an inheritance from her aunt in October 2019 and used it to make a contribution of £42,000 (gross) into a personal pension scheme in November 2019.

Basil Plum

Basil is employed by the Banana Bank plc as a fund manager. On 6 April 2019 Basil received a significant promotion and a large pay rise of £50,000, such that in the tax year 2019/20 he was paid a gross salary of £152,000.

Basil made contributions into a personal pension plan totalling £30,000 (gross) during the tax year 2016/17 and £40,000 (gross) during the tax years 2017/18 and 2018/19. During the tax year 2019/20 he also made total gross contributions of £40,000.

He is not a member of Banana Bank plc's occupational pension scheme but the bank contributed £5,000 to Basil's personal pension in the tax year 2019/20.

Chloe Pear

Chloe Pear lets out unfurnished property. For the tax year 2019/20 her taxable property income was £24,550. Chloe made contributions of £8,200 (gross) into a personal pension scheme during the tax year 2019/20.

Neither Ann nor Basil nor Chloe has any other income.

Required:

(a) For each of the three taxpayers Ann Peach, Basil Plum and Chloe Pear, state, giving reasons, the amount of personal pension contributions that will have qualified for tax relief for the tax year 2019/20, and calculate their income tax liabilities for that year. ▦

Marks are allocated as follows:

Ann Peach 2 marks; Basil Plum 6 marks; and Chloe Pear 2 marks. **(10 marks)**

(b) Briefly explain:

(1) The tax implications for both Basil and the Banana Bank plc of the bank making contributions into Basil's personal pension scheme▦, and **(3 marks)**

(2) The implications for Basil's available annual allowance in 2019/20 of Banana Bank plc contributing £100,000 instead of £5,000 into Basil's personal pension in the tax year 2019/20. ▦ **(2 marks)**

(Total: 15 marks)

127 JACK (ADAPTED) *Walk in the footsteps of a top tutor*

You should assume that today's date is 15 March 2020 and that the tax rates and allowances for the tax year 2019/20 continue to apply.

Jack, aged 44, is a widower following the recent death of his wife. He has just cashed in a substantial share portfolio and is now considering what to do with the proceeds.

Gift to a trust

The value of Jack's estate is in excess of £1,000,000, and he is worried about the amount of inheritance tax which will be payable should he die. His wife's nil rate band was fully used when she died.

Jack is therefore planning to make an immediate lifetime cash gift of £300,000 to a trust with the funds then being held for the benefit of his two children aged 10 and 12. Jack has not made any previous lifetime gifts.

Personal pension contribution

The only pension contributions which Jack has made previously are a gross amount of £500 per month which he saves into a personal pension scheme. Jack has continued to make these contributions throughout the tax year 2019/20. Although Jack has been saving into this scheme for the previous 15 years, he is concerned that he is not saving enough for his retirement. Jack therefore wants to make the maximum possible amount of additional gross personal pension contribution for the tax year 2019/20, but only to the extent that the contribution will attract tax relief at the higher rate of income tax.

Jack is self-employed. His trading profit is £100,000 for the tax year 2019/20 and the previous five tax years. He does not have any other income and expects to make the same level of profit in future years.

Individual savings account (ISA)

Jack has never invested any amounts in ISAs. During the next 30 days he would like to invest the maximum possible amounts into stocks and shares ISAs.

Required:

(a)   Explain, with supporting calculations where necessary, why it is good inheritance tax planning for Jack to make the immediate lifetime cash gift of £300,000 to a trust. 🖥

        Note: You are not expected to consider taper relief.   (3 marks)

(b)   (i)   Advise Jack of the amount of additional gross personal pension contribution he can make for the tax year 2019/20 which will benefit from tax relief at the higher rate of income tax, and explain why this is a tax efficient approach to pension saving. 🖥   (4 marks)

        (ii)   Calculate the amount of unused pension annual allowances which Jack will be able to carry forward to the tax year 2020/21 if the contribution in (i) above is made. ⊞   (1 mark)

(c)   Advise Jack as to the maximum possible amount which he can invest into stocks and shares ISAs during the next 30 days. 🖥   (2 marks)

                                                                    (Total: 10 marks)

SELF-ASSESSMENT

128   PI CASSO (ADAPTED)

(a)   Pi Casso has been a self-employed artist since 2008, preparing her accounts to 30 June.

        Pi's tax liabilities for the tax years 2017/18 to 2019/20 (inclusive) are as follows:

	2017/18	2018/19	2019/20
	£	£	£
Income tax liability	3,240	4,100	2,730
Class 2 national insurance contributions	148	153	156
Class 4 national insurance contributions	1,240	1,480	990
Capital gains tax liability	0	4,880	0

Required:

(1) Prepare a schedule showing the payments on account and balancing payments that Pi will have made or will have to make during the period from 1 July 2019 to 31 March 2021, assuming that Pi makes any appropriate claims to reduce her payments on account. ⊞

Your answer should clearly identify the relevant due date of each payment.

(7 marks)

(2) State the implications if Pi had made a claim to reduce her payments on account for the tax year 2019/20 to £Nil. 💻 **(2 marks)**

(3) State the latest date by which Pi must make a claim to reduce her payments on account for the tax year 2019/20. 💻 **(1 mark)**

Assume that the tax rules for the tax year 2019/20 apply to all tax years.

(b) Turner is married to Andrea. In the tax year 2019/20 Turner had trading income of £250,000 and interest income of £5,000.

Andrea had employment income of £20,000 and dividend income of £23,000.

Required:

Explain, with supporting calculations, the maximum joint tax saving that Turner and Andrea could have made in the tax year 2019/20 by transferring investments between them. ⊞ **(5 marks)**

(Total: 15 marks)

129 ERNEST VADER (ADAPTED) *Walk in the footsteps of a top tutor*

You should assume that today's date is 30 June 2021.

You are a trainee Chartered Certified Accountant and are dealing with the tax affairs of Ernest Vader.

Ernest's self-assessment tax return for the tax year 2019/20 was submitted to HM Revenue & Customs (HMRC) on 15 May 2020, and Ernest paid the resulting income tax liability by the due date of 31 January 2021. However, you have just discovered that during the tax year 2019/20 Ernest disposed of a freehold property, the details of which were omitted from his self-assessment tax return. The capital gains tax liability in respect of this disposal is £18,000, and this amount has not been paid.

Ernest has suggested that since HMRC's right to initiate a compliance check into his self-assessment tax return for the tax year 2019/20 expired on 15 May 2021, no disclosure should be made to HMRC of the capital gain.

Required:

(a) Briefly explain the difference between tax evasion and tax avoidance, as well as the general anti-abuse rule and how HMRC would view the situation if Ernest Vader does not disclose his capital gain. 💻 **(4 marks)**

(b) Briefly explain from an ethical viewpoint how you, as a trainee Chartered Certified Accountant, should deal with the suggestion from Ernest Vader that no disclosure is made to HMRC of his capital gain. 💻 **(3 marks)**

(c)   Explain the penalties which your firm, as tax agents, could be liable to, if a compliance check is commenced by HMRC and the firm fails to supply the information requested by HMRC.   **(2 marks)**

(d)   State the period for which late payment interest will run assuming that HMRC discover the capital gain and raise an assessment on 15 July 2021 in respect of Ernest Vader's capital gains tax liability of £18,000 for the tax year 2019/20, and that this amount is then paid on 31 July 2021.   **(1 mark)**

                                                                                     (Total: 10 marks)

130   SOPHIE SHAPE (ADAPTED)

> *Question debrief*

Sophie Shape has been a self-employed sculptor since 2001, preparing her accounts to 5 April. Sophie's tax liabilities for the tax years 2018/19 and 2019/20 are as follows:

	2018/19	2019/20
	£	£
Income tax liability	5,240	6,100
Class 2 national insurance contributions	153	156
Class 4 national insurance contributions	1,820	1,910
Capital gains tax liability	0	5,280

Required:

(a)   Prepare a schedule showing the payments on account and balancing payment which Sophie Shape will have made, or will have to make, during the period from 1 April 2020 to 31 March 2021.

         Your answer should clearly identify the relevant due date of each payment.

                                                                                     (4 marks)

(b)   State the implications if Sophie Shape had made a claim to reduce her payments on account for the tax year 2019/20 to nil without any justification for doing so.
                                                                                     (2 marks)

(c)   Advise Sophie Shape of the latest date by which she can file a paper self-assessment tax return for the tax year 2019/20.   **(1 mark)**

(d)   State the period during which HM Revenue and Customs (HMRC) will have to notify Sophie Shape if they intend to carry out a compliance check in respect of her self-assessment tax return for the tax year 2019/20, and the possible reasons why such a check would be made.

         You should assume that Sophie will file her tax return by the filing date.   **(3 marks)**

                                                                                     (Total: 10 marks)

> *Calculate your allowed time and allocate the time to each separate part.*

Section 2

PRACTICE CHARGEABLE GAINS QUESTIONS

PRACTICE SECTION A OBJECTIVE TEST QUESTIONS

INDIVIDUALS – CAPITAL GAINS TAX

131 Massita is planning to dispose of several assets and wants to avoid any capital gains tax liability. He is unsure which of his assets to sell and which to retain.

Which TWO of the following assets would potentially realise a chargeable gain?

A   Qualifying corporate bonds

B   Painting by a famous artist

C   Gilt-edged securities

D   Main residence that he has always lived in

E   A car used in his trade, on which he has claimed capital allowances and which would be sold for £15,000 and realise a profit

F   A machine used in his trade, on which he has claimed capital allowances and which would be sold for £22,000 and realise a profit

132 Lexie sold a residential property, which she had never lived in, for £338,200 in the tax year 2019/20. She had acquired the building for £150,000 in 2009.

Lexie has taxable income of £54,000 for the tax year 2019/20. She sold no other assets in the tax year.

What is Lexie's capital gains tax liability?

A   £35,240

B   £49,336

C   £52,696

D   £31,716

133 Jackson acquired a holiday villa for £115,000 on 1 May 2009. He gave it to his wife Sophia on 30 September 2014 when it was worth £100,000. Sophia sold the villa for £165,000 on 1 July 2019. The villa was never the couple's main home.

Sophia had no other capital disposals in the tax year 2019/20 and has capital losses brought forward of £4,300. Her taxable income for the tax year 2019/20 is £60,000.

What is Sophia's capital gains tax payable in the tax year 2019/20?

£ [   ]

134 *September 2016 OT question*

Putting an asset into joint names with a spouse (or a partner in a registered civil partnership) prior to the asset's disposal can be sensible capital gains tax (CGT) planning.

Which of the following CANNOT be achieved as a direct result of using this type of tax planning?

A   Making the best use of annual exempt amounts

B   Deferring the CGT due date

C   Reducing the amount of CGT payable

D   Making the best use of capital losses

135 Noah sold two paintings at an auction on 14 May 2019 for £4,000 and £7,200 respectively. He had purchased the two paintings for £1,000 each on 22 May 2008.

What is Noah's total chargeable gain arising on the sale of the two paintings?

£ [   ]

136 Liam purchased an antique glass vase for £22,000 on 30 March 2004, incurring legal fees of £800.

The market for antique glassware has since slumped and Liam sold the vase for £5,500 on 1 January 2020 incurring auctioneer fees of £300.

What is Liam's allowable loss on this disposal?

A   £16,000

B   £16,800

C   £17,100

D   £17,600

137 *June 2015 OT question*

For the tax year 2019/20, Nog has a chargeable gain of £23,700 and a capital loss of £10,400. She has unused capital losses of £5,300 brought forward from the tax year 2018/19.

What amount of capital losses can Nog carry forward to the tax year 2020/21?

£ [   ]

138 *September 2015 OT question*

On 31 March 2020, Jessica sold a copyright for £28,800. The copyright had been purchased on 1 April 2014 for £21,000 when it had an unexpired life of 15 years.

What is Jessica's chargeable gain in respect of the disposal of the copyright?

A   £0

B   £20,400

C   £16,200

D   £7,800

139   Aiden bought 30 acres of land on 1 March 2012 for £300,000.

On 1 March 2014 he sold 10 acres of the land for £150,000. At this time the remaining land was worth £250,000.

On 1 January 2020 Aiden sold the remaining acres for £425,600.

Identify Aiden's chargeable gain and the due date for the capital gains tax payable thereon.

		Due date	
		31 January 2020	**31 January 2021**
Chargeable gain	£225,600	A	B
	£238,100	C	D

140 *December 2016 OT question*

Habib purchased a copyright on 30 April 2003 for £31,320. The remaining life of the copyright at the date of purchase was 30 years. On 30 April 2019, Habib sold the copyright for £27,900.

What is Habib's chargeable gain or allowable loss for the tax year 2019/20 in respect of the disposal of the copyright?

A   (£3,420)

B   £11,196

C   £0

D   £13,284

141   Cooper purchased a holiday home for £142,000 on 1 October 2013. The property was damaged in a fire on 1 January 2014.

Cooper received compensation of £60,000 from his insurance company on 31 January 2015. He spent £70,000 on restoring the home in March 2015 and it was worth £180,000 after restoration. Cooper made an election such that a part disposal did not arise in the tax year 2014/15.

Cooper sold the holiday home for £230,000 on 1 March 2020.

What is Cooper's chargeable gain on the sale?

£ ⬚

142   September 2015 OT question

On 10 January 2020, a freehold property owned by Winifred was damaged by a fire. The property had been purchased on 29 May 2007 for £73,000. Winifred received insurance proceeds of £37,200 on 23 February 2020, and she spent a total of £41,700 during March 2020 restoring the property. Winifred has elected to disregard the part disposal.

What is the base cost of the restored freehold property for capital gains tax purposes?

A   £68,500

B   £77,500

C   £114,700

D   £35,800

143   Madison gave 10,000 shares in Miles plc to her daughter during the tax year 2019/20.

The shares were quoted in the Stock Exchange Official List at 120p – 136p per share on the day of the sale.

Madison acquired 15,000 shares in Miles plc on 1 January 2014 for £4,000.

What is the chargeable gain on the gift of the 10,000 shares?

£ ☐

144   Clarissa has disposed of the following shares and securities during the tax year 2019/20:

(1)   Gilts for £8,000 which were purchased in 2017 for £2,500.

(2)   20,000 shares in Martin plc sold to her sister for £7,000.

The market value of the shares on the day of the sale was £12,300.

The shares were purchased for £8,000 in February 2017.

What is Clarissa's total chargeable gain on these disposals in the tax year 2019/20?

A   £4,500

B   £4,300

C   £5,500

D   £9,800

145 Emily had the following transactions in the shares of Elijah Plc during 2019:

		Number of shares	Cost £	Proceeds £
1 June	Purchase	22,000	88,000	
1 October	Purchase	2,000	7,440	
1 October	Sale	20,000		59,000
23 October	Purchase	3,000	10,800	

Select the share purchases which will be matched to the 20,000 shares sold on 1 October 2019.

Share purchases	Matching order
20,000 shares from the purchase on 1 June	Matched first
2,000 shares from the purchase on 1 October	Matched second
3,000 shares from the purchase on 23 October	Matched third
15,000 shares from the share pool as at 1 October	
17,000 shares from the share pool as at 1 October	
18,000 shares from the share pool as at 1 October	
20,000 shares from the share pool as at 1 October	
No further matches needed	
No further matches needed	

146 In February 2020 Siobhan, a higher rate taxpayer, sold shares in Banana Ltd, a trading company. She realised a gain of £45,000. Siobhan acquired the newly issued shares in July 2016.

Siobhan has never worked at Banana Ltd, nor has she made any previous share disposals.

What is the chargeable gains tax liability arising on the disposal of the shares in February 2020 assuming all available reliefs are claimed and Siobhan makes no other disposals in the tax year 2019/20?

£ [   ]

147 Caleb had the following transactions in Harper plc shares:

26 April 2008	Purchased 40,000 shares in Harper plc for £200,000
19 May 2011	Harper plc announced a 1:4 rights issue at £4 per share. Caleb took up his rights in full
3 May 2015	Harper plc announced a 1:5 bonus issue
25 March 2020	Caleb sold 12,500 shares for £175,000

Identify the allowable cost for capital gains tax purposes of the shares disposed of on 25 March 2020, and the due date for the capital gains tax payable thereon.

		Due date	
		31 July 2020	**31 January 2021**
Allowable cost	£50,000	A	B
	£60,000	C	D

148 Hunter purchased 50,000 shares in Grayson Ltd for £90,000 on 30 May 2009.

On 1 November 2019 Grayson Ltd was taken over by Riley plc. Grayson Ltd shareholders received £3 cash and 2 Riley plc ordinary £1 shares for every Grayson Ltd share.

Immediately after takeover Riley plc shares were worth £1.20 each.

What is Hunter's chargeable gain as a result of the takeover?

£ [   ]

149 *September 2016 OT question*

On 31 March 2020, Angus sold a house, which he had bought on 31 March 2006.

Angus occupied the house as his main residence until 31 March 2011, when he left for employment abroad.

Angus returned to the UK on 1 April 2013 and lived in the house until 31 March 2014, when he bought a flat in a neighbouring town and made that his principal private residence.

What is Angus' total number of qualifying months of occupation for principal private residence relief on the sale of the house?

A   72 months

B   54 months

C   114 months

D   96 months

150 Masuma sold her only home and realised a gain before reliefs of £120,000. She had used six of the ten rooms herself and let out the other four for the duration of her ownership.

What is her chargeable gain, assuming she claims all available reliefs?

£ [   ]

151 In October 2019 Bhavin sold his business, which he had run for nine years as a sole trader, realising chargeable gains on disposal of the business assets of £13,250,900.

Bhavin is a higher rate taxpayer and has not made any previous disposals.

What is Bhavin's capital gains tax liability for the tax year 2019/20 assuming he has made no other gains during the tax year or any previous tax years, and claims all available reliefs?

    A   £1,906,892

    B   £1,650,180

    C   £1,647,780

    D   £1,325,090

152 **The disposal of which TWO of the following assets qualifies for rollover relief?**

    A   A portable sewing machine used by a sole trader in his business

    B   Shares in an individual's personal trading company

    C   Land used by a sole trader in his business

    D   Shares in the company of which the individual is an employee

    E   A building owned by a company and let out to other businesses

    F   The goodwill in a sole trader's business

153 *June 2015 OT question*

Alice is in business as a sole trader. On 13 May 2019, she sold a freehold warehouse for £184,000, and this resulted in a chargeable gain of £38,600. Alice purchased a replacement freehold warehouse on 20 May 2019 for £143,000. Where possible, Alice always makes a claim to roll over gains against the cost of replacement assets. Both buildings have been, or will be, used for business purposes by Alice.

What is the base cost of the replacement warehouse for capital gains tax purposes?

    A   £181,600

    B   £104,400

    C   £143,000

    D   £102,000

154 In October 2008 Hitesh sold a factory for £230,574 and realised a gain of £31,083.

In May 2009 he bought a warehouse for £231,211. He then sold the warehouse in December 2019 for £270,213.

Both of the buildings were used for the purposes of his sole trader business.

What is the chargeable gain arising on the disposal of the warehouse in December 2019 assuming all available reliefs are claimed?

    £ ☐

155 Lionel owns 50% of the ordinary share capital in Giraffe Ltd and 2% of the ordinary share capital in Zebra plc. Both are trading companies and Lionel has 50% and 2% of the voting rights respectively.

Which TWO of the following would be a qualifying asset for the purposes of gift relief?

A   Part of Lionel's shareholding in Giraffe Ltd, representing 2% of the total ordinary share capital in Giraffe Ltd

B   A building owned by Lionel and used in the trade of Zebra plc

C   Lionel's entire holding of Zebra plc shares

D   A warehouse owned by Lionel and used by Giraffe Ltd for storing raw materials

156 The four shareholders of Elephant Ltd are selling their shares. They own the share capital as follows:

Amin: 32%

Ben: 32%

Camilla: 32%

Dimitri: 4%

All shares have equal voting rights. Amin has never worked for the company. Ben works part time, and Camilla and Dimitri work full time for the company. Camilla only joined Elephant Ltd six months ago and has owned her shares for three months, whereas Ben and Dimitri have worked for the company and owned their shares for five years.

Only _____ will qualify for entrepreneurs' relief on the sale of their shares.

Select the individual that appropriately fills the gap above:

A   Amin

B   Ben

C   Camilla

D   Dimitri

157 *December 2016 OT question*

 Anika sold her entire holding of 3,000 £1 ordinary shares in Distribo Ltd, a trading company, to her son, Hemi, for £53,000 on 14 July 2019. The market value of the shares on that date was £98,000. Anika had purchased the 3,000 shares on 28 October 2007 for £41,500. She has never worked for Distribo Ltd.

What is the amount of gift (holdover) relief (if any) which could be claimed in respect of the disposal of these shares, and Anika's chargeable gain for the tax year 2019/20 after taking account of any available relief?

	Gift relief	Gain
A	£0	£11,500
B	£11,500	£0
C	£45,000	£11,500
D	£56,500	£0

COMPANIES – CHARGEABLE GAINS

158 Forrest Ltd bought a warehouse for £250,000 in December 2009, incurring £20,000 legal fees in connection with the acquisition. The warehouse was sold for £800,000 in May 2019.

Assume the relevant indexation factors are as follows:

December 2009 to December 2017   0.276
December 2009 to May 2019   0.312

What is the chargeable gain arising on the sale of the warehouse?

A   £461,000

B   £455,480

C   £452,000

D   £445,760

159 Harrop Ltd sold two assets during the accounting period:

(1)   Two acres of land which it had acquired for £20,000 and sold for £45,000. The relevant indexation factor is 1.418.

(2)   A warehouse which it had acquired for £80,000 and sold for £75,000. The relevant indexation factor is 0.702.

What is the company's allowable loss for the period, assuming it sold no other assets?

A   £64,520

B   £8,360

C   £5,000

D   £61,160

160 In the year ended 30 June 2019 Lompy Ltd had a tax adjusted trading profit of £800,200 and property income of £45,000. It also realised a chargeable gain of £25,000 and a capital loss of £80,000 on assets that were used for the purposes of the property business.

In the year ended 30 June 2018 it had a tax adjusted trading profit of £520,000 and chargeable gains of £9,000.

How much, if any, of the capital loss arising in the year ended 30 June 2019 is carried forward to the year ended 30 June 2020?

£ ☐

161   Rimbo Ltd had the following transactions in the shares of Profitable Ltd, an investment company:

		Number	**£**
April 1995	Purchase	25,000	33,000
June 2019	Sale	8,000	26,000

Assume the relevant indexation factors are as follows:

April 1995 to June 2019   0.926
April 1995 to December 2017   0.866

What is the amount of the indexed cost available on the sale of the shares in June 2019?

A   £61,578

B   £20,339

C   £19,705

D   £10,560

162   On 1 October 2019 Smooth Ltd sold a factory for £850,000, realising a gain of £250,000.

On 1 November 2018 the company had purchased an immovable machine for £900,000. The machine is expected to be used by the company for at least 25 years.

The company prepares accounts to 31 December.

The company wishes to defer the gain arising on the sale of the factory by making a rollover relief election in respect of the acquisition of the machine.

For each of the following statements select whether it is true or false:

	True	**False**
The £250,000 gain which could be deferred as a result of the acquisition of the machine will become chargeable on 1 October 2029		
The company must make a rollover relief election by 31 December 2023		

PRACTICE SECTION B OBJECTIVE TEST CASES

INDIVIDUALS – CAPITAL GAINS TAX

163 MICHAEL CHIN (ADAPTED)

Michael Chin made the following disposals of assets during the tax year 2019/20:

(1) On 30 June 2019 Michael sold a business that he had run as a sole trader since 1 January 2015. He realised the following gains and losses on the chargeable assets of the business:

	£
Goodwill	60,000
Freehold property	64,000
Storage unit	(13,000)

The goodwill has been built up since 1 January 2015. The freehold property had been acquired 6 months prior to the date of disposal and the storage unit had been acquired on 1 June 2016.

(2) On 8 December 2019 Michael gave Mika, his daughter, his entire holding of 50,000 50p ordinary shares (a 60% holding) in Minnow Ltd, an unquoted trading company. The market value of the shares on that date was £180,000.

Michael had originally purchased the shares on 5 January 2019 for £87,500. On 8 December 2019 the market value of Minnow Ltd's chargeable assets was £250,000, of which £200,000 was in respect of chargeable business assets. Michael has never been employed by Minnow Ltd.

(3) On 28 February 2020 Michael sold a painting for £5,900 after auctioneer's fees of £656. He had originally acquired the painting on 1 June 2018 for £4,000.

(4) On 15 March 2020 Michael gave Mika, his daughter, the following assets:

– Necklace valued at £4,000. Acquired by Michael for £5,000.

– Boat valued at £80,000. Acquired by Michael for £70,000.

– Machine used for trading activities valued at £7,000. Acquired by Michael for £8,000.

Michael incurred a capital loss of £16,800 during the tax year 2017/18, and made a chargeable gain of £17,100 and a capital loss of £7,000 during the tax year 2018/19.

Assume that the tax rates and allowances for the tax year 2019/20 apply throughout.

1 **What is the net chargeable gain on the disposal of the sole trader business on 30 June 2019 that qualifies for entrepreneurs' relief?**

A £124,000

B £111,000

C £60,000

D £51,000

2 What amount of gift relief, if any, is available on the gift of shares in Minnow Ltd on 8 December 2019?

£ ☐

3 What is the chargeable gain, if any, arising on the sale of the painting on 28 February 2020?

A £1,244

B £0

C £1,900

D £927

4 Match the following gifts made by Michael on 15 March 2020 to the correct category, based on whether or not the gift will result in a chargeable gain or allowable loss:

Asset given

Necklace

Boat

Machine

Chargeable gain/allowable loss	Gain not chargeable/loss not allowable

5 What amount of capital losses are brought forward from the tax year 2018/19 and how should they be used? Tick the appropriate box.

Loss b/f	Use against gains qualifying for entrepreneurs' relief	Use against gains not qualifying for entrepreneurs' relief
£16,800		
£18,400		

164 BO (ADAPTED)

You are a trainee accountant and your manager has asked for your help regarding a client who disposed of assets during the tax year 2019/20.

Bo Neptune

On 31 July 2019 Bo made a gift to his son, Chi, of his entire holding of 50,000 £1 ordinary shares (a 100% holding) in Botune Ltd, an unquoted trading company. The market value of the shares on that date was £210,000. The shares had been purchased by Bo on 22 January 2012 for £94,000. Bo and Chi have elected to hold over the gain as a gift of a business asset.

Bo has taxable income in the tax year 2019/20 of £30,500 and had made a chargeable gain on the sale of a painting of £20,700. Bo has never made any other chargeable disposals.

On 30 September 2019 Bo sold a house for £282,000, resulting in a chargeable gain of £172,000. The house had been purchased on 1 October 2007.

He occupied the house as his main residence from the date of purchase until 30 September 2009. Bo then moved in with his girlfriend and the house was unoccupied between 1 October 2009 and 30 September 2019.

Throughout the period 1 October 2007 to 30 September 2019 Bo did not have any other main residence.

1 **What is the Chi's base cost in the 50,000 £1 ordinary shares in Botune Ltd?**

   A   £94,000

   B   £106,000

   C   £116,000

   D   £210,000

2 **If Bo had instead sold the shares in Botune Ltd to Chi for £160,000, for each of the following statements select whether it is true or false:**

	True	False
Bo's chargeable gain would have been £66,000		
Bo and Chi would not have been able to claim gift relief		
The base cost of the shares for Chi would be £210,000		

3 **When is the capital gains tax due date(s) for the tax year 2019/20 and by what date must Bo and Chi make the election to hold over the gain on the Botune Ltd shares? Tick the appropriate box.**

		Election date	
		5 April 2024	31 January 2025
CGT due date	31 January 2020		
	31 January 2021		

4 Assuming that no other chargeable gains arise in the tax year, how much capital gains tax would Bo pay on the disposal of the painting in the tax year 2019/20?

£ [   ]

5 How much principal private residence relief is Bo entitled to on the sale of his main residence?

A £172,000

B £93,167

C £50,167

D £46,667

165 ALPHABET LTD (ADAPTED) *Walk in the footsteps of a top tutor*

On 15 October 2019 Alphabet Ltd, an unquoted trading company, was taken over by XYZ plc. Prior to the takeover Alphabet Ltd's share capital consisted of 100,000 £1 ordinary shares and under the terms of the takeover the shareholders received either cash of £6 per share or one £1 ordinary share in XYZ plc for each £1 ordinary share in Alphabet Ltd.

The following information is available regarding three shareholders of Alphabet Ltd:

Aloi

Aloi has been the managing director of Alphabet Ltd since the company's incorporation on 1 January 2009, and she accepted XYZ plc's cash alternative of £6 per share in respect of her shareholding of 60,000 £1 ordinary shares in Alphabet Ltd. Aloi had originally subscribed for 50,000 shares in Alphabet Ltd on 1 January 2009 at their par value, and purchased a further 10,000 shares on 20 May 2010 for £18,600.

Bon

Bon has been the sales director of Alphabet Ltd since 1 February 2018, having not previously been an employee of the company. She accepted XYZ plc's share alternative of one £1 ordinary share for each of her 25,000 £1 ordinary shares in Alphabet Ltd. Bon had purchased her shareholding on 1 February 2018 for £92,200.

On 4 March 2020 Bon gave 10,000 of her £1 ordinary shares in XYZ plc to her brother for £50,000. On that date the shares were quoted on the Stock Exchange Daily Official List at £7.10 – £7.18. Gift relief is not available in respect of this disposal.

Cherry

Cherry has been an employee of Alphabet Ltd since 1 May 2010. She accepted XYZ plc's share alternative of one £1 ordinary share for each of her 3,000 £1 ordinary shares in Alphabet Ltd. Cherry had purchased her shareholding on 20 June 2011 for £4,800.

On 13 November 2019 Cherry sold 1,000 of her £1 ordinary shares in XYZ plc for £6,600.

Cherry died on 5 April 2020, and her remaining 2,000 £1 ordinary shares in XYZ plc were inherited by her daughter. On that date these shares were valued at £15,600.

1   Which of the following individuals met the qualifying conditions for entrepreneurs' relief as regards their shareholdings in Alphabet Ltd?

	Meets the conditions for entrepreneurs' relief	Does not meet the conditions for entrepreneurs' relief
Aloi		
Bon		
Cherry		

2   What is the chargeable gain, if any, arising on Aloi on the takeover of Alphabet Ltd?

£ [   ]

3   What is the chargeable gain or allowable loss on the disposal of shares in XYZ plc by Bon to her brother?

    A   £13,120 gain

    B   £34,120 gain

    C   £34,520 gain

    D   (£20,800) loss

4   By what date(s) must Bon pay any capital gains tax due as a result of the disposal of shares in XYZ plc?

    A   31 January 2021

    B   30 September 2020

    C   4 March 2021

    D   5 December 2020

5   What is the allowable cost that will be used by Cherry's daughter in the capital gains computation on a subsequent disposal of her inherited shares in XYZ plc?

    A   £15,600

    B   £4,800

    C   £2,000

    D   £3,200

166 JORGE JUNG (ADAPTED)

Jorge Jung disposed of the following assets during the tax year 2019/20:

(1)   On 30 September 2019 Jorge sold a copyright for £8,200. The copyright had been purchased on 1 October 2017 for £7,000 when it had an unexpired life of 10 years.

(2)   On 6 October 2019 Jorge sold a painting for £6,400. The painting had been purchased on 18 May 2004 for £2,200. Jorge incurred selling fees of £350 on the disposal.

(3)   On 3 December 2019 Jorge sold two acres of land for £92,000. Jorge's father had originally purchased three acres of land on 4 August 2006 for £19,500.

His father died on 17 June 2014, and the land was inherited by Jorge. On that date the three acres of land were valued at £28,600. On 1 December 2014 Jorge incurred legal fees of £500 defending his title to the three acres of land. The market value of the unsold acre of land as at 3 December 2019 was £38,000.

(4)   On 14 January 2020 Jorge disposed of 5,000 £1 ordinary shares in a UK company to another individual. The market value of the shares on that date was £64,800. Jorge had purchased the shares for £26,300.

1   **What is the amount of the chargeable gain arising on the disposal of the copyright?**

   A   £6,800

   B   £2,600

   C   £1,200

   D   £960

2   **What is the amount of the chargeable gain arising on the disposal of the painting?**

   £ [   ]

3   **What is the allowable cost used in the capital gains tax disposal computation for the sale of the two acres of land on 3 December 2019?**

   A   £20,740

   B   £14,154

   C   £20,594

   D   £19,400

4   Jorge wishes to make a holdover (gift relief) claim in respect of the gain on the disposal of the shares on 14 January 2020.

   For each of the following statements select whether it is true or false in relation to the gift relief claim:

.	True	False
The company must be an unquoted company		
The company must not own any non-business assets		
The company must be a trading company		
Jorge must have owned the shares for at least two years		

5   Assuming Jorge sold the shares on 14 January 2020 realising a chargeable gain, which TWO of the following conditions must be met for entrepreneurs' relief to be available?

A   Jorge must make a claim for the relief by 31 January 2022

B   Jorge must have worked full time for the company for at least two years prior to the disposal

C   Jorge must have owned the shares for at least two years prior to the disposal

D   Jorge must be disposing of at least 5% of the company's shares

167   ALBERT AND CHARLES (ADAPTED) *Walk in the footsteps of a top tutor*

 Question debrief

Albert and Victoria

On 12 February 2020, Albert sold a house for £840,000, which he had owned individually. The house had been purchased on 12 February 2004 for £222,900.

Throughout the period of ownership the house was occupied by Albert and his wife, Victoria, as their main residence. One-quarter of the house was always used exclusively for business purposes by the couple.

For the tax year 2019/20 Albert is a higher rate taxpayer and did not make any other disposals of assets.

For the tax year 2019/20 Victoria had taxable income of £21,240 and made chargeable gains on other disposals of £12,000.

Charles and Daphne

On 23 October 2019 Charles sold 4,000 £1 ordinary shares in Restoration plc, a quoted trading company, to his daughter, Daphne, for £20,000 when they were valued at £31,600. Gift relief is not available in respect of this gift.

The company has 4 million £1 ordinary shares in issue. Charles has never worked for the company but Daphne has worked for the company for the previous five years.

Charles acquired his shares in the company as follows:

1 March 2011   Purchased 20,000 shares for £19,800
20 July 2015   Purchased 8,000 shares for £27,800

On 4 April 2020 Daphne sold a painting for gross proceeds of £5,300. The painting had been purchased for £13,000 in September 2003. Daphne incurred auctioneer's fees of £300 in relation to the disposal.

1   What is the amount of principal private residence relief available on the disposal of the house by Albert?

   A   £154,275

   B   £462,825

   C   £477,288

   D   £453,825

2   Albert's brother Ernest has told Albert it would have been better to have transferred 50% ownership of the house to Victoria prior to its disposal. Which TWO of the following statements are correct?

   A   The transfer to Victoria would have been at nil gain/nil loss

   B   Principal private residence relief available would not have been available in relation to Victoria's gain on the disposal of the house

   C   The amount of capital gains tax that would have been saved is £4,553

   D   The amount of capital gains tax that would have been saved is £1,626

3   What is the allowable base cost used in the capital gains tax computation on Charles' sale of shares to Daphne?

   £ [   ]

4   Which of the following are valid reasons why gift relief WAS NOT available on the sale of shares to Daphne?

	Valid reason	Not a valid reason
Charles has never worked for the company		
Daphne paid Charles for the shares		
Charles did not own at least 5% of the ordinary shares and voting rights in Restoration plc		

5   What is Daphne's allowable loss, if any, in respect of the sale of the painting on 4 April 2020?

   A   (£7,300) loss

   B   (£7,000) loss

   C   £0

   D   (£8,000) loss

 Calculate your allowed time and allocate the time to each separate part.

168 ZOYLA (ADAPTED) *Walk in the footsteps of a top tutor*

Zoyla's capital gains tax (CGT) liability for the tax year 2019/20 is calculated as follows:

	Gain £
Ordinary shares in Minor Ltd	98,700
Ordinary shares in Major plc	44,100
Annual exempt amount	(12,000)
	130,800
CGT: £10,600 × 10%	1,060
£120,200 × 20%	24,040
	25,100

Minor Ltd is an unquoted trading company with an issued share capital of 200,000 £1 ordinary shares. Zoyla has been a director of this company since 1 April 2013. On 20 June 2019, Zoyla sold 20,000 of her holding of 45,000 ordinary shares in Minor Ltd. She had originally purchased 22,500 shares on 15 August 2017 for £117,000. On 12 December 2017, Minor Ltd made a 1 for 1 rights issue. Zoyla took up her allocation under the rights issue in full, paying £7.40 for each new share issued.

Major plc is a quoted trading company with an issued share capital of 2,000,000 £1 ordinary shares. Zoyla has been an employee of Major plc since 1 November 2017 when she acquired 16,000 ordinary shares in the company. On 6 March 2020, Zoyla sold her entire holding of ordinary shares in Major plc to her son for £152,000. On that date, shares in Major plc were quoted on the stock exchange at £9.62 – £9.74.

Zoyla will not make any other disposals in the foreseeable future, and her taxable income will remain unchanged.

1 Why did neither of Zoyla's share disposals during the tax year 2019/20 qualify for entrepreneurs' relief?

Company	Size of shareholding	Holding period
Minor Ltd		
Major plc		

2 What cost figure will have been used in calculating the chargeable gain on Zoyla's disposal of 20,000 ordinary shares in Minor Ltd?

A £126,000

B £104,000

C £148,000

D £252,000

3   What proceeds figure will have been used in calculating the chargeable gain on Zoyla's disposal of 16,000 ordinary shares in Major plc?

£ ☐

4   If Zoyla had delayed the sale of her 16,000 ordinary shares in Major plc until 6 April 2020, by how long would the related CGT liability have been deferred?

   A   11 months

   B   12 months

   C   1 month

   D   6 months

5   Which of the following statements about how much CGT would Zoyla have saved if she had delayed the sale of her 16,000 ordinary shares in Major plc until the following tax year are true? Assume that the tax rates and allowances for the tax year 2019/20 continue to apply.

.	True	False
Zoyla would not have saved any CGT, but would have benefited from the delayed payment date		
Zoyla would have saved CGT of £12,000 × 20% = £2,400 due to the AEA for the tax year 2020/21 being available		
Zoyla would have saved CGT of £10,600 × 20% = £2,120 due to the remaining basic rate band for the tax year 2020/21 being available		

169 HALI AND GOMA (ADAPTED)

You should assume that the tax allowances for the tax year 2019/20 applied in previous tax years.

Hali and Goma are a married couple.

Capital losses brought forward

Hali had capital losses of £39,300 for the tax year 2017/18. He had chargeable gains of £16,000 for the tax year 2018/19.

Goma had capital losses of £9,100 and chargeable gains of £6,900 for the tax year 2018/19. She did not have any capital losses for the tax year 2017/18.

Ordinary shares in Lima Ltd

On 24 July 2019, Hali sold 5,000 £1 ordinary shares in Lima Ltd, for £4.95 per share. Lima Ltd's shares have recently been selling for £5.30 per share, but Hali sold them at the lower price because he needed a quick sale.

Goma, Hali's wife, had originally subscribed for 30,000 ordinary shares in Lima Ltd at their par value of £1 per share on 28 July 2008. On 18 August 2017, she gave 8,000 ordinary shares to Hali. On that date, the market value for 8,000 shares was £23,200.

Hali and Goma will both dispose of their remaining shareholdings in Lima Ltd during the tax year 2020/21. However, they are unsure as to whether these disposals will qualify for entrepreneurs' relief.

Antique table

On 11 October 2019, an antique table owned by Hali was destroyed in a fire. The table had been purchased on 3 June 2010 for £44,000. Hali received insurance proceeds of £62,000 on 12 December 2019, and on 6 January 2020, he purchased a replacement antique table for £63,600. Hali will make a claim to roll over the gain arising from the receipt of the insurance proceeds.

Disposals by Goma during the tax year 2019/20

Goma disposed of the following assets during the tax year 2019/20, all of which resulted in gains:

1   Qualifying corporate bonds sold for £38,300

2   A motor car (suitable for private use) sold for £11,600

3   An antique vase sold for £6,200

4   A copyright (with an unexpired life of eight years when purchased) sold for £5,400

5   Quoted shares held within an individual savings account (ISA) sold for £24,700

1   What amount of unused capital losses do Hali and Goma have brought forward to the tax year 2019/20?

	Hali	Goma
A	£23,300	£9,100
B	£23,300	£2,200
C	£35,300	£9,100
D	£35,300	£2,200

2   What cost figure and what value per share (disposal value) will be used in calculating the chargeable gain on Hali's sale of 5,000 ordinary shares in Lima Ltd?

	Cost figure	Value per share
A	£5,000	£4.95
B	£14,500	£4.95
C	£14,500	£5.30
D	£5,000	£5.30

3   In deciding whether Hali and Goma's future disposals of their shareholdings in Lima Ltd will qualify for entrepreneurs' relief, which one of the following statements is correct?

A   Hali and Goma must be directors of Lima Ltd

B   Lima Ltd must be a trading company

C   Hali and Goma must have shareholdings of at least 10% each in Lima Ltd

D   The qualifying conditions must be met for a period of three years prior to the date of disposal

4 What is the base cost of Hali's replacement antique table for capital gains tax (CGT) purposes?

A £62,000

B £63,600

C £45,600

D £44,000

5 How many of the five assets disposed of by Goma during the tax year 2019/20 are exempt assets for the purposes of capital gains tax (CGT)?

A Three

B Five

C Two

D Four

COMPANIES – CHARGEABLE GAINS

170 HAWK LTD (ADAPTED) *Walk in the footsteps of a top tutor*

Hawk Ltd sold the following assets during the year ended 31 March 2020:

(1) On 15 April 2019 a freehold office building was sold for £260,000. The office building had been purchased on 2 July 1998 for £81,000. Hawk Ltd incurred legal fees of £3,200 in connection with the purchase of the office building.

(2) On 30 April 2019 a freehold factory was sold for £500,000 (before deducting legal fees of £3,840) realising an unindexed gain of £300,000 and an indexed gain of £240,000. The factory has always been used by Hawk Ltd for business purposes.

Hawk Ltd plans to reinvest some or all of the proceeds in the purchase of a new freehold factory.

(3) On 1 July 2019 White plc was taken over by Black plc. Hawk Ltd had purchased 3,000 ordinary shares in White plc for £8,000 in June 2002. On takeover, Hawk Ltd received 2 ordinary shares and 2 preference shares in Black plc for each ordinary share in White plc.

Immediately after the takeover the ordinary shares in Black plc were quoted at £3 and the preference shares at £2.

Indexation factors are as follows:

July 1998 to December 2017   0.706
July 1998 to April 2019   0.750
June 2002 to December 2017   0.578
June 2002 to July 2019   0.633

1   What is the amount of indexation allowance available on the disposal of the freehold office building on 15 April 2019?

    A   £57,186

    B   £59,445

    C   £60,750

    D   £63,150

2   For each of the following gifts select whether they are qualifying or non-qualifying assets for companies for rollover relief purposes.

	Qualifying	Non-qualifying
Goodwill acquired on the purchase of the trade and assets of another business		
Vehicle costing £150,000 with an estimated useful life of 50 years		
Land acquired for business use		
75% shareholding of an unquoted trading company		

3   What is the maximum amount of rollover relief that Hawk Ltd can claim in respect of the gain on the factory and what is the latest date by which the reinvestment must take place? Tick the appropriate box.

		Maximum rollover relief	
		£240,000	£300,000
Latest date	30 April 2022		
	31 March 2023		

4   What is the minimum amount that will have to be reinvested in qualifying replacement business assets in order for the company to claim the maximum possible amount of rollover relief in respect of the gain on the factory?

£ _____

5   What is the indexed cost of the total number of ordinary shares in Black plc on 1 July 2019?

    A   £7,574

    B   £7,838

    C   £18,000

    D   £30,000

171 KAT LTD (ADAPTED) *Walk in the footsteps of a top tutor*

Kitten is the controlling shareholder in Kat Ltd, an unquoted trading company.

Kat Ltd

Kat Ltd sold a freehold factory on 30 November 2019 for £394,000, which resulted in a chargeable gain of £131,530 in the company's year ended 31 March 2020 (after the deduction of indexation and professional fees). The factory was purchased on 1 October 2005 for £138,600, and capital improvements were made at a cost of £23,400 during December 2017. The relevant indexation factors are as follows:

October 2005 to December 2017	0.439
October 2005 to November 2019	0.505
December 2017 to November 2019	0.046

Kat Ltd is unsure how to reinvest the proceeds from the sale of the factory. The company is considering either purchasing a freehold warehouse for £302,000, or acquiring a leasehold office building on a 40-year lease for a premium of £370,000. If either reinvestment is made, it will take place on 30 September 2020.

All of the above buildings have been, or will be, used for the purposes of Kat Ltd's trade.

Kitten

Kitten sold 20,000 £1 ordinary shares in Kat Ltd on 5 October 2019, which resulted in a chargeable gain of £142,200. This disposal qualified for entrepreneurs' relief.

Kitten had originally subscribed for 90,000 shares in Kat Ltd on 7 July 2010 at their par value. On 22 September 2013, Kat Ltd made a 2 for 3 rights issue. Kitten took up her allocation under the rights issue in full, paying £6.40 for each new share issued.

Kitten also sold an antique vase on 16 January 2020, which resulted in a chargeable gain of £28,800. For the tax year 2019/20, Kitten had taxable income of £12,000.

1   What amount of indexation allowance will have been deducted in calculating the chargeable gain of £131,530 on the disposal of Kat Ltd's factory?

   A   £60,845

   B   £69,993

   C   £71,069

   D   £81,810

2   **If Kat Ltd decides to purchase the freehold warehouse and makes a claim to roll over the chargeable gain on the factory under the rollover relief rules, which of the following statements are true?**

	True	False
The base cost of the warehouse for chargeable gains purposes will be £170,470		
The claim for rollover relief against the warehouse must be made by 31 March 2025		
A further claim for rollover relief may be made if another qualifying asset is acquired by 31 March 2023		

3   **If Kat Ltd decides to acquire the leasehold office building and makes a claim to hold over the chargeable gain on the factory under the rollover relief rules, what is the latest date by which the held-over gain will crystallise?**

A   10 years from 30 November 2019

B   The date when the office building is sold

C   40 years from 30 September 2020

D   10 years from 30 September 2020

4   **What cost figure will have been used in calculating the chargeable gain on Kitten's disposal of 20,000 ordinary shares in Kat Ltd?**

£

5   **What is Kitten's capital gains tax (CGT) liability for the tax year 2019/20 and by when must it be paid? Tick the appropriate box.**

		CGT liability	
		£17,580	£18,780
Due date	31 July 2020		
	31 January 2021		

PRACTICE SECTION C CONSTRUCTED RESPONSE QUESTIONS

INDIVIDUALS – CAPITAL GAINS TAX

172 DAVID AND ANGELA BROOK (ADAPTED) *Walk in the footsteps of a top tutor*

David and Angela Brook are a married couple. They disposed of the following assets during the tax year 2019/20:

Jointly owned property

On 30 September 2019 David and Angela sold a house for £381,900. The house had been purchased on 1 October 1999 for £86,000.

David and Angela occupied the house as their main residence from the date of purchase until 31 March 2003. The house was then unoccupied between 1 April 2003 and 31 December 2006 due to Angela being required by her employer to work elsewhere in the United Kingdom.

From 1 January 2007 until 31 December 2013 David and Angela again occupied the house as their main residence. The house was then unoccupied until it was sold on 30 September 2019.

Throughout the period 1 October 1999 to 30 September 2019 David and Angela did not have any other main residence.

David Brook

On 5 May 2019 David transferred his entire shareholding of 20,000 £1 ordinary shares in Bend Ltd, an unquoted trading company, to Angela. On that date the shares were valued at £64,000. David's shareholding had been purchased on 21 June 2016 for £48,000.

Angela Brook

On 7 July 2019 Angela sold 15,000 of the 20,000 £1 ordinary shares in Bend Ltd that had been transferred to her from David. The sale proceeds were £62,400.

Neither David nor Angela has ever worked for Bent Ltd.

On 15 October 2019 Angela disposed of a small business she had been running part time for many years. The only chargeable asset in the business was a warehouse and this resulted in a gain of £3,700.

Angela has taxable income of £26,945 for the tax year 2019/20. David does not have any taxable income.

Required:

Compute David and Angela's respective capital gains tax liabilities for the tax year 2019/20. 田   **(10 marks)**

173 BILL DING *Walk in the footsteps of a top tutor*

Bill Ding has run a construction company, High Rise Ltd since he purchased the entire shareholding for £112,000 in 2001. He has worked for the company since purchase.

Bill has decided to retire and on 17 August 2019 Bill made a gift of his entire holding of High Rise Ltd shares to his daughter, Belle, who also works for the company. The market value of the shares on that date was £260,000.

On 17 August 2019 the market value of High Rise Ltd's chargeable assets was £180,000, of which £150,000 was in respect of chargeable business assets. Bill and his daughter have elected to hold over the gain on this gift of a business asset.

Belle plans to sell the shares in High Rise Ltd on 31 March 2020, when they are expected to be worth £265,000 in order to fund a new business venture.

Neither Bill nor Belle has made any previous disposals chargeable to capital gains tax, and both are higher rate taxpayers.

Required:

(a) Calculate the gains arising and capital gains tax liabilities for Bill and Belle on the gift of High Rise Ltd shares to Belle and the subsequent sale by Belle. ⊞

Assume that Bill and Belle make a joint claim for gift relief, and state the due date for this claim. **(5 marks)**

(b) Recalculate the gains arising and capital gains tax liabilities for Bill and Belle, assuming a joint claim for gift relief is not made. ⊞ **(3 marks)**

(c) Briefly conclude, including a calculation of the tax saving, on which route would be preferable for Bill and Belle. ⊞ **(2 marks)**

(Total: 10 marks)

174 JEROME (ADAPTED) *Walk in the footsteps of a top tutor*

Jerome made the following gifts to family members during the tax year 2019/20:

(1) On 28 May 2019, Jerome made a gift of a house valued at £187,000 to his wife. Jerome's uncle had originally purchased the house on 14 July 1998 for £45,900. The uncle died on 12 June 2007, and the house was inherited by Jerome. On that date, the house was valued at £112,800. Jerome has never occupied the house as his main residence.

(2) On 24 June 2019, Jerome made a gift of his entire 12% holding of 12,000 £1 ordinary shares in Reward Ltd, an unquoted trading company, to his son. The market value of the shares on that date was £98,400. The shares had been purchased on 15 March 2009 for £39,000. On 24 June 2019, the market value of Reward Ltd's chargeable assets was £540,000, of which £460,000 was in respect of chargeable business assets. Jerome and his son have elected to hold over the gain on this gift of a business asset.

(3) On 7 November 2019, Jerome made a gift of an antique bracelet valued at £12,200 to his granddaughter. The antique bracelet had been purchased on 1 September 2004 for £2,100.

(4) On 29 January 2020, Jerome made a gift of nine acres of land valued at £78,400 to his brother. He had originally purchased ten acres of land on 3 November 2008 for £37,800. The market value of the unsold acre of land as at 29 January 2020 was £33,600. The land has never been used for business purposes.

Required:

(a) Calculate Jerome's chargeable gains for the tax year 2019/20. ▦

Note: You should ignore inheritance tax. **(7 marks)**

(b) For each of the four recipients of assets (1) to (4) gifted from Jerome, state their respective base cost for capital gains tax purposes. 💻 **(3 marks)**

(Total: 10 marks)

175 GINGER AND NIGEL (ADAPTED) *Walk in the footsteps of a top tutor*

You should assume that today's date is 1 March 2020.

(a) Ginger has a holding of 10,000 £1 ordinary shares in Nutmeg Ltd, an unquoted trading company, which she had purchased on 13 February 2010 for £2.39 per share. The current value of the shares as agreed with HM Revenue and Customs is £6.40 per share, but Ginger intends to sell some of the holding to her daughter at £4.00 per share during March 2020. Ginger and her daughter will elect to hold over any gain as a gift of a business asset.

For the tax year 2019/20, Ginger will not make any other disposals, and has therefore not utilised her annual exempt amount.

Required:

Explain how many £1 ordinary shares in Nutmeg Ltd Ginger can sell to her daughter for £4.00 per share during March 2020 without incurring any capital gains tax liability for the tax year 2019/20. 💻

Your answer should be supported by appropriate calculations. **(4 marks)**

(b) Innocent and Nigel, a married couple, both have shareholdings in Cinnamon Ltd, an unquoted trading company with a share capital of 100,000 £1 ordinary shares.

Innocent has been the managing director of Cinnamon Ltd since the company's incorporation on 1 July 2010, and she currently holds 20,000 shares (with matching voting rights) in the company. These shares were subscribed for on 1 July 2010 at their par value. Nigel has never been an employee or a director of Cinnamon Ltd, and he currently holds 3,000 shares (with matching voting rights) in the company. These shares were purchased on 23 April 2014 for £46,200.

Either Innocent or Nigel will sell 2,000 of their shares in Cinnamon Ltd during March 2020 for £65,000, but they are not sure which of them should make the disposal. For the tax year 2019/20, both Innocent and Nigel have already made disposals which will fully utilise their annual exempt amounts, and they will each have taxable income of £80,000.

Required:

Calculate the capital gains tax saving if the disposal of 2,000 shares in Cinnamon Ltd during March 2020 is made by Innocent rather than Nigel. ▦ **(6 marks)**

(Total: 10 marks)

176 MICK STONE (ADAPTED) *Walk in the footsteps of a top tutor*

Mick Stone disposed of the following assets during the tax year 2019/20:

(1) On 19 May 2019, Mick sold a freehold warehouse for £522,000. The warehouse was purchased on 6 August 2006 for £258,000. In January 2012, the floor of the warehouse was damaged by flooding and had to be replaced at a cost of £63,000. The warehouse was sold because it was surplus to the business's requirements as a result of Mick purchasing a newly built warehouse during 2018. Both warehouses have always been used for business purposes in a wholesale business run by Mick as a sole trader.

(2) On 24 September 2019, Mick sold 700,000 £1 ordinary shares in Rolling Ltd, an unquoted trading company, for £3,675,000. He had originally purchased 500,000 shares in Rolling Ltd on 2 June 2010 for £960,000. On 1 December 2015, Rolling Ltd made a 3 for 2 bonus issue. Mick has been a director of Rolling Ltd since 1 January 2010.

Required:

(a) **Assuming that no reliefs are available, calculate the chargeable gain arising from each of Mick Stone's asset disposals during the tax year 2019/20.** ⊞

You are not required to calculate the taxable gains or the amount of tax payable.

(4 marks)

(b) **State which capital gains tax reliefs might be available to Mick Stone in respect of each of his disposals during the tax year 2019/20, and what further information you would require in order to establish if the reliefs are actually available and to establish any restrictions as regards the amount of relief.** ⌨

For this part of the question you are not expected to perform any calculations.

(6 marks)

(Total: 10 marks)

177 RUBY (ADAPTED) *Walk in the footsteps of a top tutor*

You should assume that today's date is 1 March 2020.

(a) On 27 August 2019, Ruby disposed of a residential investment property, and this resulted in a chargeable gain of £47,500.

For the tax year 2019/20, Ruby has taxable income of £23,315.

Required:

Calculate Ruby's capital gains tax liability for the tax year 2019/20 if this is her only disposal in that tax year. ⊞ **(2 marks)**

(b) In addition to the disposal already made on 27 August 2019, Ruby is going to make one further disposal during the tax year 2019/20. This disposal will be of either Ruby's holding of £1 ordinary shares in Pola Ltd, or her holding of 50p ordinary shares in Aplo plc.

Shareholding in Pola Ltd

Pola Ltd is an unquoted trading company, in which Ruby has a 10% shareholding. The shareholding was purchased on 14 July 2010 for £23,700 and could be sold for £61,000. Ruby has been an employee of Pola Ltd since 2008.

Shareholding in Aplo plc

Aplo plc is a quoted trading company, in which Ruby has a shareholding of 40,000 50p ordinary shares. Ruby received the shareholding as a gift from her father on 27 May 2013. On that date, the shares were quoted on the stock exchange at £2.12–£2.24. The shareholding could be sold for £59,000.

No capital gains tax reliefs are available in respect of this disposal.

Required:

Calculate Ruby's revised capital gains tax liability for the tax year 2019/20 if, during March 2020, she also disposes of either (1) her shareholding in Pola Ltd, or alternatively (2) her shareholding in Aplo plc.

Note - the following mark allocation is provided as guidance for this requirement:

Pola Ltd	**(4.5 marks)**
Aplo plc	**(3.5 marks)**

(8 marks)

(Total: 10 marks)

178 DALJEET *Walk in the footsteps of a top tutor*

Please assume today's date is 5 April 2019.

Daljeet wishes to sell personal assets to generate funds to pay his daughter's university fees and he has selected two assets that he is willing to sell. He will sell one of the assets to a third party on 31 December 2019 and will make his decision based on the asset that will generate the highest amount of net proceeds.

The assets Daljeet has identified as potential disposals are as follows:

1,000 shares in ABC Ltd

Daljeet acquired 1,000 shares in ABC Ltd, a trading company, on 7 June 2014 for £60,000 when he became an employee of the company. On 7 June 2015 ABC Ltd underwent a rights issue, offering shareholders the opportunity to purchase 2 shares for every 5 shares already held for £50 per share. Daljeet purchased the maximum amount of shares.

ABC Ltd has 20,000 shares in issue.

If Daljeet sells the ABC Ltd shares, he will sell 1,000 shares worth £100,300 on 31 December 2019.

Holiday cottage

The cottage is currently worth £110,000 and legal fees in respect of the disposal are expected to be £1,000. Repairs costing £3,500 were made to the cottage roof in December 2018 following damage caused by a storm.

Daljeet originally bought the cottage in May 2010 at a cost of £65,000. It has always been let out and Daljeet has never occupied the property as his principal private residence.

Other information

Daljeet will be a higher rate taxpayer and will make no other disposals in the tax year 2019/20.

Required:

(a) **Calculate which of the above asset disposals will result in the highest amount of proceeds, after deducting tax and any costs of sale.** ⊞

You should assume that Daljeet will claim any relevant reliefs where possible and has not previously claimed any capital gains tax reliefs.   **(8 marks)**

(b) **Briefly explain why the disposal of either the ABC Ltd shares or the holiday cottage will not be subject to inheritance tax.** 🖥   **(2 marks)**

(Total: 10 marks)

COMPANIES – CHARGEABLE GAINS

179 FORWARD LTD (ADAPTED)

Forward Ltd sold the following assets during the year ended 31 March 2020:

(1) On 31 May 2019 Forward Ltd sold a freehold office building for £290,000. The office building had been purchased on 15 July 1998 for £148,000. Assume the indexation factors are as follows:

July 1998 to May 2019   0.755

July 1998 to December 2017   0.706

Forward Ltd purchased a replacement freehold office building on 1 June 2019 for £260,000.

(2) On 30 November 2019 Forward Ltd sold 5,000 £1 ordinary shares in Backward plc for £62,500. Forward Ltd had originally purchased 9,000 shares in Backward plc on 20 April 1992 for £18,000. The company purchased a further 500 shares on 1 November 2019 for £6,500. Assume the indexation factors are as follows:

April 1992 to December 2017   1.004

April 1992 to November 2019   1.096

Forward Ltd has never owned more than 1% of the shares in Backward plc.

Forward Ltd purchased 10,000 £1 ordinary shares in Sideways plc on 1 December 2019 for £65,000.

Where possible, Forward Ltd has claimed to roll over any gains arising.

Forward Ltd's only other income for the year ended 31 March 2020 is its tax adjusted trading profit of £78,000. There are no related 51% group companies.

Required:

(a) Calculate Forward Ltd's corporation tax liability for the year ended 31 March 2020, and state by when this should be paid.

Your answer should clearly identify the amount of any gains that have been rolled over. Capital allowances should be ignored. ⊞ **(7 marks)**

(b) Explain how Forward Ltd's rollover relief claim would have altered if on 1 June 2019 it had acquired a leasehold office building on a 15-year lease for £300,000, rather than purchasing the freehold office building for £260,000. 🖥 **(3 marks)**

(Total: 10 marks)

180 LUNA LTD *Walk in the footsteps of a top tutor*

Luna Ltd had the following transactions in shares during the year ended 31 March 2020:

(1) On 29 November 2019, Luna Ltd sold its entire shareholding of £1 ordinary shares in Pluto plc for £53,400. Luna Ltd had originally purchased 16,000 shares in Pluto plc on 14 June 2011 for £36,800. On 22 May 2013, Luna Ltd sold 10,000 of the shares for £46,200. Assume the indexation factors are as follows:

June 2011 to May 2013	0.063
May 2013 to December 2017	0.112
May 2013 to November 2019	0.164

(2) On 12 February 2020, Luna Ltd's shareholding in Asteroid plc was taken over by Comet plc. Luna Ltd had originally purchased 10,000 £1 ordinary shares in Asteroid plc, and their indexed cost on 12 February 2020 was £33,000. Under the terms of the takeover, for each of its £1 ordinary shares in Asteroid plc, Luna Ltd received £6.50 in cash plus one £1 ordinary share in Comet plc. Immediately after the takeover, Comet plc's £1 ordinary shares were quoted at £4.50.

Required:

(a) Explain how the indexation allowance can be used when a company makes a capital loss, or where the indexation allowance is greater than a company's unindexed gain. 🖥 **(2 marks)**

(b) Calculate the chargeable gain arising from each of Luna Ltd's transactions in shares during the year ended 31 March 2020. When calculating the chargeable gain arising from the disposal of the shareholding in Pluto plc, you should show full workings for the share pool. ⊞ **(8 marks)**

(Total: 10 marks)

Section 3

PRACTICE INHERITANCE TAX QUESTIONS

Tutorial note

You should expect inheritance tax to be tested in both sections A and B. The 10 mark question in Section C could also test inheritance tax topics.

There is however no set minimum or maximum number of marks for inheritance tax.

PRACTICE SECTION A OBJECTIVE TEST QUESTIONS

181   Mario made a number of gifts during the tax year 2019/20:

For each of the following gifts select whether they are exempt or not exempt transfers for inheritance tax purposes.

	Exempt	Not exempt
On 7 May 2019 he gave 100,000 shares in Lahm Ltd to his wife. The shares have been valued at that date at £500,000		
On 10 August 2019 he gave 50,000 shares in Hummells Ltd to a discretionary trust. The shares have been valued at that date at £75,000		
On 6 October 2019 he gave £2,000 to his son on the occasion of his marriage		
On 9 February 2020 he gave £300 to his daughter		

182 *September 2016 OT question*

Cora made a cash gift of £300,000 to her niece on 30 April 2014.

She then made a cash gift of £500,000 to her nephew on 31 May 2015.

Both of these amounts are stated after deducting available exemptions.

Cora subsequently died on 31 October 2019.

What amount of inheritance tax was payable as a result of Cora's death in respect of the cash gift of £500,000 to her nephew?

A   £190,000

B   £110,000

C   £114,000

D   £76,000

183   Christiano made the following lifetime gifts, and agreed to pay any inheritance tax that arose as a result of the second gift.

(1)   A gift into a discretionary trust on 18 February 2018 – the gross chargeable transfer was £274,000

(2)   A cash gift of £150,000 into a discretionary trust on 20 May 2019

The nil rate band for the tax year 2017/18 was £325,000.

How much lifetime tax is paid by Christiano in respect of the gift on 20 May 2019?

£ ☐

184 *September 2016 OT question*

On 1 July 2018, Sameer made a cash gift of £2,500 to his sister.

On 1 May 2019, he made a cash gift of £2,000 to a friend.

On 1 June 2019, he made a cash gift of £50,000 to a trust. Sameer has not made any other lifetime gifts.

In respect of Sameer's cash gift of £50,000 to the trust, what is the lifetime transfer of value for inheritance tax purposes after taking account of all available exemptions?

A   £48,500

B   £44,000

C   £46,000

D   £46,500

185 Amir died on 1 February 2020. During his lifetime, he made two gifts:

(1) On 30 November 2012 he gave £200,000 to his son

(2) On 15 June 2013 he gave £350,000 to his daughter

Select the correct chargeable amount of the above gifts (i.e. value before the deduction of the nil rate band) which becomes chargeable as a result of Amir's death.

	Chargeable amount £
(1) 30 November 2012	
(2) 15 June 2013	

0

194,000

347,000

344,000

186 *September 2015 OT question*

Heng is a wealthy 45 year old who would like to reduce the potential inheritance tax liability on her estate when she dies.

Which of the following actions will NOT achieve Heng's aim of reducing the potential inheritance tax liability on her estate when she dies?

A   Changing the terms of her will so that the residue of her estate goes to her grandchildren rather than her children

B   Making lifetime gifts to trusts up to the value of the nil rate band every seven years

C   Changing the terms of her will so that the residue of her estate goes to her husband rather than her children

D   Making lifetime gifts to her grandchildren early in life

187 *June 2015 OT question (ADAPTED)*

Chan died on 8 December 2019, having made a lifetime cash gift of £500,000 to a trust on 16 October 2018. Chan paid the inheritance tax arising from this gift.

Who will be responsible for paying the additional inheritance tax arising from the gift made to the trust as a result of Chan's death, and when will this be due? Select the appropriate box in the table below.

		Paid by	
		Trustees of the trust	Personal representatives of Chan's estate
Due date	8 June 2020	A	B
	30 June 2020	C	D

188   Edin died on 16 July 2019. He made one lifetime gift on 10 November 2014 into a discretionary trust. He paid the lifetime tax of £52,250 and the gross chargeable transfer value of the gift was £586,250.

How much inheritance tax is due on the lifetime gift as a result of Edin's death?

A   £10,450

B   £62,700

C   £52,250

D   £104,500

189   Fabrice died on 20 January 2020. During his lifetime he made the following gifts:

(1)	20 February 2009	£300,000 to his son
(2)	22 March 2012	£400,000 to a discretionary trust
(3)	30 September 2018	half share in his main residence, worth £250,000 to his daughter
(4)	24 December 2019	£800,000 to his wife

Select the gift(s) on which inheritance tax will be payable as a result of Fabrice's death.

	Inheritance tax payable
20 February 2009	
22 March 2012	
30 September 2018	
24 December 2019	

190   *September 2015 OT question*

Benjamin died on 30 November 2019 leaving an estate valued at £890,000. Inheritance tax of £252,000 was paid in respect of the estate. Under the terms of his will, Benjamin left £260,000 to his wife, a specific legacy of £120,000 (free of tax) to his brother, and the residue of the estate to his grandchildren.

What is the amount of inheritance received by Benjamin's grandchildren?

A   £638,000

B   £510,000

C   £378,000

D   £258,000

191 *June 2015 OT question (ADAPTED)*

Which TWO of the following are NOT deducted when calculating the value of a person's chargeable estate for inheritance tax purposes?

A   An outstanding repayment mortgage

B   Funeral expenses

C   An outstanding interest-only mortgage

D   An outstanding endowment mortgage

E   A verbal promise to pay a friend's debt

F   Credit card debts

192 Fred died on 8 July 2019.

His estate consisted of the following assets:

(1)   A house worth £545,000 on which there is an outstanding endowment mortgage of £145,000, and

(2)   A life insurance policy with a market value of £300,000, but the proceeds paid to the executors from the policy were £350,000.

Under the terms of Fred's will £400,000 was left to his wife with the remainder of his estate to his son.

What is Fred's chargeable estate for inheritance tax purposes?

£ ☐

193 *December 2016 OT question*

Gita died on 17 May 2019. At the date of her death she owned the following assets:

	£
House	390,000
Chattels and cash	70,000
Shares held in an individual savings account (ISA)	60,000

At the date of her death, Gita owed income tax of £25,000 in respect of the tax year 2018/19.

Gita left £100,000 of her estate to her husband, with the remainder of the estate left to her daughter.

What is Gita's chargeable estate for inheritance tax purposes?

A   £335,000

B   £395,000

C   £495,000

D   £420,000

194 Joel died on 20 December 2019, and left an estate worth £1,151,000 to his daughter. Joel's main residence, valued at £300,000, was included in the total value of the estate.

Joel did not make any lifetime gifts.

How much inheritance tax is payable on Joel's death estate?

£

195 Dominic owned 7,500 shares in Halder Ltd. On 1 July 2019 he gave 3,000 shares to his son.

The company has an issued share capital of 10,000 shares.

The values of different shareholdings in the shares on 1 July 2019 are as follows:

Holding	Value per share
Up to 25%	£5
26% to 50%	£8
51% to 74%	£13
75% or more	£20

What is the transfer of value for inheritance tax purposes on the gift of the shares to his son?

£

196 On 15 September 2015 Elvis transferred £500,000 into a discretionary trust. On 15 September 2019 Elvis died.

Select the tax payable date for both the lifetime inheritance tax and any additional inheritance tax payable on death due in respect of the chargeable lifetime transfer.

Lifetime tax	15 March 2016	31 March 2016	30 April 2016
Additional tax on death	15 March 2020	31 March 2020	30 April 2020

197 Melvin died on 6 March 2020 leaving an estate worth £2,000,000. His estate included a holiday home in the UK worth £400,000 which he left to his sister. He left the rest of his estate to his daughter and appointed a friend to act as executor.

For each of the following individuals, select whether they will pay the inheritance tax due on the estate, suffer the inheritance tax payable on the estate, or neither. It is possible to select more than one individual for the same answer.

	Pays tax	Suffers tax	Neither pays nor suffers tax
Sister			
Daughter			
Executor			

198 For each of the following statements select whether it is true or false:

	True	False
An advantage of giving an appreciating asset away during lifetime is that the increase in value up to the date of death will not be subject to inheritance tax		
For capital gains tax purposes lifetime gifts are taxable but gifts on death are not		
On a lifetime gift made more than three years before death, taper relief will reduce the amount of the gift chargeable to inheritance tax on death		

199 *December 2016 OT question*

Nadia died on 13 February 2004, leaving an estate valued at £275,400 for inheritance tax purposes. Nadia left 50% of her estate to her son and 50% to her husband, Tareq.

Tareq subsequently died on 17 January 2020.

Neither Nadia nor Tareq made any lifetime gifts, nor did they ever own a main residence.

The inheritance nil rate band for the tax year 2003/04 was £255,000.

What is the maximum available nil rate band which can be used when calculating the inheritance tax payable in respect of Tareq's estate?

A   £500,500

B   £474,500

C   £442,300

D   £462,700

PRACTICE SECTION B OBJECTIVE TEST CASES

200 LEBNA AND LULU (ADAPTED)

You should assume that today's date is 1 March 2020.

Lebna and Lulu were a married couple, but, unfortunately, Lulu died on 24 January 2016.

Lulu

Lulu left an estate valued at £210,000 for inheritance tax (IHT) purposes. The estate did not include a main residence. Under the terms of her will, Lulu left a specific legacy of £40,000 to her brother, with the residue of the estate to her husband, Lebna. Lulu had made the following lifetime transfers:

Date	Type of transfer	Amount
		£
13 February 2008	Chargeable lifetime transfer	50,000
21 June 2014	Potentially exempt transfer	80,000

Both of these transfers are after taking account of all available exemptions.

The nil rate band for the tax year 2015/16 is £325,000.

Lebna's chargeable estate

Lebna has a chargeable estate valued at £980,000. His estate includes a main residence valued at £340,000 on which there is an outstanding interest-only mortgage of £152,000.

Under the terms of his will, Lebna has left his entire estate to his son.

Gift to son on 22 February 2015

On 22 February 2015, Lebna made a gift of 60,000 £1 ordinary shares in Blean Ltd, an unquoted investment company, to his son. Before the transfer, Lebna owned all of Blean Ltd's share capital of 100,000 ordinary shares. The market value of Blean Ltd's ordinary shares on 22 February 2015 was as follows:

Holding	Market value per share
40%	£4.20
60%	£6.30
100%	£7.10

Lebna had not made any previous lifetime gifts.

Gifts to friends during October 2019

Lebna made cash gifts of £85, £225, £190 and £490 to various friends during October 2019. The gifts of £85 and £190 were to the same friend.

---

1   If Lebna were to die today, 1 March 2020, how much of Lulu's nil rate band will the personal representatives of Lebna's estate be able to claim when calculating the IHT payable on his chargeable estate?

    A   £155,000

    B   £205,000

    C   £35,000

    D   £285,000

2   If Lebna were to die today, 1 March 2020, what is the total amount of residence nil rate band which will be available when calculating the IHT payable on his chargeable estate?

    A   £150,000

    B   £300,000

    C   £340,000

    D   £188,000

3   What is the amount of the potentially exempt transfer which Lebna has made to his son on 22 February 2015 (the gift of 60,000 shares in Blean Ltd) after deducting any available exemptions?

    A   £542,000

    B   £536,000

    C   £372,000

    D   £378,000

4   If Lebna were to die today, 1 March 2020, what taper relief percentage reduction would be available when calculating the IHT payable on the potentially exempt transfer which he made to his son on 22 February 2015 (the gift of 60,000 shares in Blean Ltd), and when would this IHT be due?

	Taper relief reduction	Due date
A	60%	30 September 2020
B	60%	1 September 2020
C	40%	1 September 2020
D	40%	30 September 2020

5   What amount of the cash gifts made by Lebna to his friends during October 2019 is covered by the small gifts exemption?

A	£500
B	£990
C	£225
D	£275

201 TOM (ADAPTED) *Walk in the footsteps of a top tutor*

Tom died on 1 May 2019.

He had made a gift with a chargeable amount of £450,000 (after all available exemptions) to a trust on 20 February 2013. Tom paid the inheritance tax arising on the gift. This was Tom's only gift.

Tom's estate at the date of death included the following assets as well as some cash in the bank:

(1)   A 50% share, valued at £150,000, in a successful racehorse

(2)   Cash winnings from betting on horse racing of £40,000

(3)   His main residence valued at £875,000 which has an outstanding repayment mortgage of £500,000.

The executors have determined that Tom's chargeable estate for IHT purposes was £2,000,000 and they filed their account of the estate assets with HM Revenue and Customs on 3 January 2020.

Tom left all of his estate to his children. His wife is still alive.

The nil rate band for the tax year 2012/13 was £325,000.

1   What was the GROSS chargeable amount, for the purpose of calculating any additional tax as a result of Tom's death, in respect of Tom's gift of £450,000 to the trust on 20 February 2013?

A   £475,000

B   £450,000

C   £481,250

D   £473,750

2   If Tom had also made cash gifts of £5,500 to his daughter and £400 to his granddaughter on 20 December 2011 what would have been the amount of annual exemption available on the gift into the trust on 20 February 2013?

£ ☐

3   In respect of the gift to the trust on 20 February 2013, what rate of taper relief is applied to the IHT payable on Tom's death and who is liable to pay this additional IHT arising on death? Select the appropriate box in the table below.

		Liability for tax	
		Trustees	Executors
Taper relief	20%	A	B
	80%	C	D

4   What is the net value of the estate assets (1)–(3) that will be included in Tom's chargeable death estate for IHT purposes?

		Net value
(1)	50% share in a racehorse	
(2)	Cash winnings	
(3)	Main residence	

Potential answers

£0

£40,000

£150,000

£225,000

£375,000

£725,000

£875,000

5   How much IHT is payable on Tom's death estate?

A   £610,000

B   £670,000

C   £740,000

D   £800,000

202   AFIYA (ADAPTED) *Walk in the footsteps of a top tutor*

 Question debrief

Afiya died on 29 November 2019. She had made a number of gifts during her lifetime as follows:

(1)   Afiya's first gift was made on 14 September 2014, when she gave 6,500 £1 ordinary shares in Cassava Ltd, an unquoted investment company, to her daughter.

       Before the transfer Afiya owned 8,000 shares out of Cassava Ltd's issued share capital of 10,000 £1 ordinary shares. On 14 September 2014, Cassava Ltd's shares were worth £3 each for a holding of 15%, £7 each for a holding of 65%, and £8 each for a holding of 80%.

(2)   Afiya then made various other gifts such that as at 26 January 2019 the total gross chargeable value of all transfers made in the previous seven years was £220,000 comprising potentially exempt transfers of £100,000 and chargeable lifetime transfers of £120,000.

(3)   On 27 January 2019, Afiya made a transfer of value (after all exemptions) of £400,000 to a trust. Afiya paid the inheritance tax arising from this gift.

Afiya's husband had died on 1 June 2008 leaving an estate valued at £200,000. He left £46,800 to his daughter and the balance to Afiya. He had never made any gifts during lifetime.

On her death Afiya left an estate valued at £525,000, including her main residence worth £375,000, to her children.

The nil rate band for the tax year 2008/09 is £312,000 and it is £325,000 thereafter.

1   What is the gross chargeable transfer value (after all exemptions) of Afiya's gift to her daughter on 14 September 2014?

A   £59,500

B   £39,500

C   £53,500

D   £45,500

2   How much lifetime IHT is payable on the gift to the trust on 27 January 2019?

£ ☐

3   Which FOUR of the following items will be included in, or deducted from, Afiya's chargeable death estate for inheritance tax purposes?

   A   Her main residence

   B   Funeral expenses

   C   Unpaid gambling debts

   D   Shares held in an Individual Savings Account

   E   £10,000 held in Gilts

   F   Endowment mortgage on her buy to let property

4   What is the total amount of nil rate band(s) that Afiya could claim in respect of unused nil rate band(s) on the death of her husband?

   A   £265,200

   B   £276,250

   C   £415,200

   D   £426,250

5   For both the lifetime inheritance tax on the gift to the trust on 27 January 2019 and the tax arising on Afiya's estate select the due date of payment from the following list.

Dates	Lifetime tax on gift to trust	Tax on estate
30 April 2019		
27 July 2019		
31 July 2019		
30 April 2020		
29 May 2020		
31 May 2020		

 Calculate your allowed time and allocate the time to each separate part.

203 ROMAN (ADAPTED) *Walk in the footsteps of a top tutor*

Roman died on 7 August 2019, and his wife Paris died on 18 February 2020.

The couple had attempted to mitigate their inheritance tax (IHT) liabilities when they both made substantial gifts during 2017. These gifts made full use of their respective nil rate bands of £325,000, but unfortunately neither Roman nor Paris then survived long enough for any of the gifts to benefit from taper relief. Neither Roman nor Paris had made any previous lifetime gifts or owned a main residence.

Roman

On 4 March 2017, Roman made a cash gift of £210,000 to his daughter. On 26 August 2017, he made a cash gift of £190,000 to a trust. No lifetime IHT arose in respect of the gift to the trust.

Roman's estate for IHT purposes was valued at £560,000. Under the terms of his will, Roman left £300,000 to Paris (his wife) and the residue of his estate to his daughter.

Paris

On 12 December 2017, Paris made a gift of 75,000 £1 ordinary shares in Capital Ltd, an unquoted investment company, to her son. Before the transfer, Paris owned 100,000 of Capital Ltd's 250,000 ordinary shares. The market value of Capital Ltd's ordinary shares on 12 December 2017was as follows:

Holding	Market value per share
10%	£5
30%	£6
40%	£8

Paris also made cash gifts of £80, £210, £195 and £460 to various friends during February 2018. The gifts of £80 and £195 were to the same friend.

Paris' estate for IHT purposes was valued at £840,000, including the inheritance from Roman (her husband). Under the terms of her will, Paris left a specific legacy of £20,000 to a friend and the residue of her estate to her grandchildren.

1   **How much IHT will be payable in respect of the gift made to the trust by Roman as a result of his death?**

   A   £26,400

   B   £30,000

   C   £27,600

   D   £13,200

2   **Who will be responsible for paying the IHT arising from Roman's gift to the trust as a result of his death, and when will the tax be due? Select the appropriate box in the table below.**

		Liability for tax	
		Trustees	**Personal representatives of Roman's estate**
Due date	**28 February 2020**	A	B
	30 April 2020	C	D

3   For IHT purposes, what was the amount of the transfer of value as a result of Paris' gift of 75,000 ordinary shares in Capital Ltd?

A   £450,000

B   £600,000

C   £675,000

D   £425,000

4   What is the amount of the cash gifts made by Paris to her friends during February 2018 NOT covered by the small gifts exemption?

£ [   ]

5   What is the amount of IHT payable in respect of Roman's and Paris' estates on death? Tick the appropriate boxes.

		Roman's estate	Paris' estate
IHT payable	£104,000		
	£224,000		
	£328,000		
	£336,000		

204 ADANA (ADAPTED) *Walk in the footsteps of a top tutor*

Adana died on 17 March 2020, and inheritance tax (IHT) of £566,000 is payable in respect of her chargeable estate. Under the terms of her will, Adana left her entire estate, which does not include a main residence, to her children.

At the date of her death, Adana had the following debts and liabilities:

(1)   An outstanding interest-only mortgage of £220,000.

(2)   Income tax of £43,700 payable in respect of the tax year 2019/20.

(3)   Legal fees of £4,600 incurred by Adana's sister which Adana had verbally promised to pay.

Adana's husband had died on 28 May 2006, and only 20% of his inheritance tax nil rate band was used on his death. The nil rate band for the tax year 2006/07 was £285,000.

On 22 April 2008, Adana had made a chargeable lifetime transfer of shares valued at £500,000 to a trust. Adana paid the lifetime IHT of £52,250 arising from this gift. If Adana had not made this gift, her chargeable estate at the time of her death would have been £650,000 higher than it otherwise was. This was because of the subsequent increase in the value of the gifted shares.

1   What is the maximum nil rate band which will have been available when calculating the IHT of £566,000 payable in respect of Adana's chargeable estate?

A   £325,000

B   £553,000

C   £390,000

D   £585,000

2   What is the amount of liabilities (1)-(3) which will be deducted in calculating Adana's chargeable estate for IHT purposes?

		Deductible
(1)	Interest-only mortgage	
(2)	Income tax payable	
(3)	Sister's legal fees	

Potential answers

£0

£4,600

£43,700

£220,000

3   Select who will be responsible for paying the IHT of £566,000 in respect of Adana's chargeable estate, and the due date for the payment of this liability.

	Tax payable		
Payable by:	30 September 2020	17 September 2020	17 March 2021
Beneficiaries (her children)	A	B	C
Personal representatives	D	E	F

4   How much of the IHT payable in respect of Adana's estate would have been saved if, under the terms of her will, Adana had made specific gifts of £400,000 to a trust and £200,000 to her grandchildren, instead of leaving her entire estate to her children?

A   £240,000

B   £160,000

C   £0

D   £80,000

5   How much IHT did Adana save by making the chargeable lifetime transfer of £500,000 to a trust on 22 April 2008, rather than retaining the gifted investments until her death?

£ _____

PRACTICE SECTION C CONSTRUCTED RESPONSE QUESTIONS

205   BLU (ADAPTED) *Walk in the footsteps of a top tutor*

(a)   Red Perry died on 6 November 2019, at which point his estate was valued at £800,000. The estate included a main residence valued at £290,000.

Red's wife had died on 11 May 2014, leaving her entire estate to Red. She made no gifts during her lifetime.

Red left his estate to his brother, Sonny.

Red's only lifetime gift was a gift to his son of £211,000 (after exemptions) in January 2017.

Required:

(1)   Calculate the inheritance tax payable in respect of Red's estate. ⊞

(2)   Explain how your answer would be different if, instead of leaving the estate to his brother, Red left his estate to his son. 💻

You are not required to do calculations for requirement (a)(2).   **(4 marks)**

(b)   On 15 January 2020 Blu Reddy made a gift of 200,000 £1 ordinary shares in Purple Ltd, an unquoted investment company, to a trust. Blu paid the inheritance tax arising from this gift.

Before the transfer Blu owned 300,000 shares out of Purple Ltd's issued share capital of 500,000 £1 ordinary shares.

On 15 January 2020 Purple Ltd's shares were worth £2 each for a holding of 20%, £3 each for a holding of 40%, and £4 each for a holding of 60%.

Blu has not made any previous gifts.

Required:

Calculate the inheritance tax that will be payable as a result of Blu Reddy's gift to the trust, and the additional inheritance tax that would be payable if Blu were to die on 31 May 2024. ⊞

You should ignore annual exemptions, and should assume that the nil rate band remains unchanged from that for the tax year 2019/20.   **(6 marks)**

(Total: 10 marks)

206 JACK AND TOM (ADAPTED) *Walk in the footsteps of a top tutor*

(a) On 3 October 2019 Jack Monkton sold his entire holding of shares in Corinthian Ltd, an unquoted trading company, for £151,107. He had subscribed for the shares and paid in full in cash on 23 May 2016 for £13,119. Jack has never worked for Corinthian Ltd and has made no other gains during the tax year 2019/20 but has a capital loss of £1,872 from a less successful investment in Burn Ltd.

Required:

Explain why the disposal of the shares in Corinthian Ltd qualifies for investors' relief and calculate Jack's capital gains tax liability for the tax year 2019/20. 🖥

(5 marks)

(b) Tom Tirith made a cash gift of £200,000 to his daughter on 20 December 2018. He is now going to make a cash gift of £450,000 to a trust on 20 February 2020. The nil rate band for the tax year 2018/19 is £325,000.

Required:

(1) Calculate the lifetime inheritance tax that will be payable in respect of Tom Tirith's gift of £450,000 to a trust if: ⊞

(1) the trust pays the tax arising from the gift, or

(2) Tom pays the tax arising from the gift,

and in the case of (2) only state the value of the gross chargeable transfer.

The total marks will be split equally between each part. **(3 marks)**

(2) Explain how your answer would be different if, instead of making a cash gift to his daughter on 20 December 2018, Tom made the same gift to a trust. 🖥

You are not required to do calculations for requirement (b)(2). **(2 marks)**

(Total: 10 marks)

207 PERE JONES (ADAPTED) *Walk in the footsteps of a top tutor*

On 23 August 2014, Pere Jones made a gift of a house valued at £416,000 to his nephew, Phil Jones. This was a wedding gift when Phil got married.

Pere Jones

Pere died on 20 March 2020 aged 76, at which time his estate was valued at £880,000. Under the terms of his will, Pere divided his estate equally between his wife and his nephew, Phil. Pere had not made any gifts during his lifetime except for the gift of the house to Phil.

The nil rate band for the tax year 2014/15 is £325,000.

Phil Jones

The house which Phil received as a wedding gift from Pere, his uncle, was always let out unfurnished until it was sold on 5 April 2020.

The following income and outgoings relate to the property for the tax year 2019/20:

	£
Sale proceeds	504,000
Cost of new boundary wall around the property (there was previously no boundary wall)	(9,300)
Cost of replacing the property's chimney	(2,800)
Legal fees paid in connection with the disposal	(8,100)
Property insurance	(2,300)

Phil has earnings from employment of £80,000 in the tax year 2019/20.

Required:

(a) **Calculate the inheritance tax that will be payable as a result of Pere Jones' death.**

(6 marks)

(b) **Calculate Phil Jones' capital gains tax liability for the tax year 2019/20.** **(4 marks)**

(Total: 10 marks)

208 KENDRA OLDER (ADAPTED) *Walk in the footsteps of a top tutor*

You should assume that today's date is 1 January 2020.

Kendra Older, aged 93, is unfortunately in poor health with just a few months left to live. She has made the following gifts during her lifetime:

(1) On 20 June 2012, Kendra made a gift to a trust with a gross chargeable transfer value of £140,000. No inheritance tax arose in respect of this gift.

(2) On 5 October 2018, Kendra made a cash gift of £253,000 to her children.

Kendra owns the following assets:

(1) A residential property valued at £970,000. The property is an investment property that has always been rented out and never occupied by Kendra. If the property were disposed of during the tax year 2019/20 the disposal would result in a chargeable gain of £174,000.

(2) A life assurance policy on her own life. The policy has an open market value of £210,000, and proceeds of £225,000 will be received following Kendra's death.

None of the above valuations are expected to change in the near future.

Under the terms of her will, Kendra has left her entire estate to her children.

The nil rate band of Kendra's husband was fully utilised when he died ten years ago.

The nil rate band for the tax years 2012/13 and 2018/19 is £325,000.

For the tax year 2019/20, Kendra will pay income tax at the higher rate.

Required:

(a) Calculate the inheritance tax which would be payable if Kendra Older were to die on 31 March 2020. ⊞ **(7 marks)**

(b) Advise Kendra Older why it would not be beneficial to make an immediate lifetime gift of the property valued at £970,000 to her children. 💻

Notes:

(1) Your answer should take account of both the capital gains tax and the inheritance tax implications of making the gift.

(2) For this part of the question you should ignore the capital gains tax annual exempt amount and inheritance tax annual exemptions. **(3 marks)**

(Total: 10 marks)

209 JAMES (ADAPTED) *Walk in the footsteps of a top tutor*

James died on 22 January 2020. He had made the following gifts during his lifetime:

(1) On 9 October 2012, a cash gift of £35,000 to a trust. No lifetime inheritance tax was payable in respect of this gift.

(2) On 14 May 2018, a cash gift of £420,000 to his daughter.

(3) On 2 August 2018, a gift of a property valued at £260,000 to a trust. No lifetime inheritance tax was payable in respect of this gift because it was covered by the nil rate band. By the time of James' death on 22 January 2020, the property had increased in value to £310,000.

On 22 January 2020, James' estate was valued at £870,000. Under the terms of his will, James left his entire estate to his brother as his children already have considerable assets. James believes his nephew will benefit from his estate in the future.

The nil rate band of James' wife was fully utilised when she died ten years ago.

The nil rate band for the tax years 2012/13 and 2018/19 is £325,000.

Required:

(a) Calculate the inheritance tax which will be payable as a result of James' death, and state who will be responsible for paying the tax. ⊞ **(6 marks)**

(b) Explain why it might have been beneficial for inheritance tax purposes if James had left a portion of his estate to his nephew rather than to his brother. 💻 **(2 marks)**

(c) Explain why it might be advantageous for inheritance tax purposes for a person to make lifetime gifts even when such gifts are made within seven years of death. 💻

Notes:

(1) Your answer should include a calculation of James' inheritance tax saving from making the gift of property to the trust on 2 August 2018 rather than retaining the property until his death.

(2) You are not expected to consider lifetime exemptions in this part of the question. **(2 marks)**

(Total: 10 marks)

210 MARCUS *WALK IN THE FOOTSTEPS OF A TOP TUTOR*

(a) Inheritance tax legislation does not actually contain a definition of who is, and who is not, a chargeable person.

Required:

(1) Explain whether or not a married couple is treated as a chargeable person for inheritance tax purposes. 🖥 **(1 mark)**

(2) State the special inheritance tax measures which are applicable to married couples. 🖥 **(2 marks)**

(b) Marcus died on 31 December 2019. He had made the following gifts during his lifetime:

(1) On 14 January 2009, Marcus made a chargeable lifetime transfer of £315,000 to a trust. The trustees paid the lifetime inheritance tax of £600 which arose in respect of this gift.

(2) On 3 December 2015, Marcus made a chargeable lifetime transfer of £395,000 to another trust. In addition to the gift, Marcus paid the related lifetime inheritance tax of £96,250 on this gift.

(3) On 1 January 2016, Marcus made a gift (a potentially exempt transfer) of 30,000 £1 ordinary shares in Scarum Ltd, an unquoted investment company, to his daughter.

Before the transfer, Marcus owned all of Scarum Ltd's issued share capital of 100,000 £1 ordinary shares. On 1 January 2016, Scarum Ltd's shares were worth £5 each for a holding of 30%, £9 each for a holding of 70%, and £12 each for a holding of 100%.

The nil rate band for the tax year 2008/09 is £312,000, and for the tax year 2015/16 it is £325,000.

Under the terms of his will, Marcus left his entire estate to his wife.

Required:

Calculate the inheritance tax which will be payable as a result of Marcus's death.

Note: You should ignore the inheritance tax annual exemption. ⊞ **(7 marks)**

(Total: 10 marks)

Section 4

PRACTICE CORPORATION TAX QUESTIONS

PRACTICE SECTION A OBJECTIVE TEST QUESTIONS

CORPORATION TAX BASICS AND ADMINISTRATION

211 **Which of these options identify when a company's accounting period for corporation tax purposes will come to an end? You can tick more than one box.**

	Accounting period ends
At the end of a company's period of account	
The end of the tax financial year	
Twelve months after the beginning of the accounting period	
The date the company begins or ceases to trade	

212 **December 2016 OT question**

Somily Ltd filed its self-assessment corporation tax return for the year ended 31 December 2019 on 15 March 2021.

What is the deadline for HM Revenue and Customs (HMRC) to start a compliance check enquiry into Somily Ltd's corporation tax return for the year ended 31 December 2019?

A   30 April 2022

B   31 December 2021

C   15 March 2022

D   31 January 2022

213 *September 2015 OT question (ADAPTED)*

Indicate with a tick in the relevant box which of the following companies will be treated as resident in the UK for corporation tax purposes.

	Resident	Not resident
A Ltd, a company incorporated in the UK, with its central management and control exercised in the UK		
B Ltd, a company incorporated overseas, with its central management and control exercised in the UK		
C Ltd, a company incorporated in the UK, with its central management and control exercised overseas		
D Ltd, a company incorporated overseas, with its central management and control exercised overseas		

214 *September 2016 OT question*

Lili Ltd commenced trading on 1 January 2019. The company incurred the following expenditure prior to 1 January 2019:

		£
30 November 2011	Initial market research	15,000
6 June 2014	Research into competitors	12,000
31 July 2018	Entertaining potential customers and suppliers	8,000
15 December 2018	Donation to local school fair in exchange for advertising	2,000

What is the amount of Lili Ltd's deductible pre-trading expenditure in respect of the year ended 31 December 2019?

A   £10,000

B   £14,000

C   £27,000

D   £29,000

215 You have been given some work to complete, which includes a draft calculation of taxable total profits for a client, Trains Ltd.

Your manager has asked you to check the following calculation and make any corrections necessary.

Year ended 31 December 2019	£
Tax adjusted trading profit	50,000
Property income	6,000
Dividends received from Track Ltd	5,400
Interest received	1,800
Taxable total profits	63,200

The amount of interest receivable for the year was £2,000. In addition the company realised a chargeable gain of £12,000.

What is the correct amount of taxable total profits for Trains Ltd for the year ended 31 December 2019?

£ ☐

216 In the year ended 31 December 2019 Biscuit Ltd had tax adjusted trading profits of £1,200,000. In addition, Biscuit Ltd had property income of £250,000, received dividends of £52,200 and paid a qualifying donation to a national charity of £7,000.

What is the corporation tax liability of Biscuit Ltd for the year ended 31 December 2019?

A   £284,088

B   £285,418

C   £275,500

D   £274,170

217 Shed Ltd had a tax adjusted trading profit for the year ended 31 March 2020 of £250,000. The company also received dividends of £5,000.

During the year the company sold a painting it had held as an investment for £110,000 realising a chargeable gain of £60,000. The directors had not been expecting the painting to sell for more than £50,000 so they decided to make a qualifying charitable donation with the excess proceeds of £60,000.

What is the corporation tax payable by Shed Ltd for the year ended 31 March 2020?

£ ☐

218 December *2016 OT question*

Three unconnected companies have the following results for corporation tax purposes:

Company	Current accounting period	Number of 51% group companies	Taxable total points (TTP)	TTP for previous 12 month period
			£	£
Asher Ltd	Year ended 31 March 2020	3	700,000	600,000
Barton Ltd	Four month period ended 31 December 2019	0	600,000	1,600,000
Chelfry Ltd	Year ended 30 November 2019	0	1,600,000	1,400,000

All the companies have had the same number of 51% group companies for many years.

Which of the three companies will NOT have to pay corporation tax by quarterly instalments for the current accounting period?

A   Asher Ltd

B   Barton Ltd only

C   Chelfry Ltd only

D   Barton Ltd and Chelfry Ltd

219 In the year ended 30 June 2019, the accounts of Chelsea Ltd included the following two amounts:

(1) £1,000 spent on a Christmas party for the company's five employees

(2) £2,000 for car lease payments. The leased car has CO_2 emissions of 145g/km and has been leased by the company since 1 July 2018. During the year the car was used by one of the company's directors who drove 4,000 personal miles and 16,000 business miles in the car.

What adjustments are needed when calculating the trading profit for Chelsea Ltd for the year ended 30 June 2019? Select the appropriate box in the table below.

		Christmas party	
		£0	£1,000
Car lease	£300	A	B
	£400	C	D

220 During the year ended 31 March 2020, Swiss Ltd purchased a new car for £8,000, which has CO_2 emissions of 50g/km. It is used by an employee 30% of the time for private purposes and 70% of the time for business purposes.

On 1 April 2019, Swiss Ltd had a tax written down value brought forward on the main pool of £35,000.

What are the maximum capital allowances that Swiss Ltd could claim in the year ended 31 March 2020?

A £7,740

B £14,300

C £11,900

D £7,308

221 *December 2016 OT question*

Modal Ltd lets out an unfurnished investment property.

During the year ended 31 December 2019, the company had rental income of £3,000 per month and electricity expenses (relating to the rental property) of £200 per month. The electricity payment for December 2019 was not paid until 30 January 2020.

Modal Ltd also paid interest of £1,200 per month on a loan taken out to finance the purchase of the rental property.

What amount of property income will be included in Modal Ltd's corporation tax computation for the year ended 31 December 2019?

£ [   ]

RELIEF FOR TRADING LOSSES

222 *September 2016 OT question*

Oblong Ltd has had the following results:

	Year ended 31 March 2019 £	Year ended 31 March 2020 £
Trading profit/(loss)	79,400	(102,800)
Property business income	6,800	10,100
Qualifying charitable donations	(1,600)	(1,300)

If Oblong Ltd makes a claim to relieve its trading loss of £102,800 for the year ended 31 March 2020 against total profits for the year ended 31 March 2019, how much of this loss will remain unrelieved?

A £6,500

B £16,600

C £9,400

D £23,400

223 Hobart Ltd has had the following results:

	Year ended 31 March 2019	Year ended 31 March 2020
	£	£
Tax adjusted trading profit/(loss)	40,000	(50,000)
Property income	15,000	21,000
Qualifying charitable donations paid	(6,000)	(14,000)

What are Hobart Ltd's taxable total profits, if any, in the year ended 31 March 2019 assuming the company makes a claim to carry back the trading loss to the year ended 31 March 2019?

£ ☐

224 Tasman Ltd has had the following results:

	Year ended 30 June 2018	9 months ended 31 March 2019	Year ended 31 March 2020
	£	£	£
Tax adjusted trading profit/(loss)	40,000	22,000	(60,000)
Interest income	4,000	3,000	5,000

What is the amount of loss, if any, which is available to carry forward as at 31 March 2020 assuming Tasman Ltd claims to use the trading loss as soon as possible?

A £0

B £30,000

C £19,000

D £24,000

225 Cairns Ltd has had the following results:

	Year ended 30 June 2019	Year ended 30 June 2020
	£	£
Tax adjusted trading profit/(loss)	(40,000)	25,000
Chargeable gains	9,000	45,000
Qualifying charitable donations paid	(2,000)	(3,000)

The company wishes to claim relief for the trading loss as soon as possible.

For each of the following statements concerning the loss relief claimed by Cairns Ltd select whether it is true or false:

	True	False
Cairns Ltd's taxable total profits in the year ended 30 June 2020 are £27,000		
The trading loss may not be offset against chargeable gains.		
Cairns Ltd must make a claim for any loss relief claimed by 30 June 2021.		

226 Perth Ltd has had the following results:

	Year ended 30 April 2019	Year ended 30 April 2020
	£	£
Tax adjusted trading profit/(loss)	(120,000)	61,000
Property income/(loss)	(28,000)	27,000
Interest income	30,000	30,000
Qualifying charitable donations paid	(10,000)	(10,000)

Assuming that Perth Ltd claims loss relief in the most efficient way, select the correct amount of brought forward property and trading losses which will be offset in the year ended 30 April 2020.

	Property loss claimed in y/e 30 April 2020	Trading loss claimed in y/e 30 April 2020
A	£0	£108,000
B	£0	£118,000
C	£8,000	£100,000
D	£8,000	£110,000

227 Adelaide Ltd has had the following results:

Year ended 31 March	2018	2019	2020
	£	£	£
Tax adjusted trading profit	16,000	20,000	25,000
Property income/(loss)	5,000	(65,000)	10,000
Qualifying charitable donations paid	(800)	(900)	(1,100)

What is the amount of the unused property loss as at 31 March 2020 assuming Adelaide claims relief in the most efficient way?

£ [   ]

228 Darwin Ltd ceased to trade on 31 March 2020. Its recent results have been as follows:

Year ended 31 March	2017	2018	2019	2020
	£	£	£	£
Tax adjusted trading profit/(loss)	45,000	32,000	10,000	(100,000)
Chargeable gain	5,000	–	9,000	14,000

What are the company's taxable total profits for the year ended 31 March 2017 assuming the company makes a terminal loss relief claim?

A £0

B £6,000

C £1,000

D £15,000

WITH GROUP ASPECTS

229 *June 2015 OT question*

Ten Ltd is the parent company for a group of companies. The group structure is as follows:

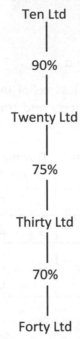

Ten Ltd

|
90%
|

Twenty Ltd

|
75%
|

Thirty Ltd

|
70%
|

Forty Ltd

Each percentage holding represents a holding of ordinary share capital.

What is the group relationship between Forty Ltd and Ten Ltd?

A   They form a group for both group relief and chargeable gains purposes

B   They form a group for group relief purposes but not for chargeable gains purposes

C   They form a group for chargeable gains purposes but not for group relief purposes

D   They do not form a group for either group relief or chargeable gains purposes

230 Computer Ltd owns 75% of Chair Ltd, 60% of Bin Ltd and 100% of Paper Inc. Paper Inc owns 75% of Cardboard Ltd. All companies are resident in the UK except Paper Inc which is resident in the US.

Computer Ltd suffered a trading loss during its most recent accounting period.

Indicate with a tick in the relevant box to which companies Computer Ltd's trading loss could be surrendered.

	Loss can be surrendered to
Chair Ltd	
Bin Ltd	
Paper Inc	
Cardboard Ltd	

231 *December 2016 OT question*

Acasta Ltd owns 75% of the ordinary share capital of Barge Ltd and 100% of the ordinary share capital of Coracle Ltd. Barge Ltd owns 75% of the ordinary share capital of Dhow Ltd. Coracle Ltd owns 51% of the ordinary share capital of Eight Ltd.

Which companies, along with Coracle Ltd, are within Acasta Ltd's chargeable gains group?

A   Barge Ltd, Dhow Ltd and Eight Ltd

B   Barge Ltd only

C   Barge Ltd and Dhow Ltd only

D   None of the other companies

232 Brazil Ltd owns 100% of Germany Ltd and 75% of Holland Ltd. Germany Ltd owns 65% of Belgium Ltd and Holland owns 75% of Russia Ltd.

Indicate with a tick in the relevant box which companies form a capital gains group for corporation tax purposes.

	Capital gains group
Brazil Ltd	
Germany Ltd	
Holland Ltd	
Belgium Ltd	
Russia Ltd	

233 Battery Ltd owns 100% of Watch Ltd. During the year ended 31 March 2020 Battery Ltd had a trading loss of £100,000. During the 6 month period ended 30 June 2020 Watch Ltd had trading income of £50,000 and property income of £30,000.

What is the maximum loss that Watch Ltd can claim from Battery Ltd for the period ended 30 June 2020? You should ignore any brought forward group losses.

A   £50,000

B   £25,000

C   £40,000

D   £80,000

234 Apple Ltd owns 75% of Grape Ltd. Apple Ltd transferred a property with a market value of £300,000 to Grape Ltd. The original cost of the asset was £100,000 and the relevant indexation allowance was £50,000.

What is the deemed acquisition cost for chargeable gains purposes for Grape Ltd?

£ [   ]

235 Telephone Ltd prepares accounts to 31 March each year. Throughout the year ended 31 March 2020 Telephone Ltd owned 62% of Desk Ltd, 75% of Chair Ltd, 55% of Table Ltd (a dormant company) and 100% of Window Inc (resident overseas). Telephone Ltd acquired 60% of the share capital of Curtain Ltd on 1 January 2020.

What is the total number of companies for the purposes of adjusting the £1,500,000 augmented profits threshold of Telephone Ltd for the year ended 31 March 2020?

A   2

B   3

C   4

D   5

236 Novak Ltd owns 80% of Roger Ltd. Roger Ltd owns 70% of Rafael Ltd and Rafael Ltd owns 55% of Andy Ltd. The group structure has been the same for a number of years.

What are the profits thresholds for determining if Novak Ltd should pay corporation tax by instalments for the year ended 31 March 2020?

A   £375,000

B   £750,000

C   £1,500,000

D   £500,000

237 Custard Ltd started trading on 1 August 2019 and prepared its first set of accounts to 31 March 2020. The company's taxable total profits for the period to 31 March 2020 are £190,000.

Custard Ltd has three related 51% group companies from which it received dividends of £70,000. The company also received dividends from one non-related company of £27,000.

What is the amount of the augmented profits threshold that will be used to determine whether Custard Ltd is a large company for the period ended 31 March 2020?

A   £250,000

B   £375,000

C   £200,000

D   £333,333

238 Bourbon Ltd prepares annual accounts to 31 January. In the year ended 31 January 2020, the company had the following income:

	£
Trading income	1,450,000
Chargeable gain	100,000

Bourbon Ltd received dividends of £50,000 from related 51% group companies and dividends of £20,000 from non-51% related companies.

What are the augmented profits of Bourbon Ltd for the year ended 31 January 2020?

£ [   ]

239 *September 2015 OT question (ADAPTED)*

During the year ended 31 March 2020, Luck Ltd received the following dividends:

	£
From unconnected companies	4,680
From a company in which Luck Ltd has a 80% shareholding	3,870
From a company in which Luck Ltd has a 45% shareholding	1,260

What is the amount that is included in Luck Ltd's augmented profits for the year ended 31 March 2020?

A   £5,940

B   £9,810

C   £3,870

D   £4,680

240 Hound Ltd started to trade on 1 June 2019 and prepared its first set of accounts for the 15 month period to 31 August 2020.

On which date(s) must Hound Ltd submit a corporation tax return in respect of the 15 month period of account? You can tick more than one box.

	Corporation tax return due
1 March 2021	
31 May 2021	
1 June 2021	
31 August 2021	

241 *Specimen exam June 2015*

For the year ended 31 March 2019, Sizeable Ltd had a corporation tax liability of £384,000, and for the year ended 31 March 2020 it had a liability of £456,000. Sizeable Ltd is a large company, and is therefore required to make instalment payments in respect of its corporation tax liability. The company's profits have accrued evenly throughout each year.

What is the amount of each instalment payable by Sizeable Ltd in respect of its corporation tax liability for the year ended 31 March 2020?

A   £228,000

B   £114,000

C   £96,000

D   £192,000

242 All of the following companies are NOT large companies for the purposes of paying corporation tax.

Which of the companies have a due date in respect of corporation tax of 1 April 2020? You can tick more than one box.

	Corporation tax due on 1 April 2020
W Ltd – prepared accounts for the year ended 30 June 2019	
X Ltd – prepared accounts for the 15 months ended 30 September 2019	
Y Ltd – prepared accounts for the year ended 31 March 2019	
Z Ltd – prepared accounts for the 8 months to 30 June 2019	

243 *September 2015 OT question*

Mammoth Ltd commenced trading on 1 January 2017. The company's augmented profits have been as follows:

Period	£
Year ended 31 December 2017	524,000
Year ended 31 December 2018	867,000
Year ended 31 December 2019	912,000

Throughout all of these periods, Mammoth Ltd had one related 51% group company.

What is the first year for which Mammoth Ltd will be required to pay its corporation tax liability by quarterly instalments?

A   Year ended 31 December 2018

B   None of the years ended 31 December 2017, 2018 or 2019

C   Year ended 31 December 2019

D   Year ended 31 December 2017

244 *September 2015 OT question (ADAPTED)*

For the year ended 30 June 2019, Forgetful Ltd had a corporation tax liability of £166,250, which it did not pay until 31 July 2020. Forgetful Ltd is not a large company.

How much interest will Forgetful Ltd be charged by HM Revenue and Customs (HMRC) in respect of the late payment of its corporation tax liability for the year ended 30 June 2019?

£ [   ]

245 Gerber Ltd has been a large company for the purposes of paying its corporation tax liability for a number of years.

In 2019 it changed its accounting date and prepared an 8 month set of accounts to 31 December 2019.

When is the final corporation tax instalment in respect of the 8 month accounting period ended 31 December 2019 due?

A   14 February 2020

B   14 April 2020

C   14 May 2020

D   14 August 2020

PRACTICE SECTION B OBJECTIVE TEST CASES

CORPORATION TAX BASICS AND ADMINISTRATION

246   GREENZONE LTD (ADAPTED) *Walk in the footsteps of a top tutor*

Greenzone Ltd is a trading company.

Year ended 31 March 2020

Included in the company's statement of profit or loss for the year ended 31 March 2020 were the following expenses:

	£
Repairs and renewals	
Repainting the exterior of the company's office building	8,390
Legal fees for renewing a 20 year lease on the office building	19,800
Entertaining expenses	
Entertaining UK customers	3,600
Entertaining overseas customers	1,840
Gifts and donations	
Political donations	740
Donation to a small, local charity where Greenzone Ltd received free advertising in the charity's newsletter.	430
Gifts to customers:	
– pens costing £30 each, not displaying Greenzone Ltd's name	660
– clocks costing £65 each and displaying Greenzone Ltd's name	910

Plant and machinery

On 1 April 2019 the tax written down value of Greenzone Ltd's main pool was £48,150.

The following motor cars were purchased during the year ended 31 March 2020:

	Date of purchase	Cost £	CO_2 emission rate
New motor car (1)	10 April 2019	10,800	48 grams per kilometre
New motor car (2)	10 June 2019	20,400	108 grams per kilometre

The following motor car was sold during the year ended 31 March 2020:

	Date of sale	Proceeds £	Original cost £
Motor car (3)	8 March 2020	9,100	8,500

The original cost of motor car (3) has previously been added to the main pool.

Period ended 30 September 2020

Greenzone Ltd changed its year end and prepared accounts for the six month period to 30 September 2020.

On 1 April 2020 the tax written down value of Greenzone Ltd's special rate pool was £9,200. During the six month period to 30 September 2020 the company installed a new air conditioning system throughout its offices at a cost of £550,000, which is expected to last 30 years.

1   **What amount must be added back in the adjustment of trading profits computation in respect of repairs and renewals and entertaining expenses? Select the appropriate box in the table below.**

		Entertaining expenses	
		£1,840	£5,440
Repairs and renewals	£0	A	B
	£19,800	C	D

2   **What amount must be added back in the adjustment of trading profits computation in respect of gifts and donations?**

A   £2,310

B   £2,740

C   £1,650

D   £660

3   **Assuming that Greenzone Ltd always claims the maximum capital allowances, what is the tax written down balance of the main pool at 31 March 2020?**

£ [   ]

4 Assuming that Greenzone Ltd always claims the maximum capital allowances, what capital allowances would be claimed in respect of the special rate pool for the six months ended 30 September 2020?

A £500,000

B £501,776

C £503,552

D £550,552

5 Assuming that Greenzone Ltd is a large company for the purposes of paying its corporation tax, on what dates are instalments of its corporation tax liability for the 6 months ended 30 September 2020 payable? You can tick more than one box.

	Instalment date
14 July 2020	
14 October 2020	
14 January 2021	
14 April 2021	

RELIEF FOR TRADING LOSSES

247 LOSER LTD (ADAPTED)

Loser Ltd 's recent results, together with a forecast for the year ended 31 March 2021 are:

	y/e 30.6.16 £	y/e 30.6.17 £	y/e 30.6.18 £	9 months ended 31.3.19 £	y/e 31.3.20 £	y/e 31.3.21 £
Trading profit/(loss)	15,800	10,600	15,700	24,300	(78,300)	60,000
Property income	5,200	1,200	6,600	8,100	5,600	3,000
Qualifying charitable donations	(1,300)	(1,400)	(800)	(1,200)	(1,100)	(1,300)

The future prospects of Loser Ltd are currently uncertain.

Loser Ltd does not own shares in any other company.

1 Which of the following factors are relevant to Loser Ltd's decision when choosing which loss relief claims to make?

	Relevant	Not relevant
Timing of relief		
Extent to which losses will be wasted		
Extent to which QCD relief will be wasted		

2 Assuming that Loser Ltd decided to carry the trading loss forward and offset it in the next period as efficiently as possible, what would be the amount of unrelieved loss at 31 March 2021?

A £18,300

B £16,600

C £15,300

D £11,000

3 Assuming that Loser Ltd elects to offset the loss as soon as possible what would be the amount of unrelieved loss at 31 March 2020?

£ [   ]

4 Assuming that Loser Ltd wishes to make a current year loss relief claim in respect of the trading loss, select whether the following statements are true or false.

	True	False
The amount of loss used in the current year can be restricted to avoid wasting QCD relief		
The claim must be made by 31 March 2022		

5 Assuming that Loser Ltd had ceased trading on 31 March 2020 and claimed terminal loss relief in respect of its trading loss, what would be the amount of unrelieved loss at 31 March 2020?

A £950

B £5,775

C £6,200

D £23,750

WITH GROUP ASPECTS

248 DEUTSCH LTD (ADAPTED) *Walk in the footsteps of a top tutor*

Deutsch Ltd has held shares in four trading companies for a number of years. All four companies prepare accounts to 31 March.

Year ended 31 March 2020

The following information is available for the year ended 31 March 2020:

	Eins Ltd	Zwei Ltd	Drei Ltd	Vier Co
Residence	UK	UK	UK	Overseas
Percentage shareholding	60%	20%	90%	70%
Trading profit/(loss)	£(74,800)	£68,900	£(52,700)	£22,600
Property income	£10,000	–	–	–
Chargeable gains		£204,400		
Qualifying charitable donations paid	–	–	£(12,000)	–

In the year ended 31 March 2020 Deutsch Ltd had a tax adjusted trading profit of £277,700 and no other income or gains.

Zwei Ltd

The remaining 80% of the Zwei Ltd shares are held by Berlin Ltd.

On 15 March 2020 Zwei Ltd sold a building for its market value of £500,000 to an independent third party. It had acquired the building for £200,000 in May 2006. The indexed cost of the building at 15 March 2020 was was £281,400. On 1 August 2019 Zwei Ltd acquired a factory at a cost of £460,000.

1   Which of the four trading companies will be treated as related 51% group companies of Deutsch Ltd? You can tick more than one box.

	Related 51% group company
Eins Ltd	
Zwei Ltd	
Drei Ltd	
Vier Co	

2   What is the maximum amount of group relief that Deutsch Ltd can claim for the year ended 31 March 2020?

    A   £64,700

    B   £52,700

    C   £139,500

    D   £47,430

3   **What is the amount of gain arising on the sale of the building by Zwei Ltd that can be rolled over into the acquisition of the factory?**

£ [   ]

4   **If instead of selling the building to an independent third party Zwei Ltd had sold it to Berlin Ltd for £450,000 on 15 March 2020, what would have been the capital gains base cost of the building for Berlin Ltd?**

A   £281,400

B   £500,000

C   £200,000

D   £450,000

5   **What are the dates by which Deutsch Ltd must make a group relief claim in respect of the year ended 31 March 2020 and Zwei Ltd must make a rollover relief claim in respect of the disposal of the building in the year ended 31 March 2020?**

		Group relief	
		31 March 2022	31 March 2024
Rollover relief	31 March 2022	A	B
	31 March 2024	C	D

PRACTICE SECTION C CONSTRUCTED RESPONSE QUESTIONS

CORPORATION TAX BASICS AND ADMINISTRATION

249   TENTH AND ELEVENTH LTD (ADAPTED) *Walk in the footsteps of a top tutor*

Mable is a serial entrepreneur, regularly starting and disposing of businesses. On 31 July 2019, Tenth Ltd, a company owned by Mable, ceased trading. On 1 October 2019, Eleventh Ltd, another company owned by Mable, commenced trading. The following information is available:

Tenth Ltd

(1)   For the final four month period of trading ended 31 July 2019, Tenth Ltd had a tax adjusted trading profit of £52,400. This figure is before taking account of capital allowances.

(2)   On 1 April 2019, the tax written down value of the company's main pool was £12,400. On 3 June 2019, Tenth Ltd purchased a laptop computer for £1,800.

On 31 July 2019, the company sold all of the items included in the main pool at the start of the period for £28,200 and the laptop computer for £1,300. None of the items included in the main pool was sold for more than its original cost.

(3)   On 31 July 2019, Tenth Ltd sold the company's freehold office building for £179,549. The building was purchased on 3 May 2013 for £150,100 and its indexed cost on 31 July 2019 was £166,911.

(4) During the four month period ended 31 July 2019, Tenth Ltd let out one floor of its freehold office building which was always surplus to requirements. The floor was rented at £1,200 per month, but the tenant left owing the rent for July 2019 which Tenth Ltd was unable to recover. The total running costs of the office building for the four month period ended 31 July 2019 were £6,300, of which one third related to the let floor. The other two thirds of the running costs have been deducted in calculating Tenth Ltd's tax adjusted trading profit of £52,400.

(5) During the four-month period ended 31 July 2019, Tenth Ltd made qualifying charitable donations of £800.

Eleventh Ltd

(1) Eleventh Ltd's operating profit for the six month period ended 31 March 2020 is £122,900. Depreciation of £2,580 and amortisation of leasehold property of £2,000 (see note (2) below) have been deducted in arriving at this figure.

(2) On 1 October 2019, Eleventh Ltd acquired a leasehold office building, paying a premium of £60,000 for the grant of a 15 year lease. The office building was used for business purposes by Eleventh Ltd throughout the six month period ended 31 March 2020.

(3) On 1 October 2019, Eleventh Ltd purchased two motor cars. The first motor car cost £12,600, and has a CO_2 emission rate of 110 grams per kilometre. This motor car is used as a pool car by the company's employees. The second motor car cost £13,200, and has a CO_2 emission rate of 40 grams per kilometre. This motor car is used by Mable, and 45% of the mileage is for private journeys.

(4) On 1 October 2019, Mable made a loan of £100,000 to Eleventh Ltd at an annual interest rate of 5%. This is a commercial rate of interest, and no loan repayments were made during the period ended 31 March 2020. The loan was used to finance the company's trading activities.

Required:

(a) Calculate Tenth Ltd's taxable total profits for the four month period ended 31 July 2019. ⊞ **(7 marks)**

(b) Calculate Eleventh Ltd's tax adjusted trading profit for the six month period ended 31 March 2020. ⊞ **(8 marks)**

(Total: 15 marks)

250 AOEDE LTD, BIANCA LTD AND CHARON LTD (ADAPTED)

You are a trainee chartered certified accountant dealing with the tax affairs of three unrelated limited companies, Aoede Ltd, Bianca Ltd and Charon Ltd.

Aoede Ltd

Aoede Ltd commenced trading on 1 April 2018. The company's results are:

	Year ended 31 March 2019	Year ended 31 March 2020
	£	£
Trading profit/(loss)	(111,300)	67,800
Property business income/(loss)	(26,400)	23,400
Chargeable gains	5,800	16,200
Qualifying charitable donations	(6,000)	(6,600)

Aoede Ltd owns 100% of the ordinary share capital of Moon Ltd. Moon Ltd commenced trading on 1 April 2019 and for the year ended 31 March 2020 made a trading profit of £19,700.

Bianca Ltd

Bianca Ltd commenced trading on 1 April 2019. The company's tax adjusted trading profit based on the statement of profit or loss for the year ended 31 March 2020 is £256,300. This figure is **before** making any adjustments required for:

1   Advertising expenditure of £5,800 incurred during January 2018 to promote Bianca Ltd's new business. This expenditure has not been deducted in calculating the profit of £256,300.

2   Leasing costs of £9,300, which have been deducted in arriving at the profit of £256,300. The leasing costs relate to two motor cars, which have been leased since 1 April 2019. The first motor car has CO_2 emissions of 105 grams per kilometre and is leased at an annual cost of £4,200. The second motor car has CO_2 emissions of 120 grams per kilometre and is leased at an annual cost of £5,100.

3   Capital allowances.

On 1 April 2019, Bianca Ltd purchased four laptop computers at a discounted cost of £1,000 per laptop. The original cost of each laptop was £1,800, but Bianca Ltd was given a discount because they were damaged.

Bianca Ltd also purchased two second hand motor cars on 1 April 2019. Details are:

	Cost £	CO_2 emission rate
Motor car [1]	12,400	35 grams per kilometre
Motor car [2]	13,900	120 grams per kilometre

Charon Ltd

During the year ended 31 March 2020, Charon Ltd disposed of two investment properties.

The first property was sold for £368,000 during January 2020. This property was purchased for £147,000 during October 1996, and was extended at a cost of £39,000 during June 2019.

The second property was sold for £167,000 during January 2020. This property was purchased for £172,000 during December 2018.

Indexation factors are:

October 1996 to December 2017	0.808
October 1996 to January 2020	0.901
December 2018 to January 2020	0.024
June 2019 to January 2020	0.019

Required:

(a)   (i)   **On the basis that Aoede Ltd claims relief for its losses as early as possible, calculate the taxable total profits of Aoede Ltd for the years ended 31 March 2019 and 31 March 2020, and of Moon Ltd for the year ended 31 March 2020.** 🎛   **(5 marks)**

   (ii)   **Explain which aspect of Aoede Ltd's loss relief claim made in part (i) is not beneficial for the company to make.** 💻   **(1 mark)**

(b)   **Calculate Bianca Ltd's revised tax adjusted trading profit for the year ended 31 March 2020.** 🎛   **(5 marks)**

(c)   **Calculate Charon Ltd's chargeable gains and capital losses, if any, for the year ended 31 March 2020.** 🎛   **(4 marks)**

                                (Total: 15 marks)

251 SOLO LTD   *Walk in the footsteps of a top tutor*

Solo Ltd's results for the previous two periods of trading are:

	Year ended 31 December 2018	Three-month period ended 31 March 2019
	£	£
Trading profit	35,900	12,300
Property business income	12,100	4,200
Chargeable gains/(capital losses)	(3,300)	(2,100)
Qualifying charitable donations	(1,200)	(1,600)

The following information is available in respect of the year ended 31 March 2020:

Trading loss

The draft tax adjusted trading loss for the year ended 31 March 2020 is £151,300. This figure is before making any adjustments required for:

(1)   A premium paid to acquire a leasehold office building on an eight-year lease.

(2)   Capital allowances.

Premium paid to acquire leasehold office building

On 1 April 2019, Solo Ltd acquired a leasehold office building, paying a premium of £20,000 for the grant of an eight-year lease. The office building was used for business purposes by Solo Ltd throughout the year ended 31 March 2020.

Plant and machinery

The tax written down value of the plant and machinery main pool as at 1 April 2019 was £0. During the year ended 31 March 2020, Solo Ltd sold equipment for £4,300. The equipment was originally purchased during the year ended 31 March 2015 for £22,400, with this expenditure qualifying for the 100% annual investment allowance.

Property business income

Solo Ltd lets out a warehouse which is surplus to requirements. The building was empty from 1 April to 31 July 2019, but was let from 1 August 2019 onwards. The following income and expenditure was received or incurred during the year ended 31 March 2020:

Date received/paid		£
1 April 2019	Insurance for the year ended 31 March 2020	(920)
1 August 2019	Rent for the six months ended 31 January 2020	7,800
1 August 2019	Security deposit equal to two months' rent	2,600
1 March 2020	Rent for the six months ended 31 July 2020	7,800

Disposal of shareholding in Multiple plc

On 12 December 2019, Solo Ltd sold 6,500 £1 ordinary shares in Multiple plc for £31,200. Solo Ltd had originally purchased 20,000 shares (less than a 1% shareholding) in Multiple plc on 18 June 2007 for £27,000, and purchased a further 1,000 shares on 8 December 2019 for £4,600. Indexation factors are:

June 2007 to December 2017	0.342
June 2007 to December 2019	0.407

Required:

(a) Calculate Solo Ltd's revised tax adjusted trading loss for the year ended 31 March 2020. ⊞

Note: You should assume that the company claims the maximum available capital allowances. **(3 marks)**

(b) On the basis that Solo Ltd claims relief for its trading loss against its total profits for the year ended 31 March 2020, prepare a corporation tax computation for this year showing taxable total profits. ⊞ **(8 marks)**

(c) On the basis that Solo Ltd claims relief for the remainder of its trading loss as early as possible, calculate the company's taxable total profits for the year ended 31 December 2018 and the three-month period ended 31 March 2019. ⊞ **(4 marks)**

(Total: 15 marks)

252 ONLINE LTD (ADAPTED) *WALK IN THE FOOTSTEPS OF A TOP TUTOR*

The following information is available in respect of Online Ltd for the year ended 31 March 2020:

Operating profit

Online Ltd's operating profit for the year ended 31 March 2020 is £896,700. Depreciation of £21,660 and amortisation of leasehold property of £9,000 (see below) have been deducted in arriving at this figure.

Leasehold property

On 1 April 2019, Online Ltd acquired a leasehold office building, paying a premium of £90,000 for the grant of a ten-year lease. The office building was used for business purposes by Online Ltd throughout the year ended 31 March 2020.

Plant and machinery

On 1 April 2019, the tax written down values of plant and machinery were as follows:

	£
Main pool	56,700
Special rate pool	13,433

The following transactions took place during the year ended 31 March 2020:

		£
14 May 2019	Sold a motor car	(18,100)
18 July 2019	Sold all items included in the special rate pool	(9,300)
27 January 2020	Purchased a motor car	13,700

The motor car sold on 14 May 2019 for £18,100 was originally purchased during the year ended 31 March 2019 for £17,200. This expenditure was added to the main pool.

The motor car purchased on 27 January 2020 for £13,700 has a CO_2 emission rate of 90 grams per kilometre. The motor car is used as a pool car by the company's employees.

Qualifying charitable donations

During the year ended 31 March 2020, Online Ltd made qualifying charitable donations of £6,800. These were not included in arriving at the operating profit above.

Disposal of shareholding in Network plc

On 20 March 2020, Online Ltd sold its entire shareholding of £1 ordinary shares in Network plc for £90,600. Online Ltd had originally purchased 40,000 shares (less than a 1% shareholding) in Network plc on 24 June 2012 for £49,300. On 7 October 2015, Online Ltd sold 22,000 of the shares for £62,200.

Indexation factors are as follows:

June 2012 to October 2015	0.073	June 2012 to December 2017	0·150
October 2015 to March 2020	0·133	October 2015 to December 2017	0·072

Brought forward losses

As at 1 April 2019, Online Ltd had the following brought forward amounts of unused losses:

	£
Capital loss	4,700
Property business loss	12,500

Online Ltd wishes to utilise the property loss in the current period.

Planned acquisition

Online Ltd currently does not have any 51% group companies. However, Online Ltd is planning to acquire a 60% shareholding in Offline Ltd in the near future. Offline Ltd is profitable and will pay regular dividends to Online Ltd.

Required:

(a)   Calculate Online Ltd's taxable total profits for the year ended 31 March 2020. ▦

(13 marks)

(b)   Briefly explain how the acquisition of Offline Ltd will affect the calculation and payment of Online Ltd's corporation tax liability in future years. 🖳   (2 marks)

(Total: 15 marks)

253 STRETCHED LTD (ADAPTED)

Stretched Ltd has always prepared its accounts to 31 December, but has decided to change its accounting date to 31 March. The company's results for the 15-month period ended 31 March 2020 are as follows:

(1) The tax adjusted trading profit is £642,500. This figure is before taking account of capital allowances.

(2) Until January 2020 the company has never been entitled to capital allowances as all assets were leased. On 15 January 2020 the company bought office equipment for £50,000, and a car with CO_2 emissions of 102 grams per kilometre for £7,500.

(3) There is a property business profit of £45,000 for the 15-month period ended 31 March 2020.

(4) On 15 April 2019 the company disposed of some investments, and this resulted in a chargeable gain of £44,000. On 8 February 2020 the company made a further disposal, and this resulted in a capital loss of £6,700.

(5) Dividend income of £30,000 was received on 10 September 2019.

(6) A qualifying charitable donation of £5,000 was made on 31 March 2020.

As at 1 January 2019 Stretched Ltd had unused trading losses of £330,000, and unused capital losses of £3,000. Stretched will make a claim to relieve these losses as soon as possible where necessary.

In the year ended 31 December 2018 the company had taxable total profits of £300,000 and no dividend income.

Stretched Ltd has no related 51% group companies.

Required:

(a) Calculate Stretched Ltd's corporation tax liabilities in respect of the 15-month period ended 31 March 2020, and advise the company by when these should be paid. ⊞ **(13 marks)**

(b) State the advantages for tax purposes of a company having an accounting date of 31 March instead of 31 December. 💻 **(2 marks)**

(Total: 15 marks)

254 STARFISH LTD (ADAPTED) *Walk in the footsteps of a top tutor*

Starfish Ltd, a retailer of scuba diving equipment, was incorporated on 15 October 2015, and commenced trading on 1 December 2015. The company initially prepared accounts to 31 March, but changed its accounting date to 31 December by preparing accounts for the nine-month period ended 31 December 2019. Starfish Ltd ceased trading on 31 March 2020, and a resolution was subsequently passed to commence winding up procedures.

Starfish Ltd's results for each of its periods of account up to 31 December 2019 are:

	Tax adjusted trading profit	Bank interest	Qualifying charitable donations
	£	£	£
Four-month period ended 31 March 2016	2,600	600	(800)
Year ended 31 March 2017	51,600	1,400	(1,000)
Year ended 31 March 2018	53,900	1,700	(900)
Year ended 31 March 2019	14,700	0	(700)
Nine-month period ended 31 December 2019	49,900	0	(600)

The company's summarised statement of profit or loss for its final three-month period of trading ended 31 March 2020 is as follows:

	Notes	£	£
Gross profit			16,100
Expenses			
Depreciation		34,400	
Donations	1	1,650	
Impairment loss in respect of a trade debt		2,000	
Other expenses	2	168,050	
			(206,100)
Loss before taxation			(190,000)

Note 1 – Donations

Donations were made as follows:	£
Donation to a political party	300
Qualifying charitable donation	1,350
	1,650

Note 2 – Other expenses

Other expenses are as follows:	£
Entertaining customers	3,600
Entertaining employees	1,840
Counselling services provided to employees who were made redundant	8,400
Balance of expenditure (all allowable)	154,210
	168,050

Note 3 – Plant and machinery

On 1 January 2020 the tax written down values of the company's plant and machinery were:

	£
Main pool	23,600
Special rate pool	13,200

On 10 January 2020 Starfish Ltd purchased a laptop computer for £3,120. This figure is inclusive of value added tax (VAT).

On 31 March 2020 the company sold all of the items included in the main pool for £31,200, and the laptop computer for £1,800.

The only item in the special rate pool was a car which had been acquired for £16,000 and which was sold on 31 March 2020 for £9,600. The car was used by the managing director, and 20% of the mileage was for private journeys.

Starfish Ltd is registered for VAT. All of the above figures are inclusive of VAT where applicable. None of the items included in the main pool was sold for more than its original cost, and all of the items in the main pool were standard-rated.

Required:

(a) Calculate Starfish Ltd's tax adjusted trading loss for the three-month period ended 31 March 2020. ▦

Your computation should commence with the loss before taxation figure of £190,000, and should also list all of the items referred to in notes (1) to (3) indicating by the use of zero (0) any items that do not require adjustment.

(10 marks)

(b) Assuming that Starfish Ltd claims relief for its trading loss on the most beneficial basis, calculate the company's taxable total profits for the four-month period ended 31 March 2016, the years ended 31 March 2017 to 2019 and the nine-month period ended 31 December 2019. ▦

(5 marks)

(Total: 15 marks)

255 HEAVY LTD (ADAPTED) *Walk in the footsteps of a top tutor*

Heavy Ltd runs a music publishing business. On 1 April 2019 Heavy Ltd acquired 100% of the ordinary share capital of Soft Ltd, a company that runs a music recording studio. Neither company has any other related companies.

Heavy Ltd has prepared accounts for the year ended 31 July 2020. The following information is available:

(1) The operating profit for the year is £433,100. Depreciation (£12,880) and a health and safety fine (£9,000) have been deducted in arriving at this figure.

(2)   On 1 August 2019 the tax written down values of Heavy Ltd's plant and machinery were as follows:

	£
Main pool	900
Short life asset (1) – machine acquired May 2016	15,100
Short life asset (2) – plant acquired August 2016	13,200
Special rate pool	24,833

The following purchases and disposals of plant and machinery took place during the year ended 31 July 2020:

		Cost/(Proceeds)
		£
23 March 2020	Purchased office equipment	22,400
24 April 2020	Purchased new motor car	16,000
1 June 2020	Purchased computers	25,000
19 July 2020	Sold short life asset (2)	(4,600)
28 July 2020	Sold all the items included in the special rate pool	(12,300)

The motor car purchased on 24 April 2020 has CO_2 emissions of 50 grams per kilometre and is used by the managing director of Heavy Ltd, and 60% of the mileage is for private journeys.

The cost of the computers acquired on 1 June 2020 includes software costs of £5,000.

Short life asset (2) sold on 19 July 2020 originally cost £19,631.

(3)   On 18 May 2020 Heavy Ltd sold a freehold office building to Soft Ltd for £113,600. The indexed cost of the office building on that date was £102,800.

(4)   On 1 March 2020 Heavy Ltd sold half of its car park for £45,000. The company purchased the entire car park for £10,000 in May 2004. The market value of the remaining half of the car park on 1 March 2020 is £50,000.

(5)   The company rents out a building that is now surplus to its requirements. It made a property business loss of £10,000 during the year to 31 July 2020 due to significant redecoration costs.

(6)   During the year ended 31 July 2020 Heavy Ltd received the following dividends:

Company paying the dividend:	£
An unrelated UK company	27,000
Soft Ltd	6,300

Required:

Calculate Heavy Ltd's corporation tax liability for the year ended 31 July 2020. ▦

The indexation factors are as follows:

May 2004 to December 2017   0.491

May 2004 to March 2019   0.525

Ignore VAT. Assume that tax rates and allowances for FY2019 continue into the future.

(15 marks)

256 SOFTAPP LTD (ADAPTED) *Walk in the footsteps of a top tutor*

 Question debrief

Softapp Ltd is a software developer. The company's summarised statement of profit or loss for the year ended 31 March 2020 is as follows:

	Notes	£
Operating profit	1	913,000
Other income		
Income from property	2	36,700
Loan interest receivable	3	8,100
Profit on disposal of shares	4	64,900
Finance costs		
Interest payable	5	(67,200)
Profit before taxation		955,500

Note 1 – Operating profit

Depreciation of £8,170 and amortisation of leasehold property of £2,500 have been deducted in arriving at the operating profit of £913,000.

Note 2 – Income from property

Since 1 November 2019, Softapp Ltd has let out one floor of a freehold office building which is surplus to requirements (see Note 5).

The income from property figure of £36,700 is made up of the following income and expenditure:

		£
23 October 2019	Advertising for tenants	(600)
25 October 2019	Security deposit of two months' rent	10,400
25 October 2019	Rent for the quarter ended 31 January 2020	15,600
1 November 2019	Insurance for the year ended 31 October 2020	(1,200)
2 February 2020	Rent for the quarter ended 30 April 2020	15,600
20 March 2020	Repairs following a flood	(12,800)
4 April 2020	Insurance claim in respect of the flood damage	9,700
		36,700

Note 3 – Loan interest receivable

The loan was made for non-trading purposes on 1 July 2019. Loan interest of £5,600 was received on 31 December 2019, and interest of £2,500 was accrued at 31 March 2020.

Note 4 – Profit on disposal of shares

The profit on disposal of shares is in respect of the sale of Softapp Ltd's entire (2%) shareholding in Networked plc on 28 February 2020. The disposal resulted in a chargeable gain of £61,300. This figure is after taking account of indexation.

Note 5 – Interest payable

The interest payable is made up as follows:

(1)   £42,200 in respect of the company's 4% debenture loan stock. Interest of £21,100 was paid on 30 September 2019 and again on 31 March 2020. The loan stock was used to finance the company's trading activities.

(2)   £25,000 in respect of a loan to acquire the freehold office building. The building has five floors, one of which is let out (see Note 2).

Additional information

The tax written down value of Softapp Ltd's plant and machinery as at 1 April 2019 was £9,000.

During October 2019 Softapp refurbished part of its freehold office building, which is used by the company's employees as a staff room.

The total cost is made up as follows:

	£
Integral to the building	
Heating system	93,600
Ventilation system	75,600
Not integral to the building	
Furniture and furnishings	38,400
Refrigerator and microwave cooker	1,400
	209,000

The full annual investment allowance is available to Softapp Ltd.

Subsidiary company

Softapp owns 100% of the ordinary share capital of Byte Size Ltd.

Required:

Calculate Softapp Ltd's corporation tax liability for the year ended 31 March 2020 and state the date it is due for payment. Assume that Softapp was not a large company in the previous accounting period ▦

Your computation should commence with the operating profit figure of £913,000.

(15 marks)

 Calculate your allowed time and allocate the time to the separate parts.

257 E-COMMERCE PLC (ADAPTED) *Walk in the footsteps of a top tutor*

You are a trainee Chartered Certified Accountant, and your firm has recently completed its audit of E-Commerce plc's financial statements for the year ended 31 March 2020. The company runs an internet-based retail business.

E-Commerce plc prepared its own corporation tax computations for the year ended 31 March 2020, and your colleague has completed your firm's tax audit of these figures.

E-Commerce plc's original corporation tax computation, along with references to your colleague's queries, is as follows.

E-Commerce plc – Corporation tax computation for the year ended 31 March 2020

	Queries	£
Operating profit	1	2,102,300
Deduction for lease premium	2	(14,400)
Capital allowances	3	(209,200)
		————
Trading profit		1,878,700
Property income	4	156,700
Loan interest receivable	5	42,400
		————
Taxable total profits		2,077,800
		————
Corporation tax at 19%		394,782
		————

Your colleague has raised some queries in regard to E-Commerce plc's corporation tax computation. Apart from any corrections arising from your colleague's queries, the corporation tax computation prepared by E-Commerce plc does not contain any errors.

Query 1 – Legal fees

E-Commerce plc has treated all of the company's legal expenditure as allowable when calculating its operating profit. However, legal expenses include the following:

(1)   Legal fees of £80,200 in connection with an issue of £1 preference shares.

(2)   Legal fees of £92,800 in connection with the issue of loan notes. The loan was used to finance the company's trading activities.

(3)   Legal fees of £14,900 in connection with the renewal of a 99-year lease of property.

(4)   Legal fees of £4,700 in connection with an action brought against a supplier for breach of contract.

(5)   Legal fees of £8,800 in connection with the registration of trade marks.

Query 2 – Deduction for lease premium

The amount assessed on the landlord has been correctly calculated, but the life of the lease should be 15 years and not the 12 years used by E-Commerce plc. The lease commenced on 1 April 2019.

Query 3 – Capital allowances

There are two issues here:

(1) E-Commerce plc purchased four motor cars during the year ended 31 March 2020, and all four motor cars have been included in the plant and machinery main pool. Details are as follows:

	Cost £	CO$_2$ emission rate
Motor car [1]	20,300	102 grams per kilometre
Motor car [2]	24,900	104 grams per kilometre
Motor car [3]	51,750	245 grams per kilometre
Motor car [4]	19,800	43 grams per kilometre

(2) Four years ago, E-Commerce plc purchased computer equipment on which a short-life asset election has been made. For the year ended 31 March 2020, the writing down allowance claimed on this equipment was £1,512, calculated at the rate of 18%. However, the computer equipment was actually scrapped, with nil proceeds, on 10 December 2019.

Query 4 – Property income

There are two issues here:

(1) E-Commerce plc has claimed a deduction for repairs of £95,300 in respect of a warehouse which was purchased on 21 May 2019. The warehouse was purchased in a dilapidated state, and could not be let until the repairs were carried out. This fact was represented by a reduced purchase price.

(2) E-Commerce plc did not receive the rent due of £16,200 in respect of this warehouse for the quarter ended 31 May 2020 until 1 April 2020. None of this amount has been taken into account in calculating the property business profit for the year ended 31 March 2020.

Query 5 – Loan interest receivable

The accrual at 31 March 2020 has been calculated at £4,800, but because of falling interest rates the accrual should actually be £3,500.

Other information

For the year ended 31 March 2019, E-Commerce plc had augmented profits of £1,360,000, and has forecast that its augmented profits for the year ended 31 March 2021 will exceed £2,000,000.

E-Commerce plc does not have any related 51% group companies.

Required:

(a) **Prepare a revised version of E-Commerce plc's corporation tax computation for the year ended 31 March 2020 after making any necessary corrections arising from your colleague's queries.** ⊞

Note: Your calculations should commence with the operating profit figure of £2,102,300, and you should indicate by the use of zero (0) any items referred to in queries (1) to (5) which do not require adjustment. **(12 marks)**

(b) Explain why E-Commerce plc will not have been required to make quarterly instalment payments in respect of its corporation tax liability for the year ended 31 March 2020, but will have to do so for the year ended 31 March 2021.

(3 marks)

(Total: 15 marks)

258 LUCKY LTD *WALK IN THE FOOTSTEPS OF A TOP TUTOR*

Lucky Ltd was incorporated on 20 July 2019, and commenced trading on 1 December 2019. The following information is available for the four-month period 1 December 2019 to 31 March 2020

(1) The operating profit for the four month period ended 31 March 2020 is £532,600. Advertising expenditure of £4,700 (incurred during September 2019), depreciation of £14,700, and amortisation of £9,000 have been deducted in arriving at this figure.

The amortisation relates to a premium which was paid on 1 December 2019 to acquire a leasehold warehouse on a 12-year lease. The amount of premium assessed on the landlord as income was £46,800. The warehouse was used for business purposes by Lucky Ltd throughout the period ended 31 March 2020.

(2) Lucky Ltd purchased the following assets during the period 20 July 2019 to 31 March 2020:

		£
19 August 2019	Computer	6,300
22 January 2020	Integral features	41,200
31 January 2020	Office equipment	32,900
17 March 2020	Motor car	12,800

The integral features of £41,200 are in respect of expenditure on electrical systems, a ventilation system and lifts which are integral to a freehold office building owned by Lucky Ltd.

The motor car has a CO_2 emission rate of 47 grams per kilometre.

(1) Lucky Ltd made a loan to another company for non-trading purposes on 1 February 2020. Loan interest income of £700 was accrued at 31 March 2020.

(2) Lucky Ltd made the following donations during the period 1 December 2019 to 31 March 2020:

		£
19 December 2019	Toys given to a local children's hospice as Christmas gifts	274
22 February 2020	Online donation to a registered national charity chosen by the employees of Lucky Ltd	835

Required:

(a) State when an accounting period starts for corporation tax purposes. 🖥️ (2 marks)

(b) Calculate Lucky Ltd's corporation tax liability for the four month period ended 31 March 2020. ▦

Note: Your computation should commence with the operating profit of £532,600, and should also indicate by the use of zero (0) any items referred to in the question for which no adjustment is required. Ignore VAT. (11 marks)

(c) Advise Lucky Ltd as to how long it must retain the records used in preparing its self-assessment corporation tax return for the four month period ended 31 March 2020, and the potential consequences of not retaining the records for the required period. 🖥️ (2 marks)

(Total: 15 marks)

RELIEF FOR TRADING LOSSES

259 LAST-ORDERS LTD *Walk in the footsteps of a top tutor*

Last-Orders Ltd ceased trading on 31 January 2020, having traded profitably for the previous ten years. The ordinary share capital of Last-Orders Ltd is owned 80% by Gastro Ltd and 20% by Gourmet Ltd.

Last-Orders Ltd's summarised statement of profit or loss for the ten-month period ended 31 January 2020 is as follows:

	Note	£
Revenue		176,790
Operating expenses		
Depreciation		(9,460)
Employee costs	1	(142,400)
Lease of motor car	2	(1,600)
Other expenses	3	(299,810)
Operating loss		(276,480)
Other income		
Property business income	4	11,500
Profit on disposal of freehold office building	5	47,400
Loss before taxation		(217,580)

Note 1 – employee costs

Employee costs are as follows:

	£
Counselling services provided to employees who were made redundant	5,200
Pension contributions paid on behalf of employees	12,200
Employer class 1 national insurance contributions (NICs)	11,890
Employer class 1A NICs payable on benefits provided for employees	1,160
Employee bonuses declared but unpaid – these will not be paid during 2020	10,400
Balance of expenditure (all allowable)	101,550
	———
	142,400
	———

Note 2 – lease of motor car

The lease is in respect of a motor car with CO_2 emissions of 105 grams per kilometre.

Note 3 – other expenses

Other expenses are as follows:

	£
Entertaining UK suppliers	1,920
Entertaining overseas customers	440
Qualifying charitable donation	800
Balance of expenditure (all allowable)	296,650
	———
	299,810
	———

Note 4 - property business income

Last-Orders Ltd let out a freehold office building. The following income and expenditure was received or incurred during the final 12 months of trading:

Date received/(paid)		£
1 February 2019	Rent for the six months ended 31 July 2019	19,200
1 February 2019	Insurance for the 12 months ended 31 January 2020	(1,800)
1 August 2019	Rent for the six months ended 31 January 2020	19,200
21 November 2019	Repairs following a fire (not covered by insurance)	(7,700)

Note 5 - disposal of freehold office building

The office building was sold on 31 January 2020. The profit has been calculated as disposal proceeds of £126,800 less cost of £79,400. The indexation allowance is £12,900. The office building was never used for business purposes.

Additional information - Plant and machinery

On 1 April 2019, the tax written down value of Last-Orders Ltd's main pool was £24,200. All of the items included in the main pool were sold for £13,600 on 31 January 2020, with none of the items sold for more than their original cost.

Last-Orders Ltd has previously always made up its accounts to 31 March. Both Gastro Ltd and Gourmet Ltd are profitable and make up their accounts to 31 March.

Required:

(a) Calculate Last-Orders Ltd's tax adjusted trading loss for the ten-month period ended 31 January 2020. ⊞

Notes:

(1) Your computation should commence with the operating loss figure of £276,480, and should also list all of the items referred to in notes (1) to (3), indicating by the use of zero (0) any items which do not require adjustment.

(2) You should assume that Last-Orders Ltd claims the maximum possible amount of capital allowances. **(6 marks)**

(b) Assuming that Last-Orders Ltd claims relief for its trading loss against its total profits for the ten-month period ended 31 January 2020, calculate the company's taxable total profits for this period. ⊞

Note: Your answer should show the amount of unused trading loss at 31 January 2020. **(5 marks)**

(c) Explain the alternative ways in which Last-Orders Ltd's unused trading loss for the ten-month period ended 31 January 2020 could be relieved. 💻 **(4 marks)**

(Total: 15 marks)

260 WRETCHED LTD (ADAPTED) *Walk in the footsteps of a top tutor*

Wretched Ltd commenced trading on 1 August 2019, preparing its first accounts for the eight month period ended 31 March 2020.

Wretched Ltd is incorporated in the United Kingdom, but its three directors are all non-resident in the United Kingdom. Board meetings are always held overseas.

The following information is available:

Trading loss

The trading loss based on the draft accounts for the eight month period ended 31 March 2020 is £141,200. This figure is **before** making any adjustments required for:

(1) Advertising expenditure of £7,990 incurred during April 2019. This expenditure has not been deducted in arriving at the trading loss for the eight month period ended 31 March 2020 of £141,200.

(2) The premium which was paid to acquire a leasehold office building on a ten year lease.

(3) Capital allowances.

Premium paid to acquire a leasehold office building

On 1 August 2019, Wretched Ltd paid a premium to acquire a leasehold office building on a ten year lease. The amount of premium assessed on the landlord as income was £34,440. The office building was used for business purposes by Wretched Ltd throughout the eight month period ended 31 March 2020.

Plant and machinery

On 1 August 2019, Wretched Ltd purchased three laptop computers at a discounted cost of £400 per laptop. The original price of each laptop was £850, but they were sold at the discounted price because they were ex-display.

Wretched Ltd also purchased three second hand motor cars on 1 August 2019. Details are:

	Cost £	CO_2 emissions rate
Motor car (1)	8,300	44 grams per kilometre
Motor car (2)	12,300	110 grams per kilometre
Motor car (3)	18,800	145 grams per kilometre

Property income

Wretched Ltd lets out a warehouse which is surplus to requirements. The warehouse was let out from 1 August to 31 October 2019 at a rent of £1,400 per month. The tenant left on 31 October 2019, and the warehouse was not re-let before 31 March 2020.

During the eight month period ended 31 March 2020, Wretched Ltd spent £2,100 on advertising for tenants.

Due to a serious flood, Wretched Ltd spent £5,900 on repairs during January 2020. The damage was not covered by insurance.

Loss on the disposal of shares

On 20 March 2020, Wretched Ltd sold its entire 1% shareholding of £1 ordinary shares in Worthless plc for £21,400. Wretched Ltd had purchased these shares on 5 August 2019 for £26,200. The indexation factor for the period August 2019 to March 2020 is 0.02.

Other information

Wretched Ltd does not have any 51% group companies. Wretched Ltd will continue to trade for the foreseeable future.

Required:

(a) State, giving reasons, whether Wretched Ltd is resident or not resident in the United Kingdom for corporation tax purposes. 🖥 **(1 mark)**

(b) Assuming that Wretched Ltd is resident in the United Kingdom, calculate the company's trading loss, property income loss and capital loss for the eight month period ended 31 March 2020. ⊞

Note: You should assume that the company claims the maximum available capital allowances. **(11 marks)**

(c) Explain how Wretched Ltd will be able to relieve its trading loss, property income loss and capital loss for the eight month period ended 31 March 2020. 🖥 **(3 marks)**

(Total: 15 marks)

261 RETRO LTD *Walk in the footsteps of a top tutor*

Retro Ltd's summarised statement of profit or loss for the year ended 31 March 2020 is as follows:

	Note	£	£
Gross profit			127,100
Operating expenses			
Depreciation		27,240	
Gifts and donations	1	2,300	
Impairment loss	2	1,600	
Leasing costs	3	4,400	
Other expenses	4	205,160	
			(240,700)
Finance costs			
Interest payable	5		(6,400)
Loss before taxation			(120,000)

Note 1 – Gifts and donations

Gifts and donations are as follows:

	£
Gifts to employees (food hampers costing £60 each)	720
Gifts to customers (calendars costing £8 each and displaying Retro Ltd's name)	480
Political donations	420
Qualifying charitable donations	680
	2,300

Note 2 – Impairment loss

On 31 March 2020, Retro Ltd wrote off an impairment loss of £1,600 relating to a trade debt. This was in respect of an invoice which had been due for payment on 10 November 2019.

Note 3 – Leasing costs

The leasing costs of £4,400 are in respect of a motor car lease which commenced on 1 April 2019. The leased motor car has CO_2 emissions of 145 grams per kilometre.

Note 4 – Other expenses

The figure of £205,160 for other expenses includes a fine of £5,100 for a breach of health and safety regulations, and legal fees of £4,860 in connection with the defence of Retro Ltd's internet domain name. The remaining expenses are all fully allowable.

Note 5 – Interest payable

The interest payable is in respect of the company's 5% loan notes which were repaid on 31 July 2019. Interest of £9,600 was paid on 31 July 2019, and an accrual of £3,200 had been provided for at 1 April 2019. The loan notes were issued in order to finance the company's trading activities.

Additional information

Plant and machinery

On 1 April 2019, the tax written down value of the plant and machinery main pool was £39,300.

The following vehicles were purchased during the year ended 31 March 2020:

	Date of purchase	Cost	CO_2 emission rate
		£	
Motor car (1)	8 June 2019	14,700	108 grams per kilometre
Delivery van	3 August 2019	28,300	162 grams per kilometre
Motor car (2)	19 October 2019	12,400	42 grams per kilometre

Previous results

Retro Ltd commenced trading on 1 September 2017. The company's results for its two previous periods of trading are as follows:

	Year ended 31 August 2018	Period ended 31 March 2019
	£	£
Tax adjusted trading profit	56,600	47,900
Bank interest receivable	1,300	0
Qualifying charitable donations paid	(540)	(330)

Future results

Retro Ltd is expected to return to profitability in the year ended 31 March 2021 and to continue to be profitable in subsequent years.

Required:

(a)   Calculate Retro Ltd's tax adjusted trading loss for the year ended 31 March 2020. ▦

Your computation should commence with the loss before taxation figure of £120,000, and should also list all of the items referred to in notes (1) to (5), indicating by the use of zero (0) any items which do not require adjustment.

(9 marks)

(b)   Assuming that Retro Ltd claims relief for its trading loss as early as possible, calculate the company's taxable total profits for the year ended 31 August 2018 and for the seven-month period ended 31 March 2019. ▦   (4 marks)

(c)   Identify the amount of unrelieved trading loss which Retro Ltd will have at 31 March 2020, and state how this can be relieved. ▦   (2 marks)

(Total: 15 marks)

WITH GROUP ASPECTS

262   MUSIC PLC (ADAPTED)

Music plc is the holding company for a group of companies. The group structure is as follows:

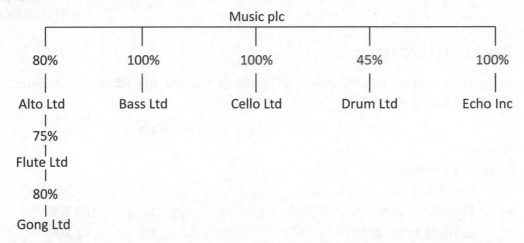

Music plc's shareholding in Bass Ltd was disposed of on 31 December 2019, and the shareholding in Cello Ltd was acquired on 1 January 2020. The other shareholdings were all held throughout the year ended 31 March 2020.

Echo Inc is resident overseas. The other companies are all resident in the United Kingdom.

For the year ended 31 March 2020 Music plc had a tax adjusted trading profit of £92,000. During the year Music plc received dividend income of £15,000 from an unconnected company, bank interest of £12,000 and a dividend of £5,400 from Bass Ltd.

As at 31 March 2019 Music plc had unused capital losses of £32,000. On 5 January 2020 the company sold a freehold office building, and this resulted in a further capital loss of £65,000. Alto Ltd sold a freehold warehouse on 10 March 2020, and this resulted in a capital gain of £120,000. An election has been made so that the gain is treated as Music plc's gain.

Year ending 31 March 2021

Music plc intends to acquire a property which it will rent out for £10,000 per annum. The company will take out a new non-trade related bank loan of £100,000 at an annual interest rate of 10% to partly fund the acquisition. Legal fees in connection with acquiring the property will be £300.

Required:

(a)   State, giving appropriate reasons, which companies in the Music plc group of companies form a group for capital gains purposes. 🖥   **(5 marks)**

(b)   Explain why Music plc has five related 51% group companies for the purposes of adjusting the augmented profits threshold for the year ended 31 March 2020. 🖥

Your answer should identify the five related companies.   **(5 marks)**

(c) Calculate Music plc's corporation tax liability for the year ended 31 March 2020. ⊞

(2 marks)

(d) Explain how the interest costs, legal fees and rent receivable will be treated for tax purposes if Music plc acquires a property in the year ended 31 March 2021. 💻

(3 marks)

(Total: 15 marks)

263 JUMP LTD (ADAPTED)

Jump Ltd's summarised statement of profit or loss for the three-month period ended 31 March 2020 is as follows:

	Note	£	£
Revenue			264,900
Operating expenses			
Depreciation		8,100	
Employee costs	1	189,700	
Lease of motor car	2	1,200	
Professional fees	3	7,800	
Other expenses	4	202,800	
			(409,600)
Operating loss			(144,700)
Bank interest receivable			0
Loss before taxation			(144,700)

Note 1 – Employee costs

Employee costs are as follows:

	£
Employee training courses	3,400
Employee pension contributions paid	11,600
Cost of annual staff party (for eight employees)	1,500
Balance of expenditure (all allowable)	173,200
	189,700

Note 2 – Lease of motor car

The lease is in respect of a motor car with CO_2 emissions of 189 grams per kilometre.

Note 3 – Professional fees

Professional fees are as follows:

	£
Accountancy	2,200
Legal fees in connection with the issue of share capital	3,800
Legal fees in connection with the renewal of a 20-year property lease	1,800
	7,800

Note 4 – Other expenses

Other expenses are as follows:

	£
Entertaining UK customers	1,700
Entertaining overseas customers	790
Political donations	800
Balance of expenditure (all allowable)	199,510
	202,800

Additional information

Plant and machinery

On 1 January 2020, the tax written down values of Jump Ltd's plant and machinery were as follows:

	£
Main pool	12,100
Special rate pool	5,700

The following motor cars were sold during the three-month period ended 31 March 2020:

	Date of sale	Proceeds	Original cost
		£	£
Motor car [1]	7 January 2020	9,700	9,300
Motor car [2]	29 March 2020	6,100	13,200

The original cost of motor car [1] was added to the special rate pool when it was purchased, and the original cost of motor car [2] was added to the main pool when it was purchased.

Previous results

Jump Ltd's results for its two previous periods of trading are as follows:

	Year ended 31 May 2019	Period ended 31 December 2019
	£	£
Tax adjusted trading profit	78,600	42,400
Bank interest receivable	1,200	0

Group companies

Jump Ltd owns 80% of the ordinary share capital of Hop Ltd and 60% of the ordinary share capital of Skip Ltd.

Hop Ltd commenced trading on 1 August 2019, and for the eight-month period ended 31 March 2020 has taxable total profits of £63,000.

Skip Ltd has been trading for several years and has taxable total profits of £56,000 for the year ended 31 March 2020.

Required:

(a) Calculate Jump Ltd's tax adjusted trading loss for the three-month period ended 31 March 2020. ⊞

Notes:

(1) Your computation should commence with the operating loss figure of £144,700, and should list all of the items referred to in notes (1) to (4), indicating by the use of zero (0) any items which do not require adjustment.

(2) You should assume that the company claims the maximum available capital allowances. **(10 marks)**

(b) (1) State ONE factor which will influence Jump Ltd's choice of loss relief or group relief claims. 🖥 **(1 mark)**

(2) Advise Jump Ltd as to the maximum amount of its trading loss which can be relieved against its total profits for the year ended 31 May 2019 and the seven-month period ended 31 December 2019. 🖥 **(2 marks)**

(3) Advise Jump Ltd as to the maximum amount of its trading loss which can be surrendered as group relief. 🖥 **(2 marks)**

(Total: 15 marks)

264 ASH LTD (ADAPTED) *Walk in the footsteps of a top tutor*

You are a trainee chartered certified accountant assisting your manager with the tax affairs of three unconnected limited companies, Ash Ltd, Beech Ltd and Cedar Ltd.

Ash Ltd

Ash Ltd was incorporated in the UK on 1 December 2017 and immediately opened a non-interest bearing bank account. The company commenced trading on 1 February 2018, preparing its first accounts for the 14-month period ended 31 March 2019. Accounts were then prepared for the year ended 31 March 2020.

At the date of incorporation, all three of Ash Ltd's directors (who each own one-third of the company's ordinary share capital) were based in the UK. However, on 1 October 2019, two of the directors moved overseas. The directors have always held Ash Ltd's board meetings in the UK, and will continue to do so despite two of them moving overseas.

Beech Ltd

Beech Ltd's summarised statement of profit or loss for the year ended 31 January 2020 is as follows:

	Note	£
Gross profit		565,800
Operating expenses		
Depreciation		(14,700)
Gifts and donations	1	(4,600)
Impairment loss	2	(3,700)
Leasing costs	3	(12,600)
Other expenses	4	(217,700)
Finance costs Interest payable	5	(7,000)
Profit before taxation		305,500

Note 1 – Gifts and donations

Gifts and donations of £4,600 comprise:

	£
Gifts to customers (pens costing £70 each and displaying Beech Ltd's name)	3,500
Qualifying charitable donations	1,100
	4,600

Note 2 – Impairment loss

On 31 January 2020, Beech Ltd wrote off an impairment loss of £3,700 relating to a trade debt. This was in respect of an invoice which had been due for payment on 15 October 2019.

Note 3 – Leasing costs

The leasing costs of £12,600 are in respect of four motor car leases which commenced on 1 February 2019. Each of the four leased motor cars has CO_2 emissions of 160 grams per kilometre.

Note 4 – Other expenses

The other expenses of £217,700 include a fine of £6,400 for a breach of data protection law, and legal fees of £5,700 in connection with the renewal of a 15-year property lease. The remaining expenses are all fully allowable.

Note 5 – Interest payable

The interest payable of £7,000 is in respect of the company's 4% loan notes which were issued on 1 July 2019. Interest of £6,000 was paid on 31 December 2019, with an accrual of £1,000 provided for at 31 January 2020. The loan notes were issued in order to finance the company's trading activities.

Capital allowances

No capital allowances are available for the year ended 31 January 2020.

Cedar Ltd

Cedar Ltd is a 100% subsidiary company of Timber Ltd. The following information is available in respect of the two companies for the year ended 31 March 2020:

(1) For the year ended 31 March 2020, Cedar Ltd made a trading loss of £19,700.

(2) On 28 December 2019, Cedar Ltd sold its entire shareholding of 25,000 £1 ordinary shares in Forest plc for £6.00 per share. Cedar Ltd had originally purchased 20,000 shares in Forest plc on 1 July 2010 for £24,800. On 20 July 2010, Forest plc made a 1 for 4 rights issue. Cedar Ltd took up its allocation under the rights issue in full, paying £1.15 for each new share issued. The indexation factor from July 2010 to December 2017 is 0.244.

(3) For the year ended 31 March 2020, Timber Ltd made:

	£
Trading loss	20,800
Capital loss	8,800

There is no possibility of Cedar Ltd or Timber Ltd offsetting their trading losses against prior year profits. The group has a policy of utilising losses at the earliest opportunity.

Required:

(a) (i) Identify Ash Ltd's accounting periods throughout the period 1 December 2017 to 31 March 2020. 🖥 **(2 marks)**

(ii) Explain Ash Ltd's residence status throughout the same period. 🖥 **(2 marks)**

(b) Calculate Beech Ltd's corporation tax liability for the year ended 31 January 2020. ⊞

Note: Your computation should commence with the profit before taxation figure of £305,500, and should also list all of the items referred to in notes (1) to (5), indicating by the use of zero (0) any items which do not require adjustment.

(6 marks)

(c) On the basis that all available claims and elections are made, calculate Cedar Ltd's taxable total profits for the year ended 31 March 2020. ⊞

(5 marks)

(Total: 15 marks)

265 CLUELESS LTD (ADAPTED) *Walk in the footsteps of a top tutor*

(a) You are a trainee accountant and your manager has asked you to correct a corporation tax computation that has been prepared by the managing director of Clueless Ltd, a company which manufactures children's board games.

The corporation tax computation is for the year ended 31 March 2020 and contains a significant number of errors:

Clueless Ltd – Corporation tax computation for the year ended 31 March 2020

	£
Trading profit (working 1)	453,782
Loan interest received (working 2)	32,100
Chargeable gain (working 3)	50,000
	535,882
Dividends received (working 4)	28,700
	564,582
Corporation tax (£564,582 × 19%)	107,271

Working 1 – Trading profit

	£
Profit before taxation	382,610
Depreciation	15,740
Client entertaining	400
Qualifying charitable donations paid	900
Gifts to customers:	
- portable power banks and displaying Clueless Ltd's name (£10 each)	920
- boxes of chocolates displaying Clueless Ltd's name (£15 each)	1,650
Capital allowances (working 5)	51,562
Trading profit	453,782

Working 2 – Loan interest received

	£
Loan interest receivable	32,800
Accrued at 1 April 2019	10,600
Accrued at 31 March 2020	(11,300)
Loan interest received	32,100

The loan was made for non-trading purposes.

Working 3 – Chargeable gain

The gain relates to the sale of a building to an unconnected party for £200,000 on 1 March 2020. The office had been acquired by Clever Ltd (a 100% UK subsidiary) for £70,000 on 1 April 2003. Clever Ltd had sold the building to Clueless Ltd on 1 June 2011 for £150,000, which was its market value at that date.

Working 4 – Dividends received

	£
From unrelated companies	20,700
From Clever Ltd (a 100% UK subsidiary company)	8,000
	————
Dividends received	28,700
	————

Working 5 – Capital allowances

	Main pool £	Motor car £	Special rate pool £	Allowances £
TWDV b/f	12,400		13,500	
Additions				
Computers	42,300			
Motor car		11,800		
	————			
	54,700			
AIA	(54,700)			54,700
Disposal proceeds			(9,300)	
			————	
			4,200	
Balancing allowance			(4,200)	(4,200)
			————	
WDA (18%)		(2,124) × 50%		1,062
	————	————		
TWDV c/f	0	9,676		
	————	————		————
Total allowances				51,562
				————

Notes:

(1)   The motor car has a CO_2 emission rate of 145 grams per kilometre. This motor car is used by the sales manager and 50% of the mileage is for private journeys.

(2)   All of the items included in the special rate pool at 1 April 2019 were sold for £9,300 during the year ended 31 March 2020 The original cost of these items was £16,200.

Required:

(a) Prepare a corrected version of Clueless Ltd's corporation tax computation for the year ended 31 March 2020.

You should indicate by the use of zero any items in the computation of the trading profit for which no adjustment is required.

The indexation factors are:

April 2003 to June 2011	0.298
April 2003 to December 2017	0.535
April 2003 to March 2020	0.623
June 2011 to December 2017	0.182
June 2011 to March 2020	0.250

(11 marks)

(b) The managing director of Clueless Ltd understands that the company has to file its self-assessment corporation tax returns online, and that the supporting accounts and tax computations have to be filed using the inline eXtensible Business Reporting Language (iXBRL). The managing director is interested in the options regarding how the company can produce documents in this format.

Required:

(1) State the date by which Clueless Ltd's self-assessment corporation tax return for the year ended 31 March 2020 should be filed. (1 mark)

(2) Explain the options available to Clueless Ltd regarding the production of accounts and tax computations in the iXBRL format. (3 marks)

(Total: 15 marks)

266 LONG LTD AND ROAD LTD (ADAPTED) *Walk in the footsteps of a top Tutor*

(a) Long Ltd owns 100% of the ordinary share capital of Road Ltd. Long Ltd and Road Ltd are both trading companies.

Long Ltd's shareholding in Road Ltd was acquired on 15 January 2019 when that company was incorporated. Long Ltd has prepared accounts for the year ended 31 March 2020, whilst Road Ltd has prepared accounts for the period 1 January 2020 (when the company commenced trading) to 31 March 2020.

The following information is available:

Long Ltd

(1) The operating profit for the year ended 31 March 2020 is £384,400. Depreciation of £43,050, amortisation of £5,000 and leasing costs of £3,600 have been deducted in arriving at this figure. The amortisation relates to a premium which was paid on 1 August 2015 to acquire a leasehold office building on a 20-year lease. The amount of premium assessed on the landlord as income was £68,200. The office building was used for business purposes by Long Ltd throughout the year ended 31 March 2020. The leasing costs relate to a motor car with a CO_2 emission rate of 142 grams per kilometre, which was leased from 1 April 2019.

(2)   On 1 April 2019, the tax written down value of the plant and machinery main pool was £44,800. On 10 June 2019, Long Ltd purchased a lorry for £36,800 and a motor car for £15,700. The motor car has a CO_2 emission rate of 102 grams per kilometre. The motor car is used by the managing director of Long Ltd, and 40% of the mileage is for private journeys.

(3)   On 1 February 2020, Long Ltd disposed of a 2% shareholding in an unconnected company. The disposal resulted in a capital loss of £21,300.

Road Ltd

(1)   The operating loss for the three-month period ended 31 March 2020 is £26,100. Donations of £2,800 have been deducted in arriving at this figure. The donations consist of political donations of £400, and qualifying charitable donations of £2,400.

(2)   On 3 October 2019, Road Ltd purchased a motor car for £11,600. The motor car has a CO_2 emission rate of 50 grams per kilometre.

(3)   For the three-month period ended 31 March 2020, loan interest receivable was £4,300. The loan was made for non-trading purposes.

(4)   On 18 March 2020, Road Ltd disposed of a 1% shareholding in an unrelated company. The disposal resulted in a chargeable gain of £29,800. This figure is after taking account of indexation.

Other information

Road Ltd is not expected to be profitable for the foreseeable future, and Long Ltd and Road Ltd claim maximum possible group relief where group relief is available.

Required:

On the assumption that any available reliefs are claimed as soon as possible, calculate the corporation tax liability of Long Ltd for the year ended 31 March 2020, and of Road Ltd for the three-month period ended 31 March 2020.   **(12 marks)**

(b)   Road Ltd's recently appointed bookkeeper understands that the company must report PAYE information to HM Revenue and Customs in real time. However, the bookkeeper does not know how PAYE real time reporting works in practice, having previously only produced payroll manually.

Road Ltd pays its employees at the end of each calendar month, with some employees receiving taxable benefits. Road Ltd has chosen not to tax the benefits through the payroll system.

Required:

Explain how and when Road Ltd will have to report real time PAYE information to HM Revenue and Customs, and state what forms, if any, will have to be provided to employees or submitted to HM Revenue and Customs following the end of the tax year.   **(3 marks)**

(Total: 15 marks)

Section 5

PRACTICE VALUE ADDED TAX QUESTIONS

PRACTICE SECTION A OBJECTIVE TEST QUESTIONS

267 Fred began trading as a sole trader on 1 January 2020 but did not register for VAT when he commenced to trade. He has made the following sales so far in 2020, all of which are standard-rated:

	£
January	2,000
February	3,500
March	4,000
April	3,200
May	1,400
June	90,000
July	5,000
August	4,000

All of the sales in June relate to an order which was received on 1 June for goods to be delivered by 30 June.

When must Fred notify HMRC that he is required to register for VAT, and when must he start charging VAT to his customers?

		Notify	
		30 June 2020	30 July 2020
Charge VAT from	1 June 2020	A	B
	1 August 2020	C	D

268 Layla started trading on 4 January 2019.

Taxable supplies for 2019 are as follows:

3 months to 31 March	£3,000 per month
3 months to 30 June	£9,000 per month
3 months to 30 September	£30,000 per month
3 months to 31 December	£50,000 per month

What is the effective date of registration for VAT, assuming that Layla waits until her turnover exceeds the registration threshold before registering?

A   1 February 2020

B   1 October 2019

C   1 July 2019

D   1 September 2019

269 Betty, a retailer, decides to voluntarily register for VAT.

Which TWO of the following statements, concerning supplies made to Betty before the date of VAT registration, are TRUE?

A   Betty can reclaim input VAT on a car that she purchased six months ago, which she still uses for both private and business purposes

B   Betty cannot reclaim input VAT on the petrol used in her car, for both private and business purposes, in the month prior to the date of VAT registration

C   Betty can reclaim input VAT on a van purchased for the business two years ago which she still uses in the business

D   Betty can reclaim input VAT on accountancy services she purchased one year ago in connection with setting up the business

E   Betty can reclaim input VAT on the cost of goods bought for resale two months ago, which she sold the week before registration

270 Fergus owns shares in a number of companies as set out below.

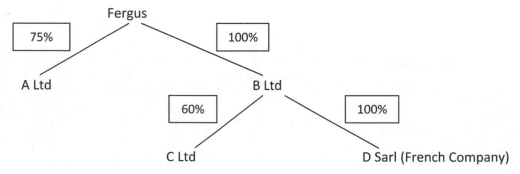

D Sarl's only place of business is in France.

Tick the appropriate box(es) to show which of the above companies can be in a VAT group.

	Can be in VAT group
A Ltd	
B Ltd	
C Ltd	
D Sarl	

271 *September 2015 OT question*

Yui commenced trading on 1 April 2019, and registered for value added tax (VAT) from 1 January 2020. Her first VAT return is for the quarter ended 31 March 2020. During the period 1 April 2019 to 31 March 2020, Yui incurred input VAT of £110 per month in respect of the hire of office equipment.

How much input VAT, in respect of the office equipment, can Yui reclaim on her VAT return for the quarter ended 31 March 2020?

    A   £660

    B   £990

    C   £330

    D   £1,320

272 Vikram ceased trading on 17 June 2019.

For each of the following statements concerning his responsibilities in relation to VAT select whether it is true or false:

	True	False
Vikram should have notified HM Revenue and Customs that he had ceased to make taxable supplies by 30 July 2019		
Vikram must account for output tax on the value of non-current assets and inventory held at the date of deregistration and on which a deduction for input tax has previously been claimed, unless this would result in a liability below £83,000.		

273 Padma Ltd received an order for goods on 20 October 2019. The goods were delivered to the customer on 20 December 2019 and Padma Ltd sent the invoice for £1,000 on 15 January 2020, which the customer paid on 5 February 2020.

What is the tax point of the transaction for VAT?

    A   20 October 2019

    B   20 December 2019

    C   15 January 2020

    D   5 February 2020

274 Barney is VAT registered and only makes standard-rated supplies. On 31 March 2020 he wrote off two irrecoverable debts in his VAT account. The first for £800 (VAT inclusive) was due for payment on 1 June 2019 and despite being chased has still not been paid. The second for £1,000 (VAT inclusive) relates to a company that Barney has recently been informed has gone into liquidation. The debt was due for payment on 1 December 2019.

How much input VAT will Barney be able to recover, in respect of the irrecoverable debts, in his VAT return for the quarter to 31 March 2020?

£ ☐

275 *June 2015 OT question*

Violet Ltd provides one of its directors with a company motor car which is used for both business and private mileage. For the quarter ended 31 March 2020, the total cost of petrol for the car was £600, of which 30% was for private use by the director. The relevant quarterly scale rate is £354. Both these figures are inclusive of value added tax (VAT).

What output VAT and input VAT entries will Violet Ltd include on its VAT return for the quarter ended 31 March 2020 in respect of the company motor car?

A   Output VAT of £59 and input VAT of £71

B   Output VAT of £0 and input VAT of £71

C   Output VAT of £0 and input VAT of £100

D   Output VAT of £59 and input VAT of £100

276 West Ltd is registered for VAT and makes standard-rated supplies.

The company incurs the following costs:

(1)   £650 (VAT inclusive) on entertaining new suppliers based in France

(2)   £3,000 (VAT inclusive) on car leasing costs. The car has CO_2 emission of 120g/km and is used by a director for both private (20% of the time) and business purposes.

How much input VAT can the company recover on the above costs?

		Entertaining suppliers	
		£0	£108
Car leasing	£100	A	B
	£250	C	D

277 *December 2016 OT question*

Emil is registered for value added tax (VAT). For the quarter ended 31 March 2020, the input VAT incurred on his purchases and expenses included the following:

	£
Entertaining overseas customers	320
Purchase of new office equipment	1,250
Purchase of a new motor car for business and private use by one of Emil's employees	3,000

What is the amount of input VAT recoverable by Emil in the quarter ended 31 March 2020 in respect of the entertaining, office equipment and motor car?

A   £1,250

B   £320

C   £1,570

D   £4,570

278   Tobias is VAT registered and only makes standard-rated supplies.

In the quarter to 31 March 2020 he had the following transactions:

(1)   Sales of £30,000 and purchases of goods for resale of £16,800. Both figures are VAT inclusive.

(2)   He gave samples of his products to a potential customer which he would normally sell for £100 (VAT exclusive).

How much VAT is payable by Tobias for the quarter ended 31 March 2020?

£ _____

279   Blessing is VAT registered.

In the quarter to 31 March 2020 Blessing's accounts include the total cost of fuel for her car, which she uses 20% for private purposes, of £1,200 (VAT inclusive). The relevant VAT scale rate for the car is £414.

How much net VAT (i.e. output VAT less input VAT) is reclaimable by Blessing for the quarter ended 31 March 2020 in respect of the fuel for her car?

A   £200

B   £157

C   £131

D   £69

280 For each of the following statements concerning less detailed VAT invoices select whether it is true or false.

	True	False
The date of the supply is not required on a less detailed VAT invoice.		
A description of goods and services is required on a less detailed VAT invoice.		
A less detailed VAT invoice can be provided when the consideration for the supply is less than £1,000.		
The amount of VAT payable on the supply is not required on a less detailed VAT invoice.		

281 Having always filed VAT returns on time, Chimney Ltd's VAT return for the quarter ended 31 October 2019 was submitted on 13 December 2019 along with the VAT due. For the quarter ended 31 January 2020 the return and VAT of £26,000 was filed on 23 March 2020.

What are the VAT consequences when the 31 January 2020 VAT return is filed late?

A   A surcharge liability period will run for the 12 months until 31 January 2021 but no penalty will be charged

B   A surcharge liability period will run for the 12 months until 31 January 2021 and a penalty of £520 will be charged

C   A surcharge liability period will run for the 12 months until 23 March 2020 but no penalty will be charged

D   A surcharge liability period will run for the 12 months until 23 March 2020 and a penalty of £520 will be charged

282 For the VAT quarter ended 30 June 2019 Beach Ltd has a taxable turnover of £380,000. It subsequently finds it has under-declared output tax of £8,000 on its VAT return for that quarter.

How must Beach Ltd notify HM Revenue and Customs (HMRC) of the error and what are the consequences for Beach Ltd? You may tick more than one box.

		Correction of error	
		Beach Ltd can correct the error on the next VAT return	Beach Ltd must separately notify HMRC of the error
Penalties and interest	Beach Ltd will be charged a penalty for an incorrect VAT return		
	Beach Ltd will be charged default interest		

283 *September 2016 OT question*

Triangle Ltd is registered for value added tax (VAT) and uses the annual accounting scheme. For the year ended 31 December 2019, the net VAT payable by Triangle Ltd was £73,500. For the year ended 31 December 2018, the net VAT payable by Triangle Ltd was £47,700.

What monthly payments on account of VAT must Triangle Ltd make in respect of the year ended 31 December 2019 prior to submitting its VAT return for that year?

A   Nine monthly payments of £7,350

B   Nine monthly payments of £4,770

C   Ten monthly payments of £4,770

D   Ten monthly payments of £7,350

284 **For each of the following statements concerning the VAT cash accounting scheme select whether it is true or false:**

	True	False
Input tax cannot be claimed until the invoice is paid which delays recovery of input VAT		
Traders using the scheme do not have to pay output VAT to HMRC until they receive it from customers		
To join the scheme the trader's expected taxable turnover (excluding VAT) for the next twelve months must not exceed £150,000		
The cash accounting scheme cannot be used where a trader issues an invoice in advance of supplying goods		

285 *Specimen exam June 2015 OT question*

For the quarter ended 31 March 2020, Zim had standard-rated sales of £59,700 and standard-rated expenses of £27,300. Both figures are inclusive of value added tax (VAT). Zim uses the flat rate scheme to calculate the amount of VAT payable, with the relevant scheme percentage for her trade being 12%.

How much VAT will Zim have to pay to HM Revenue and Customs (HMRC) for the quarter ended 31 March 2020?

A   £8,597

B   £3,888

C   £6,480

D   £7,164

286 Petr has standard-rated sales of £80,000 excluding VAT, zero-rated sales of £15,000 and exempt sales of £10,000 for the quarter ended 30 June 2019. He has standard-rated expenses including VAT of £8,400. Petr uses the flat rate scheme for VAT and the flat rate for his business is 13%.

What is Petr's VAT liability for the quarter ended 30 June 2019?

£ [   ]

287 Marina is a UK VAT registered trader making only standard-rated supplies purchased goods worth £10,000 (VAT exclusive) from a VAT registered trader situated elsewhere within the European Union. The goods would be classed as standard-rated if they were supplied in the UK. The standard rate in the EU country the good are supplied from is 5%.

What is the net effect on the VAT position of the UK trader?

A   £0

B   £2,000 to pay to HM Revenue and Customs

C   £2,000 to reclaim from HM Revenue and Customs

D   £500 to pay to HM Revenue and Customs

PRACTICE SECTION B OBJECTIVE TEST CASES

288 THIDAR (ADAPTED)

You should assume that today's date is 25 April 2020.

Thidar commenced trading as a builder on 1 January 2019. She voluntarily registered for value added tax (VAT) on 1 January 2019.

Sales

Thidar's sales for the first 15 months of trading have been:

Month	Standard rated	Zero rated	Month	Standard rated	Zero rated
	£	£		£	£
1	3,400	0	9	8,800	6,300
2	0	1,900	10	2,900	7,300
3	5,700	2,100	11	0	0
4	6,800	0	12	0	2,600
5	9,500	1,200	13	2,800	900
6	7,900	2,200	14	3,200	1,700
7	0	3,700	15	22,200	3,600
8	12,100	0			

Pre-registration expenditure

Thidar paid for the following standard rated services prior to registering for VAT on 1 January 2019:

Date	Cost of service	Description
	£	
10 June 2018	1,800	Advertisement for the building business
8 December 2018	300	Advertisement for the building business

Both figures are exclusive of VAT. Thidar paid for the advertisement of £300 by cash, and she does not have any evidence of this transaction (such as a VAT invoice).

VAT return for the quarter ended 30 September 2019

Thidar's VAT return for the quarter ended 30 September 2019 was filed by the submission deadline of 7 November 2019 and the related VAT liability was paid on time.

However, on 15 February 2020, Thidar discovered that the amount of VAT paid was understated by £1,200 as a result of incorrectly treating a standard rated sale as zero rated. Given that the underpayment does not exceed £10,000, Thidar is permitted to correct this error on her VAT return for the quarter ended 31 March 2020, and this is what she will do. Thidar will file this VAT return by the submission deadline of 7 May 2020 and pay the related VAT liability (including the underpaid £1,200) on time.

VAT return for the quarter ended 31 March 2020

Thidar is currently completing her VAT return for the quarter ended 31 March 2020 and is unsure as to how much input VAT is non-deductible in respect of two items:

During the quarter ended 31 March 2020, Thidar spent £800 on entertaining UK customers.

During the quarter ended 31 March 2020, Thidar leased a motor car at a cost of £700. The motor car is used by Thidar and 75% of the mileage is for private journeys.

Both figures are exclusive of VAT.

1   **In which month did Thidar exceed the VAT threshold for compulsory registration?**

    A   Month 14

    B   Month 15

    C   Month 13

    D   Not yet exceeded

2   **What amount of pre-registration input VAT was Thidar able to recover in respect of expenditure incurred prior to registering for VAT on 1 January 2019?**

    A   £360

    B   £60

    C   £420

    D   £0

3   **Within what period must Thidar issue a VAT invoice after making a standard rated supply, and for how long must these VAT invoices then normally be retained by Thidar?**

	VAT invoices	Retention
A	Within 14 days	Four years
B	Within 30 days	Six years
C	Within 30 days	Four years
D	Within 14 days	Six years

4 Why will VAT default (or penalty) interest not be charged on Thidar's underpayment of VAT of £1,200 for the quarter ended 30 September 2019?

A Because Thidar corrected the error within 12 months

B Because the error was not deliberate

C Because separate disclosure of the VAT underpayment was not required

D Because Thidar paid the underpayment of £1,200 by the submission deadline of 7 May 2019

5 For the quarter ended 31 March 2020, what is the amount of non-deductible input VAT in respect of entertaining UK customers and the leasing cost of the motor car?

	Entertaining UK customers	Leasing cost
A	£0	£105
B	£160	£105
C	£160	£70
D	£0	£70

289 CANDY APPLE AND SUGAR PLUM (ADAPTED) *Walk in the footsteps of a top tutor*

 Question debrief

Candy Apple

Candy Apple began a trading business on 1 April 2019. Her sales since the commencement of trading have been as follows:

April to July 2019	£10,500 per month
August to November 2019	£14,400 per month
December 2019 to March 2020	£21,500 per month

These figures are stated exclusive of value added tax (VAT). Candy's sales are all standard-rated and arise evenly over the month.

As her accountant you have advised Candy in writing that she should be registered for VAT, but she has refused to register because she thinks her net profit is insufficient to cover the additional cost which would be incurred.

Sugar Plum

Sugar Plum began trading on 1 April 2019 and registered for VAT on 1 May 2019 to avoid late registration penalties. The following information is available in respect of Sugar Plum's VAT for the quarter ended 31 July 2019:

(1) Invoices were issued for standard-rated and zero-rated sales of £53,700 and £23,100 respectively. These figures are exclusive of VAT.

---

(2) Sugar uses a room at her home as her office. The house has seven main rooms. The VAT charged on the electricity bill for the whole house for the quarter is estimated as £49.

During the quarter, Sugar also purchased several items of furniture for her office for a total of £1,500 exclusive of VAT. A 5% discount was applied to this amount as Sugar had purchased two items or more.

(3) Prior to starting business, Sugar engaged a consultancy firm to undertake some market research. Sugar paid the consultancy firm £250 on 1 August 2018 and £375 on 1 January 2019. Sugar also purchased £2,500 worth of inventory on 1 January 2019, of which £1,000 was unsold by 1 May 2019. These figures are exclusive of VAT.

1 **From what date was Candy Apple compulsorily required to charge VAT on her taxable supplies and by what date must she notify HM revenue and customs that she is required to register for vat?**

		Charge VAT from	
		1 November 2019	**1 December 2019**
Notify	31 October 2019	A	B
	30 November 2019	C	D

2 **For each of the following statements concerning the consequences of late VAT registration select whether it is true or false:**

	True	False
A default surcharge penalty will be charged for late registration		
Candy must account to HM Revenue and Customs for output tax at 20/120 of the value of sales from the date that she should have been registered from		
Candy must issue VAT invoices charging her customers the VAT that she should have charged on sales from the date she should have been registered by		

3 **What is the amount of output VAT payable by Sugar Plum in respect of her sales for the quarter ended 31 July 2019?**

£ [ ]

4 **What is the amount of input VAT claimable by Sugar in respect of the electricity and furniture costs for the quarter ended 31 July 2019?**

A £292

B £334

C £245

D £307

5   **What is the amount of input VAT claimable by Sugar in respect of the consultancy fees and inventory costs incurred prior to the commencement of trade?**

A   £625

B   £200

C   £325

D   £275

 Calculate your allowed time and allocate the time to the separate parts.

290 LITHOGRAPH LTD (ADAPTED)

Lithograph Ltd runs a printing business, and is registered for VAT. Because its annual taxable turnover is only £250,000, the company uses the annual accounting scheme so that it only has to prepare one VAT return each year. The annual VAT period is the year ended 31 March. Unless stated otherwise all of the figures below are exclusive of VAT.

Year ended 31 March 2019

The results for the year ended 31 March 2019 include the following:

(1)   Standard-rated expenses of £28,000. This includes £3,600 for entertaining overseas customers.

(2)   On 1 May 2018 Lithograph Ltd purchased a motor car costing £18,400 for the use of its managing director. The manager director is provided with free petrol for private mileage, and the cost of this petrol is included in the standard-rated expenses in Note (1). The relevant annual scale rate is £1,952. Both figures are inclusive of VAT.

(3)   During the year ended 31 March 2019 Lithograph Ltd purchased machinery for £24,000, and sold office equipment for £8,000. Input VAT had been claimed when the office equipment was originally purchased.

Year ended 31 March 2020

In the year ended 31 March 2020 Lithograph Ltd wrote off two debts which were due from customers. The first debt of £4,800 was in respect of an invoice that was due for payment on 31 August 2019. The second debt of £6,400 was in respect of an invoice that was due for payment on 12 October 2019. Both these figures are VAT inclusive.

1   In which months would Lithograph Ltd have been required to pay payments on account (POA) of VAT in respect of the year ended 31 March 2019? You can tick more than one box.

	POA due
April 2018	
May 2018	
June 2018	
July 2018	
August 2018	
September 2018	
October 2018	
November 2018	
December 2018	
January 2019	
February 2019	
March 2019	
April 2019	

2   By reference to which VAT liability were the payments on account for the year ended 31 March 2019 calculated and by when must the annual VAT return for the year ended 31 March 2019 be submitted to HM Revenue and Customs?

		VAT liability	
		Estimated for year ended 31 March 2019	Actual for year ended 31 March 2018
Due date for return	7 May 2019	A	B
	31 May 2019	C	D

3   How much output tax is payable by Lithograph Ltd in respect of the items (1) – (3) included in the results for the year ended 31 March 2019?

A   £325

B   £390

C   £1,925

D   £1,990

4   How much input tax is reclaimable by Lithograph Ltd in respect of the items (1) – (3) included in the results for the year ended 31 March 2019?

£ [   ]

KAPLAN PUBLISHING

189

5 How much VAT is reclaimable by Lithograph Ltd in the VAT year to 31 March 2020 in respect of the two impaired debts written off?

A £1,867

B £2,240

C £960

D £800

291 ALISA (ADAPTED) *Walk in the footsteps of a top tutor*

Alisa commenced trading on 1 January 2019. Her sales since commencement have been as follows:

January to April 2019	£7,500 per month
May to August 2019	£10,000 per month
September to December 2019	£15,500 per month

The above figures are stated exclusive of value added tax (VAT). Alisa only supplies services, and these are all standard-rated for VAT purposes. Alisa notified her liability to compulsorily register for VAT by the appropriate deadline.

For each of the eight months prior to the date on which she registered for VAT, Alisa paid £240 per month (inclusive of VAT) for website design services and £180 per month (exclusive of VAT) for advertising. Both of these supplies are standard-rated for VAT purposes and relate to Alisa's business activity after the date from when she registered for VAT.

After registering for VAT, Alisa purchased a motor car on 1 January 2020. The motor car is used 60% for business mileage. During the quarter ended 31 March 2020, Alisa spent £456 on repairs to the motor car and £624 on fuel for both her business and private mileage. The relevant quarterly scale rate is £296. All of these figures are inclusive of VAT.

All of Alisa's customers are registered for VAT, so she appreciates that she has to issue VAT invoices when services are supplied.

1 From what date would Alisa have been required to be compulsorily registered for VAT and therefore have had to charge output VAT on her supplies of services?

A 30 September 2019

B 1 November 2019

C 1 October 2019

D 30 October 2019

2 What amount of pre-registration input VAT would Alisa have been able to recover in respect of inputs incurred prior to the date on which she registered for VAT?

A £468

B £608

C £536

D £456

3   What is the maximum amount of input VAT which Alisa can reclaim in respect of her motor expenses for the quarter ended 31 March 2020?

£ _____

4   How and by when does Alisa have to pay any VAT liability for the quarter ended 31 March 2020?

		How the liability is paid	
		Any payment method	Electronically
Due date	30 April 2020	A	B
	7 May 2020	C	D

5   Which of the following items of information is Alisa required to include on a valid VAT invoice? You can tick more than one box.

	Include
The customer's VAT registration number	
An invoice number	
The customer's address	
A description of the services supplied	

292   THE WHITLOCK SISTERS (ADAPTED)   *Walk in the footsteps of a top tutor*

Sisters Beth and Amy Whitlock trade as a partnership.

(1)   The partnership has been registered for VAT for many years and on 1 January 2020 it began using the flat rate scheme to calculate the amount of VAT payable. The relevant flat rate scheme percentage for the partnership's trade is 13%.

(2)   For the quarter ended 31 March 2020 the partnership had standard-rated sales of £50,000 and exempt sales of £10,000. For the same period standard-rated expenses amounted to £27,300. All figures are stated inclusive of VAT.

(3)   The partnership has two private rooms in its premises that can be hired by customers. Such customers can book the rooms up to two months in advance, at which time they have to pay a 25% deposit.

An invoice is then given to the customer on the day after the room hire, with payment of the balance of 75% required within seven days. For VAT purposes, the renting out of the rooms is a standard-rated supply of services.

(4)   Beth and Amy are planning to make significant changes to the partnership's accounts payable and accounts receivable processes and plan to take key suppliers and clients out for dinner to explain the changes. The VAT inclusive cost of this in the quarter to 30 June 2020 will be as follows:

UK customers	£250
UK suppliers	£100
Overseas customers	£775
Overseas suppliers	£650

1   **How much VAT is payable by the partnership for the quarter ended 31 March 2020 if the flat rate scheme is used?**

    A   £6,500

    B   £4,251

    C   £2,951

    D   £7,800

2   **How much VAT would be payable by the partnership for the quarter ended 31 March 2020 if the flat rate scheme was NOT used?**

    £ [   ]

3   **For each of the following statements concerning the VAT flat rate scheme select whether it is true or false:**

	True	False
To join the scheme expected taxable turnover (including VAT) for the next 12 months must not exceed £150,000		
The scheme can only be used by small unincorporated businesses		
A business must leave the scheme if total VAT inclusive turnover exceeds £230,000		
VAT must still be charged on standard-rated sales invoices at the rate of 20%		

4   **Select the actual tax point date in respect of the 25% deposit and 75% balancing payment in respect of the room hire.**

Dates	Deposit	Balancing payment
When the deposit is paid	[ ]	[ ]
Invoice date		
Day of the room hire		
When the balance is paid		

5   **What is the amount of input VAT reclaimable in the quarter to 30 June 2020 on the proposed dinner expenses?**

    A   £238

    B   £296

    C   £108

    D   £129

293 KNIGHT LTD (ADAPTED) *Walk in the footsteps of a top tutor*

Knight Ltd is a UK resident trading company. The following information is available in respect of Knight Ltd's value added tax (VAT).

(1)   For the quarter ended 31 March 2020 Knight Ltd had the following transactions:

(a)   Output VAT of £38,210 was charged in respect of sales. This figure includes output VAT of £400 on a deposit received on 29 March 2020, which is in respect of a contract that is due to commence on 20 April 2020.

(b)   The managing director of Knight Ltd is provided with free fuel for private mileage driven in his company motor car. The relevant quarterly scale rate is £265. This figure is inclusive of VAT.

(c)   Input VAT of £12,770 was incurred in respect of sundry expenses as follows:

	£
Entertaining UK customers	210
Entertaining overseas customers	139
Extending the office building in order to create a new reception area	3,300
Other sundry expenses (all recoverable)	9,121
	12,770

(2)   In the following quarter to 30 June 2020, the following information is available in respect of outstanding customer debts:

Customer	Invoice date	Payment due date	Output VAT
			£
Armour Ltd	1 November 2015	30 November 2015	640
Jousting Ltd	1 October 2019	1 November 2019	555
Marion Ltd	15 December 2019	31 January 2020	759

All of the above debts have been written off in Knight Ltd's accounts except for the debt due from Jousting Ltd, as Knight Ltd is still hopeful that the debt will be paid.

(3)   On 1 July 2020 Knight Ltd acquired 100% of the shares in Are Ltd and Can Ltd, which are both UK resident VAT registered companies. Knight Ltd will make standard-rated supplies to both companies.

(4)   Knight Ltd was late in submitting the following VAT returns and in paying the related VAT:

Return period	VAT due
	£
3 months ended 31 December 2017	20,000
3 months ended 30 September 2019	30,000
3 months ended 30 June 2020	21,000

All of the company's other VAT returns have been submitted on time, and the related VAT liabilities have been paid on time.

1   How much output tax is payable by Knight Ltd for the quarter to 31 March 2020?

   A   £38,254

   B   £37,854

   C   £38,263

   D   £37,863

2   How much input tax is recoverable in respect of the sundry expenses incurred in the quarter to 31 March 2020?

   A   £9,260

   B   £12,421

   C   £12,560

   D   £12,631

3   How much relief for impairment losses can Knight Ltd claim in respect of the quarter to 30 June 2020?

   £ [   ]

4   For each of the following statements concerning the VAT groups select whether it is true or false:

	True	False
If Knight Ltd forms a VAT group it will include both Are Ltd and Can Ltd		
Standard-rated supplies made by Knight Ltd to other VAT group members will be ignored for VAT purposes		
Knight Ltd will be the representative member of the VAT group and will be required to submit one VAT return for the whole group		
Each group member will remain liable for its share of the VAT payable		

5   As a result of the late submission of the VAT return and late payment of VAT in respect of the 3 months ended 30 June 2020, what is the total amount of the default surcharge payable, and to when will the surcharge period will be extended?

		Default surcharge	
		£400	£420
Surcharge period end date	30 June 2021	A	B
	30 September 2021	C	D

294 ARDENT (ADAPTED) *Walk in the footsteps of a top tutor*

Ardent Ltd was incorporated on 1 April 2019 and commenced trading on 1 January 2020. The company voluntarily registered for valued added tax (VAT) on 1 January 2020, preparing its first VAT return for the quarter ended 31 March 2020. Ardent Ltd's sales have been as follows:

		Standard-rated	Zero-rated
		£	£
2020	January	24,800	30,100
	February	42,600	28,700
	March	58,300	22,700
		125,700	81,500

Where applicable, the above figures are stated exclusive of VAT.

During the period 1 April to 31 December 2019, Ardent Ltd incurred input VAT of £120 each month in respect of payments made for advertising services. The company also incurred input VAT totalling £400 (£200 each) in respect of the purchase of two laptop computers on 10 July 2019. One of the laptop computers was scrapped on 30 November 2019 at a nil value, and the other laptop was not used until Ardent Ltd commenced trading on 1 January 2020.

During the quarter ended 31 March 2020, Ardent Ltd received standard-rated invoices totalling £56,400 (inclusive of VAT) in respect of purchases and expenses. As at 31 March 2020, £11,400 (inclusive of VAT) of the purchases was unsold and therefore included in inventory.

Ardent Ltd was late in submitting its VAT return for the quarter ended 31 March 2020, and in paying the related VAT liability. The company currently does not use either the VAT cash accounting scheme or the annual accounting scheme.

1   For each of the following statements concerning Making Tax Digital (MTD) select whether it is true or false:

	True	False
MTD software is used to print out returns which can then be sent to HMRC		
The usual VAT return and payment submission dates apply		
Although returns are produced automatically, the business is still responsible for checking them		
The rules apply to all VAT registered businesses, including those with taxable supplies below the VAT registration threshold		

2 What amount of pre-registration input VAT was Ardent Ltd able to recover in respect of the inputs incurred prior to it registering for VAT on 1 January 2020?

		Advertising	
		£720	£1,080
Laptops	£200	A	B
	£400	C	D

3 Ignoring pre-registration input VAT, what amount of VAT should Ardent Ltd have paid to HM Revenue and Customs in respect of the quarter ended 31 March 2020?

£ _____

4 How and by when should Ardent Ltd have filed its VAT return for the quarter ended 31 March 2020?

A   Either by paper or electronically by 30 April 2020

B   Electronically by 7 May 2020

C   Electronically by 30 April 2020

D   Either by paper or electronically by 7 May 2020

5 For what period after 31 March 2021 will Ardent Ltd need to avoid further defaults in order to revert to a clean default surcharge record, and which VAT scheme may help in avoiding such further defaults? Tick the relevant box.

		Period	
		6 months	12 months
VAT scheme	Annual accounting		
	Cash accounting		
	Flat rate		

PRACTICE SECTION C CONSTRUCTED RESPONSE QUESTIONS

295 GARFIELD (ADAPTED) *Walk in the footsteps of a top tutor*

Garfield has been registered for valued added tax (VAT) since 1 April 2013. Garfield makes taxable supplies in excess of the VAT registration threshold each year. Garfield has previously completed his VAT returns himself, but for the quarter ended 31 March 2020 there are some items for which he is unsure of the correct VAT treatment.

Garfield's partly completed VAT computation for the quarter ended 31 March 2020 is shown below. All of the completed sections of the computation are correct, with the omissions marked as outstanding (O/S).

	Note	£
Output VAT		
Sales (all standard-rated)		22,500
Discounted sale	1	O/S
Equipment	2	O/S
Fuel scale rate		60
Input VAT		
Purchases (all standard-rated)		(11,200)
Motor car (purchased on 1 January 2020)		0
Equipment	2	O/S
Impairment losses	3	O/S
Entertaining – UK customers		0
– Overseas customers	4	O/S
Motor expenses	5	O/S
VAT payable		O/S

Unless otherwise stated, all of the figures in the following notes are stated exclusive of VAT.

Note 1 – Discounted sale

On 10 February 2020, a sales invoice for £4,300 was issued by Garfield in respect of a standard-rated supply. To encourage this previously late paying customer to pay promptly, Garfield offered a 10% discount for payment within 14 days of the date of the sales invoice. The customer paid within the 14-day period.

This invoice has not been taken into account in calculating the output VAT figure of £22,500, and this is the only sale for which Garfield has offered a prompt payment discount.

Note 2 – Equipment

During the quarter ended 31 March 2020, Garfield acquired some new equipment at a cost of £12,400 from a VAT registered supplier situated in the European Union.

Note 3 – Impairment losses

On 31 March 2020, Garfield wrote off three impairment losses. Details are as follows:

Amount	Invoice date	Payment due date
£1,400	30 July 2019	29 August 2019
£2,700	12 September 2019	12 October 2019
£1,900	4 October 2019	3 November 2019

Note 4 – Entertaining

During the quarter ended 31 March 2020, Garfield spent £960 on entertaining overseas customers. This figure is inclusive of VAT.

Note 5 – Motor expenses

The motor car purchased on 1 January 2020 is used by Garfield 60% for business mileage. During the quarter ended 31 March 2020, Garfield spent £1,008 on repairs to the motor car and £660 on fuel for both his business and private mileage. Both of these figures are inclusive of VAT.

Additional information

Garfield would like some information on making tax digital (MTD). He is aware the system has been implemented by HMRC and he would like to know more about it and whether it is relevant to small businesses.

Required:

(a) Calculate the amount of value added tax (VAT) payable by Garfield for the quarter ended 31 March 2020. ▦ (7 marks)

(b) Give a brief explanation of Making Tax Digital and state whether it applies to Garfield's business. ⌨

(3 marks)

(Total: 10 marks)

296 VICTOR STYLE (ADAPTED)

Victor Style has been a self-employed hairdresser since 1 January 2017.

His sales from the date of commencement of the business to 31 December 2019 were £5,800 per month.

On 1 January 2020 Victor increased the prices that he charged customers, and from that date his sales have been £9,500 per month. Victor's sales are all standard-rated.

Concerned about the registration thresholds, Victor voluntarily registered for VAT on 1 January 2020.

As none of his customers are VAT registered, it was not possible to increase prices any further as a result of registering for VAT.

Victor's standard-rated purchases are £400 per month.

Where applicable, the above figures are inclusive of VAT.

Required:

(a) Calculate the total amount of VAT payable by Victor during the year ended 31 December 2020. ⊞ **(3 marks)**

(b) Advise Victor why it would have been beneficial to have used the VAT flat rate scheme from 1 January 2020. 💻

Your answer should include a calculation of the amount of VAT that Victor would have saved for the year ended 31 December 2020 by joining the scheme.

The flat rate scheme percentage for hairdressing for Victor in the year ended 31 December 2020 is 13%. **(3 marks)**

(c) Calculate the effect of the price increase on 1 January 2020 and subsequent VAT registration on Victor's net profit for the year ended 31 December 2020. ⊞ **(4 marks)**

(Total: 10 marks)

297 DENZIL DYER (ADAPTED)

Denzil Dyer has been a self-employed printer since 2008. He has recently registered for value added tax (VAT).

Denzil's sales consist of printed leaflets, some of which are standard-rated and some of which are zero-rated. He sells to both VAT registered customers and to non-VAT registered customers.

Customers making an order of more than £500 are given a discount of 5% from the normal selling price. Denzil also offers a discount of 2.5% of the amount payable to those customers that pay within one month of the date of the sales invoice.

All of Denzil's printing supplies are purchased from a VAT registered supplier. He pays by credit card and receives a VAT invoice. However, Denzil also purchases various office supplies by cash without receiving any invoices.

Denzil does not use the annual accounting scheme, the cash accounting scheme or the flat rate scheme.

Required:

(a) Explain why it is important for Denzil to correctly identify whether a sale is standard-rated or whether it is zero-rated. 💻 **(2 marks)**

(b) Explain the VAT implications of the two types of discount that Denzil gives or offers to his customers. 💻 **(2 marks)**

(c) Advise Denzil of the conditions that will have to be met in order for him to recover input VAT. 💻

You are not expected to list those goods and services for which input VAT is non-recoverable. **(3 marks)**

(d) State the circumstances in which Denzil is and is not required to issue a VAT invoice, and the period during which such an invoice should be issued. 💻 **(3 marks)**

(Total: 10 marks)

298   SILVERSTONE LTD (ADAPTED) *Walk in the footsteps of a top tutor*

Silverstone Ltd is registered for value added tax (VAT), but currently does not use any of the special VAT schemes. The company has annual standard-rated sales of £1,200,000 and annual standard-rated expenses of £550,000. Both these figures are exclusive of VAT and are likely to remain the same for the foreseeable future.

Silverstone Ltd is up to date with all of its tax returns, including those for corporation tax, PAYE and VAT. It is also up to date with its corporation tax, PAYE and VAT payments. However, the company often incurs considerable overtime costs due to its employees working late in order to meet tax return filing deadlines.

Silverstone Ltd pays its expenses on a cash basis, but allows customers two months credit when paying for sales. The company does not have any impairment losses.

Silverstone Ltd is planning to purchase some new machinery at a cost of £22,000 (exclusive of VAT). The machinery can either be purchased from an overseas supplier situated outside the European Union, or from a VAT registered supplier situated inside the European Union. Silverstone Ltd is not a regular importer and so is unsure of the VAT treatment for this purchase.

Required:

(a)   Explain why Silverstone Ltd is entitled to use both the VAT cash accounting scheme and the VAT annual accounting scheme, and why it will probably be beneficial for the company to use both schemes. 🖥 **(6 marks)**

(b)   Explain when and how Silverstone Ltd will have to account for VAT in respect of the new machinery if it is purchased from: 🖥

   (1)   a supplier situated outside the European Union, or

   (2)   a VAT registered supplier situated within the European Union.

(4 marks)

(Total: 10 marks)

299   TARDY PLC *Walk in the footsteps of a top tutor*

You are a trainee Chartered Certified Accountant, and your firm has recently completed its audit of Tardy plc's financial statements for the year ended 31 March 2020. The company runs an internet-based retail business.

For the previous three value added tax (VAT) quarters, Tardy plc has been late in submitting its VAT returns and in paying the related VAT liabilities. The company is therefore currently serving a default surcharge period.

As part of your firm's tax audit for the year ended 31 March 2020, you have discovered that Tardy plc has been careless in incorrectly treating the supply of standard-rated services received from VAT registered businesses situated elsewhere within the European Union. This careless incorrect treatment has resulted in an underpayment of VAT to HM Revenue and Customs of £8,200 for the year ended 31 March 2020.

Required:

(a) Advise Tardy plc of the default surcharge implications if during the current default surcharge period it is late in paying a further VAT liability, and what the company will need to do in order to revert to a clean default surcharge record. 🖥 **(3 marks)**

(b) Explain when and how a UK VAT registered business should account for VAT in respect of the supply of services received from VAT registered businesses situated elsewhere within the European Union. 🖥 **(3 marks)**

(c) Explain why Tardy plc will be permitted to disclose the underpayment of VAT of £8,200 by entering this amount on its next VAT return, and state whether or not default interest will be due. 🖥 **(2 marks)**

(d) Advise Tardy plc as to the maximum amount of penalty which is likely to be charged by HM Revenue and Customs in respect of the underpayment of VAT of £8,200, and by how much this penalty would be reduced as a result of the company's unprompted disclosure. 🖥 **(2 marks)**

(Total: 10 marks)

300 SMART LTD *Walk in the footsteps of a top tutor*

Smart Ltd commenced trading on 1 September 2019. The company's sales for the first four months of trading were as follows:

	£
September 2019	26,000
October 2019	47,000
November 2019	134,000
December 2019	113,000

On 1 November 2019, the company signed a contract valued at £86,000 for completion during November 2019.

All of the above figures are stated exclusive of value added tax (VAT). Smart Ltd only supplies services and all of the company's supplies are standard-rated.

Smart Ltd allows its customers 60 days credit when paying for services, and it is concerned that some customers will default on the payment of their debts. The company pays its purchase invoices as soon as they are received.

Smart Ltd does not use either the VAT cash accounting scheme or the annual accounting scheme.

Required:

(a) State, giving reasons, the date from which Smart Ltd was required to register for value added tax (VAT), and by when it was required to notify HM Revenue and Customs (HMRC) of the registration. 🖥️ **(3 marks)**

(b) State how and when Smart Ltd will have to submit its quarterly VAT returns and pay any related VAT liability. 🖥️

Note: You are not expected to cover substantial traders or the election for monthly returns. **(2 marks)**

(c) State the circumstances when a VAT registered business like Smart Ltd, which is not using the VAT cash accounting scheme, would still have to account for output VAT at the time that payment is received from a customer. 🖥️ **(2 marks)**

(d) Advise Smart Ltd as to why it should be beneficial for the company to use the VAT cash accounting scheme. 🖥️ **(3 marks)**

(Total: 10 marks)

301 ZIA *Walk in the footsteps of a top tutor*

Zia has been registered for value added tax (VAT) since 1 April 2009.

The following information is available for the year ended 31 March 2020:

(1) Sales invoices totalling £126,000 were issued, of which £115,200 were in respect of standard-rated sales and £10,800 were in respect of zero-rated sales. None of Zia's customers are VAT registered.

(2) On 31 March 2020, Zia wrote off two impairment losses which were in respect of standard-rated sales.

The first impairment loss was for £780, and was in respect of a sales invoice which had been due for payment on 15 August 2019.

The second impairment loss was for £660, and was in respect of a sales invoice which had been due for payment on 15 September 2019.

(3) Purchase invoices totalling £49,200 were received, of which £43,200 were in respect of standard-rated purchases and £6,000 were in respect of zero-rated purchases.

(4) Rent of £1,200 is paid each month. During the year ended 31 March 2020, Zia made 13 rental payments because the invoice dated 1 April 2020 was paid early on 31 March 2020. This invoice was in respect of the rent for April 2020.

(5) During the year ended 31 March 2020, Zia spent £2,600 on mobile telephone calls, of which 40% related to private calls.

(6) During the year ended 31 March 2020, Zia spent £1,560 on entertaining customers, of which £240 was in respect of overseas customers.

All of the above figures are inclusive of VAT where applicable. The expenses referred to in notes (4), (5) and (6) are all standard-rated.

Zia does not use either the cash accounting scheme or the flat rate scheme.

He has forecast that for the year ended 31 March 2021, his total sales will be the same as for the year ended 31 March 2020.

Required:

(a)   Calculate the amount of value added tax (VAT) payable by Zia for the year ended 31 March 2020. ⊞

You should indicate by the use of zero any items referred to in notes (1) to (6) where there is no VAT impact.   **(6 marks)**

(b)   Explain why Zia will be permitted to use the VAT flat rate scheme from 1 April 2020, and state the circumstances in which he will have to leave the scheme. 🖥

(2 marks)

(c)   Explain whether or not it would have been beneficial for Zia to have used the VAT flat rate scheme for the year ended 31 March 2020. 🖥

Notes:

(1)   You should assume that the relevant flat rate scheme percentage for Zia's trade would have been 12% throughout the whole of the year ended 31 March 2020.

(2)   Your answer for this part of the question should be supported by appropriate calculations.   **(2 marks)**

(Total: 10 marks)

Section 6

ANSWERS TO PRACTICE INCOME TAX AND NATIONAL INSURANCE QUESTIONS

PRACTICE SECTION A OBJECTIVE TEST QUESTIONS

INCOME TAX BASICS AND EMPLOYMENT INCOME

1

	Taxable	Exempt
£400 in shares in the company he works for	✓	
£1,000 in an Individual Savings Account		✓
£800 in a NS&I investment account	✓	
£500 purchasing a NS&I certificate		✓

Income generated from an Individual Savings Account and a NS&I certificate is exempt from income tax.

Income generated from shares (dividends) and from a NS&I investment account (interest) is subject to income tax.

2   B

	£
Personal allowance	12,500
Restriction (£111,900 − £800 − £100,000) = £11,100 ÷ 2	(5,550)
	———
Restricted personal allowance	6,950
	———

3   £9,350

		£
Trading income		106,800
Dividend		1,500
Net income		108,300

	£	£
PA		12,500
Net income	108,300	
Less: Gross gift aid	(2,000)	
Adjusted net income	106,300	
Less: Income limit	(100,000)	
	6,300	
Reduction of PA (50% × £6,300)		(3,150)
Adjusted PA		9,350

4   C

		Non-savings income
		£
Rental income = net income		40,650
Less: PA		(12,500)
Taxable income		28,150

Income tax liability:	£		
Non-savings income – basic rate	28,150	× 20%	5,630
Less: Marriage allowance	1,250	× 20%	(250)
Income tax liability			5,380

5

	Deductible	Not deductible
A contribution into a personal pension scheme		✓
A charitable gift aid donation		✓
A contribution into an employer's HM Revenue and Customs' registered occupational pension scheme	✓	
A charitable donation made under the payroll deduction scheme	✓	

6   D

	£	£
Child benefit received		1,789
Trading income = Adjusted net income	53,000	
Less: Lower limit	(50,000)	
	————	
	3,000	
	————	

1% per £100 of £3,000 = 30%

Child benefit tax charge = 30% of £1,789 (rounded down)   536

Tutor's top tips

The method for calculating the child benefit income tax charge is included in the tax rates and allowances provided to you in the examination.

7

	Qualifying interest	Not qualifying
Interest paid on a loan he incurred to purchase a laptop for use in his employment	✓	
Interest paid on the mortgage for his principal private residence		✓
Interest paid on an amount he borrowed to finance the acquisition of 2,000 shares in a quoted company		✓
Interest paid on a loan he took to invest capital in a partnership in order to become a partner	✓	

Tutorial note

Relief is given for interest paid on loans to finance expenditure for a qualifying purpose, which includes:

- *The acquisition of plant and machinery by an employed person for use in his employment.*

- *The purchase of shares in an employee-controlled trading company by a full-time employee.*

- *The purchase of a share in a partnership, or the contribution to a partnership of capital or a loan. The borrower must be a partner in the partnership.*

- *The purchase of plant and machinery for use in the partnership, by a partner.*

8   C

Tutor's top tips

The number of ties needed for an individual to be UK resident depending on the number of days spent in the UK in a particular tax year is included in the tax rates and allowances provided to you in the examination.

This question could have been answered quickly and easily provided that you understood how to interpret the table!

9

	Resident	Not resident
Bao		✓
Min	✓	

Bao is treated as automatically non-UK resident, as he has spent less than 46 days in the UK in the tax year 2019/20 and has not been treated as UK resident in any of the three previous tax years (having spent less than 46 days in the UK each tax year).

Minh is treated as automatically resident in the UK as, although he has been here for less than 183 days, he works full time in the UK.

10   D

> *Tutorial note*
>
> The circumstances described in options A, B and C would each lead to Harper meeting one of the automatic UK residency tests. The circumstances described in option D would result in Harper meeting two of the sufficient ties tests, but not an automatic UK residency test.

11   £645

	£	£
Child benefit received		1,076
Trading income	56,500	
Less: Gross gift aid (£400 × 100/80)	(500)	
Adjusted net income	56,000	
Less: Lower limit	(50,000)	
	6,000	

1% per £100 of £6,000 = 60%
Child benefit tax charge = 60% of £1,076 (rounded down)   645

12   D

	£
Interest received 30 June 2019 (£200,000 × 1% × 6/12)	1,000
Interest accrued (1 July 2019 - 30 November 2019)	
(£200,000 × 1% × 5/12)	833
Total interest income	1,833

> *Tutorial note*
>
> Gilt interest is assessed like other interest income on the receipts basis. However, under the accrued income scheme when gilts are sold interest is effectively allocated to the vendor and purchaser on the accruals basis up to the date of sale.
>
> Matthew did not receive any interest on 31 December 2019 but will be taxed on £833 representing the interest accruing in the interest period for which he owned the gilts.

13

	True	False
Eric is automatically not resident in the UK	✓	
Fran is automatically not resident in the UK		✓

Tutorial note

Eric – less than 46 days and not previously resident.

Fran – resident during the previous three years, so to be automatically not resident she must be in the UK for less than 16 days.

14   A

	£
Interest received 30 September 2019 (£10,000 × 2% × 6/12)	100
Less: Interest accrued prior to purchase (1 April 2019 – 31 May 2019) (£10,000 × 2% × 2/12)	(33)
Interest accrued (1 October 2019 – 29 February 2020) (£10,000 × 2% × 5/12)	83
	———
Total interest income	150
	———

Tutorial note

Gilts are subject to the accrued income scheme. On a disposal interest is effectively, allocated between the vendor and purchaser on the accruals basis in relation to their period of ownership.

15

	Taxable	Exempt
NS&I investment account interest	✓	
Gilt edged security interest	✓	
NS&I savings certificate interest		✓

16   A

	£
Property income	21,150
Interest from UK Government securities (Gilts)	2,400
Dividends	1,250
Net income	24,800
Less: Personal allowance	(12,500)
Taxable income	12,300

Analysis of income:

Non-savings income = £8,650 (£21,150 – £12,500), savings income = £2,400, dividend income = £1,250.

£			
8,650	× 20%	(Non-savings income)	1,730
1,000	× 0%	(SNRB)	0
1,400	× 20%	(Savings income)	280
1,250	× 0%	(DNRB)	0
12,300			
Income tax liability			2,010

Tutorial note

Basic rate taxpayers are entitled to a £1,000 savings nil rate band (SNRB), whereas higher rate taxpayers are only entitled to a £500 SNRB, and additional rate taxpayers do not receive a SNRB at all.

A dividend nil rate band of £2,000 is available to all taxpayers regardless of the amount of their taxable income.

17 **£4,921**

	£
Dividends	56,950
Less: PA	(12,500)
Taxable income	44,450

	£
Income tax liability:	
Dividend income – nil rate band (£2,000 × 0%)	0
Dividend income – basic rate band (£35,500 × 7.5%)	2,662
Dividend income - higher rate (£6,950 × 32.5%)	2,259
Income tax liability	4,921

Tutorial note

The dividend nil rate band is £2,000. This uses the basic and higher rate bands.

18 **A**

	£
Premium	82,000
Less: £82,000 × 2% × (15 – 1)	(22,960)
Property income	59,040

Alternative calculation = £82,000 × (51 – 15)/50 = £59,040

19 **A**

	£	£
Child benefit received		1,789
Employment income	55,000	
Bank interest	3,000	
Adjusted net income	58,000	
Less: Lower limit	(50,000)	
	8,000	

1% per £100 of £8,000 = 80%

	£
Child benefit tax charge = 80% of £1,789 (rounded down)	1,431

20   A

	£
Normal assessment:	
Rental income (£750 × 12)	9,000
Expenses (£475 × 12)	(5,700)
Property income	3,300
Alternative:	
Rental income	9,000
Rent-a-room relief	(7,500)
	1,500

Tutorial note

Rent-a-room relief of £7,500 should be deducted instead of the actual expenses incurred as this produces a lower taxable amount than the normal property income calculation.

21   £23,520

	£
Premium	42,000
Less: £42,000 × 2% × (23 – 1)	(18,480)
Property income	23,520

Alternative calculation = £42,000 × (51 – 23)/50 = £23,520

22   B

	£	£
Rent received		9,600
Less: Expenses paid		
Council tax	900	
Insurance	540	
Refrigerator	870	
		(2,310)
Property income		7,290

Tutorial note

Property income should be calculated on the cash basis in the examination unless you are told otherwise. The deduction for insurance is calculated by reference to the date paid, the period covered is irrelevant under the cash basis. A deduction can be taken for the cost of replacing furniture, furnishings, appliances (including white goods) and kitchenware provided for use in a dwelling.

23   £21,500

	£	£
Net property income before adjustments		25,000
Less: Expenses		
Replacement kitchen unit (repair to fitted kitchen)	500	
Interest payable (£12,000 × 25%)	3,000	
	———	(3,500)
		———
Property income		21,500
		———

Tutorial note

Tax relief for interest paid on a loan to acquire a residential property that is let out, is restricted for the tax year 2019/20 as follows:

1   25% of the finance costs are an allowable deduction from property income

2   Tax relief is given on the remaining 75% of costs at the basic rate (20%) by deduction from the taxpayer's final income tax liability.

Note that details of the basic rate restriction that applies to 75% of finance costs is given in the Tax Rates and Allowances provided in the examination.

24   A

	£	£
Salary		55,000
Mileage allowance:		
Amount received (14,500 × 43p)	6,235	
AMAP rates:		
10,000 × 45p	(4,500)	
4,500 × 25p	(1,125)	
	———	
Excess mileage allowance		610
		———
Employment income		55,610
		———

25   £650

The assessable benefit is the cost of the medical insurance to Christos' employer. The other benefits are both exempt.

26   A

The original cost did not exceed £75,000, therefore it is not considered to be an 'expensive' accommodation. The only benefit is the basic charge based on the annual value of £2,600. Jo contributes more than the annual value (£250 × 12 = £3,000) and therefore the assessable benefit is nil.

27   £9,497

CO_2 emissions = 158g/km (rounded down to 155), available for 11 months

	%
Diesel (meets RDE2 standard so no additional 4%)	23
Plus: $(155 - 95) \times {}^1/_5$	12
	—
Appropriate percentage	35
	—
	£
Car benefit (£28,000 × 35% × 11/12)	8,983
	—

28   B

Average method	£	£
Loan at start of tax year	100,000	
Loan at end of tax year	60,000	
	———	
	160,000	
	———	
Average loan (£160,000 ÷ 2)	80,000	
	———	
Assessable benefit (£80,000 × 2.5%)		2,000
Less Interest paid		
(£100,000 × 1% × 4/12)	333	
(£60,000 × 1% × 8/12)	400	
	———	(733)
		———
		1,267
		———

29

	Taxable in tax year 2019/20	Not taxable in tax year 2019/20
Bonus of £2,800 received on 6 April 2019 in respect of the year to 31 December 2018	✓	
Bonus of £3,300 received on 3 April 2020 in respect of the year to 31 December 2019.	✓	

Tutorial note

Employment income is assessed on the receipts basis (i.e. income received in the tax year).

30 D

	£	£
Higher of:		
(i) MV at date of transfer	1,400	
	———	
(ii) MV when made available for private use	2,000	
Less: Annual value for 2018/19 for use of asset (£2,000 × 20%)	(400)	
	———	
	1,600	
	———	
Taxable benefit		1,600
		———

Tutorial note

The benefit on 6 April 2019 when Max was given the camera is the higher of the market value at the time of gift and the market value when it was first made available to Max less amounts previously taxed.

31   C, D

Tutorial note

Where an employee is reimbursed expenses by the employer, the amount received is taxable income. However, an exemption applies where the employee would be able to claim a tax deduction for the business related expenses.

The reimbursement of Albert's professional subscription fees and train fares are therefore exempt income.

INCOME TAX BASICS AND INCOME FROM SELF-EMPLOYMENT

32   £600

The £450 spent on food hampers needs to be added back as gifts of food are disallowable. Costs relating to the acquisition of a short lease are disallowable so £150 must be added back. The costs of renewing a short lease would be allowable.

Employee parking fines incurred on business and amounts spent on staff entertaining (regardless of the amount) are allowable deductions from trading profits.

Tutorial note

Annual events which cost the employer more than £150 per head are a taxable benefit for the employee, but the cost is still deductible for the employer.

33   B

Haniful is treated as making a sale to himself at selling price. As no adjustment has been made in the accounts to reflect the goods taken for personal use the full selling price must be added to the trading profits.

Tutorial note

If Haniful had already made an adjustment in the accounts to remove the cost of the goods taken out of the business (by adding back the cost of £850) then only the profit element of £250 would need to be added to the trading profits for tax purposes.

34   £775

Firstly the amount taxable on the landlord as property income must be calculated:

	£
Premium	25,000
Less: £25,000 × 2% × (20 – 1)	(9,500)
Property income	15,500

Alternative calculation = £25,000 × (51 – 20)/50 = £15,500

Fleur can take an annual deduction for the property income element, spread evenly over the period of the lease:

(£15,500 ÷ 20) = £775.

As Fleur acquired the lease on 1 January 2019 the full annual amount of £775 is deductible when calculating the tax adjusted trading profits for the year ended 31 December 2019.

35   C

	Main pool £	Allowances £
TWDV b/f	6,200	
Addition: Computer	1,600	
	7,800	
Disposal	(9,800)	
	(2,000)	
Balancing charge	2,000	(2,000)
Total allowances	0	(2,000)

Tutorial note

In the period of account in which the business permanently ceases, the AIA, WDAs and FYAs are not available. Additions and disposals are added to/deducted from the relevant pool and a balancing charge or allowance is calculated.

36   C and F

Any asset with private use by the owner of the business is allocated to a private use asset column rather than the main pool.

Cars with CO_2 emissions in excess of 110g/km are allocated to the special rate pool rather than the main pool.

Long life assets (those with an expected life of 25 years or more, with a total cost of £100,000 in a twelve month period) are added to the special rate pool. Assets with an expected working life of less than 25 years are not treated as long life assets and are added to the main pool.

37   £14,420

A new car with CO_2 emissions up to 50g/km qualifies for a first year allowance of 100%. The FYA is never time apportioned irrespective of the length of the period of account.

The tax written down value brought forward in the main pool is entitled to WDA at 18% time apportioned for 8 months therefore:

	£	Main pool £	Allowances £
TWDV b/f		18,000	
WDA (18% × 8/12)		(2,160)	2,160
Addition (with FYA)			
Motor car	12,260		
FYA (100%)	(12,260)		12,260
	——		
		0	
		——	
TWDV c/f		15,840	
		——	
Total allowances			14,420
			——

Tutorial note

In Section A, marks are not available for your workings. If you are confident with capital allowances you may find it quicker for straightforward questions such as this to calculate the allowances available for each pool without using the pro forma:

(£12,260 × 100%) = £12,260

(£18,000 × 18%) = £3,240 × 8/12 = £2,160

Total = (£12,260 + £2,160) = £14,420

38   D

In the final period of account, no AIA, WDA or FYA is available; only balancing adjustments arise.

		Main pool	Allowances
		£	£
TWDV b/f		15,000	
Additions		4,500	
Disposals	– pool items	(14,550)	
Disposals	– laptop retained personally	(4,150)	
		———	
		800	
Balancing allowance		(800)	800
		———	———

The laptop is treated as having been disposed of at market value.

39   £16,500

> **Tutorial note**
>
> *Jacinta started trading on 1 August 2019 and so the tax year 2019/20 is the first tax year of her trade.*
>
> *In the first tax year, the profits taxed are the actual profits arising from the first day of trade up to the following 5 April.*
>
> *This is an eight month period and will include all the profits for the five months to 31 December 2019 and three months (1 January to 5 April 2020) from the next set of accounts.*
>
> *£10,500 + (3/12 × £24,000) = £16,500.*

40   C

Lee ceased to trade on 31 January 2020, which falls into the tax year 2019/20.

Up to that tax year Lee has been taxed on the current year basis therefore in 2018/19, Lee was taxed on the profits of the accounting period ending in that year i.e. y/e 30 April 2018.

In the tax year in which he ceases to trade he is taxed on any trading profits not taxed in previous years less his overlap profits that arose when he started his business, i.e.:

	£
y/e 30 April 2019	10,000
p/e 31 January 2020	14,000
Less: Overlap profits	(3,000)
	———
Trading income assessment – 2019/20	21,000
	———

PARTNERSHIPS

41   D

y/e 31 December 2019	Total £	Henry £
p/e 31 July 2019 (£120,000 × 7/12) = £70,000		
PSR (70:30)	70,000	21,000
p/e 31 December 2019 (£120,000 × 5/12) = £50,000		
Salary (£24,000 × 5/12)	10,000	10,000
PSR (80:20)	40,000	8,000
	———	———
Allocation of profit	120,000	39,000
	———	———

42   £39,850

2019/20 – y/e 30 September 2019	Total £	Albert £	Jolene £
Salary	25,000	25,000	
Interest on capital			
(4% × £50,000/£40,000)	3,600	2,000	1,600
Balance (1:3)	51,400	12,850	38,550
	———	———	———
Allocation of profit	80,000	39,850	40,150
	———	———	———

43   B

y/e 31 December 2019	Total £	Tim £
1.1.19 – 31.5.19 (£360,000 × 5/12) = £150,000		
Salary (£15,000 × 5/12)	6,250	6,250
PSR (1/6)	143,750	23,958
	———	———
Allocation of profit	150,000	30,208
	———	———

Tutorial note

You could have calculated the profit allocated to each of the three partners for the whole year ended 31 December 2019. However, only the profit allocated to Tim for the 5 months that he was a partner was required. It was not necessary to calculate how the remaining profit was allocated to the other two partners and would have wasted valuable time in the examination.

44   B, D, E

y/e 31 October 2019	Total £	Fabiola £
1.6.19 – 31.10.19 (£240,000 × 5/12)		
PSR (1:5)	100,000	20,000
y/e 31 October 2020		
PSR (1:5)	300,000	60,000

2019/20 – First tax year
Actual basis 1.6.19 – 5.4.20

	Fabiola
1.6.19 – 31.10.19	20,000
1.11.19 – 5.4.20 (£60,000 × 5/12)	25,000
Trading income assessment	45,000

2020/21 – Second tax year
Current year basis y/e 31 October 2020

Trading income assessment	60,000

Overlap

1.11.19 – 5.4.20 (£60,000 × 5/12)	25,000

TRADING LOSSES

45   A

Prior year loss relief claim

	£
Set against trading profits (unrestricted)	24,000
Set against non-trading profits (restricted to maximum)(note)	50,000
Maximum loss relief claim	74,000

Tutorial note

Only losses set against non-trading income of earlier years are restricted to the maximum amount; losses set against prior year trading profits are not restricted. The cap on income tax reliefs is included in the tax rates and allowances provided to you in the examination.

46   £13,000

	2019/20
	£
Trading income	12,000
Less: Losses b/f	(12,000)
Dividends	9,000
Furnished holiday accommodation	4,000
NS&I certificate interest	exempt
Net income	13,000

Tutorial note

The trading loss is carried forward to the next tax year and offset against the first available trading profits from the same trade. Profits from qualifying furnished holiday accommodation are not treated as trading income for the purposes of offsetting trading losses.

47   D

	2018/19	2019/20
	£	£
Trading income	55,000	0
Bank interest	14,000	14,000
Total income	69,000	14,000
Less: Loss relief	(69,000)	(14,000)
Net income	0	0

Loss memorandum:

	£
Loss arising in 2019/20	90,000
Used in 2018/19 – Prior year	(69,000)
Used in 2019/20 – Current year	(14,000)
Loss carried forward to 2020/21	7,000

Tutorial note

A current and prior year loss relief claim is against total income in the tax years 2019/20 and/or 2018/19. It cannot be restricted to prevent the loss of the personal allowance.

The loss offset in the tax year 2018/19 is not restricted to £50,000 as the restriction only applies to losses offset against other income, not income from the same trade.

48 £10,417

Tax year	Basis period	Available loss
		£
2017/18	1.11.17 – 5.4.18	
	(5/12 × £25,000)	10,417
		———
2018/19	y/e 31.10.18	25,000
Less: Used in 2017/18		(10,417)
		———
		14,583
		———

Tutorial note

The loss of £10,417 is a loss in the first four tax years of trading and can be offset against total income in the tax years 2014/15, 2015/16 and 2016/17 in that order.

49 D

	£
Available loss is lower of:	
(i) Remaining trading loss following current year claim against total income (£45,000 - £8,000)	37,000
	———
(ii) CY chargeable gains	32,000
Less: CY capital losses	(4,000)
Less: Capital losses b/f	(18,000)
	———
	10,000
	———
Available loss	10,000
	———

Tutorial note

The maximum amount of trading loss that can be offset against chargeable gains is the lower of:

(i)   the remaining loss, or

*(ii)   chargeable gains in the year after the deduction of current year capital losses and brought forward capital losses. Brought forward capital losses are **not** restricted to preserve the annual exempt amount in this calculation.*

*The maximum trading loss is then offset against current year chargeable gains, after current year capital losses but before brought forward capital losses. The offset of brought forward capital losses **is** restricted to preserve the annual exempt amount.*

50   £30,000

Terminal loss	£	£
6 April before cessation to date of cessation		
6.4.19 – 30.9.19 (£24,000 × 6/8)		18,000
12 months before cessation to 5 April before cessation		
1.2.19 – 5.4.19 (£24,000 × 2/8)	6,000	
1.10.18 – 31.1.19 (£39,000 × 4/12)	(13,000)	
	———	
Profit – ignore	(7,000)	0
Plus: Overlap profits		12,000
		———
Terminal loss		30,000
		———

Tutorial note

A terminal loss is the loss of the last 12 months of trading. The result arising in the period from the 12 months before the date of cessation to 5 April 2019 is a profit. It is therefore ignored in the terminal loss calculation.

PENSIONS AND NIC

51   C

Tutorial note

Class 2 and class 4 national insurance contributions are paid by self-employed individuals in respect of trading profits.

52

	Paid by Hamid to HMRC	Suffered by Hamid
Employee class 1 primary	✓	
Employer's class 1 secondary	✓	✓
Class 1A	✓	✓
Class 2	✓	✓
Class 4	✓	✓

Tutorial note

Hamid must pay class 2 and class 4 NICs in respect of his sole trader profits, employer's class 1 secondary NICs in respect of his employee's salary and class 1A NICs in respect of the company car benefit for the employee.

Although Hamid is required to pay over the employee class 1 primary NIC to HMRC, he will deduct this from the salary paid to his employee so it is not a cost that is suffered by him.

53   C

	£
Employed – Class 1 (£36,000 – £8,632) × 12%	3,284
Self-employed – Class 4 (£36,000 – £8,632) × 9%	(2,463)
– Class 2 (£3.00 × 52)	(156)
	665

54   £5,618

	£
(£50,000 – £8,632) × 12%	4,964
(£82,700 – £50,000) × 2%	654
	5,618

Tutorial note

Employment benefits are subject to class 1A NIC, not class 1 NIC.

55   A

	£
(£50,000 – £8,632) × 12%	4,964
(£63,000 – £50,000) × 2%	260
Class 1 employee NICs	5,224

Tutorial note

Subsidised on-site canteen facilities are an exempt benefit, provided they are available for all employees.

56   £5,792

Class 1 employer's NICs	£
(£50,600 – £8,632) × 13.8%	5,792

Working: Earnings liable to class 1 NIC

	£
Salary	50,000
Excess mileage allowance (12,000 × (50p – 45p))	600
	50,600

Tutorial note

Occupational pension scheme contributions are not deductible from earnings for NIC purposes.

The excess mileage allowance above the AMAP of 45p per mile (regardless of the number of business miles) is subject to class 1 NICs.

57 D

	£
(£50,000 – £8,632) × 9%	3,723
(£58,000 – £50,000) × 2%	160
	3,883

Tutorial note

Paloma is assessed on the 'current year basis' as she has been trading for a number of years.

58 A

	£
Class 1A NIC	
£3,450 × 13.8%	476

Working: Car benefit
CO_2 emissions = 99g/km (rounded down to 95)

	%
Appropriate percentage – base level of emissions	23

	£
Car benefit (£15,000 × 23%)	3,450

59 C

	£
Trading profits	70,000
Less: Trading loss b/f	(20,000)
Assessable profits for class 4 NICs	50,000

Tutorial note

If trading losses are carried forward they are offset against the first available trading profits arising from the same trade.

A sole trader pays class 4 NIC on trading profits only, not on any other income.

60

	Class 2 NICs payable	Class 2 NICs not payable
Mohammed	✓	
Nicole		✓

Tutorial note

Mohammed will pay class 2 NICs for the tax year as his tax adjusted trading profit for the tax year is more than the small profits threshold.

Nicole does not pay class 2 NICs for the tax year as she is above the state pension age.

61   £1,113

	£
1.1.19 – 31.12.19	
6 months ended 30 June 2019	8,800
6 months to 31 December 2019 (6/12 × £24,400)	12,200
	———
Assessable profits	21,000
	———
Class 4 NICs	
(£21,000 – £8,632) × 9%	1,113
	———

Tutorial note

2019/20 is the second tax year of trading and Sanjay's period of account ending in that tax year is < 12 months long. Therefore the assessment is based on the first 12 months of trading i.e. the 12 months ended 31 December 2019.

62 C and E

The annual summer event is a taxable benefit as the cost exceeds £150 per head, and the sports club membership fee is also a taxable benefit. As non-cash benefits they are subject to class 1A NIC.

Occupational pension scheme contributions paid by the employer, car parking spaces at or near the workplace and the provision of one mobile phone are all exempt benefits for NIC purposes.

The mileage allowance paid for normal commuting is a taxable cash benefit, which is subject to class 1 NICs, not class 1A NICs.

63 £17,500

Isaac's income tax basic rate band is extended by the grossed up contribution as follows:

£37,500 + (£40,000 × 100/80) = £87,500

Income tax of £17,500 (£87,500 × 20%) is payable at the basic rate.

The contribution is lower than Isaac's relevant earnings for the year (£110,000) and therefore tax relief is available on the full amount.

Tutorial note

Isaac's gross contributions exceed the annual allowance threshold of £40,000 for the tax year 2019/20. Therefore, although his basic rate band is extended by his total gross contributions of £50,000, some tax relief may be clawed back via an annual allowance charge depending on the availability of unused annual allowances to carry forward from the previous three tax years.

64 C

	£
Annual allowance	40,000
Add: brought forward allowances (w)	15,000
	———
Maximum contributions	55,000
	———

Working: Unused AA B/f

		£
2016/17	(Exceeds £40,000)	0
2017/18	(£40,000 – £37,000)	3,000
2018/19	(£40,000 – 28,000)	12,000
		———
AA b/f from earlier years		15,000
		———

Tutorial note

Unused annual allowances can be brought forward from the previous three tax years.

There is no unused AA for 2016/17 as the gross contributions in that year exceeded the AA of £40,000.

The excess would have been matched against earlier years and would not reduce the later AA available. Therefore this year has no impact on the answer to this question.

65

	Fully tax relievable pension contributions	**Not fully tax relievable pension contributions**
Austin	✓	
Petra		✓

Austin's total gross pension contributions are £28,000 (£22,400 × 100/80). They are less than his relevant earnings of £51,200 and less than the annual allowance. His contributions are fully tax relievable.

Petra's gross contributions of £62,500 (£50,000 × 100/80) exceed the annual allowance of £40,000 for the tax year 2019/20. She has no unused annual allowances brought forward as she was not a member of a pension scheme in previous years. She will obtain tax relief at source on the contributions, as they are less than her relevant earnings. However, part of the tax relief will be clawed back through an annual allowance charge.

Tutorial note

An employed individual can make pension contributions into either an occupational pension scheme or a personal pension scheme or both. Contributions are fully tax relievable provided total gross contributions do not exceed their total relevant earnings and the annual allowance.

66 D

	£
Salary	50,000
Furnished holiday accommodation income	5,000
Relevant earnings	55,000

Tutorial note

Tax relief for both personal pension contributions and gift aid donations is made by extending the basic and higher rate bands by the gross contribution/donation.

There is no need to adjust relevant earnings for gift aid donations – this was included to mislead you!

67   £142,100

	£
Salary	145,000
Less: Occupational pension contributions (2% × £145,000)	(2,900)
Net income	142,100

Tutorial note

Employer pension contributions are an exempt benefit.

Tax relief for occupational pension scheme contributions is given at the employee's marginal rate of tax by deducting them from employment income.

Basic rate tax relief for personal pension scheme contributions is given at source. Tax relief at higher rates is given by extending the basic rate and higher rate tax bands.

68   B

	£
Trading income	100,000
Less: PA	(12,500)
Taxable income	87,500

Income tax liability		£
£87,500 × 20%		17,500
Annual allowance charge	£10,000 × 40%	4,000
		21,500

Working: Extended basic rate band	£
Basic rate band	37,500
Gross personal pension contributions	50,000
	87,500

Tutorial note

The annual allowance charge is taxed at the taxpayer's highest marginal rate. In this case there is no remaining basic rate band so all of the annual allowance charge is taxed at 40%.

ADMINISTRATION AND ETHICS

69

	Capital tax	Revenue tax	Neither type
Value added tax			✓
Inheritance tax	✓		
National insurance contributions		✓	
Capital gains tax	✓		

Tutorial note

VAT is neither a capital nor a revenue tax. VAT is an example of a 'sales tax' suffered by consumers.

70   B

Tutorial note

The term tax evasion summarises any action taken to avoid or reduce tax by illegal means, for example providing HM Revenue and Customs with deliberately false information.

71

	True	False
Corporation tax is a direct tax on the turnover of companies		✓
National insurance is a direct tax suffered by employees, employers and the self-employed on earnings	✓	
itance tax is a direct tax on transfers of income by individuals		✓
Value added tax is a direct tax on the supply of goods and services by businesses		✓

Tutorial note

Corporation tax is a tax on the profits of companies, not the turnover. Inheritance tax is a tax on the transfer of assets not income. VAT is an indirect tax not a direct tax.

72   B and E

The other options refer to tax avoidance.

73   B

A tax adviser must not assist a client to plan or commit any offence.

Tutorial note

A tax adviser may have a legal or professional right or duty to disclose information about a client without their authority (e.g. in the case of money laundering).

If the adviser becomes aware that a client has committed an offence they must discuss the irregularity with the client and ensure proper disclosure is made to HMRC.

A tax adviser has duties and responsibilities towards both his client and HMRC (e.g. they must ensure that all information provided to HMRC is accurate and complete).

74

	Could be expected	Unacceptable
Reporting under the money laundering regulations	✓	
Advising the client to make disclosure	✓	
Ceasing to act for the client	✓	
Informing HMRC of the non-disclosure		✓
Warning the client that your firm will be reporting the non-disclosure		✓
Notifying HMRC that your firm has ceased to act for the client	✓	

Tutorial note

Members should not disclose information about the client to third parties (including HMRC) unless they have authorisation from the client or there is a legal or professional right or duty to disclose (e.g. money laundering).

Where a money laundering report is made the client should not be informed as this may amount to tipping off, which is an offence.

75   A

Tutorial note

The legality of extra-statutory concessions was successfully challenged in 2005, so they are gradually being withdrawn or made law. HM Revenue and Customs (HMRC) issue Notices and Guidance Notes, aimed at tax agents and advisers, to provide additional detail in relation to the general principles set out in legislation. HMRC's interpretation of tax legislation and clarification or detail of how it should be applied is given in statements of practice. Guidance provided to HMRC staff in interpreting and applying tax legislation is also available to the public.

76   A

77   C

Tutorial note

If a taxpayer submits a paper return on time, they can ask HMRC to calculate the tax due. Tax returns submitted electronically automatically calculate the tax due.

78

	Phillip	Harriet
31 January 2022		
31 January 2025		
31 January 2026	✓	✓

Tutorial note

Taxpayers who are in business, which for this purpose includes the letting of a property, must keep their records until five years after the 31 January filing date (i.e. 31 January 2026 for a 2019/20 return).

79   D

Tutorial note

Taxpayers with a business must keep their records until 5 years after the 31 January filing date. A business for these purposes includes property income.

Other taxpayers are generally required to keep their records for 12 months from the 31 January filing deadline.

80   B

Tutorial note

The taxpayer can amend the return within 12 months of the 31 January filing date. For the tax year 2018/19, amendments must therefore be made by 31 January 2021. HMRC must give written notice before commencing a compliance check. The written notice must be issued within 12 months of the actual date the return is filed with HMRC.

81   D

Payments on account (POAs) for the tax year 2019/20 are based on the relevant amount for the tax year 2018/19 = (£300 + £320) = £620.

As this does not exceed £1,000, POAs are not required in the tax year 2019/20.

82   B

2019/20	£
Income tax liability	25,000
Less: PAYE	(5,400)
Income tax payable (relevant amount)	19,600
Payments on account (POA)	(18,000)
CGT liability	5,000
Balancing payment due 31 January 2021	6,600

Tutorial note

CGT is payable in full on 31 January following the tax year and must therefore be included in the balancing payment. The first payment on account for the tax year 2020/21 is also due on 31 January 2021, making the total payable £16,400.

83   B

Tutorial note

The balancing payment is due on 31 January following the end of the tax year.

For the tax year 2019/20 this is 31 January 2021.

Where the balancing payment is made:

- *more than one month late, penalty = 5%*
- *more than six months late = an additional 5% is charged (total of 10%)*
- *more than 12 months late = a further 5% is charged (total of 15%).*

84

	True	False
Belinda will have to pay interest on late paid tax from 31 January 2020 to 10 March 2020	✓	
Belinda will have to pay a £100 fixed penalty because the payment is late		✓
Belinda will have to pay a 5% penalty because the payment is more than 30 days late	✓	

Tutorial note

The tax was due on 31 January 2020 and not actually paid until 10 March 2020. Interest on late paid tax runs from the due date until the date of payment, therefore the first statement is true. A 5% penalty is charged if the tax is paid more than 30 days late, therefore the third statement is true. Fixed penalties are only charged on the late submission of returns, not the late payment of tax.

85 D

Tutorial note

A taxpayer can make a claim to reduce their payments on account if they expect their actual income tax and class 4 liability for the tax year to be lower than the previous tax year. The payments on account will each be 50% of the expected liability for the tax year 2019/20 i.e. £4,840/2 = £2,420

86 £1,225

	£
Daily penalties as 3 months late for max. 90 days (£10 × 90)	900
6 months late (£6,500 × 5%)	325
	⎯⎯
Maximum penalty	1,225
	⎯⎯

Tutorial note

The return was filed more than 6 months but less than 12 months late.

87   D

Tutorial note

Interest will be charged from 1 February 2021 to 30 June 2021:

£1,200 × 3% × 5/12 = £15

A penalty will be imposed since the payment is more than 30 days late:

£1,200 × 5% = £60

88

	True	False
Under the Real Time Information PAYE system, Welan Ltd must submit income tax and NIC information in respect of the monthly salary payments to HM Revenue & Customs electronically by the 15th day of each month	✓	
If Welan Ltd pays the income tax and NIC due on the monthly salary payments to HM Revenue & Customs electronically it must make the payment by the 22nd of the month following the month the salaries are paid	✓	
Welan Ltd must provide each employee with a year-end summary form (P60) for the tax year 2019/20 by 6 July 2020		✓

Tutorial note

Under the RTI PAYE system information must be submitted electronically to HMRC on or before the date of payment.

The due date for electronic payments is 17 days after the end of the tax month (i.e. by the 22nd of the month following the month of payment). Employers with more than 250 employees must pay their PAYE payments electronically. Smaller employers have the choice to pay electronically.

An employer must provide an employee with a P60 by 31 May following the tax year.

PRACTICE SECTION B OBJECTIVE TEST CASES

INCOME TAX BASICS AND EMPLOYMENT INCOME

89   PHILIP & CHARLES (ADAPTED) *Walk in the footsteps of a top tutor*

Key answer tips

This case OT involves the income tax position for two individuals with different circumstances. It tests income tax, knowledge of NIC and pension contributions. All the topics are covered at a basic level and should therefore have been manageable.

1   A

	Total income £	Non-savings income £	Savings income £
Pension income	15,000	15,000	
Building society interest	14,600		14,600
Total income/Net income	29,600	15,000	14,600
Less: PA	(12,500)	(12,500)	
Taxable income	17,100	2,500	14,600

Income tax	£
2,500 × 20% Non-savings	500
2,500 × 0% Savings	0
1,000 × 0% Savings	0
11,100 × 20% Savings	2,220
17,100	
Income tax liability	2,720

Tutorial note

Savings income falling in the first £5,000 of taxable income is taxed at the starting rate of 0%. In addition, basic rate taxpayers are entitled to a nil rate band of £1,000 for savings income. The starting rate band and the savings income nil rate band use the basic rate and higher rate bands.

2   B

Charles's personal allowance is adjusted as follows:

	£	£
Personal allowance		12,500
Total income = net income	112,400	
Less: Gross gift aid	(800)	
	————	
ANI	111,600	
Less: Income limit	(100,000)	
	————	
Reduction of PA	11,600 × 50%	(5,800)
	————	————
Adjusted PA		6,700
		————

Tutorial note

1   Charitable donations under gift aid are grossed up before being used in the adjusted personal allowance computation. The gross figure is given in the question so there is no need to gross up the figure given.

2   As the adjusted net income exceeds £100,000 the allowance is reduced by £1 for every £2 it exceeds the limit. Net income for these purposes is adjusted (i.e. reduced) for both gross gift aid and gross personal pension contributions made in the year.

---

3   £4,971

	£
(£50,000 – £8,632) = £41,368 × 9%	3,723
(£112,400 – £50,000) = £62,400 × 2%	1,248
	———
	4,971
	———

4   A

Unused annual allowances:	£
2016/17 (Not a member of a scheme)	0
2017/18 (£40,000 – £25,000)	15,000
2018/19	40,000
	———
Total unused allowances b/f	55,000
Allowance for 2019/20	40,000
	———
	95,000
	———

Tutorial note

The total available annual allowance is the allowance for the current tax year plus unused allowances from the previous three tax years, provided the individual was a member of a registered pension scheme in the tax year.

Tutor's top tips

Always check carefully whether you have been given payments gross or net.

5

	True	False
His basic rate band for the tax year 2019/20 would have been increased by £8,600 in relation to this contribution	✓	
His taxable income for the tax year 2019/20 would have been reduced by £8,600		✓
HM Revenue and Customs would have paid £1,376 into the pension fund on his behalf		✓
His personal allowance would have increased by £4,300 in the tax year 2019/20	✓	

Tutorial note

Statement (2) is incorrect because personal pension contributions do not affect taxable income. Instead basic rate tax relief is given at source and higher rate relief is given by extending the basic and higher rate bands by the amount of the gross contribution of £8,600 (£6,880 × 100/80).

Statement (3) is incorrect because HM Revenue and Customs would have contributed £1,720 i.e. the basic rate tax deducted at source (£6,880 x 20/80).

Statement (1) is correct because the basic rate band for 2019/20 is extended by the gross amount of the personal pension contributions (£6,880 x100/80= £8,600). This reduces the income falling in the higher rate band by £8,600.

Statement (4) is correct as Charles' adjusted net income would have been £8,600 lower as a result of deducting the gross personal pension contribution of £8,600. This would increase the personal allowance by £8,600 × 50% = £4,300 as the ANI in excess of £100,000 has decreased.

90 KIM BAXTER (ADAPTED) *Walk in the footsteps of a top tutor*

Key answer tips

This case OT involves the employment income rules, including benefits and deductions of expenses. It also covers qualifying interest payments and the marriage allowance. Benefits are a highly examinable area and the detailed rules must be learnt.

1   A

Ordinary commuting (i.e. travel between home and the permanent workplace) does not qualify for relief. The travel to a temporary workplace qualifies as it is for a period lasting less than 24 months.

Business mileage is therefore 10,500 miles (9,200 + 1,300).

	£
Amount reimbursed (10,500 miles at 36p)	3,780
Less: Approved mileage allowance:	
10,000 miles at 45p	(4,500)
500 miles at 25p	(125)
Allowable deduction	(845)

2   D

	£
Interest payable at official rate (£14,600 × 2.5% × 10/12)	304
Less: Interest actually paid (£14,600 × 1% × 10/12)	(122)
Taxable benefit	182

Tutor's top tips

Where a benefit has only been available for part of the tax year, it must be time apportioned.

---

3   £590

	£	£	£
Higher of:			
Market value when gifted		200	
Market value when first made available	800		
Less: Use of asset benefit:			
2018/19 (£800 × 20%)	(160)		
		640	
			640
Less: Price paid			(50)
Taxable benefit			590

4   A

	Total
	£
Employment income = total income	25,650
Less: Relief for interest paid (Note)	(140)
Net income	25,510
Less: PA	(12,500)
Taxable income	13,010

Tutorial note

The loan interest paid of £140 is eligible for relief since the loan was used by Kim to finance expenditure for a qualifying purpose.

5

	Richard	Kim
Personal allowance reduced by £800		
Personal allowance reduced by £1,190	✓	
Personal allowance increased by £800		
Personal allowance increased by £1,190		
Income tax liability reduced by £160		
Income tax liability reduced by £238		✓

Tutorial note

The effect of the marriage allowance election is that the:

- *transferring spouse's PA is reduced by the fixed amount of £1,250 (for the tax year 2019/20)*

- *the recipient spouse's income tax liability is reduced by a maximum of £250 (£1,250 MA × 20% BR income tax)*

Note that there is no provision for transferring less than the fixed amount.

INCOME TAX BASICS AND INCOME FROM SELF-EMPLOYMENT

91 FOO DEE (ADAPTED)

Key answer tips

This question covers both the rules for income from employment and self-employment.

It requires a simple adjustment of profit and capital allowances computation which should not have caused any problems if you remembered that it is a 9 month accounting period and therefore the maximum AIA and WDAs are time apportioned.

1   B, E

CO_2 emissions rounded down to 135g/km, available 9 months

	%
Diesel	27
Plus: $(135 - 95) \times 1/5$	8
	───
Appropriate percentage	35
	───
Car benefit $(£19,000 \times 35\% \times 9/12)$	4,987
Fuel benefit $(£24,100 \times 35\% \times 9/12)$	6,326

2   B

	£
Overnight expenses paid when working away in the UK $(£6 \times 14)$	84
Employer pension contributions (6%)	0
	─────
	84
	─────

Tutorial note

The expenses paid to Foo exceed £5 per night therefore the full amount is a taxable benefit. If the amount paid to cover overnight expenses in the UK was ≤£5 per night it is fully exempt.

Pension contributions made by an employer are an exempt employment benefit.

3   £138,954

Trading profit – 9 m/e 30 September 2020

	£
Net profit	130,854
Depreciation	3,500
Legal fees (capital re acquisition of restaurant)	1,400
Private accommodation (£12,800 × 1/4)	3,200
Trading profit before capital allowances	138,954

4   A

Capital allowances – nine months ended 30 September 2020

	Private use car £		Allowances £
Additions (no AIA)			
Car (51 – 110g/km)	14,600		
WDA (18% × 9/12)	(1,971)	× 70%	1,380
TWDV c/f	12,629		
Total allowances			1,380

Tutorial note

(1)   The WDA is time apportioned by 9/12 as the accounting period is only 9 months long.

(2)   Capital allowances on car purchases are calculated based on CO_2 emissions.

As the car purchased in this question has CO_2 emissions of between 51 – 110g/km, it is eligible for a WDA at 18%. The WDA then needs to be adjusted for the short accounting period and for the private use by Foo Dee, as only the business use proportion of the allowance can be claimed.

5   B

Tutorial note

Foo starts to trade on 1 January 2020 which is in the tax year 2019/20. The basis period for the first tax year of trading is therefore 1 January 2020 to 5 April 2020.

The time limit for notifying HM Revenue and Customs of chargeability is six months from the end of the tax year in which the liability arises i.e. 5 October 2020.

The filing date for the tax return is 31 January following the end of the tax year i.e. 31 January 2021 for the tax year 2019/20.

PRACTICE SECTION C CONSTRUCTED RESPONSE QUESTIONS

INCOME TAX BASICS AND EMPLOYMENT INCOME

92 ARRAY LTD (ADAPTED) *Walk in the footsteps of a top tutor*

Key answer tips

This question is a classic employee benefits question which should be straightforward provided you have revised this topic. Remember to learn the reporting deadline for forms P11D as this point is often tested as part of a question on employment benefits.

Part (b) required knowledge of the payment due date for class 1A. The calculation of class 1A is also a common requirement so make sure you are prepared for this.

(a) Details of employees' taxable benefits are reported to HM Revenue and Customs using a form P11D for each employee.

The P11D submission deadline for the tax year 2019/20 is 6 July 2020.

(b) Alice

	£
Car benefit (£19,600 × 25%) (W)	4,900
Fuel benefit (£24,100 × 25%)	6,025

Working: Car benefit

CO_2 emissions = 108g/km (rounded down to 105g/km), available all year

	%
Petrol	23
Plus: $(105 - 95) \times {}^{1}/_{5}$	2
Appropriate percentage	25

	£
List price	24,600
Less: Capital contribution (maximum £5,000)	(5,000)
	19,600

Tutorial note

The amount of capital contribution which can be used to reduce the list price when calculating a car benefit is restricted to £5,000.

The proportion of business mileage is not relevant to the calculation of a company car benefit.

Buma

Average method	£	£
Loan at start of year	30,000	
Less: Repaid during year (£1,000 × 12)	(12,000)	
Loan at end of year	18,000	
Average loan (£30,000 + £18,000) ÷ 2)	24,000	
Assessable benefit (£24,000 × 2.5%)		600
Less: Interest paid		(240)
Taxable benefit		360

Claude

The provision of one mobile telephone does not give rise to a taxable benefit even if the telephone is a smartphone.

The taxable benefit for the use of the home entertainment system is £160 (£3,200 × 20% × 3/12).

Tutorial note

The home entertainment system has not been given to Claude, so the market value at the end of the tax year is irrelevant. The use of asset benefit is calculated based on the market value of the asset when it is first made available to the employee for private use.

Denise

Only £8,000 of the relocation costs are exempt, so the taxable benefit is £2,400 (£10,400 – £8,000).

The payment of medical costs of up to £500 does not result in a taxable benefit provided the medical treatment is to assist an employee to return to work following a period of absence due to ill-health or injury.

(c)   The employer's class 1A NIC payable by Array Ltd for the tax year 2019/20 is £1,911 (W). If paid electronically, this would have been payable by 22 July 2020.

Working: Class 1A

Benefits subject to class 1A:

	£
Alice: car benefit	4,900
Alice: fuel benefit	6,025
Buma: loan benefit	360
Claude: use of the home entertainment system	160
Denise: excess relocation costs	2,400
	13,845
Class 1A at 13.8%	1,911

Examiner's report

This was the income tax question. It was well answered, and involved an employer company that had provided various benefits to four of its employees.

For part (a), many candidates appreciated that reporting is done using form P11D, but the submission deadline was often not known. Less well prepared candidates often discussed (at length) submission details for self-assessment tax returns.

Part (b). There were many exceptional answers to this section. Common mistakes included:

–   For the car and fuel benefits, not ignoring the fuel cost and the mileage figures – both of which were irrelevant to the benefit calculations.

–   For the beneficial loan, not commencing calculations with the amount of the loan outstanding at the start of the tax year – this figure was given – but instead trying to work from the original loan amount.

–   For the home entertainment system, using the value at the start of tax year rather than the original purchase price.

Note: The examiner's report has been edited to remove comments on elements of the question that have been deleted due to changes in legislation.

ACCA marking scheme		
		Marks
(a)	P11D	2.0
(b)	**Taxable benefits**	
	Car benefit	3.0
	Fuel benefit	1.0
	Beneficial loan	3.0
	Mobile telephone	1.0
	Home entertainment system	1.0
	Relocation	1.0
	Medical costs	1.0
		───
		11.0
		───
(c)	**Class 1A NIC**	
	Amount	1.0
	Due date	1.0
		───
		2.0
		───
Total		**15.0**
		───

93 MARTIN (ADAPTED) *Walk in the footsteps of a top tutor*

(a) **Martin – Taxable income 2019/20**

Key answer tips

It is important in part (a) to set up your pro forma to work out the different types of income in the question that need to be brought together to work out taxable income.

Remember to put zeros into your answer where you come across exempt income to ensure you score all the marks available.

It is likely that some parts of the section C questions will test some admin and there are four marks allocated here. Try and break these questions down as there is often more than one issue that needs to be discussed to get the marks available.

	£
Employment income	
Salary	144,000
Bonuses (£21,400 + £13,700) (Note 1)	35,100
Car benefit (£16,400 × 26% (W1) × 9/12)	3,198
Car benefit (£36,400 × 16% × 3/12)	1,456
Beneficial loan (Note 2)	0
Home entertainment system (£7,400 × 20%)	1,480
Charitable payroll deductions	(1,000)
Professional subscription	(560)
Health club membership	0
	183,674
Trading profit (W2)	20,930
Property income (£9,200 – £7,500)	1,700
Dividend income	440
Interest from savings certificate	0
	206,744
Personal allowance (Note 3)	0
Taxable income	206,744

Tutorial note

1   *The bonus of £18,200 will have been treated as being received during the tax year 2018/19 because Martin became entitled to it during that tax year.*

2   *There is no taxable benefit in respect of the beneficial loan because it did not exceed £10,000 at any time during the tax year.*

3   *No personal allowance is available because Martin's adjusted net income exceeds £125,000.*

Workings

(W1) Car benefit

CO_2 emissions = 113g/km (rounded down to 110g/km), available all year

	%
Petrol	23
Plus: (110 – 95) × $^1/_5$	3
Appropriate percentage	26

(W2) Trading profit

	£
1 January to 30 September 2019	
£54,600 × 9/12 × 40%	16,380
1 October to 31 December 2019	
£54,600 × 3/12 × 1/3	4,550
	20,930

(b) **(i)** Martin's deadline for amending his self-assessment tax return for the tax year 2019/20 will be 31 January 2022 (12 months from the latest (electronic) filing date for the return of 31 January 2021).

Should additional tax become payable, then interest will be charged from 31 January 2021 to the date when the additional tax is paid.

(ii) If HMRC intend to carry out a compliance check into Martin's self-assessment tax return for the tax year 2019/20, then they will have to notify him by 26 December 2021 (12 months after they receive his tax return).

HMRC will carry out a compliance check because of a suspicion that income has been undeclared or deductions have been incorrectly claimed.

ACCA marking guide			
			Marks
(a)		Salary and bonuses	1.5
		Car benefits	2.0
		Other benefits	1.5
		Deductions	1.5
		Trading profit	2.0
		Other income	2.0
		PA	0.5
			11.0
(b)	(i)	Amendment	2.0
	(ii)	Compliance check	2.0
Total			**15.0**

Examiner's report

This income tax question involved Martin who was employed by Global plc and was also a member of a partnership. In addition, Martin rented out one furnished room of his main residence, received dividends and interest on the maturity of savings certificates from NS&I (National Savings and Investments).

Part (a) for 11 marks required a calculation of Martin's taxable income. This section was very well answered, and there were many perfect responses. However, the following points should be noted when answering this style of question:

- Candidates should think carefully about which workings can be included as one-line calculations within the main computation and which need their own separate working. For example, there were two car benefit calculations which were easily included within the main computation. The only aspect which warranted a separate working here was the partnership trading profit.

- When calculating Martin's share of the partnership's trading profit, it was only necessary to deal with his share. The allocations made to the other two partners were not relevant.

- Practise as many computations as possible. If this is done, basic mistakes such as claiming capital allowances rather than applying the motor car benefit rules can be avoided.

- As stated in the requirements, candidates should always clearly indicate (by the use of a zero) any items which do not require adjustment. The beneficial loan and the interest on the maturity of savings certificates were exempt, but this needed to be indicated.

- With computations containing both additions and deductions, candidates should be very careful to indicate which is which. A single column approach with deductions shown in brackets avoids any confusion.

- Candidates should appreciate that if expenses are paid privately by an employee, then they cannot possibly be taxable benefits – only a potential deduction against taxable income. In this case, Martin had paid a professional subscription (which was relevant to his employment with Global plc) and a membership fee to a health club (which he used to entertain Global plc's clients). It was clearly stated that Global plc did not reimburse Martin for either of these costs.

- Being aware of which benefits are exempt, such as the beneficial loan not exceeding £10,000, will avoid spending time on unnecessary calculations.

- Reading and understanding a question's requirements will avoid spending a lot of time calculating an income tax liability when it is not needed. The requirement was just to calculate Martin's taxable income.

Part (b)(i) for 2 marks was to advise Martin of the deadline for making an amendment to his self-assessment tax return and to state how HM Revenue and Customs (HMRC) will calculate interest if such an amendment results in additional tax becoming payable. This section was not answered particularly well. The deadline was 31 January 2022, but too many candidates gave a date of 12 months following the submission of Martin's self-assessment tax return.

Answers need to be precise, so the explanation how HMRC will calculate interest should have said that this will be from the original due date (31 January 2021) to the date that the additional tax is paid. A general discussion of how HMRC charges interest was not sufficient.

Part (b)(ii) for 2 marks was to state the latest date by which HMRC will have to notify Martin if they intend to carry out a compliance check in respect of his self-assessment tax return, and (assuming the check is not made on a completely random basis) the possible reasons why such a check would be made. Although this was better answered than part (b)(i), too many candidates wrote everything they knew on compliance checks rather than focusing on the information given – it being clearly stated that this was not a random check.

Candidates should note that detailed answers are not required where just a few marks are involved as was the case for both aspects of part (b).

94   KAYA *Walk in the footsteps of a top tutor*

Key answer tips

This question is a typical 'new style' question requiring the comparison of two alternative forms of profit extraction.

Fairly straightforward computations were required to calculate the income tax and NICs under each option.

Additional director's remuneration

Kaya's revised income tax liability will be:

	£
Director's remuneration (£30,000 + £25,000)	55,000
Dividend income	45,000
	100,000
Personal allowance	(12,500)
Taxable income	87,500

Income tax	£
£	
37,500 × 20% (non-savings income)	7,500
5,000 × 40% (non-savings income)	2,000
2,000 × 0% (dividend income)	0
43,000 × 32.5% (dividend income)	13,975
87,500	
Income tax liability	23,475

Kaya's revised employee class 1 national insurance contributions (NICs) will be:

	£
(£50,000 – £8,632) × 12%	4,964
(£55,000 – £50,000) × 2%	100
Class 1 employee NICs	5,064

Hoppi Ltd's revised employee class 1 NICs will be:

	£
Per question	2,949
Bonus (£25,000 × 13.8%)	3,450
Total class 1 employer's NICs	6,389

Hopi Ltd's revised corporation tax liability is as follows:

	£
Forecast trading profit	80,000
Less: Bonus	(25,000)
Less: Employer's NICs on bonus	(3,450)
Revised profit	51,550
CT liability (£51,550 × 19%)	9,794

Additional dividend income

Kaya's revised income tax liability will be:

	£
Per question	12,975
Income tax on additional dividend (£25,000 × 32.5%)	8,125
Total class 1 employer's NICs	21,100

The class 1 NICs for both Kaya and Hopi Ltd will remain unchanged, as will Hopi Ltd's corporation tax liability.

Tutorial note

The examining team has stated that a single column approach to an income tax computation is acceptable in the exam. This could save you time in a question with a basic computation such as Kaya's.

Dividends are not an allowable deduction from profits and they are not subject to employee or employer's NICs.

Examiner's report

Those candidates who understood basic tax rules had no difficulty answering this question. As warned in previous reports, where tax figures are given for the original scenario, candidates should never attempt to recalculate these figures for themselves. All this does is lose valuable time with candidates producing three sets of workings rather than the expected two. Candidates should always read the requirements very carefully. These types of questions often require a summary or a conclusion, but neither was necessary for this question – again those candidates who provided one lost a bit more time.

Where computations are required for two different scenarios, candidates should clearly indicate which scenario is being answered. It is much better to deal with one scenario first, then the second, rather than have a mix of computations dealing with one tax at a time, such as all the income tax and class 1 NIC computations for Kaya, then the corporation tax and class 1 NIC calculations for Hopi Ltd. Although full marks are awarded for correct answers however the information is presented, dealing with one scenario at a time can help candidates to ensure they have covered all aspects in their answers.

Some of the calculations in this question required full computations (such as Kaya's income tax liability under the additional director's remuneration alternative), whereas others (such as Kaya's income tax liability under the additional dividend alternative) could be calculated by working at the margin. Appreciating where full computations can be avoided saves time as well as reducing the complexity of the workings. Also, under the additional dividend alternative, many candidates did not appreciate that the class 1 NICs and Hopi Ltd's corporation tax liability would not change from the original figures provided.

In summary, although many candidates correctly calculated most, if not all, of the revised tax and NICs, they often took a much longer route in reaching their answer than was necessary. Working through past examination questions will help candidates familiarise themselves with the best approach to be taken when answering these types of questions. Also, it is important that candidates appreciate the interactions which can arise in these questions, and an article has been published covering many of the scenarios which could be examined.

ACCA marking scheme	
	Marks
Option 1	
Kaya's income tax computation:	
Director's remuneration	0.5
Dividend income	0.5
PA	0.5
IT on non-savings	1.0
DNRB	0.5
Tax on dividends	0.5
NICs	
Kaya's employee NICs	1.5
Hoppi Ltd's revised employer's NICs	1.0
Hoppi Ltd's revised CT liability	1.0
Option 2	
Kaya's revised income tax liability	1.5
No change to employee and employer's NICs	1.0
No change to Hoppi Ltd's CT liability	0.5
Total	**10.0**

95   PATIENCE (ADAPTED) *Walk in the footsteps of a top tutor*

Key answer tips

This question required the computation of income tax and capital gains tax for an individual with employment income, self-employment income and property income.

A calculation of the various types of income was necessary in order to complete the income tax computation.

There were two marks available for a basic capital gains computation on the disposal of the two rental properties.

Tutor's top tips

You are required to calculate employment income, self-employment income and property income for inclusion in the income tax computation. Start with your strongest of the three areas as it does not have to be completed in a set order.

Remember to clearly show your workings to enable the marker to award marks where mistakes have been made.

Patience – Income tax computation

		£
Employment income		
Salary (£3,750 × 9)		33,750
Pension contributions – Patience (£33,750 × 6%)		(2,025)
– Employer		0
		———
		31,725
School place – cost to employer (marginal cost)		540
Long-service award		0
Beneficial loan		0
		———
Employment income		32,265
Trading profit (W1)		16,100
Pensions (£1,450 + £6,000 + £3,300)		10,750
Property business profit (W3)		3,500
		———
Total income		62,615
Personal allowance		(12,500)
		———
Taxable income		50,115
		———

	£
42,000 (W4) × 20%	8,400
8,115 × 40%	3,246
50,115	
Income tax liability	11,646

Tutorial notes

(1) *A non-cash long-service award is not a taxable benefit if it is for a period of service of at least 20 years, and the cost of the award does not exceed £50 per year of service.*

(2) *There is no taxable benefit if beneficial loans do not exceed £10,000 during the tax year.*

Workings

(W1) Trading profit

	£	£
Year ended 31 July 2019		14,800
Period ended 31 December 2019	6,900	
Balancing allowance (working 2)	(1,900)	
		5,000
		19,800
Relief for overlap profits		(3,700)
		16,100

(W2) Capital allowances

	Main pool	Allowances
	£	£
TWDV brought forward	2,200	
Addition – Laptop computer	1,700	
Proceeds (£1,200 + £800)	(2,000)	
Balancing allowance	(1,900)	1,900

Tutorial notes

(1) There is no annual investment allowance, 100% FYA or writing down allowance available in the final capital allowances computation. Additions are included in the relevant pool at cost. The disposal proceeds are deducted to calculate a balancing allowance/charge on all columns on cessation of trade.

(2) The closing year basis period rules must be applied in the final tax year of trade. The final assessment includes any profits not yet assessed less overlap profits from commencement of trade.

(W3) Property business profit

	£
Rent received (£3,600 + £7,200)	10,800
Expenditure (£4,700 + £2,600)	(7,300)
Property business profit	3,500

(W4) Basic rate band

	£
Basic rate band	37,500
Add: Gross personal pension contributions (£3,600 × 100/80)	4,500
Extended basic rate band	42,000

Patience – capital gains tax computation

		£	£
Property 1:	Proceeds	122,000	
	Less: Cost	(81,400)	
			40,600
Property 2:	Proceeds	98,000	
	Less: Cost	(103,700)	
			(5,700)
Net gains			34,900
Annual exempt amount			(12,000)
Taxable gain			22,900
Capital gains tax (£22,900 × 28%)			6,412

Tutorial note

Gains on residential properties are taxed at higher rates than other gains, the rates are provided in the tax tables. Patience is a higher rate taxpayer so the gain is all taxed at 28%.

Examiner's report

This was the income tax question. It was well answered, and involved a taxpayer who had retired during the tax year, ceasing both employment and self-employment. The requirement was to calculate the income tax and capital gains tax liabilities for the tax year.

Two aspects to this question caused particular difficulty. Firstly, many candidates treated the pension income (state pension, employer's occupational pension scheme and a private pension) as exempt income. Secondly, the format in which information was given for two properties caused a certain amount of confusion, with the information relevant for income tax and the capital gains tax details being shown within the one table; candidates being required to separate out the relevant information for income tax and capital gains tax purposes. Here figures were often duplicated, with, for example, revenue expenditure being (correctly) deducted as an expense in calculating the property business profit, but then also (incorrectly) deducted in calculating chargeable gains.

ACCA marking scheme	
	Marks
Salary less employee pension contributions	1.0
Employer's pension contributions exempt	0.5
School place	1.0
Long service award	0.5
Beneficial loan	0.5
Trading profit year ended 31.7.19	0.5
Trading profit period ended 31.12.19	0.5
Deduct overlap profits	1.0
Capital allowances – TWDV b/f	0.5
Capital allowances – addition	0.5
Capital allowances – disposal proceeds	1.0
Capital allowances – balancing allowance	1.0
Property income – rental income	0.5
Property income – expenses	0.5
Pension income	1.0
Personal allowance	0.5
Extend BRB	1.0
IT	1.0
Gain on property 1	0.5
Gain on property 2	0.5
AEA	0.5
CGT at 28%	0.5

Total	**15.0**
	----

96   ALIMAG LTD   *Walk in the footsteps of a top tutor*

Key answer tips

This question is a typical 'new style' question requiring the comparison of two alternative forms of profit extraction.

Fairly straightforward computations were required to calculate the total tax under the revised basis of extraction.

An easy mark was available for comparing the total tax under the original basis with the total tax calculated under the revised basis.

Gamila's income tax liability

	£
Director's remuneration	25,000
Dividend income	75,000
	————
Total income	100,000
Less: PA	(12,500)
	————
Taxable income	87,500
	————

Income tax

£	
12,500 × 20% (non-savings income)	2,500
2,000 × 0% (dividend income)	0
23,000 × 7.5% (dividend income)	1,725
————	
37,500	
50,000 × 32.5%	16,250
————	
87,500	
————	
Income tax liability	20,475
	————

Tutorial note

The examining team has stated that a single column approach is acceptable in the exam. This could save you time in a question with a basic income tax computation such as Gamila's.

Magnus' income tax liability

	£
Dividend income	25,000
Less: PA	(12,500)
Taxable income	12,500

Income tax

	£	
2,000 × 0% (dividend income)		0
10,500 × 7.5% (dividend income)		787
12,500		

Income tax liability	787

Gamila's class 1 NICs

	£
(£25,000 – £8,632) × 12%	1,964

There will be no class 1 NIC for Magnus because he will not have any earnings.

Alimag Ltd's class 1 NICs

	£
(£25,000 – £8,632) × 13.8%	2,259

Alimag Ltd's corporation tax

	£
Trading profit	180,000
Director's remuneration	(25,000)
Employer's class 1 NIC	(2,259)
Taxable income	152,741
Corporation tax (£152,741 × 19%)	29,021

The overall savings of taxes and NICs if the revised basis of profit extraction is used instead of the profit extraction is £17,916 (£72, 422 – £54,506).

	Original £	Revised £
Provided in question	72,422	
Income tax – Gamila		20,475
Income tax – Magnus		787
Class 1 employee		1,964
Class 1 employer's		2,259
Corporation tax		29,021
Maximum claim against non-trade income	72,422	54,506

Examiner's report

There were many perfect answers to this question, although other candidates had difficulty with various aspects. This scenario is covered in the Higher Skills article which has been published, and candidates are advised to work carefully through the examples contained in the article. It is important that candidates appreciate the interactions involved in this type of higher skills question. For example, director's remuneration reduces a company's taxable total profits, but the payment of dividends does not. Most candidates forgot to deduct the employer's NICs when calculating Alimag Ltd's profits. Another fairly common mistake was to apply NICs to the dividends received.

Tax and NIC figures were provided for the original basis of profit extraction. Candidates should never attempt to recalculate these figures for themselves, since all this does is waste a lot of time. Where there are several computations forming part of the same question, then candidates should always use appropriate headings to indicate which aspect is being answered. The tax computations were relatively straightforward, so there was no need, for example, to have separate columns for director's remuneration and dividends. The same went for the NIC computations given that the 2% rate was not applicable. The calculation of the overall tax and NICs saving was often omitted. This was a very easy one mark to obtain given that candidates simply had to use figures already calculated.

ACCA marking scheme		
		Marks
Gamila's income tax computation:		
Director's remuneration		0.5
Dividend income		0.5
PA		0.5
IT on non-savings		0.5
DNRB		0.5
Tax on dividends		1.0
Magnus' income tax computation:		
Dividend income		0.5
PA		0.5
DNRB		0.5
Tax on dividends		0.5
Gamila's employee class 1		0.5
Nil for Magnus		0.5
Employer's NICs		0.5
Trading profit		0.5
Director's remuneration		0.5
Employer's NICs		0.5
Corporation tax		0.5
Overall saving		1.0
		———
Total		**10.0**
		———

97   DILL *Walk in the footsteps of a top tutor*

Key answer tips

Part (a) tests the residence rules for individuals. The tax rates and allowances show the required number of ties based on the time spent in the UK. You could have passed this part of the question using this information. In the answer the highlighted words are key phrases that markers are looking for

Part (b) has a very straightforward computation of taxable income including a classic employee benefit section.

(a)   Dill was resident in the UK during the three previous tax years, and was in the UK between 46 and 90 days, so did not meet any of the automatic tests in the tax year 2018/19.

She had two UK ties, which are having a house in the UK (which she made use of in the tax year 2018/19) and being in the UK for more than 90 days during the previous two tax years.

Dill was therefore not resident in the UK in the tax year 2018/19 because she had fewer than three UK ties.

(b) **Dill – taxable income**

	£
Employment income	
Salary	270,000
Occupational pension contribution	(10,000)
Bonuses (£16,200 + £29,300)	45,500
Company gym	0
Home entertainment system (£5,900 × 20%)	1,180
Workplace nursery	0
Beneficial loan (£80,000 × 2.5% × 10/12)	1,667
Health club membership	990
Mileage allowance (W)	(1,625)
Professional subscription	(560)
Golf club membership	0
	307,152
Premium bond prize	0
Interest from savings certificate	0
	307,152
Total income	307,152
Less: Loss relief	(58,000)
	249,152
Less: PA	(0)
Taxable income	249,152

Working: Mileage allowance

The mileage allowance received will be tax-free, and Dill can make the following expense claim:

	£
Approved mileage allowance:	
10,000 miles at 45p	4,500
4,500 miles at 25p	1,125
	5,625
Less: Mileage allowance received (16,000 at 25p)	(4,000)
Allowable deduction	1,625

Tutorial note

Exempt benefits must be stated as such in your answer or shown as a benefit of nil in order to score the marks available.

Relief for employee occupational pension contributions is given by reducing employment income, which is a different method of relief from personal pension contributions where the basic rate band is extended.

As Dill has adjusted total income in excess of £210,000 and has not been a member of a pension scheme in previous tax years she is only entitled to relief on the minimum amount of £10,000 before incurring an annual allowance charge.

Bonuses are taxed on the earlier of the receipts and the entitlement basis. In this question the entitlement is earlier in both cases and consequently both bonuses are taxable in the tax year 2019/20.

Dill is entitled to relief for her business mileage only using the approved mileage rate scheme.

Loss relief claimed in the current year is capped at the higher of £50,000 and 25% of adjusted total income (25% × £307,152 = £76,788). Thus there is full relief for the £58,000 loss against total income.

Examiner's report

Part (a) for 3 marks required candidates to explain why Dill was treated as not resident in the UK for the previous tax year. Although reasonably well answered, very few candidates managed to pick up all the available marks for this section. For example, most candidates simply stated that Dill had been in the UK for 60 days, rather than indicating that this fell in the 46 to 90 day band from the tax tables. A number of candidates wasted time by explaining the automatically resident and not resident tests, when it was obvious that these were not relevant. Then when discussing UK ties, some candidates focused on those ties which were not met, rather than those which were. The three marks available should have been a clear indication that a long, detailed, explanation was not required.

Part (b) for 12 marks required candidates to calculate Dill's taxable income. This section was generally answered very well, with many candidates achieving high marks. Common problems included:

- Not appreciating that the benefit of a workplace nursery is an exempt benefit.

- Treating subscriptions as benefits rather than as deductions.

- Omitting the personal allowance. Even when shown, it was obvious (given the level of Dill's income) that the personal allowance was not available, so all that was needed was a zero entry. There was no need for an explanation or a calculation of the reduction to nil.

- If a question requires just a calculation of taxable income, then that is where candidates should stop. Calculating the income tax liability just wastes valuable time.

- As stated in the requirements, candidates should always clearly indicate (by the use of a zero) any items which are not taxable or deductible – such as exempt benefits, non-deductible expenses and exempt income.

- Where a computation contains additions and deductions, candidates should be very careful to indicate which is which. A single column approach with deductions shown in brackets avoids any confusion.

- Candidates should think carefully about which workings can be included as one-line calculations within the main taxable income computation, and which need their own separate working. The only aspects which warranted a separate working here was the mileage allowance.

- The use of abbreviated numbers such as 45.5k instead of 45,500 for the bonuses should be avoided.

ACCA marking scheme		Marks
(a)	Automatic tests not met	1.0
	Two UK ties	0.5
	Identification of ties (0.5 each)	1.0
	Not UK resident as less than 3 ties	0.5
		3.0
(b)	Employment income	
	Salary	0.5
	Occupational pension contribution	1.0
	Bonuses	1.0
	Gym	0.5
	Home entertainment system	1.0
	Workplace nursery	0.5
	Beneficial loan	1.5
	Health club membership	0.5
	Mileage allowance	1.5
	Professional subscription	0.5
	Golf club membership	0.5
	Premium bond	0.5
	Interest from savings certificate	0.5
	Loss relief	1.5
	PA	0.5
		12.0
Total		**15.0**

98   RICHARD TRYER (ADAPTED) *Walk in the footsteps of a top tutor*

Key answer tips

This question requires a calculation of the income tax payable for a taxpayer who has correctly completed parts of his income tax computation, but left the following omissions:

(1)   Car and fuel benefits

(2)   Living accommodation

(3)   Property income

(4)   Income tax calculation

It is important not to be put off if a question is presented in a different format from those you have seen before; each one of these omissions tests areas that are commonly examined in TX.

Tutor's top tips

The best way to approach this question is the same as any other income tax computation question, by preparing an income tax computation in the normal columnar format. The examining team has chosen to give you some of the information you need in the body of the incomplete income tax computation. You can score easy marks by using these figures in your own computation.

You do not have to use the layout presented in the question.

There is a lot of information in the question which you must read carefully. Pay special attention to dates given to see if income and benefits are available all year or must be time apportioned.

Richard Tryer

Income tax computation – 2019/20

	Total	Non-savings income	Savings income	Dividend income
	£	£	£	£
Employment income (W1)	68,114	68,114		
Property income (W4)	7,480	7,480		
Building society interest (per Q) (Note)	1,260		1,260	
Dividends (Note 1)	5,800			5,800
	82,654	75,594	1,260	5,800
Less: PA (per Q)	(12,500)	(12,500)		
Taxable income	70,154	63,094	1,260	5,800

£		
37,500	at 20% (per Q)	7,500
25,594	at 40%	10,238
63,094		
500	at 0%	0
760	(£1,260 – £500) at 40%	304
2,000	at 0%	0
3,800	(£5,800 – £2,000) at 32.5%	1,235
70,154		

Income tax liability	19,277
Less: PAYE (per Q)	(19,130)
Income tax payable	147

Tutorial note

There is no need to consider any potential issues in relation to the building society interest or dividend because the question states that the completed parts of the income tax computation are correct.

Workings

(W1) Employment income

	£
Salary (per question)	41,000
Car benefit (W2)	3,275
Fuel benefit (W2)	4,519
Living accommodation (W3)	13,200
Furniture (£12,100 × 20%)	2,420
Running costs	3,700
	──────
Employment income	68,114
	──────

(W2) Car and fuel benefits

CO_2 emissions = 109g/km (rounded down to 105) and available all year.

	%
Petrol	23
Plus: (105 – 95)/5	2
	──────
Appropriate percentage	25
	──────

	£
List price of car	17,900
	──────

	£
Car benefit (£17,900 × 25%)	4,475
Less: Contribution for private use	(1,200)
	───────
Car benefit	3,275
	───────
Fuel benefit	
(£24,100 × 25% × 9/12)	4,519
	───────

Tutorial note

(1) *Note that the fuel benefit is only given for part of the tax year (unlike the car itself which is available all year). Hence the fuel benefit must be time apportioned.*

(2) *The cost of providing the fuel and the percentage that relates to private use is irrelevant for the purposes of calculating the fuel benefit.*

(W3) Living accommodation

- The benefit for the living accommodation is the higher of the annual value of £8,600 and the rent paid of £13,200 (£1,100 × 12).

- There is no additional benefit because Prog plc does not own the property.

Tutor's top tips

The examining team has included the market value of the living accommodation. This is not needed to calculate the benefit because the property is rented by the employer and not owned.

This information is included to test that you understand this point, so do not fall into the examining team's trap and try to use the market value.

(W4) Property income

	£	£
Premium received		12,000
Less: £12,000 × 2% × (30 − 1)		(6,960)
		5,040
Rent received (£664 × 5)		3,320
		8,360
Roof replacement	0	
Ceiling repairs (£8,600 − £8,200)	400	
Insurance paid	480	
		(880)
Property income		7,480

Tutorial note

The initial replacement cost of the shop's roof is capital in nature, as the building was not in a usable state when purchased and this fact was reflected in the reduced purchase price. Remember that property income for an individual is always calculated using the cash basis unless the question specifies otherwise.

ACCA marking scheme	
	Marks
Salary	0.5
Car benefit	2.0
Fuel benefit	1.5
Living accommodation	2.0
Furniture	0.5
Running costs	0.5
Assessment on premium	1.5
Rent received	1.0
Roof replacement	0.5
Ceiling repairs	1.0
Insurance	1.0
Building society interest & dividends	0.5
Income tax payable	2.5
Total	**15.0**

99 PETULA (ADAPTED) *Walk in the footsteps of a top tutor*

Key answer tips

This question covers the situation where an individual is employed and also earns property income.

Part (a) should have provided easy marks for the calculation of employment income as it contained core areas. The property income calculation was also straightforward, providing you were familiar with replacement furniture relief.

The accrued income scheme is based on the accruals principle so providing you practise questions on this area it shouldn't pose a problem.

Part (b) involved the calculation of the annual allowance available to carry forward. You must ensure you look out for individuals with a high level of adjusted income as the annual allowance is tapered from 2017/18 onwards where adjusted income is greater than £150,000.

(a) **Taxable income**

	£
Employment income	
Salary	230,000
Bonuses (£18,600 + £22,400)	41,000
Mileage allowance (W1)	8,350
Employer pension contributions (exempt benefit)	0
Professional subscription	(630)
Golf club membership	0
	———
Employment income	278,720
Property income (W2)	11,340
Savings income (£250,000 at 3% x 4/12)	2,500
	———
Total income	292,560
Qualifying interest paid	(140)
	———
Net income	292,420
Personal allowance	0
	———
Taxable income	292,420
	———

Tutorial notes:

The bonus of £21,200 will have been treated as being received during the tax year 2018/19 because Petula became entitled to it during that tax year.

Under the accrued income scheme, Petula must include the accrued interest from the gilts as savings income for 2019/20, even though she has not received any actual interest.

No personal allowance is available because Petula's adjusted net income of £292,420 exceeds £125,000.

Workings

(W1) Mileage allowance

	£
Reimbursement (26,000 × 60p)	15,600
Tax free amount:	
10,000 miles × 45p	(4,500)
11,000 miles × 25p	(2,750)
	———
Taxable benefit	8,350
	———

(W2) Property income

	£
Rent received	12,000
Replacement furniture relief:	
- Washing machine	(420)
- Dishwasher	0
Other expenses	(1,640)
	9,940
Furnished room (£8,900 – £7,500)	1,400
Property income	11,340

Tutorial notes:

No relief is given for that part of the cost of the washer-dryer which represents an improvement over the original washing machine. Relief is therefore restricted to the cost of a similar washing machine.

No relief is available for the cost of the dishwasher because this is the initial cost of a new asset rather than the cost of a replacement.

Claiming rent-a-room relief in respect of the furnished room is more beneficial than the normal basis of assessment (£8,900 – £2,890 = £6, 010).

(b) Petula has unused pension annual allowances of £10,000 from the tax year 2018/19 available to carry forward to the tax year 2020/21.

Tax year	Annual allowance	Contribution	Unused/(Excess)
	£	£	£
2019/20	10,000	30,000	(20,000)
2018/19	40,000	30,000	10,000
2017/18	40,000	30,000	10,000
2016/17	40,000	30,000	10,000

Tutorial notes

Petula's adjusted income for the tax year 2019/20 exceeds £210,000, so she is only entitled to the minimum tapered annual allowance of £10,000 for this year.

The pension contributions in the tax year 2019/20 utilised the restricted allowance in full and also the unused annual allowances of the tax years 2016/17 and 2017/18. She has £10,000 unused from the tax year 2018/19 to carry forward to the tax year 2020/21.

Examiner's report

Computation of an individual's taxable income

With this type of question, candidates should think carefully about which workings can be included as one-line calculations within the main computation, and which need their own separate working. Workings should always have a heading or be obviously identifiable, rather than just (for example) be referenced to the bullet list numbers from the question. The use of abbreviated numbers such as 8.35k instead of 8,350 should be avoided.

Where a computation contains additions and deductions, candidates should be very careful to indicate which is which. A single column approach with deductions shown in brackets avoids any confusion. Any items which do not require adjustment or where the entry is nil, should always be shown by the use of a zero. And if a result is obvious, such as a nil personal allowance due to a very high level of income, all that is needed is a zero entry – there is no need for an explanation or a calculation of the reduction to nil.

Candidates need to appreciate that each source of income is self-contained. It is not correct to show all the receipts from each source first (such as rent received), and then all the various expenses lumped together (such as property income deductions). For example, there should a working for property income, with the one figure then included in the main income tax computation.

Pension annual allowances

When calculating the amount of unused annual allowances, candidates should appreciate that they might need to take account of various factors such as:

–   The tapering of the annual allowance to a minimum of £10,000 where income exceeds £210,000.

–   The three-year restriction for the carry forward of unused allowances.

–   The fact that an employer's pension contributions utilise the annual allowance.

If a separate section of a question, then the marks available should be a good indication as to the complexity of a requirement.

ACCA marking scheme		Marks
(a)	**Employment income**	
	Salary	0.5
	Bonuses	1.0
	Mileage	1.5
	Pension contributions – no benefit	0.5
	Professional subscription	0.5
	Golf membership	0.5
	Property income	
	Rental income	0.5
	Washing machine cost deducted	1.0
	No deduction for dishwasher	1.0
	Other expenses	0.5
	Furnished room	1.0
	Accrued income	2.0
	Qualifying interest	1.0
	Personal allowance fully abated	0.5
		———
		12.0

ACCA marking scheme		
		Marks
(b)	Restriction to £10k in 2019/20	1.0
	Amounts b/f and used in 2019/20	1.5
	Carry forward of £10k from 2018/19	0.5
		–––––
		3.0
		–––––
Total		**15**
		–––––

INCOME TAX BASICS AND INCOME FROM SELF-EMPLOYMENT

100 CAROL COURIER (ADAPTED)

Key answer tips

A straightforward purely computational question dealing with the income tax and national insurance consequences of being employed and self-employed.

Part (c) requires a comparison of the net disposable income arising from the two options.

(a) Carol's income tax liability – continues to be employed

	£
Salary	44,000
Less: Pension contributions (£44,000 × 5%)	(2,200)
	–––––––
Employment income	41,800
Less: PA	(12,500)
	–––––––
Taxable income	29,300
	–––––––
Income tax liability (£29,300 × 20%)	5,860
	–––––––

Class 1 NICs – Employee's primary contributions

(£44,000 – £8,632) × 12%	4,244
	–––––––

(b) Carol's income tax liability – accepts self-employed contract

	£
Income (£47,000 + £13,000)	60,000
Less: Expenses (£4,400 + £2,800)	(7,200)
	–––––––
Trading income	52,800
Less: PA	(12,500)
	–––––––
Taxable income	40,300
	–––––––
Income tax liability (£40,300 × 20%) (Working)	8,060
	–––––––

Class 4 NICs

(£50,000 – £8,632) × 9%	3,723
(£52,800 – £50,000) × 2%	56
	3,779

Class 2 NICs

(£3 for 52 weeks)	156

Working: Extension of the basic rate band

	£
Basic rate band	37,500
Plus: Gross pension contributions	3,000
Extended basic rate band	40,500

All of Carol's taxable income falls into this extended basic rate band and is therefore taxed at 20%.

(c) **Benefit of accepting self-employed contract**

	Employed	Self employed
	£	£
Salary	44,000	0
Trading income	0	52,800
Pension contributions paid (Note)	(2,200)	(2,400)
NIC – Classes 1 and 4	(4,244)	(3,779)
NIC – Class 2	0	(156)
Income tax	(5,860)	(8,060)
Net disposable income	31,696	38,405

It is therefore beneficial for Carol to accept the offer to provide delivery services on a self-employed basis as her net income will increase by £6,709 (£38,405 – £31,696).

Tutorial note

Carol will pay personal pension contributions net of basic rate tax. If self-employed she will therefore pay £2,400 (£3,000 × 80%).

Tutor's top tips

When calculating the net disposable income think just in terms of cash and identify all cash coming in and all cash payments going out.

Cash payments obviously include the tax liabilities but also include other expenses such as pension contributions.

101   IDRIS WILLIAMS *Walk in the footsteps of a top tutor*

Key answer tips

This question has been written to test the rules on the cash basis as well as the choice of accounting date.

Students should be familiar with the factors that influence the choice of accounting date and the advantages and disadvantages of choosing an accounting date early or late in the tax year.

The cash basis rules are examinable to a limited extent. This question tests all the rules which could be examined.

The highlighted words in the written sections are key phrases that markers are looking for.

Tutor's top tips

There are four marks available for part (a), therefore four clear points should be made.

(a)   **Advantages of a 5 April accounting date**

- If Idris chooses to prepare his accounts to 5 April, the application of the basis period rules will be simplified.

- Idris will not have any overlap profits on the commencement of trade. If he prepares his accounts to 30 June, nine months of overlap profits will arise and these would not be relieved until the cessation of trading.

Advantages of a 30 June accounting date

- If Idris prepares his accounts to 30 June the interval between earning profits and paying the related tax liability will be 9 months longer than with an accounting date of 5 April.

- An accounting date of 30 June would make it easier to implement tax planning measures as there is a longer period over which to plan.

(b) (1) Tax adjusted trading profit – accruals basis

Tutor's top tips

This question does not specifically request that you start with the net profit figure and adjust for any disallowable items, but this is the most obvious approach to take.

Always show your workings if the figure you are adjusting for is not clear from the question.

When using the normal accruals basis no adjustment should be made for any revenue not received or purchases not actually paid for during the year.

	£	£
Net profit	20,175	
Food, utilities, etc. (personal use)	4,500	
Depreciation	1,250	
Motor expenses (£9,340 × 7,000/20,000)	3,269	
Capital allowances (W)		4,553
	29,194	4,553
	(4,553)	
Tax adjusted trading profit	24,641	

Tutorial note

The usual presentation of an adjustment of profits is produced above. However, an alternative method of calculating the same taxable trading profit figure is to reproduce the accounts just deducting the expenses which are allowable, as opposed to adding back those that are not allowable to the net profit. This alternative presentation is given below as it provides a more direct comparison of the difference in the treatment when the cash basis is used.

	£	£
Revenue		*49,910*
Food, utilities and other household goods (£17,660 – £4,500)		*(13,160)*
		36,750
Depreciation	*0*	
Motor expenses (£9,340 × 13,000/20,000)	*6,071*	
Other expenses	*1,485*	
Capital allowances (W)	*4,553*	
		(12,109)
		24,641

Working: Capital allowances

	Main pool £	Private use car £		Allowances £
Additions (no AIA)				
Car (51 – 110g/km)		9,000		
Additions (with AIA)				
Furniture	3,500			
AIA	(3,500)			3,500
	———	0		
WDA (18%) (Note)		(1,620)	× 65%	1,053
		———		
TWDV c/f	0	7,380		
	———	———		———
Total allowances				4,553
				———

Tutorial note

Capital allowances on car purchases are calculated based on the CO_2 emissions.

As the car purchased in this question has CO_2 emissions of between 51 – 110g/km, it is eligible for a WDA at 18%. The WDA then needs to be adjusted for the private use by Idris, as only the business use proportion of the allowance can be claimed.

The business mileage is 13,000 out of 20,000 miles (i.e. 65%).

(2) Cash basis

Idris is entitled to use the cash basis as his total cash receipts are not greater than £150,000 for the year.

Tutor's top tips

When operating the cash basis adjustments need to be made for any revenue not received or purchases not actually paid for during the year (i.e. receivables and payables).

The examining team has stated that where the cash basis is used you should assume that flat rate expenses are claimed for motor expenses and private use of business premises.

The motor expenses deduction is calculated using the HMRC approved mileage allowances. The private use of business premises flat rate adjustment covers the private use of food, utilities and other household goods and services.

Capital purchases are deductible in full in the year of purchase; however, no deduction is available for the purchase of a motor car as this is covered by the approved mileage allowance.

Note that the cash basis revenue limit is given in the Tax Rates and Allowances provided in the examination.

	£	£
Revenue (£49,910 – £10,275)		39,635
Less: Food, utilities, etc. (£17,660 × 95%)		(16,777)
		———
		22,858
Plus: Flat rate private use adjustment		4,200
Less: Depreciation	0	
Capital expenditure	3,500	
Motor expenses (W)	5,250	
Other expenses (£1,485 – £400)	1,085	
	———	(9,835)
		———
Tax adjusted trading profit		17,223
		———

Working: Motor expenses

Idris is entitled to claim a deduction for his business mileage of 13,000 miles at the approved mileage rates.

	£
10,000 miles at 45p	4,500
3,000 miles at 25p	750
	———
	5,250
	———

(3)   More beneficial basis

Using the cash basis will result in Idris being taxed on £7,418 (£24,641 – £17,223) less than under the accruals basis.

102   ETHEL *Walk in the footsteps of a top tutor*

Key answer tips

Part (a) tests cash accounting and flat rate basis rules.

The highlighted words are key phrases that markers are looking for.

Part (b) has a very straightforward computation of taxable trading profit using the accruals basis.

Tutor's top tips

You do not have to answer this question in the order set. Provided you clearly indicate which part you are answering, you can answer in any order. Hence you might prefer to start with part (b) on the accruals basis as this may be more familiar.

However, do take care when attempting a question out of order, as sometimes the answer to part (a) is required in part (b), and so on.

(a) **Ethel Brown – Calculation of tax adjusted trading profit using cash basis with flat rate expense adjustments**

	£	£
Revenue (£74,500 – £10,000) (Note 1)		64,500
Less: Food, utilities, etc.	(25,000)	
Plus: Flat rate private use adjustment (Note 2)	7,800	
	———	(17,200)
Less: Mileage (Note 3)		(4,750)
Equipment (Note 4)		0
		———
Tax adjusted trading profit		42,550
		———

Notes:

(1) **Income**

• The income of £10,000 outstanding at the year-end is excluded when calculating the profit using the cash basis. When using cash accounting, income is only included if it has been received during the period.

(2) **Business premises used partly for private purposes**

• The total payments of £25,000 can be deducted from the trading profit but the flat rate private use adjustment of £7,800 must be added to the trading profit for tax purposes.

• A net deduction from trading profits of £17,200 can therefore be claimed for tax purposes.

(3) **Car used for private and business purposes**

• The cash payments in respect of the purchase and running costs of the car totalling £17,000 (£14,000 + £3,000) are not deductible from the trading profit and capital allowances are not available.

- Instead a tax deduction for the car is allowed using the approved mileage allowances for the business mileage as follows:

	£
First 10,000 miles at 45p/mile	4,500
1,000 miles at 25p/mile	250
Allowable deduction	4,750

(4)   Kitchen equipment

- A tax deduction can be claimed from the trading profits for the full cost of the kitchen equipment when the invoice is paid.

- No tax deduction is therefore allowed in the accounts for the year to 5 April 2020 but Ethel will obtain a tax deduction of £350 from trading profits in the following year to 5 April 2021.

Tutorial note

(1)   *The question states that Ethel opts to use the cash basis and the flat rate expense adjustments. Note that the examining team have stated that whilst the use of flat rate expenses is optional it should be assumed in any question involving the cash basis that flat rate expenses are claimed.*

(2)   *Where a business premises is used partly for private purposes (e.g. a bed and breakfast or small care home), a private use adjustment must be made for tax purposes if the full cost of food, utilities and other household goods have been included in the accounts. The HMRC flat rate private use adjustments are based on the number of occupants and will be provided as part of the question in the examination. Any information regarding actual private expenses is irrelevant.*

(3)   *The flat rate expense adjustment in respect of cars is based on the HMRC approved mileage allowances. These are the same rates that are used to calculate the taxable benefit/allowable deduction where employees use their own cars for business purposes. The rates are given in the tax tables provided in the examination.*

(4)   *Under the cash basis a 100% trading deduction is given for the acquisition cost of items of plant and machinery (other than cars) rather than capital allowances.*

(b)   Ethel Brown – Calculation of tax adjusted trading profit using accruals basis

	£	£
Revenue		74,500
Less: Food, utilities, etc. (£25,000 × 65%)		(16,250)
		58,250
Less: Motor running costs (£3,000 × 60%)	1,800	
Equipment	0	
Capital allowances (W)	1,862	
		(3,662)
Tax adjusted trading profit		54,588

Working: Capital allowances

	£	Main pool £	Private use car £		Allowances £
Additions (no AIA)					
Car (51 – 110g/km)			14,000		
Additions (with AIA)					
Equipment	350				
AIA	(350)				350
		0			
WDA (18%) (Note)			(2,520)	× 60%	1,512
TWDV c/f		0	11,480		
Total allowances					1,862

Tutorial note

Capital allowances on car purchases are calculated based on the CO_2 emissions.

As the car purchased in this question has CO_2 emissions of between 51 – 110g/km, it is eligible for a WDA at 18%. The WDA then needs to be adjusted for the private use by Ethel as only the business use proportion of the allowance can be claimed.

103   SAM WHITE (ADAPTED)   *Walk in the footsteps of a top tutor*

Key answer tips

A classic self-employed scenario. The adjustment of profits was straightforward, except that some may not have known what to do with the patent royalties. In fact, if you did nothing, that was the right thing to do!

Be careful with the calculation of the private use/business use proportion of the car and remember the impact private use has on both the adjustment of profits computation and capital allowances.

Tutor's top tips

The key to success when you are doing an adjustment of profits is to think about what, if anything has already been included in the statement of profit or loss.

If an expense is disallowable and has been deducted, you need to add it back. If it hasn't been deducted you do nothing. Conversely, if an expense is allowable and has been deducted, you include it with a zero adjustment. If it hasn't been deducted, you need to deduct it.

Read the question carefully here! As the question just asks you to 'calculate', you do not need to explain why you are making adjustments, although you do need to make sure you label your answers so that the marker can see which expenses you are adding back or deducting. It is also important to include all the major items of expenditure in the question, showing a zero for the adjustment figure where the expenditure is allowable.

Always show your workings if the adjustment figure is not clear from the question.

Sam White – trading profit

	£	£
Net profit	100,000	
Depreciation	7,600	
Motor expenses (£8,800 × 20%) (W1)	1,760	
Patent royalties (Note 1)	0	
Breach of contract fees (Note 2)	0	
Accountancy fees (Note 2)	0	
Personal capital gains tax advice	320	
Gifts to customers (£560 + £420) (Note 3)	980	
Use of office (£5,120 × 1/8)		640
Private telephone (£1,600 × 25%)		400
Own consumption (Note 4)	1,480	
Capital allowances (W2)		3,634
	112,140	4,674
	(4,674)	
Trading profit	107,466	

Tutorial note

(1)   Patent royalties are allowed as a deduction when calculating the trading profit, because they are for the purposes of the trade. As they have already been deducted in arriving at the profit, no adjustment is required.

(2)   The fees incurred for accountancy and the breach of contract defence are allowable as incurred wholly and exclusively for the purposes of the trade.

(3)   Gifts to customers are an allowable deduction if they cost less than £50 per recipient per year, are not of food, drink, tobacco or vouchers exchangeable for goods and carry a conspicuous advertisement for the company making the gift.

(4)   Goods for own consumption must be treated as a sale at full market value. As no entries have been made in the accounts, the full sale proceeds are added back. Had the cost of the goods been accounted for already, only the profit element would need to be added back.

Workings

(W1) Private/business mileage

	Total	Private	Business
Total miles	25,000		
Visiting suppliers	(5,000)		5,000
Allocate (25:75)	20,000	5,000	15,000
		5,000	20,000
(5,000/25,000)		20%	
(20,000/25,000)			80%

Tutor's top tips

A familiar full blown capital allowances computation is given in the workings to this answer to show clearly how the allowances are calculated.

However, where there are not many transactions it is perfectly acceptable to do one or two lines and just calculate the allowances available on each asset acquired rather than a full computation.

If you do this however, be careful and make sure you explain your calculations clearly.

(W2) Capital allowances

	Main pool £	Private use car £	Allowances £
TWDV b/f	14,800	20,200	
WDA (18%)	(2,664)		2,664
WDA (6%)(Note)		(1,212) × 80%	970
TWDV c/f	12,136	18,988	
Total allowances			3,634

Tutorial note

The motor car is a high emission car (CO_2 emissions exceed 110g/km) and is eligible for a WDA at 6%.

Examiner's report

This question was very well answered by the majority of candidates.

The adjustments for use of office, business use of a private telephone and own consumption caused the most problems, with a number of candidates being unsure as to whether adjustments should be added or subtracted in order to arrive at the tax adjusted trading profit.

Note: *The examiner's report has been edited to remove comments on elements of the question that have been deleted due to changes to the examination format.*

ACCA marking scheme		
		Marks
Net profit		0.5
Depreciation		0.5
Motor expenses		1.5
Patent royalties		0.5
Professional fees		1.5
Gifts to customers		1.0
Use of office		1.0
Private telephone		1.0
Own consumption		0.5
Capital allowances	– Pool	1.0
	– Motor car	1.0
		―――
Total		**10.0**
		―――

104 GEORGE *Walk in the footsteps of a top tutor*

Key answer tips

A classic examination question on self-employed versus employed which was not difficult, but presented in a scenario requiring the application of knowledge to the particular situation given.

This is a newer style of question for students, comparing the income tax and NIC liabilities on the same amount of income for both an employee and a sole trader. This is useful preparation for those planning to move on to ATX.

Tutor's top tips

It is important to learn the rules for determining whether an individual is self-employed.

However, it is not enough here to simply state those rules; instead they must be applied to the situation given.

The question requirement specifically asks only for those factors that indicate employment rather than self-employment.

The answer must therefore focus on those factors, not any factors you can remember and not those that would clearly suggest self-employment rather than employment.

Even without detailed knowledge of the rules here, common sense suggestions should enable students to pick up some marks.

The answer below gives six factors for tutorial purposes but you were only required to provide four in your answer.

(a)   **Factors indicating employment**

- The contract is for a relatively long period of time
- George is required to do the work personally
- Xpee plc exercises control over George via the weekly meetings and instructions
- George will not incur any significant expenses in respect of the contract
- George will only be working for Xpee plc.
- George is not taking any significant financial risk

Tutor's top tips

Part (b) involves straightforward income tax and NIC calculations, which you should be able to score well on, regardless of your answer to part (a).

Don't miss the opportunity to gain these easy marks by being put off by the first part of the question, or by running out of time.

(b)   **Income tax liability**

	£
Income	41,000
Capital allowances (£3,600 × 100% AIA)	(3,600)
	———
Trading profit	37,400
Personal allowance	(12,500)
	———
Taxable income	24,900
	———

Income tax

£	
24,900 × 20%	4,980
———	

National insurance contributions

	£
Class 2 NICs	
(£3 × 52)	156
	———
Class 4 NICs	
(£37,400 – £8,632) × 9%	2,589
	———

(c) **(1)** If George is treated as employed in respect of his contract with Xpee plc, then the company will be required to deduct tax under PAYE every time that George is paid during 2019/20.

If treated as self-employed, George's income tax liability for 2019/20 would not be payable until 31 January 2021.

(2) If George is treated as employed in respect of his contract with Xpee plc, then his class 1 national insurance contributions for 2019/20 will be:

	£
Class 1 employee NIC	
(£41,000 – £8,632) × 12%	3,884
	————

The additional amount of national insurance contributions which he will suffer is therefore £1,139 (£3,884 – £156 – £2,589).

Tutorial note

For income tax purposes, capital allowances will reduce employment income in the same way that they are deducted in calculating the trading profit. However, there is no deduction for capital allowances when it comes to calculating class 1 national insurance contributions.

Examiner's report

Part (a) required four factors which were indicators of the taxpayer being treated as an employee in relation to their contract rather than as self-employed. Most candidates missed the fact that the taxpayer would not incur any significant expenses in respect of the contract and would not be taking any significant financial risk. Many candidates incorrectly gave the payment of tax under PAYE for the previous year as an indicator.

Part (b) required a calculation of the taxpayer's income tax liability and national insurance contributions if they were treated as self-employed in respect of the one-year contract. This was well answered, but many candidates produced extremely long answers for what should have been a simple set of workings. For example, the capital allowance was simply a 100% annual investment allowance on the purchase of a new asset and did not require a detailed capital allowances computation.

Part (c) required (1) an explanation why the taxpayer's income tax liability would be payable earlier if they were treated as being an employee instead of self-employed, and (2) a calculation of the additional amount of national insurance contributions which would be suffered. As regards the payment aspect, most candidates just referred to PAYE without any further relevant detail. Very few appreciated that the due date under the self-employed basis was simply 31 January following the tax year - payments on account not being required because the previous year's tax liability was collected under PAYE.

ACCA marking scheme			Marks
(a)		The contract is for a long period of time	0.5
		Required to do the work personally	0.5
		Xpee exercises control over George	0.5
		George won't incur significant expenses	0.5
		Only working for Xpee	0.5
		No financial risk	0.5
			———
		Maximum	2.0
			———
(b)		**Treated as self employed**	
		Contract fee	0.5
		Capital allowances	1.0
		Personal allowance	0.5
		Income tax	0.5
		Class 2	0.5
		Class 4	1.0
			———
			4.0
			———
(c)	(1)	If employed – PAYE	1.0
		Self- employed 31 January 2021	1.0
	(2)	Class 1 employee	1.5
		Additional NIC	0.5
			———
			4.0
			———
		Total	**10.0**
			———

105 SOPHIA WONG (ADAPTED) *Walk in the footsteps of a top tutor*

Key answer tips

Part (a) is a relatively straightforward comparison of the tax cost of trading as either a sole trader or through a company.

The cost of trading as a sole trader is given in the question so detailed calculations are in fact only required for the cost of extracting profits from a company as either remuneration or dividends. The examining team provide a lot of guidance in the question; giving figures for the amount of salary and dividends to use in the calculations and telling you the calculations that are required in the notes to the requirement. So if you follow the instructions carefully the calculations are relatively easy.

Part (b) covered a topic that is no longer in the syllabus and has therefore been replaced with a new topic.

Tutor's top tips

Make sure you set out your answer clearly and logically, using headings so it is clear which calculations relate to each scenario.

In part (1) consider the implications, for both Sophia of receiving employment income and for the company of paying remuneration. Likewise in part (2) consider the implications for both parties of paying a dividend. Consider what tax consequences there may be, such as:

Is the payment tax deductible for the company?

Is it subject to NIC?

For each part work through the calculations specified in the notes to the requirements. And don't forget to summarise the total costs for each alternative and conclude on whether it is more or less than the cost of being self-employed – there are easy marks to be gained here.

(a)   (1)   Profits withdrawn as director's remuneration

- Employer's class 1 NIC will be = (£80,000 – £71,346) = £8,654

Tutorial note

If all of the profits of £80,000 are withdrawn as director's remuneration (including the employer's class 1 NIC) and the gross remuneration is £71,346 (per the question) then the employer's class 1 NIC must be the difference of £8,654.

The examining team has taken this 'short cut' approach, however if you were unsure of this approach you could prepare the usual NIC calculation as follows:

(£71,346 – £8,632) × 13.8% = £8,654

The £3,000 NIC employment allowance is not available as Sophia is a director and the sole employee of the company.

- Sophia's income tax liability for the tax year 2019/20 will be:

	£
Director's remuneration	71,346
Less: PA	(12,500)
Taxable income	58,846

Income tax	£	
37,500 × 20%		7,500
21,346 × 40%		8,538
58,846		
Income tax liability		16,038

- Sophia's employee class 1 NIC for the tax year 2019/20 will be as follows:

	£
(£50,000 – £8,632) × 12%	4,964
(£71,346 – £50,000) × 2%	427
	5,391

- There is no corporation tax liability for the new company as the profits are entirely withdrawn as director's remuneration.

- The total tax and NIC cost if all of the new company's profits are withdrawn as director's remuneration is as follows:

	£
Employer's NIC	8,654
Sophia's income tax	16,038
Sophia's employee NIC	5,391
	30,083

This is more than the cost on a self-employed basis.

(2) Profits withdrawn as dividends

- There will be no class 1 NIC.

- The corporation tax liability of the new company for the year ended 5 April 2020 will be £15,200 (£80,000 – £64,800).

Tutorial note

If all of the profits of £80,000 are withdrawn as dividends (after allowing for corporation tax) and the dividends are £64,800 (per the question) then the corporation tax liability must be the difference of £15,200.

The examining team has taken this 'short cut' approach, however if you were unsure of this approach you could prepare the usual corporation tax calculation as follows:

(£80,000 × 19%) = £15,200.

Remember that dividends are not tax deductible.

- The income tax liability of Sophia for the tax year 2019/20 will be:

	£
Dividends	64,800
Less: PA	(12,500)
Taxable income	52,300

Income tax

£		£
2,000 × 0%		0
35,500 × 7.5%		2,662
14,800 × 32.5%		4,810
52,300		
Income tax liability		7,472

Tutorial note

The first £2,000 of dividend income is taxed at 0%. This uses the basic and higher rate bands.

- The total tax and NIC cost if all of the new company's profits are withdrawn as dividends are as follows:

	£
Corporation tax	15,200
Sophia's income tax	7,472
	22,672

This is £1,307 (£23,979 – £22,672) less than the cost on a self-employed basis.

(b) **(1)** **Sophia Wong**

Capital gains tax liability – 2019/20

	Not qualifying for ER	Qualifying for ER
	£	£
Qualifying for entrepreneurs' relief (Note 1)		
Sale of business: Goodwill (£150,000 – £0)		150,000
Not qualifying for entrepreneurs' relief		
Necklace	12,053	
	———	———
Chargeable gains	12,053	150,000
Less: Annual exempt amount (Note 2)	(12,000)	(0)
	———	———
Taxable gains	53	150,000
	———	———

	£
Capital gains tax liability	
Qualifying for ER (£150,000 × 10%)	15,000
Not qualifying for ER (£53 × 20%) (Note 3)	11
	———
	15,011
	———

(2) **Election**

An election for entrepreneurs' relief must be submitted by 31 January 2022. (i.e. within 12 months of the 31 January following the tax year in which the disposal is made).

Tutorial note

(1) *Where an individual sells the whole or part of a business which they have owned for at least two years they can elect for entrepreneurs' relief to apply such that the net chargeable gains (up to a lifetime maximum of £10 million) arising on the disposal are taxed at a lower rate of 10%.*

(2) *The annual exempt amount is set against the chargeable gain from the sale of the necklace as it does not qualify for entrepreneurs' relief and therefore this saves CGT at the higher rate of 20% rather than 10%.*

(3) *The gains qualifying for entrepreneurs' relief have to be taxed first and they utilise the remaining BR band, therefore the gain on the necklace is taxed at 20%.*

Examiner's report

Part (a) as a whole was very badly answered, often as a result of being attempted last with inadequate time remaining. Many students did not seem to notice that they had been given some of the information (employer's NIC when withdrawing profits as director's remuneration, and corporation tax when withdrawing profits as dividends) and wasted time trying to calculate the figures themselves.

As regards withdrawing profits as director's remuneration, very few candidates appreciated that there would be no taxable profit and hence no corporation tax liability. As regards withdrawing profits as dividends, far too many candidates did not appreciate that no NIC would be payable. Some candidates even attempted to answer this section with just one calculation combining the director's remuneration and dividend, and very few marks were available with this approach.

Part (b) has been replaced with a new question as the original topic is no longer in the syllabus. So the examiner's comments for this part are not relevant.

ACCA marking scheme			Marks
(a)	(1)	Profits withdrawn as director's remuneration	
		Employer's class 1 NIC	1.0
		Sophia's income tax liability	
		Personal allowance	0.5
		Tax at 20%	0.5
		Tax at 40%	0.5
		Sophia's employee class 1 NIC	1.5
		No corporation tax liability	1.0
		Summary of cost and conclusion	1.0
			–––
			6.0
			–––
	(2)	Profits withdrawn as dividends	
		No class 1 NIC	0.5
		Corporation tax liability	1.0
		Sophia's income tax payable	
		Personal allowance	0.5
		Tax at 0%	0.5
		Tax at 7.5%	1.0
		Tax at 32.5%	0.5
		Summary of cost and conclusion	1.0
			–––
			5.0
			–––
(b)	(1)	Gain on goodwill	0.5
		Gain on necklace - not qualifying for ER	0.5
		Annual exempt amount offset against gain on necklace	1.0
		CGT calculation	1.0
			–––
			3.0
			–––
	(2)	Date of entrepreneurs' relief election	1.0
			–––
Total			**15.0**
			–––

106 FERGUS *Walk in the footsteps of a top tutor*

Key answer tips

This question guides you through comparing whether a particular individual should remain self-employed or incorporate his business and be employed by his own company.

Note that no marks are available for considering issues other than the relevant taxes mentioned in the requirement. The notes at the end of the requirement give clear guidance on which taxes you need to calculate.

Make sure you follow the guidance given and give a clear conclusion that follows from your calculations.

Tutor's top tips

When asked to compare two situations from a tax perspective it is sensible to present your answer in a summary table supported by workings.

	Self-employed	Incorporated
	£	£
Income tax payable by Fergus (W1)		6,850
Class 1 employee NICs – payable by Fergus (W2)		1,364
Class 1 employer's NICs – payable by the company (W2)		1,569
Corporation tax liability of the company (W3)		14,902
Total tax and NIC cost	32,379	24,685

Conclusion

If Fergus incorporated his business there would be an overall saving of tax and NIC of £7,694 (£32,379 – £24,685) compared with continuing on a self-employed basis.

Workings

(W1) Fergus – Income tax liability – 2019/20

	£
Director's remuneration	20,000
Dividends	40,000
Total income	60,000
Less: Personal allowance	(12,500)
Taxable income	47,500

Income tax

	£	£
7,500 × 20% (Non-savings)		1,500
2,000 × 0% (Dividends)		0
28,000 × 7.5% (Dividends)		2,100
37,500		
10,000 × 32.5% (Dividends)		3,250
47,500		
Income tax liability		6,850

(W2) National insurance contributions (NICs) – 2019/20

	£
Employee – class 1 employee (primary) NICs	
(£20,000 – £8,632) × 12%	1,364
Employer's – class 1 employer's (secondary) NICs	
(£20,000 – £8,632) × 13.8%	1,569
Less: Employment allowance (Note)	(0)
	1,569

Tutorial note

The employment allowance is not available in this scenario as Fergus is both a director and the sole employee of the company.

(W3) Corporation tax liability of the new limited company – year ended 5 April 2020

	£
Trading profit	100,000
Less: Director's remuneration	(20,000)
Employer's class 1 secondary NICs	(1,569)
Taxable total profits	78,431
Corporation tax × 19%	14,902

ACCA marking scheme	
	Marks
Income tax liability	
Director's remuneration	0.5
Dividend	0.5
PA	0.5
Income tax on non-savings income at 20%	0.5
Income tax on dividend income at 0%	0.5
Income tax on dividend income at 7.5%	0.5
Income tax on dividend income at 32.5%	0.5
NICs	
Employee class 1	1.5
Employer class 1	1.5
No deduction for employment allowance	0.5
Corporation tax	
Trading profit	0.5
Deduction of director's remuneration	0.5
Deduction or employer's class 1 national insurance	0.5
Corporation tax at 19%	0.5
Total tax and NIC cost	0.5
Conclusion	0.5

Total	**10.0**

107 DEMBE (ADAPTED)

Key answer tips

This question is a typical 'higher skills' question and may initially appear quite daunting as it requires you to consider a number of different taxes. However, each part is only for three or four marks, so does not require an extensive answer. If you are unsure how to answer any part make an attempt and move quickly on.

Part (a) required a good understanding of the tax relief available to an individual making contributions into a personal pension. You should familiarise yourself with the necessary adjustments and the calculations required.

Part (b) focussed on husband and wife tax planning in relation to capital gains tax. This was a fairly straightforward requirement involving the savings available as a result of using Dembe's spouse's annual exempt amount and remaining basic rate band.

Part (c) involved a basic death estate computation and some IHT planning. The availability and transfer of nil rate bands is regularly tested therefore this shouldn't have posed a problem.

(a)

		£
Extension of basic rate tax band		
£40,000 (£32,000 × 100/80) at 20%	(40% – 20%)	8,000
Reinstatement of personal allowance		
£12,500 at 40%		5,000
		————
Reduction in income tax liability		13,000
National insurance contributions (NICs)		0
		————
Total tax reduction		13,000
		————

Tutorial notes

1   *Before making the personal pension contribution, Dembe's adjusted net income of £130,000 exceeds £125,000, so no personal allowance is available. The personal pension contribution will reduce Dembe's adjusted net income to less than £100,000 (£130,000 – £40,000 = £90,000), so the personal allowance will be fully reinstated.*

2   *Pension contributions have no impact on NICs.*

(b)

	£	£
Disposal made by Dembe		
£67,000 at 28%		18,760
Disposal made by Kato		
£16,350 (£37,500 – £21,150) at 18%	2,943	
£36,650 (£65,000 – £12,000 – £16,350) at 28%	10,262	
	————	
		(13,205)
		————
Capital gains tax (CGT) saving		5,555
Additional legal fees		(2,000)
		————
Overall saving		3,555
		————

(c) On the first death, there will be no inheritance tax (IHT) liability because of the spouse exemption.

There will also be no IHT liability on second death because the couple's residence nil rate bands and nil rate bands will exceed the value of the combined chargeable estate:

	£
Combined chargeable estate	880,000
Residence nil rate bands (£150,000 × 2)	(300,000)
Nil rate bands (£325,000 × 2)	(650,000)
Chargeable at 40%	0

Even if IHT were payable (for example, if the value of the estate increases faster than the available nil rate bands), then there is no advantage to leaving assets to children on the first death. This is because unused nil rate bands can be transferred to the surviving spouse.

ACCA marking guide		Marks
(a)	Pension	4
(b)	Property	3
(c)	IHT	3
Total		**10**

108 FANG, HONG AND KANG *Walk in the footsteps of a top tutor*

Key answer tips

A question covering three different scenarios all concerned with self-employed individuals.

Part (a) is a straightforward question involving the opening year basis of assessment rules and the deductibility of pre-trading expenditure for an individual starting a business. The highlighted words in the written sections are key phrases that markers are looking for.

Part (b) involves an established trader who has incurred trading losses. This is not a difficult question but involves a number of loss offsets and therefore needs to be approached in a methodical manner.

Part (c) involves a partnership where one of the partners is retiring. This is a commonly tested scenario and should not have caused any difficulties.

(a)   **Fang**

(1)   **Assessments**

		£
2017/18	Actual (1 August 2017 to 5 April 2018) (£45,960 × 8/12)	30,640
2018/19	CYB (Year ended 31 July 2018)	45,960
2019/20	CYB (Year ended 31 July 2019)	39,360

In the tax year 2018/19 there are overlap profits of £30,640 (i.e. the eight-month period 1 August 2017 to 5 April 2018).

(2)   **Pre-trading expenditure**

- The trading expenditure will be treated as incurred on 1 August 2017 provided it was incurred within the previous seven years and would have been allowable if the trade had already commenced.

- The computer equipment which Fang already owned will be an addition for capital allowances purposes based on its market value at 1 August 2017.

(b)   **Hong**

Tutor's top tips

There is a lot of information in this relatively short question which can appear daunting so it is important to approach the question in a methodical manner.

You are asked to calculate taxable income, taxable gains and the amount of trading loss carried forward – so layout your pro formas and start by filling in the easy numbers.

Then consider the trading losses – dealing with the earliest loss first. You are told how to offset the loss for the year ended 5 April 2019 in the question so you do not need to decide how best to use the loss – just follow the instructions!

Taxable income – 2018/19

	£
Trading profit	29,700
Less: Loss relief b/f	(2,600)
	27,100
Property income	3,900
	31,000
Total income	31,000
Less: Loss relief – c/b from 2019/20	(31,000)
Net income	0
Less: Personal allowance	(wasted)
Taxable income	0

Taxable gain – 2018/19

	£
Chargeable gain	17,800
Less: Trading loss relief (W1)	(11,600)
	6,200
Less: Annual exempt amount (part wasted)	(6,200)
	0
Less: Capital loss b/f (Note)	(0)
Taxable gain	0

The trading loss carried forward is £3,200 (W2).

Tutorial note

Relief for trading losses against total income and net chargeable gains is 'all or nothing' (i.e. the relief cannot be restricted to preserve the PA for income tax or the AEA for CGT).

However, capital losses brought forward are offset after deducting the AEA. Therefore, in this case, capital losses brought forward would not be utilised and would be carried forward to set against future net chargeable gains.

Workings

(W1) Trading loss relief

The trading loss relief claim against the chargeable gain = Lower of:

- Chargeable gain less capital loss brought forward

  = (£17,800 – £6,200) = £11,600, and

- Trading loss remaining = (£45,800 – £31,000) = £14,800

  Therefore, can only offset £11,600 against gains

(W2) Loss memorandum

	£
Loss – 2017/18	2,600
Less: Set off against trading profits – 2018/19	(2,600)
Loss – 2019/20	45,800
Less: Carry back against 2018/19 income	(31,000)
Loss relief extended to capital gains in 2018/19 (W1)	(11,600)
Loss carried forward	3,200

Tutorial note

The loss brought forward from the tax year 2017/18 must be set against the first available trading profits in subsequent years (i.e. 2018/19). The loss is offset before losses arising in later years.

The loss arising in the tax year 2019/20 can be offset against total income in the tax year(s) 2018/19 and/or 2019/20. Once a claim has been made to offset the loss against the total income of a particular tax year (e.g. 2018/19) a claim can also be made to offset any remaining trading losses against chargeable gains of the same tax year.

(c)   **Kang, Ling and Ming**

Allocation of profits

	Total £	Kang £	Ling £	Ming £
Year ended 30 June 2018				
(£148,800 × 1/3)	148,800	49,600	49,600	49,600
Year ended 30 June 2019				
1 July 2018 to 31 October 2018				
(£136,800 × 4/12 × 1/3)	45,600	15,200	15,200	15,200
1 November 2018 to 30 June 2019				
(£136,800 × 8/12 × ½)	91,200	45,600	45,600	0
	136,800	60,800	60,800	15,200

Trading income assessments

	Kang £	Ling £	Ming £
2018/19			
Year ended 30 June 2018 – CYB	49,600	49,600	
Cessation rules:			
Year ended 30 June 2018			49,600
Period ended 31 October 2018			15,200
			64,800
Less: Relief for overlap profits			(29,400)
			35,400
2019/20			
Year ended 30 June 2019 – CYB	60,800	60,800	0

Tutorial note

The cessation rules apply to Ming for the tax year 2018/19 since she ceased to be a partner on 31 October 2018. Her basis period for the tax year 2018/19 runs from the end of the basis period for the tax year 2017/18 to the date of cessation (i.e. 1 July 2017 to 31 October 2018).

ACCA marking scheme			Marks
(a)	(1)	2017/18 assessment	1.0
		2018/19 assessment	0.5
		2019/20 assessment	0.5
		Overlap profits	1.0
			3.0
	(2)	Pre-trading revenue expenditure	1.0
		Addition for capital allowance purposes at MV	1.0
			2.0
(b)		Taxable income	
		Trading profit	0.5
		Less trading losses b/f	0.5
		Property business profit	0.5
		Less loss of 2019/20 against total income	0.5
		PA = £0	0.5
		Taxable gain	
		Chargeable gain less trading loss relief	0.5
		AEA	0.5
		Trading loss c/f	0.5
		Maximum loss relief against chargeable gain	1.0
			5.0
(c)		Allocation of profits	
		Year ended 30.6.18	0.5
		Year ended 30.6.19	1.5
		Assessments	
		2018/19 – year ended 30.6.18	0.5
		2018/19 – plus period ended 31.10.18 for Ming	1.0
		Ming overlap relief	1.0
		2019/20	0.5
			5.0
Total			**15.0**

109 NA STYLE (ADAPTED) *Walk in the footsteps of a top tutor*

Key answer tips

This question is a classic self-employed individual scenario, testing opening year's basis of assessment and the compilation of an income tax computation. There is also an element of self-assessment at the end.

The first part is relatively easy to score highly on.

Part (b) was straightforward provided the self-assessment rules had been learnt and applied to the information given.

Tutor's top tips

Remember to read the requirement carefully.

This question has clear mark allocations, which should be used to allocate the time spent on each section. You need to adopt a logical approach, using the requirements to break down the information and plan your answer.

The first part just requires the application of the opening year rules to figures given in the question. It is possible to score very well on this sort of question, which is not technically difficult, as long as you do not panic.

Be sure to explain your answer; clearly showing the tax year, basis of assessment and calculation so that method marks can be given even if the maths goes awry!

Don't forget to highlight the overlap profits as they are specifically asked for and will therefore earn a mark.

(a)   Assessable trading profits – first four tax years

Tax year	Basis of assessment	£
2016/17	Actual basis	
	(1 January 2017 to 5 April 2017)	
	(£25,200 × 3/6)	12,600
2017/18	First 12 months trading	
	(1 January 2017 to 31 December 2017)	
	£25,200 + (£27,600 × 6/12)	39,000
2018/19	Current year basis	
	(Year ended 30 June 2018)	27,600
2019/20	Current year basis	
	(Year ended 30 June 2019)	31,315

Overlap profits

Tax year	Profits taxed twice	£
2017/18	(1 January 2017 to 5 April 2017)	
	(£25,200 × 3/6)	12,600
2018/19	(1 July 2017 to 31 December 2017)	
	(£27,600 × 6/12)	13,800
		26,400

Tutorial note

The assessment for the second tax year (2017/18) is the first 12 months of trading as the accounting period ending in that year is less than 12 months long.

(b)   (1)   Income tax computation – 2019/20

Tutor's top tips

For part (b) a systematic approach is needed. Remember not to ignore exempt income, as credit is given for stating that it is exempt, even though you do NOT include the figure in your computation. Part (b)(2) goes on to require the balancing payment after taking account of payments on account (POAs) already paid, and then requires the POAs to be paid in the following year.

	£
Trading profit	31,315
Building society interest	700
Interest from ISA (exempt)	0
Interest from NS&I savings certificate (exempt)	0
Interest from government stocks	370
Dividends	5,200
Total income	37,585
Less: PA	(12,500)
Taxable income	25,085

Analysis of income (Note)

Dividends = £5,200;

Savings (£700 + £370) = £1,070;

Non-savings income (£31,315 – £12,500) = £18,815.

Income tax	£
£	
18,815 × 20% (non-savings income)	3,763
1,000 × 0% (savings income)	0
70 × 20% (savings income)	14
2,000 × 0% (dividend income)	0
3,200 × 7.5% (dividend income)	240
25,085	
Income tax payable	4,017

Tutorial note

There is nothing wrong in presenting your computation using one column for all sources of income (rather than different columns for non-savings, savings and dividend income) if you prefer.

However, you do need to be able to break down the taxable income into the different types of income, namely: dividends, savings and non-savings income, in order to apply the correct rates of tax to each type of income.

Basic rate taxpayers are entitled to a £1,000 nil rate band for savings income.

A £2,000 nil rate band is also available to all taxpayers for dividend income.

(2) **Tax payments**

- Na's balancing payment for the tax year 2019/20 due on 31 January 2021 is £817 (£4,017 – £3,200).

- Her payments on account for the tax year 2020/21 will be £2,009 and £2,008 (£4,017 × 50%). These will be due on 31 January 2021 and 31 July 2021.

Examiner's report

This question was very well answered, and there were many high scoring answers.

In part (a) some candidates lost marks because they did not show the relevant tax years in which profits were assessable.

As regards the balancing payment and payments on account, candidates were often not aware of the relevant dates.

Note: The examiner's report has been edited to remove comments on elements of the question that have been deleted due to changes to the examination format.

			ACCA marking scheme		
					Marks
(a)		2016/17			1.0
		2017/18	– Assessment		1.0
			– Overlap profits		1.0
		2018/19	– Assessment		1.0
			– Overlap profits		1.0
		2019/20	– Assessment		1.0
					———
					6.0
					———
(b)	(1)	Income tax computation			
		Trading profit			0.5
		Building society interest			0.5
		Individual savings account			0.5
		Interest from NS&I savings certificate			0.5
		Interest from government stocks			0.5
		Dividends			0.5
		Personal allowance			0.5
		Income tax			2.5
					———
					6.0
					———
	(2)	Tax payments			
		Balancing payment			1.5
		Payments on account			1.5
					———
					3.0
					———
Total					**15.0**
					———

110 ZHI (ADAPTED) *Walk in the footsteps of a top tutor*

Key answer tips

This question is a typical 'higher skills' question and may initially appear quite daunting as it requires you to consider a number of different taxes. However, each part is only for two or three marks, so does not require an extensive answer. If you are unsure how to answer a part make an attempt and move quickly on.

The common theme of all the parts is the amount of tax that can be saved by different courses of action. So make sure you focus on this and compare your revised computation to the original liability.

Ensure you look out for opportunities to 'work in the margin' as in part (d) where a full computation of the revised PAYE and NIC is not necessary. You could save considerable time in the examination by realising that you simply needed to calculate the tax on the bonus at the appropriate rate of tax/NIC depending on the taxpayer's circumstances i.e. basic rate or higher rate taxpayer.

(a) (1) The balancing payment for the tax year 2018/19 due on 31 January 2020 cannot be reduced.

(2) A claim can be made to reduce the payment on account for the tax year 2019/20 due on 31 January 2020 by £5,040:

	£
Current POA (£27,600 + £4,204) x 50%	15,902
Revised POA (£18,000 + £3,724) x 50%	(10,862)
Reduction	5,040

(b)

	£	£
Current CGT liability		12,860
Revised CGT liability		
Proceeds not reinvested (£210,000 – £164,000)	46,000	
Annual exempt amount	(12,000)	
	34,000	
CGT: £34,300 x 20%		(6,800)
Reduction		6,060

Tutorial note:

Equivalent marks will be awarded if the reduction is alternatively calculated as £30,000 (£76,000 – (£210,000 – £164,000)) at 20% = £6,000.

(c) (1) The basic tax point for goods is the date when they are made available to the customer, which in the case of Zhi's sale is 12 December 2019.

(2) An invoice date of 1 February 2020 will not affect this because the invoice will not have been issued within 14 days of the basic tax point.

(3) Zhi therefore cannot reduce the amount of VAT payable on 7 February 2020.

(d)

	£
First employee	
PAYE (£1,500 × 20%)	300
NIC:	
Employee (£1,500 × 12%)	180
Employer (£1,500 × 13·8%)	207
Second employee	
PAYE (£5,000 × 40%)	2,000
NIC:	
Employee (£5,000 × 2%)	100
Employer (£5,000 × 13·8%)	690
Reduction	3,477

The postponed PAYE and NICs of £3,477 will be payable one month later on 22 February 2020.

Examiner's report

Basic tax planning

Where a question is just for two or three marks, candidates should realise that long, detailed, computations or written answers are not expected.

Questions of this nature often require candidates to work at the margin. It is much easier (and quicker) to work out, for example, that the tax reduction if a higher rate taxpayer's income falls by £5,000 is £5,000 at 40% = £2,000, rather than producing full before and after tax computations.

If a tax figure is given as part of a question, then candidates gain nothing by then calculating this figure for themselves.

A suggested tax planning strategy might not necessarily be effective, and candidates need to have the courage to base their answer on this conclusion if led there based on the application of basic principles. In such situations, too many candidates want to answer the question that they wish had been set, rather than the one that has been set.

ACCA marking scheme		
		Marks
(a)	**Income tax and national insurance**	
	2018/19 balancing payment can't be reduced	0.5
	2019/20 payment on account reduction	1.5
		–––
		2.0
(b)	**Capital gains tax (CGT)**	
	Current CGT liability	0.5
	Proceeds not reinvested	1.0
	Annual exempt amount	1.0
	CGT @ 20%	0.5
		–––
		3.0
(c)	**Value added tax (VAT)**	
	Basic tax point	0.5
	Invoice raised after 14 days	1.0
	NO reduction possible	0.5
		–––
		2.0
(d)	**PAYE and NICs**	
	First employee:	
	PAYE	0.5
	Employee and employer's NIC	0.5
	Second employee:	
	PAYE	0.5
	Employee and employer's NIC	1.0
	Payment delayed by 1 month	0.5
		–––
		3.0
Total		10.0
		–––

111 TIM BURR (ADAPTED)   *Walk in the footsteps of a top tutor*

Key answer tips

A short, but complex question involving a new person joining a sole trader business part way through the accounting period and tax year, either as an employee or partner.

The employment NIC calculations were not straightforward as the annual thresholds need to be apportioned before they can be applied to the 4 months of earnings. In addition, the trading income assessments need to be very carefully calculated by allocating the partnership profits first, then applying the opening year rules.

The self-employment NIC calculations are however straightforward and should not cause difficulties.

Part (b)(2) requires figures brought forward from the previous part. However it is important to remember that full credit will still be given in this part even if the earlier part is calculated incorrectly.

(a) **National insurance – if Hazel is employed**

Class 1 – primary employee contributions – paid by Hazel

(£3,300 – £719 (W)) × 12% × 4 months = £1,239

Class 1 – secondary employer contributions – paid by Tim

(£3,300 – £719 (W)) × 13.8% × 4 months = £1,425

As Hazel is the only employee the employer's class 1 secondary liability will be fully covered by the £3,000 employment allowance reducing the class 1 employer's liability to £nil.

Working: Monthly earnings thresholds

Employee class 1 NIC

Primary earnings threshold (PET) = (£8,632 × 1/12) = £719

Upper earnings limit = (£50,000 × 1/12) = £4,167

Hazel's monthly earnings are £3,300 which falls in between these limits.

For each month that Hazel is employed, she is therefore liable to class 1 NICs at 12% on the excess over the PET.

Employer's class 1 NIC

Secondary earnings threshold (SET) = (£8,632 × 1/12) = £719

Tim, as Hazel's employer, is liable to class 1 NICs at 13.8% on the excess over the SET.

Hazel will be employed for 4 months of the tax year (December to March inclusive).

Tutor's top tips

Usually in the examination, for simplicity, NICs are calculated on an annual basis using the annual limits. In this question however the individual has only been employed for four months in the tax year. Accordingly, the annual limits need to be time apportioned.

This is because NICs are actually calculated on an earnings period basis. This means that if an individual is paid monthly, the monthly limits are used; if they are paid on a weekly basis, the weekly limits are used.

The examining team have confirmed that the alternative approach of using the annual earnings threshold and then taking 4/12ths of an annual NIC figure was acceptable in the examination.

(b) **(1)** **Trading income assessments**

Allocation of partnership profits

	Total £	Tim £	Hazel £
y/e 30.9.20			
1.10.19 to 30.11.19 (2 months)			
All profits to Tim	36,000	36,000	
1.12.19 to 30.09.20 (10 months)			
PSR (80%:20%)	180,000	144,000	36,000
	216,000	180,000	36,000
y/e 30.9.21			
PSR (80%:20%)	240,000	192,000	48,000

Applying basis of assessment rules

If Hazel joins the partnership on 1 December 2019, the opening year rules will apply to her profit share as follows:

Tax year	Basis of assessment	£	£
2019/20	Actual basis		
	(1.12.19 to 5.4.20)		
	(£36,000 × 4/10) (Note)		14,400
2020/21	First 12 months trading		
	(1.12.19 to 30.11.20)		
	10 m/e 30.9.20	36,000	
	y/e 30.9.21 × 2/12 (£48,000 × 2/12)	8,000	
			44,000

Tutorial note

The partnership profits should be allocated to the partners according to the partnership agreement in the accounting period.

The basis of assessment rules are then applied to each partner's share of profits separately.

Tim was a sole trader and becomes a partner. However he will continue to be assessed on a current year basis (CYB).

The commencement rules will apply to Hazel's share of profits for the tax year 2019/20 since she will join as a partner on 1 December 2019.

(2) **NICs – 2019/20**

Paid by Hazel – self employed

Class 2 NICs (Note 1) = (18 weeks × £3) = £54

Class 4 NICs (Note 2) = (£14,400 − £8,632) × 9% = £519

Paid by Tim

There are no NIC implications for Tim in relation to Hazel's trading income assessments (Note 3).

Tutorial note

(1) *Class 2 NICs are £3 per week. If Hazel joins the partnership on 1 December 2019, in the tax year 2019/20 she will be a partner for 126 days (31 + 31 + 28 + 31 + 5), which is 18 weeks (126 days ÷ 7).*

(2) *Class 4 NICs are calculated using the full annual lower profits limit, which is not time apportioned as the opening year rules produce an assessment for the full tax year 2019/20.*

This trading income assessment figure comes from the previous part. However, full credit would be given for this part even if the assessment was calculated incorrectly provided you calculated the NICs correctly based on your figure.

(3) *The question asks for the NICs to be paid by Tim, but only in relation to Hazel's trading income assessment. The question specifically states that his own NICs are not to be calculated.*

Examiner's report

In part (a) it was pleasing to see several candidates correctly restricted NIC contributions to the four months of employment.

Although there were also many good answers to part (b), there were also a lot of candidates who wasted time by doing NIC calculations for both the taxpayer and the new person, or NIC calculations for both years, instead of just the one required.

Note: *The examiner's report has been edited to remove comments on elements of the question that have been deleted due to changes to the examination format.*

ACCA marking scheme		Marks
(a)	Monthly earnings thresholds	1.0
	Employee class 1 NIC	1.0
	Employer's class 1 NIC	1.0
	Employment allowance reduces class 1 secondary to £0	1.0
		4.0
(b)	Trading income assessments	
	2019/20	1.5
	2020/21	2.5
		4.0
	NIC re Hazel	
	Class 2 NIC	0.5
	Class 4 NIC	1.0
	Tim	0.5
		2.0
Total		10.0

112 RICHARD FEAST (ADAPTED) *Walk in the footsteps of a top tutor*

Key answer tips

Part (a) is a fairly straightforward adjustment of trading profit computation, which should not have caused any problems.

Part (b) requires employer's NIC calculations for an employee. It was important to limit your answer to just the classes of NIC required.

Part (c) requires knowledge of basic self-assessment administration issues and should not have caused any problems. The highlighted words in the written sections are key phrases that markers are looking for.

(a)   Trading profit – year ended 5 April 2020

Tutor's top tips

This straightforward adjustment of profit computation is presented in a familiar format, with a statement of profit or loss followed by a number of notes.

As is common with this type of question you are instructed to start your computation with the net profit figure and list all items in the question, using a zero if no adjustment is necessary. Note that marks are available for correctly showing zero for a non-adjusting item, so do not lose easy marks by ignoring these items. Work methodically through the statement, referring to the notes where appropriate, and entering each item in your computation as you go.

Remember to adjust for private use by the proprietor, but not an employee.

	£
Net profit	32,200
Motor expenses – Richard (£4,710 × 70%)	3,297
Motor expenses – Chef	0
Parking fines	280
Property expenses (£16,200 × 1/5)	3,240
Decorating – Restaurant	0
– Apartment	1,320
Other expenses – Legal fees (capital)	2,590
	42,927
Less: Capital allowances (W)	(3,780)
Trading profit	39,147

Working: Capital allowances

	Main pool £	Private use car £	Business use %	Allowances £
Additions not qualifying for AIA:				
Private use car (51 – 110g/km)		14,000		
Car (51 – 110g/km)	16,800			
WDA (18%)		(2,520)	× 30%	756
WDA (18%)	(3,024)			3,024
TWDV c/f	13,776	11,480		
				3,780

Tutorial note

Both motor cars have CO_2 emissions between 51 and 110 grams per kilometre and therefore qualify for writing down allowances at the rate of 18%.

The private use of a motor car by an employee is irrelevant, since such usage will be assessed on the employee as a benefit.

(b)   Employer national insurance contributions

Tutor's top tips

This question only requires the calculation of the employer's NIC liabilities, so do not waste time calculating employee NICs.

Make sure that you clearly identify the different classes of NIC payable (i.e. class 1 and class 1A) and the different income on which they are charged.

	£	£
Employer's class 1 NIC		
(£46,000 – £8,632) × 13.8%	5,157	
Less: NIC employment allowance (Note)	(3,000)	
	———	2,157
Employer's class 1A NIC		
£4,032 (W1) × 13.8%		556
		———
Total NICs		2,713
		———

Tutorial note

As the chef is the only employee the employment allowance will be offset against the employer's class 1 NIC liability on his salary.

Workings

(W1) Car benefit

CO_2 emissions = 103g/km (rounded down to 100g/km) available for the full tax year

	%
Petrol	23
Plus: $(100 - 95) \times 1/5$	1
Appropriate percentage	24

List price (same as cost)	£16,800
Car benefit ($£16,800 \times 24\%$)	£4,032

(c) **Self-assessment**

- Unless the notice to file a return is issued late, the latest date that Richard can file a paper self-assessment tax return for the tax year 2019/20 is 31 October 2020.

- However, he has until 31 January 2021 to file his self-assessment tax return for the tax year 2019/20 online.

Compliance checks

- If HM Revenue and Customs intend to carry out a compliance check into Richard's 2019/20 tax return, they will have to notify him within 12 months of the date that they receive the return.

- HM Revenue and Customs have the right to carry out a compliance check as regards the completeness and accuracy of any return, and such a check may be made on a completely random basis.

- However, compliance checks are generally carried out because of a suspicion that income has been undeclared or because deductions have been incorrectly claimed. For example, where accounting ratios are out of line with industry norms.

			Marks
	ACCA marking scheme		
(a)	Motor expenses – Richard		1.0
	Motor expenses – Chef		0.5
	Parking fines		0.5
	Property expenses		1.0
	Decorating – Restaurant		0.5
	Decorating – Apartment		0.5
	Legal fees – Purchase of property		0.5
	Working – Capital allowances		
	– Private use (PU) car – in own column		0.5
	– Car 2 – in main pool		0.5
	WDA on PU car		1.0
	WDA on Car 2		0.5
			————
			7.0
			————
(b)	Employer's class 1 calculation		1.0
	Deducting employment allowance		0.5
	Class 1A calculation		0.5
	Car benefit calculation		1.0
			————
			3.0
			————
(c)	(i)	Paper return date	1.0
		Online return date	1.0
			————
			2.0
			————
	(ii)	Notify within 12 months of date received return	1.0
		Right to carry out compliance check on any return	1.0
		Generally carried out if suspicion of errors in return	1.0
			————
			3.0
			————
Total			**15.0**
			————

113   TONIE (ADAPTED)

Key answer tips

Part (a) tests the residence rules for individuals. The tax rates and allowances show the required number of ties based on the time spent in the UK. You could have passed this part of the question using this information.

Part (b) asks for four factors that indicate Tonie will be treated as employed, rather than self-employed. The requirement asks you to 'list' four factors so don't waste time providing unnecessary explanations.

Part (c) requires the calculation of taxable income. This is a standard requirement and you should be familiar with the various income and expenses included in this calculation.

(a) Tonie was previously resident and was in the UK between 46 and 90 days. She therefore needed three UK ties or more to be treated as UK resident.

Tonie only had two UK ties, which were being in the UK for more than 90 days during the previous tax year, and spending more time in the UK than in any other country during 2018/19.

(b) The contract was for a relatively long period of time.

Tonie did not take any financial risk.

Tonie only worked for Droid plc.

Tonie was required to do the work personally.

Droid plc exercised control over Tonie via the weekly meetings and instructions.

(c) **Tonie – Taxable income 2019/20**

	£
Employment income	
Salary (£6,200 × 12)	74,400
Mileage allowance (2,300 at 15p (60p – 45p))	345
Leasing costs (£180 × 12)	(2,160)
Property income (W)	8,620
Savings income (£100,000 at 3% × 5/12)	1,250
Premium bond prize	0
Interest from savings certificate	0
	82,455
Personal allowance	(12,500)
Taxable income	69,955

Tutorial note

Under the accrued income scheme, Tonie must include the accrued interest from the gilts as savings income for 2019/20, even though she has not received any actual interest.

Working – Property income

	£
Rent received	10,080
Mortgage interest (£4,200 × 25%)	(1,050)
Replacement furniture relief	
Washing machine	(380)
Dishwasher	0
Other expenses	(1,110)
	7,540
Furnished room (£8,580 – £7,500)	1,080
Property income	8,620

Tutorial notes

1   *No relief is given for that part of the cost of the washer-dryer that represents an improvement over the original washing machine. Relief is therefore restricted to the cost of a similar washing machine.*

2   *No relief is available for the cost of the dishwasher because this is an initial cost rather than the cost of a replacement.*

3   *Claiming rent-a-room relief in respect of the furnished room is more beneficial than the normal basis of assessment (£8,580 – £870 = £7,710).*

ACCA marking guide		
		Marks
(a)	Residence	2.0
(b)	Factors	2.0
(c)	Employment	2.5
	Other income	3.0
	Property	4.0
	Room	1.0
	PA	0.5
		11.0
Total		**15.0**

114 DANH *Walk in the footsteps of a top tutor*

Key answer tips

Part (a) tests the residence rules for individuals. The tax rates and allowances show the required number of ties based on the time spent in the UK. You could have passed this part of the question using this information. The highlighted words in the answer are key phrases that markers are looking for.

Part (b) has a straightforward computation of income tax including a classic adjustment of profit section. The qualifying interest and share of the partnership loss are not popular topics but it was possible to achieve a pass in the question without knowledge of these areas.

(a)   2017/18

Danh was not resident in the UK. Danh was permitted two UK ties because he was in the UK between 91 and 120 days and was not resident in the UK during the three previous tax years. Danh only had two UK ties, which were having a house in the UK (which was made use of) and doing substantive work in the UK.

2018/19

Danh was resident in the UK. Danh had three UK ties for this year because he was also in the UK for more than 90 days during the previous tax year.

(b)   Danh – Income tax computation 2019/20

	£
Trading profit (W1)	73,176
Property income (W2)	11,670

Total income	84,846
Interest paid	(875)
Partnership loss (£12,600 × 7/12 × 20%)	(1,470)
Net income	----------
	82,501
Personal allowance	(12,500)

Taxable income	70,001

	£
37,500 × 20% (non-savings income)	7,500
32,501 × 40% (non-savings income)	13,000
70,001	
Interest relief (£5,000 × 75%) × 20%	(750)
Income tax liability	19,750

Workings

(W1) Trading profit for the eight-month period ended 5 April 2020

	£
Net profit	70,200
Depreciation	2,300
Motor expenses (£3,300 × 4,000/12,000)	1,100
Accountancy	0
Legal fees in connection with the grant of a new lease	1,460
Use of office (£4,200 × 1/6)	(700)
Capital allowances (£14,800 × 18% × 8/12 × 8,000/12,000)	(1,184)
Trading profit	73,176

(W2) Property income

	£
Rent received	14,400
Allowable mortgage interest paid (£5,000 × 25%) (Note)	(1,250)
Other expenses paid	(1,480)
	11,670

Tutorial note

The deduction from property income for interest paid is restricted to 25% in the tax year 2019/20. The remaining 75% of interest paid is restricted to basic rate relief by way of a deduction from the income tax liability.

Examiner's report

Part (a) for 3 marks required candidates to explain whether Danh was treated as resident or not resident in the UK for two tax years. This section was reasonably well answered although a number of candidates did not appreciate that there would be one additional UK tie for the second tax year. This is often the case where a question covers two tax years since for the second year a taxpayer will have the additional UK tie of being in the UK for more than 90 days during the previous tax year.

Where a question makes it clear that that the tests of automatic residence and automatic non-residence are not relevant, then there is nothing to be gained from explaining why this is the case. It should have been quite obvious from reading the question that only residence based on UK ties needed to be considered. The three marks available for this section was a good indication as to the length of answer required.

Part (b) for 12 marks required candidates to calculate Danh's income tax liability. This section was very well answered, and there were many perfect responses. However, the following points should be noted when answering this style of question:

– Candidates should think carefully about which workings can be included as one-line calculations within the main computation and which need their own separate working. For example, the partnership loss calculation of £12,600 x 7/12 x 20% = 1,470 was easily included within the main computation which would have saved candidates time. Similarly, as Danh acquired only one asset a single line working for capital allowances is acceptable and saves time in the examination. The only aspects which warranted separate workings here were the trading profit and property income.

– As mentioned above, the calculation for the partnership loss was fairly straightforward. There was no need to work out the loss allocations for the other partners and such workings simply used valuable time.

– Practice as many computations as possible. If this is done, basic mistakes such as applying the motor car benefit rules rather than claiming capital allowances should be avoided.

– As stated in the requirements, candidates should always clearly indicate (by the use of a zero) any items which do not require adjustment – the accountancy fees were deductible when calculating the trading profit, but this needed to be indicated.

– With computations containing both additions and deductions, candidates should be very careful to indicate which is which. A single column approach with deductions shown in brackets should avoid any confusion.

– Candidates need to appreciate that each source of income is self-contained. It is not technically correct to show all the receipts from each source first (such as rent receivable), and then the various deductions shown later in the main computation (such as property income deductions). With a separate working for property income, just the one figure for property income should then be included in the main taxable income computation.

ACCA marking scheme		
		Marks
(a)		
	Conclude non-resident and identify two UK ties in 2017/18	2.0
	Resident due to three ties in 2018/19	1.0
		———
		3.0
		———
(b)	Trading profit:	
	Depreciation	0.5
	Private motor expenses	1.0
	Accountancy	0.5
	Legal fees	0.5
	Use of office	1.0
	Capital allowances	2.0
	Property income:	
	Rent receivable	0.5
	Mortgage interest	1.0
	Other expenses	0.5
	Interest paid	0.5
	Partnership loss	1.5
	PA	0.5
	Income tax	1.0
	Deduction of 75% interest at basic rate	1.0
		———
		12.0
		———
Total		**15.0**
		———

TRADING LOSSES

115 NORMA (ADAPTED)

Key answer tips

The first part required the computation of taxable income for five tax years before considering loss relief. Marks should have been gained here in laying out pro forma computations and filling in the easy numbers before applying the opening and closing year rules to establish the trading income assessments. A loss arises in the final tax year and so the trading income assessment in that year is £0.

The second part involved consideration of the options available for loss relief, including a terminal loss.

It is important to communicate to the examining team that you know the loss relief rules; however you must apply the knowledge to the specific facts of the question.

The highlighted words in the written sections are key phrases that markers are looking for.

(a) Taxable income and gains before loss relief

	2015/16 £	2016/17 £	2017/18 £	2018/19 £	2019/20 £
Trading income (W)	27,750	27,000	16,900	9,835	0
Employment income (£11,400 × 10/12)					9,500
Interest income	3,250	3,250	3,250	3,250	3,250
Total income	31,000	30,250	20,150	13,085	12,750
Less: PA	(12,500)	(12,500)	(12,500)	(12,500)	(12,500)
Taxable income	18,500	17,750	7,650	585	250
Taxable gain				38,000	

Working: Trading income

Tax year	Basis of assessment	£	£
2015/16	Actual basis (1.5.15 – 5.4.16)		
	Period to 31.12.15	21,000	
	1.1.16 – 5.4.16 (£27,000 × 3/12)	6,750	
			27,750
2016/17	Year ended 31.12.16		27,000
2017/18	Year ended 31.12.17		16,900
2018/19	Year ended 31.12.18		9,835
2019/20	Year of cessation		
	Period to 31 May 2019	(11,000)	
	Less: Overlap profits (1.1.16 – 5.4.16)		
	(£27,000 × 3/12)	(6,750)	
	Trading loss/Trading assessment	(17,750)	0

Tutorial note

If the trader does not have a 31 March (or 5 April) year end you should be looking for overlap profits.

The overlap profits increase the loss of the final tax year and is included in the calculation of the terminal loss.

(b) **Options available to utilise trading loss**

(1) **Relief against total income**

The loss arising in the tax year 2019/20 can be set against total income in the same and/or previous tax year, in either order.

(1) Setting the loss against total income of the tax year 2019/20 first (i.e. employment income and bank interest) would reduce total income to £0, would waste the personal allowance and save no tax (see Tutorial Note).

The remaining loss of £5,000 (£17,750 – £12,750) could be offset against total income of the tax year 2018/19, wasting part of the personal allowance and saving no tax (see Tutorial Note).

(2) Setting the loss against total income of the tax year 2018/19 first would reduce total income to £0, would waste the personal allowance and save no tax.

The remaining loss of £4,665 (£17,750 – £13,085) could be offset against total income of the tax year 2019/20, which would waste part of the personal allowance and save no tax.

Tutorial note

The rate of tax saving when offsetting the loss against total income is 0% because Norma's taxable income is savings income which will fall into the first £5,000 of taxable income in those years.

(2) **Relief against chargeable gains**

Alternatively, once a claim has been made to offset trading losses against total income in the tax year 2018/19, a claim can be made to offset any remaining losses against chargeable gains in the same tax year.

Accordingly, the £4,665 loss remaining after the offset against total income in the tax year 2018/19 could be set against the chargeable gain arising in June 2018, which will save tax at 10% on some of the gain and 20% on the remaining gain (see Tutorial Note).

Tutorial note

Currently, before loss relief, there is £36,915 (£37,500 – £585) of gain in the basic rate band and £1,085 (£38,000 – £36,915) in the higher rate band.

So using £4,665 of loss against the gain would save 20% on the top £1,085 of the gain, and 10% on £3,580 (£4,665 – £1,085).

(3) **Terminal loss relief**

The loss arising in the final 12 months of trading can be set against:

* available trading profits

* in the tax year of cessation, and

* the three preceding tax years

* on a last-in-first-out (LIFO) basis.

Calculation of terminal loss

				£
(1)	6 April before cessation to date of cessation (6.4.19 – 31.5.19) (£11,000 loss × 2/5)			4,400

(2) 12 months before cessation to 5 April before cessation

	£	
1.6.18 – 31.12.18 (£9,835 profit × 7/12)	5,737	Profit
1.1.18 – 5.4.18 (£11,000 loss × 3/5)	(6,600)	Loss
	(863)	Net Loss

		863

(3)	Overlap profits 1.1.16 – 5.4.16 (£27,000 × 3/12)	6,750
	Terminal loss	12,013

Utilisation of terminal loss

Norma has no trading profits in the tax year of cessation.

The terminal loss can therefore be carried back against the trading profits arising in the preceding three years, on a LIFO basis, as follows:

	2016/17 £	2017/18 £	2018/19 £
Trading income	27,000	16,900	9,835
Less: Terminal loss relief	(0)	(2,178)	(9,835)
	27,000	14,722	0
Interest income	3,250	3,250	3,250
Net income	30,250	17,972	3,250
Less: PA	(12,500)	(12,500)	(12,500)
Taxable income	17,750	5,472	0

The terminal loss reduces taxable income in the tax year 2018/19 to £0, wasting part of the personal allowance and saving no tax.

The remaining loss of £2,178 (£12,013 – £9,835) is then offset against the trading income in the tax year 2017/18, saving tax at 20% on £2,178 (£7,650 – £5,472).

116 ASHURA (ADAPTED) *Walk in the footsteps of a top tutor*

Key answer tips

This question covers the situation where an individual is employed then also sets up a business, which is initially loss making. This type of scenario is common in examination questions.

Part (a) should have provided easy marks for stating the advantages of a 5 April year end.

The calculation of the loss in part (b) was straightforward provided you remembered to time apportion the writing down allowance in the opening period of account.

(a) (1) The application of the basis period rules is more straightforward.

(2) There will be no overlap profits.

(3) The basis period in the year of cessation will be a maximum of 12 months in length, rather than the potential 23 months that could arise with a 30 April year end.

(b) **Ashura – Trading loss for the nine-month period ended 5 April 2020**

	£
Draft tax adjusted trading loss	(1,996)
Use of office (£4,350 × 1/5)	(870)
Capital allowances (W)	(2,859)
Advertising	(800)
	———
Tax adjusted trading loss	(6,525)
	———

Working – Capital allowances

		Main pool	Private use car		Allowances
	£	£	£		£
Additions (no AIA)					
Car (>110g/km)			19,200		
Additions (with AIA)					
Laptop computer	2,600				
AIA – 100%	(2,600)				2,600
	———	0			
WDA – 6% × 9/12 (Note)			(864)	× 30%	259
		———	———		———
TWDV c/f		0	18,336		2859
		———	———		———

Tutorial notes

(1) Ashura's motor car has CO_2 emissions over 110 grams per kilometre, and therefore only qualifies for writing down allowances at the rate of 6%. The business mileage is 2,400 out of 8,000 miles (i.e. 30%).

(2) The laptop computer purchased on 10 June 2019 is pre-trading capital expenditure, and is therefore treated as incurred on 1 July 2019.

(c) (1) The trading loss would be relieved against total income for the tax years 2016/17 to 2018/19, using the income of the earliest year first.

(2) Ashura's total income for the tax year 2016/17 of £10,400 is already covered by her personal allowance so a loss relief claim against this year would use the entire loss but would not result in any tax saving.

(d) **Ashura – Taxable income 2019/20**

	£
Employment income	
Salary	56,200
Mileage allowance (3,400 × 10p (55p – 45p))	340
Pension contributions – Occupational (£56,200 × 5%)	(2,810)
– Personal pension	0
Subscriptions – Professional	(320)
– Health club	0
Total income	53,410
Loss relief	(6,525)
Net income	46,885
Personal allowance	(12,500)
Taxable income	34,385

Tutorial notes

(1) The personal pension scheme contribution does not affect the calculation of taxable income, but will instead extend Ashura's basic rate tax band by £3,400.

(2) The health club subscription is not an allowable deduction because membership is not necessary for Ashura to carry out her duties of employment.

(3) The loss relief cap does not apply because Ashura's trading loss is less than the greater of £50,000 and 25% of her total income.

Examiner's report

This was the income tax question. It was well answered, and involved a taxpayer who was employed and had also commenced self-employment during the tax year (making a trading loss).

For part (a), the requirement was to state two advantages of the taxpayer choosing 5 April as an accounting date rather than a date early in the tax year such as 30 April. There were three obvious advantages, and many candidates correctly explained that the application of the basis period rules is more straightforward and that there will be no overlap profits. Less well prepared candidates instead covered the advantages of a 30 April accounting date, so not surprisingly did not achieve high marks.

Part (b) has been significantly altered so the examiner's comments for this question are not relevant.

For part (c), candidates had to explain why it was not beneficial for the taxpayer to claim loss relief under the provisions giving relief to a loss incurred in the early years of trade. It should have been fairly obvious that such a claim would have wasted the personal allowance and not resulted in any tax saving. This section was not as well answered, with many candidates not appreciating that the loss could only be carried back for three years. Some candidates actually explained why a claim would be beneficial.

Part (d) required a calculation of the taxpayer's taxable income (on the basis that loss relief was claimed against total income). This section was generally well answered, although many candidates wasted time by calculating the tax liability. The occupational pension scheme contribution was often grossed up (such contributions are not paid net of tax). Many candidates made things more difficult than they needed to be by attempting this section before section (b).

ACCA marking scheme		Marks
(a) **Advantages of basis period**		
Basis periods more straightforward		1.0
No overlap profits		1.0
Shorter basis period in final tax year		1.0
		3.0
	Maximum	2.0
(b) **Trading loss**		
Advertising expenditure deducted		1.0
Use of office deducted		1.0
Capital allowances deducted		0.5
Laptop included in main pool		0.5
AIA offset against laptop		1.0
Car in separate column		0.5
WDA on car		1.5
		6.0
(c) **Early year loss relief**		
Relieved against 2016/17 – 2018/19 total income FIFO		1.0
2016/17 income covered by PA therefore no tax saving		1.0
		2.0

ACCA marking scheme		
(d)	**Taxable income**	
	Salary	0.5
	Mileage	1.0
	Pension	1.0
	Subscriptions	1.0
	Loss	1.0
	Personal allowance	0.5
		———
		5.0
		———
Total		**15.0**
		———

117 DEE ZYNE (ADAPTED) *Walk in the footsteps of a top tutor*

Key answer tips

An individual that is employed for part of the tax year, then sets up a business which is initially loss-making, is a common scenario in examination questions.

The calculation of the adjusted loss was straightforward provided you remembered to time apportion WDAs in the opening period of account.

Part (b) required consideration of alternative claims for Dee's trading loss, which is a common requirement in loss relief questions and you should therefore make sure that you are well prepared for this.

The highlighted words in the written sections are key phrases that markers are looking for.

Tutor's top tips

In this question, Dee has 5 April as her year end, so the capital allowances are calculated for the period ended 5 April 2020.

However, where a sole trader chooses a different year end, remember that the capital allowances are always calculated for the period of account before matching profits or losses to tax years.

(a)   Tax adjusted trading loss – 2019/20

	£
Trading loss	(11,653)
Patent royalties (Note)	(500)
Capital allowances (W)	(5,477)
	———
	(17,630)
	———

Tutorial note

The patent royalties were incurred for trade purposes and are therefore deductible in computing the tax adjusted trading loss. As the question says they have not been accounted for in arriving at the loss given in the question, they must be adjusted for and will increase the loss.

Working: Capital allowances	Main Pool	PU car	Allowances
	£	£	£	£
Additions (no AIA)				
Car (between 51 – 110g/km)		10,400		
Car (> 110g/km) (Note 1)			17,800	
Additions (with AIA)				
Computer	1,257			
Office furniture	2,175			
	———			
	3,432			
AIA (Note 2)	(3,432)			3,432
	———	0		
WDA (18% × 9/12)		(1,404)		1,404
WDA (6% × 9/12) (Note 3)			(801) ×80%	641
		———	———	
TWDV c/f		8,996	16,999	
		———	———	———
Total allowances				5,477
				———

Tutorial note

(1) Capital allowances on purchases of cars are calculated based on their CO_2 emissions.

The car with CO_2 emissions of between 51 – 110g/km is put in the main pool and is eligible for a writing down allowance at 18%.

The car with CO_2 emissions of > 110g/km is a private use car, has its own column and is eligible for a writing down allowance at 6%.

(2) The maximum AIA and the WDAs are time apportioned because Dee's period of account is only nine months' in length. However, the maximum AIA clearly exceeds the total qualifying expenditure so all of the expenditure is eligible for relief.

(3) Only private use by the owner restricts capital allowances. Private use of the employee's motor car therefore does not affect the capital allowance claim, but will instead result in an assessable employment benefit for that employee.

(b)   Alternative uses of trading loss

Tutor's top tips

When you are describing use of losses, you must be very specific about exactly what the loss can be set against, and when. For example, don't just say 'the loss can be set off in the current year'. Specify in which tax year that is, and state that the loss can be set against total income.

The examining team have stated that the use of section numbers is not required and is not encouraged at the expense of explaining the relief.

- The loss could have been claimed against total income for the tax year(s) 2018/19 and/or 2019/20.

- By claiming loss relief against her total income (£29,875) for the tax year 2019/20, Dee has relieved the loss entirely at the basic rate of 20% and reduced her income tax liability by £3,526 (£17,630 × 20%).

- If the loss is carried back to the tax year 2018/19 when Dee's total income was £80,000, Dee could relieve the loss entirely at the higher rate of 40% and reduced her income tax liability by £7,052 (£17,630 × 40%).

- The loss is incurred within the first four tax years of trading, so a claim for special opening year loss relief could have been made against total income for the three tax years 2016/17 to 2018/19, earliest first.

- As Dee's total income in the tax years 2016/17 to 2018/19 was £80,000, this would also have relieved the loss at the higher rate of 40%, and resulted in an income tax refund of £7,052 (£17,630 × 40%).

118   SAMANTHA FABRIQUE (ADAPTED)   *Walk in the footsteps of a top tutor*

Key answer tips

This is a losses question that requires you to choose the best use of the loss.

Given the information about gains it should be fairly obvious that you need to consider a claim against capital gains. However, remember that this only saves tax at 10% or 20% (for a higher rate taxpayer) and can only happen after a claim against total income has been made first in the same tax year.

Be careful to consider the loss relief restriction which applies to loss claims against total income other than the profits of the same trade. This restriction did not apply in the question as originally set, as these rules did not exist then.

Part (a) should have provided easy marks listing the factors a taxpayer takes into account when deciding what to do with a loss.

(a)   **Factors influencing choice of loss relief claims**

- The rate of income tax or capital gains tax at which relief will be obtained, with preference being given to income charged at the higher rate of 40% or additional rate of 45%.

- The timing of the relief obtained, with a claim against total income/chargeable gains of the current tax year or preceding tax year resulting in earlier relief than a claim against future trading profits.

- The extent to which personal allowances, the capital gains annual exempt amount and the savings and dividend nil rate bands may be wasted.

Tutor's top tips

As long as you addressed the factors influencing the choice of relief, not what the relief options are, you should have scored well here.

(b)   **Taxable income**

	2018/19 £	2019/20 £	2020/21 £
Trading income	21,600	0	11,650
Interest	52,100	3,800	1,850
	73,700	3,800	13,500
Less: Loss relief		(0)	
– against trading (no restriction)	(21,600)		
– against other income (restricted)	(50,000)		
	2,100	3,800	13,500
Less: PA	(restricted)	(restricted)	(12,500)
Taxable income	0	0	1,000

Taxable gains

	2018/19 £	2019/20 £	2020/21 £
Chargeable gains	53,300	0	12,200
Less: Trading loss relief	(10,300)		
	43,000	0	12,200
Less: AEA	(12,000)	(wasted)	(12,000)
	31,000	0	200
Less: Capital loss b/f			(200)
Taxable gains	31,000	0	0

Tutorial note

The loss relief in the previous tax year against total income is restricted due to the cap on income tax reliefs. The losses offset against profits from the same trade are not restricted; therefore £21,600 of loss can be set against trading income. A further £50,000 of loss relief is available as this is the higher of £50,000 and 25% of total income (£73,700 × 25% = £18,425).

Although these two claims are both set off against total income in the computation, you may find it helpful to separate them out to ensure you relieve the correct amount of loss.

Key answer tips

Where loss questions require you to set off a loss against income and gains, make sure that you keep your income tax computation and CGT computation **separate**.

This is not only technically correct, but will also make it easier for you to see where best to set off the losses and apply your PA and AEA, and much easier for the marker to mark your answer!

The highlighted words are key words or phrases that markers are looking for.

Loss memorandum

	£
Trading loss in the tax year 2019/20	81,900
Less: Relief against total income	
current year (no claim as income covered by PA)	(0)
prior year – total claim	(71,600)
Loss remaining	10,300
Less: Relief against chargeable gains in prior year	(10,300)
Loss carried forward	0

Utilisation of losses

Trading loss

Loss relief has been claimed:

- against total income for the tax year 2018/19,

- then against the chargeable gains of the same tax year.

This gives relief at the earliest date and at the highest rates of tax.

Capital loss

The capital loss for the tax year 2019/20 is carried forward and set against the chargeable gains for the following tax year.

The use of brought forward capital losses is after the annual exempt amount, which avoids wasting any of the annual exempt amount.

The balance of the loss £3,200 (£3,400 – £200) is carried forward against future gains.

Tutorial note

For the tax year 2018/19, if relief is claimed, the personal allowance is partially wasted in that year and the tax saving will be at 40% and 20% for income tax and 20% for capital gains.

Offsetting losses in the tax year 2019/20 however would utilise £3,800 of the loss, would waste the personal allowance and would not save any tax.

A claim against total income must be made before relief against chargeable gains can be considered.

Carrying all of the loss forward would use £11,650 of the loss in the tax year 2020/21 (as could only carry forward against future trading profits from the same trade), would waste most of the personal allowance and would save no tax.

The taxable income (before loss relief) of £1,000 represents savings income. All of the savings income falls in the nil rate starting rate band of £5,000 so no tax would be saved. The remaining loss would not be relieved until subsequent years.

The optimum relief is therefore to claim against total income for the tax year 2018/19, then against the chargeable gains of the same tax year, since this gives relief at the earliest date and at the highest rates of tax.

Examiner's report

This question was generally not answered well.

Although it was technically the most demanding question in the exam, requiring a bit more thought than the other four questions, it was quite short and should not have presented too many difficulties for reasonably well prepared candidates.

In part (a) many candidates explained the loss reliefs that were available rather than the factors that must be taken into account when deciding which loss reliefs to actually claim.

In part (b) it was extremely disappointing to see the vast majority of candidates include the capital gains in their computation of taxable income. The capital gains annual exempt amount was often then deducted against the combined figure of taxable income and taxable gains.

Many candidates claimed loss relief against the total income for the year of the loss despite this income clearly being covered by the personal allowance.

Very few candidates, even if they showed the capital gains separately, claimed loss relief against capital gains.

	ACCA marking scheme		
			Marks
(a)	Rate of tax		1.0
	Timing of relief		1.0
	Personal allowance, annual exempt amount, nil rate bands		1.0
			——
			3.0
			——
(b)	Trading income		0.5
	Building society interest		0.5
	Loss relief against total income		2.0
	Personal allowance		0.5
	Capital gains		1.5
	Loss relief against capital gains		1.0
	Capital loss carried forward		1.0
	Explanation of most beneficial route		5.0
			——
			12.0
			——
Total			**15.0**
			——

119 MICHAEL AND SEAN *Walk in the footsteps of a top tutor*

Key answer tips

Part (a) offered four easy marks to identify the reliefs available for individual savings accounts, pensions, gift aid, entrepreneurs' relief and capital allowances.

Part (b) was tricky and the hardest part of the whole examination. It involved opening and closing year losses.

Consideration of the optimum use of the losses was required together with the identification of the rates at which tax would be saved. A good knowledge of the loss relief rules and a lot of practice at application prior to sitting the examination was needed to score well on this part in the time given.

In order to score well in part (b) computations alone showing the different loss reliefs were not enough; explanations of how the reliefs work and advice on the most beneficial course of action were also needed.

The highlighted words are key words or phrases that markers are looking for.

Tutor's top tips

When you need to explain how tax policies can encourage individuals to take certain actions, always think about how those actions can save tax for the individual.

By opening an ISA, individuals can save income tax on the interest.

By saving money in a pension fund, individuals can save income tax by either reducing their employment income or extending their basic and higher rate bands.

By donating money to a charity, the individual can save income tax by either reducing their employment income (payroll deduction scheme) or extending their basic and higher rate bands (gift aid donations).

When the sole trader buys plant and machinery he gets capital allowances that reduce trading profits saving income tax.

(a) **Government tax policies**

(1) **Individuals to save**

Saving is encouraged by offering individuals tax incentives such as tax-free individual savings accounts (ISAs) and tax relief on pension contributions. In addition, the savings income nil rate bands encourage basic and higher rate taxpayers to save by providing tax free savings income.

(2) **Individuals to support charities**

Charitable support is encouraged by giving individuals tax relief on donations made through the gift aid scheme or the payroll deduction scheme.

(3) **Entrepreneurs to build businesses and invest in plant and machinery**

Entrepreneurs are encouraged to build their own businesses through various capital gains tax reliefs such as entrepreneurs' relief.

Investment in plant and machinery is encouraged through capital allowances.

(b) **Michael**

Tutor's top tips

It is difficult to comment on loss relief by just reading the scenario. Set up the income tax computations for each tax year involved, bringing in the figures given in the question.

This will give a clear picture of the position and will help to decide on the appropriate reliefs for the loss. It will also make it easier to comment on the tax savings and possible wastage of the personal allowance.

Loss relief available

(1) Special opening year loss relief

The loss of £24,600 arising in the tax year 2018/19 (W1) can be claimed against total income for the three preceding tax years, earliest first, since it is incurred in the first four tax years of trading.

Amount of loss claim

The loss relief claim will therefore be £17,200 in the tax year 2015/16 and £7,400 (£24,600 – £17,200) in the tax year 2016/17.

Tax saving

For the tax year 2015/16 this will waste Michael's personal allowance, with the balance of the claim of £4,700 (£17,200 – £12,500) (W2) saving income tax at the basic rate of 20%.

For the tax year 2016/17 Michael has income of £1,000 (£51,000 – £12,500 – £37,500) subject to income tax at the higher rate of 40%, so the claim of £7,400 will save tax at the higher rate on the first £1,000. The remaining £6,400 will save tax at 20%.

(2) Carry loss forward

Alternatively, Michael could have carried the trading loss forward against future trading profits, but the trading profit of £7,100 for the tax year 2019/20 is less than the personal allowance, and therefore no tax is saved in that year. There is no information available regarding future trading profits.

Most beneficial

Claim special opening year loss relief.

Tutorial note

A standard loss relief claim against total income in the tax year of the loss (2018/19) and/or the preceding tax year (2017/18) is not possible since Michael does not have any income for either of these years.

Special opening year loss relief is one claim for all three years (if there is sufficient loss) on a FIFO basis, it is not possible to only claim in one year, and it is an 'all or nothing relief' (i.e. cannot restrict the offset to preserve the personal allowance).

Note that the limit on the amount of loss relief that can be deducted from other income in any tax year does not need to be considered in this question, as the loss is not sufficiently high for it to be an issue.

Workings

(W1) Opening year assessments

	£
2018/19 – Actual basis	
1.7.18 – 5.4.19 Loss of £24,600	0
2019/20 – Current year basis	
Year ended 5.4.20	7,100

(W2) Taxable income (ignoring loss relief)

	2015/16 £	2016/17 £	2017/18 £	2018/19 £	2019/20 £
Employment income	17,200	51,000	0	0	0
Trading income				0	7,100
Less: PA	(12,500)	(12,500)	0	0	(restricted)
Taxable income	4,700	38,500	0	0	0
Basic rate band		(37,500)			
Taxed at higher rate		1,000			

The loss carried back is offset against income before the personal allowance is deducted. This means that £12,500 of the loss each year does not actually save tax as it merely replaces the personal allowance. This working enables you to see how much of the loss actually saves tax and at what rate.

Sean

Amount of the loss

The unused overlap profits brought forward are added to the loss for the year ended 31 December 2019, so the total loss for the tax year 2019/20 is £26,700 (£23,100 + £3,600).

Loss relief available

(1) Terminal loss relief

The whole of the loss can be claimed as a terminal loss since it is for the final 12 months of trading.

The claim is against trading income for the tax year of the loss and the three preceding tax years, latest first.

Amount of loss claim

The terminal loss claim will therefore be £3,700 in the tax year 2018/19, £18,900 in 2017/18 and £4,100 (£26,700 − £3,700 − £18,900) in the tax year 2016/17.

Tax saving

The property business profits are sufficient to utilise Sean's personal allowance for each year, so the loss relief claims will save income tax at the basic rate of 20%.

(2) Standard loss relief against total income

Alternatively, Sean could have initially claimed loss relief against his total income for the tax year(s) 2019/20 and/or 2018/19, but this would have wasted his personal allowance for either or both of those years.

Most beneficial

Claim terminal loss relief.

Tutorial note

A claim against future trading profits is not available since the business is ceasing and a trading loss can only be carried forward against future trading profits of the same trade.

A terminal loss claim is against trading profits only, on a LIFO basis, and is an 'all or nothing' relief (i.e. cannot restrict the offset to preserve the personal allowance).

The terminal loss is the loss of the last 12 months of trading. It is normally calculated as follows:

	£
6 April before cessation to the date of cessation	
Actual trading loss in this period (£23,100 × 9/12)	*17,325*
Overlap profits not yet relieved	*3,600*
12 months before cessation to 5 April before cessation	
Actual trading loss in this period (£23,100 × 3/12)	*5,775*
Terminal loss	*26,700*

However when the final period of account is 12 months long it is unnecessary to prepare this detailed working and it is acceptable to take the examining team's approach of simply adding the unused overlap profits to the trading loss for the final 12 month period.

Examiner's report

Part (a) was generally well answered, although candidates should note that where just one or two marks are available for a requirement then just a short sentence is required – not a detailed explanation.

Not surprisingly, part (b) was the section of the exam that caused the most problems.

For Michael, the claims should have been fairly straightforward given that he only had one source of income for each year. However, some candidates were not even aware that a claim could be made against total income.

For Sean, a few candidates suggested that the loss be carried forward despite the trade ceasing. In both cases, it was generally not appreciated that the most advantageous choice of loss relief claims would generally preserve the benefit of personal allowances.

ACCA marking scheme			
			Marks
(a)	(i)	Saving	1.0
	(ii)	Charitable support	1.0
	(iii)	Build businesses: CGT reliefs	1.0
		Plant and machinery: CAs	1.0
			———
			4.0
			———
(b)	**Michael**		
	Relief against total income – opening year loss relief		1.0
	Amount of loss claims		1.0
	Rate of tax saved – 2015/16		1.0
	– 2016/17		1.0
	Carry forward		1.0
	Sean		
	Available loss		1.0
	Terminal loss relief		1.0
	Amount of loss claim		1.0
	Rate of tax saved		1.5
	Relief against total income		1.5
			———
			11.0
			———
Total			**15.0**
			———

PARTNERSHIPS

120   PETER, QUINTON AND ROGER (ADAPTED)   *Walk in the footsteps of a top tutor*

Key answer tips

A loss making partnership presents a tricky problem and it is important to approach the computation in part (b) with care.

Firstly, profits/(losses) need to be allocated to each partner and then the opening year rules applied for each partner according to the date they joined the firm.

There are many loss relief options available. A brief mention of each is all you have time for in the examination. Be careful not to go into too much detail and there is no need to discuss the relative merits of each option in this question.

It is much better to mention all the reliefs available and applicable to the question succinctly than to talk about any one relief in great detail.

The highlighted words are key words or phrases that markers are looking for.

(a)   Basis of assessment – Joining partners

- Each partner is treated as a sole trader running a business.

- The commencement rules therefore apply when a partner joins the partnership, with the first year of assessment being on an actual basis (i.e. date of commencement to the following 5 April).

(b) **Trading income assessments**

	Peter	Quinton	Roger
	£	£	£
2016/17			
Peter and Quinton			
Actual basis (1 January 2017 to 5 April 2017)			
(£40,000 × 1/2 × 3/12)	5,000	5,000	
	——	——	
2017/18			
Peter and Quinton			
CYB (y/e 31 December 2017)			
(£40,000 × 1/2)	20,000	20,000	
	——	——	
Roger			
Actual basis (1 January 2018 to 5 April 2018)			
(£90,000 × 1/3 × 3/12)			7,500
			——
2018/19			
All partners – CYB (y/e 31 December 2018)			
(£90,000 × 1/3)	30,000	30,000	30,000
	——	——	——

Tutorial note

The commencement rules apply to:

- *Peter and Quinton from the tax year 2016/17, as the partnership started on 1 January 2017.*

- *Roger from the tax year 2017/18, since he joined as a partner on 1 January 2018.*

(c) **Possible methods of relieving trading loss for the tax year 2019/20**

- Peter, Quinton and Roger each have a tax adjusted trading loss of £10,000 (£30,000 × 1/3) for the tax year 2019/20.

- Peter resigned as a partner on 31 December 2019. His unrelieved overlap profits of £5,000 (1 January 2017 to 5 April 2017) will therefore increase his loss to £15,000 (£10,000 + £5,000).

- **Carry forward relief:**

  Quinton and Roger can carry their share of the loss forward against their first available future trading profits arising in the same trade.

- **Relief against total income:**

  Peter, Quinton and Roger can claim relief against their total income for the tax year(s) 2019/20 and/or 2018/19.

- **Special opening year loss relief:**

  Peter, Quinton and Roger can carry back their share of the loss against their total income for the tax year(s) 2016/17 to 2018/19, earliest year first.

- **Terminal loss relief:**

  Peter can carry back his share of the loss of the last 12 months trading against his trading profits for the tax year 2018/19.

  He has insufficient losses to carry back the loss any further. If he had more losses, he could carry back the loss and make a claim in respect of the tax years 2017/18 and 2016/17, in that order.

Tutor's top tips

The requirement is to 'State the possible ways to relieve the losses'. Therefore there will be no marks for discussing in detail the relative merits of each claim and which would be the most beneficial.

Remember that it is much better to mention all the reliefs available and applicable to the question succinctly than to talk about any one relief in great detail.

121 AE, BEE, CAE, AND DEE (ADAPTED) *Walk in the footsteps of a top tutor*

Key answer tips

This question tests the basis of assessment rules, but with the application of the rules to partnerships, and includes the opening year rules and overlap profits.

A well prepared student should have been able to secure good marks on this question and each part is independent.

Part (b) of this question has been amended due to syllabus changes.

The highlighted words are key words or phrases that markers are looking for.

Tutor's top tips

Part (a) deals with both the partnership profit sharing rules together with straightforward opening year rules. Opening year rules can be tricky, but are commonly tested so you should make sure that you are prepared for a question on this topic.

(a) **Ae, Bee & Cae**

Tax year	Basis of assessment	Ae £	Bee £	Cae £
2017/18	Actual basis 1 July 2017 to 5 April 2018 £54,000 × 9/12 × 1/2	20,250	20,250	
2018/19	CYB (y/e 30 June 2018) £54,000 × 1/2	27,000	27,000	
2019/20	CYB (y/e 30 June 2019) £66,000 × 1/2	33,000	33,000	
	Actual basis 1 July 2019 to 5 April 2020 £87,000 × 9/12 × 1/3			21,750

Tutorial note

The commencement rules apply for Ae & Bee in the tax year 2017/18 and for Cae in the tax year 2019/20, as these are the tax years in which each partner started to trade.

In the case of Cae, the fact that the partnership had been trading in the years before is not relevant.

(b) **(1)** **Dee – Relief for losses**

Key answer tips

Part (b) has been rewritten due to syllabus changes since the question was originally set. It now tests the new cap on loss reliefs against total income and loss reliefs in a partnership.

Dee can claim relief against her total income in the tax year 2019/20 (the year of the loss), and/or the tax year 2018/19 (the previous tax year). As she has no trading profits in either year, any loss relief will be claimed against other income and the cap on income tax reliefs will apply. The maximum claim is therefore £50,000 in each year as this is greater than 25% of Dee's adjusted total income of £85,000 (i.e. 25% × £85,000 = £21,250). The remaining loss must then be carried forward for relief against her share of any future trading profit from the partnership.

It is likely that she will obtain relief for some of the carried forward loss in the tax year 2021/22 when she anticipates that the business will become profitable again. The fact that the business will then be a partnership does not prevent the future loss relief.

Loss memorandum

	£
Loss in 2019/20	165,000
Less: Relief against total income	
2019/20 (maximum)	(50,000)
2018/19 (maximum)	(50,000)
Carried forward against future trading profits	65,000

Tutorial note

It is assumed that the £5,000 loss for the tax year 2018/19 has been carried back to the tax year 2017/18 and set off against the savings income in that year.

Tutor's top tips

Since the question asked you to 'explain' the loss reliefs available, it is important to write narrative describing the loss reliefs as well as calculating the amount of loss relief that will be claimed.

---

(2)   Eae – relief for losses

Eae will be entitled to claim relief for her share of the partnership's trading loss in the year ended 5 April 2021 as follows.

- The loss could be claimed against total income for 2020/21 (the tax year of the loss) and/or 2019/20 (the previous tax year).

- Since Eae has just joined the partnership, the loss is incurred within the first four tax years of trading from her perspective; therefore a claim for special opening year loss relief could be made against total income for the three tax years 2017/18 to 2019/20, starting with the earliest first.

Tutorial note

Since the question refers to a 'small' loss, it can be assumed that the cap on income tax reliefs is not relevant in this part.

Examiner's report

This question was extremely well answered by the majority of candidates, many of whom scored maximum marks.

One of the main problems in the answers of poorer candidates was not showing the appropriate tax years, thus losing a lot of marks throughout.

Note: The final part of the examiner's report is not included here as it referred to the original part (b) which is no longer examinable following syllabus changes.

ACCA marking scheme				
				Marks
(a)		Ae, Bee & Cae – 2017/18		1.5
		– 2018/19		1.0
		– 2019/20 Ae & Bee		1.0
		– 2019/20 Cae		1.5
				–––––
				5.0
				–––––
(b)	(i)	Dee	– 2019/20 claim	1.0
			– 2018/19 claim	1.0
			– loss carried forward	1.0
	(ii)	Eae	– total income claim	1.0
			– opening years relief	1.0
				–––––
				5.0
Total				**10.0**
				–––––

122 AUY MAN AND BIM MEN (ADAPTED) *Walk in the footsteps of a top tutor*

Key answer tips

This question was unusual in that the scenario was a partnership. However, this should not have caused concern as there were many easy marks to be gained.

Part (a) may have caused some problems if the definition of residence status had not been learnt, however it was only worth 2 marks. The rules regarding the definition of residence have been amended since this question was set and are now more complicated.

Parts (b) and (c) involved preparing familiar adjustment of profits and capital allowances computations, followed by a straightforward allocation of profits between the partners and class 4 NIC calculations.

The highlighted words are key words or phrases that markers are looking for.

Tutor's top tips

Remember to read the requirement carefully.

This question has clear mark allocations, which should be used to allocate the time spent on each section. Don't overrun on parts which carry only a few marks.

The first part required the application of the residence status rules. Note that just stating the rules would not have gained full marks. You must apply the knowledge to the facts of the specific individuals.

(a)   Residence status

- Auy will be treated as resident in the United Kingdom (UK) for the tax year 2019/20 as she was present in the UK for 190 days and therefore she meets the first automatic UK residency test (i.e. in the UK for at least 183 days in the tax year).

- Bim will be treated as resident in the UK for the tax year 2019/20 as she was previously resident in the UK, was present here for between 91 and 120 days and she meets two of the sufficient ties tests.

    She has a home in the UK which she makes use of for 100 days during the tax year (the 'accommodation' test) and she has spent 90 days or more in the UK during both of the previous tax years (the 'days in UK' test).

Tutorial note

When considering residence it is important to approach a question systematically.

*You should firstly consider whether the individual meets one of the automatic non-residence tests. However, it is clear that these are not relevant here as the examining team has told you in the question that both individuals **are** resident in the UK.*

Secondly, you should consider whether the individual meets one of the automatic residence tests. This is the case for Auy in this question.

Finally, if neither of the automatic tests are applicable, you should consider how many days the individual has spent in the UK, whether they were resident in the UK within the previous three tax years, and how many of the sufficient ties tests are met. The table showing the number of ties which must be met is provided in the examination.

These rules are now more complex than they were when this question was originally set.

(b)   Tax adjusted trading profit – year ended 5 April 2020

Tutor's top tips

Part (b) gives you clear guidance on the approach that is needed for an adjustment of profits, and you should follow this – starting with the net profit and then making the necessary adjustments.

Work through the notes and the plant and machinery information in order. Ensure you have dealt with every single item, and shown, as stated in the requirement, nil in the profits adjustment where an adjustment is not necessary, as marks are given for this.

If you are not sure how to deal with an item, make a sensible assumption and move on, but do not ignore it, or waste unnecessary time.

Note that as the question has asked you to 'calculate' the adjusted profits you do not need to explain each adjustment that you make, but you should show any workings.

	£	£
Net profit	87,780	
Depreciation	3,400	
Entertaining employees (Note 1)	0	
Appropriation of profit (Note 2)	4,000	
Capital allowances (W)		12,938
	95,180	12,938
	(12,938)	
Tax adjusted trading profit	82,242	

Tutorial note

(1)   The only exception to the non-deductibility of entertainment expenditure is when it is in respect of employees.

(2)   Salaries paid to a partner are not allowable. They merely represent an agreed form of allocation of the partnership profits in the partnership agreement. Appropriations of profit (i.e. drawings such as partner's salaries) need to be added back to profit.

Allocation of profits – year ended 5 April 20120

Tutor's top tips

Once the tax adjusted trading profit of the partnership has been calculated, it must be allocated between the partners in accordance with the partnership agreement in force in the accounting period.

Note that full marks can be obtained for this part in showing clearly how you have allocated the amounts; even if your tax adjusted trading profit figure from part (a) is incorrect.

	Total	Auy Man	Bim Men
	£	£	£
Salary	4,000		4,000
Interest (£56,000/£34,000 at 5%)	4,500	2,800	1,700
Balance (80%/20%)	73,742	58,994	14,748
	82,242	61,794	20,448

Trading income assessments – tax year 2019/20

	£
Auy Man	61,794
Bim Man	20,448

Tutorial note

The profit share for each partner must now be assessed in the correct tax year. The basis of assessment rules need to be applied to determine in which tax year the profits are assessed.

However, in this question the partnership has a 5 April year end and therefore the rule is simple: the actual profits for the year ended 5 April 2020 will be assessed in the tax year 2019/20.

Working – Capital allowances

Tutor's top tips

A standard capital allowances computation is required; however it is slightly unusual in that the only transactions in the year involve cars. There are no other additions and therefore there is no AIA.

The rules for cars need to be known in detail and applied carefully here. Each of the cars has a different CO_2 emissions rate so these need to be considered carefully to determine the correct available capital allowances. Also watch out for 'private use' adjustments.

		Main pool	Motor car (1)	Special rate pool		Allowances
	£	£	£	£		£
TWDV b/f			3,100	21,000		
Additions (no AIA)						
Motor car (3)			14,200			
Motor car (4)				11,600		
			17,300	21,000	11,600	
WDA (18%)			(3,114)			3,114
WDA (6%)				(1,260)	× 80%	1,008
WDA (6%)				(696)		696
Addition (with FYA)						
Motor car (2)		10,150				
FYA (100%)		(10,150)			× 80%	8,120
		0				
TWDV c/f			14,186	19,740	10,904	
Total allowances						12,938

Tutorial note

(1)   *Capital allowances on car purchases are calculated based on the CO_2 emissions of the car as follows:*

  —   *New car with CO_2 emissions of ≤ 50g/km:*
      eligible for a FYA of 100% (i.e. Motor car (2))

  —   *CO_2 emissions of between 51 – 110g/km:*
      put in main pool and eligible for a WDA at 18% (i.e. Motor car (3))

  —   *CO_2 emissions of > 110g/km:*
      put in special rate pool and eligible for a WDA at 6% (i.e. Motor car (4))

However, cars with an element of private use by a partner (i.e. owner of the business) are given a separate column and only the business use percentage of the allowances can be claimed.

Note that motor car (2) is a depooled asset as it has private use by the owner of the business. In practice it should be given a separate column and carried forward at a tax written down value of £0. When it is sold it will result in a balancing charge, but only the business proportion will be taxed.

(2)   *Motor car (1), which was owned at the beginning of the year, has CO_2 emissions of > 110g/km and is therefore eligible for a WDA at 6%. This must then be adjusted for private use.*

(c)   Class 4 national insurance contributions – 2019/20

Tutor's top tips

Straightforward computations are required for this part.

Remember that full marks can be obtained for this part, even if your allocation of profit to the partners is incorrect, provided that you use the partners' profit allocations which you have calculated in part (b) as the basis of your national insurance calculations. Just make sure that you clearly show the method of calculation.

Auy Man

	£
(£50,000 – £8,632) × 9%	3,723
(£61,794 – £50,000) × 2%	236
	3,959

Bim Men

(£20,448 – £8,632) × 9%	1,063

ACCA marking scheme		
		Marks
(a)	Auy Man	1.0
	Bim Men	1.0
		2.0
(b)	**Trading profit**	
	Depreciation	0.5
	Entertaining employees	0.5
	Appropriation of profit	0.5
	Deduction of capital allowances	0.5
	Capital allowances – Main pool	1.0
	– Motor car (1)	1.5
	– Special rate pool	1.5
	– FYA	1.5
	Trading income assessments	
	Salary	0.5
	Interest on capital	1.0
	Balance of profits	1.0
		10.0
(c)	Auy Man	2.0
	Bim Men	1.0
		3.0
Total		**15.0**

123 DANIEL, FRANCINE AND GREGOR *Walk in the footsteps of a top tutor*

Key answer tips

This question comprises three separate parts, each related to a different area of income tax.

Part (a) tests the popular examination topic of basis periods.

Part (b) tests the calculation of a beneficial loan benefit. Employment benefits are a good opportunity for some easy marks, but care must be taken here as the loan is made part way through a tax year and the loan is not interest free.

Part (c) tests trading losses and you should think carefully before beginning to answer. The requirement asks you to calculate the remaining loss to carry forward and not net income after loss relief, as you may have been expecting.

Tutor's top tips

This question is made up of three separate scenarios which could be attempted in any order.

One strategy is to attempt the parts that you are most confident with first, ensuring you stick to the appropriate time allocation. Then use the remaining time for the question to attempt any parts that you are less confident about.

(a)   **Daniel – Trading income assessment 2019/20**

	£
1 May 2019 to 31 October 2019	
(£96,000 × 1/4 × 6/12)	12,000
1 November 2019 to 5 April 2020	
(£180,000 × 1/4 × 5/12)	18,750
	———
	30,750
	———

Tutorial note

Daniel joined as a partner on 1 May 2019, so the commencement rules apply to him for the tax year 2019/20. The basis period is the 11 month period from 1 May 2019 to 5 April 2020 (using the actual basis).

(b) **Francine – Beneficial loan**

	£	£
Average method		
Loan on 1 August 2019		96,000
Loan at end of 2019/20 tax year		110,000
		206,000
Average loan (£206,000 ÷ 2)		103,000
Taxable benefit (£103,000 × 2.5% × 8/12)		1,717
Less: Interest paid (£96,000 × 1.5% × 2/12)	240	
(£110,000 × 1.5% × 6/12)	825	
		(1,065)
Taxable benefit		652

Tutor's top tips

It is specifically stated in the question that the beneficial loan benefit should be calculated using the average method. It is important to follow this instruction as calculating an alternative benefit using the precise method will not score marks and will waste time that you could use elsewhere.

(c) **Gregor – Loss memorandum**

	£
Loss – 2019/20	68,800
Loss: Set off against total income 2018/19 (W1)	(20,600)
Loss: Set off against total income 2019/20 (W1)	(900)
Loss: Extended to chargeable gains 2019/20 (W2)	(14,500)
Loss carried forward	32,800

Workings

(W1) Income tax computations

	2018/19	2019/20
	£	£
Trading income	14,700	0
Property income	4,600	0
Interest income	1,300	900
Total income	20,600	900
Less: Loss relief – current year		(900)
– prior year	(20,600)	
Net income	0	0

Tutorial note

The property loss of £2,300 in the tax year 2019/20 is carried forward against future property income. It cannot be offset against 2019/20 total income nor carried back against any income from the tax year 2018/19.

(W2) Trading loss relief against chargeable gains

The trading loss relief claim against the chargeable gain = Lower of:

• Chargeable gain less capital loss brought forward

= (£17,400 – £2,900) = £14,500, and

• Trading loss remaining = (£68,800 – £20,600 – £900) = £47,300

Therefore the maximum loss that can be offset against chargeable gains is £14,500.

Tutorial note

Gregor wishes to relieve his trading loss of £68,800 as early as possible so after a claim against total income is made in 2019/20, a claim against capital gains is made. The loss relief claim against the chargeable gain is restricted by the capital loss brought forward from 2018/19.

ACCA marking scheme		
		Marks
(a)	**Daniel – Trading income assessment 2019/20**	
	1 May 2019 to 31 October 2019	1.5
	1 November 2019 to 5 April 2020	1.5
		3.0
(b)	**Francine – Beneficial loan 2019/20**	
	Interest at official rate (average method)	1.5
	Interest actually paid	1.5
		3.0
(c)	**Gregor – Trading loss carried forward**	
	2018/19 – claim against total income	1.0
	2019/20 – claim against total income	1.0
	2019/20 – claim against chargeable gains	1.5
	Loss carried forward	0.5
		4.0
Total		**10.0**

PENSIONS AND NIC

124 JOHN BEACH (ADAPTED) *Walk in the footsteps of a top tutor*

Key answer tips

Part (a) required the computation of the income tax liability of an employed individual with several employment benefits and both an occupational and personal pension scheme.

Straightforward marks were available for calculating the employment benefits. The pension scheme contributions were a little trickier and required knowledge of how tax relief is obtained for both types of contribution and the operation of the annual allowance, including tapering of the allowance for high earners.

The NIC computations in part (b) were relatively straightforward provided the key facts about national insurance contributions had been learnt.

Tutor's top tips

For part (a) a systematic approach is needed, taking one note at a time, and therefore breaking up the information given into smaller, manageable chunks.

Make the marker your friend, if you keep your calculations clear and easy to read you will score much higher marks. Always ensure your workings are clearly labelled.

(a)   Income tax computation – 2019/20

	£
Director's remuneration	144,000
Mileage allowance (W1)	1,425
	145,425
Occupational pension contributions (Note 1)	(28,000)
	117,425
Beneficial loan (W2)	530
Long service award (gold watch) – exempt	0
Total income = Net income	117,955
Less: PA (W4)	(3,784)
Taxable income	114,171

Income tax	£
£	
38,023 × 20% (W5)	7,605
76,148 × 40%	30,459
114,171	
Income tax liability	38,064

Tutorial notes

(1)   Tax relief for contributions to occupational pension schemes is given by deduction from employment income. Contributions made by an employer are an exempt employment benefit.

(2)   Long service awards are exempt where there has been at least 20 years of service by the employee and where the cost is £50 or less for each year of service.

(3)   The personal allowance is restricted as John's ANI exceeds the limit of £100,000 (see W4).

Workings

(W1) Mileage allowance

	£
Amount received by John (5,960 miles × 60p)	3,576
Less: Approved mileage allowance (4,270 + 510) × 45p	(2,151)
Taxable benefit	1,425

Tutorial note

Travel between home and office is ordinary commuting which does not qualify for tax relief.

(W2) Beneficial loan

John repaid £24,000 (£12,000 + £12,000) of the loan during the tax year so the outstanding balance at 5 April 2020 is £60,000 (£84,000 – £24,000).

Tutor's top tips

The question states that the average method is used to calculate the taxable benefit, so do not waste time also preparing calculations using the precise (or accurate) method which will score no marks.

The benefit calculated using the average method is:

	£
((£84,000 + £60,000) ÷ 2) × 2.5%	1,800
Less: Interest paid	(1,270)
Taxable benefit	530

(W3) Personal pension contributions

Tutor's top tips

You must compare the amount of personal pension contributions paid by John in the tax year with the available annual allowance. Read the question carefully as this provides some hints on how to approach the calculation.

Remember that ALL contributions count towards the available annual allowance. Once you have calculated the available annual allowance for the tax year 2019/20, you will need to consider the unused allowances from the three prior tax years.

The annual allowance for the tax year 2019/20 is subject to tapering as John's adjusted income (net income plus employee's occupational pension contributions and employer's contributions) of £117,955 + £28,000 + £11,000 = £156,955 is above the income limit of £150,000.

	£	£
Annual allowance – 2019/20	40,000	
Less: 50% × (£156,955 – £150,000)	(3,477)	
		36,523
Unused allowances b/f from previous three tax years:		
(Per Q £1,000 × 3)		3,000
Maximum annual allowance for the tax year 2019/20		39,523
Less: Employee occupational scheme contributions		(28,000)
Employer occupational scheme contributions		(11,000)
Remaining available annual allowance = PPCs made		523

Tutorial note

(1) *Both employee and employer pension contributions count towards the annual allowance.*

(2) *Unused annual allowances can be carried forward for three years.*

(3) *The annual allowance is the maximum gross amount that can be contributed into pension schemes in a tax year without incurring an annual allowance charge. The £523 is therefore the gross amount of contributions made by John into the personal pension scheme.*

(4) *Higher and additional rate tax relief for personal pension scheme contributions is given by the extension of the basic and higher rate tax bands (W5).*

(5) *Remember that the PPCs also affect John's adjusted net income (ANI) for the purposes of calculating the PA available.*

(W4) Personal allowance

	£	£
Total income = net income	117,955	
Less: Gross PPCs (W3)	(523)	
ANI	117,432	
Personal allowance		12,500
Less: 50% × excess ANI		
(£117,432 – £100,000) × 50%		(8,716)
Revised PA		3,784

(W5) Extension of basic and additional rate bands

	Basic rate	Additional rate
	£	£
Basic rate band threshold	37,500	150,000
Plus: Gross PPCs	523	523
Extended basic and additional rate bands	38,023	150,523

(b) National Insurance contributions – 2019/20

Tutor's top tips

You are asked to calculate the class 1 national insurance contributions payable by both John Beach and Surf plc. Make sure you present your answer so that it is clear which contributions are paid by whom.

John Beach

- Class 1 employee's primary NICs payable:

Cash earnings = (£144,000 salary + £1,425 mileage allowance) = £145,425

	£
(£50,000 – £8,632) × 12%	4,964
(£145,425 – £50,000) × 2%	1,908
	6,872

Tutorial note

Class 1 NICs are assessed on cash earnings without any allowable deductions. Accordingly pension contributions are not deductible and non-cash benefits are not subject to class 1 NICs.

Note that the taxable mileage allowance paid in respect of home to office travel is cash earnings and is subject to class 1 NIC.

Surf plc

- Class 1 employer's secondary NICs payable:

   Also payable on cash earnings of £145,425.

	£
(£145,425 − £8,632) × 13.8%	18,877

Examiner's report

Part (a) was generally very well answered, and the only aspect that caused problems was the calculation of the personal pension contributions. A common mistake was to gross up the contributions.

Part (b) was well answered by the majority of candidates.

Note: *The examiner's report has been edited to remove comments on elements of the question that have been deleted due to changes to the exam format.*

ACCA marking scheme		Marks
(a)	Director's remuneration	0.5
	Mileage allowance received	0.5
	Approved mileage allowance	1.0
	Taxable benefit on mileage	0.5
	Occupational pension contributions	1.0
	Outstanding balance on loan	1.0
	Loan interest at official rate	1.0
	Interest paid	0.5
	Long service award	0.5
	Personal allowance	1.0
	Income tax liability	1.0
	Unused annual allowance for 2019/20	1.5
	Total available annual allowance	1.0
	Extension of basic and higher rate bands	1.0
		12.0
(b)	Employee class 1 NIC	2.0
	Employer class 1 NIC	1.0
		3.0
Total		**15.0**

125   KAT (ADAPTED) *Walk in the footsteps of a top tutor*

(a)   **Property purchased personally**

Key answer tips

In this question you are required to work out the tax savings that result from holding property either directly as an individual or through a company.

The corporation tax is provided for you and you must ensure you do not repeat calculations that have already been performed.

The key to passing this question is to ensure you set out two separate calculations, one with the dividends being the income that will be taxed via the company and the other with the property income directly taxed via a personal holding of the property.

When working out the property income for the option where the property is owned personally try and remember that only 25% of the mortgage expense is allowable in the property income calculation with the other 75% being given basic income tax relief at the bottom of the income tax calculation.

Don't ignore part b) as there is an easy mark for acknowledging that the annual exempt amount is only available to individuals

Property purchased personally	£
Employment income	60,650
Property income (working)	23,600
	84,250
Personal allowance	(12,500)
Taxable income	71,750

Income tax
£

37,500 × 20% (Non-savings)	7,500
34,250 × 40% (Non-savings)	13,700
71,750	
	21,200
Interest relief (£12,000 × 75% ×20%)	(1,800)
Income tax liability	19,400

Working – Property income

	£
Rent receivable (£2,600 × 12)	31,200
Mortgage interest (£12,000 × 25%)	(3,000)
Other expenses	(4,600)
Property income	23,600

Property purchased via a limited company

	£
Employment income	60,650
Dividend income	6,000
	66,650
Personal allowance	(12,500)
Taxable income	54,150

Income tax

£	
37,500 × 20% (Non-savings)	7,500
10,650 × 40% (Non-savings)	4,260
2,000 × 0% (Dividends)	0
4,000 × 32.5% (Dividends)	1,300
54,150	
Income tax liability	13,060

Conclusion

If Kat purchases the property via a limited company, then the overall tax saving will be £3,566 compared to purchasing the property personally:

	£
Purchased personally	19,400
Purchased via a limited company (£2,774 + £13,060)	(15,834)
Tax saving	3,566

Tutorial note

The comparison ignores the fact that not all of the profits are withdrawn under the company purchase option. However, profits might typically be retained within a company to repay the mortgage borrowing or to fund a future property purchase.

(b) The annual exempt amount will not be available if the gain occurs within a limited company.

Tutorial note

A limited company would not benefit from an indexation allowance as the property would be purchased after December 2017.

ACCA marking guide (adapted)		
		Marks
(a)	**Kat – Income tax**	
	Employment income	0.5
	Personal allowance	0.5
	Tax at 20%	0.5
	Tax at 40%	0.5
	Interest relief	1.0
	Kat – Property income	
	Rent received	0.5
	Interest	1.0
	Other expenses	0.5
	Company – Income tax	
	Dividend income	0.5
	Employment income	0.5
	Personal allowance	0.5
	Tax at 20%	0.5
	Tax at 40%	0.5
	Tax at 0%	0.5
	Tax at 32.5%	0.5
	Tax saving	0.5
		——
		9.0
		——
(b)	AEA available to individuals	**1.0**
		——
Total		**10.0**
		——

Examiner's report

This question involved an individual who was planning to purchase a residential freehold property which was going to be let out. She was unsure whether to purchase the property personally or via a limited company. The limited company would be incorporated for the sole purpose of purchasing and letting out the property, and Kat would hold all of the shares in the company. The company's corporation tax liability was provided in the question.

Part (a) for 9 marks required candidates to determine if there would be an overall saving of tax if Kat purchased the property via a limited company rather than purchasing it personally. Those candidates who made sure that they understood the scenario and worked carefully through each calculation had no difficulty answering this section.

As warned in previous reports, where a tax figure is given for one of the scenarios (in this case, the corporation tax figure), candidates should never attempt to recalculate the figure for themselves. All this does is use up valuable time. As regards the conclusion, this should have just been a calculation of the tax difference between the two scenarios. There was no need for a detailed explanation.

Where computations are required for two different scenarios, candidates should clearly indicate which scenario is being answered. This is particularly important where some of the same information is used in both scenarios. In this case employment income and the personal allowance were common across both scenarios. Some candidates attempted to answer this question with just the one computation; impossible given that property income formed part of the first computation, with dividend income included in the second.

It should have been quite clear from the information provided that full computations were necessary for both scenarios. Those candidates who calculated the tax liability for a personal purchase and then attempted to adjust the figures for a corporate purchase invariably ended up with a very confused answer.

The personal purchase required candidates to apply the restriction whereby relief for 75% of property income finance costs is restricted to the basic rate.

Working through past examination questions will help candidates familiarise themselves with the best approach to be taken when answering questions which examine more than one tax. Also, it is important that candidates appreciate the interactions that can arise in such questions, and an article has been published covering many of the scenarios which could be examined.

Part (b) for 1 mark required an explanation of one way in which the calculation of a future taxable gain on a property disposal made by the limited company would differ from the calculation of a taxable gain on a disposal made personally by Kat. Although there were many good answers to this section, some candidates discussed the finance costs restriction when this has nothing to do with taxable gains. All that was required was a brief mention (not a detailed answer) of the annual exempt amount.

126 ANN, BASIL AND CHLOE (ADAPTED) *Walk in the footsteps of a top tutor*

Key answer tips

This question covers the pension relief available to three different individuals. This should be a straightforward question provided the rules had been learnt.

Relief for pension contributions is a key area of the syllabus that is tested regularly.

Note that this question has been adapted in light of the new syllabus and part (b) is a new addition to the question to test the annual allowance rules introduced in the pension legislation since the date of the sitting when this examination question was set.

The highlighted words are key words or phrases that markers are looking for.

Tutor's top tips

This question is classic in style with individuals in different situations contributing to a personal pension scheme.

The key is to:

- *Remember the definition of 'relevant earnings'*

- *Compare the gross contributions paid with the 'relevant earnings' (or £3,600 if this is higher) to decide the maximum tax allowable amount*

- *Consider the annual allowance limit charge and tapering where necessary.*

Note that the maximum contribution allowable for a person without any relevant earnings in the tax year (£3,600) and the annual allowance limit are given in the examination.

(a)   (1)   Ann Peach

Amount of pension contributions qualifying for relief

Ann can obtain relief for the lower of:

(1)   Gross contributions of £42,000

(2)   Higher of:

    (i)   £3,600

    (ii)   Relevant earnings of £38,650

Therefore, £38,650 qualifies for tax relief.

Her taxable income falls below the basic rate band even before extension due to pension contributions; therefore her income is taxed at 20%.

Income tax liability

	£
Trading profit	38,650
Less: PA	(12,500)
Taxable income	26,150
Income tax liability (£26,150 × 20%)	5,230

Tutorial note

The annual allowance charge is not applicable to Ann, as although she has made pension contributions in excess of £40,000, she has only received tax relief for contributions of £38,650. The annual allowance charge is intended to claw back tax relief for contributions in excess of the limit, which is not applicable here.

(2) Basil Plum

Amount of pension contributions qualifying for relief

Basil can obtain relief for the lower of:

(1) Gross contributions of £40,000

(2) Higher of:

(i) £3,600

(ii) Relevant earnings of £152,000

Therefore, £40,000 will qualify for tax relief and his basic rate band is extended to £77,500 (W2).

Tutorial note

Note that this scenario differs from the treatment for Ann (above) as Ann had contributed more than 100% of her relevant earnings into a scheme, whereas Basil has contributed less than 100% of his relevant earnings into the scheme.

Income tax liability

	£
Employment income	152,000
Less: PA (W1)	(6,500)
Taxable income	145,500

Income tax:		£
£		
77,500 × 20% (W2)		15,500
68,000 × 40%		27,200
————		
145,500		
————		
Income tax liability		42,700

Workings

(W1) Personal allowance

Basil's adjusted net income is in excess of £100,000, therefore his personal allowance is restricted.

His ANI is calculated as follows:

	£
Employment income = Total income = Net income	152,000
Less: Gross PPC	(40,000)
	————
ANI	112,000
	————
Personal allowance	12,500
Less: 50% × excess ANI (112,000 – 100,000) × 50%	(6,000)
	————
	6,500
	————

(W2) Extension of basic rate band

	£
Basic rate band	37,500
Plus: Gross PPC	40,000
	————
Extended basic rate band	77,500
	————

(W3) Annual allowance

	£	£
Net income		152,000
Add: Employer's pension contributions		5,000
Adjusted income		157,000
Annual allowance – 2019/20	40,000	
Less: 50% × (£157,000 – £150,000)	(3,500)	
		36,500
Unused AA b/f from previous three tax years:		
2017/18 and 2018/19 ((£40,000 – £40,000) × 2)		0
2016/17 (£40,000 – £30,000)		10,000
Maximum annual allowance for 2019/20		46,500

Basil's gross contributions of £40,000 combined with his employer's contributions of £5,000 are within the available annual allowance. Basil will not be subject to an annual allowance charge.

Tutorial note

Basil's adjusted income for the purposes of tapering the annual allowance for the tax year 2019/20 exceeds £150,000. His allowance is reduced by £1 for every £2 of adjusted income in excess of £150,000. His net income (£152,000 - £50,000) plus personal pension contributions in the tax years prior to 2018/19 did not exceed £150,000 so the available annual allowance in each year is £40,000.

(3)   Chloe Pear

Amount of pension contributions qualifying for relief

Property income does not qualify as relevant earnings (unless it relates to qualifying furnished holiday accommodation).

Therefore, as Chloe has no relevant earnings, she will only receive tax relief on £3,600 of her pension contributions.

Her taxable income falls below the basic rate band even before extension due to pension contributions; therefore her income is taxed at 20%.

Income tax liability

	£
Property income	24,550
Less: PA	(12,500)
Taxable income	12,050
Income tax (£12,050 × 20%)	2,410

(b) (i) Tax implications of Banana Bank plc contributing into Basil's pension fund

If Basil's employer contributes into his personal pension scheme, the employer contributions are:

- a tax free benefit
- a tax allowable deduction in Banana Bank plc's corporation tax computation
- combined with Basil's contributions and compared to the available annual allowance in the tax years 2016/17 to 2019/20.

Where the annual allowance is exceeded a tax charge is levied on the individual.

(ii) Implications for Basil's available annual allowance of Banana Bank plc contributing £100,000 into Basil's pension fund

The annual allowance of £40,000 is tapered where the individual's adjusted income is greater than £150,000, subject to a minimum of £10,000 where adjusted income is £210,000 or more.

Basil's adjusted income would now be £252,000 (£152,000 + £100,000) such that his annual allowance for 2019/20 would be reduced to the minimum amount of £10,000.

Examiner's report

This question was reasonably well answered, although there were few first-rate answers.

For the second taxpayer the basic rate band was often extended by the amount of annual allowance rather than the contributions.

Very few candidates stated that the third taxpayer would have received tax relief up to £3,600 of her contributions.

Note: This question has been adapted in light of the new syllabus and part (b) is a new addition to the question.

ACCA marking scheme		
		Marks
(a) **Ann Peach**		
Taxable income		0.5
Income tax		0.5
Amount qualifying for tax relief		1.0
		2.0
Basil Plum		
Taxable income		0.5
Personal allowance		2.0
Extension of basic rate band		1.5
Income tax		1.0
Amount qualifying for tax relief		1.0
		6.0
Chloe Pear		
Taxable income		0.5
Income tax		0.5
Amount qualifying for tax relief		1.0
		2.0
(b) Employer contributions		
Tax free benefit		0.5
Tax allowable deduction for corporation tax		1.0
Combined with Basil's contributions re annual allowance (AA)		0.5
Unused AA b/f 3 years		0.5
If annual allowance exceeded tax charge levied		0.5
AA tapered to minimum of £10,000		1.0
Adjusted net income now £252,000		1.0
		5.0
Total		**15.0**

127 JACK (ADAPTED) *Walk in the footsteps of a top tutor*

Key answer tips

This question is really three separate questions. Requirements (a) and (c) are straightforward, whereas requirement (b) is a bit tricky, so you may want to leave this part until last.

Part (a) required basic inheritance tax planning knowledge but in a written context. Don't forget you may need to explain tax implications in the examination as well as calculate them!

Part (b) required a good understanding of tax relief for pension contributions and the availability of the annual allowance. The annual allowance is included in the tax rates and allowances provided to you in the examination. Part (b)(ii) in particular was tricky but remember it is only worth one mark – have a quick go and move on!

Part (c) required basic tax planning in relation to ISAs. The maximum investment per tax year is included in the tax rates and allowances provided to you in the examination.

(a) The gift will be a chargeable lifetime transfer of £294,000 (£300,000 less annual exemptions of £3,000 for the tax years 2019/20 and 2018/19).

No lifetime inheritance tax will be payable because this is less than the nil rate band of £325,000, and if Jack survives for seven years, there will also be no inheritance tax liability on Jack's death.

The value of Jack's estate will therefore be reduced by £300,000, which will mean an eventual inheritance tax saving of £120,000 (£300,000 at 40%).

Tutorial note

Although no IHT will be payable on Jack's gift to a trust due to the availability of his nil rate band, the chargeable amount of £294,000 will have to be taken into account when calculating the nil rate band available to set against any further chargeable lifetime transfers (i.e. gifts to trusts) which are be made within the following seven years.

(b) **(i)** **(1)** For the tax year 2019/20, £44,000 (W1) of Jack's income is currently taxable at the higher rate of income tax.

(2) This is less than the available annual allowances of £136,000 (W2) for the tax year 2019/20.

(3) Restricting the amount of personal pension contributions to the amount qualifying for tax relief at the higher rate will minimise the cost of pension saving because each £100 saved will effectively only cost £60 (£100 less 40% tax relief).

(W1) Amount of income subject to tax at the higher rate

	£
Net income	100,000
Less: Personal allowance	(12,500)
Taxable income	87,500
Less: Basic rate band (£37,500 + (£500 × 12))	(43,500)
Amount of income falling in the higher rate band	44,000

(W2)   Amount of annual allowance available

	£
Annual allowance 2019/20	40,000
Brought forward allowances:	
2018/19	40,000
2017/18	40,000
2016/17	40,000
Total available allowances	160,000
Less: Contributions made (£500 × 12 × 4)	(24,000)
Remaining allowance for 2019/20 contributions	136,000

Tutorial note

Unused annual allowances can be carried forward for up to three years.

It wasn't necessary to restrict Jack's annual allowance as his adjusted income is ≤ £150,000.

Although Jack's approach to pension saving will maximise the available tax relief, it will mean that some carried forward annual allowances are wasted.

(ii)   Jack will have unused allowances of £34,000 (£40,000 − £6,000) from both of the tax years 2017/18 and 2018/19 to carry forward to 2020/21, so total allowances of £68,000 (£34,000 × 2).

Tutorial note

This requirement was only worth one mark so the examining team were expecting you to build on your calculations from the previous part and use your technical knowledge of how brought forward annual allowances are utilised. A proof of the answer is as follows:

Remaining allowance for 2019/20 contributions		*£136,000*
Less: Additional contribution in 2019/20		*(£44,000)*
Less: Unused 2016/17 allowance no longer c/f		
Remaining allowance (£40,000-£6,000)	*£34,000*	
Utilised by additional contribution		
(£44,000 - £34,000*)	*(£10,000)*	
	———	
		(£24,000)
		———
Allowance remaining to carry forward to 2020/21		*£68,000*
		———

* £34,000 of the additional contribution will utilise the remaining allowance from the current year (2019/20). The remaining £10,000 of the additional contribution will utilise the unused allowance carried forward from 2016/17. The unused allowances from the tax years 2017/18 and 2018/19 are not needed to allow tax relief on the additional contribution and are carried forward to 2020/21.

(c) Jack can invest in an ISA for the tax year 2019/20 until 5 April 2020, and another ISA for the tax year 2020/21 between 6 April 2020 and 5 April 2021.

The maximum possible amount which he can invest into stocks and shares ISAs during the next 30 days is therefore £40,000 (£20,000 × 2).

Examiner's report

This question proved difficult for many candidates, with some aspects consistently causing problems.

As regards part (a), long, detailed, computations were often provided when the answer was quite straightforward. For example, the gift would have reduced the taxpayer's death estate by £300,000, so the inheritance tax saving was simply £120,000 (£300,000 at 40%). There was no need for before and after computations.

As regards part (b), few candidates appreciated that restricting the amount of personal pension contributions to the amount qualifying for tax relief at the higher rate minimises the cost of pension saving because each £100 saved effectively only costs £60 (£100 less 40% tax relief).

As regards part (c), very few candidates realised that the 30 day period fell into two tax years, so the taxpayer could invest £20,000 by 5 April 2020, and then another £20,000 on or after 6 April 2020.

ACCA marking scheme		
		Marks
(a)	**Inheritance tax**	
	Chargeable lifetime transfer	1.0
	Inheritance tax	1.0
	Value of estate	1.0
		―――
		3.0
		―――
(b)	**Pension contributions**	
	(i) Income at higher rate	1.5
	Annual allowances at £40,000 – £6,000 each year b/f	1.5
	Conclusion	1.0
		―――
		4.0
		―――
	(ii) Unused allowances 2017/18 –2019/20	1.0
		―――
(c)	**ISA**	
	Timing	1.0
	Limit ×2	1.0
		―――
		2.0
		―――
Total		**10.0**
		―――

SELF-ASSESSMENT

128   PI CASSO (ADAPTED)

Key answer tips

The first part of requirement (a) of this question involves detailed calculations to work out the income tax, class 4 NICs and CGT payable under self-assessment and when the payments are due.

The remaining two parts require wholly written answers on two common self-assessment topics.

These are marks which are easy to gain if you have done your work, but easy to lose if you do not invest the time in learning the self-assessment rules.

Part (a)(3) of the original question has been changed and part (4) has been deleted to reflect changes to the structure of the examination.

Part (b) is a new part that has been added to the original question to test the implications for tax planning for married couples of the savings and dividend income nil rate bands.

The highlighted words are key words or phrases that markers are looking for.

(a) **(1)** **Due dates of payment of tax under self-assessment**

Due date	Tax year	Payment	£
31 July 2019	2018/19	Second payment on account (W1)	2,240
31 January 2020	2018/19	Balancing payment (W2)	6,133
31 January 2020	2019/20	First payment on account (W3)	1,860
31 July 2020	2019/20	Second payment on account (W3)	1,860
31 January 2021	2019/20	Balancing payment (W4)	156
31 January 2021	2020/21	First payment on account (W5)	1,860

Workings

(W1) Second payment on account – 2018/19

The second payment on account for the tax year 2018/19 is based on Pi's income tax and class 4 NIC liability for the previous tax year as follows:

	£
Income tax	3,240
Class 4 NICs	1,240
	———
	4,480
	———
Payments on account (50%)	2,240
	———

(W2) Balancing payment – 2018/19

	£
Income tax	4,100
Class 4 NICs	1,480
Class 2 NICs	153
Capital gains tax (see Tutorial Note)	4,880
	———
	10,613
Less: POAs (£2,240 × 2)	(4,480)
	———
Balancing payment	6,133
	———

(W3) Payments on account – 2019/20

Pi will make a claim to reduce her total payments on account for the tax year 2019/20 as follows:

	£
Income tax	2,730
Class 4 NICs	990
	———
	3,720
	———
Payments on account (50%)	1,860
	———

(W4) Balancing payment – 2019/20

	£
Income tax and class 4 NICs	3,720
Class 2 NICs	156
Capital gains tax	0
	3,876
Less: POAs (£1,860 × 2)	(3,720)
Balancing payment	156

(W5) First payments on account – 2020/21

The first payment on account for the tax year 2020/21 is based on Pi's income tax and class 4 NIC liability for the previous tax year as follows:

	£
Income tax	2,730
Class 4 NICs	990
	3,720
Payments on account (50%)	1,860

Tutorial note

Class 2 NICs and capital gains tax are collected via self-assessment and are payable all in one payment on 31 January following the end of the tax year along with the balancing payment for income tax and class 4 NICs.

Payments on account are not required for class 2 NICs and CGT.

---

(2) Reduction of payments on account to £0

- If Pi's payments on account for the tax year 2019/20 were reduced to £0, then she would be charged late payment interest on the payments due of £1,860 from the relevant due date to the date of payment.

- A penalty will be charged if the claim to reduce the payments on account to £0 was made fraudulently or negligently.

(3) Claim to reduce payment on accounts

- Pi must submit a claim to reduce her payments on account for the tax year 2019/20 by 31 January 2021 (i.e. by 31 January following the tax year).

(b) **Turner and Andrea tax savings**

- Turner is an additional rate taxpayer in the tax year 2019/20. Therefore he does not have any savings nil rate band and has paid tax on his interest income at 45%.

- Andrea is a basic rate taxpayer in the tax year 2019/20. She did not use her savings nil rate band of £1,000 but had dividend income in excess of her £2,000 dividend nil rate band. She paid tax at 7.5% on the dividend income above £2,000.

- Their total tax liability for the tax year 2019/20 would have been reduced if:

  - Turner had transferred all of his interest income to Andrea. This would have utilised her savings nil rate band and the balance of the interest would have been taxed at 20% instead of 45%

  - Andrea had transferred £2,000 of dividend income to Turner to utilise his dividend nil rate band

- The total tax saving would have been:

	£
Interest income £1,000 × 45%	450
Interest income £4,000 × 25% (45% - 20%)	1,000
Dividend income £2,000 × 7.5%	150
	———
	1,600
	———

Examiner's report

This question was generally not well answered, and the impression given was that candidates had struggled with time management and had a lack of time remaining for this question.

Part (a)(1) caused the most problems, with the vast majority of candidates not being able to demonstrate how payments are calculated and paid under the self-assessment system.

In part (a)(2) most candidates appreciated that interest would be due, but very few mentioned the potential penalty that could be charged.

Note: *The examiner's report has been edited to remove comments on elements of the question that have been deleted due to changes to the examination format. Note that part (b) was not in the original question.*

		ACCA marking scheme	
			Marks
(a)	(1)	Second payment on account for 2018/19	1.5
		Balancing payment for 2018/19	2.0
		Claim to reduce payments on account	1.0
		Payments on account for 2019/20	1.0
		Balancing payment for 2019/20	0.5
		First payment on account for 2020/21	1.0
			7.0
	(2)	Interest	1.0
		Penalty	1.0
			2.0
	(3)	Claim date	1.0
(b)		Turner additional rate taxpayer	0.5
		No savings nil rate band	0.5
		Andrea basic rate taxpayer	0.5
		Unused savings nil rate band £1,000	0.5
		Dividends exceed £2,000 nil rate band	0.5
		Transfer all interest income to Andrea	0.5
		Transfer £2,000 dividends to Turner	0.5
		Calculation of tax saving	1.5
			5.0
Total			**15.0**

129 ERNEST VADER (ADAPTED) *Walk in the footsteps of a top tutor*

Key answer tips

This is an unusual and tricky question requiring substantial written explanations and statements about ethical issues and self-assessment.

Detailed knowledge is required to score highly on this question; however the application of some basic common sense would also gain quite a few marks.

The highlighted words are key words or phrases that markers are looking for.

The legislation regarding the general anti-abuse rule and dishonest conduct by tax agents did not exist when this question was first written, and have been added since to test these areas. The original part (c) tested HMRC's information powers, which are no longer in the syllabus and this part has therefore been removed.

Part (d) has been amended to reflect changes to the examination structure.

Tutor's top tips

Remember to read the requirement carefully and allocate the time spent on each section.

Part (a) covers the classic topic of tax evasion and tax avoidance, but care must be taken to apply your knowledge to Ernest's particular problem. This part also tests awareness of the general anti-abuse rule.

Part (b) requires the application of common sense if the specific guidelines have not been learnt.

Parts (c) and (d) are straightforward if the self-assessment rules have been learnt, difficult if not learnt.

(a)   Tax evasion and tax avoidance

- Tax evasion is illegal and involves the reduction of tax liabilities by not providing information to which HMRC is entitled, or deliberately providing HMRC with false information.

- In contrast, tax avoidance involves the minimisation of tax liabilities by the use of any lawful means. However, certain tax avoidance schemes must be disclosed to HMRC.

- The general anti-abuse rule is a rule to counter artificial and abusive schemes where arrangements (which cannot be regarded as a reasonable course of action) are put in place deliberately to avoid tax.

- If Ernest makes no disclosure of the capital gain then this will be viewed as tax evasion as his tax liability for the tax year 2019/20 will be understated by £18,000.

(b)   Failure to disclose information to HMRC

- How to deal with the failure to disclose is a matter of professional judgement, and a trainee Chartered Certified Accountant would be expected to act honestly and with integrity.

- Ernest should therefore be advised to disclose details of the capital gain to HMRC.

- If such disclosure is not made by Ernest, you would be obliged to report under the money laundering regulations, and you should also consider ceasing to act for Ernest.

- In these circumstances you would be advised to notify HMRC that you no longer act for him although you should not provide any reason for this.

(c)   Penalties for tax agent

- A civil penalty may be payable by the firm if they have engaged in dishonest conduct, which may be the case if they have failed to supply the information HMRC have requested.

- The potential penalty is up to £50,000.

 KAPLAN PUBLISHING

(d)   Interest payable

*   Late payment interest will run from the due date of 31 January 2021 to the payment date of 31 July 2021.

Examiner's report

This question was not well answered, with many candidates attempting it as their final question or omitting it altogether. This was disappointing given that several sections covered recent tax management changes which have been covered in my Finance Act articles.

In part (a) most candidates knew the difference between tax evasion and tax avoidance, but many failed to score an easy mark by not stating that the taxpayer's actions would be viewed as tax evasion.

Part (b) caused problems for most candidates but a common sense approach would have gained most of the available marks. Unfortunately, far too many candidates instead just incorrectly explained that it would be necessary to inform HMRC themselves.

The examiner's comments on the original parts (c) and (d) have been deleted as they are no longer relevant to the amended question.

ACCA marking scheme		
		Marks
(a)	Tax evasion	1.0
	Tax avoidance	1.0
	General anti-abuse rule	1.0
	Non-disclosure of disposal	1.0
		4.0
(b)	Professional judgement	0.5
	Advise disclosure	1.0
	Report under Money Laundering Regulations	0.5
	Cease to act and inform HMRC that ceased	1.0
		3.0
(c)	Civil penalty for dishonest conduct	1.0
	£50,000 penalty	1.0
		2.0
(d)	Interest period	1.0
Total		**10.0**

130 SOPHIE SHAPE (ADAPTED)

Key answer tips

Occasionally the examining team do include a section C question solely testing administration aspects of taxation such as this 10 mark personal tax question.

Parts (a) and (b) test the popular examination topic of payments on account. Part (c) tests tax return due dates for 1 mark. Part (d) tests compliance checks.

Provided you have revised the administration chapter, this question should be straightforward.

(a) Schedule of tax payments

Due date	Tax year	Payment	£
31 July 2020	2019/20	Second payment on account £7,060 (£5,240 + £1,820) × 50%	3,530
31 January 2021	2019/20	Balancing payment £13,438 (£6,100 + £1,910 + £156 + £5,280) – £7,060 (£3,530 × 2)	6,386
31 January 2021	2020/21	First payment on account £8,010 (£6,100 + £1,910) × 50%	4,005

Tutorial note

(1)   The second payment on account for the tax year 2019/20 is based on Sophie's income tax and class 4 NIC liability for the previous tax year.

(2)   The balancing payment for the tax year 2019/20 includes the class 2 NIC and capital gains tax liabilities for that year.

(3)   The first payment on account for the tax year 2020/21 is based on Sophie's income tax and class 4 NIC liabilities for the previous tax year.

(b) Reduction of payments on account

If Sophie's payments on account for the tax year 2019/20 were reduced to £0, then she would be charged interest on the payments due of £3,530 from the relevant due date to the date of payment.

A tax geared penalty will be charged as the claim to reduce the payments on account to £0 would appear to be made fraudulently or negligently.

(c) Filing a paper tax return

Unless the notice to file a return is issued late, the latest date when Sophie can file a paper self-assessment tax return for the tax year 2019/20 is 31 October 2020.

(d) **Compliance check**

If HM Revenue and Customs (HMRC) intend to carry out a compliance check into Sophie's 2019/20 tax return they will have to notify her within 12 months of the date when they receive the return.

HMRC has the right to carry out a compliance check as regards the completeness and accuracy of any return, and such a check may be made on a completely random basis.

However, compliance checks are generally carried out because of a suspicion that income has been undeclared or because deductions have been incorrectly claimed. For example, where accounting ratios are out of line with industry norms.

Section 7

ANSWERS TO PRACTICE CHARGEABLE GAINS QUESTIONS

PRACTICE SECTION A OBJECTIVE TEST QUESTIONS

INDIVIDUALS – CAPITAL GAINS TAX

131   B and F

Qualifying corporate bonds, gilt-edged securities, a main residence (which has always been lived in by the owner) and all cars (regardless of any business use), are all exempt from CGT.

A painting is a non-wasting chattel. A non-wasting chattel is a chargeable asset unless it is bought and sold for less than £6,000 which is unlikely to be the case for a painting by a famous artist.

Assets used in the trade are still chargeable assets and will potentially realise a chargeable gain if they are sold at a profit. The wasting chattel rules do not apply to assets on which capital allowances have been claimed.

132   B

	£
Sale proceeds	338,200
Less: Cost	(150,000)
Chargeable gain	188,200
Less: AEA	(12,000)
Taxable gains	176,200
Capital gains tax liability (£176,200 × 28%)	49,336

Tutorial note

Lexie has taxable income of £54,000 and is therefore a higher rate taxpayer. Her capital gains will therefore be subject to the higher tax rate for residential properties of 28%. Remember that higher rates of CGT apply when you are taxing a gain in relation to a residential property.

133 £9,436

	£
Disposal proceeds	165,000
Less: Deemed acquisition cost	(115,000)
Chargeable gain	50,000
Less: AEA	(12,000)
	38,000
Less: Capital losses b/f	(4,300)
Taxable gains	33,700
Capital gains tax payable (£33,700 × 28%)	9,436

Tutorial note

A transfer between spouses is a no gain/no loss transfer. Sophia's deemed acquisition cost is equal to the deemed proceeds on the transfer from her husband. This is equal to his acquisition cost.

134 B

Tutorial note

The CGT due date will be the same whether the asset is split between spouses (or civil partners) or not.

135 £2,000

	£
Painting 1	
Non-wasting chattel bought and sold for < £6,000	Exempt
Painting 2	
Sale proceeds	7,200
Less: Cost	(1,000)
	─────
Chargeable gain	6,200
	─────
Gain cannot exceed:	
5/3 × (£7,200 – £6,000)	2,000
	─────
Total chargeable gain (£0 + £2,000)	2,000
	─────

Tutorial note

The two paintings disposed of in this question are non-wasting chattels.

If non-wasting chattels are bought and sold for £6,000 or less they are exempt.

If bought for £6,000 or less but are sold for more than £6,000, the gain is restricted to:

5/3 × (gross proceeds – £6,000).

136 C

	£
Deemed sale proceeds	6,000
Less: Allowable selling costs (legal fees)	(300)
	─────
Net sale proceeds	5,700
Less: Allowable expenditure	
Cost	(22,000)
Incidental costs of acquisition	(800)
	─────
Allowable loss	(17,100)
	─────

Tutorial note

The vase disposed of in this question is a non-wasting chattel.

If a non-wasting chattel cost more than £6,000 but is sold for £6,000 or less, the allowable loss is calculated using deemed gross sale proceeds of £6,000.

137 £4,000

	£
Chargeable gain	23,700
Less: Current year capital losses	(10,400)
	———
Net current year gains	13,300
Less: AEA	(12,000)
	———
	1,300
Less: Capital losses b/f (restricted)	(1,300)
	———
Taxable gains	0
	———

Capital loss c/f

	£
2018/19 Loss	5,300
Utilised – 2019/20	(1,300)
	———
Loss c/f	4,000
	———

Tutorial note

The offset of capital losses brought forward is restricted to preserve the annual exempt amount.

138 C

	£
Sale proceeds	28,800
Less: Allowable element of acquisition cost (W)	(12,600)
Chargeable gain	16,200

Working: Allowable element of acquisition cost

Remaining life at disposal = 9 years

Estimated useful life = 15 years

Allowable cost = £21,000 × 9/15 = £12,600

139 D

	£
Sale proceeds	425,600
Deemed cost of remainder (£300,000 – £112,500(W))	(187,500)
Chargeable gain	238,100
Capital gains tax payable by:	31 January 2021

Working: Part disposal March 2014

Deemed cost of 10 acres disposed of:

£300,000 × £150,000/(£150,000 + £250,000)   £112,500

140 D

	£
Proceeds	27,900
Cost (£31,320 × 14/30)	(14,616)
Chargeable gain	13,284

Tutorial note

The copyright is a wasting asset as it has an expected life of ≤ 50 years. The allowable expenditure is restricted to take account of the asset's natural fall in value.

The asset's fall in value is deemed to occur on a straight line basis over its useful life.

141 £78,000

	£
Sale proceeds	230,000
Less: Cost (W)	(152,000)
Chargeable gain	78,000

Working: Restored asset base cost

	£
Original cost	142,000
Plus: Restoration expenditure	70,000
Less: Insurance proceeds	(60,000)
Revised base cost	152,000

Tutorial note

Where insurance proceeds are received in respect of an asset that has been damaged there is a part disposal.

However, if all of the insurance proceeds are used in restoring the asset the taxpayer may claim to deduct the proceeds from the cost of the asset rather than be treated as having made a part disposal of the asset.

Remember to include the amount spent restoring the asset in the revised base cost.

142 B

	£
Original cost	73,000
Plus: Restoration expenditure	41,700
Less: Insurance proceeds	(37,200)
Revised base cost	77,500

143 £10,133

	£
Sales proceeds (W)	12,800
Cost (£4,000 × 10,000/15,000)	(2,667)
Chargeable gain	10,133

Working: Average of quoted prices

(120p + 136p) ÷ 2   128p

Sales proceeds = £12,800 (128p × 10,000)

Tutor's top tips

The share prices quoted in the question are given in pence, but you are required to provide your answer in pounds. Be careful when entering your answer that you have done this if the question requires you to!

144 B

	£
Gilts	Exempt
Martin plc shares:	
Proceeds – Market value	12,300
Less: Cost	(8,000)
Chargeable gain	4,300

Tutorial note

Where an asset is transferred to a connected party, market value is substituted for actual gross proceeds.

145

Matching order

Matched first	2,000 shares from the purchase on 1 October
Matched second	3,000 shares from the purchase on 23 October
Matched third	15,000 shares from the share pool as at 1 October

Tutorial note

The matching rules require that shares disposed of by an individual are matched against shares acquired in the following order:

(1)   Shares purchased on the same day as the date of disposal; then

(2)   Shares purchased within the following 30 days; then

(3)   Shares in the share pool (made up of shares acquired before the date of disposal).

146 £3,300

	£
Chargeable gain	45,000
Less: AEA	(12,000)
	————
Taxable gain	33,000
	————
Capital gains tax (£33,000 × 10%)	3,300
	————

Tutorial note

The gain on the shares is taxed at 10% as the disposal is eligible for Investors' relief (IR). IR applies to the disposal of:

- *unlisted ordinary shares in a trading company (including AIM shares)*

- *subscribed for (i.e. newly issued shares) on/after 17 March 2016*

- *which have been held for a minimum period of 3 years starting on 6 April 2016*

- *by an individual that is not an employee of the company.*

Siobhan had not made any previous disposals, therefore the £10 million lifetime limit is available.

147 B

The allowable cost is £50,000 (W) and the capital gains tax is due on 31 January 2021.

Working: Share pool

		Number	Cost
			£
April 2008	Purchase	40,000	200,000
May 2011	Rights issue (1:4) @ £4 per share	10,000	40,000
		————	————
		50,000	240,000
May 2015	Bonus issue (1:5)	10,000	0
		————	————
		60,000	240,000
March 2020	Sale (12,500/60,000 × £240,000)	(12,500)	(50,000)
		————	————
		47,500	190,000
		————	————

148 £100,000

The total consideration provided by Riley plc is:

	MV	Cost
	£	£
Cash (50,000 × £3)	150,000	50,000
Shares (50,000 × 2 × £1.20)	120,000	40,000
	270,000	90,000

Hunter has made a part disposal in relation to the cash consideration.

	£
Disposal proceeds (cash: 50,000 × £3)	150,000
Less: Original cost (£150,000/£270,000 × £90,000)	(50,000)
Chargeable gain	100,000

149 C

Date	Explanation	Total months	Exempt months	Chargeable months
31.3.06 to 31.3.11	Actual occupation	60	60	
1.4.11 to 31.3.13	Empty	24	24	
1.4.13 to 31.3.14	Actual occupation	12	12	
1.4.14 to 31.3.20	Empty	72	18	54
		168	114	54

Tutorial note

Any period of employment overseas is exempt, providing there is actual occupation at some point before and at some point after the period of employment.

The last 18 months of ownership are exempt as the property was Angus' main residence at some point.

150 £8,000

	£
Chargeable gain before reliefs	120,000
Less: PPR relief (£120,000 × 6/10)	(72,000)
	48,000
Less: Letting relief (W)	(40,000)
Chargeable gain	8,000

Working: Letting relief

Lowest of:

(1) Maximum = £40,000

(2) PPR relief = £72,000

(3) Gain on letting = £48,000

Tutorial note

PPR is available on 6/10 of the gain as Masuma has always occupied six out of the ten rooms in the house. Masuma cannot benefit from the rules of deemed occupation on the remaining four rooms as she has never used them as part of her main residence.

151 C

	£
Qualifying for ER	
Gain on sale of business	13,250,900
Less: AEA	(12,000)
Taxable gain	13,238,900
Capital gains tax:	
£10,000,000 × 10%	1,000,000
£3,238,900 × 20%	647,780
	1,647,780

Tutorial note

Entrepreneurs' relief is available as Bhavin is disposing of his sole trader business that he has operated for at least two years prior to disposal.

Entrepreneurs' relief is subject to a lifetime limit of £10 million. Chargeable gains in excess of this are subject to capital gains tax at a rate of 20% as Bhavin is a higher rate taxpayer. Even if Bhavin had not utilised his basic rate band, the chargeable gains in excess of the £10 million lifetime limit would still all be taxed at 20% as the gains qualifying for entrepreneurs' relief are deemed to utilise any remaining basic rate band.

152 C and F

Only fixed (i.e. not movable) plant and machinery qualifies for rollover relief.

Shares are not qualifying assets.

Assets must be used for trading purposes to qualify for rollover relief.

Goodwill qualifies for rollover relief provided it is disposed of by a sole trader and not a company.

153 C

Disposal on 13 May 2019

Chargeable gain is the lower of:

(1)   All of the chargeable gain = **£38,600**

(2)   Sale proceeds not reinvested

(£184,000 – £143,000) = £41,000

As all of the gain is chargeable in the tax year 2019/20, no rollover relief claim is possible.

Accordingly, the base cost of the replacement asset is the actual cost of £143,000.

154   £70,085

	£	£
Sale of warehouse		
Sale proceeds		270,213
Less: Cost	231,211	
Less: ROR on factory (Note)	(31,083)	
	———	(200,128)
		———
Chargeable gain		70,085
		———

Tutorial note

The proceeds from the sale of the factory were fully reinvested in the warehouse.

Therefore, the gain on the factory of £31,083 can be fully rolled over against the acquisition cost of the warehouse.

155 A and D

Unquoted shares in a trading company are qualifying assets for gift relief irrespective of the percentage shareholding.

Quoted shares are only qualifying assets if they are in the donor's personal trading company.

A company qualifies as a donor's personal trading company for the purposes of gift relief if at least 5% of the voting rights are held by the individual. However, unlike for entrepreneurs' relief, there is no minimum holding period and no requirement for the individual to work for the company.

Assets used by a donor's personal trading company are also qualifying assets for the purposes of gift relief but only if the company uses the asset in their trade.

156 B

Ben will qualify for entrepreneurs' relief as he has worked for the company, and has owned at least 5% of the shares, for at least two years prior to the disposal. The others do not meet all of these conditions.

157 C

	£
Proceeds (MV)	98,000
Less: Cost	(41,500)
Gain before relief	56,500
Gift relief (balancing figure)	(45,000)
Chargeable gain (£53,000 − £41,500)	11,500

Tutorial note

The full gain cannot be deferred using gift relief where there are actual proceeds in excess of cost (i.e. the donor has made a profit). In this case the actual proceeds of £53,000 exceeded the cost by £11,500. Therefore £11,500 of the gain is chargeable immediately and only the balance can be deferred using gift relief.

There is no requirement for the donor to work at the company or to have held the shares for a minimum time period when claiming gift relief in relation to shares. These are requirements for entrepreneurs' relief.

COMPANIES – CHARGEABLE GAINS

158 B

	£
Sale of warehouse	
Sale proceeds	800,000
Less: Cost (£250,000 + £20,000)	(270,000)
Unindexed gain	530,000
Less: Indexation allowance (Note)	
Cost (£270,000 × 0.276)	(74,520)
Chargeable gain	455,480

Note: Indexation has been frozen at December 2017.

159 C

	£
Land	
Sale proceeds	45,000
Less: Cost	(20,000)
Unindexed gain	25,000
Less: Indexation allowance (W)	
Cost (£20,000 × 1.418) – restricted	(25,000)
Chargeable gain	0

Warehouse

	£
Sale proceeds	75,000
Less: Cost	(80,000)
Unindexed loss	(5,000)
Less: Indexation allowance (Note)	0
Allowable loss	(5,000)

Tutorial note

The indexation allowance cannot increase or create a loss.

160 £55,000

	£
Year ended 30 June 2019	
Capital loss	80,000
Offset against current year chargeable gain	(25,000)
Loss carried forward	55,000

Tutorial note

Capital losses can only be offset against chargeable gains arising in the same accounting period. Any remaining loss is then carried forward against future capital gains.

Capital losses cannot be offset against current year total profits nor carried back and offset against income or gains from previous accounting periods.

161 C

The indexed cost on the disposal of shares is £19,705 (W).

Working: Share pool

		Number	Cost £	Indexed cost £
April 1995	**Purchase**	25,000	33,000	33,000
IA to December 2017 (Note)	0.866 × £33,000			28,578
		25,000	33,000	61,578
June 2019	**Sale**			
	(8,000/25,000 × £33,000/£61,578)	(8,000)	(10,560)	(19,705)
		17,000	22,440	41,873

Note: Indexation has been frozen at December 2017.

162

	True	False
The £250,000 gain which could be deferred as a result of the acquisition of the machine will become chargeable on 1 October 2029		✓
The company must make a rollover relief election by 31 December 2023	✓	

The election must be made within four years of the later of the end of the accounting period in which the old asset is sold and the new asset is acquired.

Tutorial note

The deferred gain of £250,000 will become chargeable 10 years after the replacement asset is acquired (i.e. on 1 November 2028).

PRACTICE SECTION B OBJECTIVE TEST CASES

INDIVIDUALS – CAPITAL GAINS TAX

163 MICHAEL CHIN (ADAPTED)

Key answer tips

A typical examination question on capital gains tax with a series of disposals covering a variety of topics. Remember to use the market value as the proceeds in the computation of the gains when the disposal is a gift.

1 B

	£
Disposal of business	
Goodwill	60,000
Freehold property	64,000
Storage unit	(13,000)
	————
Net chargeable gains qualifying for entrepreneurs' relief	111,000
	————

Tutorial note

*The **net chargeable gains** on the disposal of an unincorporated business qualify for entrepreneurs' relief provided the business has been owned by the sole trader for two years prior to the disposal. The period of ownership of the individual assets is irrelevant.*

2 £74,000

Ordinary shares in Minnow Ltd	£
Deemed proceeds = MV	180,000
Less: Cost	(87,500)
	————
	92,500
Less: Gift relief (W)	(74,000)
	————
Chargeable gain	18,500
	————

Working

The gift relief in respect of the ordinary shares in Minnow Ltd is restricted because the shares are in Michael's personal trading company (i.e. he owns > 5%) and the company has investment assets.

The proportion of gain eligible for gift relief is the proportion of chargeable business assets to chargeable assets, calculated as follows:

Gift relief = (£92,500 × £200,000/£250,000) = £74,000

Tutorial note

Gift relief is available as ordinary shares in an unquoted trading company are qualifying assets for gift relief purposes. However full relief is not available as the shares are in Michael's personal trading company and the company holds investments.

3 D

	£	£
Painting		
Gross proceeds (£5,900 + £656)	6,556	
Less: Selling costs	(656)	
Net proceeds	5,900	
Less: Cost	(4,000)	
Gain	1,900	
Chargeable gain restricted to maximum of:		
5/3 × (£6,556 − £6,000)	927	927

Tutorial note

It is important to be able to recognise when an asset is a chattel (i.e. tangible and movable) and therefore that the disposal is subject to special rules.

4

Chargeable gain/allowable loss	Gain not chargeable/loss not allowable
	Necklace
	Boat
	Machine

Tutorial note

It is important to be able to recognise when an asset is a chattel (i.e. tangible and movable) and therefore that the disposal is subject to special rules.

The necklace is a chattel that was bought and sold for less than £6,000. It is therefore an exempt chattel and the loss is not an allowable loss.

The boat is exempt as a wasting chattel and the gain is therefore not chargeable.

The machine is a wasting chattel, but as it has been used for trading activities it is not an exempt disposal. However, the capital loss is not allowable as relief will be given through the capital allowances computation instead.

5

Loss b/f	Use against gains qualifying for entrepreneurs' relief	Use against gains not qualifying for entrepreneurs' relief
£16,800		✓
£18,400		

Loss left to c/f to 2019/20

	£
Capital loss – 2017/18	16,800
Less: Used in 2018/19 (W)	0
	——
Loss c/f to 2019/20	16,800
	——

In order to maximise the tax saved, the loss should be use against gains not qualifying for entrepreneurs' relief.

Working – Capital loss brought forward

	£
Chargeable gain – 2018/19	17,100
Less: Current year capital loss	(7,000)
	——
Net current year gains	10,100
Less: AEA (restricted)	(10,100)
	——
Taxable gain	0
	——

Tutorial note

The capital loss brought forward is not used in the tax year 2018/19 as the AEA already covers the net gains.

164 BO (ADAPTED)

Key answer tips

This case covers an individual making disposals eligible for reliefs. The first two questions relate to a gift of a business asset and the application of gift relief, followed by a basic calculation of capital gains tax. The third question tests payment and claim dates – it is important to learn the administration rules and to be able to apply them to a given scenario. The fourth question looks again at gift relief, but this time where there is a sale at undervalue.

The last question relates to a separate individual and tests the rules regarding PPR relief.

1   A

Since no consideration has been paid for the shares, all of Bo's chargeable gain can be held over (i.e. deferred) with a gift relief claim. The base cost of Chi's 50,000 £1 ordinary shares in Botune Ltd is:

	£
MV of shares acquired	210,000
Less: Gift relief (W)	(116,000)
Base cost of shares	94,000

Working: Gift relief

	£
Deemed proceeds = MV	210,000
Less: Cost	(94,000)
	116,000
Less: Gift relief	(116,000)
Chargeable gain	0

2

	True	False
Bo's chargeable gain would have been £66,000	✓	
Bo and Chi would not have been able to claim gift relief		✓
The base cost of the shares for Chi would be £210,000		✓

Bo and Chi would not have been able to claim gift relief as the consideration paid for the shares would be less than the market value. Bo's chargeable gain would have been calculated as follows:

	£
Deemed proceeds = MV	210,000
Less: Cost	(94,000)
	———
	116,000
Less: Gift relief (β)	(50,000)
	———
Chargeable gain (£160,000 – £94,000)	66,000
	———

The base cost of the shares for Chi would be £160,000.

	£
MV of shares acquired	210,000
Less: Gift relief (W)	(50,000)
	———
Base cost of shares	160,000
	———

3

		Election date	
		5 April 2024	31 January 2025
CGT due date	31 January 2020		
	31 January 2021	✓	

Tutorial note

Capital gains tax is due under self-assessment, with the balancing payment for income tax, on 31 January following the tax year i.e. 31 January 2021 for the tax year 2019/20.

A gift relief claim must be made within four years of the end of tax year of the gift i.e. 5 April 2024 for a disposal in the tax year 2019/20.

4 **£1,040**

	£
Chargeable gain	20,700
Less: AEA	(12,000)
Taxable gain	8,700

CGT payable:	£
Remaining BRB (£37,500 – £30,500) = £7,000	
£7,000 × 10%	700
£1,700 (£8,700 – £7,000) × 20%	340
	1,040

5 **C**

Working: PPR relief

	Total months	Exempt months	Note	Chargeable months
1.10.07 to 30.9.09 (occupied)	24	24		
1.10.09 to 31.03.18	102	0	1	102
1.04.18 to 30.09.19	18	18	2	
	144	42		102

PPR exemption = (£172,000 × 42/144) = £50,167

Tutorial note

(1) Bo can't use 'three years for any reason' as a period of 'deemed occupation' as she did not reoccupy the property.

(2) The last 18 months are always allowable provided the property was the taxpayer's PPR at some time.

165 ALPHABET LTD (ADAPTED) *Walk in the footsteps of a top tutor*

Key answer tips

This is a familiar style capital gains tax question involving three individuals making disposals. All of them had shares in a company which is taken over.

Takeovers can be complicated where there is mixed consideration and many students may have been put off by the opening paragraph. However, in this question, there is no mixed consideration and it is quite straightforward.

They are disposing of their existing shares and have a choice of either cash or shares, but not a mixture of the two.

Of the three individuals, one chooses cash and therefore they just have a straightforward disposal of shares for cash.

The other two choose shares, which is just a share for share exchange with no capital gains tax consequences at that time. The new shares just 'stand in the shoes' of the old shares and are deemed to have been acquired at the same cost and at the same time as the original shares. They then dispose of some of the new shares.

For the first part, detailed knowledge of the entrepreneurs' relief conditions is required.

1

	Meets the conditions for entrepreneurs' relief	Does not meet the conditions for entrepreneurs' relief
Aloi	✓	
Bon		✓
Cherry		✓

Aloi

Aloi acquired her shareholding and became a director on 1 January 2009, so the qualifying conditions were met for the 24 months prior to the date of the takeover.

Bon

Bon acquired her shareholding and became a director on 1 February 2018, so the qualifying conditions were not met for the 24 months prior to the date of the takeover.

Cherry

Cherry owned 3,000 shares out of the 100,000 shares in the company, which is a 3% shareholding.

This is less than the minimum required holding of 5% to qualify for the relief.

Tutorial note

To qualify for entrepreneurs' relief, the company must be trading and the individual must:

- Own 5% or more of the shares, and

- Work for the company, and

- Must satisfy both of these conditions for 24 months prior to the date of disposal.

Note that the question specifically asks whether the individuals meet the qualifying conditions in relation to their shares in Alphabet Ltd, i.e. before the date of the takeover.

2   £291,400

	£
Ordinary shares in Alphabet Ltd	
Disposal proceeds (60,000 × £6)	360,000
Cost (£50,000 + £18,600)	(68,600)
Chargeable gain	291,400

3   C

	£
Ordinary shares in XYZ plc	
Disposal proceeds (£7.14 × 10,000)(W)	71,400
Cost (£92,200 × 10,000/25,000)	(36,880)
Chargeable gain	34,520

Working: Valuation of quoted shares

The disposal is to a connected party (her brother) and market value is therefore used as the proceeds in the capital gains computation.

The shares in XYZ plc are valued using the mid-price (i.e. average) of the quoted prices in the Stock Exchange Daily Official List:

(£7.10 + £7.18) × 1/2) = £7.14

Total value is 10,000 × £7.14 = £71,400

Tutorial note

Following the takeover Bon received 25,000 ordinary shares in XYZ plc.

Where there is a share for share exchange, the cost of the original shareholding is treated as the cost of the new shareholding acquired on the takeover.

The cost of the new shares disposed of is therefore a proportion of the original cost of the Alphabet Ltd shares.

4   A

5   A

Tutorial note

Transfers on death are exempt disposals for CGT purposes. The daughter's cost of acquisition on a subsequent disposal is the probate value i.e. the market value of the shares at the date of death.

166   JORGE JUNG (ADAPTED)

Key answer tips

This is a fairly typical capital gains tax question involving a number of disposals. It tests the rules for wasting assets which are not chattels, the marginal rules for chattel disposals and part disposals. The last two questions then test gift relief and entrepreneurs' relief, and in particular look at the conditions for each relief to apply. It is important to learn the conditions for each relief and the differences between them.

1   B

	£
Copyright	
Disposal proceeds	8,200
Less: Depreciated cost (£7,000 × 8/10)	(5,600)
Chargeable gain	2,600

Tutorial note

The copyright is a wasting asset. The cost of £7,000 must therefore be depreciated based on an unexpired life of ten years at the date of acquisition and an unexpired life of eight years at the date of disposal.

2   £667

	£
Painting	
Disposal proceeds	6,400
Less: Selling costs	(350)
Net proceeds	6,050
Less: Cost	(2,200)
Chargeable gain	3,850
Restricted to 5/3 × (£6,400 – £6,000)	667

Tutorial note

The painting is a non-wasting chattel that was sold for more than £6,000 but purchased for less than £6,000. The gain is restricted to 5/3 x (gross proceeds – £6,000).

---

3   C

	£
Land – part disposal	
Allowable cost	
£28,600 × (£92,000/(£92,000 + £38,000))	20,240
Legal fees	
£500 × (£92,000/(£92,000+£38,000))	354
Total cost	20,594

Tutorial note

The cost of the land for Jorge is £28,600 which is the value when his father died. Remember that where an individual inherits an asset the cost of acquisition is the market value at the date of death (i.e. the probate value). In addition he incurred £500 on legal fees defending his title to the land, which is an allowable cost of acquisition. His total base cost is therefore £29,100 (£28,600 + £500).

The proportion of the legal fees and the allowable cost of acquisition that can be deducted on the part disposal by Jorge are shown as separate calculations in the computation. It would be equally correct to show this as one calculation based on the total base cost of £29,100 as follows:

£29,100 × (£92,000/(£92,000 + £38,000)) = £20,594

4

.	True	False
The company must be an unquoted company		√
The company must not own any non-business assets		√
The company must be a trading company	√	
Jorge must have owned the shares for at least two years		√

Tutorial note

The company can be a quoted company provided that it is the individual's personal trading company (i.e. Jorge owns at least 5% of the voting rights).

If the company owns non-business assets a gift relief claim can be made but the relief will be restricted if the shares are in the individual's personal company.

There are no minimum ownership period requirements for gift relief.

5   A and C

Tutorial note

The individual can work part time for the company.

Jorge must own at least 5% of the shares of the company – but he can sell a smaller shareholding out of a shareholding of at least 5%

167   ALBERT AND CHARLES (ADAPTED) *Walk in the footsteps of a top tutor*

Key answer tips

A typical capital gains question with two distinct parts. The first part tests the rules for PPR relief and husband and wife transfers. The second part tests the valuation of a gift, the share matching rules and the composition of the share pool.

1   B

One quarter of Albert's house was always used exclusively for business purposes, so the principal private residence relief is restricted to £462,825 (£840,000 − £222,900) × 3/4).

Tutorial note

*The last 18 months exemption does not apply to the whole house as one quarter has **always** been used for business purposes. If the business use had only been for part of the period of ownership the last 18 months would have applied to the whole house.*

2   A, D

Principal private residence relief available would have been available to Victoria as married couples must have a single principal private residence.

Transferring 50% ownership of the house to Victoria prior to its disposal would have enabled her to use her remaining lower rate tax band of 18% for residential properties. There is no saving in respect of her annual exempt amount which has already been used by her other disposals in the tax year. The capital gains tax saving would have been calculated as:

	£
Gains falling into the BRB for Victoria (£37,500 − £21,240) = £16,260	
– lower residential rate of CGT applied (£16,260 × 10% (28% − 18%))	1,626

Tutorial note

The tax saving could be calculated by computing the tax payable by Albert at 28%, and then computing the tax payable by Albert and Victoria sharing the gain equally. However, with only 2 marks available, there is insufficient time to perform all of these calculations. Therefore, the examining team expects you to be able to see the effect of the planning on the computations and perform a two line short cut calculation.

3   £6,800

Share pool	Number	Cost
		£
Purchase 1 March 2011	20,000	19,800
Purchase 20 July 2015	8,000	27,800
	———	———
	28,000	47,600
Disposal 23 October 2019 (£47,600 × 4,000/28,000)	(4,000)	(6,800)
	———	———
Balance c/f	24,000	40,800
	———	———

4

.	Valid reason	Not a valid reason
Charles has never worked for the company		√
Daphne paid Charles for the shares		√
Charles did not own at least 5% of the ordinary shares and voting rights in Restoration plc	√	

Tutorial note

There is no requirement for an individual to work for the company in order to claim gift relief.

The donee paying for the asset does not prevent gift relief being available. However, if the amount paid exceeds the cost to the donor, the gift relief must be restricted so that any actual capital profit made by the donor at the time of the sale will be immediately chargeable.

5 A

	£
Sale of painting – April 2020	
Deemed proceeds	6,000
Less: Cost of disposal	(300)
	————
Net proceeds	5,700
Less: Cost	(13,000)
	————
Allowable capital loss	(7,300)
	————

Tutorial note

You were required to apply the rules for non-wasting chattels. In this situation the gross proceeds were <£6,000 and the cost was ≥£6,000. This requires the use of deemed gross proceeds of £6,000 in the computation to determine the allowable capital loss.

168 ZOYLA (ADAPTED) *Walk in the footsteps of a top tutor*

1

Company	Size of shareholding	Holding period
Minor Ltd		√
Major plc	√	

Tutorial note

The shares in Minor Ltd had not been owned for the 24 months required for claiming entrepreneurs' relief.

Major wasn't Zoyla's personal company i.e. she didn't own ≥5%.

2   A

		Number of shares	£
15.8.17	Purchase	22,500	117,000
12.12.17	Rights issue (1:1) @ £7.40 per share	22,500	166,500
		45,000	283,500
20.6.19	Sale (£283,500 × 20,000/45,000)	(20,000)	(126,000)
		25,000	157,500

3   £154,880

	£
Mid-price per share (£9.62 + £9.74)/2	9.68
Total value of shares sold (£9.68 × 16,000)	154,880

Tutorial note

The actual proceeds received must be substituted with market value at the date of the disposal as Zoyla and her son are connected for capital gains tax.

The market value is determined by taking the mid-price of the prices quoted on the stock exchange on the date of disposal.

4   B

Tutorial note

The disposal would have fallen into the tax year 2020/21 rather than the tax year 2019/20 and the due date of payment of the resultant CGT would accordingly have been 31 January 2022 rather than 31 January 2021.

5

	True	False
Zoyla would not have saved any CGT, but would have benefited from the delayed payment date		√
Zoyla would have saved CGT of £12,000 × 20% = £2,400 due to the AEA for the tax year 2020/21 being available	√	
Zoyla would have saved CGT of £10,600 × 20% = £2,120 due to the remaining basic rate band for the tax year 2020/21 being available		√

Tutorial note

Zoyla would have saved CGT of £10,600 × (20% − 10%) = £1,060 due to the remaining basic rate band for the tax year 2020/21 being available.

169   HALI AND GOMA (ADAPTED)

Key answer tips

A typical examination question on capital gains tax covering a variety of topics.

The first question tests capital losses, which are regularly tested, therefore you should ensure that you learn the rules in relation to both current year and brought forward losses.

The second and fourth questions require you to identify the base cost of shares and a chattel respectively. The second question includes an asset transfer between husband and wife, which is automatically on a no gain / no loss basis. The fourth question requires knowledge of the treatment of compensation received for a destroyed asset, including the impact of reinvestment of the proceeds in a replacement asset.

The third and fifth questions are relatively quick questions to answer. Question three tests the conditions in relation to entrepreneurs' relief. Question five asks you to identify the exempt assets from a list. If you are unsure, try to eliminate some of the answers if possible, then make a sensible attempt and move on.

1   D

Hali	2018/19
	£
Chargeable gain	16,000
Less: AEA	(12,000)
	4,000
Less: Capital losses b/f (restricted)	(4,000)
Taxable gains	0

Capital loss c/f

	£
2017/18 Loss	39,300
Utilised – 2018/19	(4,000)
Loss c/f	35,300

Goma	2018/19
	£
Chargeable gain	6,900
Less: Current year capital loss	(6,900)
Net gain	0

Capital loss c/f

	£
2018/19 Loss	9,100
Utilised – 2018/19	(6,900)
Loss c/f	**2,200**

2   A

Hali's deemed cost is equal to Goma's acquisition cost of £5,000 (£1 × 5,000).

The selling price of £4.95 is the value per share. Given the need for a quick sale, there is no reason to believe that this is not a bargain at arm's length.

3   B

4 **C**

	£
Insurance proceeds	62,000
Less: Cost	(44,000)
Chargeable gain	18,000

	£
Cost of replacement table	63,600
Less: Gain deferred (Note)	(18,000)
Base cost	45,600

Note: The insurance proceeds were fully reinvested within 12 months, therefore the gain can be deferred in full.

5 **A**

Qualifying corporate bonds, motor cars and shares held in an ISA are all exempt assets for the purposes of capital gains tax.

COMPANIES – CHARGEABLE GAINS

170 HAWK LTD (ADAPTED) *Walk in the footsteps of a top tutor*

Key answer tips

The only capital gains relief available to companies is rollover relief and therefore it is not surprising to see it in this question as it is often tested in corporation tax questions.

---

1 **B**

	£
Indexation allowance	
On cost (July 1998 to December 2017)	
0.706 × £84,200 (£81,000 + £3,200)	59,445

Tutorial note

Indexation has been frozen at December 2017.

2

	Qualifying	Non-qualifying
Goodwill acquired on the purchase of the trade and assets of another business		√
Vehicle costing £150,000 with an estimated useful life of 50 years		√
Land acquired for business use	√	
75% shareholding of an unquoted trading company		√

Tutorial note

Assets which qualify for rollover relief are:

– *Land and buildings used for the purposes of the trade*

– *Fixed plant and machinery*

Goodwill is a qualifying asset for individuals but not for companies.

A vehicle is not fixed (i.e. immovable) plant and machinery.

3

		Maximum rollover relief	
		£240,000	£300,000
Latest date	30 April 2022	√	
	31 March 2023		

Tutorial note

The gain rolled over is the indexed gain.

The reinvestment must take place by 30 April 2022 (i.e. three years after the date of sale).

4 **£496,160**

The factory was sold for £496,160 (net of disposal expenses). Therefore this is the amount that Hawk Ltd will have to reinvest in order to claim the maximum possible amount of rollover relief.

Tutorial note

HM Revenue and Customs allow full rollover relief provided the net sale proceeds are reinvested in qualifying assets. It is not necessary to reinvest the gross sale proceeds.

5 **A**

Indexed cost of ordinary shares: £18,000/£30,000 × £12,624 = £7,574

Workings

(W1) Share pool – White plc	**Number**	**Cost**	**Indexed cost**
		£	**£**
Purchase – June 2002	3,000	8,000	8,000
Indexation to takeover – July 2019 (restricted to Dec 2017) (£8,000 × 0.578)			4,624
	3,000	8,000	12,624

(W2) Consideration received on takeover	**MV**
	£
6,000 ordinary shares @ £3	18,000
6,000 preference shares @ £2	12,000
	30,000

Tutorial note

Indexation allowance has been frozen at December 2017.

171 KAT LTD (ADAPTED) *Walk in the footsteps of a top tutor*

1 A

	£
Cost (October 2005)	138,600
Add: Capital improvements (December 2017)	23,400
	162,000
Indexation: October 2005 to December 2017	
0.439 × £138,600	60,845

Tutorial note

An indexation allowance is not available on the capital improvements as the cost was incurred in December 2017. Indexation has been frozen at December 2017.

2

.	True	False
The base cost of the warehouse for chargeable gains purposes will be £140,470		√
The claim for rollover relief against the warehouse must be made by 31 March 2024		√
A further claim for rollover relief may be made if another qualifying asset is acquired by 31 March 2023		√

The base cost of the warehouse for chargeable gains purposes will be £262,470:

Cost	302,000
Less: Gain rolled over (W)	(39,530)
Base cost	262,470

Working: rollover relief

	£
Gain	131,530
Rollover relief (β)	(39,530)
Chargeable gain = Proceeds not reinvested (£394,000 – £302,000)	92,000

The claim for rollover relief against the warehouse must be made within four years of the later of the end of the accounting period in which the asset is sold (year ended 31 March 2020) and replaced (year ended 31 March 2021). Therefore, the claim for rollover relief must be made by 31 March 2025.

A further claim for rollover relief may be made if another qualifying asset is acquired by 30 November 2022 (three years after the disposal).

Tutorial note

The gain can't be rolled over in full as the proceeds are only partially reinvested. The gain which is chargeable immediately is the lower of:

− *the gain on the qualifying asset disposed of, and*

− *the proceeds not reinvested in the replacement asset.*

The balance of the gain can be deferred by rolling it into the base cost of the replacement asset.

---

3   D

Tutorial note

The leasehold building is a depreciating asset as it has an expected life of no more than 60 years.

The gain will crystallise at the earliest of:

− *the date the replacement asset is disposed of*

− *the date the replacement asset ceases to be used for trade purposes, and*

− *ten years from the date of the replacement asset's acquisition.*

The latest date is therefore ten years from the date of the leasehold office building's acquisition on 30 September 2020.

---

4   £63,200

	Number	Cost
	£	£
7.7.10	90,000	90,000
22.9.13 (90,000 × 2/3 = 60,000 × £6.40)	60,000	384,000
Balance at 5.10.19	150,000	474,000
Disposal (20,000/150,000 × £474,000)	(20,000)	(63,200)
Balance carried forward	130,000	410,800

5

		CGT liability	
		£17,580	£18,780
Due date	31 July 2020		
	31 January 2021	√	

2019/20	ER gains £	Non-ER gains £
Kat Ltd shares	142,200	
Vase		28,800
Chargeable gains	142,200	28,800
AEA		(12,000)
Taxable gain	142,200	16,800
Capital gains tax at 10%/20%	14,220	3,360
Total CGT payable (£14,220 + £3,360)		£17,580

Tutorial note

Kitten has some of her basic rate band remaining. However, gains qualifying for entrepreneurs' relief are treated as using up any remaining basic rate band in priority to other gains. This means that the gain on the vase is taxed at the higher rate of capital gains tax. The annual exempt amount should be offset against gains that don't qualify for entrepreneurs' relief in order to save tax at a higher rate.

PRACTICE SECTION C CONSTRUCTED RESPONSE QUESTIONS

INDIVIDUALS – CAPITAL GAINS TAX

172 DAVID AND ANGELA BROOK (ADAPTED) *Walk in the footsteps of a top tutor*

Key answer tips

A classic question involving the calculation of capital gains tax liabilities of a husband and wife, with a joint asset and assets held personally.

Tutor's top tips

Predictably a husband and wife no gain/no loss transfer is included, with the subsequent disposal by the recipient spouse.

Remember to consider entrepreneurs' relief on the disposal of shares and the business.

David Brook

Capital gains tax liability – 2019/20

	£
House (W1)	31,439
Shares in Bend Ltd (W3)	0
	———
Total chargeable gains	31,439
Less: AEA	(12,000)
	———
Taxable gain	19,439
	———
Capital gains tax (£19,439 × 18%)	3,499
	———

Tutorial note

David has no taxable income. All of his gains therefore fall into his basic rate band and are taxed at the CGT rate applicable to gains on residential properties falling within the basic rate band. Entrepreneurs' relief is not available on any of his gains.

Angela Brook

Capital gains tax liability – 2019/20

	Entrepreneurs' relief £	Other gains £	Residential property £
House (W1)			31,439
Ordinary shares in Bend Ltd (W4)		26,400	
Warehouse	3,700		
Total chargeable gains	3,700	26,400	31,439
Less: AEA			(12,000)
Taxable gain	3,700	26,400	19,439
		£	£
Gains qualifying for entrepreneurs' relief:		3,700 × 10%	370
Other gains:		6,855 × 10% (W5)	685
		19,545 × 20%	3,909
		26,400	
Residential property gains		19,439 × 28%	5,443
		49,839	
Capital gains tax liability			10,407

Tutorial note

The AEA should be offset against gains on residential property in priority to other gains in order to save the maximum amount of tax.

Angela has taxable income that uses some of, but not all of, her basic rate band. £3,700 of this is automatically used by the entrepreneurs' relief gains first, leaving £6,855 to set against the other gains.

Workings

(W1) House

Tutor's top tips

If an asset is jointly owned by husband and wife, all you need to do is calculate the gain as usual and then split it 50:50.

Make sure you show your working for the calculation of principal private residence relief. Even if you can't count months, you will still be given marks for applying the correct principles!

	£
Disposal proceeds	381,900
Less: Cost	(86,000)
	295,900
Less: Principal private residence exemption (W2)	(233,021)
Chargeable gain	62,879

David and Angela will each be assessed on 50% of the chargeable gain:

Chargeable gain each = (£62,879 × 50%) = £31,439

(W2) Occupation of the house

The total period of ownership of the house is 240 months (189 + 51), of which 189 months qualify for exemption as follows:

		Total months	Exempt months	Chargeable months
1.10.99 to 31.3.03	(occupied)	42	42	
1.4.03 to 31.12.06	(working in UK)	45	45	
1.1.07 to 31.12.13	(occupied)	84	84	
1.1.14 to 31.03.18	(unoccupied)	51		51
1.04.18 to 30.9.19	(final 18 months)	18	18	
		240	189	51

PPR relief = (189/240 × £295,900) = £233,021

Tutor's top tips

Make sure that you include a brief explanation for the periods you allow as exempt due to the deemed occupation rules – as the examining team has said that such explanations are required to obtain maximum marks in these questions.

(W3) Shares in Bend Ltd – gift by David

Tutor's top tips

Remember that the market value at the time of the inter-spouse gift is a red herring and irrelevant. The transfer will be at no gain/no loss.

Transfers between husband and wife are no gain/no loss transfers.

David makes no gain and Angela takes over David's cost of £48,000.

(W4) Shares in Bend Ltd – Sale by Angela

	£
Disposal proceeds	62,400
Less: Cost (£48,000 × 15,000/20,000)	(36,000)
Chargeable gain	26,400

Tutorial note

It is not clear what percentage interest Angela has in Bend Ltd and whether it is her personal trading company (i.e. she holds 5% interest or more). However, even if she does hold at least 5%, entrepreneurs' relief is not available as Angela does not work for the company.

(W5) Remaining basic rate band

	£
Basic rate band	37,500
Less: Taxable income	(26,945)
	10,555
Utilised by ER gains	(3,700)
Remaining basic rate band	6,855

Examiner's report

Although there were some very good answers to this question from well prepared candidates, it caused problems for many and was often the reason that they failed to achieve a pass mark.

The jointly owned property caused particular difficulty. Only a few candidates correctly calculated the principal private residence exemption.

Some candidates did not allocate the resulting chargeable gain between the couple but instead deducted an annual exempt amount and calculated a separate tax liability.

Note: The examiner's report has been edited to remove comments on elements of the question that have been deleted due to changes to the examination format.

ACCA marking scheme		Marks
Jointly owned property – House – Proceeds		0.5
– Cost		0.5
– Period of exemption		2.0
– Exemption		1.0
– Division of gain		0.5
David Brook – Bend Ltd		0.5
– Annual exempt amount		0.5
– Capital gains tax		0.5
Angela Brook– Bend Ltd – Proceeds		0.5
– Cost		0.5
– Warehouse gain qualifies for entrepreneurs' relief		0.5
– Annual exempt amount		0.5
– Capital gains tax		2.0
Total		**10.0**

173 BILL DING *Walk in the footsteps of a top tutor*

Key answer tips

This is a tricky question, examining three capital gains tax reliefs. A good knowledge of the conditions for all three reliefs and the way that they are applied is needed to score well here, and this should be a good test of whether you are well prepared for these topics!

In section (a) a father gifts shares qualifying for entrepreneurs' relief to his daughter, and they make a joint claim for gift relief. The daughter then sells the shares before two years have elapsed, meaning her disposal does not qualify for entrepreneurs' relief. In section (b) you are asked to not apply gift relief, in order for the father to benefit from entrepreneurs' relief on the full gain.

In section (c) you are asked to compare sections (a) and (b). This style of requirement has become a frequent feature of the examination, so you should make sure that you are prepared for it.

(a)   **Bill and Belle make a joint claim for gift relief**

Bill

Capital gains tax liability – 2019/20

	£
Deemed proceeds (Market value)	260,000
Less: Cost	(112,000)
	148,000
Less: Gift relief (W)	(123,333)
Chargeable gain	24,667
Less: AEA	(12,000)
Taxable gain	12,667
Capital gains tax (£12,667 × 10%) (Note)	1,267

A gift relief claim must be made by both Bill and Belle by 5 April 2024 (i.e. within four years of the end of the tax year of the gift)

Working: Gift relief on shares in High Rise Ltd

Gift relief is available on these shares as they are in an unquoted trading company. However, the gift relief in respect of the shares in High Rise Ltd is restricted because the shares are in Bill's personal trading company (i.e. he owns ≥ 5%) and the company has investment assets.

The proportion of gain eligible for gift relief is the proportion of chargeable business assets to chargeable assets, calculated as £148,000 × £150,000/£180,000 = £123,333.

Belle

Capital gains tax liability – 2019/20

	£
Proceeds	265,000
Less: Cost (£260,000 – £123,333)	(136,667)
Chargeable gain	128,333
Less: AEA	(12,000)
Taxable gain	116,333
Capital gains tax (£116,333 × 20%)	23,267

Tutorial note

(1) *High Rise Ltd qualifies as Bill's personal company, as he holds at least 5% of the shares. As he has both worked for the company and held the shares for at least two years prior to disposal, entrepreneurs' relief is available.*

(2) *High Rise Ltd also qualifies as Belle's personal company. However, she has not held the shares for two years and therefore does not qualify for entrepreneurs' relief. As she is an employee of High Rise Ltd she does not qualify investors' relief irrespective of the ownership period.*

(3) *As a joint claim for gift relief has been made, the cost for Belle is reduced by the amount of relief claimed.*

(b) **Bill and Belle do not make a joint claim for gift relief**

Bill

Capital gains tax liability – 2019/20

	£
Deemed proceeds (Market value)	260,000
Less: Cost	(112,000)
	———
Chargeable gain qualifying for entrepreneurs' relief	148,000
Less: AEA	(12,000)
	———
Taxable gain	136,000
	———
Capital gains tax (£136,000 × 10%)	13,600
	———

Belle

Capital gains tax liability 2019/20

	£
Proceeds	265,000
Less: Cost	(260,000)
	———
Chargeable gain	5,000
Less: AEA	(5,000)
	———
Taxable gain	0
	———

(c)   Comparison capital gains tax payable under options (a) and (b)

	Option (a) £	Option (b) £
Bill	1,267	13,600
Belle	23,267	0
	———	———
Total	24,534	13,600
	———	———

Conclusion of best option

- Total capital gains tax payable is £10,934 lower under option (b) (£24,534 – £13,600) as more of the gain is taxable on Bill, who pays tax at 10% as the disposal qualifies for entrepreneurs' relief.

- Bill however, may prefer option (a) as his own capital gains tax payable is £12,333 (£13,600 - £1,267) lower due to the claim for gift relief.

Tutor's top tips

In part (c) you are asked to summarise the capital gains tax liabilities that you have calculated in parts (a) and (b) and conclude on the most favourable option.

Provided that you use the capital gains tax figures that you have calculated in the earlier parts of the question, and come to a sensible conclusion, you will score marks here, even if your answers to parts (a) and (b) are incorrect.

---

174   JEROME (ADAPTED) *Walk in the footsteps of a top tutor*

Key answer tips

This question tests basic chargeable gains computations for individuals, along with a key relief: gift relief.

It also required calculations of the base costs for the recipients of the assets gifted in the tax year.

You do not have to deal with disposals in chronological order. The disposal of the bracelet was relatively straightforward and would have been a good place to start. You should be familiar with the chattels rules which apply to this disposal.

(a)

Tutor's top tips

Don't forget that disposals of assets between husband and wife and civil partners are automatically on a no gain/no loss basis. If you are provided with the market value or any actual proceeds they are merely there to distract you.

When dealing with a part disposal of land, the market value of the part disposed of and the remainder should be used to determine the cost for the computation. Don't be tempted to use the proportion of asset being disposed of i.e. 9/10 acres.

Jerome – Chargeable gains 2019/20

House

The gift of the house does not give rise to any gain or loss because it is a transfer between spouses.

Reward Ltd

	£
Deemed proceeds	98,400
Cost	(39,000)
	59,400
Gift relief (W)	(50,600)
Chargeable gain	8,800

Working – Gift relief

Gift relief is restricted to £50,600 (£59,400 × £460,000/£540,000), being the proportion of chargeable business assets to chargeable assets.

Antique bracelet

	£
Disposal proceeds	12,200
Cost	(2,100)
Chargeable gain	10,100

This is lower than the maximum gain of £10,333
(5/3 × (12,200 – 6,000)).

Land

	£
Disposal proceeds	78,400
Cost (W)	(26,460)
Chargeable gain	51,940

Working – Cost

The cost relating to the nine acres of land gifted is £26,460
(£37,800 × £78,400/(£78,400 + £33,600)).

Tutorial note

The gift relief computation tested the restriction on gift relief that applies in a very specific scenario. When an individual makes a gift of shares in their personal company (i.e. owns ≥5% of the shares), the gift relief is restricted by reference to the proportion of the company's chargeable business assets to its chargeable assets.

The disposal of land is a part disposal requiring the application of A/(A+B) to the full cost of the land. Any cost not included in the computation is the base cost of the remaining land.

(b) (1) The house has a base cost of £112,800

(2) The 12,000 £1 ordinary shares in Reward Ltd have a base cost of £47,800 (£98,400 – £50,600).

(3) The bracelet has a base cost of £12,200.

(4) The nine acres of land have a base cost of £78,400.

Examiner's report

This question was on capital gains tax, and was generally very well answered. A taxpayer had made various gifts to family members during the tax year. These were (1) a no gain or loss gift of a house to their spouse, (2) a gift of shares in an unquoted trading company which qualified for gift relief, (3) the gift of a non-wasting chattel, and (4) a part disposal of land.

Part (a) required a calculation of the taxpayer's chargeable gains for the tax year. The only aspect which consistently caused problems was the gift relief, with relief being restricted to the proportion of the company's chargeable business assets to chargeable assets.

Part (b) required the base cost taken over by each recipient. Although relatively straightforward, this requirement often resulted in detailed, incorrect, workings. The gift to the spouse caused particular problems, with the base cost being the value at the time it was inherited by the taxpayer – not the value at the time of the gift.

ACCA marking scheme		
		Marks
(a)	No gain/no loss	0.5
	Reward shares proceeds	0.5
	Reward shares cost	0.5
	Gift relief – CBA/CA	1.5
	Antique bracelet proceeds	0.5
	Antique bracelet cost	0.5
	Max – 5/3 rule	1.0
	Land proceeds	0.5
	Land cost A/A+B	1.5
		–––––
		7.0
		–––––
(b)	House base cost	1.0
	Reward shares base cost	1.0
	Bracelet base cost	0.5
	Land base cost	0.5
		–––––
		3.0
		–––––
Total		**10.0**
		–––––

175 GINGER AND NIGEL (ADAPTED) *Walk in the footsteps of a top tutor*

Key answer tips

This question tests two important capital gains tax reliefs: gift relief and entrepreneurs' relief.

Part (a) tested gift relief but in a slightly unusual way which required the application of the modified gift relief rules for sales at an undervaluation, and a calculation of the maximum number of shares that can be gifted without a capital gains tax liability arising.

If you are ever unsure of how to deal with part of a question it is important to make a sensible attempt and move on, rather than waste time, or potentially miss easy marks by not attempting to answer the part.

The highlighted words are key words or phrases that markers are looking for.

Part (b) compares the CGT payable by a husband or wife on the disposal of shares. Again easy marks were available for the basic gains computation in each case and the calculation of the difference in tax payable by the two individuals.

(a)   Ginger

Tutor's top tips

Remember that where there is a disposal at an undervalue (as opposed to an outright gift) then part of the gain may be chargeable now and cannot be held over (deferred).

The examining team has given you a hint in the question as to how to approach the answer by stating that Ginger has not utilised her annual exempt amount.

- The disposal is at an undervalue, so only the 'gift' element of the gain can be held over.

- The consideration paid for each share will be immediately chargeable to capital gains tax to the extent that it exceeds the allowable cost.

- The chargeable amount is therefore £1.61 (£4.00 – £2.39) per share.

- Ginger's annual exempt amount for the tax year 2019/20 is £12,000.

- She can therefore sell 7,453 shares (£12,000/£1.61) to her daughter without this resulting in any capital gains tax liability for the tax year 2019/20.

Tutorial note

This method may have proved quite challenging to some students. If you are unsure how to tackle the question, then make sure you write down what you do know.

One mark was available for simply stating how to calculate the gain on a transfer at an undervalue and another half mark for stating the amount of the annual exempt amount!

Proof of the calculation:

	£
MV of shares (7,453 × £6.40)	*47,699*
Less: Cost (7,453 × £2.39)	*(17,813)*
Capital gain	*29,886*
Less: Gift relief (7,453 × (£6.40 – £4.00))	*(17,887)*
Chargeable gain (7,453 × (4.00 – £2.39)) (excess actual proceeds received)	*11,999*
Less: Annual exempt amount (£1 remains unused)	*(11,999)*
Taxable gain	*0*

(b)   **Innocent and Nigel**

Tutor's top tips

Clearly, the CGT is not going to be the same for both Innocent and Nigel, so you need to look out for the differences in their circumstances. You are given a lot of information concerning their total shareholdings and employment position. As this is different for each of them this should give you a hint that you should consider how this is relevant for determining their CGT liability.

- If Innocent makes the disposal, then her CGT liability for 2019/20 will be:

	£
Disposal proceeds	65,000
Less: Cost (2,000 × £1)	(2,000)
Chargeable gain	63,000
Capital gains tax (£63,000 × 10%)	6,300

Innocent pays CGT at 10% as the disposal qualifies for entrepreneurs' relief.

- If Nigel makes the disposal, then his CGT liability for 2019/20 will be:

	£
Disposal proceeds	65,000
Less: Cost (£46,200 × 2,000/3,000)	(30,800)
Chargeable gain	34,200
Capital gains tax (£34,200 × 20%)	6,840

Nigel pays CGT at 20% because he is a higher rate taxpayer and the disposal does not qualify for entrepreneurs' or investors' relief.

- The capital gains tax saving if Innocent makes the disposal rather than Nigel is therefore £540 (£6,840 – £6,300).

Tutorial notes

(1)   A disposal by Innocent will qualify for entrepreneurs' relief as she is the managing director of Cinnamon Ltd, the company is a trading company, her shareholding of 20% (20,000/100,000) is more than the minimum required holding of 5% and she has held the shares and worked for the company for more than two years. The gain is therefore taxed at 10%.

(2)   A disposal by Nigel will not qualify for entrepreneurs' relief as he is not an officer or an employee of Cinnamon Ltd and his shareholding is only 3% (3,000/100,000). As Nigel is a higher rate taxpayer (taxable income £80,000) the gain is taxed at the higher rate.

(3)   A disposal by Nigel will not qualify for investors' relief as he acquired the shares before 17 March 2016.

Examiner's report

Although there were a number of correct answers to part (a), it caused difficulty for many candidates. The main problem was not appreciating that the annual exempt amount should be used, despite a fairly heavy hint to this effect being given in the question.

Part (b) was another well answered section, with many candidates achieving maximum marks.

Note: *The examiner's report has been edited to remove comments on elements of the question that have been deleted due to changes to the examination format.*

	ACCA marking scheme		
			Marks
(a)	Consideration paid in excess of cost is chargeable		1.0
	Chargeable amount per share		1.0
	Identifying available annual exempt amount		0.5
	Maximum number of shares that can be sold		1.5
			⎯
			4.0
			⎯
(b)	**Innocent**		
	Disposal proceeds		0.5
	Cost		1.0
	Identifying ER applies and capital gains tax		1.5
	Nigel		
	Disposal proceeds		0.5
	Cost		1.0
	Capital gains tax		1.0
	CGT saving		0.5
			⎯
			6.0
			⎯
Total			**10.0**
			⎯

176   MICK STONE (ADAPTED)   *Walk in the footsteps of a top tutor*

Key answer tips

This 10 mark question requires the calculation of the chargeable gains arising from the disposal of two different assets by an individual.

In part (a) the calculations must be done assuming that no reliefs are available, and then part (b) requires an explanation of the capital gains tax reliefs that might be available for each disposal. You also need to state what further information you would require to decide if the reliefs are actually available, and whether there would be any restrictions on the amount of relief available. The highlighted words in the answer to part (b) below are key phrases that markers are looking for.

Tutor's top tips

As you read through the question and think about your answer, it makes sense to consider parts (a) and (b) at the same time. However, it is best to present your answer as two separate parts.

(a)   Chargeable gains – 2019/20

Tutor's top tips

If an item is not an allowable deduction (like the repair to the floor), then include it in your computation as £0 rather than just leaving it out. If you don't include the item the marker will not know if you have left it out deliberately or not so will not be able to give you a mark.

Freehold warehouse

		£
Disposal proceeds		522,000
Less: Cost		(258,000)
Enhancement expenditure	– Floor	(0)
Chargeable gain		264,000

Tutorial note

The cost of replacing the warehouse's floor is revenue expenditure and is therefore not deductible from proceeds when the warehouse is sold. As a repair, it would have instead been deductible from trading profits when the replacement was made.

Rolling Ltd

	£
Disposal proceeds	3,675,000
Less: Cost (W)	(537,600)
Chargeable gain	3,137,400

Working: Share pool

		Number of shares	Cost £
June 2010	Purchase	500,000	960,000
December 2015	Bonus issue (3:2)		
	(500,000 × 3/2)	750,000	0
		1,250,000	960,000
September 2019	Disposal		
£960,000 × (700,000/1,250,000)		(700,000)	(537,600)
Balance c/f		550,000	422,400

(b) **Reliefs available**

Tutor's top tips

Think about the conditions for the relevant reliefs to help you decide what extra information you would require in order to establish whether the relief is available.

No calculations are required so do not waste time by including them.

Freehold warehouse

Possible relief

- Rollover relief may be available in respect of the chargeable gain arising on the disposal of the freehold warehouse.

Further information

- The acquisition date of the replacement warehouse is required, since relief will only be available if this is after 19 May 2018 (one year before the date of disposal).

- The cost of the replacement warehouse is required, since relief will be restricted if the sale proceeds of £522,000 have not been fully reinvested.

Rolling Ltd

Possible relief

- Entrepreneurs' relief may be available in respect of the chargeable gain arising on the disposal of the shares in Rolling Ltd.

Further information

- Details of Rolling Ltd's share capital are required, since relief will only be available if Mick had the minimum required holding (and voting rights) of 5%.

- Details of any previous entrepreneurs' relief claims made by Mick are required, since there is a lifetime limit of £10 million of gains.

Examiner's report

Part (a) was extremely well answered, with many candidates attaining full marks. The only aspect that consistently caused problems was on the disposal of the freehold warehouse, where expenditure on repairing the floor following a flood should have been treated as revenue expenditure – and therefore not a cost in calculating the chargeable gain.

Part (b) caused a few more problems, with many candidates wasting time writing about reliefs that were not applicable.

ACCA marking scheme		Marks
(a) Mick Stone – Chargeable gains		
Freehold warehouse		
Disposal proceeds		0.5
Cost		0.5
Revenue expenditure – Floor		0.5
Rolling Ltd		
Disposal proceeds		0.5
Share pool		
Purchase		0.5
Bonus issue		1.0
Disposal		0.5
		———
		4.0
		———
(b) Freehold warehouse		
ROR may be available		1.0
Acquisition date required		1.0
Cost of replacement warehouse required		1.0
Rolling Ltd		
ER may be available		1.0
Rolling Ltd's share capital required		1.0
Previous ER claims required		1.0
		———
		6.0
		———
Total		**10.0**

177 RUBY (ADAPTED) *Walk in the footsteps of a top tutor*

Key answer tips

This 10 mark question tests the calculation of CGT liability and the treatment of two alternative share disposals.

In part (a) you are required to perform a basic CGT liability calculation.

In part (b) you are required to consider the impact on the CGT liability of two alternative share disposals. This is an unusual approach by the examining team but the calculations themselves are straightforward.

(a)   Ruby – Capital gains tax liability 2019/20

		£
Chargeable gain on investment property		47,500
Less: AEA		(12,000)
		–––––––
		35,500
		–––––––

£		
14,185	× 18% (W)	2,553
21,315	× 28%	5,968
–––––––		
35,500		
–––––––		

		–––––––
Capital gains tax liability		8,521
		–––––––

Working: Remaining basic rate band

	£
Basic rate band	37,500
Less: Taxable income	(23,315)
	–––––––
Remaining basic rate band	14,185
	–––––––

Tutor's top tips

Part (a) of this question is straightforward so you should aim to score well in this section.

Note that with only one disposal being made in the tax year, the full AEA is available to reduce the chargeable gain, and the remaining basic rate band can be used to tax some of the taxable gain at 18%.

Remember that higher CGT rates apply to a gain on residential property. Gains in the basic rate band are taxed at 18%, rather than the 10% rate used for other gains.

(b) **Disposal of shareholding in Pola Ltd**

	Qualifying for ER	Not qualifying for ER
	£	£
Ordinary shares in Pola Ltd (W1)	37,300	
Residential investment property		47,500
Less: AEA	(0)	(12,000)
	———	———
Taxable gains	37,300	35,500
	———	———
(£37,300 × 10%)		3,730
(£35,500 × 28%)		9,940
		———
CGT liability		13,670
		———

Tutorial note

For the purposes of determining the rate of CGT payable the remaining basic rate band of £14,185 is set against the gain qualifying for entrepreneurs' relief of £37,300 even though this has no effect on the 10% rate. So CGT is payable at 28% on the full amount of the residential gain not qualifying for entrepreneurs' relief.

Disposal of shareholding in Aplo plc

	£	£
Ordinary shares in Aplo plc		
Sale proceeds	59,000	
Cost (W2)	(87,200)	
	———	
Capital loss		(28,200)
Chargeable gain on residential investment property		47,500
		———
Net chargeable gains		19,300
Annual exempt amount		(12,000)
		———
Taxable gains		7,300
		———
Capital gains tax liability		
(£7,300 × 18%)		1,314
		———

Workings

(W1) Chargeable gain on ordinary shares in Pola Ltd

	£
Sale proceeds	61,000
Cost	(23,700)
Chargeable gain	37,300

(W2) Cost of shares in Aplo plc

Average of the two quoted prices: (£2.12 + £2.24) × 1/2 = £2.18

£2.18 × 40,000 = £87,200

Examiner's report

Part (a) of the question was well answered, requiring a calculation of the taxpayer's capital gains tax liability for the tax year if the investment property was their only disposal in that tax year.

Part (b) The main problem here was that candidates did not appreciate that both disposals would impact on the capital gains tax payable in respect of the disposal of the investment property. The disposal of the shares in the unquoted trading company (qualifying for entrepreneur's relief) would utilise the remaining basic rate tax band, meaning that the 28% rate was now applicable. The capital loss arising on the disposal of the shares in the quoted trading company would be offset against the chargeable gain on the investment property. Another common problem was the 50p nominal value of the shares in the quoted trading company. This did not impact on the calculation of the capital loss, although many candidates incorrectly divided their cost figure by two.

ACCA marking scheme		Marks
(a)	**Ruby – Capital gains tax liability**	
	Annual exempt amount	0.5
	Capital gains tax at 18%	1.0
	Capital gains tax at 28%	0.5
		2.0
(b)	**Disposal of shareholding in Pola Ltd**	
	Gain on shareholding in Pola Ltd	1.0
	Gain on residential property	0.5
	AEA	1.0
	Capital gains tax at 10%	1.0
	Capital gains tax at 28%	1.0
	Disposal of shareholding in Aplo plc	
	Cost of shares	1.0
	Loss on shareholding in Aplo plc	1.0
	Gain on residential property	0.5
	AEA	0.5
	Capital gains tax at 18%	0.5
		8.0
Total		10.0

178 DALJEET *Walk in the footsteps of a top tutor*

Key answer tips

This 10 mark capital gains tax question tests share disposals, entrepreneurs' relief and the calculation of after tax proceeds. You are required to consider two alternative disposals and decide which one results in higher after tax proceeds.

It is becoming more common for examination questions to require the consideration of alternatives and the comparison of different outcomes so it is important that you practise questions in this style before your examination.

Tutor's top tips

When calculating after tax proceeds, start with the gross proceeds received and deduct any expenses of sale. The most obvious deduction is the tax, but remember to look out for any incidental amounts such as the legal costs in relation to the cottage. This will also be payable out of Daljeet's proceeds, therefore reducing the after tax proceeds available.

(a)   After-tax proceeds

	ABC plc shares	Holiday cottage
Shares	£	£
Disposal proceeds	100,300	110,000
Less: Selling costs		(1,000)
Less: CGT (W1)(W3)	(3,116)	(8,960)
	———	———
Net proceeds	97,184	100,040
	———	———

Daljeet should sell the holiday cottage as this will generate the higher net proceeds.

Tutor's top tips

If a question requires you to make a conclusion there will be credit given for a sensible conclusion based on your workings, even if errors in your calculations have led you to a different conclusion from the model answer.

(W1) Disposal of ABC Ltd shares

	£
Disposal proceeds	100,300
Less: Cost (W2)	(57,143)
Chargeable gain	43,157
Less: Annual exempt amount	(12,000)
Taxable gain	31,157
Capital gains tax (£31,157 × 10%)	3,116

Tutorial note

The disposal of the ABC Ltd shares qualifies for entrepreneurs' relief as for the 24 months prior to disposal, the following conditions are met:

- *ABC Ltd is a trading company,*

- *Daljeet is an employee of ABC Ltd, and*

- *Daljeet has a shareholding of ≥ 5%*

(W2) Cost of ABC Ltd shares – share pool

	Number	Cost
		£
Purchase 7 June 2014	1,000	60,000
Rights issue 7 June 2015		
(1,000 × 2/5) (£50 × 400)	400	20,000
	1,400	80,000
Disposal 31 December 2019		
(£80,000 × 1,000/1,400)	(1,000)	(57,143)
Balance c/f	400	22,857

(W3) Disposal of holiday cottage

	£
Disposal proceeds	110,000
Less: Selling costs	(1,000)
Net disposal proceeds	109,000
Less: Cost	(65,000)
Repairs	0
Chargeable gain	44,000
Less: Annual exempt amount	(12,000)
Taxable gain	32,000
Capital gains tax (£32,000 × 28%)	8,960

Tutorial note

The repairs are not an allowable deduction in the CGT computation, as they are a revenue expense.

Daljeet is a higher rate taxpayer and no reliefs are available for this disposal, therefore the gain has been taxed at the higher rate for residential properties of 28%.

(b)   Inheritance tax

Inheritance tax is charged on a transfer of value of chargeable property by a chargeable person. A transfer of value is a gift of any asset which results in a reduction in value of the donor's estate.

Daljeet is going to sell either the ABC Ltd shares, or the holiday cottage at arm's length and receive consideration in return. He does not intend to make a gift of either asset, so there is no transfer of value for inheritance tax purposes.

COMPANIES – CHARGEABLE GAINS

179 FORWARD LTD (ADAPTED)

Key answer tips

This question requires the calculation of the corporation tax liability of a company, however before that can be calculated two chargeable gains need to be calculated.

Remember that companies are entitled to an indexation allowance and that rollover relief for replacement of business assets is a key relief available for companies. No other reliefs are available. Note that the effect of reinvesting in a depreciating asset as in part (b) must be understood as this is an area that is often tested.

The highlighted words in the answer to part (b) below are key phrases that markers are looking for.

(a) **Corporation tax liability – year ended 31 March 2020**

	£
Trading profit	78,000
Net chargeable gains (£30,000 (W1) + £40,094 (W3))	70,094
Taxable total profits	148,094
Corporation tax liability FY 2019 (£148,094 × 19%)	28,138
Due date	1 January 2021

Workings

(W1) Freehold office building

	£
Disposal proceeds	290,000
Less: Cost	(148,000)
Unindexed gain	142,000
Less: Indexation allowance (frozen at December 2017) £148,000 × 0.706	(104,488)
Chargeable gain before reliefs	37,512
Less: Roll over relief (W2)	(7,512)
Chargeable gain	30,000

(W2) Rollover relief

The sale proceeds of the office building are not fully reinvested.

The chargeable gain which cannot be rolled over is calculated as follows:

	£
Disposal proceeds	290,000
Less: Reinvested in qualifying business asset	(260,000)
Sale proceeds not reinvested = chargeable now	30,000

The remaining gain of £7,512 (£37,512 – £30,000) can be deferred with a rollover relief claim.

(W3) Ordinary shares in Backward plc

	£
Disposal proceeds	62,500
Less: Cost (W4)	(12,895)
Unindexed gain	49,605
Less: Indexation allowance (£22,406 – £12,895) (W4)	(9,511)
Chargeable gain	40,094

Tutorial note

The gain cannot be rolled over into the acquisition of the shares in Sideways plc as shares are not qualifying assets for the purpose of rollover relief.

(W4) Share pool – Backward plc

		Number	Cost £	Indexed cost £
April 1992	Purchase	9,000	18,000	18,000
Indexation to December 2017				
£18,000 × 1.004				18,072
				36,072
November 2019	Purchase	500	6,500	6,500
		9,500	24,500	42,572
November 2019	Disposal			
Cost × (5,000/9,500)		(5,000)	(12,895)	(22,406)
Balance c/f		4,500	11,605	20,166

(b) **Reinvestment in leasehold office building**

- The freehold office building's sale proceeds of £290,000 will be fully reinvested, and so the whole of the gain of £37,512 is eligible for rollover relief.

- The leasehold office building is a depreciating asset, so its base cost will not be adjusted.

- The base cost of the 15 year lease will therefore be its actual cost of £300,000.

- The gain will be deferred until the earliest of:

  - ten years from the date of acquisition of the leasehold building,

  - the date that it is disposed of, or

  - the date that it ceases to be used for trading purposes.

180 LUNA LTD *Walk in the footsteps of a top tutor*

Key answer tips

As this question concerns chargeable gains for companies, be careful to ensure that your answer does not refer to individuals, an annual exempt amount or capital gains tax. A company pays corporation tax on its net chargeable gains and there is no annual exempt amount available for companies.

Part (a) is a deceptively straightforward written part about the indexation allowance and the fact that it cannot create nor increase a capital loss.

The highlighted words in the answer are the key phrases that markers are looking for.

Part (b) requires two calculations in relation to share disposals, which could be attempted in either order.

The first is a straightforward share disposal but potentially time consuming.

The second is more demanding and involves a takeover with mixed consideration, and a gain arising in respect of the cash received.

(a) **Indexation allowance**

Tutor's top tips

The requirement for part (a) is split into two parts so make sure your answer clearly sets out your explanation for each part separately.

- Where a company makes a capital loss, then no indexation allowance is available because it cannot be used to increase a loss.

- Where the indexation allowance is greater than a company's unindexed gain, then the gain is simply reduced to nil because the allowance cannot be used to create a loss.

(b)   Chargeable gains – year ended 31 March 2020

Tutor's top tips

In the absence of guidance on the split of marks you should assume equal weighting is given between the two disposals, and allocate your time accordingly.

It would be easy to spend too long on the first calculation you choose to tackle and miss easy marks on the second.

Pluto plc shares

	£
Disposal proceeds	53,400
Less: Cost (W1)	(13,800)
Unindexed gain	39,600
Less: Indexed allowance (£16,312 – £13,800) (W1)	(2,512)
Chargeable gain	37,088

Asteroid plc takeover – gain in respect of cash proceeds received

	£
Cash received on takeover	65,000
Less: Deemed cost (W2)	(19,500)
Chargeable gain	45,500

Tutorial note

On a takeover, no chargeable gain arises in respect of the £1 ordinary shares in Comet plc received as it is a paper for paper transaction. A new share pool is opened with the deemed cost calculated in respect of the shares on takeover as the base cost.

Workings

(W1) Share pool – Pluto plc

	Number	Cost £	Indexed cost £
Purchase June 2011	16,000	36,800	36,800
Add: Indexation to May 2013			
£36,800 × 0.063			2,318
			39,118
Less: Disposal May 2013			
(£36,800/£39,118 × 10,000/16,000)	(10,000)	(23,000)	(24,449)
	6,000	13,800	14,669
Add: Indexation to December 2017 (Note)			
£14,669 × 0.112			1,643
			16,312
Less: Disposal November 2019	(6,000)	(13,800)	(16,312)

Tutorial note

Remember to index the share pool before each operative event (i.e. purchase and sale) or December 2017 if earlier. The indexation allowance was frozen at December 2017.

(W2) Asteroid plc – takeover consideration and allocation of original cost

Consideration received	MV of takeover consideration £	Allocation of indexed cost £
£1 ordinary shares in Comet plc		
(10,000 × £4.50)	45,000	
£33,000 × (£45,000/£110,000)		13,500
Cash		
(10,000 × £6.50)	65,000	
£33,000 × (£65,000/£110,000)		19,500
	110,000	33,000

Examiner's report

Part (a) All that was required here was a very short statement to the effect that the indexation allowance cannot increase or create a capital loss, but many candidates produced half-page explanations of everything to do with indexation and the use of capital losses.

Part (b) Answers to this section were very mixed. There were many good answers, but other candidates struggled with the workings of the share pool, and the basis of allocating the indexed cost following a takeover. This type of question is where revision question practice is essential, since it will mean that the various rules are understood and also that answers can be laid out as efficiently as possible. There is a standard approach to laying out the workings for a share pool, and candidates are advised to follow this to save confusion.

		Marks
	ACCA marking scheme	
(a)	Capital loss	1.0
	IA greater than unindexed gain	1.0
		───
		2.0
		───
(b)	**Pluto plc**	
	Disposal proceeds	0.5
	Share pool working	
	– purchase June 2011	0.5
	– indexation June 2011 – May 2013	1.0
	– disposal May 2013	1.0
	– indexation May 2013 – December 2017	1.0
	– disposal November 2019	0.5
	Asteroid plc	
	Disposal proceeds	1.0
	Indexed cost attributable to cash element	2.5
		───
		8.0
		───
	Total	**10.0**
		───

ANSWERS TO PRACTICE INHERITANCE TAX QUESTIONS

PRACTICE SECTION A OBJECTIVE TEST QUESTIONS

181

	Exempt	Not exempt
On 7 May 2019 he gave 100,000 shares in Lahm Ltd to his wife. The shares have been valued at that date at £500,000	✓	
On 10 August 2019 he gave 50,000 shares in Hummells Ltd to a discretionary trust. The shares have been valued at that date at £75,000		✓
On 6 October 2019 he gave £2,000 to his son on the occasion of his marriage	✓	
On 9 February 2020 he gave £300 to his daughter		✓

The gift to Mario's wife is exempt as the inter spouse exemption applies.

A lifetime transfer up to £5,000 given from parent to child on the occasion of the child's marriage is exempt, so the gift of £2,000 to Mario's son is exempt.

The gift into the trust is a chargeable lifetime transfer and is therefore not exempt.

The gift to Mario's daughter is more than £250 and therefore the small gifts exemption does not apply.

182 C

	£	£
Gross chargeable amount		500,000
NRB (2019/20)	325,000	
Less: GCTs < 7 years before gift (31.5.08 – 31.5.15)	(300,000)	
		(25,000)
Taxable amount		475,000
IHT payable @ 40%		190,000
Less: Taper relief		
(31.5.15 – 31.10.19) (4 – 5 years before death) (40%)		(76,000)
IHT payable on death		114,000

183 £23,250

		CLT 20.05.2019
		£
Transfer of value		150,000
AE – Current year	(2019/20)	(3,000)
Previous year	(2018/19)	(3,000)
Chargeable amount		144,000
NRB at date of gift		
2019/20	325,000	
Less: GCTs in 7 years pre-gift		
(20.05.2012 – 20.05.2019)	(274,000)	
		(51,000)
Taxable amount		93,000
Lifetime IHT due (donor pays tax)		
(£93,000 × 25%)		23,250

184 A

	£
Transfer of value	50,000
Annual exemption	
– 2019/20 (£3,000 – £2,000)	(1,000)
– 2018/19 (£3,000 – £2,500)	(500)
Gross chargeable transfer	48,500

Tutorial note

The annual exemption is set against PETs, even if they never become chargeable. The annual exemption is offset against the earliest gift in the tax year automatically. The 2019/20 annual exemption is therefore reduced by the amount given to Sameer's friend, as this was before the gift to the trust.

The current year's annual exemption must be offset prior to the offset of any brought forward amounts.

Any unused amounts can be carried forward one tax year, so the remaining annual exemption from 2018/19 can also be offset.

185

	Chargeable amount £
30 November 2012	0
15 June 2013	347,000

Date of death: 1.2.2020

7 years before: 1.2.2013

PET on 30 November 2012 is more than 7 years before death so no IHT payable on death.

	£
PET 15.6.2013	350,000
Less: Annual exemption – 2013/14	(3,000)
– 2012/13	(0)
Chargeable amount	347,000

Tutorial note

Although the PET made on 30 November 2012 does not become chargeable on death, it still utilises the annual exemption for the tax year of the gift (2012/13). This annual exemption is therefore not available to reduce the PET made in the tax year 2013/14 that becomes chargeable on death.

186 A

Tutorial note

Option A describes the common inheritance tax planning technique of 'skipping a generation'. This technique can maximise the inheritance available to future generations as a charge to inheritance tax will only arise once, on the passing of the estate residue to Heng's grandchildren. If the residue had been left to Heng's children and they subsequently gifted the assets to their children, two charges to inheritance tax would arise.

This being said, skipping a generation would not reduce Heng's potential inheritance tax liability on death as legacies left to both children and grandchildren are equally chargeable to inheritance tax.

187 C

		Paid by	
		Trustees of the trust	**Personal representatives of Chan's estate**
Due date	**8 June 2020**	A	B
	30 June 2020	C	D

Tutorial note

The IHT payable on lifetime gifts as a result of death is always paid by the recipient of the gift. The extra tax is due six months after the end of the month of death.

188   A

	£	£
Gross chargeable amount		586,250
NRB (2019/20)	325,000	
Less: GCTs < 7 years before gift (10.11.2007 – 10.11.2014)	(0)	
		(325,000)
Taxable amount		261,250
IHT payable @ 40%		104,500
Less: Taper relief		
(10.11.2014 – 16.7.2019) (4 – 5 years before death) (40%)		(41,800)
		62,700
Less: IHT paid in lifetime		(52,250)
IHT payable on death		10,450

189

	Inheritance tax payable
20 February 2009	
22 March 2012	
30 September 2018	✓
24 December 2019	

Date of death: 20.1.2020

7 years before: 20.1.2013

The gifts to the son and the discretionary trust are more than 7 years before death so no IHT is payable as a result of death.

The gift to the daughter is a PET which has become chargeable as a result of death. The available nil rate band is fully used by the CLT (gift to the trust) made in the 7 years before the date of the gift, so there will be an IHT liability on the gift to the daughter.

The gift to the wife is exempt under the inter spouse exemption.

190 D

	£
Value of estate	890,000
Less: Legacy to wife	(260,000)
Legacy to brother	(120,000)
	510,000
Less: Inheritance tax payable	(252,000)
Residue of estate after inheritance tax	258,000

191 D, E

Tutorial note

An endowment mortgage is not deductible since it is automatically repaid on the owner's death. Repayment and interest-only mortgages are deductible.

A verbal promise to pay a friend's debt is not legally enforceable and therefore not deductible.

Funeral expenses and credit card debts are deductible.

192 £495,000

	£
House (Note)	545,000
Life insurance policy (proceeds received)	350,000
	895,000
Less: Spousal legacy	(400,000)
Chargeable amount	495,000

Tutorial note

Endowment mortgages are not deductible as they are automatically repaid on the owner's death.

193 B

	£
House	390,000
Chattels and cash	70,000
Shares in an ISA	60,000
Income tax owed	(25,000)
Total estate	495,000
Less: Spousal legacy	(100,000)
Chargeable amount	395,000

Tutorial note

Transfers between spouses are exempt from inheritance tax in lifetime and on death.

Tax liabilities of the deceased are allowable deductions from the death estate with the exception of the inheritance tax due on the death estate.

*Assets held in an ISA are exempt assets for capital gains tax but **not** for inheritance tax. They are a common feature in death estate questions for this reason!*

194 £270,400

Death estate	£	£
Gross chargeable estate		1,151,000
NRB at death (2019/20)	325,000	
Add: RNRB (2019/20)	150,000	
		(475,000)
Taxable amount		676,000
IHT on chargeable estate (£676,000 × 40%)		270,400

Tutorial note

Where an individual's main residence is included in their estate and passed on to a direct descendant, the RNRB of £150,000 (or the value of the property if lower) is available to offset against the estate in addition to the standard nil rate band.

195 £114,000

	£
Value of estate before transfer (£20 × 7,500)	150,000
Value of estate after transfer (£8 × 4,500)	(36,000)
Transfer of value	114,000

196 H

Lifetime tax	15 March 2016	31 March 2016	**30 April 2016**
Additional tax on death	15 March 2020	**31 March 2020**	30 April 2020

For a CLT made between 6 April and 30 September the lifetime inheritance tax is due by 30 April in the following year.

The additional tax due on CLTs as a result of death is due 6 months after the end of the month of death.

197

	Pays tax	Suffers tax	Neither pays nor suffers tax
Sister			✓
Daughter		✓	
Executor	✓		

Inheritance tax due on the death estate is paid by the executors but is suffered/borne by the residual legatee (i.e. the daughter).

198

	True	False
An advantage of giving an appreciating asset away during lifetime is that the increase in value up to the date of death will not be subject to inheritance tax	✓	
For capital gains tax purposes lifetime gifts are taxable but gifts on death are not	✓	
On a lifetime gift made more than three years before death, taper relief will reduce the amount of the gift chargeable to inheritance tax on death		✓

Taper relief reduces the **IHT payable on death** provided the donor survives for more than three years following the gift; it does not reduce the chargeable amount on death.

199 B

	£
Nil rate band (NRB) at Nadia's death	255,000
Band utilised on Nadia's death (£275,400 × 50%)	(137,700)
Unused NRB on Nadia's death	117,300
Percentage of NRB unused (£117,300/£255,000)	46%
Tareq's NRB in 2019/20	325,000
Transfer of Nadia's unused NRB (£325,000 × 46%)	149,500
Total NRB available	474,500

Tutorial note

*The unused **percentage** (rather than amount) of nil rate band on the death of the first spouse is applied to the nil rate band at the date of the death of the second spouse to determine the additional amount of nil rate band available.*

PRACTICE SECTION B OBJECTIVE TEST QUESTIONS

200 LEBNA AND LULU (ADAPTED)

Key answer tips

This IHT question starts by covering the transfer of the unused nil rate band and residence nil rate band from a spouse.

Question three requires knowledge of the diminution in value rule for inheritance tax.

The fourth question was straightforward. The correct taper relief percentage is included in the tax rates and allowances and the IHT payment due date is commonly tested.

The final question concerned the small gifts exemption, again, this is commonly tested and provides easy marks.

1   B

	£
Lulu's NRB	325,000
Specific legacy (to brother)	(40,000)
PET within seven years of death	(80,000)
Unused NRB available to transfer (Note)	205,000

Note: The unused percentage of the nil rate band is available to transfer to a spouse. The nil rate band was the same amount in the tax year of death of both Lulu and Lebna, therefore the unused amount is the same as the unused percentage of the current nil rate band.

2   D

The available RNRB is the lower of:

– Lebna's RNRB of £300,000 (W1)

– The value (net of repayment mortgage) of the main residence of £188,000 (W2)

Working 1 – RNRB

	£
Lebna's RNRB	150,000
100% Lulu's RNRB (Note)	150,000
Total RNRB available to Lebna	300,000

Note: The unused percentage of the RNRB is available to transfer to a spouse. Lulu died before 6 April 2017, therefore her full RNRB is available to transfer to Lebna.

Working 2 – Value of main residence

	£
Value of Lebna's main residence	340,000
Less: Outstanding interest-only mortgage	(152,000)
Total RNRB available to Lebna	188,000

3   B

	£
Value pre transfer (100,000 × £7.10)	710,000
Value post transfer (40,000 × £4.20)	(168,000)
Transfer of value	542,000
Less: AE CY	(3,000)
AE PY	(3,000)
Gross chargeable amount	536,000

4   A

Death is between five and six years of when the PET was made, so taper relief of 60% is available. The due date for the IHT is six months after the end of the month in which the donor dies.

5   C

The gifts of £275 (£85 + £190) to the same person total more than the £250 limit. The gift of £490 also exceeds the exemption.

201 TOM (ADAPTED) *Walk in the footsteps of a top tutor*

Key answer tips

This is a typical IHT question covering various aspects of lifetime gifts and then the death estate. The question doesn't test any peripheral topics and therefore should be relatively straightforward.

1   C

	£	£
Chargeable amount (after all exemptions)		450,000
NRB at date of gift	325,000	
Less: GCTs < 7 years before gift	(0)	
	———	
NRB available		(325,000)
		———
Taxable amount		125,000
		———
IHT payable × 25%		31,250
		———
Gross chargeable amount (£450,000 + £31,250)		481,250
		———

2   **£3,000**

	PETs 20 Dec 2011	CLT 20 Feb 2013
	£	£
Transfers of value	5,900	
Less: AE – 2011/12	(3,000)	
– 2010/11 b/f	(2,900)	
Less: AE – 2012/13		(3,000)
– 2011/12 b/f		0
	———	———

Tutorial note

The AE:

- *exempts the first £3,000 of lifetime transfers in any one tax year*

- *is applied chronologically to the first gift in the tax year, then (if there is any left) the second gift and so on*

- *must be applied to the first gift each year, even if the first gift is a PET and never becomes chargeable.*

Any unused AE can only be carried forward one tax year.

3   C

4

	Net value
(1) 50% share in a racehorse	£150,000
(2) Cash winnings	£40,000
(3) Main residence	£375,000

Tutor top tips

Gambling winnings and wasting chattels (e.g. a racehorse) are exempt assets for the purposes of capital gains tax. It is common for these types of assets to be included in a death estate in an examination question to test if you have remembered that there are no exempt assets for inheritance tax. Therefore, it is important that you have a clear understanding of what assets or income are exempt for each tax!

Note that the RNRB is applied to the entire estate not the main residence, so the value needed here is the market value of £875,000 less the outstanding repayment mortgage of £500,000.

5   C

	£	£
Value of estate		2,000,000
NRB at death	325,000	
Less: GCTs in previous 7 years > £325,000 (Note)	(325,000)	
NRB available		(0)
RNRB available		(150,000)
Taxable amount		1,850,000
IHT × 40%		740,000

Tutorial note

There is no nil rate band remaining as the gross chargeable transfer on 20 February 2013, which is within the seven years before death, is greater than £325,000.

Tom is leaving his main residence to his children, therefore the additional residence nil rate band of £150,000 is available to deduct from the estate. Note that this is not reduced by gross chargeable transfers in the seven years before death.

202 AFIYA (ADAPTED) *Walk in the footsteps of a top tutor*

Key answer tips

This IHT question starts by looking at two lifetime gifts, (one PET and one CLT). It then moves on to consider what is included in the death estate. The last two questions cover the transfer of the unused nil rate band from the spouse and the due dates of lifetime tax and tax on the death estate.

1   C

Working: PET – 14 September 2014

	£
Value of shares held before the transfer (8,000 × £8)	64,000
Less: Value of shares held after the transfer (1,500 × £3)	(4,500)
Transfer of value	59,500
Less: AE – 2014/15	(3,000)
– 2013/14	(3,000)
Gross chargeable transfer	53,500

Tutorial note

The loss to the donor (or diminution in value) principle applies when calculating the transfer of value for IHT purposes. This is particularly relevant when valuing shares where a majority shareholding has a higher value per share than a minority shareholding in a company.

The transfer of value is the amount by which Afiya's estate has diminished and not the market value of the asset gifted.

Prior to the transfer Afiya had 8,000 shares (an 80% (8,000/10,000) shareholding) in the company and the shares are valued at £8 per share.

After the transfer Afiya owns 1,500 shares (a 15% shareholding) and the shares are valued at £3 per share.

2   £48,750

Working: CLT – 27 January 2019

	£	£
Transfer of value (after all exemptions)		400,000
NRB at date of gift	325,000	
Less: GCTs in last 7 years (CLTs only)	(120,000)	
	———	(205,000)
		———
Taxable amount		195,000
		———
Lifetime IHT (donor pays tax)	(× 25%)	48,750
		———

Tutorial note

When calculating lifetime tax on a CLT, the available nil rate band is reduced by the value of CLTs in the previous seven years. PETs are ignored even if they subsequently become chargeable.

3   A, B, D AND E

Tutorial note

Debts are only deductible if they were outstanding at the date of death and had been incurred for valuable consideration (i.e. not gambling debts) or were imposed by law.

Endowment mortgages are not deductible as the endowment element of the policy should cover repayment of the mortgage.

4   D

Husband's death estate

	£
NRB at death	312,000
Chargeable estate (to daughter)	(46,800)
Unused NRB	265,200

% of NRB at death £265,200/£312,000 = 85%

	£
Available NRB (£325,000 × 85%)	276,250
Unused residence nil rate band	150,000
	426,250

Tutorial note

The husband did not leave a main residence to direct descendants on his death so 100% of his residence nil rate band (RNRB) is unused and could be transferred to Afiya. Note that the husband does not need to have died after 5 April 2017 in order for the RNRB to be transferred to the surviving spouse.

5

Lifetime tax on gift to trust	Tax on estate
31 July 2019	31 May 2020

Tutorial note

As the lifetime gift was made between 1 October and 5 April in the tax year 2018/19, the due date for the lifetime IHT on the CLT to the trust is 31 July 2019, being six months from the end of the month in which the gift was made.

The due date for the IHT on the estate is 31 May 2020, being six months after the end of the month in which Afiya died.

---

203   ROMAN (ADAPTED) *Walk in the footsteps of a top tutor*

1   A

	CLT – Gift to trust 26 August 2017	
	£	£
Transfer of value		190,000
AE 2017/18		(3,000)
AE 2016/17 b/f		(0)
		_____
Chargeable amount		187,000
NRB @ death	325,000	
Less: Chargeable transfers ≤ 7 years of this gift (26.8.10 to 26.08.17) (i.e. PET on 4.3.17)	(204,000)	
	_____	
NRB available		(121,000)
		_____
Taxable amount		66,000
		_____
IHT payable (£66,000 × 40%)		26,400
		_____

Tutorial note

The annual exemption for the tax year 2016/17 had already been utilised by the PET to Roman's daughter on 4 March 2017.

The PET also reduced the available nil rate band for the gift to the trust. The transfer of value in respect of the PET would be reduced by the 2015/16 and 2016/17 annual exemptions, resulting in a chargeable amount of £204,000 (£210,000 – £6,000).

2   A

Tutorial note

The trustees of the trust are responsible for paying the IHT arising on the trust on death. The IHT is due to be paid 6 months from the end of the month of death.

3   C

	£
Value of a 40% shareholding pre gift (100,000 × £8)	800,000
Value of a 10% shareholding post gift (25,000 × £5)	(125,000)
Diminution in value	675,000

Tutorial note

The fall in the value of the donor's estate must be calculated in order to determine the value of the gift for IHT purposes. Roman had a 40% shareholding (100,000/250,000) prior to making the gift and a 10% shareholding (25,000/250,000) after making the gift.

The rule is different to capital gains tax where the value of a 30% shareholding in isolation would be used as the value of the gift in the computation.

4   £735

Tutorial note

Gifts of up to £250 per recipient per tax year are exempt from IHT under the small gifts exemption. Accordingly, the gift of £210 is the only gift eligible for the small gift exemption. The gifts of £80 and £195 are made to the same friend and must be considered in total when determining whether the small gifts exemption applies.

The gifts that don't qualify = £80 + £195 + £460 = £735

5

		Roman's estate	Paris' estate
IHT payable	£104,000	✓	
	£224,000		
	£328,000		
	£336,000		✓

	£
IHT on estate:	
Roman	
Chargeable estate	560,000
Less: Exempt legacy - spouse	(300,000)
Taxable estate	260,000
IHT payable at 40% (£260,000 × 40%)	104,000
Paris	
Chargeable estate = taxable estate	840,000
IHT payable at 40% (£840,000 × 40%)	336,000

204 ADANA (ADAPTED) *Walk in the footsteps of a top tutor*

1 D

	£
Adana's NRB	325,000
Add: Husband's unused % × current NRB	
(80% × £325,000)	260,000
	585,000

Tutorial note

*The unused **percentage** (rather than amount) of nil rate band on the death of the first spouse is applied to the nil rate band at the date of the death of the second spouse to determine the additional amount of nil rate band available.*

2

		Deductible
(1)	Interest-only mortgage	£220,000
(2)	Income tax payable	£43,700
(3)	Sister's legal fees	£0

Tutorial note

The legal fees are not deductible as the debt is not legally enforceable.

Mortgages are allowable deductions with the exception of endowment mortgages, which will be repaid with the endowment element of the policy.

Outstanding taxes such as income tax and capital gains tax can be deducted in the estate, although the IHT itself is not deductible.

3   D

	Tax payable		
	30 September 2020	17 September 2020	17 March 2021
Beneficiaries (her children)			
Personal representatives			

Tutorial note

The personal representatives of the donor's estate are responsible for paying any IHT on the death estate and the IHT must be paid within six months from the end of the month of death.

4   C

Tutorial note

The assets would still have been subject to inheritance tax; therefore no tax would have been saved.

Assets left to a spouse are exempt from inheritance tax but assets left to other beneficiaries are taxable as normal.

5   £207,750

		£
Value of shares at 17 March 2020		650,000
IHT at 40% (£650,000 × 40%)		260,000
Less: Lifetime tax paid		(52,250)
IHT saved		**207,750**

PRACTICE SECTION C CONSTRUCTED RESPONSE QUESTIONS

205   BLU (ADAPTED) *Walk in the footsteps of a top tutor*

Key answer tips

Part (a) tests a basic calculation of IHT due on an estate. It is important to consider whether there is an opportunity to utilise the unused proportion of the deceased spouse's nil rate band and/or residential nil rate band when dealing with the death of the second spouse.

Part (b) is a very straightforward IHT question requiring the calculation of the lifetime and death tax on one CLT.

Tutor's top tips

You do not have to answer this question in the order set. Provided you start each part on a separate page and clearly indicate which part you are answering, you can answer in any order. Hence you might prefer to start with part (b) if you are more familiar with lifetime gifts.

However, do take care when attempting a question out of order, as sometimes the answer to part (a) is required in part (b), and so on. This is clearly not the case in this question as each part involves a different individual.

(a) (1) **Red Perry – Death estate**

	£
Gross chargeable estate	800,000
Less: NRB (W)	(439,000)
Taxable estate	361,000
IHT payable (£361,000 × 40%)	144,400

Working: Nil rate band

	£
Nil rate band at death	325,000
Less: Gross chargeable transfers < 7 years before death	
(6.11.12 – 6.11.19)	(211,000)
Available NRB	114,000
Add: Spouse's unused NRB (100% × £325,000)	325,000
Total NRB	439,000

Tutorial note

Red's wife made no lifetime gifts and left her entire estate to Red, leaving 100% of her NRB unused. This unused proportion is available to transfer to Red, and is applied to the NRB in force at the date of his death, i.e. (100% × £325,000).

The residence nil rate band is not available as Red is not leaving his estate to a direct descendant e.g. children, grandchildren.

(2) **Estate left to Red's son**

If Red left the estate to his son, a residence nil rate band of £150,000 would be available to reduce the value of the estate.

This only applies if a main residence is left to a direct descendant such as a child or grandchild.

In addition to his own residence nil rate band, Red would also be able to utilise his wife's unused residence nil rate band of £150,000.

Tutorial note

Red's wife did not leave a main residence to direct descendants on her death so 100% of her residence nil rate band (RNRB) is unused and could be transferred to Red. Note that the wife does not need to have died after 5 April 2017 in order for the RNRB to be transferred to the surviving spouse.

If Red had left the main residence to his son the IHT payable would have been reduced by £120,000 ((£150,000 + £150,000) × 40%).

(b) **Blue Reddy**

Inheritance tax computation

Lifetime tax on lifetime gift – 15 January 2020

	£	£
Value of shares held before the transfer (300,000 × £4)		1,200,000
Value of shares held after the transfer (100,000 × £2)		(200,000)
Transfer of value (Note 1)		1,000,000
Less: AE (ignore per question)		(0)
Chargeable transfer (Net)		1,000,000
NRB at time of gift	325,000	
GCTs in 7 years pre gift (15.1.2013 – 15.1.2020)	(0)	
		(325,000)
Taxable amount		675,000
IHT liability (£675,000 × 25%) (Note 2)		168,750
Gross chargeable transfer c/f (£1,000,000 + £168,750)		1,168,750

Additional death tax due on lifetime gift – 15 January 2020
(assuming death occurs 31 May 2024)

	£	£
Gross chargeable transfer		1,168,750
NRB at time of death	325,000	
GCTs in 7 years pre death (31.5.2017 – 31.5.2024)	(0)	
		(325,000)
Taxable amount		843,750
IHT liability (£843,750 × 40%)		337,500
Less: Taper relief		
(15.1.2020 – 31.5.2024) (4 – 5 years) (40%)		(135,000)
		202,500
Less: Lifetime IHT paid		(168,750)
Additional IHT payable on death		33,750

Tutorial note

(1) *The transfer of value is calculated by reference to the diminution in the value of the donor's estate. The value of the 40% shareholding transferred (i.e. 200,000 shares at £3 for a 40% shareholding) is irrelevant for IHT purposes. This is particularly relevant in this situation, where company shares are involved, where the diminution in value of Blu's estate from reducing his interest in the company from 60% to 20% (i.e. £1,000,000) is far greater than valuing a 40% shareholding in isolation (£600,000).*

(2) *Remember that where the donor pays the tax the appropriate tax rate is 25% as their estate has been diminished not just by the gift but also by the IHT paid. The gross chargeable transfer is the value of the gift plus the tax paid.*

Examiner's report

Candidates were helped in part (b) by being told to ignore annual exemptions, but many also ignored these instructions.

They were not penalised for this, but it made the calculations a bit more complicated than was necessary.

When calculating the additional liability arising on death many candidates had problems computing the amount of brought forward gross chargeable transfer, and taper relief was often calculated and deducted at the wrong point in the computation.

Candidates should also appreciate that examinations are not quite the same as real life.

With a six mark section it should be obvious that the value of the transfer was more than the nil rate band of £325,000 – many candidates calculating the transfer as (200,000 × £1) = £200,000. Using any of the other values would have enabled some marks to be obtained.

However, there were many perfect answers to part (b), with the six marks obtained often being the difference between a pass and a fail.

Note: The examiner's report has been edited to remove comments on elements of the question that have been deleted due to changes to the examination format.

Part (a) has been added since the question was originally set.

ACCA marking scheme			
			Marks
(a)	(1)	Red's NRB	1.0
		100% NRB transferred from spouse	1.0
		IHT payable at 40%	0.5
	(2)	RNRB available	0.5
		Left to direct descendant	0.5
		Wife's RNRB available in full	0.5
			———
			4.0
			———
(b)		**Lifetime transfer**	
		Value transferred	2.0
		IHT liability	1.5
		Additional liability arising on death	
		Gross chargeable transfer	0.5
		IHT liability	0.5
		Taper relief	1.0
		IHT already paid	0.5
			———
			6.0
			———
Total			**10.0**
			———

206   JACK AND TOM (ADAPTED)   *Walk in the footsteps of a top tutor*

Key answer tips

This question involves two separate topics. The requirements and mark allocation are very clear. Make sure that you allocate your time in relation to the mark allocation. Part (a) tests investors' relief and was not part of the original question. Part (b) is a straightforward IHT question testing the fundamentals of IHT. It deals with the lifetime tax payable on a chargeable lifetime gift.

The highlighted words are key phrases that markers are looking for.

(a) Jack

The disposal of the shares in Corinthian Ltd qualifies for investors' relief as the following conditions have been met:

– He has sold ordinary shares in an unlisted trading company.

– The shares were subscribed for after 17 March 2016.

– They were held for more than three years starting after 6 April 2016.

– Jack is not an employee or officer of the company.

– Investors' relief has its own £10m lifetime limit (separate from that for entrepreneurs' relief). Due to third point above, Jack cannot have used any of this limit prior to this disposal.

Capital gains tax liability – 2019/20

	£
Proceeds	151,107
Less: Cost	(13,119)
Chargeable gain qualifying for investors' relief	137,988
Less: Current year capital loss	(1,872)
Less: AEA	(12,000)
Taxable gain	124,116
Capital gains tax (£124,116 × 10%)	12,412

Tutorial note

(1) If an individual has other gains that don't qualify for investors' (or entrepreneurs') relief the annual exempt amount and any capital losses should be used against those other gains first. However, if, as in this case, the only gain does qualify for investors' relief then the current year capital loss and annual exempt amount must be offset against that gain.

(2) Jack must make a claim for investors' relief by 12 months after 31 January following the end of the tax year of disposal, i.e. 31 January 2022.

(b) Tom Tirith

Tutor's top tips

The only difference between the two computations in this part will be the rate of tax paid on the gift. Remember that if Tom pays the tax his estate will be reduced by the value of the gift and the associated tax – this is reflected in the rate of tax paid on the gift.

(1) **Inheritance tax (IHT) paid by donee (the trust)**

	£	£
Value transferred		450,000
Annual exemption – 2019/20		(3,000)
– 2018/19		0
		———
Gross chargeable transfer		447,000
NRB at date of gift	325,000	
Less: GCTs < 7 years before gift	(0)	
	———	
NRB available		(325,000)
		———
Taxable amount		122,000
		———
IHT payable × 20%		24,400
		———

IHT paid by donor (Tom)

	£
Taxable amount (as above)	122,000
	———
IHT payable × 25%	30,500
	———
Gross chargeable transfer (£447,000 + £30,500)	477,500
	———

Tutorial note

The potentially exempt transfer made on 20 December 2018 utilises the annual exemption for the tax year 2018/19 but does not use any of the nil rate band as Tom is still alive.

(2) **Effect of gift on 20 December 2018 being to a trust**

- If Tom had made a gift to a trust rather than to his daughter, it would have been a chargeable lifetime transfer rather than a potentially exempt transfer.

- No inheritance tax would be payable on the gift on 20 December 2018, as it is below the nil rate band for the tax year 2018/19.

- It would however reduce the nil rate band available for the chargeable lifetime transfer on 20 February 2020, resulting in more of the second gift being chargeable to inheritance tax in Tom's lifetime.

Examiner's report

Most candidates answered part (b)(i) extremely well, often gaining all of the available marks. However, the PET was sometimes incorrectly included in the workings for the first requirement – not only losing marks, but also complicating the otherwise straightforward calculations.

Note: The examiner's report has been edited to remove comments on elements of the question that have been deleted due to changes to the examination format.

	ACCA marking scheme	
		Marks
(a)	Jack Monkton	
	Conditions (0.5 per condition, capped at four conditions)	2.0
	Calculation of capital gains tax	3.0
		———
		5.0
		———
(b)	Tom Tirith	
	(1) Inheritance tax (IHT) paid by donee (the trust)	
	Annual exemption	0.5
	IHT liability	1.0
	IHT paid by donor (Tom)	
	IHT liability	0.5
	Gross chargeable transfer	1.0
		———
		3.0
		———
	(2) Gift would be a CLT rather than a PET	0.5
	No IHT due as bellow NRB	0.5
	Reduces NRB available for second CLT and increases IHT	1.0
		———
		2.0
		———
Total		10.0
		———

207 PERE JONES (ADAPTED) *Walk in the footsteps of a top tutor*

Key answer tips

This 10 mark question involved knowledge of two taxes: inheritance tax (IHT) and capital gains tax.

Part (a) required a calculation of the IHT that would be payable on a PET and the estate, as a result of death. This involved a straightforward IHT computation with the only trickier points being remembering to include taper relief and including it in the correct place in the computation.

Part (b) required a calculation of an individual's capital gains tax liability. The key skill was in distinguishing between capital and revenue income/expenditure.

(a) **Pere Jones**

Inheritance tax (IHT) arising on death

Lifetime transfer – 23 August 2014

	£	£
Value transferred		416,000
Less: Marriage exemption		(1,000)
Annual exemptions – 2014/15		(3,000)
– 2013/14		(3,000)
Potentially exempt transfer		409,000
NRB at death	325,000	
Less: GCTs in previous 7 years	(0)	
NRB available		(325,000)
Taxable amount		84,000
IHT × 40%		33,600
Less: Taper relief (23.8.2014 to 20.3.2020) (5 – 6 years) (60%)		(20,160)
Less: Lifetime IHT paid (£0 – as it is a PET)		(0)
IHT payable		13,440

Tutorial note

The gift is a potentially exempt transfer that becomes chargeable as a result of Pere dying within seven years of making it.

Pere died more than five but less than six years after the date of the gift so taper relief of 60% is available. The taper relief table is given in the Tax Rates and Allowances provided in the examination.

Death estate

	£	£
Value of estate		880,000
Less: Inter spouse exemption (£880,000 ÷ 2)		(440,000)
Chargeable estate		440,000
NRB at death	325,000	
Less: GCTs in previous 7 years (20.3.2013 to 20.3.2020)	(409,000)	0
Taxable amount		440,000
IHT liability × 40% (Note)		176,000

Tutorial note

There is no nil rate band available to set against the death estate as it has been fully utilised against the lifetime gift to Phil, which was within seven years of Pere's death.

Where, as in this case there is no available nil rate band make sure that you either show how the nil rate band has been used (as in the above computation) or include a note to your answer stating that the available nil rate band of £325,00 has been fully utilised by the PET of £409,000 on 23 August 2014. If you just ignore the nil rate band the marker will not know whether you understand that it has been fully utilised by the PET or you have just forgotten it.

(b) **Phil Jones**

Capital gains tax computation – 2019/20

	£
House	
Disposal proceeds	504,000
Less: Incidental costs of disposal	(8,100)
Net disposal proceeds	495,900
Less: Cost (MV at date of gift)	(416,000)
Enhancement expenditure (boundary wall)	(9,300)
Replacement of chimney (Note 1)	0
Chargeable gain	70,600
Less: Annual exempt amount	(12,000)
Taxable gain	58,600
Capital gains tax liability	
(£58,600 × 28%) (Note 2)	16,408

Tutorial note

(1) *The cost of replacing the property's chimney is revenue expenditure as the chimney is a subsidiary part of the house. The cost of the new boundary wall is capital expenditure as the wall is a separate, distinct, entity.*

(2) *Phil is a higher rate taxpayer as he has earnings from employment of £80,000 in the tax year. He therefore has no basic rate band remaining and all of his chargeable gain on residential property is taxable at the higher rate of 28%.*

Examiner's report

Part (a) was generally very well answered, with many candidates achieving maximum marks. The only aspect that consistently caused problems was taper relief, with either the incorrect rate being used or relief being given at the wrong point in the computation.

Note: *The examiner's report has been edited to remove comments on elements of the question that have been deleted due to changes to the examination format.*

ACCA marking scheme		Marks
(a)	Lifetime transfer	
	Marriage exemption	1.0
	Annual exemptions	1.0
	Potentially exempt transfer	0.5
	Nil rate band	0.5
	IHT liability at 40%	0.5
	Taper relief	1.0
	Death estate	
	Spouse exemption	1.0
	IHT liability at 40% (no NRB)	0.5
		——
		6.0
		——
(b)	**Capital gains tax**	
	Disposal proceeds	0.5
	Cost	1.0
	Enhancement expenditure	1.0
	Incidental costs of disposal	0.5
	Annual exempt amount	0.5
	CGT at 28%	0.5
		——
		4.0
		——
Total		**10.0**
		——

208 KENDRA OLDER *Walk in the footsteps of a top tutor*

Key answer tips

This question is primarily about inheritance tax, although you are also required to consider the capital gains tax implications of a gift in part (b). It can be daunting when a question requires you to think about two different taxes, and the best way to approach it is to decide on your answer for one tax, and then think about the second tax independently.

Part (b) is a written requirement. The highlighted words in the answer to part (b) are key phrases that markers are looking for.

(a)   Kendra Older – Inheritance tax arising on death

Tutor's top tips

You may find it helpful to draw a timeline showing the lifetime gifts, the assumed date of death and the date seven years prior to death to help you visualise the scenario.

Lifetime transfer within seven years of death

Date of death:	31 March 2020
7 years before:	31 March 2013

Therefore only the PET on 5 October 2018 becomes chargeable on death.

PET – 5 October 2018

	£
Transfer of value	253,000
Less: Annual exemptions 2018/19	(3,000)
2017/18 b/f	(3,000)
	————
Gross chargeable transfer	247,000
	————
NRB available (W)	(185,000)
	————
Taxable amount	62,000
	————
IHT payable (£62,000 × 40%)	24,800
Less: Taper relief (< 3 years before death)	(0)
Lifetime IHT paid (£0 as a PET)	(0)
	————
	24,800
	————

Tutor's top tips

Do not be put off by the fact that the question includes the nil rate bands for the earlier tax years: these are not needed in your answer.

The 2012/13 figure is not needed as the question states that there is no inheritance tax on the CLT on 20 June 2012 and we are given the gross chargeable transfer value of the gift.

The 2018/19 figure is not needed because the inheritance tax on a PET is always calculated using the nil rate band for the year of death and not the year of the gift. In this case the nil rate bands for the year of the gift and at death are the same, but this will not always be the case so you do need to remember this rule.

Death estate

	£	£
Investment property		970,000
Proceeds of life assurance policy		225,000
		———
Gross chargeable estate		1,195,000
Less: Nil rate band on death (31 March 2020)	325,000	
GCTs in 7 years before death		
(31.3.2013 – 31.3.2020)	(247,000)	
	———	
		(78,000)
		———
Taxable amount		1,117,000
		———
IHT payable (£1,117,000 × 40%)		446,800
		———

Tutorial note

The chargeable lifetime transfer made on 20 June 2012 is not relevant when calculating the inheritance tax on the death estate as it was made more than seven years before the date of Kendra's assumed death. Only the potentially exempt transfer made on 5 October 2018 is taken into account, and this utilises £247,000 of the nil rate band for the tax year 2019/20.

The residence nil rate band is not available as the property has always been let out and has never been Kendra's main residence.

Working: Potentially exempt transfer

	£
Nil rate band on death (31 March 2020)	325,000
Less: GCTs in 7 years before gift (5.10.2011 – 5.10.2018) CLT – 20 June 2012	
Gross chargeable transfer value	(140,000)
Nil rate band available	185,000

Tutorial note

You are given the gross chargeable transfer value of the CLT on 20 June 2012. This figure is after the deduction of any exemptions. So this figure can simply be deducted from the nil rate band available to the PET without any further calculations.

(b) Immediate lifetime gift of property

Tutor's top tips

It is important to leave sufficient time to address the written parts of questions. It is easy to get caught up with the computational parts, but often written elements provide easy marks.

This part is asking you to think about the advantages of a death gift compared to a lifetime gift. Lifetime gifts can be advantageous if the donor lives for 7 years after the PET is made as then no inheritance tax will be payable but this is not the case here.

With three marks available it is always best to aim to make three good points. However, in this question it may be difficult to think of three points to include and the mark scheme actually allocated 1.5 marks to the two main points.

- As the property is not expected to increase in value in the near future, there is no inheritance tax benefit in making a lifetime gift.

- Kendra would need to live for three more years for taper relief to be available.

- Also, a lifetime gift would result in a capital gains tax liability of £48,720 (£174,000 at 28%) in the tax year 2019/20, whereas a transfer on death would be an exempt disposal.

Examiner's report

Part (a) was generally very well answered. Some candidates did not appreciate that the chargeable gain was irrelevant to this section of the question given that the property was not disposed of. Also, the valuation of the life assurance policy sometimes caused problems, and one common mistake was to only include the difference between the open market value and the proceeds.

Very few candidates were able to correctly answer part (b), with the main problem being the lack of appreciation that there was no IHT advantage to making a lifetime gift. This was because Kendra would not live long enough to benefit from taper relief, and also because the property's value was not going to change. Even when CGT was mentioned, most candidates did not realise that holding the property until death would eliminate any liability.

		ACCA marking scheme	Marks
(a)		PET – 5 October 2018	
		Transfer of value	0.5
		Annual exemptions	1.0
		Available nil rate band	
		Nil rate band on death	0.5
		CLT – 20 June 2012	0.5
		IHT payable	1.0
	Death estate		
		Property	0.5
		Proceeds of life assurance policy	1.0
		Nil rate band available	1.5
		Inheritance tax liability at 40%	0.5
			7.0
(b)		No IHT benefit	1.5
		CGT liability arises	1.5
			3.0
Total			10.0

209 JAMES (ADAPTED) *Walk in the footsteps of a top tutor*

Key answer tips

Part (a) for six marks was a standard IHT question requiring the calculation of the tax payable on two lifetime gifts and the death estate as a result of the donor's death. This part also tested the knowledge of who is responsible for making the payments of IHT on both the lifetime gifts and the death estate.

Parts (b) and (c) involved basic IHT planning – this had to be applied to the scenario.

Tutor's top tips

The focus of this question was on lifetime gifts. Don't be put off by the fact there are three lifetime gifts made by the donor in the question.

Inheritance tax requires you to deal with the gifts in chronological order. Start with the earliest gift and apply any available exemptions. You can then consider which gifts will be subject to inheritance tax on the donor's death; any gifts more than seven years prior to the donor's death will not be subject to IHT on death.

(a) **James – Inheritance tax arising on death**

Lifetime transfers within seven years of death
14 May 2018

		£
Value transferred		420,000
Annual exemptions	2018/19	(3,000)
	2017/18	(3,000)
		————
Potentially exempt transfer		414,000
		————
Inheritance tax liability	£296,000 (W) × nil%	0
	£118,000 × 40%	47,200
		————
		47,200
		————

James' daughter will be responsible for paying the inheritance tax of £47,200.

2 August 2018

	£
Chargeable lifetime transfer (no annual exemptions remaining)	260,000
	————

Inheritance tax liability:
No nil rate band remaining – used by CLT on 9.10.12 and PET on 14.5.18

£260,000 × 40%	104,000
	————

The trust will be responsible for paying the inheritance tax of £104,000.

Death estate

	£
Chargeable estate	870,000
	————
Inheritance tax liability £870,000 × 40% (no nil rate band remaining)	348,000
	————

The personal representatives of James' estate will be responsible for paying the inheritance tax of £348,000.

Working – Available nil rate band

	£	£
Nil rate band		325,000
Chargeable lifetime transfer 9 October 2012		
Value transferred	35,000	
Annual exemptions 2012/13	(3,000)	
2011/12	(3,000)	
		(29,000)
		296,000

Tutorial notes

The gift in October 2012 was made more than seven years before the donor's death and as such there was no IHT due as a result of James' death. This was a gift into a trust however, which means it was chargeable to IHT immediately. As this gift was within 7 years of the next two lifetime gifts, the nil rate band available to these gifts is reduced accordingly.

(b)   Skipping a generation avoids a further charge to inheritance tax when his brother dies. Gifts will then only be taxed once before being inherited by his nephew, rather than twice.

(c)   (1)   Even if the donor does not survive for seven years, taper relief will reduce the amount of IHT payable after three years.

   (2)   The value of potentially exempt transfers and chargeable lifetime transfers are fixed at the time they are made.

   (3)   James therefore saved inheritance tax of £20,000 ((£310,000 – £260,000) at 40%) by making the lifetime gift of property.

Examiner's report

This question was on inheritance tax (IHT), and candidates found this to be a challenging area.

The requirement for part (a) was to calculate the IHT payable as a result of a taxpayer's death, and to state who was responsible for paying the tax. The taxpayer had made (1) a chargeable lifetime transfer (more than seven years before death), (2) a potentially exempt transfer and (3) another chargeable lifetime transfer. A quick review of the information given should have indicated that no lifetime tax would have been paid (this fact was actually stated in respect of the second chargeable lifetime transfer) and that taper relief was not relevant (given that none of the gifts were between four and seven years of death). However, many candidates dedicated a lot of time to establishing this. Candidates should read through the question carefully before they begin their calculations.

Part (b) required an explanation as to why it might have been beneficial if the taxpayer had left a portion of their estate to his nephew rather than to his brother. This aspect was well answered, with most candidates appreciating the basic IHT planning of avoiding a double charge to tax.

The IHT planning in part (c) was less well understood. It was necessary to explain why it might be advantageous to make lifetime gifts even when such gifts are made within seven years of death. The main advantage here is that the value of the gift is fixed at the time it is made, so no IHT is payable on the increase in value between making the gift and the time of death. Taper relief may also be available.

ACCA marking scheme		Marks
(a)	PET – 14 May 2018	
	Annual exemptions	1.0
	Nil rate band £325,000	0.5
	Less: CLT – AEs	1.0
	IHT at 40%	0.5
	Daughter responsible	0.5
	CLT – 2 August 2018	
	Transfer of value (no nil rate band)	0.5
	IHT at 40%	0.5
	Trust responsible	0.5
	Death estate	
	IHT at 40% (no nil rate band)	0.5
	PRs responsible	0.5
		——
		6.0
		——
(b)	IHT planning	
	Skipping a generation reduces IHT	1.0
	Gifts only taxed once	1.0
		——
		2.0
		——
(c)	IHT saving	
	Taper relief after 3 years	0.5
	Gifts lock in value	0.5
	IHT saving	1.0
		——
		2.0
		——
Total		10.0
		——

210 MARCUS *Walk in the footsteps of a top tutor*

Key answer tips

Part (a) for three marks tests your knowledge of how the inheritance tax rules apply to married couples. It is important to be brief and to the point in this section, to maximise the time available to spend on the remainder of the question.

Part (b) also tests inheritance tax, this time in relation to the tax due on lifetime gifts as a result of the donor's death. This is a commonly tested scenario.

The highlighted words in the answer are key phrases that markers are looking for.

(a) Inheritance tax for married couples

Tutor's top tips

Make sure that you pay close attention to the number of marks available for short written requirements such as these; one mark for part (1) suggests only a brief answer is required, whereas two marks for part (2) suggests that you need to state two special inheritance tax measures which are applicable to married couples.

(1) A married couple (and registered civil partnerships) is not a chargeable person for inheritance tax (IHT) purposes, because each spouse (or civil partner) is taxed separately.

(2) Gifts to spouses (and registered civil partners) are exempt from IHT. This exemption applies both to lifetime gifts and transfers on death.

   Any unused normal nil rate band and unused residence nil rate band on a person's death can be transferred to their surviving spouse (or registered civil partner).

(b) Marcus – Additional IHT liability arising on death

Tutor's top tips

It is important to read the information carefully. The examining team has indicated that the annual exemption should be ignored and the lifetime tax is given in the question. Make sure you do not waste time allocating annual exemptions or trying to recalculate the lifetime tax.

It has become more common in the examination for a question to bring you in part-way through calculations you may be used to doing in full. You need to be prepared for this approach.

IHT on CLTs and PET becoming chargeable on death

14 January 2009

			£
Chargeable lifetime transfer			315,000
– more than seven years prior to death			————

	£	CLT 3.12.15 £	PET 1.1.16 £
Transfer of value			
= chargeable amount (W)		395,000	570,000
Lifetime tax (paid by Marcus)		96,250	
		————	
Gross chargeable transfer		491,250	
NRB at death	325,000		
Less: GCTs in last 7 years			
(03.12.08 – 03.12.15)	(315,000)		
	————		
		(10,000)	
NRB at death	325,000		
Less: GCTs in last 7 years			
(1.01.09 – 1.01.16)			
(£315,000 + £491,250)	(806,250)		
	————		
			(0)
		————	————
Taxable amount		481,250	570,000
		————	————
IHT due on death × 40%		192,500	228,000
Less: Taper relief			
(3.12.15 – 31.12.19 = 4 – 5 years) (40%)		(77,000)	
(1.1.16 – 31.12.19 = 3 – 4 years) (20%)			(45,600)
Less: IHT paid in lifetime		(96,250)	
		————	————
IHT payable on death		19,250	182,400
		————	————

Working: Transfer of value

	£
Value of shares held before the transfer (100,000 × £12)	1,200,000
Value of shares held after the transfer (70,000 × £9)	(630,000)
	————
Transfer of value	570,000
	————

Tutorial note

(1) Although the CLT on 14 January 2009 was made more than seven years prior to Marcus's death, and is therefore not chargeable on death, it still reduces the nil rate band available to set against the CLT and PET made in 2015 and 2016 as it was made within seven years of these gifts.

(2) Although no details are given, there would be no IHT liability in respect of Marcus's estate because this is left entirely to his spouse.

(3) Prior to the transfer Marcus had 100,000 shares (a 100% holding) in the company and the shares are valued at £12 per share. After the transfer Marcus owns 70,000 shares (a 70% holding) and the shares are valued at £9 per share. The transfer of value is the amount by which Marcus' estate has diminished and not the market value of the asset gifted.

ACCA marking scheme			
			Marks
(a)	(1) Not chargeable person		1.0
	(2) Special measures – Exempt transfers between spouses		1.0
	– Transferable NRB and RNRB		1.0
			–––
			3.0
			–––
(b)	CLT – 14 January 2009		
	No further IHT		1.0
	CLT – 3 December 2015		
	GCT		1.0
	NRB		1.0
	IHT at 40%		0.5
	Taper relief		1.0
	IHT already paid		0.5
	PET – 1 January 2016		
	Value of shares held before the transfer		0.5
	Value of shares held after the transfer		1.0
	IHT liability		0.5
			–––
			7.0
			–––
Total			**10.0**
			–––

Section 9

ANSWERS TO PRACTICE CORPORATION TAX QUESTIONS

PRACTICE SECTION A OBJECTIVE TEST QUESTIONS

CORPORATION TAX BASICS AND ADMINISTRATION

211

	Accounting period end
At the end of a company's period of account	✓
The end of the tax financial year	
Twelve months after the beginning of the accounting period	✓
The date the company begins or ceases to trade	✓

Tutorial note

An accounting period is the period for which a charge to corporation tax is made.

A company's period of account is the period for which it prepares accounts.

The tax financial year runs from 1 April to 31 March and is identified by the year in which it begins. The rate of corporation tax is fixed by reference to the financial year. A company may have an accounting period which straddles 31 March, for example if they prepare accounts for the year ended 31 December.

212 A

Tutorial note

If a company files its return on time HMRC has 12 months from the date of actual delivery of the return to give notice of a compliance check.

If the return is submitted late, notice must be given within 12 months from the 31 January, 30 April, 31 July or 31 October next following the actual date of delivery of the tax return to HMRC (i.e. within 12 months of the next 'quarter day').

213

	Resident	Not resident
A Ltd, a company incorporated in the UK, with its central management and control exercised in the UK	✓	
B Ltd, a company incorporated overseas, with its central management and control exercised in the UK	✓	
C Ltd, a company incorporated in the UK, with its central management and control exercised overseas	✓	
D Ltd, a company incorporated overseas, with its central management and control exercised overseas		✓

214 B

Tutorial note

Lili Ltd can deduct the research into competitors incurred on 6 June 2014 (£12,000) and the donation to the local school on 15 December 2018 (£2,000), i.e. a total of £14,000.

It cannot deduct the initial market research as it was incurred more than seven years before the commencement of trade, nor the costs of entertaining customers and suppliers as this is disallowable expenditure under the normal rules.

215 **£70,000**

Taxable total profits – y/e 31 December 2019

	£
Tax adjusted trading profit	50,000
Property income	6,000
Interest income	2,000
Chargeable gain	12,000
Taxable total profits	70,000

Tutorial note

Interest income is taxable on an accruals basis (i.e. amount receivable for the accounting period) not on the receipts basis.

Taxable total profits should include a company's worldwide income (excluding dividends) and net chargeable gains.

Remember companies pay corporation tax on their chargeable gains and not capital gains tax.

---

216 **D**

Corporation tax liability – y/e 31 December 2019

	£
Tax adjusted trading profit	1,200,000
Property income	250,000
Total profits	1,450,000
Less: Qualifying charitable donations	(7,000)
Taxable total profits	1,443,000
Corporation tax	
£1,443,000 × 19%	274,170

217 £47,500

Corporation tax liability – y/e 31 March 2020

	£
Tax adjusted trading profit	250,000
Chargeable gain	60,000
Total profits	310,000
Less: Qualifying charitable donations	(60,000)
Taxable total profits	250,000
Corporation tax liability (£250,000 × 19%)	47,500

218 C

Tutorial note

Chelfry Ltd is a large company for the first time in its current accounting period, so does not have to pay its corporation tax by quarterly instalments.

Asher Ltd has a reduced profit threshold of £500,000 (£1,500,000/3) as there are three 51% group companies. The TTP of £700,000 exceeds the threshold and Asher Ltd was large in the previous year. Therefore the corporation tax must be paid by instalments.

Barton Ltd has a reduced profit threshold of £500,000 (£1,500,000 × 4/12) as the accounting period is < 12 months. The TTP of £600,000 exceeds the threshold and it was a large company in the previous accounting period. Therefore the corporation tax must be paid by instalments.

219 A

Tutorial note

Where the CO_2 emissions of a leased car exceed 110g/km 15% of the lease charges are disallowed.

Remember that there are no private use adjustments for a company. The lease payments are therefore allowed in full, irrespective of any private use, subject to the 15% restriction.

220 B

	£	Main pool £	Allowances £
y/e 31 March 2020			
TWDV b/f		35,000	
WDA (18%)		(6,300)	6,300
Low emission car			
($CO_2 \leq 50g/km$)	8,000		
FYA (100%)	(8,000)		8,000
	———	0	
TWDV c/f		28,700	
		———	———
Total allowances			14,300
			———

Tutorial note

Remember that there are no private use adjustments for a company. The employee who uses the car privately will have a taxable employment benefit instead.

221 £33,600

	£
Rental income (£3,000 × 12)	36,000
Electricity (£200 × 12)	(2,400)
	———
Property income	33,600
	———

Tutorial note

Property income for a company is always assessed on an accruals basis, therefore the payment of electricity consumed during the accounting period but paid for after the end of the accounting period is still included as an expense.

Interest payable in relation to an investment property (i.e. mortgage interest) is not deductible from property income for companies. Instead, the interest payable is deductible from interest income as it relates to a non- trading activity.

*The treatment for individuals is different; interest payable on an investment property **is** partly deductible from property income and partly deductible at the basic tax rate from the income tax liability.*

RELIEF FOR TRADING LOSSES

222   A

Loss memorandum

	£
Trading loss for the y/e 31.3.20	102,800
Loss against total profits	
– Current period (y/e 31.3.20)	(10,100)
12 month carry back:	
– y/e 31.3.19 (£79,400 + £6,800)	(86,200)
Unrelieved loss at 31.3.20	6,500

Tutorial note

The loss must be offset against the current period first to enable a 12 month carry back. The loss is deducted from total profits, prior to the deduction of qualifying charitable donations.

223   £20,000

Year ended 31 March	**2019**	**2020**
	£	£
Trading profit	40,000	0
Property income	15,000	21,000
Total profits	55,000	21,000
Less: Loss relief – current year		(21,000)
– carry back (£50,000 – £21,000)	(29,000)	
Total profits	26,000	0
Less: QCDs	(6,000)	Wasted
Taxable total profits	20,000	0

Tutorial note

A claim to carry back losses against total profits (i.e. before QCDs) of the previous year can only be made if a claim has been made to offset the loss against current year total profits first.

224 C

Loss memorandum

	£
Loss of year ended 31.3.20	60,000
Less: Used in current year – y/e 31.3.20	(5,000)
Less: Used in 12 month carry back	
– 9 m/e to 30.3.19 (W)	(25,000)
– y/e 30.6.18	
Lower of:	
(1) Total profits × 3/12 = (3/12 × 44,000) = £11,000	
(2) Remaining loss = £30,000	(11,000)
Loss carried forward	19,000

Working: Loss relief

	y/e 30 June 2018	9 m/e 31 March 2019	y/e 31 March 2020
	£	£	£
Trading profit	40,000	22,000	0
Interest income	4,000	3,000	5,000
Total profits	44,000	25,000	5,000
Loss relief:			
Current year			(5,000)
12 month carry back		(25,000)	
12 month carry back (£44,000 × 3/12)	(11,000)		
TTP	33,000	0	0

Tutorial note

A loss can be carried back against the total profits of the previous 12 months (provided a current year claim has been made first).

Where an accounting period falls partly into the 12 month carry back period the total profits must be time apportioned and only those falling in the 12 month carry back period can be relieved.

225

	True	False
Cairns Ltd's taxable total profits in the year ended 30 June 2020 are £27,000		✓
The trading loss may not be offset against chargeable gains.		✓
Cairns Ltd must make a claim for any loss relief claimed by 30 June 2021.		✓

Year ended 30 June	2019	2020
	£	£
Trading profit	0	25,000
Chargeable gain	9,000	45,000
	————	————
Total profits	9,000	70,000
Less: Loss relief		
Current year	(9,000)	
Brought forward		(31,000)
	————	————
	0	39,000
Less: QCDs	Wasted	(3,000)
	————	————
Taxable total profits	0	36,000
	————	————

Loss memorandum

	£
Loss of year ended 30 June 2019	40,000
Less: Loss relief	
Current year	(9,000)
Carried forward to y/e 30 June 2020	(31,000)
	————
Loss carried forward at 30 June 2020	0
	————

Tutorial note

Cairns Ltd's taxable total profits in the year ended 30 June 2020 are £36,000 as the trading loss must be offset against chargeable gains where a current year claim is made in year ended 30 June 2019.

A claim to set-off of brought forward losses against the total profits of the year ended 30 June 2020 must be made within two years of the end of the accounting period in which the loss is relieved i.e. by 30 June 2022. However, a claim to set-off of trading losses against total profits of the year ended 30 June 2019 must be made within two years of the end of the accounting period in which the loss arose i.e. by 30 June 2021.

When loss relief is claimed against total profits in the current year, losses must be offset in full, even if this means wasting QCDs. Losses carried forward are offset against total profits before QCDs (although a lower relief can be claimed to avoid wasting QCDs).

226 A

Loss relief

Year ended 30 April	2019	2020
	£	£
Trading profit	0	61,000
Property income	0	27,000
Interest income	30,000	30,000
Total profits	30,000	118,000
Less: Property loss relief – current year	(28,000)	(0)
Trading loss relief – brought forward		(108,000)
	2,000	10,000
Less: QCDs	(2,000)	(10,000)
Taxable total profits	0	0

Loss memorandum

	£
Property loss of year ended 30 April 2019	28,000
Less: Loss relief	
Current year	(28,000)
Loss carried forward at 30 April 2019	0

	£
Trading loss of year ended 30 April 2019	120,000
Less: Loss relief	
Carried forward to y/e 30 April 2020	(108,000)
Loss carried forward at 30 April 2020	12,000

Tutorial note

Property losses are automatically offset in the current year against total profits before QCDs, which may lead to the wastage (or part wastage as here) of the QCDs.

Trading losses do not need to be offset in the current year (and would not be in this case, as this would waste QCDs and not save any tax). When trading losses are carried forward they are offset against total profits before QCDs, but partial claims are possible to avoid the wastage of QCDs.

227 £11,100

Loss memorandum

	£
Loss of year ended 31.3.19	65,000
Less: Loss relief	
Used in current year claim – y/e 31.3.19 (W)	(20,000)
Carried forward – y/e 31.3.20 (W) restricted to preserve QCDs	(33,900)
Loss not utilised as at 31.3.20	11,100

Working – Loss relief

Year ended 31 March	2018	2019	2020
	£	£	£
Trading profit	16,000	20,000	25,000
Property income	5,000	0	10,000
Total profits	21,000	20,000	35,000
Less: Loss relief			
Current year		(20,000)	
Brought forward			(33,900)
Total profits	21,000	0	1,100
Less: QCDs	(800)	wasted	(1,100)
Taxable total profits	20,200	0	0

Tutorial note

A property loss is automatically (no choice available) set against the total profits (before QCDs) of the current year. Any unused loss is carried forward and a claim can be made to offset it against future total profits (before QCDs). A partial claim is possible, which avoids wasting QCDs. Property losses cannot be carried back.

228 D

Loss memorandum

	£
Loss of year ended 31.3.20	100,000
Less: Loss relief	
Current year	(14,000)
Terminal loss relief (Previous 3 years on LIFO basis):	
y/e 31.3.19	(19,000)
y/e. 31.3.18	(32,000)
y/e. 31.3.17 (balance)	(35,000)
Loss not utilised	0

Working – Loss relief

Year ended 31 March	2017	2018	2019	2020
	£	£	£	£
Trading profit	45,000	32,000	10,000	0
Chargeable gain	5,000	0	9,000	14,000
Total profits	50,000	32,000	19,000	14,000
Less: Loss relief				
Current year				(14,000)
Terminal loss relief (LIFO):				
First			(19,000)	
Second		(32,000)		
Third	(35,000)			
Taxable total profits	15,000	0	0	0

Tutorial note

A loss in the final 12 months of trading can be set against the total profits of the three preceding years on a LIFO basis, provided a claim has been made against current year total profits first.

WITH GROUP ASPECTS

229 D

Tutorial note

Forty Ltd is not a 75% subsidiary of Thirty Ltd.

Accordingly, regardless of indirect percentage interests, Forty Ltd and Ten Ltd cannot form a group for group relief or chargeable gains purposes.

230

	Loss can be surrendered to
Chair Ltd	✓
Bin Ltd	
Paper Inc	
Cardboard Ltd	✓

A group relief loss group consists of a company and directly/indirectly owned companies where there is a shareholding of at least 75%. Therefore, Bin Ltd is not in the loss group as Computer Ltd's direct shareholding is only 60%.

Computer Ltd has a direct holding of 75% in Chair Ltd and 100% in Paper Inc and an indirect 75% holding, through Paper Inc, in Cardboard Ltd (100% × 75%).

An overseas company can be part of the loss group structure but it cannot itself claim or surrender losses, so losses cannot be surrendered to Paper Inc.

231 C

Tutorial note

A capital gains group comprises the parent company and its 75% subsidiaries and also, the 75% subsidiaries of the first subsidiaries and so on.

The parent company must have an effective interest of over 50%, in ALL companies

Acasta Ltd has a 75% interest in Barge Ltd and greater than 50% effective interest in Dhow Ltd. Eight Ltd is not in the capital gains group as although it is an effective 51% subsidiary of Acasta Ltd, it is not a direct 75% subsidiary of Coracle Ltd.

232

	Capital gains group
Brazil Ltd	✓
Germany Ltd	✓
Holland Ltd	✓
Belgium Ltd	
Russia Ltd	✓

A capital gains group comprises the parent company and its 75% (direct or indirect) subsidiaries and also, the 75% subsidiaries of the first subsidiaries and so on. However the parent company must have an effective interest of over 50% in all group companies.

Brazil Ltd has a direct 100% holding in Germany Ltd and a direct 75% holding in Holland Ltd. Russia also forms part of the group as Brazil Ltd has an overall effective interest of over 50% (75% × 75% = 56.25%).

Belgium Ltd does not form part of the group as it is not a 75% subsidiary of Germany Ltd.

233 B

Where the companies in a loss group have non-coterminous accounting periods, the available profits and losses must be time apportioned, to find the relevant amounts falling within the corresponding accounting period.

In this situation, the maximum loss that can be surrendered = lower of:

- Allowable loss in the surrendering (loss making) company for the corresponding accounting period = £25,000 (3/12 × £100,000).

- Taxable total profits in the claimant company for the corresponding accounting period = £40,000 (3/6 × £80,000).

234 £150,000

The deemed acquisition cost is £150,000.

This is made up of the original cost of the asset to Apple Ltd (£100,000) plus indexation allowance (£50,000).

Tutorial note

When an asset is transferred between companies in a gains group the asset is deemed to be transferred at a price that gives rise to neither a gain or loss to the company transferring the asset.

The deemed transfer price becomes the deemed acquisition cost for the transferee.

235 C

There are 4 related 51% group companies (Telephone Ltd, Desk Ltd, Chair Ltd, and Window Inc) for the purposes of adjusting the augmented profits threshold for the year ended 31 March 2020.

Related 51% group companies are those companies which are 51% subsidiaries of Telephone Ltd (i.e. Telephone Ltd owns, either directly or indirectly, more than 50% of the company's ordinary share capital).

The augmented profits threshold is adjusted for the number of related 51% group companies at the end of the previous accounting period. Therefore, Curtain Ltd is not included for the purposes of adjusting the limit for the year ended 31 March 2020.

Overseas companies are included but dormant companies are excluded.

236 D

Novak Ltd has two related 51% group companies (Roger Ltd and Rafael Ltd). The augmented profits threshold will therefore be £500,000 (£1,500,000/3).

Rafael Ltd is included as Novak Ltd indirectly owns > 51% of the shares (i.e. 80% × 70% = 56%). Andy Ltd is not included as Novak Ltd only owns (indirectly) 30.8% (i.e. 80% × 70% × 55%) of the company's shares.

237 A

Corporation tax – 8 m/e 31 March 2020

	£
Augmented profits threshold	1,500,000
Adjusted for 8 month accounting period and four related companies (Custard Ltd plus three 51% subsidiaries) £1,500,000 × 8/12 × 1/4	250,000

238 £1,570,000

Augmented profits – y/e 31 January 2020

	£
TTP (£1,450,000 + £100,000)	1,550,000
Plus: Dividend income from non-51% related companies	20,000
Augmented profits	1,570,000

239 A

£5,940 (£4,680 + £1,260)

Tutorial note

Dividends received from related companies are excluded from augmented profits. As Luck Ltd does not own more than 50% of the third company from which dividends of £1,260 are received, the two companies are not related 51% group companies.

240

	Corporation tax return due
1 March 2021	
31 May 2021	
1 June 2021	
31 August 2021	✓

Tutorial note

If a period of account is split into two accounting periods, the related corporation tax return must be submitted within 12 months of the end of the period of account, not the end of the accounting periods.

241 B

£456,000/4 = £114,000

242

	Corporation tax due on 1 April 2020
W Ltd – prepared accounts for the year ended 30 June 2019	✓
X Ltd – prepared accounts for the 15 months ended 30 September 2019	✓
Y Ltd – prepared accounts for the year ended 31 March 2019	
Z Ltd – prepared accounts for the 8 months to 30 June 2019	✓

Companies which are not large (i.e. augmented profits do not exceed £1,500,000) are required to pay their corporation tax 9 months and 1 day after the end of the accounting period.

W Ltd and Z Ltd both have an accounting period ending on 30 June 2019 so the due date for payment of corporation tax is 1 April 2020.

X Ltd's 15 month period of account contains two accounting periods for tax purposes, the year ended 30 June 2019 and the 3 months ended 30 September 2019. Therefore it also has a due date for payment of corporation tax of 1 April 2020 in respect of the year ended 30 June 2019.

Y Ltd's due payment date in respect of the year ended 31 March 2019 is 1 January 2020.

243 C

Tutorial note

Large companies are required to pay corporation tax in instalments from the accounting period following the first accounting period in which they are a large company.

A large company is one whose profits exceed the augmented profit threshold of £1,500,000. This limit must be divided by the number of 51% group companies.

Mammoth Ltd has one related 51% group company and therefore the relevant augmented profit threshold is £750,000 (£1,500,000/2). Mammoth's augmented profits exceed this threshold in the year ended 31 December 2018 and therefore quarterly instalment payments will be required from the year ended 31 December 2019.

244 £1,801

£166,250 × 3.25% × 4/12 = £1,801 (period 1 April 2020 to 31 July 2020)

245 B

Tutorial note

A large company is required to pay its final instalment of corporation tax by the 14th day of the 4th month after the end of the accounting period (AP). Note that for a 12 month AP this is 16 months after the start of the AP.

Where an AP is less than 12 months, the first instalment is due by the 14th day of the 7th month after the start of the AP. Subsequent instalments are due at 3 monthly intervals thereafter, until the date of the final instalment is reached.

For an eight month AP instalments of 3/8 × corporation tax liability are payable on 14 November 2019 (14th day of month 7 of the AP) and 14 February 2020 (3 months later). The final instalment of 2/8 × corporation tax liability is due on 14 April 2020 (the 14th day of the 4th month after the end of the AP.

PRACTICE SECTION B OBJECTIVE TEST CASES

CORPORATION TAX BASICS AND ADMINISTRATION

246   GREENZONE LTD (ADAPTED) *Walk in the footsteps of a top tutor*

Key answer tips

This ten mark question concerns the adjustments to a company's tax adjusted trading profit, capital allowances computations and company payment dates.

1   B

		Entertaining expenses	
		£1,840	£5,440
Repairs and renewals	£0	A	B
	£19,800	C	D

Tutorial note

(1)   *The legal fees on the renewal of the short (≤50 years) lease are allowable.*

(2)   *For corporation tax purposes all entertaining expenditure is disallowed unless it relates to employees.*

Top tutor tips

For VAT purposes, input VAT can be reclaimed on the expense of entertaining overseas customers, but not on the expense of entertaining UK customers. Because of this, students often get confused about whether the expense of entertaining overseas customers is an allowable deduction against trading profits for income tax and corporation tax. Remember, for income tax and corporation tax purposes, only employee entertaining is deductible.

2   A

	£
Gifts and donations	
Political donations	740
Non-qualifying charitable donations (Note 1)	0
Gifts to customers – Pens (Note 2)	660
– Clocks (Note 2)	910
	2,310

Tutorial note

(1)   The charitable donation is an allowable expense against trading profits as it is local and reasonable in size in relation to the business and is wholly and exclusively incurred for trading purposes (i.e. advertising).

(2)   Gifts to customers are only an allowable deduction if they cost less than £50 per recipient per year, are not of food, drink, tobacco or vouchers exchangeable for goods and carry a conspicuous advertisement for the company making the gift.

3   £49,241

	FYA	Main pool	Allowances
		£	£
TWDV b/f		48,150	
Addition qualifying for 100% FYA			
Motor car (1)	10,800		
100% FYA	(10,800)		10,800
		0	
Addition not qualifying for AIA			
Motor car (2)		20,400	
		68,550	
Proceeds – Motor car (3)		(8,500)	
		60,050	
WDA (18%)		(10,809)	10,809
TWDV c/f		49,241	
			21,609

Tutorial note

(1) Motor car (1) is a new car and has CO_2 emissions of 50 grams per kilometre or less and therefore qualifies for the 100% first year allowance (FYA).

(2) Motor car (2) has CO_2 emissions between 51 and 110 grams per kilometre and therefore qualifies for writing down allowances at the rate of 18%.

(3) The amount deducted on disposal of motor car (3) is restricted to the original cost figure of £8,500.

4   B

	£	Special rate pool £	Allowances £
6 months to 30.9.20			
TWDV b/f		9,200	
Addition qualifying for AIA			
– special rate addition	550,000		
AIA (Max £1,000,000 × 6/12)	(500,000)		500,000
	———		
Balance to special rate pool		50,000	
		———	
		59,200	
WDA (6% × 6/12)		(1,776)	1,776
		———	
TWDV c/f		57,424	
		———	
			501,776
			———

Tutorial note

The AIA and WDA must be adjusted to reflect the short accounting period of 6 months.

5

	Instalment date
14 July 2020	
14 October 2020	✓
14 January 2021	✓
14 April 2021	

Tutorial note

Where the accounting period is less than 12 months:

- *First instalment due by: 14th day of 7th month after the start of the accounting period (as normal).*

- *Subsequent instalments are due at 3 monthly intervals thereafter, until the date of the final instalment (see below) is reached.*

- *Last instalment due by: 14th day of 4th month after the end of the accounting period. Earlier instalments (as above) are only due if they fall before the date of the final instalment.*

RELIEF FOR TRADING LOSSES

247 LOSER LTD (ADAPTED)

Key answer tips

A fairly straightforward corporation tax loss question testing the different reliefs available.

1

	Relevant	Not relevant
Timing of relief	✓	
Extent to which losses will be wasted	✓	
Extent to which QCD relief will be wasted	✓	

Tutorial note

The timing of the relief obtained is relevant as a claim against total profits in the current year and previous 12 months will result in earlier relief than a claim to carry a loss forward, and such a claim will normally result in a tax repayment as well.

Losses may be lost on a cessation of trade if they have not previously been utilised, so this is a relevant factor.

The extent to which relief for qualifying charitable donations will be lost is relevant, since these cannot be carried forward.

2   B

	y/e 31.3.20	y/e 31.3.21
	£	£
Trading profit	0	60,000
Property income	5,600	3,000
Total profits	5,600	63,000
Less: Loss b/f		(61,700)
Less: QCD relief	(1,100)	(1,300)
Taxable total profits	4,500	0

Loss memorandum

	£
Trading loss for the y/e 31.3.20	78,300
Loss against future total profits	(61,700)
Unrelieved loss at 31.3.21	16,600

Tutorial note

It is possible to make a partial claim when offsetting trading losses from earlier periods. Loser Ltd will therefore restrict the claim to avoid wasting QCDs.

3   £34,725

	y/e 30.6.18	9 m/e 31.3.19	y/e 31.3.20
	£	£	£
Trading profit	15,700	24,300	0
Property profit	6,600	8,100	5,600
Total profits	22,300	32,400	5,600
Less: Loss relief			
– Current period			(5,600)
– 12 months c/b	(5,575)	(32,400)	
	16,725	0	0
Less: QCD relief	(800)	wasted	wasted
Taxable total profits	15,925	0	0

Loss memorandum

	£
Trading loss for the y/e 31.3.20	78,300
Loss against total profits	
– Current period (y/e 31.3.20)	(5,600)
12 month carry back (p/e 31.3.19)	(32,400)
12 month carry back (y/e 30.6.18) (£22,300 × 3/12)	(5,575)
Unrelieved loss at 31.3.20	34,725

4

	True	False
The amount of loss used in the current year can be restricted to avoid wasting QCD relief		✓
The claim must be made by 31 March 2022	✓	

5   A

	y/e 30.6.16	y/e 30.6.17	y/e 30.6.18	9 m/e 31.3.19	y/e 31.3.20
	£	£	£	£	£
Trading profit	15,800	10,600	15,700	24,300	0
Property profit	5,200	1,200	6,600	8,100	5,600
Total profits	21,000	11,800	22,300	32,400	5,600
Less: Loss relief					
– Current period					(5,600)
– 36 months c/b	(5,250)	(11,800)	(22,300)	(32,400)	
	15,750	0	0	0	0
Less: QCD relief	(1,300)	wasted	wasted	wasted	wasted
Taxable total profits	14,450	0	0	0	0

Loss memorandum

	£
Trading loss for the y/e 31.3.20	78,300
Loss against total profits	
– Current period (y/e 31.3.20)	(5,600)
36 month carry back:	
– p/e 31.3.19	(32,400)
– y/e 30.6.18	(22,300)
– y/e 30.6.17	(11,800)
– y/e 30.6.16 (£21,000 × 3/12)	(5,250)
Unrelieved loss at 31.3.20	950

Tutorial note

The trading loss for the final twelve months of trading can be relieved against total profits for the previous 36 months under the terminal loss relief rules.

WITH GROUP ASPECTS

248 DEUTSCH LTD (ADAPTED) *Walk in the footsteps of a top tutor*

Key answer tips

This corporation tax question involves a company with shareholdings in a number of other companies. Provided the relevant group definitions had been learnt there were easy marks available for identifying the related 51% group companies and calculating the maximum group relief claim.

1

	Related 51% group company
Eins Ltd	✓
Zwei Ltd	
Drei Ltd	✓
Vier Co	✓

Tutorial note

Two companies are related 51% group companies if:

–   One is a 51% subsidiary of the other, or

–   Both are 51% subsidiaries of a third company

A 51% subsidiary is one where more than 50% of the ordinary share capital is directly or indirectly owned.

It does not matter where a company is resident so overseas companies are included in the definition.

2 A

Tutor's top tip

Your first step should be to identify which companies are in a group relief group with Deutsch Ltd. You can then identify how much group relief is available.

- Deutsch Ltd cannot claim group relief from Eins Ltd as this company is not a 75% subsidiary. However, Drei Ltd and Deutsch Ltd are in a group relief group.

- The maximum amount of group relief that can be claimed is £64,700 being Drei Ltd's trading loss of £52,700 plus the unrelieved qualifying charitable donations of £12,000.

Tutorial note

- *The surrendering company may surrender any amount of its current period losses.*

- *There is no requirement for the surrendering company to relieve the loss against its own profits first*

- *The current period losses which may be surrendered are trading losses, unrelieved QCDs and unrelieved property losses.*

3   £178,600

	£
Sales proceeds	500,000
Less: Indexed cost	(281,400)
Chargeable gain	218,600
Less: Rollover relief	(178,600)
Gain chargeable (proceeds not reinvested £500,000 – £460,000)	40,000

4   A

Tutorial note

Berlin Ltd owns more than 75% of Zwei Ltd. The two companies therefore form a group for capital gains purposes.

Assets transferred within a gains group are automatically transferred at no gain/no loss (i.e. without a chargeable gain or allowable loss arising).

The transfer is deemed to take place at a price that does not give rise to a gain or a loss (i.e. the indexed cost at the date of the transfer).

The transferor's deemed proceeds figure is also the deemed cost of the acquiring company.

5   C

The claim for group relief must be made by Deutsch Ltd (the claimant company) on its corporation tax return by 31 March 2022 (within two years of the end of the accounting period).

The claim for rollover relief must be made within four years of the later of the end of the accounting period in which the asset is sold and replaced i.e. 31 March 2024.

Tutor's top tip

Time limits for claims and elections should represent easy marks provided that you have learnt them prior to the examination.

PRACTICE SECTION C CONSTRUCTED RESPONSE QUESTIONS

CORPORATION TAX BASICS AND ADMINISTRATION

249 TENTH LTD AND ELEVENTH LTD (ADAPTED) *Walk in the footsteps of a top tutor*

Key answer tips

This question is really two separate corporation tax questions.

Part (a) required the calculation of taxable total profits for a company that had ceased trading. The capital allowances computation could have caused problems as the rules are different in the final accounting period. In the final period, writing down allowances, the annual investment allowance and first year allowances are not available. A balancing adjustment is calculated for all columns at the date of disposal.

Part (b) involved the calculation of tax adjusted trading profits for a short accounting period. Time apportionment is crucial in this situation, with the exception of 100% first year allowances.

(a)   Tenth Ltd – Taxable total profits for the four month period ended 31 July 2019

	£
Trading profit	52,400
Balancing charge (W1)	15,300
Revised trading profit	67,700
Property income (W2)	1,500
Chargeable gain (£179,549 – £166,911)	12,638
Total profits	81,838
Qualifying charitable donations	(800)
Taxable total profits	81,038

Workings

(W1) Balancing charge

	Main pool	Allowances
	£	£
TWDV brought forward	12,400	
Addition	1,800	
Proceeds (£28,200 + £1,300)	(29,500)	
	(15,300)	
Balancing charge	15,300	(15,300)

(W2) Property income

	£
Rent receivable (£1,200 × 4)	4,800
Impairment loss	(1,200)
Running costs (£6,300 × 1/3)	(2,100)
	_____
Property income	1,500
	_____

Tutorial note

Property income for a company is always assessed on an accruals basis. Therefore the company is assessed on the rent receivable for the four month period with impairment relief available for the rent which is not recoverable.

(b) **Eleventh Ltd – Tax adjusted trading profit for the six month period ended 31 March 2020**

	£
Operating profit	122,900
Depreciation	2,580
Amortisation	2,000
Deduction for lease premium (W1)	(1,440)
Interest payable (£100,000 × 5% × 6/12)	(2,500)
Capital allowances (W2)	(14,334)
	_____
Trading profit	109,206
	_____

Workings

(W1) Deduction for lease premium

	£
Premium paid	60,000
Less: £60,000 x 2% × (15 −1)	(16,800)
	_____
Amount assessed on the landlord as income (Note)	43,200
	_____
Deduction (£43,200/15 years × 6/12)	1,440

Tutorial note

Alternatively, the amount assessed on the landlord as income could be calculated as:

£60,000 × ((51 − 15)/50) = £43,200.

(W2) Capital allowances

	£	Main pool £	Allowances £
Additions (no AIA)			
Car 1 (51 – 110g/km)		12,600	
WDA – 18% × 6/12		(1,134)	1,134
Addition qualifying for FYA			
Car 2	13,200		
FYA (100%)	(13,200)		13,200
		0	
TWDV c/f		11,466	
Total allowances			14,334

Tutorial notes

(1) The first motor car has CO_2 emissions between 51 and 110 grams per kilometre, and therefore qualifies for writing down allowances at the rate of 18%.

(2) The second motor car has CO_2 emissions up to 50 grams per kilometre, and therefore qualifies for the 100% first year allowance. In the absence of any other information always assume that cars purchased are new cars (not second hand). The private use of the motor car is irrelevant because there are no private use adjustments in respect of a company.

Examiner's report

Part (a) was generally very well answered, requiring a calculation of the first company's taxable total profits for the final period of trading. The only consistent problem here was the capital allowances, with many candidates not appreciating that neither the annual investment allowance (a laptop computer had been purchased during the period) nor writing down allowances are given in the period of cessation. A few candidates ignored the cessation altogether and therefore did not calculate a balancing charge.

Part (b) was also well answered on the whole, requiring a calculation of the second company's tax adjusted trading profit for the initial period of trading. Some candidates attempted to calculate benefits in respect of the motor cars and loan which, although correct as regards the motor cars, had no relevance to the requirement. Perhaps not surprisingly, the deduction for the lease premium caused quite a few problems. Although the numerical aspects of this question were well answered, most candidates achieved lower marks for this question than for question one, despite this question being five marks longer.

ACCA marking scheme		
		Marks
(a)	Tenth Ltd	
	Add balancing charge	0.5
	Chargeable gain	1.0
	QCDs	1.0
	Capital allowances:	
	Main pool addition	1.0
	Proceeds	1.0
	Balancing charge	1.0
	Property income:	
	Rent receivable	0.5
	Impairment loss	0.5
	Running costs	0.5
		–––
		7.0
		–––
(b)	Eleventh Ltd	
	Trading profit	0.5
	Depreciation	0.5
	Amortisation	0.5
	Lease premium:	
	Amount assessed on landlord as property income	2.0
	Trading deduction	0.5
	Interest payable	1.0
	Capital allowances:	
	Main pool car	1.0
	WDA time apportioned	1.0
	FYA – no private use adjustment	1.0
		–––
		8.0
		–––
Total		**15.0**
		–––

250 AOEDE LTD, BIANCA LTD AND CHARON LTD (ADAPTED)

Key answer tips

This question covers various aspects of corporation tax.

Part (a) requires a calculation of taxable total profits for two periods. This part of the question also required the application of property and trading loss relief within a single company. In addition to this, there was a small element of group loss relief. These areas are commonly tested in the examination.

Part (b) involves a basic adjustment of trading profits computation with the standard requirement to calculate capital allowances. The discount awarded in relation to the laptops is something you may not have encountered before. However, the correct conclusion could be drawn by following the usual process of including the cost of the asset in the computation.

Part (c) requires the calculation of gains and losses on disposal of two properties by a company. A good understanding of the differences when calculating gains for companies rather than individuals is required in order to score well in this section.

(a)   (i)   Aoede Ltd – Taxable total profits

	Year ended 31 March 2019 £	Year ended 31 March 2020 £
Trading profit	0	67,800
Property business income	0	23,400
Chargeable gains	5,800	16,200
Total profits	5,800	107,400
Property loss relief – Current year	(5,800)	0
Loss relief – Carry forward	0	(100,800)
Qualifying charitable donations	0	(6,600)
Taxable total profits	0	0

Moon Ltd – Taxable total profits

	Year ended 31 March 2020 £
Trading profit	19,700
Group relief	(19,700)
Taxable total profits	0

Working – loss memorandum

	£
Property loss – y/e 31.3.19	26,400
Used in y/e 31.3.19	(5,800)
Property loss c/f	20,600
Add: Trading loss c/f	111,300
Total losses carried forward to y/e 31.3.20	131,900
Used in y/e 31.3.20	(100,800)
Surrendered to Moon Ltd	(19,700)
Carried forward	11,400

(ii) It is not beneficial for Aoede Ltd to make the loss relief claim against total income for the year ended 31 March 2019 because the income would have otherwise been covered by the qualifying charitable donations of £6,000.

Tutorial note

Although the loss relief claim in the year ended 31 March 2019 is not beneficial, it would not be possible for Aoede Ltd to avoid offsetting the loss in this way, as current year property loss claims are not optional. If the company only had a trading loss, the full loss could be carried forward to avoid wasting current year QCDs, as current year trading loss relief is optional and must be claimed.

(b) Bianca Ltd – Tax adjusted trading profit for the year ended 31 March 2020

	£
Trading profit	256,300
Advertising expenditure	(5,800)
Lease of motor cars (£5,100 × 15%)	765
Capital allowances	
Laptops (£1,000 × 4 × 100%)	(4,000)
Motor car [1] (£12,400 × 18%)	(2,232)
Motor car [2] (£13,900 × 6%)	(834)
Revised trading profit	244,199

Tutorial notes

1   *The advertising expenditure incurred during January 2018 is pre-trading, and is therefore treated as incurred on 1 April 2019.*

2   *The original cost of the laptops is irrelevant.*

3   *Although motor car [1] has CO_2 emissions up to 50 grams per kilometre, it is second hand and therefore does not qualify for the 100% first year allowance. It instead qualifies for writing down allowances at the rate of 18%.*

4   *Motor car [2] has CO_2 emissions over 110 grams per kilometre and therefore qualifies for writing down allowances at the rate of 6%.*

(c)   Charon Ltd – Chargeable gains and capital losses for the year ended 31 March 2020

First property

	£
Disposal proceeds	368,000
Cost	(147,000)
Enhancement expenditure	(39,000)
	————
	182,000
Indexation allowance	
£147,000 × 0.808	(118,776)
	————
Chargeable gain	63,224
	————

Second property

	£
Disposal proceeds	167,000
Cost	(172,000)
Indexation allowance	0
	————
Capital loss	(5,000)
	————

Tutorial note

There is no indexation allowance for the first property's enhancement expenditure of £39,000 because this was incurred after December 2017.

ACCA marking guide				
				Marks
(a)	(i)	Aoede Ltd		4.0
		Moon Ltd		1.0
				———
				5.0
				———
	(ii)	Explanation		1.0
				———
(b)	Adjustments			2.0
	Capital allowances			3.0
				———
				5.0
				———
(c)	First property			2.5
	Second property			1.5
				———
				4.0
				———
Total				**15.0**
				———

251 SOLO LTD *WALK IN THE FOOTSTEPS OF A TOP TUTOR*

Key answer tips

This question covers corporation tax aspects of a loss making company.

Part (a) involves a basic adjustment of trading profits computation with the standard requirement to calculate capital allowances. In this scenario the main pool balance became negative as the result of a disposal in the period, resulting in a balancing charge.

Part (b) requires a calculation of taxable total profits for the period. A basic calculation was required for both property income and chargeable gains. This part of the question also required the application of both capital and trading loss relief, both of which are commonly tested in the examination.

Part (c) requires a carry back of the remainder of the trading loss against total profits in the previous twelve months. This should not have posed a problem as it is an area often tested in corporation tax questions.

Tutor's top tips

Once you have calculated your trading loss in part (a) you have to use it in the calculation of loss relief in part (b). Remember that even if your answer to part (a) is incorrect you will get marks for applying the rules correctly in part (b).

(a)   **Solo Ltd – Trading loss for the year ended 31 March 2020**

	£
Trading loss	(151,300)
Deduction for lease premium (W)	(2,150)
Balancing charge	4,300
	(149,150)

Working – Deduction for lease premium

	£
Premium received	20,000
Less: 20,000 × 2% × (8 – 1)	(2,800)
	17,200
Deduction £17,200/8 =	2,150

Tutorial note

The alternative calculation (£20,000 × ((51 – 8)/50)/8) = £2,150 would gain equal credit.

(b)   Solo Ltd – Corporation tax computation for the year ended 31 March 2020

	£	£
Property business income (W1)		9,480
Chargeable gain (W2)	16,636	
Capital losses brought forward (£3,300 + £2,100)	(5,400)	
	———	11,236
		———
		20,716
Less: Loss relief (CY)		(20,716)
Taxable total profits		———
		0
		———

Tutorial note

Capital losses can only be offset against chargeable gains. The relief is automatic against gains in the period during which the loss arose, then the first available future chargeable gains. A restriction of the amount of loss offset is not permitted.

Workings

(W1) Property business income

	£
Rent receivable (£7,800 + (£7,800 × 2/6))	10,400
Security deposit	0
Insurance	(920)
	———
Property business income	9,480
	———

Tutorial note

Property income is assessed on the accruals basis for companies therefore the payment and receipt dates are irrelevant.

A security deposit is initially not treated as income when received, and its repayment is not treated as an expense.

(W2) Chargeable gain

	£	£
Purchase 8 December 2019		
Disposal proceeds (£31,200 × 1,000/6,500)	4,800	
Cost	(4,600)	
Chargeable gain		200
Share pool		
Disposal proceeds (£31,200 × 5,500/6,500)	26,400	
Indexed cost (W3)	(9,964)	
		16,436
Chargeable gain		16,636

(W3) Share pool

	Number	Indexed cost
		£
Purchase June 2007	20,000	27,000
Indexation to December 2017 (£27,000 × 0.342)		9,234
		36,234
Disposal December 2019 (£36,234 × 5,500/20,000)	(5,500)	(9,964)
Balance carried forward	14,500	26,270

Tutorial note
Indexation is frozen at December 2017.

(c)   Solo Ltd – Taxable total profits

	Year ended 31 December 2018	Period ended 31 March 2019
	£	£
Trading profit	35,900	12,300
Property business income	12,100	4,200
Chargeable gains	0	0
Total profits	48,000	16,500
Less: Loss relief (PY) (W)	(36,000)	(16,500)
	12,000	0
Qualifying charitable donations	(1,200)	wasted
Taxable total profits	10,800	0

Working - Loss relief

Year ended 31 December 2018

£48,000 × 9/12 = £36,000

Examiner's report

Part (a) for 3 marks required candidates to calculate Solo Ltd's revised tax-adjusted trading loss. This section was quite well answered. However, when dealing with a trading loss, candidates need to be very careful that adjustments are correctly added or deducted. Treating the loss as a negative means that there is no need to change the approach from that used for a trading profit. A number of candidates did not appreciate that there was a balancing charge because the disposal proceeds for the plant and machinery main pool exceeded the written down value brought forward.

Part (b) for 8 marks asked candidates to prepare a corporation tax computation showing taxable total profits. This was on the basis that Solo Ltd claimed relief for its trading loss against its total profits. The requirement meant that candidates had to calculate property business income, calculate a chargeable gain on a share disposal, deduct brought forward capital losses from the gain, and then deduct the trading loss so that taxable total profits were nil. This section was again well answered. One aspect which consistently caused difficulty was candidates not preparing a separate gain calculation for the share purchase made during the preceding nine days. A number of candidates incorrectly restricted the insurance deduction in the property business income calculation to 8/12ths because the building was unoccupied from 1 April to 31 July.

Information was provided in date order, and candidates often tried to use the details provided for the year ended 31 December 2018 and the period ended 31 March 2019 in this section of the question. The only details which were relevant were the capital losses, and these were often omitted in any case.

Part (c) for 4 marks required candidates to calculate Solo Ltd's taxable total profits for the year ended 31 December 2018 and the three-month period ended 31 March 2019. This was on the basis that the company claimed relief for the remainder of its trading loss as early as possible. This section was very well answered, and it was pleasing to see most candidates correctly restricting the trading loss set off for the year ended 31 December 2018 to 9/12ths of the total profits. Candidates should note that where two accounting periods are involved, then a two-column approach avoids the need to write out descriptions twice.

ACCA marking scheme		Marks
(a)	Deduction for lease premium	2.0
	Balancing charge	1.0
		3.0
(b)	Property income:	
	Rent receivable	1.0
	Security deposit	0.5
	Insurance	1.0
	Chargeable gain:	
	Dec 19 proceeds	0.5
	Dec 19 cost	0.5
	Share pool proceeds	0.5
	Share pool acquisition Jun 07	0.5
	Indexation to December 17	1.0
	Disposal	1.0
	Losses:	
	Capital losses b/f	1.0
	Trading loss relief	0.5
		8.0
(c)	Trading profit	0.5
	Property income	0.5
	Chargeable gains	0.5
	Loss carry back 12 months	1.5
	QCDs	1.0
		4.0
Total		**15.0**

252 ONLINE LTD (ADAPTED) *Walk in the footsteps of a top tutor*

Key answer tips

Part (a) included adjustments for depreciation and amortisation; both appear regularly in adjustment of profit computations in the examination.

The capital allowances computation contained many standard areas. However, all items in the special rate pool were disposed of during the period. A common mistake here would be to calculate a balancing allowance on the unrelieved expenditure. A balancing allowance only applies to the main pool and the special rate pool in the period of cessation.

Part (b) was a short section on tax administration for companies. This required knowledge of the impact of 51% group companies when determining whether corporation tax should be paid by instalments.

(a)   Online Ltd – Corporation tax computation for the year ended 31 March 2020

	£
Operating profit	896,700
Depreciation	21,660
Amortisation	9,000
Deduction for lease premium (W1)	(7,380)
Capital allowances (W2)	(9,824)
Trading profit	910,156
Chargeable gain (W3)	60,381
Total profits	970,537
Property business loss brought forward	(12,500)
Qualifying charitable donations	(6,800)
Taxable total profits	951,237

Workings

(W1) Deduction for lease premium

	£
Premium paid	90,000
Less: £90,000 x 2% x (10 – 1)	(16,200)
Amount assessed on the landlord	73,800
Deduction (£73,800/10)	7,380

Tutorial note

Alternatively, the amount assessed on the landlord as income could be calculated as:

£90,000 × ((51 − 10)/50) = £73,800.

(W2) Capital allowances

	Main pool	Special rate pool	Allowances
	£	£	£
TWDV b/f	56,700	13,433	
Addition – no AIA			
Motor car (51 – 110g/km)	13,700		
Disposals:			
Motor car	(17,200)		
SR pool		(9,300)	
	———	———	
	53,200	4,133	
WDA (£53,200 × 18%)	(9,576)		9,576
WDA (£4,133 × 6%)		(248)	248
	———	———	
TWDV c/f	43,624	3,885	
	———	———	
Total allowances			9,824
			———

Tutorial notes

The motor car purchased has CO_2 emissions between 51 and 110 grams per kilometre, and therefore qualifies for writing down allowances at the rate of 18%.

The proceeds for the motor car which was sold are restricted to the original cost figure of £17,200.

Although all of the items included in the special rate pool have been sold, there is no balancing allowance because the business has not ceased.

(W3) Chargeable gain

	£
Disposal proceeds	90,600
Indexed cost (W4)	(25,519)
	———
	65,081
Capital loss brought forward	(4,700)
	———
Chargeable gain	60,381
	———

(W4) Share pool

Purchase/sale	Number £	Indexed cost £
Purchase June 2012	40,000	49,300
Indexation to October 2015		
(£49,300 × 0.073)		3,599
	———	———
Balance at October 2015	40,000	52,899
Disposal October 2015 (W5)	(22,000)	(29,094)
	———	———
	18,000	23,805
Indexation to December 2017		
(£23,805 × 0.072)		1,714
	———	———
	18,000	25,519
Disposal March 2020	(18,000)	(25,519)
	———	———
Balance c/f	0	0
	———	———

(W5) Disposal October 2015

£52,899 × (22,000/40,000) = £29,094

(b) **(1)** The augmented profit threshold for establishing whether Online Ltd is a large company will be reduced to £750,000 (£1,500,000/2), so it is likely that the company's corporation tax will have to be paid by quarterly instalments.

(2) The dividends received from Offline Ltd, being group dividends, will not form part of Online Ltd's augmented profits.

Examiner's report

Computation of taxable total profits for a company

Again, with this type of question, candidates need to think carefully about where to show workings. In particular, candidates should not attempt to take short-cut approaches when it comes to capital allowance and share pool workings.

It is important that candidates appreciate basic tax rules. For example, even though all of the items included in a capital allowances pool may have been sold, there will be no balancing allowance unless a business has ceased trading.

Candidates need to be very careful regarding dates. For example, if a share pool involves a prior disposal (which may be several years before the current period), then that disposal obviously should not be included as part of the gain for the current period.

Acquisition of a 51% group company

Another example of where too many candidates wanted to answer the question that they wish had been set (discussing 75% groups), rather than the one set.

If a single 51% subsidiary is acquired, then the profit threshold for establishing large company status will be reduced to £750,000 (1,500,000/2). Corporation tax might then be payable by quarterly instalments. There is no need to go on and explain in detail quarterly instalments – the requirement would make this clear if this was required.

Generally not appreciated was that dividends received from the 51% subsidiary will not form part of a holding company's profits.

ACCA marking scheme		Marks
(a)	Depreciation	0.5
	Amortisation	0.5
	Lease deduction	2.0
	Capital allowances	4.5
	Chargeable gain	4.0
	Property loss b/f	1.0
	QCDs	0.5
		13.0
(b)	Profit threshold divided by 2, instalments likely	1.5
	Dividends from Offline excluded from augmented profits	0.5
		2.0
Total		15.0

253 STRETCHED LTD (ADAPTED)

Key answer tips

This question deals with the rules for a 15 month period of account which must be split into two accounting periods of 12 months and 3 months.

For ease, use a columnar layout to do the corporation tax computations side by side. Don't forget to pick up the easy marks for stating the due dates of payment.

The highlighted words in the answer are key phrases that markers are looking for.

(a)   Corporation tax computations

	y/e 31.12.19 £	p/e 31.3.20 £
Trading profit (12/15 : 3/15) (Note 1)	514,000	128,500
Less: Capital allowances (W1)	0	(50,338)
	514,000	78,162
Property business profit (12/15 : 3/15) (Note 1)	36,000	9,000
Chargeable gains (£44,000 – £3,000) (Note 2)	41,000	0
Total profits	591,000	87,162
Less: Loss relief b/f	(330,000)	0
Less: QCD relief	0	(5,000)
TTP	261,000	82,162
Corporation tax at 19% (Note 3)	45,590	15,611
Due dates (W2)	1.10.2020	1.1.2021

Tutorial note

(1) *Trading profits and property business profits are allocated on a time basis: 12/15 to the year ended 31 December 2019 and 3/15 to the period ended 31 March 2020.*

(2) *The capital loss of £6,700 for the period ended 31 March 2020 is carried forward, it cannot be carried back and set off against previous gains.*

(3) *The company's accounting period to 31 December 2019 straddles two financial years but the rate of tax is 19% in both, therefore a two-part computation of the corporation tax liability is not required.*

Workings

(W1) Capital allowances

		Main pool	Allowances
	£	£	£
3 months ended 31 March 2020			
TWDV b/f		0	
Addition – no AIA			
Motor car (51 – 110g/km)		7,500	
Additions (with AIA)			
Office equipment	50,000		
AIA (Max £1,000,000 × 3/12)	(50,000)		50,000
	———	0	
WDA (18% × 3/12)		(338)	338
		———	
TWDV c/f		7,162	
		———	
Total allowances			50,338
			———

Tutorial note

The AIA and WDA must be time apportioned as the accounting period is only three months in length.

(W2) Payment dates

	y/e 31.12.19 £	p/e 31.3.20 £
Taxable total profits	261,000	82,162
Plus: Dividend income	30,000	0
Augmented profits	291,000	82,162
Augmented profits threshold (£1,500,000 × 3/12)	1,500,000	375,000

The company is not a large company in either of the two accounting periods and was not a large company in the previous accounting period to 31 December 2018 (TTP and augmented profits £ 300,000). The tax is therefore due 9 months and one day after the end of the accounting period.

(b)   **Advantages of 31 March year end**

- Being aligned with the financial year will make it easier for a company to calculate its corporation tax liability, since the same rates, reliefs and legislation will apply throughout the accounting period.

- For owner-managed companies, alignment with the income tax year (the odd five days can be ignored) will make it easier as regards calculating the most tax efficient method of extracting profits from the company.

254   STARFISH LTD (ADAPTED) *Walk in the footsteps of a top tutor*

Key answer tips

This question covers corporation tax aspects of a loss making company.

Part (a) involved a basic adjustment of profits computation with the standard requirement to calculate capital allowances. However, the period is loss-making and is the period of cessation. Particular care is therefore needed in the calculation of the capital allowances, especially as you are required to deal with the impact of VAT on the additions and disposals.

Part (b) involves a terminal loss in the period of cessation. The terminal loss can be carried back 36 months rather than 12 months, but make sure you take into account the length of the previous accounting periods.

It is therefore a fairly standard loss question which is largely computational and should not have been too difficult provided the approach to losses questions had been practised. For ease, a columnar format should be used to present the loss offset and remember to show your record of the losses and how they have been relieved in a working.

Tutor's top tips

This is a long time pressured question and you need to work through it methodically. The requirements are broken down into small parts which help you to structure your answer.

(a)   **Starfish Ltd**

Tax adjusted trading loss – period ended 31 March 2020

	Notes	£	£
Loss before taxation			190,000
Depreciation		34,400	
Donation to political party		300	
Qualifying charitable donation	1	1,350	
Impairment loss		0	
Entertaining customers	2	3,600	
Entertaining employees	2	0	
Counselling services	3	0	
Capital allowances (W)			2,300
		———	———
		39,650	192,300
		(192,300)	———
		———	
Trading loss		(152,650)	
		———	

Tutorial note

(1)   *Qualifying charitable donations (QCDs) made by a company are allowable deductions, but not from trading profit. They are deductible from total profits in the main corporation tax computation. Therefore, in the adjustment of trading profits computation they need to be added back to trading profit.*

(2)   *The only exception to the non-deductibility of entertainment expenditure is when it is in respect of employees.*

(3)   *The costs of counselling services for redundant employees are allowable.*

Working – Plant and machinery

	Notes	Main pool	Special rate pool	Allowances
		£	£	£
TWDV b/f		23,600	13,200	
Addition (£3,120 × 100/120)	1, 2	2,600		
		———		
		26,200		
Sale proceeds:	2			
Main pool (£31,200 + £1,800) × 100/120		(27,500)		
Motor car	3		(9,600)	
		———	———	
		(1,300)	3,600	
Balancing charge		1,300		(1,300)
Balancing allowance			(3,600)	3,600
		———	———	
TWDV c/f		0	0	
		———	———	
Total allowances				2,300
				———

Tutorial note

(1)   The annual investment allowance and writing down allowances are not given for the period in which a trade ceases, so the addition is simply added into the main pool.

(2)   The net cost (excluding VAT) of the addition is added to the main pool as input VAT is recovered on the purchase, and the net sale proceeds (excluding VAT) relating to the sale of main pool items is deducted.

(3)   Input VAT however would not have been recovered in respect of the motor car as it was not used exclusively for business purposes. Therefore, output VAT is not due on the disposal and the gross sale proceeds are deducted in the capital allowances computation.

Tutor's top tips

Once you have calculated your trading loss in part (a) you have to use it in the calculation of loss relief in part (b). Remember that even if your answer to part (a) is incorrect you will get marks for applying the rules correctly in part (b).

(b)   Starfish Ltd – Taxable total profits

	4 m/e 31.3.16 £	y/e 31.3.17 £	y/e 31.3.18 £	y/e 31.3.19 £	9 m/e 31.12.19 £	3 m/e 31.3.20 £
Trading profit	2,600	51,600	53,900	14,700	49,900	0
Bank interest	600	1,400	1,700	0	0	0
Total profits	3,200	53,000	55,600	14,700	49,900	0
Less: CY relief						(0)
Less: Carry back relief		(13,250)	(55,600)	(14,700)	(49,900)	
	3,200	39,750	0	0	0	0
Less: QCD relief	(800)	(1,000)	wasted	wasted	wasted	wasted
TTP	2,400	38,750	0	0	0	0

Loss memorandum

	£
Tax adjusted trading loss – 3 m/e 31.3.20	152,650
Relief given in:	
– 3 m/e 31.3.20	(0)
– 9 m/e 31.12.19	(49,900)
– y/e 31.3.19	(14,700)
– y/e 31.3.18	(55,600)
– y/e 31.3.17 (3/12 × £53,000)	(13,250)
Loss unrelieved	19,200

Tutorial note

(1)   The trading loss for the period ended 31 March 2020 is a terminal loss, and can therefore be relieved against total profits:

–   firstly for the period of the loss (£0 in this case), and then

–   carried back to the previous 36 months prior to the start of the loss-making period, on a LIFO basis.

As there is a nine month accounting period in the terminal loss carry back period, the loss can be carried back into the year ended 31 March 2017 computation, but can only be set against 3/12 of the total profits in that year.

(2)   The terminal loss is offset against total profits (i.e. before QCDs). The relief for QCDs is therefore wasted in each of the last four accounting periods. The loss relief is an all or nothing claim and cannot be restricted to preserve relief for the QCDs.

Examiner's report

Part (a) was very well answered, with many very good answers.

The only aspect consistently answered incorrectly was the treatment of a purchased asset. In the final capital allowances computation no allowances are given, so the addition should simply have been added to the main pool.

In part (b) many candidates overlooked the trading loss for the final period of trading.

Note: *The examiner's report has been edited to remove comments on elements of the question that have been deleted due to changes to the examination format.*

ACCA marking scheme		
		Marks
(a)	Depreciation	0.5
	Donations	1.5
	Impairment loss	1.0
	Entertaining customers	0.5
	Entertaining employees	0.5
	Counselling services	0.5
	P & M – TWDV brought forward	0.5
	– Addition	1.5
	– Main pool proceeds	2.0
	– Special rate pool proceeds	1.0
	– Balancing adjustments	0.5
		———
		10.0
		———
(b)	Trading profit	0.5
	Bank interest	0.5
	Relief for 2020 loss – Year ended 31 March 2017	1.0
	– Other periods	2.0
	Qualifying charitable donations	1.0
		———
		5.0
		———
Total		**15.0**
		———

255 HEAVY LTD (ADAPTED) *Walk in the footsteps of a top tutor*

Key answer tips

This question required a straightforward corporation tax computation. There were easy marks available for basic pro forma and straightforward adjustments to trading profits for depreciation and capital allowances.

Heavy Ltd

Corporation tax computation – year ended 31 July 2020

		£
Operating profit		433,100
Add back:	Depreciation	12,880
	Health and safety fine	9,000
		454,980
Less: Capital allowances (W1)		(76,370)
Trading profit		378,610
Chargeable gain (W2)		37,937
Total profits		416,547
Less: Property loss		(10,000)
TTP		406,547
Corporation tax		
(£406,547 × 19%)		77,244

Tutorial note

(1)   The sale of the office building does not give rise to a chargeable gain as it is an inter-group transfer of a capital asset to Soft Ltd, a 75% group company. The transfer is therefore a no gain/no loss event.

(2)   The UK dividends are exempt from UK corporation tax and are therefore excluded from TTP.

(3)   The property business loss is automatically set against total profits of the current period.

Workings

(W1) Capital allowances

		Main pool £	SLA (1) £	SLA (2) £	Special rate pool £	Allow- ances £
TWDV b/f		900	15,100	13,200	24,833	
Addition qualifying for AIA						
Office equipment	22,400					
Computers	25,000					
AIA (100%)	(47,400)					47,400
		0				
Disposal proceeds				(4,600)	(12,300)	
		900	15,100	8,600	12,533	
Balancing allowance				(8,600)		8,600
Small pool WDA		(900)				900
WDA (18%)			(2,718)			2,718
WDA (6%)					(752)	752
Addition qualifying for FYA						
New low emission car (CO$_2$ ≤ 50g/km)	16,000					
FYA (100%)	(16,000)					16,000
		0				
TWDV c/f		0	12,382	0	11,781	
Total allowances						76,370

Tutorial note

(1) *The cost of software is specifically deemed to be plant and machinery for the purposes of capital allowances.*

(2) *The balance on the main pool is less than £1,000 so a small pool writing down allowance equal to the unrelieved expenditure can be claimed.*

(3) *Short life asset (1), being an item of plant and machinery, qualifies for a WDA at the rate of 18%. Short life asset (2) was disposed of in the year for proceeds less than its tax written down value and a balancing allowance therefore arises.*

(4) *The motor car acquired on 24 April 2019 is a new low emission car (CO$_2$ emissions ≤ 50g/km) and therefore qualifies for a 100% FYA. The private use of the motor car is irrelevant, since such usage will be assessed on the managing director as an employment benefit.*

(5) *Although all of the items included in the special rate pool have been sold, there is no balancing allowance arising as the business is a continuing business which has not ceased.*

(W2) Sale of car park

	£
Sale proceeds (March 2020)	45,000
Less: Cost (May 2004)	
£10,000 × (£45,000/(£45,000 + £50,000))	(4,737)
Unindexed gain	40,263
Less: Indexation allowance (to December 2017)	
Cost (£4,737 × 0.491)	(2,326)
Chargeable gain	37,937

Examiner's report

There were many very good answers.

The aspects that caused problems were not appreciating that:

(1) There was no chargeable gain on a disposal of an office building to Soft Ltd because of the 75% group relationship.

(2) The balance on the main capital allowances pool could be fully written off as it was less than £1,000.

(3) There was no balancing allowance on the special rate pool despite all the items included therein having been sold.

Note: The examiner's report has been edited to remove comments on elements of the question that have been deleted due to changes to the examination format.

ACCA marking scheme	
	Marks
Operating profit	0.5
Depreciation	0.5
Health and safety fine	0.5
Capital allowances – Software qualifying expenditure	0.5
– AIA	1.0
– Main pool – small pool WDA	1.0
– SLA (1)	1.0
– SLA (2)	2.0
– Special rate pool	2.0
– Low emission car	2.0
No chargeable gain on transfer to Soft Ltd	1.0
Chargeable gain on part disposal of land	1.5
Offset of property business loss	1.0
Corporation tax	0.5
Total	**15.0**

256 SOFTAPP LTD (ADAPTED) *Walk in the footsteps of a top tutor*

Key answer tips

This question includes a wide range of corporation tax topics including an adjusted trading profit computation, capital allowances computation, property business income and loan relationships. Originally the question also included the profits of an overseas branch and the calculation of double tax relief, but these are no longer examinable and have therefore been replaced.

Unusually you are instructed to start your computation with the operating profit figure, rather than the more usual approach of starting with the net profit figure. This should not cause any problems but requires care and a slightly different approach.

Tutor's top tips

This corporation tax computation is presented in a familiar format, with a statement of profit or loss followed by a number of notes.

However, note that you are instructed to start your computation with the operating profit figure, rather than the more usual approach of starting with the net profit figure. When adjusting the operating profit for tax purposes note that you will not need to make the 'usual' adjustments for items which appear below operating profit in the statement of profit or loss. For example, you do not need to deduct loan interest receivable from the operating profit as it is not been included in the £913,000 figure.

As usual work methodically through the statement, referring to the notes where appropriate, and enter each item in your computation as you go.

The capital additions are slightly unusual but the examining team has given a big clue as to their treatment by indicating which are integral to the building. The question also requires the calculation of property business income from a list of receipts and payments. Care needs to be taken to only include those items which relate to the accounting period.

Corporation tax computation – year ended 31 March 2020

	£	£
Adjustment of profits:		
Operating profit	913,000	
Depreciation	8,170	
Amortisation	2,500	
Interest payable (W1)		(62,200)
Capital allowances (W2)		(210,620)
	_____	_____
	923,670	(272,820)
	(272,820)	_____
	_____	
Trading profit	650,850	
Property income (W3)	21,800	
Interest income (W4)	3,100	
Chargeable gain	61,300	
	_____	
Taxable total profits	737,050	
	_____	
Corporation tax liability at 19%	140,039	
	_____	
Due payment date (W5)	1 January 2021	

Workings

(W1) Loan interest payable for trading purposes

	£
Debenture interest	42,200
Freehold property (£25,000 × 4/5)	20,000
	_____
	62,200
	_____

Tutorial note

Interest paid in respect of a loan used for trading purposes is deductible in calculating the trading profit. Only four of the five floors of the office building are used for trading purposes. Therefore 4/5ths of the loan interest is deductible from trading profits.

The remaining 1/5th which relates to the floor which is let out is deductible from interest income under the loan relationship rules. Note that it is not deductible from property income.

(W2) Plant and machinery – Capital allowances

	Main pool	Special rate pool	Allowances
	£	£	£
TWDV b/f	9,000	0	
Additions qualifying for AIA Integral features (Note):			
Heating system	93,600		
Ventilation system	75,600		
	169,200		
AIA (Max £1,000,000)	(169,200)		169,200
		0	
Additions qualifying for AIA Plant and machinery:			
Furniture and furnishings	38,400		
Refrigerator and cooker	1,400		
	39,800		
AIA	(39,800)		39,800
		0	
	9,000	0	
WDA (18%)	(1,620)		1,620
TWDV c/f	7,380	0	
Total allowances			210,620

Tutorial note

The expenditure which is integral to the building is included in the special rate pool. Although in this case there is sufficient AIA to cover all of the qualifying purchases, you must demonstrate to the marker that you realise it is beneficial to claim the AIA initially against the special rate pool additions before the main pool additions. (Expenditure allocated to the main pool would otherwise only qualify for writing down allowance at the rate of 6%, instead of 18% in the main pool.)

(W3) Property income

	£
Rent receivable (£15,600 + (15,600 × 2/3))	26,000
Security deposit	0
Less: Allowable expenses	
Advertising	(600)
Insurance (£1,200 × 5/12)	(500)
Repairs (£12,800 − £9,700)	(3,100)
Property income	21,800

Tutorial note

(1)   Property income for a company is calculated on the accruals basis. The rent receivable for the five months to 31 March 2020 is taxable (and not the actual rent received in the accounting period). Similarly, only the insurance payable for the 5 months to 31 March 2020 is deductible in the year to 31 March 2020.

(2)   A security deposit, less the cost of making good any damage, is returned to the tenant on the cessation of a letting. It is therefore initially not treated as income.

(3)   The insurance proceeds relate to the repair costs. As a tax deduction is available from trading profits for the repairs the associated insurance receipt is treated as taxable trading income.

(W4) Interest income

	£
Loan interest receivable (£5,600 + £2,500)	8,100
Less: Non-trading loan interest payable on let property	
(£25,000 × 1/5)	(5,000)
Interest income	3,100

Tutorial note

Interest paid in respect of a loan used for non-trading purposes (i.e. letting), is deducted from interest income under the loan relationship rules. Note that it is not deductible from property income.

(W5) Payment date

Softapp Ltd has one related 51% group company, so the augmented profits threshold is reduced to £750,000 (£1,500,000 ÷ 2).

The company's augmented profits (same as TTP) are £737,050 and the company is therefore not a large company. The due date for the payment of tax is therefore 9 months and one day after the end of the accounting period.

ACCA marking scheme	
	Marks
Trading income:	
Operating profit	0.5
Depreciation	0.5
Amortisation	0.5
Debenture interest payable deduction	0.5
Interest payable re let property	1.0
Heating system – special rate (SR) addition	0.5
Ventilation system – SR addition	0.5
AIA firstly against SR additions	1.0
Furniture – main pool addition	0.5
Fridge and cooker – main pool addition	0.5
AIA against main pool additions	0.5
WDA on main pool	0.5
Property income:	
Rent receivable	0.5
Security deposit – not taxable income	0.5
Advertising	0.5
Insurance	1.0
Repairs net of insurance proceeds	1.0
Interest income:	
Interest receivable	0.5
Freehold property interest payable deduction	1.0
Chargeable gain	0.5
Corporation tax	0.5
Payment date	1.0
Adjust augmented profits threshold	0.5
Company not large in current period	0.5
	——
Total	**15.0**

257 E-COMMERCE PLC (ADAPTED) *Walk in the footsteps of a top tutor*

Key answer tips

Part (a) involves correcting an existing tax computation, rather than preparing the computation from scratch. This is a somewhat unusual presentation, although it is not dissimilar to that seen in a previous corporation tax question. Here, however, the question is made slightly more difficult as it also involves reversing the calculations which have already been done (incorrectly) to calculate the correct figures. This question was not popular with students, many of whom did not know how to tackle it. It is important however, to attempt every question in the examination and therefore you should set out the computation, including the figures you do know, attempt the workings for those you don't (making assumptions if necessary), and then go on to calculate the corporation tax liability, for which you will get follow through marks, even if parts of your answer are wrong. This part is also only for 12 marks, so you must make sure you don't overrun on time here.

Part (b) requires you to identify why the company would not pay instalments in the current year and why they would be due in the following year. This should be straightforward provided these aspects of administration have been learnt.

The highlighted words in the answer are key phrases that markers are looking for.

(a) Revised corporation tax computation – year ended 31 March 2020

Tutor's top tips

In a challenging question such as this, it is important to maximise marks with a systematic approach, making sure you score all the easy marks (of which there are many).

Start by laying out your computation – inserting any obvious figures (such as those figures provided in the question which you know are correct) and leaving blank the more difficult ones. Then work through the gaps, doing straightforward workings on the face of the computation and more detailed ones in referenced workings underneath.

Where you are not sure you need to make a decision and move on, do not waste too much time on one small point.

For some of the figures, you need to reverse the calculations which have been carried out incorrectly (some of which are not shown in the question), before doing the revised calculations. This requires a good understanding of the way the calculations work, rather than just the ability to follow the pro forma and crunch the numbers. There are a number of ways these calculations could be presented, and this is discussed further in the tips below.

		£	£
Operating profit			2,102,300*
Legal fees	– Issue of preference shares (Note 1)	80,200	
	– Issue of loan notes (Note 2)	0	
	– Renewal of long lease (Note 3)	14,900	
	– Breach of contract (Note 4)	0	
	– Registration of trade marks (Note 5)	0	
			95,100
			2,197,400
Deduction for lease premium (£14,400 × 12/15) (Note 6)			(11,520)
Capital allowances		209,200*	
Motor car [1] (Note 7)		0	
Motor car [2] (Note 7)		0	
Motor car [3] (£51,750 × 12% (18% – 6%) (Note 8)		(6,210)	
Motor car [4] (£19,800 × 82% (100% – 18%) (Note 9)		16,236	
Short-life asset (£1,512 × 82/18) (Note 10)		6,888	
			(226,114)
Trading profit			1,959,766
Property income		156,700*	
Repairs (capital in nature)		95,300	
Rent accrual – March 2020 (£16,200 × 1/3) (Note 11)		5,400	
			257,400
Loan interest receivable		42,400*	
Accrual (£4,800 – £3,500) (Note 11)		(1,300)	
			41,100
Taxable total profits			2,258,266
Corporation tax (£2,258,266 × 19%*)			429,071

*Figures provided in question

Tutor's top tips

Whilst it would be possible to calculate the capital allowances by doing a revised capital allowances computation, not all of the figures for that computation (such as the brought forward balance on the main pool) were provided in the question. Therefore it would be necessary to do significantly more workings (to establish the missing figures) if this approach were taken. It is therefore easier to simply correct the mistakes you are aware of via short workings as shown above.

Tutorial note

(1) The issue of preference shares is not a trading expense and therefore the associated legal fees are not an allowable deduction.

(2) Legal fees in relation to the issue of loan notes will be treated in the same way as the loan they relate to. Here the loan was for trading purposes, therefore the fees are a deductible trading expense.

(3) Legal fees relating to a lease are only deductible if it is the **renewal** of a **short** (50 years or less) lease.

(4) Legal fees for breach of contract are generally deductible, since they are likely to relate to a trading purpose.

(5) Legal fees in relation to the registration of trademarks relate to the trade, and are therefore tax deductible.

(6) Since it is only the life of the lease which was incorrect in the original calculation, this can be corrected by simply multiplying the figure given by the 12 years used originally and dividing by the correct figure of 15 years. It is not necessary to try to recalculate the deduction from scratch, and this would prove very difficult as the figure for the premium paid was not provided in the question.

(7) Motor cars [1] and [2] have CO_2 emissions between 51 and 110 grams per kilometre, and qualify for writing down allowances at the rate of 18%. No adjustment is therefore required.

(8) Motor car [3] has CO_2 emissions over 110 grams per kilometre, and therefore only qualifies for writing down allowances at the rate of 6%.

(9) Motor car [4] has CO_2 emissions up to 50 grams per kilometre, and therefore qualifies for the 100% first year allowance. In the absence of any other information always assume that cars purchased are new cars (not second hand).

(10) The scrapping of the computer equipment is a disposal for capital allowances purposes. The company should therefore have received a 100% balancing allowance rather than a writing down allowance at the rate of 18%. The 82/18 adjustment represents the additional 82% (100% – 18%) of the brought forward TWDV which can be deducted.

(11) Property and interest income must be dealt with on an accruals basis, therefore an adjustment is required for the rent due in respect of the period and the correct loan interest accrual.

(b) **Quarterly instalment payments**

Tutor's top tips

Being able to determine when corporation tax is payable is a common examination requirement, and it is important to learn the rules about which companies must pay by quarterly instalments and the exceptions from that system, which are relevant here.

- Large companies have to make quarterly instalment payments in respect of their corporation tax liability. A large company is one with augmented profits exceeding £1,500,000, adjusted for short accounting periods and related 51% group companies.

- However, a company is not required to make quarterly instalment payments in the first year that it is large.

  Therefore, E-Commerce plc will not have been required to make instalment payments for the year ended 31 March 2020 as it was not a large company in the year ended 31 March 2019.

  This is because the augmented profits of £1,360,000 were less than £1,500,000.

- For the year ended 31 March 2021, this exception will not apply. Therefore, E-Commerce plc will have to make quarterly instalment payments as its augmented profits will exceed £1,500,000.

Examiner's report

Part (a) was not particularly difficult, but the information was presented in a different format to previous questions of this nature. However, candidates would have benefited from knowing the pro forma layout.

The requirement was generally reasonably well answered and there were a few highly satisfactory answers. The deduction for the lease premium caused the most problems, with many candidates not appreciating that there was no need to recalculate the amount assessed on the landlord – thereby spending quite a bit of time unnecessarily.

Part (b) was also reasonably well answered, although to score full marks it was necessary for answers to be quite precise – not, for example, just mentioning large companies, without explaining what a large company is.

	ACCA marking scheme	
		Marks
(a)	Correct figures from return – operating profit, capital allowances, property profit, loan interest receivable	1.0
	Legal fees re preference shares	0.5
	Legal fees re loan notes	0.5
	Legal fees re renewal of lease	0.5
	Legal fees re breach of contract	0.5
	Legal fees re registration of trade marks	0.5
	Deduction for lease premium	1.0
	Capital allowances – motor car [1]	0.5
	– motor car [2]	0.5
	– motor car [3]	1.0
	– motor car [4]	1.0
	– short life asset	1.0
	Repairs disallowed	1.0
	Rent accrual	1.0
	Loan interest accrual adjustment	1.0
	Corporation tax liability	0.5
		———
		12.0
		———
(b)	Companies with augmented profits exceeding £1,500,000	1.0
	No instalments if not large in previous year	1.0
	No exception in year ended 31 March 2021	1.0
		———
		3.0
		———
Total		**15.0**
		———

258 LUCKY LTD *Walk in the footsteps of a top tutor*

Key answer tips

This three part question on corporation tax is a classic section C corporation tax question.

Parts (a) and (c) test knowledge of administrative aspects of corporation tax.

Part (b) which is worth 11 out of the 15 marks available, is a straightforward corporation tax computation with marks available for adjustments to trading profit, capital allowances and the calculation of corporation tax.

The highlighted words in the answer are key phrases that markers are looking for.

Tutor's top tips

Parts (a) and (c) of this question could both be attempted before reading the scenario or carrying out the corporation tax computation in part (b). Answering both of these straightforward written parts first could help you manage your time, and ensure that you don't spend too long on part (b).

(a)   The start of accounting period

- An accounting period will normally start immediately after the end of the preceding accounting period.

- An accounting period will also start when a company commences to trade, or otherwise becomes liable to corporation tax.

Tutorial note

This is a common examination requirement and could be tested with either an objective test question or constructed response question, meaning it could feature in any one of the three examination sections.

(b)   Lucky Ltd – Corporation tax computation for the four-month period ended 31 March 2020

Tutor's top tips

Begin part (b) by setting out the corporation tax pro forma then work through the information given, inserting the more straightforward numbers first (such as the interest income). Where a working is required (for example the capital allowances) attempt these after the easier numbers, but make sure you leave time to calculate the corporation tax!

	£	£
Operating profit per question		532,600
Advertising	0	
Depreciation	14,700	
Amortisation	9,000	
Deduction for lease premium (W1)	(1,300)	
Capital allowances (W2)	(93,200)	
Donation to local charity	0	
Donation to national registered charity	835	
		(69,965)
Tax adjusted trading profit		462,635
Interest income		700
Total profits		463,335
Less: QCD relief		(835)
Taxable total profits		462,500
Corporation tax at 19%		87,875

Tutorial note

The advertising expenditure incurred during September 2019 is pre-trading expenditure. As it is incurred within seven years of the trade commencing, it is treated as being incurred on 1 December 2019. It is therefore deductible and no adjustment is required.

Workings

(W1) Deduction for lease premium

£46,800/12 × 4/12 = £1,300

Tutorial note

The steps for calculating the allowable trading deduction for a lease premium paid by a company are as follows:

- **Calculate the amount of the premium paid by the company that will be taxable for the landlord as property income.**

In this question the amount of premium assessed on the landlord as income has been given (£46,800) so do not waste time trying to calculate this figure.

- **The annual deduction available from trading profits is the property income on which the landlord is taxed, divided by the number of years of the lease.**

In this question the annual deduction is £46,800/12 but since the lease was taken out on 1 December 2019 only 4/12 of this amount is deductible for the year ended 31 March 2020.

- **Disallow any amortisation relating to the lease premium in the accounts.**

In this question the amortisation of £9,000 needs to be added back.

(W2) Capital allowances

4 m/e 31 March 2020		Main pool	Special rate pool	Allowances
	£	£	£	£
TWDV b/f		0	0	0
Additions qualifying for AIA				
Integral feature	41,200			
AIA (100%)				
Max				
(£1,000,000 × 4/12 = £333,333)	(41,200)			41,200
			0	
Computer	6,300			
Office equipment	32,900			
	39,200			
AIA (100%)	(39,200)			39,200
		0		
Addition qualifying for FYA				
Motor car	12,800			
FYA (100%)	(12,800)			12,800
		0		
TWDV c/f		0	0	
Total allowances				93,200

Tutorial notes

(1)   The computer purchased on 19 August 2019 is pre-trading expenditure as it was purchased within the seven years before the trade commenced. Therefore it is treated as purchased on 1 December 2019 for capital allowance purposes.

(2)   The motor car has CO_2 emissions up to 50 grams per kilometre, and therefore qualifies for the 100% first year allowance. In the absence of any other information always assume that cars purchased are new cars (not second hand).

(3)   The expenditure which is integral to the building is included in the special rate pool.

(c)   Retaining records

Tutor's top tips

Due dates and time limits are easily tested in any of the three sections of the examination. They are a source of easy marks provided you have learnt them!

- Lucky Ltd must retain the records used in preparing its self-assessment corporation tax return until six years after the end of the accounting period, which is 31 March 2026.

- A failure to retain records could result in a penalty of up to £3,000 per accounting period. However, the maximum penalty will only be charged in serious cases.

ACCA marking scheme		Marks
(a)	The start of accounting period	2.0
(b)	Lucky Ltd – Corporation tax computation for 4 m/e 31 March 2020	
	Advertising	0.5
	Depreciation	0.5
	Amortisation	0.5
	Deduction for lease premium	1.5
	Interest income	0.5
	Donations	1.5
	Corporation tax	0.5
	Capital allowances	
	Integral feature	1.0
	Computer	0.5
	Office equipment	0.5
	AIA	2.0
	Motor car	0.5
	FYA	1.0
		11.0
(c)	Retaining records	2.0
Total		**15.0**

RELIEF FOR TRADING LOSSES

259 LAST-ORDERS LTD *Walk in the footsteps of a top tutor*

Key answer tips

This question covers corporation tax aspects of a loss making company.

Part (a) involves a basic adjustment of profits computation with the standard requirement to calculate capital allowances. The company has ceased to trade, therefore a balancing adjustment must be calculated in place of the standard WDA etc.

Part (b) asks for taxable total profits for the period. A basic calculation was required for both property income and chargeable gains.

Part (c) requires an explanation of alternative methods of relief for the trading loss. This should not have posed a problem as it is an area often tested in the examination.

Tutor's top tips

Once you have calculated your trading loss in part (a) you have to use it in the calculation of loss relief in part (b). Remember that even if your answer to part (a) is incorrect you will get marks for applying the rules correctly in part (b).

(a) **Last-Orders Ltd – Trading loss for the ten-month period ended 31 January 2020**

	£
Operating loss	(276,480)
Depreciation	9,460
Counselling services	0
Employee pension contributions	0
Employer class 1 NICs	0
Employer class 1A NICs	0
Unpaid bonuses	10,400
Lease of motor car	0
Entertaining UK suppliers	1,920
Entertaining overseas customers	440
Qualifying charitable donations	800
Balancing allowance (£24,200 – £13,600)	(10,600)
	————
Tax adjusted trading loss	(264,060)
	————

Tutorial note

Staff costs are disallowable if they are not paid within nine months following the end of the period of account.

The deduction of lease costs is restricted if emissions are >110g/km. The car had emissions of 105g/km, therefore no adjustment is necessary.

Entertaining is disallowable with the exception of staff entertaining.

(b) **Last-Orders Ltd – Taxable total profits for the ten-month period ended 31 January 2020**

	£
Property income (W1)	22,800
Chargeable gain (W2)	34,500
	————
Total profits	57,300
Less: Trading loss	(57,300)
	————
	0
Less: QCD relief	wasted
	————
TTP	0
	————

Unrelieved loss at 31 January 2020 £206,760 (£264,060 – £57,300).

Workings

(W1) Property income

	£
Rent receivable (10/12 × (£19,200 × 2))	32,000
Less: Insurance (£1,800 × 10/12)	(1,500)
Repairs	(7,700)
	————
Property income	22,800
	————

Tutorial note

Property income is assessed on an accruals basis for companies, therefore the dates of receipt and payment are irrelevant.

(W2) Chargeable gain – office building

	£
Disposal proceeds	126,800
Less: Acquisition cost	(79,400)
Unindexed gain	47,400
Less: Indexation allowance (given)	(12,900)
Chargeable gain	34,500

(c)   The trading loss can be relieved against Last-Orders Ltd's total profits for the previous three years, latest year first, because it is a terminal loss.

The trading loss can be surrendered to Gastro Ltd because there is a 75% group relationship. The amount surrendered will be restricted to 10/12ths of Gastro Ltd's taxable total profits for the year ended 31 March 2020.

There is not a group relationship with Gourmet Ltd, so no group relief claim is possible.

Examiner's report

Part (a) for 6 marks required candidates to calculate Last-Orders Ltd's trading loss for the ten-month period. This involved adjusting for depreciation, various employee costs, the lease of a motorcar, entertainment expenditure and a qualifying charitable donation, plus calculating the balancing allowance on the cessation of trade. Although this section was very well answered by many candidates, it caused problems for others. The section did not require any detailed workings, with any adjustments easily contained within the single computation. When commencing with a loss figure, candidates should be particularly careful to indicate which adjustments are deductions and which are additions. A single column approach with deductions shown in brackets avoids any confusion. Many candidates did not show those items not requiring any adjustment, despite being instructed specifically to do so – easy marks thereby being lost. Also, candidates should appreciate that there is no need to adjust for items of income which occur in the statement of profit or loss AFTER the figure used to commence the loss adjustment. Last-Orders Ltd had ceased trading, so this meant that there was a balancing allowance. Many candidates missed this point, instead calculating capital allowances for the period.

Part (b) for 5 marks required candidates to calculate Last-Orders Ltd's taxable total profits for the ten-month period ended 31 January. This was on the assumption that relief for the trading loss was claimed against this period's income. Last-Orders Ltd's other income consisted of property business income and a chargeable gain. This section was generally well answered, with a number of perfect answers. However, candidates do not impress if they make basic mistakes such as deducting the annual exempt amount when calculating a corporate chargeable gain. Also, candidates should always be careful to follow the requirements – an easy half-mark was sometimes missed by not showing a figure for the amount of unused trading loss despite this being specifically requested.

Part (c) for 4 marks required an explanation of the alternative ways in which Last-Orders Ltd's unused trading loss could be relieved. Given that the company had ceased trading, candidates should really have realised that the loss could not be carried forward. Vague answers such as 'claim terminal loss relief' are not sufficient. Instead, candidates should have stated that relief was against total profits, for the previous three years and on a latest year first (LIFO) basis.

ACCA marking scheme		Marks
(a)	Adjustment of loss	
	Depreciation	0.5
	Counselling services	0.5
	Employee pension contributions	0.5
	Employer class 1 NICs	0.5
	Employer class 1A NICs	0.5
	Unpaid bonuses	0.5
	Lease of motor car	0.5
	Entertaining UK suppliers	0.5
	Entertaining overseas customers	0.5
	QCDs	0.5
	Balancing allowance	1.0
		────
		6.0
		────
(b)	Rent receivable	1.0
	Insurance	1.0
	Repairs	0.5
	Chargeable gain	1.0
	Loss deducted	0.5
	QCD wasted	0.5
	Loss carried forward	0.5
		────
		5.0
		────
(c)	Terminal loss relief – ½ mark per point	1.5
	Last-Orders and Gastro in a 75% group	1.0
	Group relief restricted to 10/12	1.0
	Gourmet not in 75% group	0.5
		────
		4.0
		────
Total		**15.0**
		────

260 WRETCHED LTD (ADAPTED) *Walk in the footsteps of a top tutor*

Key answer tips

The first mark available was in relation to company residence and was straightforward. You should be prepared to be tested on this topic.

The calculation of three separate losses was required; a trading loss, a property loss and a capital loss.

The capital allowances computation was the largest section of the trading loss calculation. Knowledge of the different treatment of cars based on the level of emissions was required here. This is regularly tested in the examination. Also, remember to time apportion allowances, with the exception of the first year allowance, for a short accounting period.

The calculation of property income is tested regularly. This should have been straightforward as it was a standard computation.

(a) Wretched Ltd is resident in the UK as companies which are incorporated in the UK are resident in the UK regardless of where their central management and control is exercised.

(b) **Wretched Ltd – Period ended 31 March 2020**

Trading loss

	£
Trading loss	(141,200)
Advertising expenditure	(7,990)
Deduction for lease premium ((£34,440/10) × 8/12)	(2,296)
Capital allowances (working)	(4,424)
Revised trading loss	(155,910)

Tutorial note

The advertising expenditure was incurred within seven years of the company commencing to trade so it is treated as being incurred on the first day of trading. It is therefore deductible, and an adjustment is required.

Working – Capital allowances

	Main pool	Special rate pool	Allowances
	£	£	£	£
Additions qualifying for AIA				
Laptops (£400 × 3)	1,200			
AIA – 100%	(1,200)			1,200
Additions– Motor car (1)		8,300		
– Motor car (2)		12,300		
– Motor car (3)			18,800	
		_____		
		20,600		
WDA – 18% × 8/12		(2,472)		2,472
WDA – 6% × 8/12			(752)	752
		_____	_____	
TWDV c/f		18,128	18,048	
		_____	_____	
Total allowances				4,424
				_____

Tutorial note

(1) The original cost of the laptops is irrelevant.

(2) Although motor car (1) has CO_2 emissions up to 50 grams per kilometre, it is second hand (i.e. not new) and therefore does not qualify for the 100% first year allowance. It instead qualifies for writing down allowances at the rate of 18%.

(3) Motor car (2) has CO_2 emissions between 51 and 110 grams per kilometre and therefore qualifies for writing down allowances at the rate of 18%.

(4) Motor car (3) has CO_2 emissions over 110 grams per kilometre and therefore qualifies for writing down allowances at the rate of 6%.

Property income loss

	£
Rent receivable (£1,400 × 3)	4,200
Advertising	(2,100)
Repairs	(5,900)
	_____
Property income loss	(3,800)
	_____

Capital loss

	£
Disposal proceeds	21,400
Cost	(26,200)
Indexation allowance	0
Capital loss	(4,800)

Tutorial note

The indexation allowance was frozen at December 2017 and therefore no allowance is available in respect of the shares which were acquired after this date.

Remember though that even where an indexation allowance is available it cannot be used to increase a loss.

(1)   The trading loss of £155,910 will be carried forward and a claim can be made to offset it against total profits in future.

(2)   The property income loss of £3,800 will be carried forward and a claim can be made to offset it against total profits in future.

(3)   The capital loss of £4,800 will be carried forward and relieved against the first available chargeable gains.

Examiner's report

For part (a), candidates were required to state whether the company was resident or not resident in the UK for corporation tax purposes. This requirement resulted in a very surprising amount of incorrect answers, with at least half the candidates deciding that the company was not resident because of its central management and control being exercised overseas.

Part (b) required a calculation of the company's trading loss, property business loss and capital loss. As regards the trading loss, this involved pre-trading expenditure, a deduction for a lease premium and capital allowances. This section was generally very well answered, although there were a couple of consistent problems. Firstly, it was often not appreciated that a second-hand motor car does not qualify for the 100% first year allowance. And secondly, indexation allowance was often used to increase the capital loss.

For part (c), candidates were required to explain how the company would have been able to relieve its trading loss, property business loss and capital loss. Provided candidates appreciated that it was the company's first period of trading, this section was then well answered. However, candidates who overlooked this basic fact spent a lot of time discussing all the various (irrelevant) loss reliefs, with a few candidates discussing the income tax relief for a loss incurred in the early years of a trade.

ACCA marking scheme		
		Marks
(a)	Residence	1.0
		―――
(b)	**Trading loss**	
	Advertising	1.0
	Lease premium	1.5
	Capital allowances	
	– AIA	1.5
	– Additions	2.0
	– WDA	2.0
	Property loss	
	Rent receivable	0.5
	Advertising	0.5
	Repairs	0.5
	Capital loss	
	Proceeds	0.5
	Cost	0.5
	No indexation allowance available	0.5
		―――
		11.0
		―――
	Trading loss	1.0
	Property loss	1.0
	Capital loss	1.0
		―――
		3.0
		―――
Total		**15.0**
		―――

261 RETRO LTD *Walk in the footsteps of a top tutor*

Key answer tips

This question on corporation tax losses starts with a requirement to calculate the amount of the corporation tax loss.

The remaining parts require consideration of how to relieve the loss and a calculation of the remaining loss to carry forward.

The highlighted words in part (c) are key phrases that markers are looking for.

Tutor's top tips

Make sure you follow the presentation instructions given. This is the standard approach the markers would expect to see in any adjustments to profit calculation.

(a)   Trading loss – year ended 31 March 2020

	£
Loss before taxation	(120,000)
Depreciation	27,240
Gifts to employees (Note 1)	0
Gifts to customers (Note 2)	0
Political donations	420
Qualifying charitable donations	680
Impairment loss	0
Lease of motor car (£4,400 × 15%)	660
Health and safety fine	5,100
Legal fees – Internet domain name (Note 3)	0
Interest payable (Note 4)	0
Capital allowances (W)	(50,420)
	————
Trading loss	(136,320)
	————

Tutorial note

(1)   Gifts to employees are an allowable deduction regardless of cost or the fact that the gift is food. This is because the gifts will be assessed on the employees as benefits of employment.

(2)   Gifts to customers are an allowable deduction if they cost less than £50 per recipient per year, are not of food, drink, tobacco or vouchers for exchangeable goods and carry a conspicuous advertisement for the company making the gift.

(3)   Legal fees incurred in defending the title to non-current assets (e.g. the domain name) are incurred for the purposes of the trade and are allowable trading expenses.

(4)   Interest on a loan used for trading purposes is deductible on an accruals basis.

Working: Capital allowances

	£	Main pool £	Allowances £
TWDV brought forward		39,300	
Addition – Motor car (1)		14,700	
Additions qualifying for AIA			
Delivery van	28,300		
AIA (100%)	(28,300)		28,300
		0	
		54,000	
WDA (18%)		(9,720)	9,720
Addition qualifying for FYA			
Motor car (2)	12,400		
FYA (100%)	(12,400)		12,400
		0	
TWDV c/f		44,280	
Total allowances			50,420

Tutorial note

(1) *Motor car (1) has CO_2 emissions between 51 and 110g/km, and therefore qualifies for writing down allowances at the rate of 18%.*

(2) *Motor car (2) has CO_2 emissions of ≤ 50g/km, and therefore qualifies for the 100% first year allowance. In the absence of any other information always assume that cars purchased are new cars (not second hand).*

(b) Loss relief

Tutor's top tips

It is more efficient to use a columnar format for loss relief questions.

A company cannot carry back losses unless they are offset against current year total profits first. However, only the carry back periods need to be shown in the answer as there is no other income in the loss-making period (year ended 31 March 2020) to set the losses against.

	y/e 31 August 2018	7 m/e 31 March 2019
	£	£
Trading profit	56,600	47,900
Interest income	1,300	0
Total profits	57,900	47,900
Less: Loss relief – 12 month carry back (Note)		
– 7 m/e 31.3.19		(47,900)
– y/e 31.8.18 (£57,900 × 5/12)	(24,125)	
	33,775	0
Less: QCD relief	(540)	(wasted)
TTP	33,235	0

Tutorial note

Corporation tax losses can be carried back exactly 12 months before the start of the loss-making period.

If in the 12 month carry back period there has been a change in accounting date, and there is a short period of account, the loss can be carried back to two periods. The loss is carried back on a LIFO basis.

In this question, the loss is therefore carried back against the 7 m/e 31 March 2019 first, and then against the y/e 31 August 2018.

When carried back to the year ended 31 August 2018, the remaining loss can only be set against 5/12 of the total profits of that period.

(c) Loss carried forward

Tutor's top tips

It would be equally acceptable to show the loss memorandum within your answer to parts (b) or (c).

- The amount of unrelieved trading loss at 31 March 2020 is £64,295 (W).

- The unrelieved trading loss can be carried forward and a claim can be made to offset it against future total profits.

Working: Loss memorandum

	£
Loss in y/e 31 March 2020	136,320
Less: Current period	(0)
Carry back losses 12 months (LIFO basis)	
– 7 m/e 31 March 2019	(47,900)
– 5 m/e 31 August 2018	(24,125)
Loss c/f	64,295

Examiner's report

Part (a) Most candidates had little difficulty with this section. One poor practice was the use of notes and explanations. It was a simple matter, as per the model answer, to just list all the items of expenditure (and show whether or not an adjustment was required), so the use of notes (such as for the gifts and donations) was completely unnecessary and against the guidance given in the note to the requirement. Since the requirement was for a calculation, explanations are not required, and result in wasted time. As regards the capital allowances, many candidates did not appreciate that the delivery van qualified for the 100% annual investment allowance – instead including it in the special rate pool.

Part (b) There were many perfect answers to this section, although disappointingly a few candidates tried to time-apportion profits using the opening year rules.

Note: *The examiner's report has been edited to remove comments on elements of the answer that have changed as a result of a change in finance act.*

ACCA marking scheme

		Marks
(a)	**Adjustment to profits**	
	Depreciation	0.5
	Gifts to employees	0.5
	Gifts to customers	0.5
	Political donations	0.5
	Qualifying charitable donations	0.5
	Impairment loss	0.5
	Lease of motor car	1.0
	Health and safety fine	0.5
	Legal fees – Internet domain name	0.5
	Interest payable	0.5
	Capital allowances	
	TWDV b/f	0.5
	Additions qualifying for AIA - delivery van	0.5
	AIA – 100%	0.5
	Addition – motor car (1)	0.5
	WDA – 18%	0.5
	Addition qualifying for FYA – motor car	0.5
	FYA – 100%	0.5
		9.0

ACCA marking scheme		
(b)	Trading profits	0.5
	Bank interest	0.5
	Loss relief	1.0
	Restriction of relief to 5m/e 31 August 2018	1.0
	QCD	1.0
		4.0
(c)	Amount of unrelieved trading loss	1.0
	Loss c/f	1.0
		2.0
Total		**15.0**

WITH GROUP ASPECTS

262 MUSIC PLC (ADAPTED)

Key answer tips

In this question there are 10 marks for written explanations of the gains group and related 51% group company rules. It is important to state the basic rule and then apply to the facts of the question. Be careful with the overseas company, which is included but unable to enjoy the benefits of gains group status.

The highlighted words in the answer are key phrases that markers are looking for.

(a)   Capital gains group

- Companies form a capital gains group if at each level in the group structure there is a 75% shareholding, provided the parent company has an effective interest of more than 50%.

- Alto Ltd, Bass Ltd, Cello Ltd, Echo Inc and Flute Ltd are all 75% subsidiaries, and Music plc has an effective interest of 60% (80% × 75%) in Flute Ltd. All of these companies therefore form a capital gains group.

- However, Bass Ltd and Cello Ltd will only be included in respect of assets acquired or disposed of whilst they were members of the group.

- Drum Ltd and Gong Ltd are not included as Drum Ltd is not a 75% subsidiary, and Music plc's effective interest in Gong Ltd is only 48% (80% × 75% × 80%).

- Although Echo Inc is included in the definition of the capital gains group, companies that are resident overseas are not able to take advantage of the provisions applicable to a capital gains group.

(b)   Related 51% group companies

- Music plc directly owns at least 51% of the shares in Alto Ltd, Bass Ltd, Cello Ltd and Echo Inc. Alto, Bass and Echo are related 51% group companies as Music owned the shareholdings in these companies at the end of the previous period i.e. 31 March 2019.

- Music did not own the shares in Cello Ltd at the end of the previous period therefore it will not be included as a 51% company until the year ended 31 March 2021.

- Flute Ltd is also a related 51% group company as Music Ltd indirectly owns at least 51% of the company i.e. 80% × 75% = 60%.

- Gong Ltd is not a related 51% group company as Music Ltd owns (indirectly) less than 51% of the company i.e. 80% × 75% × 80% = 48%.

- Drum Ltd is not a related 51% group company since Music plc's effective interest in this company is only 45%.

- For these purposes, it does not matter where a company is resident. Echo Inc is therefore included despite being resident overseas.

- The five related 51% group companies for the year ended 31 March 2020 are therefore Music plc, Alto Ltd, Bass Ltd, Echo Inc and Flute Ltd.

(c) **Corporation tax liability – year ended 31 March 2020**

	£
Trading profit	92,000
Interest income	12,000
Net chargeable gains (W)	23,000
Taxable total profits	127,000
Corporation tax (£127,000 × 19%)	24,130

Tutorial note

The capital gain of £120,000 is included in Music plc's taxable total profits since an election has been made with Alto Ltd to transfer the gain to Music plc. Music plc's capital losses may be set against this gain.

Working: Net chargeable gain

	£
Net chargeable gain in the year (by election)	120,000
Less: Capital losses in the year	(65,000)
	55,000
Less: Capital losses b/f	(32,000)
Net chargeable gain	23,000

(d) **Bank loan**

Under the loan relationship rules, the cost of loans used for non-trade purposes are deductible from interest income. If the loan was used to acquire a property which was to be rented out (i.e. a non-trade purpose), the interest would not be deducted from trading income, nor property business income (as for individuals), but from the company's interest income.

Legal fees

Legal fees incurred in relation to the purchase of a capital asset are not deductible from the company's trading profits. They will be deductible in the chargeable gain computation when the building is ultimately sold.

Rent receivable

The rent receivable from letting the property to a tenant will be included on an accruals basis, net of any allowable deductions, in taxable total profits as property income.

263 JUMP LTD (ADAPTED)

Key answer tips

The first part of this question involves a standard adjustment of profit computation where the company is loss making.

The second part is more difficult and requires detailed group relief knowledge and the calculation of the maximum surrender possible to a subsidiary that commenced trading during the year. The usual principles apply but the TTP and loss must be time apportioned for the period the subsidiary is part of the loss relief group.

Tutorial note

An adjustment to profits calculation is required and the fact that the company is making a loss should not change your approach in any way.

Just start with a negative figure for the loss, then make the same adjustments as you would make if it were a profit and lay out your answer in the same way.

Remember that it is important to list all the major items indicated in the question requirement, showing a zero (0) for expenditure that is allowable. This is because credit will be given for showing no adjustment where none is needed.

List the adjustments in the order they appear in the question.

If required, also add notes to show why you have not adjusted for an item, or why you have added it back. However, lengthy explanations are not required where the requirement is, as in this case, just to 'calculate' the adjusted profits, rather than to explain them.

Always show your workings if the figure you are adjusting for is not clear from the question.

(a)   Jump Ltd – Trading loss for the three-month period ended 31 March 2020

	£
Operating loss	(144,700)
Depreciation	8,100
Employee training courses (Note 1)	0
Employee pension contributions (Note 2)	0
Staff party (Note 3)	0
Lease of motor car (£1,200 × 15%) (Note 4)	180
Accountancy (Note 5)	0
Legal fees – Issue of share capital (Note 6)	3,800
– Renewal of short lease (Note 7)	0
Entertaining UK customers (Note 8)	1,700
Entertaining overseas customers (Note 8)	790
Political donations (Note 9)	800
Capital allowances (net balancing charge)	3,330
	————
Trading loss	(126,000)
	————

Tutorial note

(1)   *The cost of employee training courses is wholly and exclusively for trade purposes and therefore allowable.*

(2)   *Employer's pension contributions made in respect of employees are allowable on a paid basis.*

(3)   *The only exception to the non-deductibility of entertainment expenditure is when it is in respect of employees. The £150 limit does not apply to employers, this limit relates to employment income only.*

(4)   *The leased car has emissions of >110g/km hence 15% of the expense has been disallowed.*

(5)   *Audit and accountancy fees are allowable, as they are incurred wholly and exclusively for the purposes of the trade.*

(6)   *Legal fees in connection with the issue of share capital are not allowable, being capital in nature.*

(7)   *The cost of renewing a short-lease (less than 50 years) is specifically allowable as a trading expense.*

(8)   *The only exception to the non-deductibility of entertainment expenditure is when it is in respect of employees.*

(9)   *Political donations are specifically disallowable.*

Working – Capital allowances

	Main pool	Special rate pool	Allowances
	£	£	£
TWDV b/f	12,100	5,700	
Proceeds – Motor car [1]		(9,300)	
– Motor car [2]	(6,100)		
		(3,600)	
Balancing charge		3,600	(3,600)
	6,000	0	
WDA – 18% × 3/12	(270)		270
TWDV c/f	5,730		
Overall balancing charge			(3,330)

Tutorial note

The proceeds for motor car [1] are restricted to the original cost figure of £9,300. Note that a balancing charge can arise on the main and special rate pools at any time but a balancing allowance on these pools can only arise on the cessation of trade.

(b) (1) The main factor which will influence Jump Ltd's choice of loss relief or group relief claims is the timing of the relief obtained, with an earlier claim generally being preferable.

Tutorial note

Note that only one factor was required.

Another possible factor is the extent to which relief for qualifying charitable donations will be lost. However, this is not relevant given that Jump Ltd has not made any charitable donations.

(2) The maximum loss relief claim for the seven-month period to 31 December 2019 is £42,400, being the total profits for this period

The loss relief claim for the year ended 31 May 2019 is restricted to £33,250 ((£78,600 + £1,200) × 5/12).

(3) The maximum amount of trading loss which can be surrendered to Hop Ltd is £23,625, being the lower of Hop Ltd's taxable total profits (£63,000 × 3/8 = £23,625) and Jump Ltd's loss of £126,000.

Skip Ltd is not a 75% subsidiary of Jump Ltd, so no group relief claim is possible.

Examiner's report

Part (a) was generally well answered; requiring a calculation of the company's tax adjusted trading loss. Candidates need to appreciate that where a profit adjustment involves a loss, then they must clearly show whether adjustments are added or deducted – in particular, capital allowances which in this case were deducted due to there being an overall balancing charge. Some candidates did not appreciate that where disposal proceeds exceed a pool's brought forward written down value, then there will be a balancing charge.

Part (b) required candidates to (1) state the main factor influencing the choice of a company's loss relief or group relief claims, (2) advise the company as to the maximum amount of trading loss which could be relieved against total profits for previous periods, and (3) advise the company as to the maximum amount of trading loss which could be surrendered as group relief. For (3), it was often not appreciated that a 75% shareholding is necessary in order for a group relief claim to be possible.

ACCA marking scheme		
		Marks
(a)	Depreciation	0.5
	Employee training	0.5
	Employee pension contributions	0.5
	Staff party	0.5
	Lease	1.0
	Professional fees	1.5
	Entertaining	1.0
	Political donations	0.5
	Capital allowances add back	0.5
	TWDV b/f	0.5
	Motor car (1)	1.0
	Motor car (2)	0.5
	Balancing charge	0.5
	WDA at 18% × 3/12	1.0
		———
		10.0
		———
(b)	Main factor – Maximum 1	1.0
	Max relief 7 months ended 31.12.19	0.5
	Loss relief year ended 31.5.19	1.5
	Maximum surrender to Hop	1.5
	Skip not in group	0.5
		———
		5.0
		———
Total		**15.0**
		———

264 ASH LTD (ADAPTED) *Walk in the footsteps of a top tutor*

(a) **Ash Ltd**

Key answer tips

This question covers corporation tax for three different companies.

a) Part (a) involves explaining the residency status of a company. Make sure you don't mix up the rules that apply to individuals here.

b) Part (b) is a standard requirement looking for the corporation tax liability via an adjustment to profits starting point. Make sure you start with the correct figure here i.e. the profit before tax before making your adjustments.

c) Part (c) involved calculating a gain on shares followed by the offset of a capital loss by another group company. Make sure you index the pool before taking out the shares that are disposed of.

    (i) **Accounting periods**

        1 February 2018 to 31 January 2019

        1 February 2019 to 31 March 2019

        Year ended 31 March 2020

Tutorial notes

1   The bank account opened by Ash Ltd on 1 December 2017 is not a source of income as it does not generate interest, and therefore does not trigger the start of an accounting period.

2   An accounting period cannot be longer than 12 months, so the period of account ended 31 March 2019 must be split into two accounting periods.

3   The move overseas of a majority of Ash Ltd's director/shareholders on 1 October 2019 has no impact on the company's accounting periods.

    (ii) **Residence status**

        Ash Ltd was incorporated in the UK, so the company is therefore resident in the UK throughout the period 1 December 2017 to 31 March 2020.

        The move overseas of a majority of Ash Ltd's director/shareholders on 1 October 2019 does not have any impact on the company's residence status.

(b)   **Beech Ltd**

Corporation tax computation for the year ended 31 January 2020

	£
Profit before taxation	305,500
Depreciation	14,700
Gifts to customers	3,500
Qualifying charitable donations	1,100
Impairment loss	0
Lease of motor cars (£12,600 × 15%)	1,890
Data protection fine	6,400
Legal fees – Renewal of short lease	0
Interest payable	0
Trading profit	333,090
Qualifying charitable donations	(1,100)
Taxable total profits	331,990
Corporation tax (£331,990 × 19%)	63,078

Tutorial note

Gifts to customers are only an allowable deduction if they cost less than £50 per recipient per year, are not of food, drink, tobacco or vouchers for exchangeable goods and carry a conspicuous advertisement for the company making the gift.

15% of the car lease costs must be disallowed as the emissions exceed 110g/km.

(c)   **Cedar Ltd**

Corporation tax computation for the year ended 31 March 2020

	£
Disposal proceeds (£6 × 25,000)	150,000
Indexed cost (W)	(38,004)
Chargeable gain	111,996
Capital loss	(8,800)
Loss relief	(19,700)
Group relief	(20,800)
Taxable total profits	62,696

Working – Indexed cost

	Number	£
Purchase July 2010	20,000	24,800
Rights issue July 2010 (£1.15 × 20,000 × ¼)	5,000	5,750
	25,000	30,550
Indexation to December 2017 (£30,550 × 0.244)		7,454
		38,004
Disposal December 2017	(25,000)	(38,004)
Balance c/f	0	0

Tutorial note

Indexation allowance for companies was frozen at December 2017 so although the disposal took place in December 2019 the pool is only indexed up to December 2017.

A joint election can be made so that Cedar Ltd is treated as having incurred Timber Ltd's capital loss.

ACCA marking guide			
			Marks
(a)	(i)	Accounting periods	2.0
			———
	(ii)	UK resident due to UK incorporation	1.0
		Retain UK residence	1.0
			———
			2.0
			———
(b)		Depreciation	0.5
		Gifts to customers	0.5
		Charitable donations	0.5
		Impairment loss	0.5
		Lease restriction	1.0
		Fine	0.5
		Legal fees	0.5
		Interest	0.5
		Deduct QCDs	0.5
		Corporation tax	1.0
			———
			6.0
			———
(c)		Proceeds	0.5
		Share pool working:	
		Purchase July 2010	0.5
		Rights issue	1.0
		Indexation	1.0
		Losses	2.0
			———
			5.0
			———
Total			**15.0**
			———

Examiner's report

The corporation tax question involved three unconnected limited companies, Ash Ltd, Beech Ltd and Cedar Ltd.

Part (a)(i) for 2 marks was to identify Ash Ltd's accounting periods throughout the period 1 December 2017 (incorporation) to 31 March 2020 (the end of the first twelve month set of accounts, Ash Ltd having previously prepared accounts for the 14-month period ended 31 March 2019). This section was quite well answered. However, when considering accounting periods, it is very important not to confuse the corporate and unincorporated business rules. Applying the unincorporated business opening year rules to a limited company will obviously not achieve many marks.

If asked to identify a company's accounting periods throughout a given period candidates should make sure that all relevant periods are stated. It does not create a good impression if there are gaps between the accounting periods stated by a candidate, or if a stated period ends before it has started.

Part (a)(ii) required candidates to explain Ash Ltd's residence status throughout the same period. Again, candidates should be careful not to confuse the rules for companies with those applicable to individuals. If a limited company is incorporated in the UK, then nothing else is relevant. So, as regards the majority of Ash Ltd's director/shareholders moving overseas, candidates should just have stated that this did not have any impact on the company's residence status.

For Beech Ltd, a summarised statement of profit or loss was provided for the year ended 31 January 2020. The requirement for 6 marks was to calculate the company's corporation tax liability for this year. Various adjustments were required, but there were no capital allowances. This section was very well answered.

When making adjustments to a trading profit, candidates need to be very careful that adjustments are correctly added and not deducted.

Cedar Ltd had made a chargeable gain on the disposal of a shareholding on 28 December 2019. For the year ended 31 March 2020, the company made a trading loss. Cedar Ltd was a 100% subsidiary company of Timber Ltd, and for the year ended 31 March 2020, Timber Ltd had made a trading loss and also a capital loss.

Part (c) for 5 marks required a calculation of Cedar Ltd's taxable total profits for the year ended 31 March 2020. This was on the basis that all available claims and elections were made. This section was again well answered. When calculating chargeable gains for a corporate share disposal carefully check the dates that have been given. There was a rights issue which had taken place in the month of purchase, so there was no need to index prior to adding the new shares into the share pool.

265   CLUELESS LTD (ADAPTED) *Walk in the footsteps of a top tutor*

Key answer tips

Part (a) requires the computation of a company's corporation tax liability including an adjustment of trading profits calculation. The information is presented in a slightly unusual format as an existing corporation tax computation that contains numerous errors. However this should not prove a problem for the well prepared student.

Part (b) deals with the administrative aspects of corporation tax. There is an easy mark in part (1). However, part (2) may cause some students problems if they have not learnt this topic. As all companies must now file their tax returns electronically it is an important and topical area.

The highlighted words in the answer are key phrases that markers are looking for.

Tutor's top tips

Do not be put off by the different format in which the information is presented. Set up your corporation tax computation as usual and work through each of the workings in the question dealing with each piece of information as you go. Remember to indicate by the use of zero any items in the computation of trading profit for which no adjustment is required.

Note that the company has a wholly owned subsidiary, Clever Ltd. Remember that dividends received are not included in taxable total profits, regardless of the relationship with the paying company. However, remember there are special rules where members of a capital gains group transfer assets between each other.

(a)   **Corporation tax computation – year ended 31 March 2020**

	£
Trading profit (W1)	355,808
Loan interest receivable	32,800
Chargeable gain (W3)	92,603
	———
Taxable total profits	481,211
Less: QCD relief	(900)
	———
Taxable total profits	480,311
	———
Corporation tax liability at 19%	91,259
	———

Tutorial note

Loan interest income is assessed on the amount receivable in respect of the accounting period.

Workings

(W1) Trading profit

	£
Profit before taxation	382,610
Depreciation	15,740
Client entertaining	400
Qualifying charitable donations	900
Gifts to customers – portable power banks	0
Gifts to customers – boxes of chocolates	1,650
	401,300
Less: Capital allowances (W2)	(45,492)
Trading profit	355,808

Tutorial note

(1)   Donations to political parties are a disallowable trading expense. Qualifying charitable donations are a disallowable trading expense but are deductible from total profits.

(2)   Gifts to customers are an allowable deduction if they cost less than £50 per recipient per year, are not of food, drink, tobacco or vouchers for exchangeable goods, and carry a conspicuous advertisement for the company making the gift.

(W2) Capital allowances

		Main pool	Special rate pool	Allowances
	£	£	£	£
TWDV b/f		12,400	13,500	
Additions not qualifying for AIA				
Motor car			11,800	
Additions qualifying for AIA				
Computers	42,300			
AIA	(42,300)			42,300
	———	0		
Less: Disposal proceeds			(9,300)	
			———	
			16,000	
WDA (18%)		(2,232)		2,232
WDA (6%)			(960)	960
		———	———	
TWDV c/f		10,168	15,040	
		———	———	
Total allowances				45,492
				———

Tutorial note

(1)   The motor car has CO$_2$ emissions over 110 grams per kilometre and therefore qualifies for writing down allowances at the rate of 6%. The private use of a motor car by an employee is irrelevant, since such usage will be assessed on the employee as a benefit.

(2)   A balancing allowance only arises on the main and special rate pools on the cessation of trade, even where all of the assets in the relevant pool have been disposed of.

(W3) Chargeable gain

Clueless Ltd owns 100% of Clever Ltd and together they form a capital gains group. The transfer from Clever Ltd to Clueless Ltd takes place at no gain/no loss as follows:

	£
Cost (April 2003)	70,000
Plus: IA (April 2003 to June 2011)	
£70,000 × 0.298	20,860
	———
Deemed proceeds	90,860

When Clueless Ltd sells the building outside of the group, its deemed cost is £90,860. The chargeable gain is:

	£
Proceeds (March 2020)	200,000
Less: Deemed cost	(90,860)
Unindexed gain	109,140
Less: IA (June 2011 to December 2017) (Note)	
£90,860 × 0.182	(16,537)
Chargeable gain	92,603

Tutorial note

The indexation allowance has been frozen at December 2017.

(b)   **Self-assessment return**

Tutor's top tips

For written parts, write short succinct sentences in bullet point form and bear in mind the mark allocation for each sub-section. In general, there is usually one mark allocated for each valid point made. Do not therefore dwell on any one part too much and keep an eye on the clock. The highlighted words indicate those that the marker will be looking for.

(1)   **Filing date**

Clueless Ltd's self-assessment tax return for the year ended 31 March 2020 must be submitted by 31 March 2021.

(2)   **Options for iXBRL format**

If Clueless Ltd has straightforward accounts, it could use the software provided by HM Revenue and Customs. This automatically produces accounts and tax computations in the iXBRL format.

Alternatively, other software that automatically produces iXBRL accounts and computations could be used.

A tagging service could be used to apply the appropriate tags to the accounts and tax computations, or Clueless Ltd could use software to tag documents itself.

Examiner's report

Part (a) was generally very well answered. The only aspect that consistently caused problems was the loan interest with very few candidates appreciating that this is assessed on a receivable basis.

In part (b) it was surprising that only a few candidates were aware of the filing date for a self-assessment corporation tax return, with far too many candidates giving a 31 January date…hardly any candidates were able to provide relevant details regarding the production of accounts and computations using iXBRL.

Note: The examiner's report has been edited to remove comments on elements of the question that have been deleted due to changes to the examination format.

ACCA marking scheme			Marks
(a)	Loan interest		0.5
	Qualifying charitable donations		0.5
	Corporation tax		0.5
	Trading profit		
		Depreciation	0.5
		Donations to political parties	0.5
		Qualifying charitable donations	0.5
		Gifts to customers – pens – no adjustment	0.5
		Gifts to customers – food hampers	0.5
		Capital allowances deducted	0.5
	Capital allowances		
		TWDVs brought forward	0.5
		AIA on machinery	1.0
		Motor car addition in special rate pool	0.5
		Disposal proceeds in special rate pool	0.5
		WDA on main pool at 18%	0.5
		WDA on special rate pool at 6%	0.5
	Chargeable gain		
		Deemed proceeds on no gain/no loss transfer	1.5
		Chargeable gain on disposal outside of group	1.5
			———
			11.0
			———
(b)	(i)	Submit by 31 March 2021	1.0
			———
	(ii)	HMRC software	1.0
		Other software producing iXBRL accounts	1.0
		Tagging service/software to tag documents	1.0
			———
			3.0
			———
Total			**15.0**
			———

266   LONG LTD AND ROAD LTD (ADAPTED) *Walk in the footsteps of a top tutor*

Key answer tips

This question, about a group of two companies, is split into two unrelated areas.

Part (a) requires you to calculate the corporation tax liability for each of the companies. There are capital and trading losses to deal with.

Part (b) has two requirements: firstly to explain the reporting of real time PAYE information to HM Revenue and Customs ('HMRC'); and secondly to state which forms must be provided to employees or submitted to HMRC following the end of the tax year. The highlighted words in the answer to part (b) below are key phrases that markers are looking for.

Tutor's top tips

It is easy to overrun on part (a), so you could consider answering part (b) before part (a) to make sure that you do not run out of time to answer both parts of the question.

(a)   Corporation tax computations

Tutor's top tips

When you read the information you see that one company has a capital loss and one has a trading loss. The requirement states that reliefs must be claimed as soon as possible so you will need to consider how relief can be taken for these losses.

You were told the amount of premium assessed on the landlord as income, not the premium itself, so all that is needed to calculate the tax allowable amount is to divide this figure by the number of years in the lease.

Long Ltd – Corporation tax computation – year ended 31 March 2020

		£
Operating profit		384,400
Depreciation		43,050
Amortisation		5,000
Lease of motor car (£3,600 × 15%) (Note 1)		540
Less: Deduction for lease premium (£68,200 ÷ 20) (Note 2)		(3,410)
Less: Capital allowances (W)		(47,690)
Trading profit		381,890
Net chargeable gain (£29,800 – £21,300) (Note 3)		8,500
Total profits		390,390
Less: Group relief – from Road Ltd (Note 4)		
Lower of:		
Road Ltd's loss	£34,900	
3/12 of Long Ltd's profit (£390,390 × 3/12)	£97,598	(34,900)
Taxable total profits		355,490
Corporation tax liability		
(£355,490 × 19%)		67,543

Tutorial note

(1)   The leased motor car has CO$_2$ emissions of more than 110 grams per kilometre, so 15% of the leasing costs are disallowed.

(2)   The office building has been used for business purposes. Therefore the proportion of the lease premium assessed on the landlord as property income can be deducted from trading income, spread over the life of the lease.

(3)   A joint election can be made so that Long Ltd is treated as having made Road Ltd's capital gain. It would be equally beneficial for a joint election to be made so that Road Ltd is treated as having made Long Ltd's capital loss. In the examination equal marks would be awarded for either treatment.

(4)   Group relief is not restricted as Road Ltd's available loss is less than 3/12ths of Long Ltd's taxable total profits.

Road Ltd

Trading loss – period ended 31 March 2020

	£
Operating loss	(26,100)
Donations	2,800
Capital allowances (£11,600 × 100%)	(11,600)
Surrendered as group relief	(34,900)

Tutorial note

(1)   The motor car is purchased on 3 October 2019 before trade commences, so is treated as incurred on the first day of trading – 1 January 2020. The motor car has CO_2 emissions up to 50 grams per kilometre and therefore qualifies for the 100% first year allowance. First year allowances are never time apportioned. In the absence of any other information always assume that cars purchased are new cars (not second hand).

(2)   It is beneficial for Road Ltd to surrender its trading loss to Long Ltd as this will use the loss as soon as possible.

Road Ltd

Corporation tax computation for the period ended 31 March 2020

	£
Interest income	4,300
Less: Qualifying charitable donations	(2,400)
Taxable total profits	1,900
Corporation tax	
(£1,900 × 19%)	361

Tutorial note

The qualifying charitable donations cannot be surrendered as group relief as they are fully relieved against Road Ltd's interest income.

Working – Plant and machinery – Long Ltd

	£	Main pool £	Allowances £
TWDV b/f		44,800	
Addition not qualifying for AIA			
Motor car		15,700	
Addition qualifying for AIA			
Lorry	36,800		
AIA	(36,800)		36,800
		0	
		60,500	
WDA (18%)		(10,890)	10,890
TWDV c/f		49,610	
Total allowances			47,690

Tutorial note

The motor car has CO_2 emissions between 51 and 110 grams per kilometre, and therefore qualifies for writing down allowances at the rate of 18%.

When dealing with a company there is never any private use adjustment. The private use of the motor car will be assessed on the managing director as an employment benefit.

(b) PAYE real time reporting

Tutor's top tips

Use headings to separate the two parts of your answer which makes it easier to mark.

Real time PAYE information

- Real time PAYE information must be filed electronically, so Road Ltd will have to either run payroll software or use the services of a payroll provider.

- Road Ltd will have to send real time PAYE information to HMRC electronically by the end of each calendar month (the time when employees are paid).

Forms

- Form P60 must be provided to employees following the end of the tax year.

- Form P11D detailing the benefits provided to the employees must be submitted to HMRC following the end of the tax year, with a copy provided to the employees.

- Form P11D (b) should be submitted to HMRC detailing class 1A national insurance contributions.

Examiner's report

Part (a) was generally well answered. The only aspect that consistently caused problems was Road Ltd, where candidates often incorrectly increased the loss for donations, and decreased it for capital allowances. In some cases, the loss was simply treated as a profit.

Part (b), perhaps not surprisingly, was not generally well answered. In many cases, the only form mentioned was form P45 which is no longer relevant. Candidates often explained PAYE in general terms, rather than answering the requirements of the question.

	ACCA marking scheme	
		Marks
(a)	Long Ltd – Corporation tax computation	
	Depreciation	0.5
	Amortisation	0.5
	Lease of motor car	1.0
	Deduction for lease premium	1.0
	Net chargeable gain	1.5
	Group relief from Road Ltd	1.5
	Corporation tax	0.5
	TWDV brought forward	0.5
	Lorry	0.5
	AIA	0.5
	Motor car	0.5
	WDA – 18%	0.5
	Road Ltd – Trading loss for the period	
	Donations	0.5
	Capital allowances	1.0
	Road Ltd – Corporation tax computation	
	Interest income	0.5
	Qualifying charitable donations	0.5
	Corporation tax	0.5
		———
		12.0
		———
(b)	PAYE real time reporting	
	File electronically	1.0
	Timing	0.5
	P60	0.5
	P11D	0.5
	P11D(b)	0.5
		———
		3.0
		———
Total		**15.0**
		———

Section 10

ANSWERS TO PRACTICE VALUE ADDED TAX QUESTIONS

PRACTICE SECTION A OBJECTIVE TEST QUESTIONS

267 A

Under the future prospects test, Fred is required to register for VAT when taxable supplies in the next 30 days in isolation are expected to exceed £85,000.

Fred had grounds for expecting this to be the case on 1 June 2020 when he received an order to supply £90,000 of goods by 30 June 2020. Registration is effective from the start of the 30 day period so Fred must start charging VAT from 1 June 2020.

268 B

Taxable supplies for 7 m/e 31 July 2019 are £66,000 and for 8 m/e 31 August 2019 taxable supplies are £96,000. Layla therefore exceeds the registration threshold of £85,000 by the end of August 2019.

Layla must notify HM Revenue & Customs by 30 September 2019 and she will be registered from 1 October 2019.

269 B and C

VAT cannot be reclaimed on cars which are used for private purposes.

VAT can normally be reclaimed on fuel used partially for private purposes (although output VAT will be due based on the fuel scale rate). However, the fuel has been consumed prior to the date of registration and therefore the input tax cannot be reclaimed. Input tax can only be reclaimed on goods if they are still on hand (or not consumed) at the date of registration.

Pre-registration input VAT can only be reclaimed on services if they were supplied within six months of registration.

Pre-registration input VAT can be reclaimed on goods acquired for the business provided they are on hand (i.e. in inventory) at the date of registration.

270

	Can be in VAT group
A Ltd	✓
B Ltd	✓
C Ltd	✓
D Sarl	

Companies that are under common control (>50%) can be in a VAT group provided they all have a place of business in the UK. All of the companies are under the common control of Fergus, but D Sarl cannot be a member of the group as it does not have a place of business in the UK.

271 B

	£
1.7.19 – 31.12.19: Pre-registration (6 × 110)	660
1.1.20 – 31.3.20: Post-registration (3 × 110)	330
	———
Total input tax recoverable	990
	———

Tutorial note

Pre-registration input VAT relating to services can only be recovered if it was incurred in the six months prior to registration.

272

	True	False
Vikram should have notified HM Revenue & Customs that he had ceased to make taxable supplies by 30 July 2019		✓
Vikram must account for output tax on the value of non-current assets and inventory held at the date of deregistration and on which a deduction for input tax has previously been claimed, unless this would result in a liability below £83,000.		✓

A VAT registered trader must notify HM Revenue & Customs (HMRC) within 30 days of ceasing to make taxable supplies i.e. Vikram should have notified HMRC by 16 July 2019.

Vikram must account for output tax on the value of non-current assets and inventory held at the date of deregistration and on which a deduction for input tax has previously been claimed, unless this would result in a liability below £1,000.

273 B

The basic tax point is the date the goods are delivered. This is only overridden by an actual tax point if a tax invoice is issued or payment is made before the basic tax point or provided an actual tax point has not already arisen under the earlier rule, an invoice is issued within 14 days after the basic tax point.

274 £133

Quarter ended 31 March 2020

	£
Input tax:	
Relief for impairment losses (£800 × 1/6)	133

Tutorial note

Relief for impairment losses is only available where at least six months has elapsed since the debt was due for payment and the seller has written the debt off in their VAT account.

The VAT on the £1,000 debt (net of any recovery from the liquidator) can be recovered in the next quarter.

275 D

Input VAT: £600 × 20/120 = £100

Output VAT: £354 × 20/120 = £59

276 C

Recoverable input VAT

	£
Entertaining new suppliers	0
Car leasing (£3,000 × 1/6 × 50%)	250
	250

Tutorial note

VAT can only be recovered on entertaining staff and overseas customers.

Where any car, which has some private use, is leased only 50% of the input VAT can be recovered. The level of the car's CO_2 emissions is irrelevant.

277 C

	£
Entertaining overseas customers	320
Purchase of new office equipment	1,250
Total input VAT recoverable	1,570

Tutorial note

Input VAT incurred in relation to entertaining overseas customers is recoverable. Input VAT incurred on entertaining UK customers is irrecoverable.

Input tax on the purchase of business assets is recoverable; with the exception of cars with an element of private use.

---

278 £2,200

Quarter ended 31 March 2020

	£	£
Output tax:		
Sales (£30,000 × 1/6)	5,000	
Samples	0	
		5,000
Input tax:		
Purchases (£16,800 × 1/6)		(2,800)
VAT payable		2,200

Tutorial note

Business samples are not treated as taxable supplies and therefore no output VAT is payable in respect of them.

279 C

Quarter ended 31 March 2020

	£
Output tax:	
Fuel scale charge (£414 × 1/6)	69
Input tax:	
Fuel (£1,200 × 1/6)	(200)
VAT reclaimable	(131)

280

	True	False
The date of the supply is not required on a less detailed VAT invoice.		✓
A description of goods and services is required on a less detailed VAT invoice.	✓	
A less detailed VAT invoice can be provided when the consideration for the supply is less than £1,000.		✓
The amount of VAT payable on the supply is not required on a less detailed VAT invoice.	✓	

Tutorial note

A less detailed VAT invoice can be provided when the consideration for the supply is less than £250. A less detailed invoice need only show the following information: the supplier's name, address and VAT registration number; the date of supply; a description of the goods or services supplied; the consideration for the supply; the rate of VAT in force at the time of supply.

281 B

This is the second time the return is late. On the first offence a surcharge liability period (SLP) would start, which would end on 31 October 2020 (the 12-month anniversary of the VAT period to which the default relates.

The second offence is the first default in the SLP, the SLP is extended to 31 January 2021 and a 2% penalty of £520 (£26,000 × 2%) is charged.

282

		Correction of error	
		Beach Ltd can correct the error on the next VAT return	Beach Ltd must separately notify HMRC of the error
Penalties and interest	Beach Ltd will be charged a penalty for an incorrect VAT return	✓	
	Beach Ltd will be charged default interest		

The error is smaller than the greater of £10,000 or 1% of turnover (£3,800) and can therefore be corrected on the next quarter's VAT return. Any error that can be corrected on the next return will not attract an interest charge.

283 B

Tutorial note

The payments on account are made at the end of month's four to twelve on the annual accounting scheme.

Each payment is 10% of the VAT liability for the previous year i.e. year ended 31 December 2018.

Each payment is therefore £4,770 (£47,700 × 10%).

284

	True	False
Input tax cannot be claimed until the invoice is paid which delays recovery of input VAT	✓	
Traders using the scheme do not have to pay output VAT to HMRC until they receive it from customers	✓	
To join the scheme the trader's expected taxable turnover (excluding VAT) for the next twelve months must not exceed £150,000		✓
The cash accounting scheme cannot be used where a trader issues an invoice in advance of supplying goods	✓	

To join the scheme a trader's taxable turnover (excluding VAT and sales of capital assets) for the next twelve months must not exceed £1,350,000.

285 D

£59,700 × 12% = £7,164

286 £15,730

The flat rate scheme applies a percentage to the VAT inclusive total turnover including zero-rated and exempt sales. Expenses are not deductible.

Standard-rated sales = (£80,000 + 20% VAT) = £96,000.

Total VAT inclusive turnover = (£96,000 + £15,000 + £10,000) = £121,000

This is multiplied by the flat rate percentage to calculate the VAT due to HMRC

(£121,000 × 13%) = £15,730

287 A

Marina accounts for output VAT of £2,000 as the goods would be standard-rated if supplied in the UK. She can claim back input VAT of £2,000 on the same return as the goods are used by a trader that only makes taxable supplies. The net effect on VAT payable is therefore nil.

PRACTICE SECTION B OBJECTIVE TEST CASES

288 THIDAR (ADAPTED)

Key answer tips

This question tests knowledge of a number of VAT issues.

There were some easy marks to be gained in the first two questions for a relatively straightforward compulsory registration computation and knowledge of the recovery of pre-registration input VAT.

The next two questions cover the administration of VAT, which again, would provide easy marks if the rules had been learnt.

The final question focuses on the recovery of input VAT, an area commonly tested.

1   A

	£
Total standard rated sales for months 1 to 12	57,100
Total zero rated sales for months 1 to 12	27,300
Total taxable supplies for months 1 to 12	84,400

	£
Total taxable sales for months 1 to 12	84,400
Less: Taxable supplies in month 1 (£3,400 + £0)	(3,400)
Add: Taxable supplies in month 13 (£2,800 + £900)	3,700
Total taxable supplies for months 2 to 13	84,700

	£
Total standard rated sales for months 2 to 13	84,700
Less: Taxable supplies in month 2 (£0 + £1,900)	(1,900)
Add: Taxable supplies in month 14 (£3,200 + £1,700)	4,900
Total taxable supplies for months 3 to 14	87,700

2   D

The £1,800 advertising is more than six months prior to registration, and the £300 advertising has no VAT invoice, so there is no pre-registration VAT recoverable.

3   B

A VAT invoice must be issued within 30 days of making a taxable supply. VAT records (including VAT invoices) must normally be retained for six years.

4   C

Default interest will not be charged because separate disclosure of the VAT underpayment was not required (it was less than £10,000).

5   C

	£
Irrecoverable input VAT	
Entertaining UK customers	160
Motor car leasing (£700 × 20% × 50%)	70

289 CANDY APPLE AND SUGAR PLUM (ADAPTED) *Walk in the footsteps of a top tutor*

Key answer tips

This question is really two separate questions and tests knowledge of a number of VAT issues.

There were some easy marks to be gained in the first part for a relatively straightforward compulsory registration computation and knowledge of the implications of late registration.

The second part of the question is purely computational and tests your knowledge of output and input VAT, including the rules for pre-registration input VAT.

1   D

Candy was liable to compulsory register for VAT when her taxable supplies during any 12 month period exceeded £85,000.

This happened on 31 October 2019 when taxable supplies amounted to £85,200 (£10,500 + £10,500 + £10,500 + £10,500 + £14,400 + £14,400 + £14,400).

Candy was required to notify HMRC within 30 days of the end of the month in which the threshold was exceeded (i.e. 30 November 2019) and was registered from and required to charge VAT on taxable supplies from the first day of the second month after her taxable supplies exceeded the threshold (i.e. from 1 December 2019).

2

	True	False
A default surcharge penalty will be charged for late registration		✓
Candy must account to HM Revenue and Customs for output tax at 20/120 of the value of sales from the date that she should have been registered from	✓	
Candy must issue VAT invoices charging her customers the VAT that she should have charged on sales from the date she should have been registered by		✓

Tutorial note

A late registration penalty may be charged. A default surcharge penalty applies for filing a return and paying the related VAT late.

Output VAT must be accounted for to HM Revenue and Customs from the date that she should have been registered. Sales from the date of compulsory registration are treated as VAT inclusive (even though VAT was not actually charged to customers). Candy can try to recover the VAT that she should have charged from customers but is not required to do so by HM Revenue and Customs and indeed it may not be possible.

3   £10,740

	£
Output VAT	
Standard-rated sales (£53,700 × 20%)	10,740
Zero-rated sales (£23,100 × 0%)	0
	————
	10,740
	————

4   A

	£
Input VAT	
Electricity (£49 × 1/7)	7
Furniture (£1,500 × 95% × 20%)	285
	————
	292
	————

Tutorial note

Where services are used partly for private and partly for business use, an apportionment is made to calculate the recoverable input VAT.

5   D

	£
Pre-registration input VAT	
Consultancy fees (£375 × 20%)	75
Inventory (£1,000 × 20%)	200
	————
	275
	————

Tutorial note

Pre-registration Input VAT can be reclaimed on:

- *services supplied within the six months prior to registration, and*

- *inventory acquired for business purposes in the four years prior to registration that has not been sold at the time of registration.*

290 LITHOGRAPH LTD (ADAPTED)

Key answer tips

The first two questions in this case test your knowledge of the VAT annual accounting scheme.

The other three questions require fairly standard calculations of output VAT and input VAT, including relief for impaired debts.

1

	POA due
April 2018	
May 2018	
June 2018	
July 2018	✓
August 2018	✓
September 2018	✓
October 2018	✓
November 2018	✓
December 2018	✓
January 2019	✓
February 2019	✓
March 2019	✓
April 2019	

Lithograph Ltd will have made nine payments on account, and these will have been paid in the months of July 2018 to March 2019, being months 4 to 12 of the annual VAT return period.

2 D

The payments on account are 10% of the VAT payable for the previous year i.e. the year ended 31 March 2018.

The annual VAT return is due 2 months after the end of the VAT period i.e. 31 May 2019.

3 C

	£
Output VAT	
Motor car scale charge (£1,952 × 20/120)	325
Office equipment (£8,000 × 20%)	1,600
	———
	1,925
	———

Tutorial note

For transactions quoted inclusive of VAT, the VAT is calculated as 20/120 (or 1/6).

4 £10,400

	£
Input VAT	
Expenses (£28,000 × 20%)	5,600
Machinery (£24,000 × 20%)	4,800
	———
	10,400
	———

Tutorial note

Input VAT on business entertainment is not recoverable unless it relates to overseas customers.

Input VAT cannot be recovered in respect of the motor car as this is not used exclusively for business purposes.

5   D

	£
Recoverable VAT	
Impaired debt 1 (£4,800 × 1/6)	800
Impaired debt 2 – not recoverable	0
	800

Tutorial note

Relief for impaired debts is available where the claim is made more than six months from the time that payment was due, and the debt has been written off in the company's books.

The VAT on the second impaired debt cannot be recovered until the VAT return for the year ended 31 March 2021.

291   ALISA (ADAPTED) *Walk in the footsteps of a top tutor*

1   B

	£
January to April 2019 (£7,500 × 4)	30,000
May to August 2019 (£10,000 × 4)	40,000
September 2019	15,500
Total sales to September 2019	85,500

Tutorial note

Taxable turnover exceeded the VAT registration threshold by 30 September 2019. Alisa should therefore have notified HMRC by 30 October 2019, with registration effective from 1 November 2019.

2   D

	£
Advertising: (6 × £180 × 20%)	216
Website design: (6 × £240/6)	240
Total pre-registration input VAT recoverable	456

Tutorial note

Pre-registration input VAT is recoverable in respect of services supplied in the 6 months prior to registration.

3   £180

	£
Repairs (£456/6)	76
Fuel (£624/6)	104
Maximum input VAT recoverable	180

Tutorial note

The input VAT in respect of the fuel is recoverable in full, despite the private use element. Output tax will be payable on the fuel scale charge to account for the private use.

4   D

Tutorial note

All businesses must make their VAT payments electronically and this must be done no later than one month and seven days after the end of the quarter, i.e. 7 May 2020.

5

	Include
The customer's VAT registration number	
An invoice number	✓
The customer's address	✓
A description of the services supplied	✓

Tutorial note

A customer's VAT registration number is not required to be included on a valid VAT invoice.

292 THE WHITLOCK SISTERS (ADAPTED) *Walk in the footsteps of a top tutor*

Key Answer Tips

The first two questions test the straightforward computation of the VAT payable using the flat rate scheme percentage, and then the VAT that would have been payable if the normal basis had been used, and should have provided easy marks to a well prepared student.

Be careful to read the question carefully though to ascertain whether the figures given are inclusive or exclusive of VAT.

The third question tests more of the details regarding the flat rate scheme – this sort of question can only really be answered if the rules have been learnt.

The final two questions test tax points in respect of services and entertaining expenses.

1   D

Using the flat rate scheme to calculate its VAT liability the partnership will have paid VAT of £7,800 (£50,000 + £10,000) × 13% for the quarter.

Tutorial note

Under the flat rate scheme, VAT is calculated by applying a fixed percentage to the turnover figure inclusive of VAT and including any exempt or zero-rated supplies. Expenses and purchases are not relevant.

2   £3,783

If the partnership had used the normal basis it would have paid VAT of £3,783 ((£50,000 – £27,300) = £22,700 × 20/120).

Tutorial note

(1)   Calculate the VAT element of VAT inclusive prices using either 1/6 or 20/120 of the VAT inclusive price.

(2)   Output tax is not charged on exempt supplies.

3

	True	False
To join the scheme expected taxable turnover (including VAT) for the next 12 months must not exceed £150,000		✓
The scheme can only be used by small unincorporated businesses		✓
A business must leave the scheme if total VAT inclusive turnover exceeds £230,000	✓	
VAT must still be charged on standard-rated sales invoices at the rate of 20%	✓	

Tutorial note

To join the scheme expected taxable turnover (**excluding** VAT) for the next 12 months must not exceed £150,000.

The scheme can be used by both small unincorporated and incorporated businesses

4

Deposit	Balancing payment
When the deposit is paid	Invoice date

The basic tax point date (BTP) is the date when the service is completed, which will be the date that the room is used, i.e. the day of the room hire.

In respect of the 25% deposit the BTP is overridden by a payment before the BTP and that payment date becomes the actual tax point.

In respect of the 75% balancing payment the BTP is not overridden by either a payment or an invoice being issued before the BTP. However, as the invoice is issued within 14 days of the BTP, the invoice date becomes the actual tax point.

Tutorial note

For services, the basic tax point (BTP) is the date the service is provided/completed.

The actual tax point (ATP) can be either before or after the BTP.

The ATP will be before the BTP if:

- An invoice is issued before the BTP, or

- A payment is received before the BTP (as in this case with the deposit payments).

The ATP will be after the BTP if:

- An invoice is issued within 14 days of the BTP, or

- The business has an agreement with HMRC for a different date (typically businesses agree a month end invoicing policy so that the invoice date is usually the ATP).

5   D

Tutorial note

Input VAT incurred on business entertaining cannot be recovered, with the exceptions of staff entertaining and entertaining overseas **customers**.

293   KNIGHT LTD (ADAPTED) *Walk in the footsteps of a top tutor*

Key Answer Tips

This question covers a variety of VAT topics. Firstly it deals with the VAT return looking at output VAT and then input VAT separately. The third question looks at impairment loss relief, and tests the detailed rules regarding what is recoverable. The fourth question tests the rules regarding VAT groups. Finally, the fifth question relates to the default surcharge penalty and the specifics of when it is charged as well as the relevant rates.

1   A

	£
Output VAT	
Sales (Note 1)	38,210
Fuel scale charge (£265 × 20/120) (Note 2)	44
	38,254

Tutorial note

(1) The tax point for the deposit is the date of payment, so no adjustment is required to the output VAT figure of £38,210.

(2) The fuel scale rate is quoted inclusive of VAT. The VAT element can be calculated as 20/120 of the scale figure, or as a short cut, you can use 1/6.

2   C

Input tax – Sundry expenses

	£
Other sundry expenses (all recoverable)	9,121
Entertaining UK customers (Note 1)	0
Entertaining overseas customers (Note 1)	139
New reception area (Note 2)	3,300
	12,560

Tutorial note

(1) Input VAT on business entertainment is not recoverable unless it relates to the cost of entertaining staff or overseas customers.

(2) Input tax is recoverable on the extension (capital expenditure). There is no distinction between capital and revenue for VAT purposes.

3   £0

Tutorial note

Relief is only available for the impairment loss provided that both six months has passed from the time that payment was due and the debt has been written off in the seller's accounts.

Claims must be made within four years and six months of the payment being due.

4

	True	False
If Knight Ltd forms a VAT group it will include both Are Ltd and Can Ltd		✓
Standard-rated supplies made by Knight Ltd to other VAT group members will be ignored for VAT purposes	✓	
Knight Ltd will be the representative member of the VAT group and will be required to submit one VAT return for the whole group		✓
Each group member will remain liable for its share of the VAT payable		✓

Tutorial note

Are Ltd and Can Ltd can form a group with Knight Ltd for VAT purposes as they are under the control of Knight Ltd and all of the companies are UK resident. However, eligible companies are not automatically included in the group. Either Are Ltd or Can Ltd may be excluded.

There will be no need to account for VAT on goods and services supplied between group members. Such supplies will simply be ignored for VAT purposes.

The group must appoint a representative member which will be responsible for completing one VAT return for the group. However, the representative member could be any of the group companies.

Each group member is jointly and severally liable for the VAT payable by the whole group, not just its share.

5   B

Tutorial note

The late submission for the quarter ended 31 December 2017 is irrelevant, as it was followed by the submission of four consecutive VAT returns on time.

The late payment for the quarter ended 30 September 2019 results in the issue of a surcharge liability notice for the period up to 30 September 2020.

The late payment of VAT for the quarter to 30 June 2020 occurs during the surcharge period. Therefore, there will be a surcharge of £420 (£21,000 × 2%).

In addition, the surcharge period will be extended to 30 June 2021.

The surcharge of £420 is payable as it exceeds the de minimis amount of £400.

294 ARDENT (ADAPTED) *Walk in the footsteps of a top tutor*

Key Answer Tips

This question covers a variety of VAT topics that are frequently tested along with the recently introduced system, making tax digital (MTD). The first question deals with MTD and predominantly tests knowledge of businesses affected by the new rules. Pre-registration input VAT is a very common examination topic so make sure that you know the specific rules, as you are unlikely to be able to correctly guess them!

1

	True	False
MTD software is used to print out returns which can then be sent to HMRC		✓
The usual VAT return and payment submission dates apply	✓	
Although returns are produced automatically, the business is still responsible for checking them	✓	
The rules apply to all VAT registered businesses, including those with taxable supplies below the VAT registration threshold		✓`

Tutorial note

Most VAT registered businesses with a taxable turnover above £85,000 are required to register for 'making tax digital'. VAT registered businesses with a taxable turnover below £85,000 (i.e. voluntarily registered businesses) can choose to follow the rules but it is not compulsory to do so.

2   A

	£
Input VAT re. advertising – 1.7.19 – 31.12.19 (£120 × 6)	720
Laptop still in use at registration	200
	────
Recoverable pre-registration input VAT	920
	────

Tutorial note

*Input VAT incurred on services in the **six months** prior to registration can be recovered provided the services were supplied for business purposes. The input VAT incurred on advertising costs from 1 April to 30 June is therefore not recoverable.*

Input VAT incurred on the acquisition of goods for business purposes can be recovered provided the goods are acquired no more than 4 years prior to registration and the goods are still held at the date of registration. This rule applies equally to capital items as well as current assets such as inventory and consumables.

3   £15,740

	£
Output VAT:	
Standard-rated sales (£ 125,700 × 20%)	25,140
Input VAT:	
Standard-rated invoices (£56,400/6)	(9,400)
VAT payable	15,740

Tutorial note

The VAT incurred from the point of registration is recoverable regardless of whether the goods are still in inventory at the end of the VAT quarter. This is only relevant when determining whether pre-registration input VAT is recoverable.

4   B

Tutorial note

All businesses must file their VAT return and pay VAT electronically.

The deadline for filing and payment is one month and seven days after the end of the quarter.

5

		Period	
		6 months	12 months
VAT scheme	Annual accounting		✓
	Cash accounting		
	Flat rate		

Tutorial note

A company must submit their VAT returns on time and pay the related VAT on time for 12 months in order to break out of the surcharge period.

As the annual accounting scheme reduces the administrative compliance burden of filing quarterly returns this may help Ardent Ltd to avoid further defaults.

PRACTICE SECTION C CONSTRUCTED RESPONSE QUESTIONS

295 GARFIELD (ADAPTED) *Walk in the footsteps of a top tutor*

Tutor's top tips

Read the question carefully – there are two parts to this requirement. The first requirement is computational, requiring the VAT payable for a specific quarter.

The second part of the requirement asks you to state the potential VAT schemes available in this scenario. It asks for an explanation of which scheme would be suitable, which involves applying your knowledge to the situation in hand. Don't waste time explaining how the different schemes work as there are no marks available in relation to this as stated in the notes.

The highlighted words in the answer are key phrases that markers are looking for.

(a) **Garfield – Value added tax (VAT) return for the quarter ended 31 March 2020**

	£
Output VAT	
Sales	22,500*
Discounted sale (£4,300 × 90% × 20%)	774
Equipment (£12,400 × 20%)	2,480
Fuel scale charge	60*
Input VAT	
Purchases	(11,200)*
Motor car	0*
Equipment	(2,480)
Impairment losses (£1,400 × 20%)	(280)
Entertaining – UK customers	0*
– Overseas customers (£960 × 20/120)	(160)
Motor expenses (£1,668 (£1,008 + £660) × 20/120)	(278)
	———
VAT payable	11,416
	———

*Figures provided in question.

Tutorial notes

(1) *Relief for an impairment loss is only available if the claim is made more than six months from the time when payment was due. Therefore, relief can only be claimed in respect of the invoice due for payment on 29 August.*

(2) *Input VAT on business entertainment is recoverable if it relates to the cost of entertaining overseas customers.*

(b) Making tax digital (MTD) requires most businesses to submit their VAT returns directly to HMRC using suitable software. They must also keep digital records.

VAT returns and payments are still due to be filed within one month and seven days of the end of the relevant quarter.

Garfield must comply with MTD as he makes taxable supplies in excess of the VAT registration threshold, currently £85,000.

Tutorial notes

Most VAT registered businesses are required to use digital software to keep records and submit their returns to HMRC. If a business has taxable turnover below the registration threshold and registers for VAT voluntarily, the use of MTD software is optional.

Examiner's report

Part (a) required a calculation of the amount of VAT payable for the quarter. A partly completed VAT computation was provided, so copying this out was the obvious starting point. However, some candidates amended the given figures despite being told that these were correct. It is important to read the question carefully in order to avoid unnecessary complications. The only point which consistently caused problems was the impairment losses, with the impairment loss figure itself being included rather than the VAT thereon.

Note: The examiner's report has been edited to remove comments on elements of the question that have been amended to include a new topic.

ACCA marking scheme		Marks
(a)	Output VAT on discounted sale	1.0
	Output VAT on equipment	1.0
	Input VAT on equipment	0.5
	Input VAT on impaired debts	1.0
	Input VAT on overseas customers	1.0
	Input VAT on motor expenses	1.5
	Inclusion of amounts provided in the question	1.0
		———
		7.0
		———
(b)	Digital software for records and returns	1.0
	Submission dates for returns and payments remains the same	1.0
	Applicable to Garfield	1.0
		———
		3.0
		———
Total		10
		———

296 VICTOR STYLE (ADAPTED)

Key answer tips

This is a question covering the common issues of registration and the flat rate scheme and also asks for the effect of registration on profit. This is unusual because traders usually pass on the cost of VAT to their customers, but in this case the question clearly states that it was not possible to raise prices as a consequence of becoming registered.

Provided you work carefully through the numbers, this should be a straightforward question.

(a) **VAT payable**

• Output VAT will be £19,000 (£9,500 × 12 = £114,000 × 20/120) since Victor must absorb this himself rather than pass it on to his customers.

• Input VAT will be £800 (£400 × 12 = £4,800 × 20/120).

• The total VAT payable by Victor during the year ended 31 December 2020 is therefore £18,200 (£19,000 – £800).

(b)   **Flat rate scheme**

- The main advantage of the flat rate scheme is the simplified VAT administration. Victor will calculate his VAT liability by simply taking a percentage of his turnover rather than having to calculate output tax and input tax separately.

- If Victor had used the flat rate scheme he would have paid VAT of £14,820 (£114,000 × 13%) during the year ended 31 December 2020.

- This is a saving of £3,380 (£18,200 – £14,820) for the year.

Tutorial note

In the first 12 months of VAT registration, HMRC allow a 1% reduction in the appropriate percentage for that trade group. However, knowledge of this is not required in the examination.

Therefore, you will be given the rate that should apply in the first 12 months and you do not need to deduct 1%, just use the rate given.

(c)   **Reduction in net profit**

- If Victor had not increased his prices, his net profit for the year ended 31 December 2020 based on the information given would have been £64,800 (£5,800 – £400 = £5,400 × 12).

- As a result of increasing his prices, Victor's net profit will be as follows:

	£
Sales (£114,000 – £19,000)	95,000
Less: Expenses (£4,800 – £800)	(4,000)
Net profit	91,000

- This is an increase in net profit of £26,200 (£91,000 – £64,800).

Tutor's top tips

If the flat rate scheme had been used there would have been an increase in net profit of £29,580 (£26,200 + £3,380).

297 DENZIL DYER (ADAPTED)

Key answer tips

A question ranging over a number of VAT issues. Make sure you consider each part and write enough for each part.

Remember also to relate your answer to the specific circumstances of the business.

Numbered points or bullet points are the best way to make your answer 'marker friendly'.

(a) **Identification of the type of supply**

- Output VAT is only due in respect of standard-rated supplies. Incorrectly classifying a supply as zero-rated would not remove Denzil's liability to pay the output VAT which is calculated on the actual price charged. This would then be an additional cost to the business.

- The type of supply, whether standard-rated or zero-rated, has no effect on the recovery of input VAT for Denzil.

(b) **VAT implications of discounts**

- Where a discount of 5% is given for an order of more than £500 then output VAT is simply calculated on the revised, discounted, selling price.

- As regards the 2.5% discount offered for prompt payment, output VAT is calculated on the amount that the customer actually pays.

- For prompt payment discounts the supplier will not know, when the invoice is raised, whether the customer will qualify for the discount by paying within the required timescale. The supplier must therefore charge VAT on the invoice on the full price and either issue a credit note if the discount is taken or adjust their records to account for output tax on the amount received when the invoice is paid.

(c) **Conditions for the recovery of input VAT**

- The supply must be made to Denzil since he is the taxable person making the claim.

- The supply must be supported by evidence, normally in the form of a VAT invoice. Denzil will therefore not be able to recover any input VAT in respect of the purchases of office supplies for cash, where there is no invoice.

- Denzil must use the goods or services supplied for business purposes, although an apportionment can be made where supplies are acquired partly for business purposes and partly for private purposes.

(d) **Circumstances for issuing VAT invoices**

- Denzil must issue a VAT invoice when he makes a standard-rated supply to one of his VAT registered customers.

- A VAT invoice is not required if the supply is zero-rated or the supply is to a non-VAT registered customer (e.g. a member of the public) then an invoice need not be issued unless the customer requests.

- A simplified invoice can be issued if the supply is less than £250.

- A VAT invoice should be issued within 30 days of the date that the supply of services is treated as being made.

298   SILVERSTONE LTD (ADAPTED) *Walk in the footsteps of a top tutor*

Key answer tips

This is a classic 10 mark VAT question. A number of easy marks are available for the key facts and advantages of the VAT cash accounting and annual accounting schemes, provided they are related to the particular circumstances of Silverstone Ltd.

Part (b) covers the overseas aspects of VAT which is relatively straightforward provided the rules have been learnt.

Tutor's top tips

Part (a) – Read the requirement carefully – you are required to explain why the company can use the schemes and why they will be beneficial. Make sure that you take account of and refer to the specific circumstances of the company and do not just write about the schemes in general.

In part (b) use headings in your answer so that it is clear which points relate to each type of supplier and remember to deal with both when and how to account for the VAT for each supplier.

(a)   **Cash accounting scheme and annual accounting scheme**

- Silverstone Ltd can use both schemes because its expected taxable turnover for the next 12 months does not exceed £1,350,000 exclusive of VAT.

- In addition, for both schemes the company is up to date with its VAT payments, and for the cash accounting scheme it is up to date with its VAT returns.

- With the cash accounting scheme, output VAT will be accounted for two months later than at present since the scheme will result in the tax point becoming the date that payment is received from customers.

- The recovery of input VAT on expenses will not be affected as these are paid in cash.

- With the annual accounting scheme, the reduced administration in only having to file one VAT return each year should save on overtime costs.

(b)   **Supplier situated outside the European Union**

- Silverstone Ltd will have to pay VAT of £4,400 (£22,000 at 20%) to HM Revenue and Customs at the time of importation.

- This will then be reclaimed as input VAT on the VAT return for the period during which the machinery is imported.

Supplier situated elsewhere within the European Union

- VAT will have to be accounted for according to the date of acquisition. This will be the earlier of the date that a VAT invoice is issued or the 15th day of the month following the month in which the machinery comes into the UK.

- The VAT charged of £4,400 will be declared on Silverstone Ltd's VAT return as output VAT, but will then be reclaimed as input VAT on the same VAT return. This is known as the reverse charge procedure.

Examiner's report

The first requirement was reasonably well answered, although candidates had a tendency to write everything they knew about the two schemes rather than tailoring their answers to the information given in the question.

The second requirement caused more problems, and there was little appreciation that the two alternatives would effectively leave Silverstone Ltd in the same overall financial position.

ACCA marking scheme		Marks
(a) Both schemes – Expected taxable T/O for next 12 months ≤ £1,350,000		1.5
And up to date with VAT payments and returns		1.5
Cash accounting – output tax accounted for 2 months later		1.0
Cash accounting – input tax recovery not affected		1.0
Annual accounting – reduced admin (only one return a year)		1.0
		———
		6.0
		———
(b) (1) Supplier situated outside the European Union		
Pay at time of importation		1.0
Reclaim as input tax on VAT return in period in which imported		1.0
(2) Supplier situated elsewhere within the European Union		
Date of acquisition		1.0
Include as output and input tax on same return		1.0
		———
		4.0
		———
Total		**10.0**
		———

---

299 TARDY PLC *Walk in the footsteps of a top tutor*

Key answer tips

This question has four requirements covering various administrative aspects including default surcharges, accounting for supplies of services from the EU, disclosure of VAT errors, default interest and penalties for errors. All these aspects should be manageable provided you have learnt the detailed administration rules. However, make sure you are guided by the marks available, that you answer the specific question asked and that you base your answer on the facts in the question, not everything you know about VAT!

In the answers the highlighted words are key phrases that markers are looking for.

(a)   Default surcharge

Tutor's top tips

There are two separate requirements here – to advise of the implications of a further late payment and what the company needs to do to revert to a clean record. You must make sure you deal with both and give three clear points to get the three marks available.

Default surcharges are tested relatively frequently. The key points to grasp are that there is no penalty on the first default, penalties are payable on subsequent defaults and each default will trigger an extension of the default surcharge period.

The rates of penalties need to be learnt as they are not included in the Tax Rates and Allowances provided in the examination.

- Tardy plc has already defaulted twice during the current default surcharge period, so a further default will result in a surcharge of 10% of the amount of VAT outstanding.

- In addition, the default surcharge period will be extended to the 12-month anniversary of the VAT quarter to which the default relates.

- In order to revert to a clean default surcharge record, Tardy plc will need to submit four consecutive VAT returns on time and also pay the related VAT liabilities on time.

(b)   Supply of services within the EU

Tutor's top tips

*This part also has two requirements, **when** and **how** the VAT should be accounted for. It would be easy to miss the first part of this requirement, which is actually about tax points, rather than EU supplies. Note that the question relates to services, not goods, and therefore the tax point rules are different.*

The second requirement requires an explanation of the reverse charge procedure, by which VAT is accounted for in the country where the services are carried out.

- VAT should be accounted for on the earlier of the date when the service is completed and the date the service is paid for.

- Output VAT at the UK VAT rate should be declared on the UK business's VAT return.

   This will then be reclaimed as input VAT on the same VAT return, so the effect will be VAT neutral.

   This is known as the reverse charge procedure.

(c) **Errors on a VAT return and default interest**

Tutor's top tips

Again there are two separate requirements here. The first is explaining why the error can be disclosed on the next return, which means applying the de minimis test to the amount of the error. Since the error is less than £10,000, the company's turnover figure is not required.

The second requirement is to explain whether default interest will be charged. If you have not learnt the rules here, it may be worth a guess!

- Tardy plc will be permitted to disclose the underpayment of VAT of £8,200 by entering this amount on its next VAT return as the net error is less than the limit of £10,000.

- Default interest is not charged where voluntary disclosure can be made by entering the underpayment on the next VAT return.

(d) **VAT penalties**

Tutor's top tips

This question covers the standard penalty for an incorrect return. The same penalty system applies to income tax, NICs, corporation tax and VAT and could be tested in relation to any of those taxes. Note that the penalties for errors are included in the Tax Rates and Allowances provided in the examination.

Here you are asked for the maximum amount of the penalty, which depends upon the taxpayer's behaviour and also by how much it could be reduced by an unprompted disclosure. Again, make sure you cover both points in your answer.

- Tardy plc has been careless in its incorrect treatment of the supply of services received, so the maximum amount of penalty will therefore be 30% of the VAT underpaid (£8,200 × 30% = £2,460).

- However, this penalty could be reduced to £0 as a result of the company's unprompted disclosure to HM Revenue and Customs.

Examiner's report

This question as a whole was generally not well answered. For the first requirement, many candidates wasted time by stating everything they knew about the default surcharge rather than confining their answer to the facts of the question – what penalties had been charged in respect of the previous defaults being irrelevant. For the second requirement, candidates often confused the VAT treatment of services received with that for imports or the acquisition of goods. In the fourth requirement, candidates often explained the full range of potential penalties despite being told that the underpayment had arisen due to carelessness.

ACCA marking scheme		
		Marks
(a)	Third default – 10% surcharge	1.0
	Default surcharge period extended	1.0
	Submit and pay on time for next four returns	1.0
		3.0
(b)	Earlier of service completion and payment date	1.0
	Declare output VAT on UK VAT return	1.0
	Reclaim input VAT on same return	1.0
		3.0
(c)	Can disclose on return as less than £10,000	1.0
	No default interest	1.0
		2.0
(d)	Careless therefore maximum penalty 30%	1.0
	Can be reduced to £0	1.0
		2.0
Total		**10.0**

300 SMART LTD *Walk in the footsteps of a top tutor*

Key answer tips

This question has four requirements covering various administrative aspects of VAT, including registration tests, due dates, tax points and the cash accounting scheme. It is not uncommon for a section C VAT question to be predominantly written and you need to be prepared for questions such as this.

In the answers the highlighted words are key phrases that markers are looking for.

(a) VAT registration

Tutor's top tips

This part of the question is testing knowledge of the future registration test. However, marks would also have been given for noting that the historic test was not relevant, as it would have resulted in a later registration date.

- Smart Ltd was liable to register for VAT from 1 November 2019 because this is the date when it signed the contract valued at £86,000.

- The company would therefore have known that its taxable supplies for the following 30-day period would have exceeded £85,000. Registration is required from the start of the 30-day period.

- Smart Ltd would have had to notify HM Revenue and Customs by 30 November 2019, being the end of the 30-day period.

(b) **Return submission and payment**

Tutor's top tips

Parts (b) and (c) of the question did not require any application to the scenario so could have been attempted before parts (a) and (d) if you felt more comfortable with these parts of the question.

- Smart Ltd will have to file its VAT returns online and pay the VAT which is due electronically.

- The deadline for filing the VAT return and paying any VAT which is due is one month and seven days after the end of each quarter (for example, on or before 7 March 2020 for the quarter ended 31 January 2020).

(c) **Tax point**

- The basic tax point for services is the date when they are completed.

- Smart Ltd will have to account for output VAT at the time that payment is received if a customer pays before the basic tax point and before an invoice is issued (for example, if a deposit is paid).

(d) **Advantages of cash accounting**

Tutor's top tips

Make sure you tailor your answer to the scenario; not being able to reclaim input VAT until the invoices are actually paid is normally stated as a disadvantage of cash accounting. However, this was not relevant here as Smart Ltd pays its invoices immediately.

- Output VAT will be accounted for 60 days later than at present, because the scheme will result in the tax point becoming the date when payment is received from customers.

- The recovery of input VAT on purchase invoices will not be affected because Smart Ltd pays these immediately after they are received.

- The scheme will provide automatic relief for an impairment loss should a customer default on the payment of a debt.

ACCA marking scheme		Marks
(a)	VAT registration	
	Liable from 1 November	1.0
	Taxable supplies in next 30 days > £85,000	1.0
	Notify HMRC by 30 November	1.0
		3.0
(b)	Submission and payment	
	File online/pay electronically	1.0
	File one month and 7 days after end of return period	1.0
		2.0
(c)	Tax point	
	BTP - Date completed	1.0
	Payment date if before BTP	1.0
		2.0
(d)	Cash accounting	
	Output VAT 60 days later	1.0
	Input VAT not affected	1.0
	Automatic bad debts relief	1.0
		3.0
Total		**10.0**

301 ZIA *Walk in the footsteps of a top tutor*

Key answer tips

A classic VAT question covering the preparation of a VAT return and the flat rate scheme.

Part (a) requires the calculation of VAT payable by a sole trader for a year.

Part (b) considers why the flat rate scheme may be an option and requires knowledge of the conditions.

Part (c) requires a calculation to prove whether or not it would be advantageous to join the scheme.

The highlighted words in parts (b) and (c) are key phrases that markers are looking for.

Tutor's top tips

In this type of question, read the question carefully and find out whether the figures given are inclusive of VAT (as in this question) or exclusive of VAT.

(a)   **Value added tax (VAT) – year ended 31 March 2020**

		£	£
Output VAT			
Sales	– Standard-rated (£115,200 × 20/120)		19,200
	– Zero-rated		0
Input VAT			
Impairment losses ((£780 + £660) × 20/120)		240	
Purchases	– Standard rate (£43,200 × 20/120)	7,200	
	– Zero-rated	0	
Rent ((£1,200 × 13) × 20/120)		2,600	
Telephone (£2,600 × 60% × 20/120)		260	
Entertaining – UK customers		0	
	– Overseas customers (£240 × 20/120)	40	
		——	(10,340)
VAT payable			8,860

Tutorial note

(1)   *Relief for impairment losses is given once six months have expired from the time the payment was due. Accordingly, relief can be claimed in respect of both impairment losses.*

(2)   *Rent is a continuous supply; therefore the tax point for the April 2020 rental invoice is the date of payment. Therefore, input VAT is recoverable in respect of all 13 rental payments in the year ended 31 March 2020.*

(3)   *An apportionment is made where a service such as the use of a telephone is partly for business purposes and partly for private purposes.*

(4)   *Input VAT on business entertainment is not recoverable unless it relates to the cost of entertaining overseas customers or staff.*

(b)   **Flat rate scheme – conditions**

Tutor's top tips

Make sure you memorise the conditions and thresholds for the various VAT schemes which provide easy marks as long as you have learnt them.

This requirement has two parts (joining and leaving the flat rate scheme), so be sure that you address both parts.

- Zia can join the flat rate scheme from 1 April 2020 because his taxable turnover (excluding VAT) for the next 12 months is not expected to exceed £150,000.

- He can continue to use the scheme until his total turnover (including VAT, but excluding sales of capital assets) for the previous year exceeds £230,000.

Tutorial note

It is also necessary to leave the flat scheme if total turnover is expected to exceed £230,000 during the following 30 days.

Although candidates are not expected to be aware of this point, equivalent marks were awarded if this was given instead of the previous year limit.

(c) **Flat rate scheme – benefits**

Tutor's top tips

The notes underneath the requirement give a strong hint to recalculate the liability using the flat rate given. Remember to then conclude whether or not it would have been beneficial to have used the scheme.

- Using the flat rate scheme to calculate his VAT liability, Zia would have paid VAT of £15,120 (£126,000 × 12%) for the year ended 31 March 2020.

- It would therefore not have been beneficial to use the flat rate scheme as the additional cost of £6,260 (£15,120 − £8,860) for the year would appear to outweigh the advantage of simplified VAT administration.

Tutorial note

Under the flat rate scheme Zia would be required to pay the flat rate percentage of his VAT inclusive turnover (including zero-rated supplies) with no deductions for input VAT.

ACCA marking scheme		
		Marks
(a)	Sales – standard-rated	0.5
	Sales – zero-rated	0.5
	Impairment losses	1.0
	Purchases – standard-rated	0.5
	Purchases – zero-rated	0.5
	Rent	1.0
	Telephone	1.0
	Entertaining – UK customers	0.5
	Entertaining – overseas customers	0.5
		6.0
(b)	Taxable turnover will not exceed £150,000	1.0
	Can continue until total turnover exceeds £230,000	1.0
		2.0
(c)	Liability under flat rate scheme	1.0
	Conclusion	1.0
		2.0
Total		**10.0**

Section 11

SPECIMEN EXAM QUESTIONS

TAXATION – UNITED KINGDOM (TX UK) – SPECIMEN EXAM

Time allowed: This specimen exam is not timed.

This exam is divided into three sections:

SECTION A

- 15 objective test (OT) questions, each worth 2 marks.

- 30 marks in total.

SECTION B

- Three OT cases, each containing a scenario which relates to five OT questions, each worth 2 marks.

- 30 marks in total.

SECTION C

- Three constructed response questions, each containing a scenario which relates to one or more requirement(s).

- Each constructed response question is worth 10 or 15 marks in total.

- 40 marks in total.

All questions are compulsory

TAXATION – UNITED KINGDOM (TX UK) – SPECIMEN EXAM

SECTION A

This section of the exam contains **15 objective test (OT) questions**.

Each question is worth **2 marks** and is compulsory.

This exam section is worth **30 marks** in total.

Important:

(1)   Calculations and workings need only be made to the nearest £.

(2)   All apportionments should be made to the nearest month.

1   William is self-employed, and his tax adjusted trading profit for the year ended 5 April 2020 was £82,700. During the tax year 2019/20, William contributed £5,400 (gross) into a personal pension scheme.

What amount of class 4 national insurance contributions (NIC) will William pay for the tax year 2019/20?

A   £6,666

B   £4,377

C   £4,269

D   £3,723

2   You are a trainee Chartered Certified Accountant and your firm has a client who has refused to disclose a chargeable gain to HM Revenue and Customs (HMRC).

From an ethical viewpoint, which TWO of the following actions could be expected of your firm?

1   Reporting under the money laundering regulations.

2   Advising the client to make disclosure.

3   Informing HMRC of the non-disclosure.

4   Warning the client that your firm will be reporting the non-disclosure.

3   Martin is self-employed, and for the year ended 5 April 2020 his trading profit was £111,100. During the tax year 2019/20, Martin made a gift aid donation of £800 (gross) to a national charity.

What amount of personal allowance will Martin be entitled to for the tax year 2019/20?

£ [   ]

4   For the year ended 31 March 2020, Halo Ltd made a trading loss of £180,000.

Halo Ltd has owned 100% of the ordinary share capital of Shallow Ltd since it began trading on 1 July 2019. For the year ended 30 June 2020, Shallow Ltd will make a trading profit of £224,000.

Neither company has any other taxable profits or allowable losses.

What is the maximum amount of group relief which Shallow Ltd can claim from Halo Ltd in respect of the trading loss of £180,000 for the year ended 31 March 2020?

A   £180,000

B   £168,000

C   £45,000

D   £135,000

5   For the year ended 31 March 2019, Sizeable Ltd had taxable total profits of £820,000, and for the year ended 31 March 2020 had taxable total profits of £970,000. The profits accrue evenly throughout the year.

Sizeable Ltd has had one 51% group company for many years.

How will Sizeable Ltd pay its corporation tax liability for the year ended 31 March 2020?

A   Nine instalments of £17,311 and a balancing payment of £28,500

B   Four instalments of £46,075

C   Four instalments of £38,950 and a balancing payment of £28,500

D   One payment of £184,300

6   For the year ended 31 December 2019, Lateness Ltd had a corporation tax liability of £60,000, which it did not pay until 31 March 2021. Lateness Ltd is not a large company.

How much interest will Lateness Ltd be charged by HM Revenue and Customs (HMRC) in respect of the late payment of its corporation tax liability for the year ended 31 December 2019?

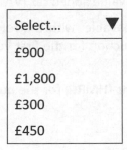

Select... ▼
£900
£1,800
£300
£450

7   On 26 November 2019, Alice sold an antique table for £8,700. The antique table had been purchased on 16 May 2015 for £3,800.

What is Alice's chargeable gain in respect of the disposal of the antique table?

A   £4,500

B   £1,620

C   £4,900

D   £0

8   On 14 November 2019, Jane made a cash gift to a trust of £800,000 (after deducting all available exemptions). Jane paid the inheritance tax arising from this gift. Jane has not made any other lifetime gifts.

What amount of lifetime inheritance tax would have been payable in respect of Jane's gift to the trust?

£ [   ]

9 During the tax year 2019/20, Mildred made four cash gifts to her grandchildren:

For each of the gifts listed below, click in the box to indicate whether the gift will be exempt or not from inheritance tax under the small gifts exemption.

£400 to Alfred	EXEMPT	NOT EXEMPT
£140 to Minnie	EXEMPT	NOT EXEMPT
A further £280 to Minnie	EXEMPT	NOT EXEMPT
£175 to Winifred	EXEMPT	NOT EXEMPT

10 For the quarter ended 31 March 2020, Zim had standard-rated sales of £49,750 and standard-rated expenses of £22,750. Both figures are exclusive of value added tax (VAT).

Zim uses the flat rate scheme to calculate the amount of VAT payable, with the relevant scheme percentage for her trade being 12%. The percentage reduction for the first year of VAT registration is not available.

How much VAT will Zim have to pay to HM Revenue and Customs (HMRC) for the quarter ended 31 March 2020?

A £5,970

B £3,888

C £5,400

D £7,164

11 Which TWO of the following assets will ALWAYS be exempt from capital gains tax?

1 A motor car suitable for private use

2 A chattel

3 A UK Government security (gilt)

4 A house

12 Winston has already invested £8,000 into a cash individual savings account (ISA) during the tax year 2019/20. He now wants to invest into a stocks and shares ISA.

What is the maximum possible amount which Winston can invest into a stocks and shares ISA for the tax year 2019/20?

A £20,000

B £12,000

C £0

D £8,000

13 Ming is self-employed.

For each of the types of records listed below, click in the box to indicate the date until which Ming must retain the records used in preparing her self-assessment tax return for the tax year 2019/20?

Business records	31 January 2022	31 January 2026
Non-business records	31 January 2022	31 January 2026

14 Moon Ltd has had the following results:

Period	Profit/(loss)
	£
Year ended 31 December 2019	(105,000)
Four-month period ended 31 December 2018	43,000
Year ended 31 August 2018	96,000

The company does not have any other income.

How much of Moon Ltd's trading loss for the year ended 31 December 2019 can be relieved against its total profits of £96,000 for the year ended 31 August 2018?

A   £64,000

B   £96,000

C   £70,000

D   £62,000

15 Nigel has not previously been resident in the UK, being in the UK for less than 20 days each tax year. For the tax year 2019/20, he has three ties with the UK.

What is the maximum number of days which Nigel could spend in the UK during the tax year 2019/20 without being treated as resident in the UK for that year?

A   90 days

B   182 days

C   45 days

D   120 days

SECTION B

This section of the exam contains **three OT cases**.

Each OT case contains a scenario which relates to **five OT questions**.

Each question is worth **2 marks** and is compulsory.

This exam section is worth **30 marks** in total.

Important

(1)   Calculations and workings need only be made to the nearest £.

(2)   All apportionments should be made to the nearest month.

The following scenario relates to questions 16–20.

Delroy and Grant

On 10 January 2020, Delroy made a gift of 25,000 £1 ordinary shares in Dub Ltd, an unquoted trading company, to his son, Grant. The market value of the shares on that date was £240,000. Delroy had subscribed for the 25,000 shares in Dub Ltd at par on 1 July 2009. Delroy and Grant have elected to hold over the gain as a gift of a business asset.

Grant sold the 25,000 shares in Dub Ltd on 18 March 2020 for £240,000.

Dub Ltd has a share capital of 100,000 £1 ordinary shares. Delroy was the sales director of the company from its incorporation on 1 July 2009 until 10 January 2020. Grant has never been an employee or a director of Dub Ltd.

For the tax year 2019/20, Delroy and Grant are both higher rate taxpayers. They have each made other disposals of assets during the tax year 2019/20, and therefore they have both already utilised their annual exempt amount for this year.

Marlon and Alvita

On 28 March 2020, Marlon sold a house for £497,000, which he had owned individually. The house had been purchased on 22 October 2004 for £152,600.

Throughout the period of ownership, the house was occupied by Marlon and his wife, Alvita, as their main residence. One-third of the house was always used exclusively for business purposes by the couple. Entrepreneurs' relief is not available in respect of this disposal.

For the tax year 2019/20, Marlon is a higher rate taxpayer, but Alvita did not have any taxable income. This will remain the case for the tax year 2020/21. Neither of them has made any other disposals of assets during the year.

16   **What is Grant's capital gains tax (CGT) liability for the tax year 2019/20 in respect of the disposal of the shares in Dub Ltd?**

A   £43,000

B   £40,600

C   £21,500

D   £20,300

17 Which TWO of the following statements would have been true in relation to the CGT implications if Delroy had instead sold the 25,000 shares in Dub Ltd himself for £240,000 on 10 January 2020, and then gifted the cash proceeds to Grant?

1   Entrepreneurs' relief would have been available.

2   The CGT liability would have been paid later.

3   The cash gift would not have been a chargeable disposal.

4   The cash gift would have qualified for holdover relief.

18 What is Marlon's chargeable gain for the tax year 2019/20?

A   £229,600

B   £0

C   £114,800

D   £344,400

19 What is the amount of CGT which could have been saved if Marlon had transferred 50% ownership of the house to Alvita prior to its disposal?

A   £3,360

B   £3,750

C   £7,110

D   £13,860

20 Why would it have been beneficial if Marlon had delayed the sale of the house until 6 April 2020?

Select...   ▼
A lower rate of CGT would have been applicable
Two annual exempt amounts would have been available
Principal private residence relief would have been greater
The CGT liability would have been paid later

The following scenario relates to questions 21 – 25.

You should assume that today's date is 15 March 2020.

Opal is aged 71, and has a chargeable estate for inheritance tax (IHT) purposes valued at £1,000,000.

She owns two properties, respectively valued at £374,000 and £442,000. The first property is her main residence and has an outstanding repayment mortgage of £160,000, and the second property has an outstanding endowment mortgage of £92,000.

Opal owes £22,400 in respect of a personal loan from a bank, and she has also verbally promised to pay legal fees of £4,600 incurred by her nephew. Opal expects the cost of her funeral to be £5,200, and this cost will be covered by the £6,000 which she has invested in an individual savings account (ISA).

Under the terms of her will, Opal has left all of her estate to her children. Opal's husband is still alive.

On 14 August 2009, Opal had made a gift of £100,000 to her daughter, and on 7 November 2019, she made a gift of £220,000 to her son. Both these figures are after deducting all available exemptions.

You should assume that both the value of Opal's estate and the nil rate band will remain unchanged for future years.

21   **What is the net value for the two properties, and related mortgages, which will have been included in the calculation of Opal's chargeable estate?**

   A   £816,000

   B   £564,000

   C   £656,000

   D   £724,000

22   **Which TWO of the following amounts will have been deducted in calculating Opal's chargeable estate?**

   1   Personal loan from a bank of £22,400

   2   Promise to pay legal fees of £4,600

   3   Funeral cost of £5,200

   4   ISA investment of £6,000

23   **What amount of IHT will be payable in respect of Opal's chargeable were she to die on 20 March 2020?**

   A   £210,000

   B   £298,000

   C   £338,000

   D   £295,600

24   By how much would the IHT payable on Opal's death be reduced if she were to live for another seven years until 20 March 2027, compared to if she were to die on 20 March 2020?

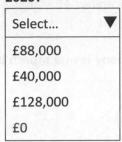

Select... ▼
£88,000
£40,000
£128,000
£0

25   Which TWO of the following conditions must be met if Opal wants to make gifts out of her income, so that these gifts are exempt from IHT?

1   The gifts cannot exceed 10% of income

2   The gifts must be habitual

3   Opal must have enough remaining income to maintain her normal standard of living

4   Opal must make the gifts monthly or quarterly

The following scenario relates to questions 26 – 30.

The following information is available in respect of Glacier Ltd's value added tax (VAT) for the quarter ended 31 March 2020:

(1)   Invoices were issued for sales of £44,600 to VAT registered customers. Of this figure, £35,200 was in respect of exempt sales and the balance in respect of standard-rated sales. The standard-rated sales figure is exclusive of VAT.

(2)   In addition to the above, on 1 March 2020 Glacier Ltd issued a VAT invoice for £8,000 plus VAT of £1,600 to a VAT registered customer in respect of a contract which will be completed on 15 April 2020. The customer paid for the contract in two instalments of £4,800 on 31 March 2020 and 30 April 2020.

(3)   The managing director of Glacier Ltd is provided with free fuel for private mileage driven in her company motor car. During the quarter ended 31 March 2020, the total cost of fuel for business and private mileage was £720, of which £270 was for private mileage. The relevant quarterly scale rate is £487. All of these figures are inclusive of VAT.

For the quarters ended 30 September 2018 and 30 June 2019, Glacier Ltd was one month late in submitting its VAT returns and in paying the related VAT liabilities. All of the company's other VAT returns have been submitted on time.

26   What is the amount of output VAT payable by Glacier Ltd in respect of its sales for the quarter ended 31 March 2020?

Select... ▼
£2,680
£3,480
£10,520
£1.880

27 **Calculate the amounts required to complete the following sentence:**

Glacier Ltd will include output VAT of £ [_____] and input VAT of £ [_____] on its VAT return for the quarter ended 31 March 2020 in respect of the managing director's company motor car.

28 **What surcharge penalty could Glacier Ltd be charged if the company is one month late in paying its VAT liability for the quarter ended 31 March 2020?**

A   5% of the VAT liability

B   2% of the VAT liability

C   There will be no penalty

D   10% of the VAT liability

29 **What is the minimum requirement which Glacier Ltd needs to meet in order to revert to a clean default surcharge record?**

A   Submit four consecutive VAT returns on time

B   Submit any four VAT returns on time and also pay the related VAT liabilities on time

C   Pay four consecutive VAT liabilities on time

D   Submit four consecutive VAT returns on time and also pay the related VAT liabilities on time

30 Glacier Ltd will be required to issue a VAT invoice in certain circumstances.

Complete the following sentence by matching one of the "types of supply" and one of the "types of customer" into each target area.

Glacier Ltd will be required to issue a VAT invoice when [_____]

is made to [_____]

Types of supply	Types of customer
a standard-rated supply	a VAT registered customer
any type of supply	any customer

SECTION C

This section of the exam contains **three constructed response questions**.

Each question contains a scenario which relates to one or more requirement(s) which may be split over multiple question screens.

Each question is worth **10 or 15 marks** and is compulsory.

This exam section is worth **40 marks** in total.

Important

(1)   Calculations and workings need only be made to the nearest £.

(2)   All apportionments should be made to the nearest month.

(3)   In your live exam please show all notes/workings that you want the marker to see within the spreadsheet or word processing answer areas. Remember, any notes/workings made on the Scratch Pad or on your workings paper will not be marked.

31   You should assume that today's date is 1 March 2019.

Sarah is currently self-employed. If she continues to trade on a self-employed basis, her total income tax liability and national insurance contributions (NIC) for the tax year 2019/20 will be £11,379.

However, Sarah is considering incorporating her business on 6 April 2019. The forecast taxable total profits of the new limited company for the year ended 5 April 2020 will be £50,000 (before taking account of any director's remuneration). Sarah will pay herself gross director's remuneration of £30,000 and dividends of £10,000. The balance of the profits will remain undrawn within the new company.

Required:

Determine whether or not there will be an overall saving of tax and national insurance contributions (NIC) for the year ended 5 April 2020 if Sarah incorporates her business on 6 April 2019.

Notes:

(1)   **You are expected to calculate the income tax payable by Sarah, the class 1 NIC payable by Sarah and the new limited company, and the corporation tax liability of the new limited company for the year ended 5 April 2020.**

(2)   **You should assume that the rates of corporation tax remain unchanged.**

(10 marks)

32 On 6 April 2019, Simon commenced employment with Echo Ltd. On 1 January 2020, he commenced in partnership with Art running a small music venue, preparing accounts to 30 April. The following information is available for the tax year 2019/20:

Employment

(1) During the tax year 2019/20, Simon was paid a gross annual salary of £24,700.

(2) Throughout the tax year 2019/20, Echo Ltd provided Simon with living accommodation. The company had purchased the property in 2009 for £89,000, and it was valued at £143,000 on 6 April 2019. The annual value of the property is £4,600. The property was furnished by Echo Ltd during March 2019 at a cost of £9,400. The living accommodation is not job-related.

(3) On 1 December 2019, Echo Ltd provided Simon with an interest-free loan of £84,000, which he used to purchase a holiday cottage.

Partnership

(1) The partnership's tax adjusted trading profit for the four-month period ended 30 April 2020 is £29,700. This figure is before taking account of capital allowances.

(2) The only item of plant and machinery owned by the partnership is a motor car which cost £25,000 on 1 February 2020. The motor car has a CO_2 emission rate of 155 grams per kilometre. It is used by Art, and 40% of the mileage is for private journeys.

(3) Profits are shared 40% to Simon and 60% to Art. This is after paying an annual salary of £6,000 to Art.

Property income

(1) Simon owns a freehold house which is let out furnished. The property was let throughout the tax year 2019/20 at a monthly rent of £660 received in advance. All rents were received on the due dates.

(2) During the tax year 2019/20, Simon paid council tax of £1,320 in respect of the property, and also spent £660 on replacement carpets.

Required:

(a) Calculate Simon's taxable income for the tax year 2019/20. (13 marks)

(b) State TWO advantages for the partnership of choosing 30 April as its accounting date rather than 5 April. (2 marks)

(Total: 15 marks)

33 (a) You are a trainee accountant and your manager has asked you to correct a corporation tax computation which has been prepared by the managing director of Naive Ltd. The corporation tax computation is for the year ended 31 March 2020 and contains a significant number of errors:

Naive Ltd – Corporation tax computation for the year ended 31 March 2020

	£
Trading profit (W1)	372,900
Loan interest received (W2)	32,100
	405,000
Corporation tax (£405,000 at 19%)	76,950

Workings

(W1) Trading profit

	£
Profit before taxation	274,530
Depreciation	15,740
Donations to political parties	400
Qualifying charitable donations	900
Accountancy	2,300
Legal fees in connection with the issue of loan notes (the loan was used to finance the company's trading activities)	5,700
Entertaining suppliers	3,600
Entertaining employees	1,700
Gifts to customers (pens costing £40 each and displaying Naive Ltd's name)	920
Gifts to customers (food hampers costing £45 each and displaying Naive Ltd's name)	1,650
Capital allowances (W3)	65,460
Trading profit	372,900

(W2) Loan interest received

	£
Loan interest receivable	32,800
Accrued at 1 April 2019	10,600
Accrued at 31 March 2020	(11,300)
Loan interest received	32,100

The loan was made for non-trading purposes.

(W3) Capital allowances

	Main pool £	Motor car £	Special rate pool £	Allowances £
TWDV brought forward	12,400		14,500	
Additions				
Machinery	42,300			
Motor car [1]	13,800			
Motor car [2]		18,100		
	68,500			
AIA	(68,500)			68,500
Disposal proceeds			(8,200)	
			4,300	
Balancing allowance			(4,300)	(4,300)
WDA – 18%		(2,520) × 50%		1,260
TWDV carried forward	0	11,480		
Total allowances				65,460

(1)   Motor car [1] has a CO_2 emission rate of 110 grams per kilometre.

(2)   Motor car [2] has a CO_2 emission rate of 155 grams per kilometre. This motor car is used by the sales manager and 50% of the mileage is for private journeys.

(3)   All of the items included in the special rate pool at 1 April 2019 were sold for £8,200 during the year ended 31 March 2020. The original cost of these items was £16,200.

Required:

Prepare a revised version of Naive Ltd's corporation tax computation for the year ended 31 March 2020.

Note: Your calculations should commence with the profit before taxation figure of £274,530, and you should indicate by the use of zero (0) any items in the computation of the trading profit for which no adjustment is required.

(12 marks)

(b)   The managing director of Naive Ltd understands that the company will have to file its self-assessment corporation tax returns online, and that the supporting accounts and tax computations will have to be filed using the inline eXtensible Business Reporting Language (iXBRL). The managing director is concerned about how the company will be able to produce documents in this format.

Required:

Explain the options available to Naive Ltd regarding the production of accounts and tax computations in the iXBRL format.

(3 marks)

(Total: 15 marks)

Section 12

ANSWERS TO SPECIMEN EXAM QUESTIONS

SECTION A

1   B

Class 4	£
£41,368 (£50,000 − £8,632) × 9%	3,723
£32,700 (£82,700 − £50,000) × 2%	654
	4,377

2   1 & 2

3   £7,350

	£
Personal allowance	12,500
Restriction (£111,100 − £800 − £100,000 = £10,300/2)	(5,150)
Restricted personal allowance	7,350

4   D

Maximum loss relief = Lower of:	£
(£180,000 × 9/12)	135,000
(£224,000 × 9/12)	168,000
Maximum loss relief	135,000

Tutorial note

Where companies do not have coterminous (matching) year ends, the available profits and losses must be time apportioned, to find the relevant amounts falling within the corresponding accounting period.

5   B

$(£970,000 × 19\%)/4 = £46,075$

Tutorial note

The profit threshold is divided by the number of 51% group companies, in this case two. Sizeable Ltd exceeded the threshold of £750,000 (£1,500,000/2) in the current period and the previous period.

As this is not the first period that Sizable Ltd is a large company, the corporation tax must be settled by paying quarterly instalments. The instalments are based on the estimated corporation tax liability for the current accounting period.

6   A

$£60,000 × 3\% × 6/12 = £900$ (period 1 October 2020 to 31 March 2021)

7   A

$£2,700 (£8,700 – £6,000) × 5/3 = £4,500$

This is less than £4,900 (£8,700 – £3,800).

Tutorial note

The chattels rules apply to the disposal of the antique table. The gross proceeds are >£6,000 and the cost is ≤£6,000 therefore the treatment is as follows:

The gain is calculated as normal i.e. Proceeds – cost

The gain must not exceed the maximum amount of 5/3 × (gross proceeds - £6,000)

8   C

	£
Gross chargeable amount	800,000
Nil rate band available at the date of the gift	(325,000)
Taxable amount	475,000
IHT payable at 25%	118,750

9   £175 TO WINIFRED IS EXEMPT
OTHER GIFTS ARE NOT EXEMPT

Tutorial note

When determining whether the small gifts exemption applies; the total gifts to each recipient during the tax year must be considered. If the total value of gifts to one individual exceeds £250, the small gifts exemption cannot be applied to any of the gifts.

10   D

£49,750 × 120/100 at 12% = £7,164

Tutorial note

The flat rate percentage is applied to total turnover, inclusive of VAT where applicable.

11   1 & 3

12   B

£20,000 – £8,000 = £12,000

13   31 JANUARY 2026 & 31 JANUARY 2026

Tutorial note

Taxpayers with a business must retain all of their records (not just business records), until 5 years from the 31 January filing date.

14   D

The maximum loss relief is the lower of:

- Remaining loss: £62,000 (£105,000 – £43,000)
- Profits for 8 months ended 31.8.18: £64,000 (£96,000 × 8/12)

15   A

SECTION B

16   A

Capital gains tax liability – 2019/20

	£
Proceeds	240,000
Less: Cost (W)	(25,000)
Gain	215,000
Less: AEA (utilised)	(0)
Taxable gain	215,000
Capital gains tax (£215,000 × 20%)	43,000

Working:	£
Deemed cost (MV at gift)	240,000
Less: Gain held over (£240,000 – £25,000)	(215,000)
Cost	25,000

17   1 & 3

18   C

	£
Proceeds	497,000
Less: Cost	(152,600)
Gain	344,400
Chargeable gain (1/3 business use)	114,800

19   C

(£12,000 at 28%) + (£37,500 at 10% (28% – 18%)) = £7,110

Tutorial note

If half of the gain had been transferred to Alvin, his previously unused annual exempt amount would have reduced the gain by £12,000. In addition, as Alvin does not have any taxable income, £37,500 of the gain falling in his unused basic rate will be taxed at the lower rate of 18% rather than 28%. Remember that the higher capital gains tax rates of 18% and 28% apply to residential property.

20   The CGT liability would have been paid later

21   C

	£
Property 1	374,000
Property 2	442,000
Gross value	816,000
Less: Repayment mortgage	(160,000)
Net value	656,000

Tutorial note

Endowment mortgages are not deducted from the value of the property, unlike repayment and interest only mortgages. The endowment element of the policy should cover the repayment of the mortgage.

22   1 & 3

Tutorial notes

The promise to pay the nephew's legal fees is not deductible as it is not legally enforceable.

An ISA investment is an asset so is not deducted from the estate.

23   B

	£	£
Gross chargeable estate		1,000,000
Less: RNRB		(150,000)
NRB at death	325,000	
Less: Gross chargeable transfers (20.3.2013 – 20.3.2020)	(220,000)	
		(105,000)
Taxable amount		745,000
IHT payable at 40%		298,000

Tutorial note

Opal's estate is reduced by the available nil rate band of £105,000 (£325,000 – £220,000). The PET made on the 7 November 2019 reduces the nil rate band available as it is within seven years of the date of death.

Opal also qualifies for the full residence nil rate band as she is leaving her main residence to her direct descendants and it is valued in excess of £150,000.

24   £88,000

£220,000 at 40% = £88,000

Tutorial note

If Opal were to live until 20 March 2027 the PET on 7 November 2019 would no longer be chargeable and would result in an additional available nil rate band on death of £220,000.

25   2 & 3

26   £3,480

(£9,400 (£44,600 – £35,200) × 20%) + £1,600 = £3,480

Tutorial note

The basic tax point for a supply of services is the date when they are completed, but if a VAT invoice is issued or payment received before the basic tax point, then this becomes the actual tax point. Therefore the tax point for the additional contract is when the VAT invoice was issued on 1 March.

27 OUTPUT VAT OF £81 AND INPUT VAT OF £120

Output VAT £487 × 20/120 = £81

Input VAT £720 × 20/120 = £120

28 A

Second default during surcharge period.

Tutorial note

Glacier Ltd was late in submitting VAT returns and paying the related VAT liability for two previous quarters. The company has not managed to revert to a clean default surcharge record by submitting four consecutive VAT returns on time.

The late payment of VAT for the quarter ended 31 March 2020 will therefore result in a surcharge of 5% of the VAT liability for that period, although this will not be collected if it is less than £400. In addition, the surcharge period will be extended to 31 March 2021.

29 D

30 STANDARD-RATED SUPPLY & VAT REGISTERED CUSTOMER

Tutorial note

Glacier Ltd must issue a VAT invoice when it makes a standard-rated supply to a VAT registered customer. However, there is no requirement to do so if the supply is exempt or if the supply is to a non-VAT registered customer.

A VAT invoice should be issued within 30 days of the date when the supply is treated as being made.

SECTION C

31   SARAH

The total tax and NIC cost if Sarah incorporates her business is £12,853 (£4,100 (W1) + £2,564 (W2) + £2,949 (W2) + £3,240 (W3)).

Therefore, if Sarah incorporated her business there would be an overall increase in tax and NIC of £1,474 (£12,853– £11,379) compared to continuing on a self-employed basis.

Workings

(W1) Sarah's income tax payable

		£
Director's remuneration		30,000
Dividends		10,000
		40,000
Less: Personal allowance		(12,500)
Taxable income		27,500

Income tax		£
£		
17,500 × 20%		3,500
2,000 × 0%		0
8,000 × 7.5%		600
27,500		
Income tax payable		4,100

(W2) National insurance contributions

	£
Employee class 1: (£30,000 – £8,632) × 12%	2,564
Employer's class 1: (£30,000 – £8,632) × 13.8%	2,949

(W3) Corporation tax liability

	£
Trading profit	50,000
Director's remuneration	(30,000)
Employer's class 1 NIC	(2,949)
Taxable total profits	17,051
Corporation tax at 19%	3,240

ACCA marking scheme	
	Marks
Sarah's income tax payable	3.5
National insurance contributions	3.0
Corporation tax liability	2.0
Total tax and NIC cost	1.0
Increase	0.5
Total	**10.0**

32 SIMON

(a) Simon – Taxable income 2019/20

	£
Employment income	
Salary	24,700
Living accommodation – Annual value	4,600
– Additional benefit (W1)	1,700
– Furniture (£9,400 × 20%)	1,880
Beneficial loan (£84,000 × 4/12 × 2.5%)	700
	33,580
Trading profit (W2)	8,220
Property income (W4)	5,940
Total income	47,740
Less: Personal allowance	(12,500)
Taxable income	35,240

Workings

(W1) Living accommodation additional benefit

(1) The benefit is based on the market value when first provided.

	£
Market value	143,000
Limit	(75,000)
	68,000

(2) The additional benefit is therefore £1,700 (£68,000 at 2.5%).

Tutorial note

The property was purchased more than six years before first being provided, so the benefit is based on the market value when first provided.

(W2) Trading profit

(1) Simon's share of the partnership's trading profit for the period ended 30 April 2020 is £10,960 calculated as follows:

	£
Trading profit	29,700
Capital allowances (W3)	(300)
	29,400
Salary paid to Art (£6,000 × 4/12)	(2,000)
	27,400
Profit share (£27,400 × 40%)	10,960

(2) Simon's trading income assessment for the tax year 2019/20 is £8,220 (£10,960 × 3/4).

Tutorial note

Simon's assessment for the tax year 2019/20 is for the period 1 January 2020 to 5 April 2020.

(W3) Capital allowances

	Motor car		Allowances
	£		£
Addition	25,000		
WDA – 6% × 4/12	(500)	× 60%	300
	————		———
TWDV c/f	24,500		
	————		

Tutorial note

The partnership's motor car has CO_2 emissions over 110 grams per kilometre and therefore qualifies for writing down allowances at the rate of 6%.

(W4) Property income

	£	£
Rent received (£660 × 12)		7,920
Council tax	1,320	
Replacement carpets	660	
	————	
		(1,980)
		————
Property income		5,940
		————

Tutorial note

The initial cost of purchasing domestic items for use by the tenant, such as carpets, is not allowable, however, the cost of replacing such items is an allowable deduction.

(b) (1) The interval between earning profits and paying the related tax liability will be 11 months longer. This can be particularly beneficial where profits are rising.

(2) It will be possible to calculate taxable profits well in advance of the end of the tax year, making it much easier to implement tax planning and make pension contributions.

	Marking scheme	
		Marks
(a)	**Calculate Simon's taxable income**	
	Employment income	5.0
	Trading profit	5.0
	Property income	2.5
	Personal allowance	0.5
		————
		13.0
		————
(b)	**Advantages of accounting date**	
	Two advantages	2.0
		————
Total		**15.0**
		————

33 NAIVE LTD

(a) Naive Ltd – Corporation tax computation for the year ended 31 March 2020

	£
Trading profit (W1)	248,340
Loan interest receivable	32,800
	————
Total profits	281,140
Qualifying charitable donations	(900)
	————
Taxable total profits	280,240
	————
Corporation tax at 19%	53,246
	————

Workings

(W1) Trading profit for the year ended 31 March 2020

	£	£
Profit before taxation	274,530	
Depreciation	15,740	
Donations to political parties	400	
Qualifying charitable donations	900	
Accountancy	0	
Legal fees	0	
Entertaining suppliers	3,600	
Entertaining employees	0	
Gifts to customers – pens	0	
Gifts to customers – food hampers	1,650	
Capital allowances (W2)		48,480
	————	————
	296,820	48,480
		————
	(48,480)	
	————	
Trading profit	248,340	
	————	

Tutorial note

(1)   The only exception to the non-deductibility of entertainment expenditure is when it is in respect of employees.

(2)   Gifts to customers are an allowable deduction if they cost less than £50 per recipient per year, are not of food, drink, tobacco or vouchers for exchangeable goods, and carry a conspicuous advertisement for the company making the gift.

(W2) Capital allowances

	Main pool	Special rate pool	Allowances
	£	£	£	£
TWDV b/f		12,400	14,500	
Additions qualifying for AIA				
Machinery	42,300			
AIA – 100%	(42,300)	0		42,300
Other additions				
Motor car [1]		13,800		
Motor car [2]			18,100	
Proceeds			(8,200)	
		26,200	24,400	
WDA – 18%		(4,716)		4,716
WDA – 6%			(1,464)	1,464
TWDV c/f		21,484	22,936	
Total allowances				48,480

Tutorial note

(1)   Motor car [1] has CO_2 emissions between 51 and 110 grams per kilometre and therefore qualifies for writing down allowances at the rate of 18%.

(2)   Motor car [2] has CO_2 emissions over 110 grams per kilometre and therefore qualifies for writing down allowances at the rate of 8%. The private use of the motor car is irrelevant, since such usage will be assessed on the employee as a benefit.

(b)   (1)   If Naive Ltd has straightforward accounts, it could use the software provided by HM Revenue and Customs. This automatically produces accounts and tax computations in the iXBRL format.

        (2)   Alternatively, other software which automatically produces iXBRL accounts and computations could be used.

        (3)   A tagging service could be used to apply the appropriate tags to the accounts and tax computations, or Naive Ltd could use software to tag documents itself.

ACCA marking scheme		Marks
(a)	**Corporation tax computation**	
	Trading profit	5.0
	Capital allowances	5.0
	Loan interest	1.0
	Qualifying charitable donations	0.5
	Corporation tax	0.5
		――
		12.0
		――
(b)	**iXBRL**	
	HMRC software	1.0
	Other software	1.0
	Tagging service	1.0
		――
		3.0
		――
Total		**15.0**
		――